Recommended by Teachers
Trusted by Toppers

All in One®

Science

CBSE Class 9

Focused Theory ▪ Practice Exercises ▪ Sample Papers

Authors
Heena Sharma *(Physics)*
Shubhankar Vats (Chemistry)
Rashmi Gupta (Biology)

arihant
SUCCESS AND NOTHING LESS

arihant
SUCCESS AND NOTHING LESS

ARIHANT PRAKASHAN
(School Division Series)

卐 ADMINISTRATIVE & PRODUCTION OFFICES

Regd. Office

'Ramchhaya' 4577/15, Agarwal Road, Darya Ganj, New Delhi -110002
Tele: 011- 47630600, 43518550; Fax: 011- 23280316

卐 *Head Office*

Kalindi, TP Nagar, Meerut (UP) - 250002, Tel: 0121-7156203, 7156204

卐 SALES & SUPPORT OFFICES

Agra, Ahmedabad, Bengaluru, Bareilly, Chennai, Delhi, Guwahati, Hyderabad, Jaipur, Jhansi, Kolkata, Lucknow, Nagpur & Pune.

PO No : TXT-XX-XXXXXXX-X-XX

Published By Arihant Publications (India) Ltd.

For further information about the books published by Arihant, log on to www.arihantbooks.com or e-mail at info@arihantbooks.com

Follow us on

卐 PRICE ₹425.00

PRODUCTION TEAM

Publishing Managers	Cover Designer	Inner Designer
Mahendra Singh Rawat & Keshav Mohan	Rakesh Rawat	Ankit Tyagi
Project Head	**Page Layouting**	**Proof Reader**
Yojna Sharma	Rajbhaskar Rana	Mansi , Ishan

Index *cum* Study Planner

Studied | Revised | Exam Ready

One Book - Endless Features
to Help you Succeed

Chapter Intro

At the start of each chapter, all the chapter topics have been listed , so that students may know what they are going to study.

CHAPTER 01

Matter In Our Surroundings

In our surroundings, we see a large variety of objects with different shapes, sizes and textures. All objects infact everything in this universe is made up of material which scientists have named 'matter'. Thus, we can say that anything that has both mass and volume and occupies space is called **matter**. The air we breathe, the food we eat, the clothes we wear, stones, clouds, stars, plants, animals and even a small drop of water or a particle of sand—everything is matter. Matter can be seen, tasted, smelled or felt.

Classification of Matter

- Early Indian philosophers classified matter into five basic elements, called the ***Panch-Tatva***. These are **air, water, earth, sky** and **fire**. According to them, everything, living or non-living, was made up of these five basic elements.
- Now-a-days, matter is classified into groups according to their physical properties and chemical nature.

  e.g. **Solid, liquid** and **gas** (based on particle arrangement or physical properties) or **elements, compounds** and **mixtures** (based on chemical nature).

Simplified Theory

It contains the necessary study material well supported by Definitions, Facts, Figures, Flow Charts, etc.

Rigidity and Fluidity

Rigid means inflexible. A solid is a rigid form of matter, hence it does not require a container to keep it. Fluid is a material which can flow easily and requires a vessel to keep it. A liquid is a fluid form of matter which takes the shape of container, while a gas is a fluid form of matter which fills the container.

Boxed Matter

Additional but informational matter related to given concept. It helps students to bring focus on important points.

Try These 1.2

1. What are the factors which are responsible for bringing a change in the physical state of substance?
2. Why inter particles start vibrating in solids on heating?
3. Convert the temperature of 70° C to the Kelvin scale.
4. What is the value of latent heat of fusion of ice?
5. How gases can be liquefy?

Try These

A set of 3-5 Questions given in between the next, helps students to remain connected with the text while studying. They can instantly assess themselves for their understanding.

One Book - Endless Features

to Help you Succeed

Illustrative Figures

To make the concepts completely visible, illustrative diagrams have been given at various place.

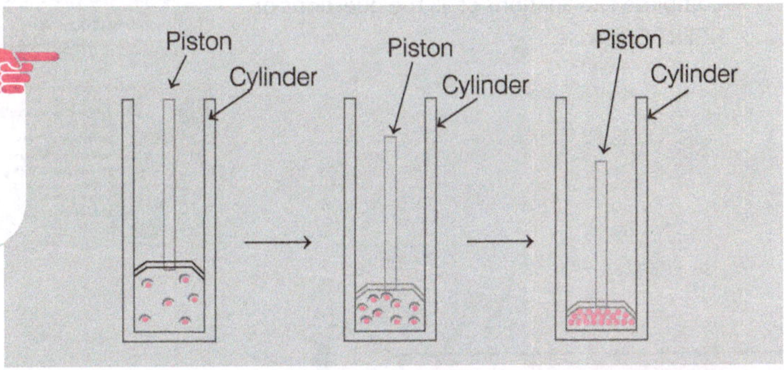

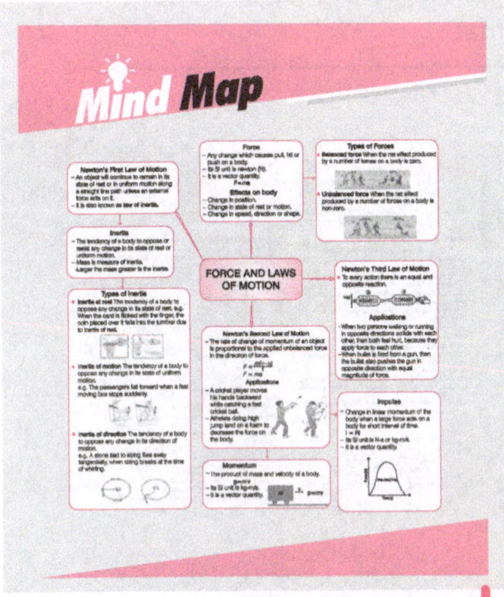

NCERT Exemplar Problems

NCERT Exemplar Problems are considered to be the best problem books for School/Board Examinations. To make students practice of exemplary questions given in this book, each chapter has selected problems from NCERT Exemplar.

9 **Which condition out of the following will increase the evaporation of water?** **NCERT Exemplar**

(a) Increase in temperature of water

(b) Decrease in temperature of water

(c) Less exposed surface area of water

(d) Adding common salt to water

Sol. (*a*) Increase in temperature of water will increase the evaporation of water. It is because, on increasing the temperature, kinetic energy of water molecules increases and more particles get enough kinetic energy to go into the vapour state.

Mind Map

A quick revision visual toll for the complete chapter.

One Book - Endless Features

to Help you Succeed

NCERT Folder

Complete explanations of all the questions of NCERT Excercise.

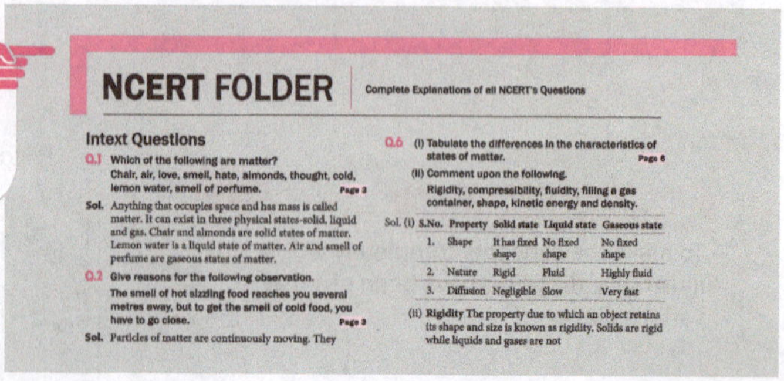

Review Excercise

Chapter exercise having all types of questions; MCQs, Assertion-Reason, Case based, VSA, SA, LA.

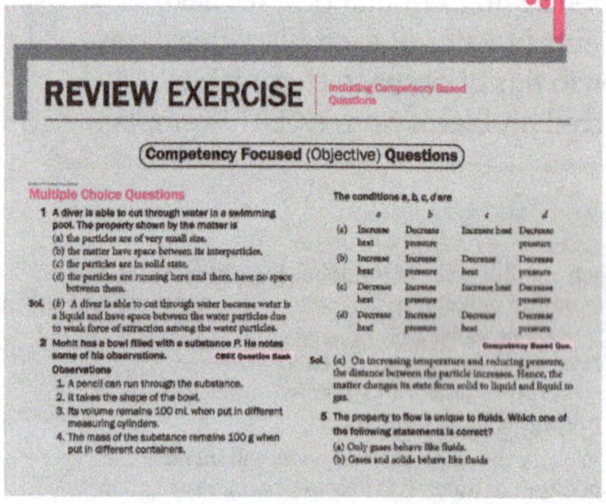

Assessment Excercise

Complete Test of chapter in Exam format.

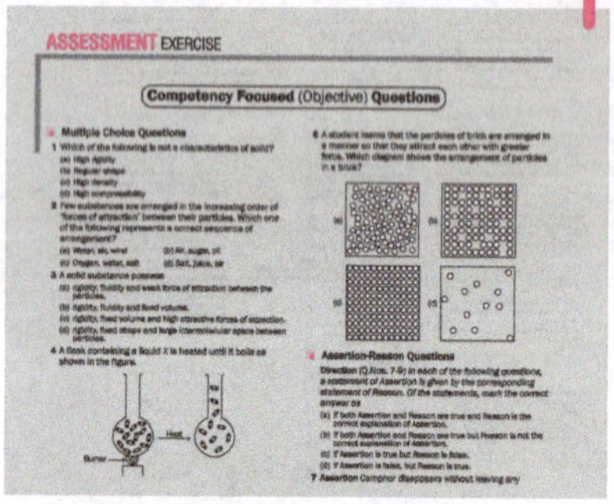

Sample Question Papers

To make students practice of examination in real sense, there are 3 Sample Question Papers at the end. All these Sample Questions Papers are exactly prepared on the latest syllabus & pattern of examination.

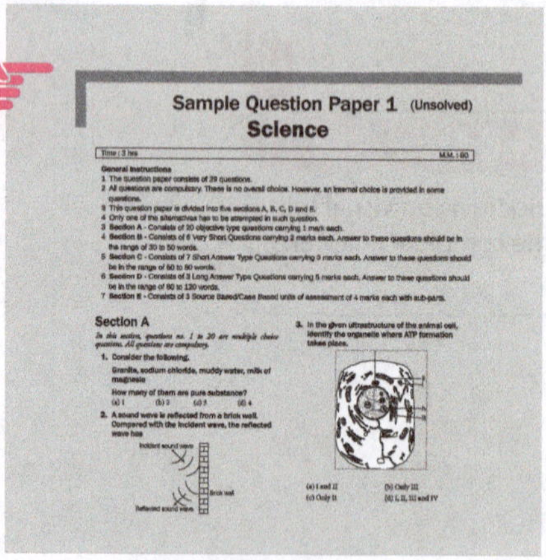

Latest Course Structure

Unit No.	Unit	Marks
I	Matter- Its Nature and Behaviour	25
II	Organisation in the Living World	22
III	Motion, Force and Work	27
IV	Food; Food Production	06
	Total	**80**
	Internal Assessment	20
	Grand Total	**100**

THEME Materials

UNIT I : Matter- Nature and Behaviour

Definition of matter; Particular Nature of Matter : Solid, Liquid and Gas and their Characteristics - Change of state-Melting (absorption of heat), Freezing, Evaporation (cooling by evaporation), Condensation, Sublimation.

IS Matter Around us Pure : Elements, Compounds and Mixtures, Heterogeneous and Homogeneous Mixtures, Colloids and Suspensions. Physical and chemical changes (excluding separating the components of a mixture). Pure and Impure Substances

Atoms and Molecules : Atoms and Molecules, Law of Chemical Combination, Chemical formula of common compounds, Atomic and Molecular Masses.

Structure of Atoms Sub-atomic Particles Electrons, Protons and Neutrons, Models of atom Valency, atomic Number and mass number, Isotopes and Isobars.

THEME The World of the Living

UNIT II : Organisation in the Living World

Cell - Basic Unit of Life Cell as a Basic Unit of Life; Prokaryotic and Eukaryotic Cells, Multicellular Organisms; Cell Membrane and Cell Wall, Cell Organelles and Cell Inclusions; Chloroplast, Mitochondria, Vacuoles, Endoplasmic Reticulum, Golgi Apparatus; Nucleus, Chromosomes - Basic Structure, Number.

Tissues, Organs, Organ System, Organism Structure and Functions of Animal and Plant Tissues (only four types of tissues in animals; Meristematic and permanent tissues in plants).

The following topics are included in the syllabus but will be assessed only formatively to reinforce understanding without adding to summative assessments. The reduces academic stress while ensuring meaningful learning. Schools can integrate these with existing chapters as they align well. Relevant NCERT textual material is enclosed for reference.

Health and Diseases: Health and its failure. Infectious and Non-infectious diseases, their causes and manifestation. Diseases caused by microbes (Virus, Bacteria and Protozoans) and their prevention; Principles of treatment and prevention. Pulse Polio programmes.

THEME Moving Things, People and Ideas

UNIT III : Motion, Force and Work

Motion Distance and Displacement, Velocity; Uniform and Non-Uniform Motion Along a Straight Line; Acceleration, Distance-time and Velocity-time Graphs for Uniform Motion and Uniformly Accelerated Motion, Elementary Idea of Uniform Circular Motion.

Force And Newton's Laws Force and Motion, Newton's Laws of Motion, Action and Reaction Forces. Inertia of a Body, Inertia and Mass, Momentum, Force and Acceleration.

The following topics are included in the syllabus but will be assessed only formatively to reinforce understanding without adding to summative assessments. The reduces academic stress while ensuring meaningful learning. Schools can integrate these with existing chapters as they align well. Relevant NCERT textual material is enclosed for reference.

Elementary idea of conservation of Momentum

Gravitation Gravitation; Universal Law of Gravitation, Force of Gravitation of the Earth (gravity), Acceleration due to Gravity; Mass and Weight; Free Fall.

Floatation Thrust and Pressure, Archimedes Principle, Buoyancy,

Work, Energy and Power Work done by a Force, Energy, Power; Kinetic and Potential Energy; Law of Conservation of Energy (excluding commercial unit of Energy)

Sound Nature of Sound and its Propagation in Various Media, Speed of Sound, Range of Hearing in Humans; Ultrasound; Reflection of Sound; Echo

THEME Food

UNIT IV : Food Production

Plant and Animal Breeding and Selection for Quality Improvement and Management; Use of Fertilizers and Manures; Protection from Pests and Diseases; Organic Farming.

List of Experiments

Practicals should be conducted alongside the concepts taught in theory classes

1. Preparation of — UNIT-I
   a. a true solution of common salt, sugar and alum
   b. a suspension of soil, chalk powder and fine sand in water
   c. a colloidal solution of starch in water and egg albumin/milk in water and distinguish between these on the basis of
      - Transparency
      - Filtration Criterion
      - Stability
2. Preparation of — UNIT-I
   a. a mixture
   b. a compound

   using iron filings and sulphur powder and distinguish between these on the basis of
   i. appearance, i.e., homogeneity and heterogeneity
   ii. behaviour towards a magnet
   iii. behaviour towards carbon disulphide as a solvent
   iv. effect of heat
3. Perform the following reactions and classify them as physical or chemical changes — UNIT-I
   a. Iron with copper sulphate solution in water
   b. Burning of Magnesium in air
   c. Zinc with dilute sulphuric acid
   d. Heating of copper sulphate crystals
   e. Sodium sulphate with barium chloride in the form of their solutions in water
4. Preparation of stained temporary mounts of (a) onion peel, (b) human cheek and to record observations and draw their labelled diagrams. — UNIT-II
5. Identification of parenchyma, Collenchyma and sclerenchyma tissues in plants, striped smooth and cardiac muscle fibers and nerve cells in animals, from prepared slides. Draw their labelled diagrams. — UNIT-II
6. Determination of the melting point of ice and the boiling point of water. — UNIT-I
7. Verification of the laws of reflection of sound. — UNIT-III
8. Determination of the density of solid (denser than water) by using a spring balance and a measuring cylinder. — UNIT-III
9. Establishing the relation between the loss in weight of a solid when fully immersed in — UNIT-III
   a. tap water
   b. strongly salty water with the weight of water displaced by it by taking at least two different solids.
10. Determination of the speed of a pulse propagated through a stretched string/slinky (helical spring). — UNIT-III
11. Verification of the law of conservation of mass in a chemical reaction. — UNIT-III

Matter In Our Surroundings

CHAPTER 01

In our surroundings, we see a large variety of objects with different shapes, sizes and textures. All objects infact everything in this universe is made up of material which scientists have named 'matter'. Thus, we can say that anything that has both mass and volume and occupies space is called **matter**. The air we breathe, the food we eat, the clothes we wear, stones, clouds, stars, plants, animals and even a small drop of water or a particle of sand—everything is matter. Matter can be seen, tasted, smelled or felt.

Classification of Matter

- Early Indian philosophers classified matter into five basic elements, called the ***Panch-Tatva***. These are **air, water, earth, sky** and **fire**.
  According to them, everything, living or non-living, was made up of these five basic elements.
- Ancient Greek philosophers had arrived at a similar classification of matter.
- Now-a-days, matter is classified into groups according to their physical properties and chemical nature.
  e.g. **Solid, liquid** and **gas** (based on particle arrangement or physical properties) or **elements, compounds** and **mixtures** (based on chemical nature).

Physical Nature of Matter

When we study the physical composition of matter, we found that

- Every matter is made up of certain particles which differ in shape, size and nature from other type of matter.
- The particles of matter are very small or tiny (beyond our imagination).

Characteristics of Particles of Matter

Some important characteristics of particles of matter are as follows

- Particles of matter have space between them. These spaces in between the particles are called **interparticle spaces.**
- Particles of matter are in a state of continuous movement. This suggests that they possess some energy, called the **kinetic energy**. As the temperature rises, the kinetic energy of the particles increases and hence, particles move faster.
- Particles of matter have a tendency to intermix on their own with each other. They do so by getting into the spaces between the particles. This intermixing of particles of two different types of matter on their own is called **diffusion**.
- Particles of matter attract each other. Thus, a force of attraction exists between the particles. This force keeps the particles together. The strength of this force of attraction varies from one kind of matter to another.

1.1 States of Matter

Matter around us exists in three different states which are **solid, liquid** and **gas**. These states of matter arise due to the variation in the characteristics of the particles of matter.

The Solid State

Solid is defined as that form of matter in which constituent particles are held very close to each other in an orderly fashion. As a result of which, less or negligible movement occurs between their particles. Magnified schematic picture of solid state is shown below.

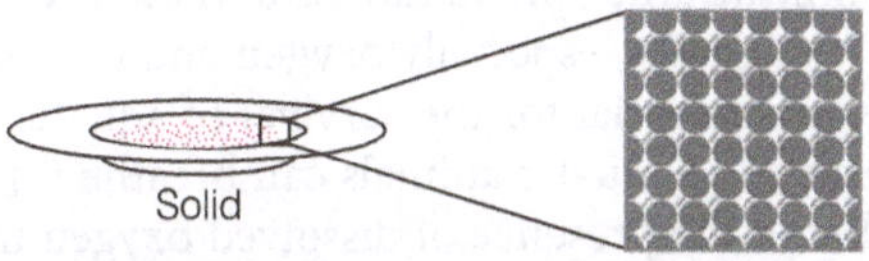

Because of such arrangement of particles, solid states of matter exhibits the following properties.

- Solids have definite shape, distinct boundaries and fixed volumes, i.e. have negligible compressibility.

  e.g. Sugar and salt take the shape of the container in which they are placed but are considered as solids. This is because the shape of each individual sugar or salt crystal remains fixed.

> **Sponge** is compressible, but considered as a solid. This is because a sponge has minute holes, in which air is trapped. When it is pressed, the air is expelled out and we are able to compress it.

- They have a tendency to maintain their shape when subjected to outside force. They may break under force, but it is difficult to change their shape, so they are considered as rigid.

  e.g. A rubber band changes its shape under force and regains the same shape when the force is removed. If excessive force is applied, it breaks.

- Generally, solids have higher densities as compared to their liquid or gaseous forms as they have very small interparticle spaces.

Note Mass per unit volume of a substance is called **density**.

The Liquid State

Liquid is defined as that form of matter in which constituent particles are arranged close to each other. However, they can move around but in a restricted way. Magnified schematic picture of liquid state is shown below.

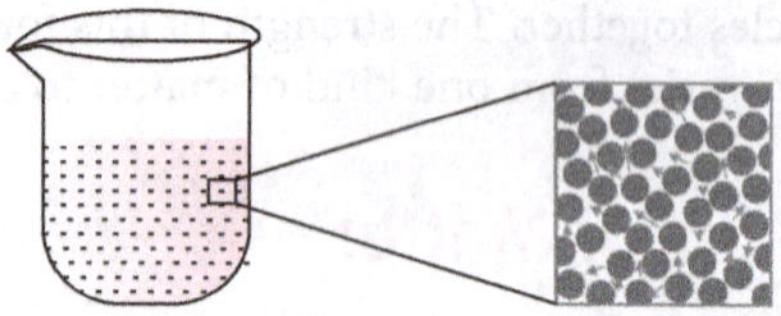

Liquid

Because of such arrangement of particles, liquid state exhibits the following properties

- Liquids have a fixed volume but do not have a definite shape, i.e. they take up the shape of the container in which they are kept.
- Liquids can flow and change shape, so they are not rigid, but can be called **fluid**.

Note In science, the common name of gases and liquids is fluid.

- Solids, liquids and gases can diffuse into liquids. The gases from the atmosphere diffuse and dissolve in water. These gases, especially oxygen and carbon dioxide, are essential for the survival of aquatic animals and plants. The aquatic animals can breathe under water due to the presence of dissolved oxygen in water.
- The rate of diffusion of liquids is higher than that of solids. This is due to the fact that in the liquid state, particles move freely and have greater space between them as compared to particles in the solid state.
- Liquids are almost incompressible.
- The attraction force between the particles of liquid is greater than that of gases, but less than that of solids.
- Density of a liquid is generally less than that of its solid form. Some exceptions are also there, e.g. solid ice is lighter than water as it floats on water.

The Gaseous State

Gases can be defined as that form of matter in which the constituent particles are far apart from each other as compared to those present in solid or liquid states. As a result of which, the movement of the constituent particles is easy and fast. Magnified schematic picture of the gaseous state is shown below

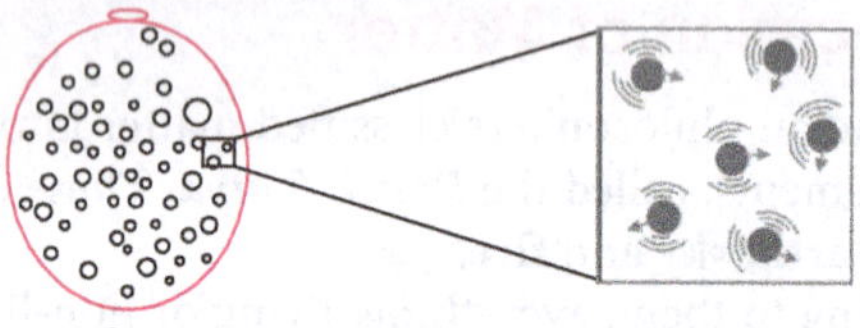

Gas

Because of such arrangement of particles, gaseous state exhibits the following properties.

- Gases have a tendency to flow as liquids do. Therefore, they are also considered as **fluids**.
- Gases show the property of diffusing very fast into other gases due to high speed of particles and large spaces between them.

  Due to the high diffusion tendency of gases, the smell of hot cooked food in the kitchen reaches us in seconds without even entering there. The particles of the aroma of food mix with the particles of air spread from the kitchen, reach us and even farther away.

- Gases are highly compressible. The **Liquefied Petroleum Gas** (LPG) cylinder used in our homes for cooking and the oxygen supplied to hospitals in cylinders is compressed gas. **Compressed Natural Gas** (CNG) is used as a fuel these days in vehicles.
- In gaseous state, the particles move randomly at high speed. Due to this random movement, gases exert pressure on the walls of the container in which they are kept. The pressure exerted by the gas is because of the force exerted by gas particles per unit area on the walls of the container.

- The density of gases is minimum as compare to other states. A gas is much lighter than the same volume of a solid or a liquid.

Comparison of Three States of Matter

Property	Solid state	Liquid state	Gaseous state
Shape	Fixed shape	No fixed shape	No fixed shape
Compressibility	Can't be compressed	Can't be compressed easily	Can be compressed easily
Nature	Rigid	Fluid	Fluid
Diffusion	Negligible	Slow	Very fast

Rigidity and Fluidity

Rigid means inflexible. A solid is a rigid form of matter, hence it does not require a container to keep it. **Fluid** is a material which can flow easily and requires a vessel to keep it. A liquid is a fluid form of matter which takes the shape of container, while a gas is a fluid form of matter which fills the container.

Try These 1.1

1. **What was the basic classification of matter in ancient time? Name them.**
2. **By which physical process the fragrance of burning incense stick spreads all around?**
3. **What property of solids that defines their ability to conduct electricity?**
4. **Why liquid and gas are called fluid?**
5. **Why solid ice floats on water?**

1.2 Change of States of Matter

In your daily life, you come across various substances which exist in three states, i.e. solid, liquid and gas, e.g. water, wax, ghee, etc. Water is the most commonly observed example that exists as ice (solid), water (liquid) as well as water vapour (gas). The states of matter are interconvertible.

Following two factors (or any one of these) make it possible to convert one state of matter into another

(i) Change in temperature. (ii) Change in pressure.

Terms Involved in Change of State

The following terms are involved in change of state.

1. Fusion (or Melting) and Melting Point

The process of conversion of a matter from its solid state to liquid state (usually by heating) is called **fusion/melting.**

The minimum temperature at which a solid melts to become a liquid at the atmospheric pressure is called the **melting point** of that solid. e.g. Melting point of ice is 0°C or 273.15 K.

The melting point of a solid indicates the strength of the force of attraction between its particles. Higher the melting point of a solid stronger are the forces of attraction between the constituents particles.

2. Boiling and Boiling Point

The process of conversion of a matter from its liquid state to vapours (gaseous state) at specific conditions of temperature and pressure is called **boiling.**

The temperature at which a liquid starts boiling at the atmospheric pressure is known as its **boiling point.**

Boiling is a bulk phenomenon because in this, the particles of the bulk of liquid gain energy and then get converted into gaseous or vapour state.

The boiling point of water is 373 K or 100°C.

3. Vaporisation

The process of conversion of a matter from its liquid state to gaseous state at specific conditions of temperature and pressure is called **vaporisation.**

4. Sublimation

The process of change of solid state directly into gaseous state without passing through the liquid state is known as **sublimation.**

The direct change of gas to solid without changing into liquid is called **deposition.**

e.g. Naphthalene, camphor, iodine, ammonium chloride, etc., are the solids that undergo sublimation.

5. Freezing and Freezing Point

The process of conversion of matter from its liquid state to solid state at specific conditions of temperature and pressure is called **freezing.** It is a reverse process of fusion/melting.

The definite temperature at which a liquid changes into solid state by giving out heat energy at 1 atm is called the **freezing point.**

6. Condensation

The process of conversion of matter from its gaseous state to liquid state at specific conditions of temperature and pressure is called **condensation.** It is a reverse process of vaporisation.

1.3 Effect of Change of Temperature

When a solid is heated, the kinetic energy of its particles increases. Due to the increase in kinetic energy, the particles start vibrating with greater speed. The energy supplied by the heat overcomes the forces of attraction between the particles.

The particles leave their fixed positions and start moving more freely. At a certain stage (i.e. at melting point), solid melts and is converted into a liquid state. The temperature of the system does not change after the melting point is reached, till all the ice melts. This happens even though we continue to supply heat. This heat gets used up in changing the state. As this heat energy is absorbed by ice without showing any rise in temperature, it is considered that it gets hidden and is known as latent heat (which is discussed below). When we continously supply heat energy, particles start moving faster. At a certain temperature, a point is reached when the particles have enough energy to break free from the forces of attraction of each other. At this temperature (i.e. boiling point), the liquid starts changing into gas.

In contrast, by decreasing the temperature (by cooling), a gas can be converted into liquid state and a liquid can be converted into solid state.

Effect of change of temperature on the physical state may be summarised as

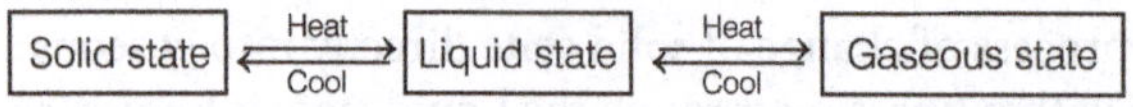

> **Difference between Gas and Vapour**
>
> A substance is said to be a gas if its boiling point is below room temperature, e.g. O_2, N_2, CO_2, etc. If the normal physical state of a substance is either a solid or a liquid, but gets converted into the gaseous state either on its own or by absorbing energy, that gaseous state is called the vapour state, e.g. vapours of water in air.

Scales of Measuring Temperature

Kelvin (K) is the SI unit of temperature.

Temperature on Kelvin scale

$$= \text{Temperature on Celsius scale} + 273$$

Temperature on Celsius scale

$$= \text{Temperature on Kelvin scale} - 273$$

$$0°\text{C} = 273.15\ \text{K} \approx 273\ \text{K}$$

Latent Heat

The heat energy which has to be supplied to change the state of substance without changing its temperature, is called its **latent heat**. In actual, the word 'latent' means 'hidden'.

Latent heat is of the following two types

Latent Heat of Fusion (Solid to Liquid Change)

The amount of heat energy that is required to change 1 kg of a solid into liquid at atmospheric pressure at its melting point is known as the **latent heat of fusion**. Particles in water at 0°C (273.16 K) have more energy as compared to particles in ice at the same temperature.

Latent Heat of Vaporisation (Liquid to Gas Change)

The amount of heat energy that is required to convert 1 kg of a liquid into gas (at its boiling point) without any rise in temperature is known as the **latent heat of vaporisation**. Particles in steam, i.e. water vapours at 373 K (100°C) have more energy than water at the same temperature.

1.4 Effect of Change of Pressure

The physical state of a substance can also be changed by changing the pressure. An increase in pressure brings the particles closer and increases the force of attraction between them, that brings about the change. As when high pressure is applied to a gas and its temperature is reduced, the gas is converted to a liquid, i.e. the gas is liquefied.

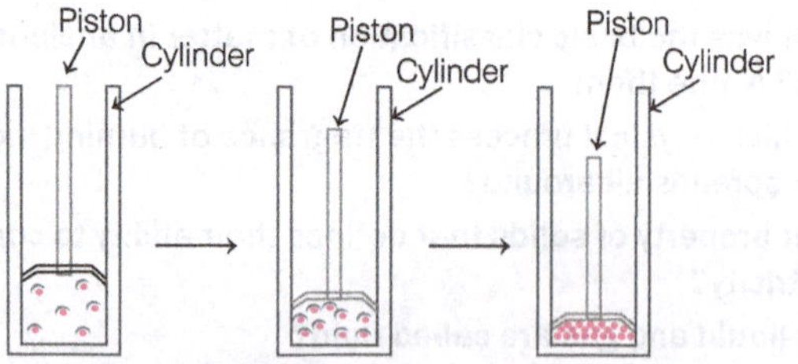

By applying pressure, particles of matter can be brought close together

e.g. Solid carbon dioxide can be stored under high pressure. Solid CO_2 gets converted directly into gaseous state on decrease of pressure to 1 atmosphere without coming into liquid state. This is the reason that solid carbon dioxide is also known as dry ice.

Thus, we can conclude that pressure and temperature determine the state of a substance, whether it will be solid, liquid or gas.

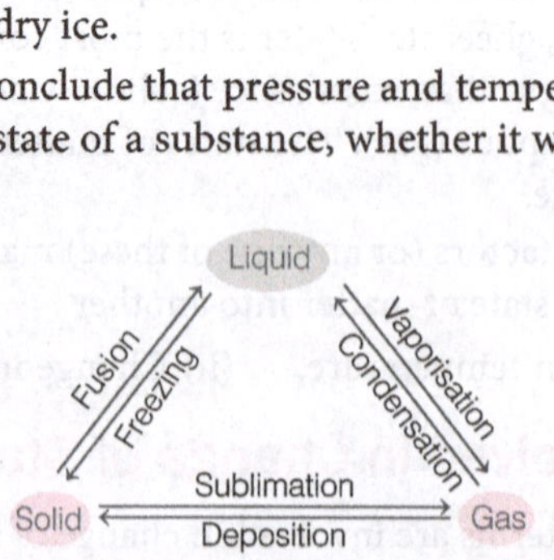

Interconversion of the three states of matter

Unit of Pressure

The unit of pressure is pascal (Pa). Atmosphere (atm) is a unit of measuring pressure exerted by a gas. The pressure of air in atmosphere is called **atmospheric pressure.** The atmospheric pressure at sea level is 1 atmosphere and is taken as the normal atmospheric pressure.

Try These 1.2

1. **What are the factors which are responsible for bringing a change in the physical state of substance?**
2. **Why inter particles start vibrating in solids on heating?**
3. **Convert the temperature of 70 °C to the Kelvin scale.**
4. **What is the value of latent heat of fusion of ice?**
5. **How gases can be liquefy?**

1.5 Evaporation

The process of conversion of a liquid into its vapour state at any temperature below its boiling point is called **evaporation.** The particles of a liquid have different amount of kinetic energies. The particles present at the surface possess comparatively higher kinetic energy as compared to those present in the bulk.

Therefore, particles at the surface with higher kinetic energy is able to break away from the forces of attraction of other particles and get converted into vapour. Water, when left uncovered, slowly changes into vapour.

Factors Affecting Evaporation

The rate of evaporation of a liquid depends upon the following factors

(i) **Surface area** Evaporation is a surface phenomenon. If the surface area is increased, the rate of evaporation increases. e.g. While putting clothes for drying up we spread them out.

(ii) **Temperature** The rate of evaporation of a liquid increases with a rise in temperature. With the increase of temperature, more number of particles get enough kinetic energy to go into the vapour state. That is why, evaporation is faster in a hot summer day than in winter or on a cloudy day.

(iii) **Humidity** It is the amount of water vapour present in air. The air around us cannot hold more than a definite amount of water vapour at a given temperature. If the humidity is high, the rate of evaporation decreases. That is why, clothes dry up faster on a dry day than on a wet (rainy) day.

(iv) **Wind speed** We know that clothes dry faster on a windy day. This is because with increase in wind speed, the particles of water vapour move away with the wind, decreasing the amount of water vapour in the surroundings.

Evaporation Causes Cooling Effect

In an open vessel, the liquid keeps on evaporating. The particles of liquid absorb energy from the surrounding to regain the energy lost during evaporation. This absorption of energy from the surroundings makes the surroundings cold.

Some daily life examples of cooling effect of evaporation are given below.

- When ice-cold water is kept in a glass tumbler for some time, water droplets are observed on its outer surface.

  Explanation This occurs as the water vapours present in the air come in contact of the surface of the glass tumbler, get cooled and condensed to form surface of the small water droplets. The formation of drops of water on the outside surface of a tumbler containing crushed ice, shows the presence of water vapour in air.

- Cotton clothes are preferred to wear during summer season.

  Explanation Cotton is a good absorber of water, so it helps to absorb sweat from our body. As it is obvious, the person sweats (perspire) more during summer due to auto temperature control mechanism. Hence, wearing of cotton clothes helps in the easy evaporation of sweat. When this sweat evaporates, it takes the latent heat of vaporisation from our body, which in turn, cools the body. Thus, a person feels comfortable.

- People sprinkle water on the roof or open ground on a hot sunny day.

  Explanation When water is sprinkled on a hot surface, it gets evaporated very quickly. As evaporated water leaves the surface cool due to the large latent heat of vaporisation of water, this technique is quite effective in summers for cooling the surface.

- Liquids like acetone (nail-polish remover) or alcohol placed on your palm give you feeling of cooling.

  Explanation Acetone and alcohol are volatile liquids. When kept on palm, their particles gain energy from the palm or surroundings and evaporate, causing the palm to feel cool.

Note The liquids which evaporate fast at room temperature are called **volatile liquids.**

Try These 1.3

1. **Why is evaporation called a surface phenomenon?**
2. **Give reason, clothes dry faster in sunlight than in cloudy day.**
3. **By which physical process wet clothes dry up?**
4. **Name the chemical compound contains in nail-polish remover.**
5. **Why do we feel cool by placing alcohol on our palm?**

Mind Map

MATTER IN OUR SURROUNDINGS

Matter is anything which has mass and occupy space. It is made up of tiny particles.

Composition of matter

Particles
These are very small in size and have mass.

Characteristics of Particles of Matter
- Have intermolecular space.
- Have force of attraction.
- Are in a state of continuous motion.
- Have a tendency to diffuse.
Property of diffusion increases with increase in temperature.

States of Matter
- **Solids**
They are rigid, have high density, definite shape and definite volume. Solids have maximum attraction force between their particles.
- **Liquids**
They have definite volume, but not definite shape. They are incompressible, have fluidity and diffusibility. The attraction force between the particles of liquid is less than that of solid.
- **Gases**
They have neither definite shape nor definite volume. They are highly compressible, diffusible and have low density. The intermolecular space between their molecules is maximum and attraction force is minimum.

Basic Quantities and its Units

Quantity	Unit	Symbol
Temperature	Kelvin	K
Length	metre	m
Mass	kilogram	kg
Weight	Newton	N
Volume	cubic metre	m^3
Density	kilogram per cubic metre	kg m^{-3}
Pressure	Pascal	Pa

Change of States of Matter

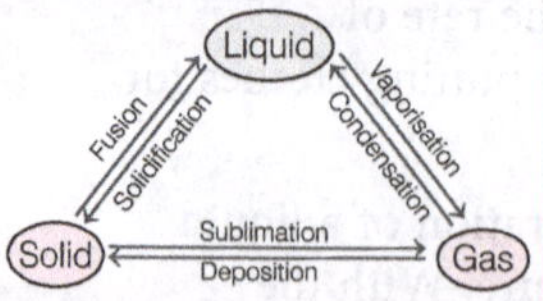

Effect of change of temperature

Increase in temperature

Melting
It is the process of conversion of solid into liquid.
Increase in temperature increases the kinetic energy of particles, they start moving freely and at one point matter change to liquid state.

Latent Heat of Fusion
It is the amount of heat that is required to change 1 kg of a solid into liquid at 1 atm at its melting point.

Melting Point
It is the temperature at which a solid starts melting at atmospheric pressure.
Melting point of ice is 0°C or 273.15 K.

Sublimation
It is the process of conversion of a solid into its vapour It is shown by naphthalene, camphor, iodine etc.
It can occur either by change in temperature or by change in pressure. e.g. conversion of dry ice into gas can be done either by increasing temperature or decreasing pressure.

Evaporation
It is the process of conversion of a liquid into its vapours at any temperature below its boiling point.
Factors affecting Evaporation
1. Exposed surface area
2. Temperature
3. Humidity
4. Wind speed

Boiling Point
It is the temperature at which a liquid starts boiling or at which vapour pressure of a liquid becomes equal to atmospheric pressure .

Vaporisation
It is the process of conversion of a liquid into its vapour state at its boiling point.

Latent Heat of vaporisation
It is the amount of heat that is required to convert 1 kg of a liquid into gas at its boiling point without any rise in temperature.

Decrease in temperature

Freezing Point
It is the temperature at which a liquid changes into solid state by giving out heat at 1 atm.

Scales of Measuring Temperature
Kelvin scale (K) and Celsius scale (°C)
$T\ (K) = t\,°C + 273.15$
or $t\,°C = T\ (K) - 273.15$

Effect of Change of Pressure

Condensation
It is the process of conversion of gas into liquid at specific conditions of temperature and pressure.

NCERT FOLDER

Complete Explanations of all NCERT's Questions

Intext Questions

Q.1 Which of the following are matter?
Chair, air, love, smell, hate, almonds, thought, cold, lemon water, smell of perfume. **Page 3**

Sol. Anything that occupies space and has mass is called matter. It can exist in three physical states-solid, liquid and gas. Chair and almonds are solid states of matter. Lemon water is a liquid state of matter. Air and smell of perfume are gaseous states of matter.

Q.2 Give reasons for the following observation.
The smell of hot sizzling food reaches you several metres away, but to get the smell from cold food you have to go close. **Page 3**

Sol. Particles of matter are continuously moving. They possess kinetic energy. As the temperature rises, the rate of diffusion increases and the particles of the aroma of hot food mix with the particles of air and reach to us several metres away, but to get an aroma or smell of cold food, we have to go close because the particles that carry smell of cold food diffuses slower as compared to particles that carry smell of hot sizzling food.

Q.3 A diver is able to cut through water in a swimming pool. Which property of matter does this observation show? **Page 3**

Sol. This observation shows that the particles of matter have spaces between them.

Q.4 What are the characteristics of the particles of matter? **Page 3**

Sol. The characteristics of particles of matter are as follows

(i) They are very small in size and have space between them.

(ii) They move faster in gaseous state as compared to solid or liquid state.

(iii) They have force of attraction between them and diffuse faster at higher temperature.

Q.5 The mass per unit volume of a substance is called density (Density = Mass/Volume).
Arrange the following in the order of increasing density. **Page 6**
Air, exhaust from chimneys, honey, water, chalk, cotton and iron.

Sol. The increasing order of density is
Air < exhaust from chimneys < cotton < water <honey < chalk < iron.

Q.6 (i) Tabulate the differences in the characteristics of states of matter. **Page 6**

(ii) Comment upon the following.
Rigidity, compressibility, fluidity, filling a gas container, shape, kinetic energy and density.

Sol. (i)

S.No.	Property	Solid state	Liquid state	Gaseous state
1.	Shape	It has fixed shape	No fixed shape	No fixed shape
2.	Nature	Rigid	Fluid	Highly fluid
3.	Diffusion	Negligible	Slow	Very fast

(ii) **Rigidity** The property due to which an object retains its shape and size is known as rigidity. Solids are rigid while liquids and gases are not.

Compressibility The property due to which a substance reduced to its lower volume when force is applied is called compressibility. Gases are the most compressible while solids and liquids are not.

Fluidity The property due to which a substance tends to flow is known as fluidity. Gases and liquids can flow, hence they are known as fluids.

Filling a gas container Particles of a gas move freely in all the directions and occupy all the space available to them. Hence, gas fills the container completely.

Shape The geometry of an object is called its shape. Solids have a definite shape while gases and liquids do not.

Kinetic energy The energy of particles of matter due to their movement is called their kinetic energy. Gases have maximum kinetic energy among the three states of matter. Kinetic energy increases with the rise in temperature and *vice-versa*.

Density The mass per unit volume of a substance is called its density.

$$\text{Density} = \frac{\text{Mass}}{\text{Volume}} \quad \text{or} \quad D = \frac{m}{V}$$

Generally, a substance has maximum density in its solid state as compared to liquid or gaseous state.
S.I. unit of density is kg m^{-3}.

Q.7 Give reasons. **Page 6**

(i) A gas fills completely the vessel in which it is kept.

(ii) A gas exerts pressure on the walls of the container.

(iii) A wooden table should be called a solid.

(iv) We can easily move our hand in air but to do the same through a solid block of wood, we need a karate expert.

Sol. (i) Particles of gas have least forces of attraction between them hence, they move freely in all directions and occupy all the space available to them. Hence, a gas fills the vessel completely in which it is kept.

(ii) Due to high kinetic energy possessed by the gas particles, they randomly move at a high speed within the container.

Due to this random movement, the particles hit each other as well as the walls of the container. The force by which these particles strike the container exerts a pressure on its walls.

(iii) A wooden table has a definite shape and volume. It is very rigid and cannot be compressed. As wood has all the characteristics of a solid, hence, a wooden table should be called solid.

(iv) Particles of air are very far apart from each other due to negligible forces of attraction between them. Therefore, our hands get sufficient space to move in air.

We also displace the air particles without much effort. But in a solid block of wood, particles are closely packed with least space between them due to strong forces of attraction between their particles. Thus, there is no possibility of moving hands through a block of wood.

Q.8 Liquids generally have lower density as compared to solids. But you must have observed that ice floats on water. Find out why? Page 6

Sol. The mass per unit volume of a substance is called density. As the volume of a substance increases, its density decreases.

Though, ice is a solid, but it has a cage-like structure in which some spaces are present between the particles of water (these spaces are left when water solidifies).

These spaces are trapped by the air particles. In fact, these spaces are larger as compared to the spaces present between the particles of water. Thus, the volume of ice is greater than that of water. Hence, the density of ice is less than that of water. A substance with lower density than water can floats on water. Thus, ice floats on water.

Q.9 Convert the following temperature to Celsius scale.

(i) 300 K (ii) 573 K Page 9

Sol. For converting Kelvin to Celsius, the formula is $K - 273 = °C$.

(i) $300\text{ K} - 273 = 27°C$

(ii) $573\text{ K} - 273 = 300°C$

Q.10 What is the physical state of water at

(i) 250 °C? (ii) 100 °C? Page 9

Sol. (i) Water vapour or steam.

(ii) Liquid water as well as water vapour, as steam and water co-exist at 100°C.

Q.11 For any substance, why does the temperature remain constant during the change of state? Page 9

Sol. During the change of state, the temperature remains constant because the heat provided is utilised for breaking the attraction forces between the particles of the substance.

Q.12 Suggest a method to liquefy atmospheric gases. Page 9

Sol. Applying high pressure or reducing temperature, helps to liquefy atmospheric (or any other) gases. Because under these conditions, the particles come closer, kinetic energy decreases and thus, gas is liquefied.

Q.13 Why does a desert cooler cool better on a hot dry day? Page 10

Sol. On a hot dry day, the temperature is high and humidity is low. The rate of evaporation increases with increase in temperature and decrease in humidity. A desert cooler functions on the principle of evaporation. The water takes heat from the hot desert cooler and evaporates. The evaporation of water cools the pads and the circulating water. As a result, the incoming air also gets cooled down.

Q.14 How does the water kept in an earthen pot (matka) become cool during summer? Page 10

Sol. Earthen pots contain tiny pores. During summer, when water is poured into an earthen pot, some of the water seeps through pores to the outer surface.

The water molecules on evaporation escape from the tiny pores of the earthen pot. The heat required for evaporation is taken from the earthen pot and the water in it. This results in lowering of the heat content of the remaining water and the water becomes cool.

Q.15 Why does our palm feel cold when we put some acetone or petrol or perfume on it? Page 10

Sol. Acetone, petrol and perfume are volatile liquids which evaporate readily. When these liquids kept on palm, their particles gain energy from the palm or surroundings and evaporate, thus causing the palm to cool.

Q.16 Why are we able to sip hot tea or milk faster from a saucer rather a cup? Page 10

Sol. A saucer and plate has more surface area in comparison to cup. Therefore, evaporation of tea occur more in the saucer rather than cup and more cooling observed in a saucer.

Q.17 What type of clothes should we wear in summer? **Page 10**

Sol. We should wear cotton clothes in summer because cotton is a good absorber of water and helps in absorbing the sweat and exposing it to the atmosphere for easy evaporation thereby, causing cooling sensation.

Exercise

Q.1 Convert the following temperatures to the Celsius scale.

(i) 293 K **(ii) 470 K**

Sol. (i) 293 K − 273 = 20°C (ii) 470 K − 273 = 197°C

Q.2 Convert the following temperatures to the Kelvin scale.

(i) 25°C **(ii) 373°C**

Sol. (i) 25°C + 273 = 298 K

(ii) 373°C + 273 = 646 K

Q.3 Give reason for the following observations:

(i) Naphthalene balls disappear with time without leaving any solid.

(ii) We can get the smell of perfume sitting several metres away.

Sol. (i) Naphthalene being a sublimable substance converts directly from solid to gaseous state by taking heat from the surroundings through the process, called sublimation. The naphthalene balls keep on forming naphthalene vapours which slowly disappears into the air. Hence, no residue is left after sometime.

(ii) The smell or aroma of perfume reaches several metres away due to the fast diffusion of the gaseous particles of perfume through air.

Q.4 Arrange the following substances in increasing order of forces of attraction between the particles–water, sugar, oxygen.

Sol. Oxygen(gas) < Water (liquid) < Sugar (solid).

Q.5 What is the physical state of water at

(i) 25 °C? **(ii) 0 °C?** **(iii) 100 °C?**

Sol. (i) Liquid state

(ii) Solid or liquid state (transition state)

(iii) Liquid or gaseous state

Q.6 Give two reasons to justify.

(i) Water at room temperature is a liquid.

(ii) An iron almirah is solid at room temperature.

Sol. (i) Water is liquid at room temperature as

(a) it has a tendency to flow.

(b) it takes the shape of the vessel in which it is filled, but its volume does not change.

(ii) An iron almirah is solid at room temperature because

(a) it has definite shape and volume.

(b) it is hard and rigid.

Q.7 Why is ice at 273 K more effective in cooling than water at the same temperature?

Sol. When ice melts, it absorbs the energy equal to the latent heat of fusion from the surroundings so, it causes cooling more effectively than the water at same temperature (because water does not absorb energy from the surroundings).

Q.8 What produces more severe burns, boiling water or steam?

Sol. Steam causes more severe burns than boiling water. The reason is that it releases the extra amount of heat (latent heat) which it has already taken during vaporisation (when the steam was formed from water).

Q.9 Name *A, B, C, D, E* and *F* in the following diagram showing change in its state.

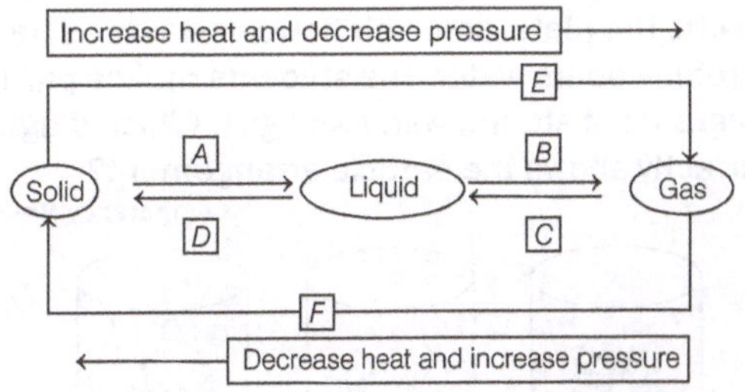

Sol. *A* = Melting or fusion, here the solid changes into liquid.

B = Evaporation or vaporisation, here the liquid changes into gas.

C = Condensation or liquefaction, here the gas changes into liquid.

D = Freezing or solidification, here the liquid changes into solid.

E = Sublimation, here solid directly changes into gas without coming in liquid state.

F = Deposition, here gas changes into solid without coming in liquid state.

To Study NCERT Activities
Scan the Code

REVIEW EXERCISE

Including Competency Based Questions

Competency Focused (Objective) Questions

Multiple Choice Questions

1 A diver is able to cut through water in a swimming pool. The property shown by the matter is

(a) the particles are of very small size.

(b) the matter have space between its interparticles.

(c) the particles are in solid state.

(d) the particles are running here and there, have no space between them.

Sol. (*b*) A diver is able to cut through water because water is a liquid and have space between the water particles due to weak force of attraction among them.

2 A student has a glass of hot water which is covered with a plate. The student wants to transfer the hot water into another glass. The student notices that as he lifts the plate, some air flows upwards as he carefully pours water. The students makes particle diagrams of steam, water and gas. Which diagram correctly shows the particle arrangement?

Competency Based Que.

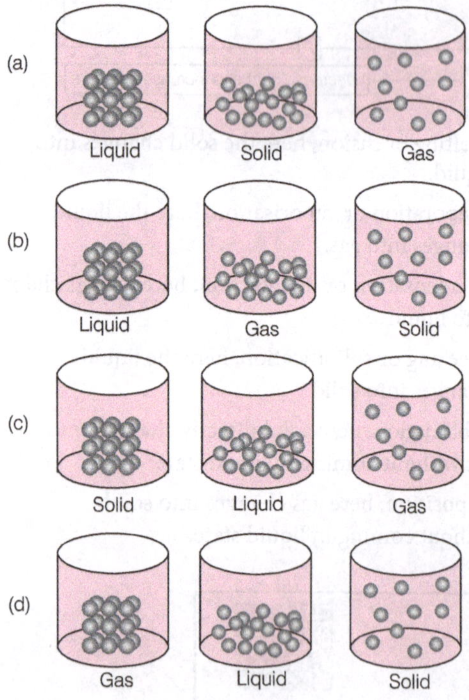

Sol. (*c*) Among the given diagrams, (c) represent the correct set of particle arrangement. Because in solid state, atoms or molecules occupy fixed positions with respect to each other and unable to move freely. Whereas, in a liquid state, particles are less tightly packed as compared to solids and in gaseous state particles are far apart, fast-moving and not organised in any particular way.

3 Match Column I with Column II and select the correct option using the given codes.

Column I	Column II
A. Particles in solids	(i) closely packed but can slide past each other.
B. Particles in liquids	(ii) tightly packed and only vibrate in place.
C. Particles in gases	(iii) maximum in gases.
D. Compressibility	(iv) Can move freely and are far apart.

(a) A-(i), B-(iii), C-(ii), D-(iv)

(b) A-(ii), B-(i), C-(iv), D-(iii)

(c) A-(i), B-(ii), C-(iv), D-(iii)

(d) A-(ii), B-(i), C-(iii), D-(iv)

Sol. (*b*) The correct match is, A-(ii), B-(i), C-(iv), D-(iii).

4 Mohit has a bowl filled with a substance *P*. He notes some of his observations. **CBSE Question Bank**

Observations

1. A pencil can run through the substance.
2. It takes the shape of the bowl.
3. Its volume remains 100 mL when put in different measuring cylinders.
4. The mass of the substance remains 100 g when put in different containers.

What can substance *P* be classified as?

(a) A gas because it has a volume.

(b) A solid because it has a fixed mass.

(c) A liquid because its shape changes.

(d) A gas because objects can pass through it.

Sol. (*c*) *P* is a liquid substance. This is because liquid has fixed volume but does not have fixed shape.

5 Liquids diffuse at the slower rate than gases because

(a) the molecules of liquid move fast.
(b) the molecules of liquid are too heavy.
(c) the gases do not have definite shape.
(d) there is strong intermolecular forces in liquids than gases.

Sol. (*d*) Liquids diffuse slowly than gases because in liquids, the intermolecular forces are stronger and intermolecular spaces are lesser than gases.

6. Masood wanted to find out which state of a substance dissolves faster in water.

He filled two similar glass jars with the same amount of water.

Masood added to following substances to the jars of water.

- 10 g of copper sulphate crystal to Jar 1.
- 10 mL of 75% copper sulphate solution to Jar 2.

The table below shows the colour of the water in each jar after specific time periods.

Jar	Colour of water in the jars		
	After 5 minutes	After 30 minutes	After 60 minutes
Jar 1	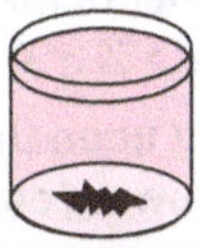	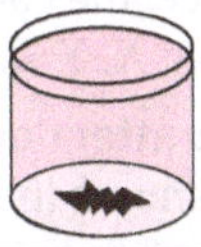	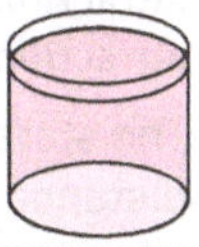
Jar 2	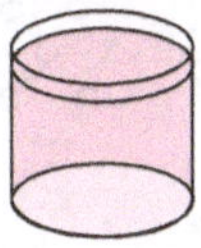	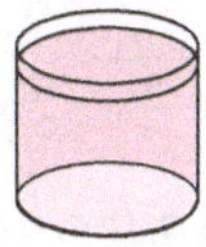	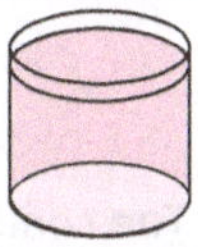

Which statement can be concluded from Masood's activity? **Competency Based Que.**

(a) Crystals dissolve partially in water.
(b) Liquids dissolve faster than solids in water.
(c) Copper sulphate dissolves faster in water than in any other liquid.
(d) Particles of a liquid have a stronger force of attraction than that of a solid.

Sol. (*b*) Liquids dissolve faster than solids in water because the particles of a liquids have a weaker force of attraction between them than that of a particles of solids.

7 The property to flow is unique to fluids. Which one of the following statements is correct?

(a) Only gases behave like fluids.
(b) Gases and solids behave like fluids.
(c) Gases and liquids behave like fluids.
(d) Only liquids are fluids. **NCERT Exemplar**

Sol. (*c*) Gases and liquids behave like fluids. Both gases and liquids tend to flow due to less force of attraction between their particles.

8 In which conversion, do particles of water lose speed? **Competency Based Que.**

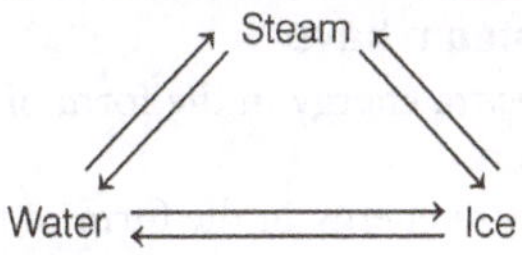

(a) Ice → Water
(b) Ice → Steam
(c) Steam → Ice
(d) Water → Steam

Sol. (*c*) Particles of water lose speed when they give out heat. Steam condenses into water and water freezes into ice. Both condensation and freezing involve loss of heat to the surroundings and hence, loss of speed in water particles.

9 Which of the following changes represents the process of deposition? **Competency Based Que.**

(a) Solid → Liquid
(b) Liquid → Gas
(c) Gas → Liquid
(d) Gas → Solid

Sol. (*d*) In the process of deposition, gas is converted to solid directly without changing into its liquid state.

10 Gases can be converted to liquid by

(a) decreasing temperature, decreasing pressure
(b) decreasing temperature, increasing pressure
(c) increasing temperature, decreasing pressure
(d) increasing temperature, increasing pressure

Sol. (*b*) By lowering the temperature or increasing the pressure, the interparticles space decreases and thus, gases can be converted into liquid.

11 The kinetic energy of interparticles is maximum in

(a) wood (b) ghee (c) table (d) oxygen

Sol. (*d*) The space between the particles of gas is maximum, thus among the given, oxygen has maximum kinetic energy.

12 The conditions under which air is liquefied are

(a) high temperature, low pressure
(b) low temperature, high pressure
(c) high temperature, high pressure
(d) low temperature, low pressure

Sol. (*b*) At low temperature and high pressure, the air can be liquefied.

13 The process of sublimation can be observed in

(a) ammonium chloride, naphthalene, ice
(b) camphor, ammonium chloride, naphthalene
(c) ice, water, camphor
(d) steam, naphthalene, sodium chloride

Sol. (*b*) Sublimation is the process of conversion of solid into gas directly. The substances like camphor, ammonium chloride and naphthalene shows sublimation process.

14 **Particles in steam at 373 K have more energy than water at the same temperature. This is because the particles in steam have**

(a) absorbed extra energy in the form of latent heat of vaporisation.
(b) released extra energy in the form of latent energy.
(c) absorbed extra energy in the form of latent heat of fusion.
(d) absorbed extra energy in the form of kinetic energy.

Sol. (*a*) Particles in steam that is, water vapour at 373 K (100°C) have more energy than water at the same temperature.

This is because the particles in steam have absorbed extra energy in the form of latent heat of vaporisation.

15 **Which of the following is not a characteristics of gas?**

(a) High rigidity (b) High compressibility
(c) Low density (d) High rate of diffusion

Sol. (*a*) Gases are not rigid at all. They are highly flexible and highly compressible.

16. **Tina found three syringes of the same size closed with rubber cork.**

She took the piston out of each syringe and filled them with coconut oil, sawdust and cotton.

Tina closed the end of each syringe with piston.

She then tried to press the piston of each syringe as much as possible. **Competency Based Que.**

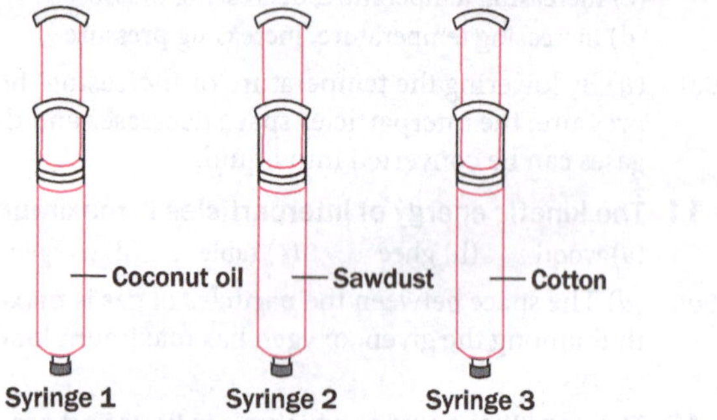

Arrange the syringes in increasing order of difficulty of pressing the piston.

key : less difficult → more difficult

(a) Syringe 1 → Syringe 2 → Syringe 3
(b) Syringe 3 → Syringe 1 → Syringe 2
(c) Syringe 1 → Syringe 3 → Syringe 2
(d) Syringe 2 → Syringe 3 → Syringe 1

Sol. (*b*) It is easier to press the piston of a syringe filled with cotton (Syringe 3) than one filled with coconut oil (Syringe 1) and one with sawdust (Syringe 2). This is because cotton is compressible, so it is easy for the piston to move. Whereas, coconut oil is a liquid, so it compresses more easily then solid objects like sawdust. However, it may provide some resistance.

17 **Which of the following statement(s) regarding S.I. units is/are not correct?**

(a) S.I. unit of temperature is Celsius.
(b) S.I. unit of pressure is Pascal.
(c) S.I. unit of density is kg/m^3.
(d) S.I. unit of volume is m^3.

Sol. (*a*) S.I. unit of temperature is Kelvin (K).

18 **Aquatic animals using oxygen dissolved in water because of the phenomenon of**

(a) osmosis (b) diffusion
(c) sublimation (d) transpiration

Sol. (*b*) Aquatic animals use oxygen dissolved in water because of the phenomenon of diffusion. The spontaneous mixing of the particles of solids or liquids or gases to form homogeneous mixtures is called diffusion.

19 **The melting point of three solids *X*, *Y* and *Z* are 280 K, 1670 K and 380 K respectively. The forces of attraction are in order of** **Competency Based Que.**

(a) $X > Y > Z$ (b) $X > Z > Y$
(c) $Y > Z > X$ (d) $Z > Y > X$

Sol. (*c*) Higher the melting point, more will be the forces of attraction. Hence, the correct order of the forces of attraction among *X*, *Y* and *Z* is $Y > Z > X$.

20 **The states of matter depending upon the interparticle distances are shown in the following diagram.**

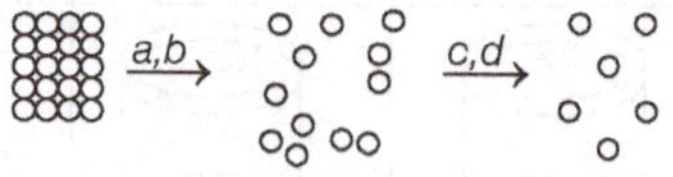

The conditions *a*, *b*, *c*, *d* are

	a	*b*	*c*	*d*
(a)	Increase heat	Decrease pressure	Increase heat	Decrease pressure
(b)	Increase heat	Increase pressure	Decrease heat	Decrease pressure
(c)	Decrease heat	Increase pressure	Increase heat	Decrease pressure
(d)	Decrease heat	Increase pressure	Decrease heat	Decrease pressure

Competency Based Que.

Sol. (*a*) On increasing temperature and reducing pressure, the distance between the particle increases. Hence, the matter changes its state form solid to liquid and liquid to gas.

21 **The boiling points of diethyl ether, acetone and *n*-butyl alcohol are 35°C, 56°C and 118°C, respectively. Which one of the following correctly represents their boiling points in Kelvin scale?** **NCERT Exemplar**

(a) 306 K, 329 K, 391 K (b) 308 K, 329 K, 392 K
(c) 308 K, 329 K, 391 K (d) 329 K, 392 K, 308 K

Sol. (*c*) The correct order of boiling points of diethyl ether, acetone and *n*-butyl alcohol in Kelvin scale is 308 K, 329 K and 391 K respectively, which can be explained as

Boiling point of diethyl ether

$$= 35°C + 273 = 308 \text{ K}$$

$$(\because T°C + 273 = T\text{K}).$$

Boiling point of acetone $= 56°C + 273 = 329$ K

Boiling point of *n*-butyl alcohol

$$= 118°C + 273 = 391 \text{ K}$$

22 Which condition out of the following will increase the evaporation of water? NCERT Exemplar

(a) Increase in temperature of water.
(b) Decrease in temperature of water.
(c) Less exposed surface area of water.
(d) Adding common salt to water.

Sol. (*a*) Increase in temperature of water will increase the evaporation of water. It is because, on increasing the temperature, kinetic energy of water molecules increases and more particles get enough kinetic energy to go into the vapour state.

23 During summer, water kept in an earthen pot becomes cool because of the phenomenon of NCERT Exemplar

(a) diffusion (b) transpiration
(c) osmosis (d) evaporation

Sol. (*d*) During summer, water kept in an earthen pot becomes cool because of the phenomenon of evaporation. Earthen pot has a large number of tiny pores in its walls and some of the water molecules continuously keep seeping through these pores to outside the pot.

24 How can the process of evaporation be increased?

(a) By decreasing surface area .
(b) By increasing temperature.
(c) By increasing humidity.
(d) By decreasing wind speed.

Sol. (*b*) The rate of evaporation of a liquid increases with increase in temperature.

25 Consider the following statements regarding change of state.

(i) During the change of state from solid to liquid and liquid to solid, temperature remains constant.
(ii) Dry ice is stored at low temperature.
(iii) Evaporation occurs faster from brine solution (water + salt) than from ordinary water.
(iv) Like naphthalene, ammonium chloride also sublimes.

The incorrect statement(s) is/are

(a) Only (i) (b) Both (i) and (iii)
(c) Only (iii) (d) (i), (ii), (iii) and (iv)

Sol. (*c*) Evaporation occurs faster in ordinary water than brine solution. Thus, statement (iii) is incorrect.

Assertion-Reason Questions

Direction (Q.Nos. 1-8) In each of the following questions, a statement of Assertion is given by the corresponding statement of Reason. Of the statements, mark the correct answer as

(a) If both Assertion and Reason are true and Reason is the correct explanation of Assertion.
(b) If both Assertion and Reason are true but Reason is not the correct explanation of Assertion.
(c) If Assertion is true but Reason is false.
(d) If Assertion is false but Reason is true.

1 Assertion (A) Smell of burning incense stick spreads all around due to the diffusion of its fumes into air.

Reason (R) Increased temperature results in increased kinetic energy of the molecules.

Sol. (*a*) Both Assertion and Reason are true and Reason is the correct explanation of Assertion.

2 Assertion (A) The smell of hot cooked food reaches us in seconds.

Reason (R) Rate of diffusion of solids is greater than that of gases.

Sol. (*c*) The smell of hot cooked food reaches us in seconds. This is because, gases show the property of diffusing into other gases very fast in high temperature.

Rate of diffusion of gases is greater than solid.

Hence, Assertion is true but Reason is false.

3 Assertion (A) Naphthalene does not leave a residue when kept open for sometime.

Reason (R) The conversion of a gas directly into solid is called condensation.

Sol. (*c*) Naphthalene being a sublimate converts directly into vapour and hence, does not leave a residue when kept open for sometime.

Conversion of a gas directly into solid (without coming into liquid state) is called sublimation while condensation is the process of conversion of a gas into its liquid form.

Hence, Assertion is true but Reason is false.

4 Assertion (A) There is no change in the temperature of a substance when it undergoes a change in its physical state.

Reason (R) The heat supplied is absorbed either as latent heat of fusion or as latent heat of vaporisation.

Sol. (*a*) Both Assertion and Reason are true and Reason is the correct explanation of Assertion.

5 **Assertion** (A) Ice cubes float on water.

Reason (R) Ice cubes are solid in nature.

Sol. (*b*) Ice cubes being a solid floats on water because the density of ice cubes is less than water.

Both Assertion and Reason are correct, but Reason is not the correct explanation for Assertion.

6 **Assertion** (A) Solids may break by applying force but it is difficult to change their shape.

Reason (R) Solids are rigid.

Sol. (*a*) Due to rigidity, the shape of solids cannot be changed easily but can be beaten or broken by applying force.

Hence, both Assertion and Reason are true and Reason is the correct explanation of Assertion.

7 **Assertion** (A) Interparticles in liquid state shows motion.

Reason (R) They possess potential energy.

Sol. (*c*) The interparticles in liquid shows motion which is due to kinetic energy.

Hence, Assertion is true but Reason is false.

8 **Assertion** (A) During evaporation of liquids, the temperature remains unaffected.

Reason (R) Kinetic energy of the particles is directly proportional to temperature.

Sol. (*d*) During evaporation of liquids the temperature increases and, thus kinetic energy of the particles also increases.

Hence, Assertion is false but Reason is true.

Case Based/Source Based Questions

Direction (1-4) Answer the questions on the basis of your understanding of the following passage and related studied concepts:

1 **A student of a class performed an experiment in a chemistry laboratory. He took a conical flask containing ice cubes and placed the flask on a burner with a thermometer suspended in it. Student recorded the following observations in his note book. The observations are**

Time (min)	0	2	4	6	10	15	20	25	30	35
Temp (°C)	−3	0	0	12	22	30	50	73	100	100

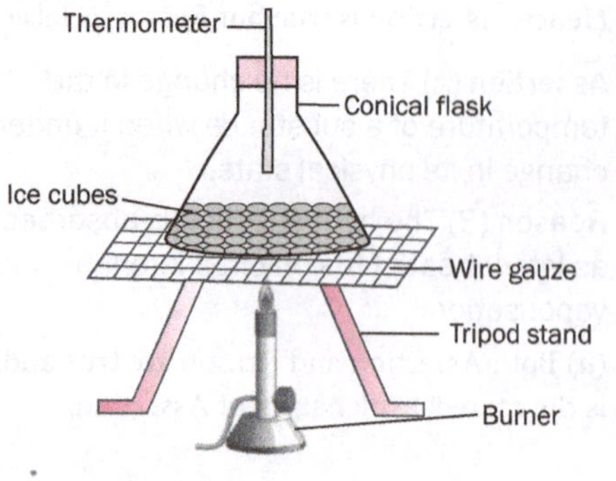

Based on the above observations, answer the following:

(i) State the change(s) observed between 2-4 minutes.

(ii) Name the process involved during the reading 2-4 minutes.

(iii) Between 30-35 minutes, the temperature remains constant. Why?

Or

Define the heat involved during 30-35 min and its SI unit.

Sol. (i) Between 2-4 minutes, ice converts into water. [1]

(ii) During 2-4 minutes, the process takes place is called fusion/melting. [1]

(iii) Between 30-35 minutes, the temperature remains constant because the heat supplied is used by the particles of liquid to break the force of attraction. [2]

Or

The heat involved during the process of 30-35 minutes is called latent heat of vaporisation. It is defined as the amount of heat energy required to change 1 kg of liquid into gas at its boiling point. Its SI unit is J/kg. [2]

2 **The rate of evaporation increases with increase in surface area, temperature, speed of wind and decrease in humidity. Evaporation causes cooling due to decrease in average kinetic energy of the remaining liquid after the surface molecules leave. Lower the boiling point of the liquid, higher is the rate of evaporation.**

(i) Why synehetic clothes are uncomfortable in summers?

(ii) The water spilled on the floor evaporates faster than the water in a glass. Explain?

(iii) You want to wear a favourite shirt to a party, but the problem is that it is still wet after a wash. Mention any two steps with reason that you would take to dry it faster.

Or

Write two factors other than temperature and surface area on which evaporation depends.

Sol. (i) Synthetic clothes are not porous and hence, they do not absorb sweat from our body. As sweat from our skin does not evaporate, the body does not lose heat energy and hence, we have an uncomfortable feeling. [1]

(ii) When the water is spilled on the floor, the surface area of water increases, hence the rate of evaporation also increases. [1]

(iii) The two steps that can dry the shirt faster are:

(a) Spread the shirt on a stand. It provides greater surface area for evaporation.

(b) Squeeze the shirt with force. By doing so, some of the moisture get removed. [2]

Or

Evaporation also depends on humidity and wind speed. Rate of evaporation increases with increase in wind speed while decreases with increase in humidity. [2]

3 A matter is anything that has mass and occupies space. Pen, paper, clips, sand, air, ice, etc., are different forms of matter. Every matter is made up of small particles. These particles are so tiny that they can't be seen with naked eyes.

Particles of matter has spaces between them and are continuously moving.

(i) Identify the matter among the following substances.
Pen, air, sense of smell, honey, water vapours

(ii) Name the energy responsible for the motion in particles of matter.

(iii) Give four examples of matter which have maximum interparticle spaces.

Or

The property of flow is unique to fluids. Explain.

Sol. (i) Pen, air, honey and water vapours come under the category of matter. [1]

(ii) Kinetic energy is responsible for the motion of particles of matter. [1]

(iii) Oxygen, air, carbon dioxide and water vapours. [2]

Or

Gases and liquids both behave like fluids because both gases and liquids tend to flow due to less force of attraction between their interparticles. [2]

4 The particles that makeup matter are constantly in motion and their motion determines the state of matter. In a solid, the particles are tightly packed and have a fixed shape and volume. In a liquid, the particles are close together but can move past each other, giving the substance a fixed volume but no fixed shape.

In a gas, the particles are far apart and move freely, allowing the substance to occupy any volume and shape.

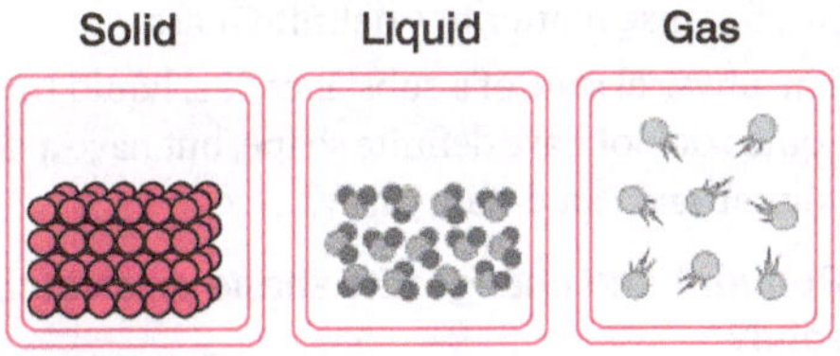

(i) How are particles arranged in a solid?

(ii) What is the behaviour of particles in a gas?

(iii) Explain why solids have fixed shape but liquids and gases do not have fixed shape.

Or Liquids and gases can be compressed but it is difficult to compress solids. Why?

Sol. (i) In solids, particles are tightly packed and have a fixed shape. [1]

(ii) The particles of gases are far apart and move freely. [1]

(iii) Solids have fixed shape due to strong force of attraction between its interparticles. On the other hand, the liquids and gases have molecules with less interparticles force of attraction and hence they can flow and take shape of the container. [2]

Or Liquids and gases have interparticles space, on applying pressure externally on them the particles can come closer thereby minimizing the space between them. But in case of solids, there is no interparticles space to do so. [2]

Constructed Response (Descriptive) Questions

Very Short Answer Type Questions

1. (i) A substance has no mass. Can we consider it as matter?

(ii) A given substance *X* has definite volume, but no definite shape and can diffuse easily. What is the physical state of a substance *X*?

Sol. (i) No, because matter has definite mass. [1]

(ii) The physical state of a substance *X* is liquid because liquids do not have definite shape, but have a definite volume and can diffuse easily. [1]

2. (i) Rubber band changes its shape on stretching. Is it solid?

(ii) Why do liquids take up the shape of the container in which they are kept?

Sol. (i) Rubber band changes its shape under force and regains its shape after removing the force, however during the process, its mass remains constant. Thus, it is a solid. [1]

(ii) Forces of attraction among the particles are not very strong in liquids which is necessary to maintain their shape. Therefore, they acquire the shape of the container in which they are kept. [1]

3. What would be the effect of

(i) temperature and

(ii) density on the rate of diffusion of liquids?

Sol. (i) On increasing temperature, the rate of diffusion of liquids increases. [1]

(ii) Rate of diffusion is more for a liquid having lower density. [1]

4. (i) Why do gases exert more pressure on the walls of the container than the solids?

(ii) Which characteristic of a gas is used in supplying oxygen cylinders to hospitals?

Sol. (i) In gases, the particles move randomly at high speed and they collide with each other and also with the walls of the container. [1]

Thus, they exert more pressure on the walls of the container than solids.

(ii) Gases are highly compressible in nature and can be liquefied. Due to these properties, gases are used in supplying oxygen cylinders to hospitals. [1]

5. (i) Why is boiling called a bulk phenomenon?

(ii) Why the temperature remains constant during sublimation?

Sol. (i) Boiling starts from the bulk, i.e. inside the liquid, therefore it is a bulk phenomenon. [1]

(ii) During the process of sublimation, heat given to the system is used up to evaporate solid into vapour at constant temperature. [1]

6. (i) What happens to the melting point of solids with the decrease in pressure?

(ii) Why should wet clothes are spread while drying?

Sol. (i) Generally, for solids like ice, melting point increases with the decrease in pressure. [1]

(ii) On spreading wet clothes, the surface area exposed to air increases and evaporation becomes faster. Thus, they dry quickly. [1]

7. (i) What is the effect of sprinkling of water on the roof or open ground on a hot sunny day?

(ii) When a solid melts, its temperature remain constant, so where does the heat energy go?

Sol. (i) The water evaporates by absorbing heat from the ground and the surrounding air. By losing heat, the roof or open ground becomes cool and people feel comfortable. [1]

(ii) When a solid melts, the heat energy given is used up to convert solid into liquid. This is called latent heat of fusion. [1]

8. Why do we sweat more in a humid day ?

Sol. In a humid day, the air around us has already contain high percentage of water vapours. Therefore, the water coming from the skin gets less opportunity to change into vapours and remain sticking to our body. Hence, we sweat more on a humid day. [2]

9. When water is cooled to a temperature *X*, it gets converted into ice by a process called *P*.

(i) What is the value of temperature *X* in Kelvin?

(ii) What is the process *P* known as?

Sol. (i) Water is converted into ice at 0°C, i.e. $(0° + 273)$ K = 273 K. [1]

(ii) The process of conversion of matter from its liquid state to solid state is called freezing. Thus, process *P* is called as freezing. [1]

10. (i) Conversion of solid to vapour is sublimation. Name the term used to denote the conversion of vapour to solid.

(ii) Conversion of solid state to liquid state is called fusion. What is meant by the latent heat of fusion?

Sol. (i) Conversion of vapour to solid without changing into liquid is known as deposition. [1]

(ii) Latent heat of fusion is the amount of heat required to convert a unit mass of the substance from a solid form to liquid form without changing the temperature. [1]

11. **(i) Solids are incompressible. Give reason.**

(ii) State one difference between gas and vapour.

Competency Based Que.

Sol. (i) Solids are incompressible because the particles are closely packed and there is negligible space for their movement. [1]

(ii) Gas is a stable state as compared to vapour which is an unstable state. [1]

12. **List any two characteristics of particulate nature of matter.**

Sol. (i) Particles of matter have space between them. [1]

(ii) Particles of matter are continuously moving. [1]

13. **(i) What do you mean by dry ice?**

(ii) What is the physical state of water at 0°C?

Sol. (i) Solid carbon dioxide is called dry ice. [1]

(ii) Physical state of water at 0°C may be solid in the forms of ice or liquid. [1]

14. **The diagram given below shows burning of an oil lamp. Draw the arrangement of particles of position of 'X' and 'Y' when the lamp is burning.**

Competency Based Que.

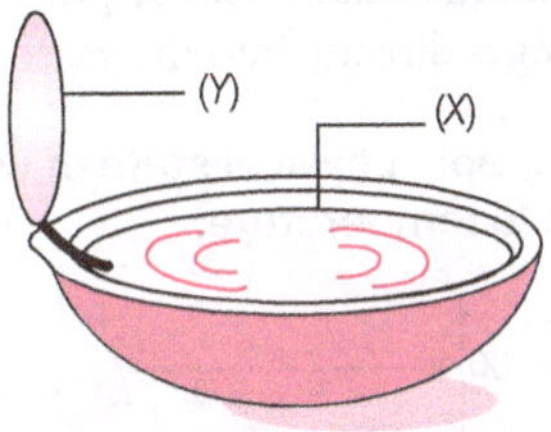

Sol.

Position (X)
This is because oil is in liquid state.

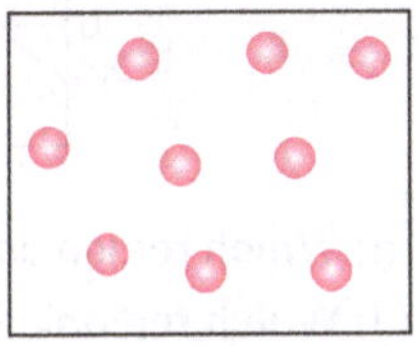

Position (Y)
This is because oil burns to produce gaseous products.

In gaseous state molecules are far apart to each other in comparision to liquid state. [2]

15. **(i) Liquids generally have lower density as compared to solids. But you must have observed that ice floats on water. Why?**

(ii) What is physical state of water at 250 °C?

Sol. (i) Ice which is solid has vacant spaces between its interparticles thus making it less dense than water. Hence, ice floats on water. [1]

(ii) Physical state of water at 250°C is a gas as its boiling point is 100°C. [1]

16. **Give reasons for the following :**

(i) Water at room temperature is a liquid.

(ii) Camphor disappear with time without leaving any solid.

Sol. (i) Water at room temperature is a liquid because it has fluidity also it has no shape but has a fixed volume that is it occupies the shape of the container in which it is kept. [1]

(ii) Camphor undergoes sublimation easily, i.e. it changes its state from solid to gas without leaving any solid. [1]

Short Answer Type Questions

1. **(i) A sponge can be compressed, yet it is a solid? Explain.**

(ii) Name the state of matter that has minimum space between particles.

(iii) Which state of matter has maximum fluidity?

Sol. (i) A sponge has minute holes, in which air is trapped, when we press it, the air is expelled out and we are able to compress it. Hence, sponge can be compressed, instead of being a solid. [1]

(ii) Solid state has minimum space between their particles among other states of matter. [1]

(iii) Gaseous state has maximum fluidity as interparticle space is maximum in it. [1]

2. **(i) Explain the interconversion of three states of matter in terms of force of attraction and kinetic energy of the particles.**

(ii) Arrange the three states of matter in the increasing order of rate of diffusion and particle motion.

Sol. (i) During the interconversion of a solid into a liquid and liquid into gas on increasing temperature, the kinetic energy of the particles increases and force of attraction among particles decreases and *vice-versa*. [2]

(ii) (a) Rate of diffusion, Solid < liquid < gas. [½]

(b) Particles motion, Solid < liquid < gas. [½]

3. **(i) How do you differentiate between, liquids and gases on the basis of their melting and boiling points?**

(ii) Kinetic energy of particles of water in three vessels A, B and C are E_A, E_B and E_C respectively and $E_A > E_B > E_C$. Arrange the temperature T_A, T_B and T_C of water in the three vessel in increasing order. **Competency Based Que.**

Sol. (i) Liquids have melting point below room temperature and boiling point above room temperature.

Gases have both melting and boiling points below room temperature. [2]

(ii) The kinetic energy of particles is greater at higher temperature.

Thus, the order is : $T_C < T_B < T_A$. [1]

4. **(i) Dry ice is compressed under high pressure. What happens to it when the pressure is released?**

(ii) A piece of chalk can be broken down into small pieces when hammered but it is not possible to do so in case of an iron bar. Explain.

(iii) Why do we feel comfortable under a fan when we are sweating on a hot summer day?

Sol. (i) On releasing the pressure, dry ice sublimes to vapour state without undergoing liquid state. [1]

(ii) The particle space between the iron bar are closely packed as compared to the piece of chalk. Thus, it is easy to break chalk into small pieces when hammered but it is not possible to do so in case of an iron bar. [1]

(iii) A fan produces feeling of comfort because our sweating evaporate rapidly due to the presence of air and make our body cool. [1]

5. **What is dry ice? How is it formed?**

Sol. Dry ice is solid carbon dioxide which sublimes to form carbon dioxide gas without undergoing into liquid state. On sublimation, vapours of carbon dioxide create a foggy dense appearance denoted by term ice. Hence, solid carbon dioxide is also termed as dry ice.

Dry ice is formed when gaseous carbon dioxide is compressed and stored under high pressure. On decreasing pressure to 1 atm, it again changes to the gaseous form without coming into liquid state. [3]

6. **(i) Draw a well-labelled diagram showing sublimation of ammonium chloride.**

(ii) What is the difference between evaporation and sublimation?

Sol. (i) Take some ammonium chloride in a China dish and place the China dish on a tripod stand. Cover the China dish with an inverted glass funnel.

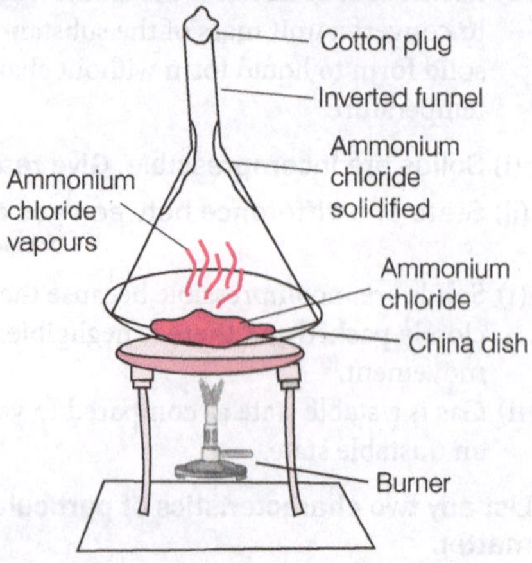

Sublimation of ammonium chloride

Put a loose cotton plug in the upper open end of the funnel to prevent the ammonium chloride vapour from escaping into the atmosphere.

The China dish is heated by using a burner. On heating, ammonium chloride changes into white vapours. These vapours rise up and get converted into solid ammonium chloride on coming in contact with the cold, inner walls of the funnel. [2]

(ii) Evaporation is the process in which the liquid state of matter changes into the gaseous state, while on the other hand, sublimation is the process in which the solid changes directly into the gaseous state of matter. [1]

7. **In the given graph, physical state of water is given with respect to temperature.**

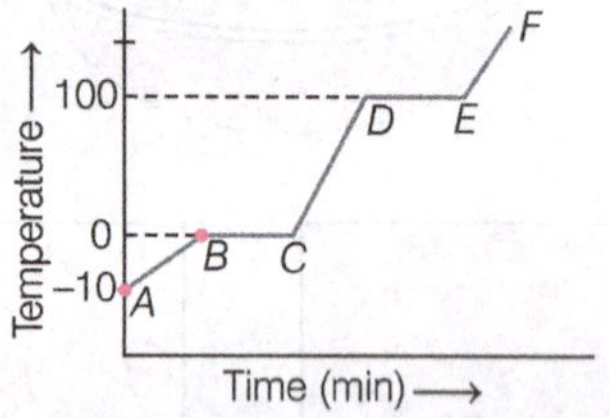

(i) Which region contains only solid?

(ii) Which region contains liquids form of water?

(iii) Which region shows latent heat of vaporisation? **Competency Based Que.**

Sol. (i) AB is the region that contains only solid in the form of ice. [1]

(ii) CD is the region that contains liquids from of water. [1]

(iii) DE is the region that shows latent heat of vaporisation. [1]

8. Substance 'A' has high compressibility and can be easily liquefied. It can take up the shape of any container. Predict the nature of the substance. Enlist four properties of this state of matter. **Competency Based Que.**

Sol. Substance 'A' is a gas.

Properties of gases are as follows

(i) They have high diffusion tendency.

(ii) They are highly compressible.

(iii) In gaseous state, the particles move about randomly at high speed.

(iv) They have minimum density. [1 × 3]

9. (i) Which factors determine the state of a substance?

(ii) Convert 30℃ into Kelvin.

(iii) Water droplets are observed on the outer surface of a glass tumbler containing ice cold water. Give reason.

Sol. (i) Temperature and pressure determine the state of a substance. [1]

(ii) 30℃ = 273 + 30 = 303 K [1]

(iii) Water droplets are observed on glass tumbler because water vapours present in the air get condensed on the cold surface of the glass which appears as water droplets. [1]

10. Give reason for the following:

(i) Butter is generally wrapped in wet cloth during summer if no refrigeration is available?

(ii) When sugar crystals dissolve in water, the level of water does not rise appreciably.

Sol. (i) In summer, the weather is quite high (hot). As a result, water present in wet cloth readily evaporates.

Since, cooling is caused during evaporation, the temperature of butter gets lowered and it does not give any foul odour. [1½]

(ii) Since, water is a liquid, there are interparticles space in it. Sugar particles occupy these spaces. As a result, water level does not rise appreciably. [1½]

11. (i) List any two properties that liquids have in common with gases.

(ii) Give two reasons to justify that a piece of wood is a solid at room temperature.

(iii) Distinguish between solids and gases on the basis of interparticle distance.

Sol. (i) (a) Gases and liquids do not have fixed shape they occupies the shape of containers in which they are kept. [½]

(b) Gases and liquids flow easily. [½]

(ii) A piece of wood is a solid at room temperature as,

(a) It is a rigid body and can't be compressed easily. [½]

(b) It has a definite shape. [½]

(iii) In solids, interparticle distance is small while in gases interparticle distance is maximum. [1]

12. Give reason : **Competency Based Que.**

(i) Solids have a fixed geometrical shape.

(ii) Gases are compressible but liquids are not.

(iii) Steam at 100 °C is better for heating than water at 100 °C.

Sol. (i) In solids, the interparticles forces are very strong. Therefore, solids have fixed geometrical shape. [1]

(ii) Interparticles space is very large in gases whereas it is very less in liquids. Thus, gases are compressible while liquids are not. [1]

(iii) Steam is better for heating than water because it possesses the additional heat i.e. latent heat of vaporisation. [1]

13. With the help of an example, explain how diffusion of gases in water is important?

Sol. The gases from the atmosphere diffuse and dissolve in water. Gases like oxygen and carbon dioxide diffuse in water, are essential for the survival of aquatic animals and plants. Animals breathe in oxygen dissolved in water for their survival and plants use carbon dioxide dissolved in water for photosynthesis. [3]

14. When a crystals of potassium permanganate is placed in a beaker containing water, its purple colour spreads throughout the water. What do you conclude from this observation about the nature of potassium permanganate and water? **Competency Based Que.**

Sol. When a few crystals of potassium permanganate are placed in a beaker containing water, we get two different layers, one is colourless water at the top and second is pink colour at the bottom. After few minutes, pink colour spreads and whole solution turns pink due to diffusion. As potassium permanganate is a solid substance, it does not possess so much space. While water particles due to liquid states, collide with solid particles and intermixes due to sufficient space between particles. [3]

15. (i) Why do the doctors advise to put strips of wet cloth on the forehead of a person having high fever?

(ii) Why do people sprinkle water on the roof in summer?

Sol. (i) When a person is suffering from fever, his body temperature becomes more than the normal body temperature. If we put strips of wet cloth on the forehead of a person suffering from high fever, the water evaporates taking heat from the body. Thus, moist strips will lower his body temperature. [1½]

(ii) Water sprinkled on the roof evaporates because of the large latent heat of vaporisation from the ground. This makes the place cool and comfortable. [1½]

16. Cotton clothes are comfortable to wear in summers. Which feature of cotton explains why cotton is comfortable to wear in summers?

Circle 'Yes' or 'No' for each row.

Why cotton is comfortable to wear in summers?	Yes or No
(a) Cotton has strong fibres.	Yes/No
(b) Cotton is a natural fabric.	Yes/No
(c) Cotton absorbs water and has pores.	Yes/No

Sol. (a) No [1]

(b) No [1]

(c) Yes, cotton easily absorbs sweat from the body due to presence of pores. Cotton clothes have fine threads which easily allow air to pass through when compared to woolen clothes. With more air flowing through the clothes, the sweat from the body and clothes gets evaporated easily, which leaves the cooling effect. [1]

17. Tina found a syringe in her science lab.

The mouth of the syringe was closed with a rubber cork.

Tina tried to press the piston of the syringe as much as possible.

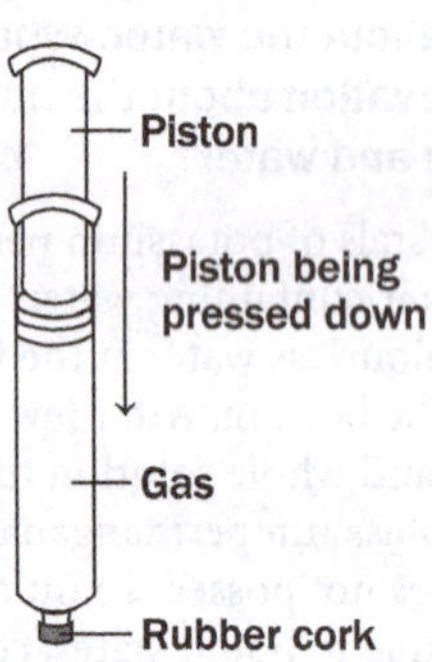

Tina found that it was difficult to press the piston as it moved deeper.

Explain the reason with reference to the change in space between the particles. **Competency Based Que.**

Sol. The difficulty experienced by Tina in pressing the piston of the syringe as it moved deeper because of the change in the space between particles of air present within the syringe.

This change in space is attributed to the concept of gas compression. Compression of a substance gets difficult when there is less space between the particles. [3]

18. (i) Ghee freezes at room temperature and mustard oil does not during winter time.

(ii) You are given a mixture of sand, sodium chloride and ammonium chloride. Write the names of two methods used to separate the components of the mixture.

Sol. (i) Since, ghee freezes at room temperature and mustard oil does not during winter time, it shows that interparticles forces of ghee are stronger as compared to those of mustard oil. [2]

(ii) (a) Ammonium chloride is separated from its mixture, with sand and sodium chloride by the process of sublimation. [½]

(b) Sodium chloride and sand are separated by the process of evaporation. [½]

19. Comment on the following statements:

(i) Evaporation produces cooling.

(ii) Rate of evaporation of an aqueous solution decreases with increase in humidity.

(iii) Sponge though compressible is a solid.

NCERT Exemplar

Sol. (i) Evaporation of liquid produces cooling because liquid takes away the heat from the surroundings, thereby producing a cooling effect. [1]

(ii) If humidity is high, then air is already saturated with water vapour, i.e. it has a lot of water vapour. Therefore, it will not take more water vapour easily. Hence, rate of evaporation decreases. [1]

(iii) Sponge has minute holes in which air is trapped. The material is also not so rigid. On pressing this, air is expelled out, that is why, it can be compressed, but it is solid as it has a definite shape and volume and does not change its shape unless compressed. [1]

20. Look at the following figures and suggest in which of the vessels *A*, *B*, *C* or *D*, the rate of evaporation will be the highest? Explain.

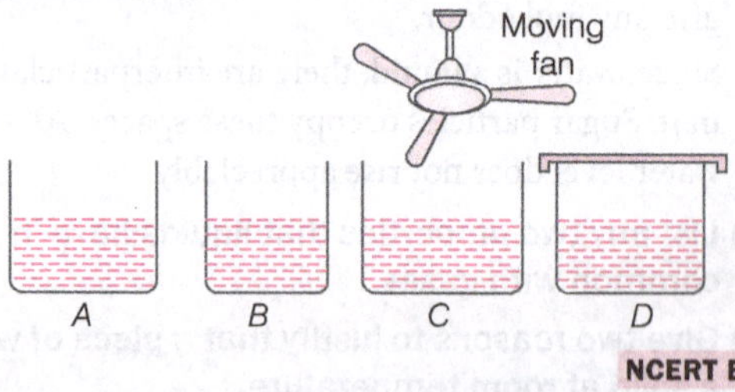

NCERT Exemplar

Sol. The rate of evaporation will be highest in vessel *C* as the surface area exposed for evaporation is larger than *B* (smaller size). The moving fan increases the wind speed which also increases the rate of evaporation. Although, *A* and *D* are also equal in size to that of *C*, but *A* is at a greater distance from the fan and *D* is covered with a lid. [3]

21. **(i) How does the change in temperature and humidity affect the rate of evaporation?**

(ii) Name the factors other than temperature and humidity which affect the rate of evaporation.

Sol. (i) When the temperature of a liquid is increased by heating, more particles of the liquid get enough kinetic energy to go into vapour state. This increases the rate of evaporation.

When the humidity of air is low, then the rate of evaporation is high and water evaporates rapidly. When the humidity of air is high then the rate of evaporation is low and water evaporates very slowly. [2]

(ii) The factors other than temperature and humidity which affect the rate of evaporation are [1]

(a) Surface area (b) Wind speed

22. **(i) It is a hot summer day. Priyanshi and Ali are wearing cotton and nylon clothes, respectively. Who do you think would be more comfortable and why?**

(ii) How evaporation depends on surface area?

Competency Based Que.

Sol. (i) Priyanshi would be more comfortable. The reason is that cotton absorbs sweat from the body and provides a larger surface area for evaporation which causes more cooling effect.

Nylon being a bad absorber of water does not absorb sweat. Thus, the sweat does not evaporate from the body and Ali would feel uncomfortable. [2]

(ii) Evaporation increases with increase in the surface area of substance. [1]

23. **Write the three differences between evaporation and boiling.**

Sol.

Evaporation	Boiling
Evaporation is a normal process that occurs when the liquid state changes into the gaseous state while causing an increase in temperature.	Boiling is an unnatural process where the liquid gets heated up and vaporised due the pressure or heating of the liquid. [1]
Evaporation usually occurs on the surface of the liquid being heated up.	Boiling usually occurs on the entire mass of the liquid that gets heated up. [1]
The process of evaporation is usually slower and carried out more as compared to boiling.	The process of boiling is usually much quicker and the process happens quite rapidly as well. [1]

24. **Mention the factors that affect evaporation.**

Sol. (i) An increase of surface area leads to increase the rate of evaporation. [1]

(ii) By increasing temperature, the evaporation process becomes faster. [1]

(iii) With an increase in wind speed, the rate of evaporation increases. [1]

Long Answer Type Questions

1 **(i) Out of boiling and evaporation which is a surface phenomenon?**

(ii) If refrigerator is not available, butter is kept wrapped in a wet cloth during summer. Why?

(iii) Ice cream feels colder than water at same temperature (say 273 K). Give reason.

Sol. (i) Out of boiling and evaporation, evaporation is a surface phenomenon.

Particles from the surface gain enough energy to overcome the force of attraction present in the liquid and change into vapour state. [2]

(ii) Due to wet cloth, the temperature is comparatively lower than room temperature. [1]

(iii) Ice cream at 273 K, which take latent heat from the medium to convert itself into liquid at 273 K and then into liquid at higher temperature but in water such condition is not possible. [2]

2 **(i) Explain the term density. Arrange different states of matter in increasing order of density.**

(ii) Explain how ice floats on water?

Sol. (i) The mass per unit volume of a substance is called density. Density depends upon the volume of the substance. Substance with small interparticle spaces have small volumes and high densities.

The increasing order of space between the particles in the different states of matter is solid < liquid < gas. Thus, the increasing order for their density would be gas <liquid<solid. [2½]

(ii) Ice is a solid, but it has a cage-like structure in which some spaces are present between the particles of water. These spaces are trapped by the air particles.

These spaces are larger as compared to the spaces present between the particles of water. Thus, the volume of ice is greater than that of water. Hence, the density of ice is less than water and it floats on water. [2½]

3 **(i) What determines the state of a substance?**

(ii) Convert 40°C into Kelvin.

(iii) Water droplets are observed on the outer surface of a glass tumbler containing ice cold water. Give reason.

(iv) What is the physical state of water at

(a) 250°C? **(b) 90°C?**

Sol. (i) The state of a substance is determined by temperature and pressure. [1]

(ii) Temperature in Kelvin = Temperature in Celsius + 273

i.e. $273 + 40 = 313$ K [1]

(iii) Water droplets are observed on glass tumbler because water vapours get condensed on the cold surface of the glass. [1]

(iv) (a) At 250°C water is in gaseous state, since it is beyond its boiling point i.e. 100°C. [1]

(b) At 90°C, water is in liquid state as its boiling point is 100°C. [1]

4 **(i) What is matter? Write two properties of solids and liquids each.**

(ii) Why does ice at 0°C appear colder in the mouth than water at 0°C?

(iii) A patient suffering from fever is advised to put the strips of wet cloth on the forehead. Explain why?

Sol. (i) Matter is a substance which has mass and occupies space.

(a) In solids, force of attraction between particles is strongest and space between its particles is very less.

(b) In liquids, force of attraction is relatively less and space between the particles is more in comparison to solids. [2]

(ii) As ice absorbs the latent heat of fusion from the mouth and therefore, it feels colder than the water at the same temperature, i.e. 0°C. [1]

(iii) As the temperature of the patient's body is high, the water from the wet strips evaporates by absorbing the heat from the body.

This lowers the body temperature of the patient. That is why, patient is advised to put the strips of wet cloth on his forehead during high fever. [2]

5 **The temperature-time graph given below shows the heating curve for pure wax.**

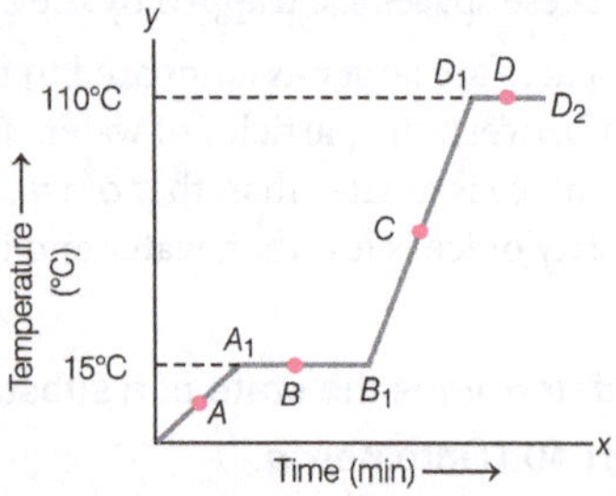

From the graph, answer the following:

(i) What is the physical state of the substance at the points *A*, *B*, *C*, and *D*?

(ii) What is the melting point of the wax?

(iii) What is its boiling point?

(iv) Which portions of the graph indicate that change of state is taking place?

(v) Name the terms used for heat absorbed during change of states involved in the above processes.

Competency Based Que.

Sol. (i) At point A = Solid wax

At point B = Solid as well as liquid wax (Melting continues)

At point C = Liquid wax

At point D = Liquid as well as vapour state (Boiling continues) [1]

(ii) Melting point of wax = 15°C [1]

(iii) Boiling point of wax = 110°C [1]

(iv) Straight lines in the curve parallel to time-axis (x-axis) indicates the change of state. These portions are A_1 to B_1 (solid to liquid) and D_1 to D_2 (liquid to vapour state). [1]

(v) Latent heat of fusion is the amount of heat required to convert a unit mass of solid into liquid at its melting point.

Latent heat of vaporisation is the amount of heat required to convert a liquid into gas at constant temperature. [1]

6 **(i) What temperature in Kelvin scale is equal to 50°C?**

(ii) Describe an activity to show that rate of evaporation increases with surface area.

Sol. (i) Temp. in Kelvin = Temp. in Celsius + 273

50°C + 273 = 323 K [1]

(ii) **Activity** Take little amount of water in three containers which have different surface areas. Keep them in sunlight for 2 h. Measure the volume of water left in all three containers. [2]

Observation The amount of water left will be least in container having largest surface area among them. [1]

Conclusion Greater the surface area, more will be the rate of evaporation. [1]

7 **(i) Name the state of matter in which**

(a) layers of particle can slip and slide over one another easily.

(b) particles just move around randomly because of very weak force of attraction.

(ii) Define density and give its SI unit.

(iii) Can a rubber band change its shape on stretching? Is it a solid?

Sol. (i) (a) Liquid state (b) Gaseous state [1]

(ii) Density of a substance is the mass per unit volume. Its SI unit kg m^{-3}. [2]

(iii) Yes, rubber band change its shape under force and regains the same shape when the force is removed. It breaks on applying excessive force. Yes it is a solid. [2]

ASSESSMENT EXERCISE

Competency Focused (Objective) Questions

Multiple Choice Questions

1 Which of the following is not a characteristics of solid?
(a) High rigidity
(b) Regular shape
(c) High density
(d) High compressibility

2 Few substances are arranged in the increasing order of 'forces of attraction' between their particles. Which one of the following represents a correct sequence of arrangement?
(a) Water, air, wind
(b) Air, sugar, oil
(c) Oxygen, water, salt
(d) Salt, juice, air

3 A solid substance possess
(a) rigidity, fluidity and weak force of attraction between the particles.
(b) rigidity, fluidity and fixed volume.
(c) rigidity, fixed volume and high attractive forces of attraction.
(d) rigidity, fixed shape and large intermolecular space between particles.

4 A flask containing a liquid *X* is heated until it boils as shown in the figure.

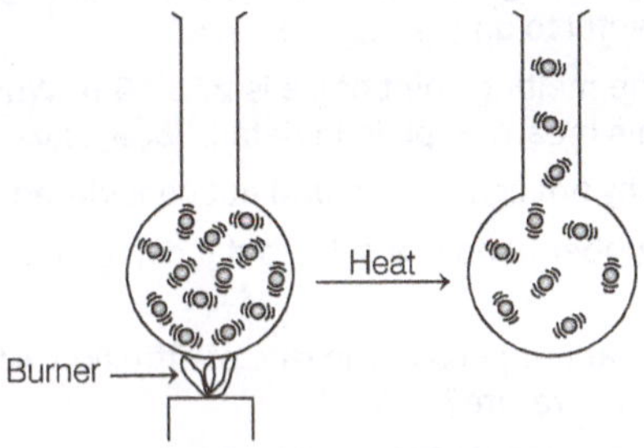

Choose the incorrect statement about the particles of the substance during the process.
(a) Energy is absorbed by particles in the liquid *X*.
(b) The particles lose kinetic energy.
(c) Eventually, the particles throughout the liquid have enough energy to overcome the forces holding them together.
(d) Both (a) and (b)

5 On converting 25°C, 38°C and 66°C to Kelvin scale, the correct sequence of temperature will be
(a) 298 K, 311 K and 339 K
(b) 298 K, 300 K and 338 K
(c) 273 K, 278 K and 543 K
(d) 298 K, 310 K and 338 K

6 A student learns that the particles of brick are arranged in a manner so that they attract each other with greater force. Which diagram shows the arrangement of particles in a brick?

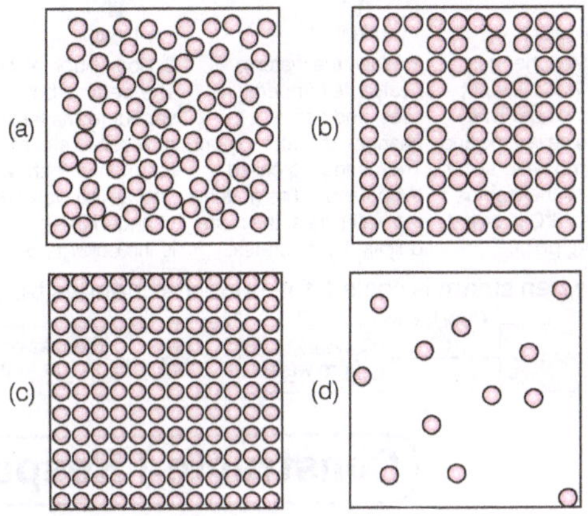

Assertion-Reason Questions

Direction (Q.Nos. 7-9) *In each of the following questions, a statement of Assertion is given by the corresponding statement of Reason. Of the statements, mark the correct answer as*
(a) If both Assertion and Reason are true and Reason is the correct explanation of Assertion.
(b) If both Assertion and Reason are true but Reason is not the correct explanation of Assertion.
(c) If Assertion is true but Reason is false.
(d) If Assertion is false, but Reason is true.

7 **Assertion** (A) Camphor disappears without leaving any residue.
Reason (R) Camphor undergoes sublimation.

8 **Assertion** (A) A sponge is the solid matter which can be easily compressed by our hand.
Reason (R) The matter around us exists in three different states i.e. solid, liquid and gas.

9 **Assertion** (A) Liquids diffuse less easily as compared to gases.
Reason (R) Forces between the particles are greater in gases than liquids.

Answers

1. (d)	**2.** (c)	**3.** (c)	**4.** (b)	**5.** (a)
6. (c)	**7.** (a)	**8.** (b)	**9.** (c)	

Case Based/Source Based Questions

Direction : (i - iii) *Answer the questions on the basis of your understanding of the following paragraph and related studied concepts:*

10 Consider the following change of state by heating or cooling.

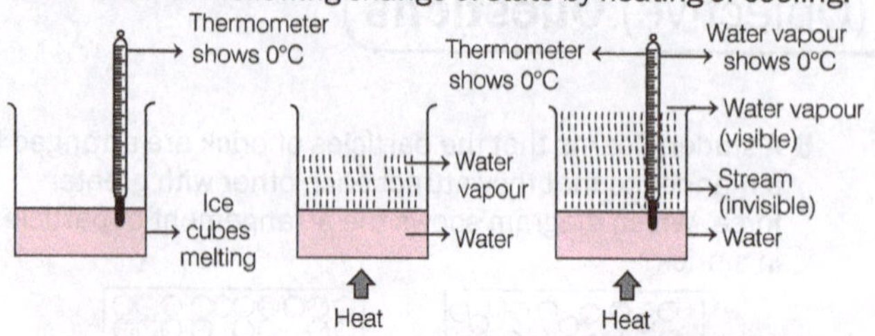

1. Ice slowly changes to water, when it is put in a warm place. This change is called melting. The thermometer show 0°C until all the ice has melted, so 0°C is called its melting point.

2. When the water is heated its temperature rises, and some of it changes to water vapour. This change is called evaporation. The hotter the water gets, the more quickly it evaporates.

3. Soon bubbles appear. The water is boiling. Water vapour forms faster. It is now called steam. The thermometer shows 100°C until all the water has changed to steam, 100°C is the boiling point to water.

And when steam is cooled, the opposite changes take place:

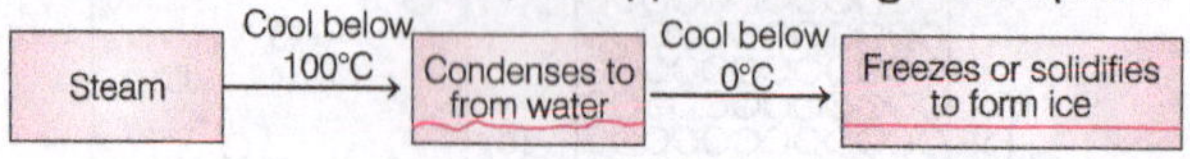

A few substances change straight from solid to gas without becoming liquid, when they are heated, the change is called sublimation. Carbon dioxide and iodine both sublime.

(i) The image shows two changes.

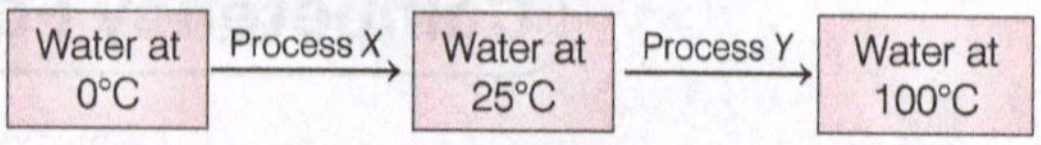

Identify process *X* and *Y*.

(ii)

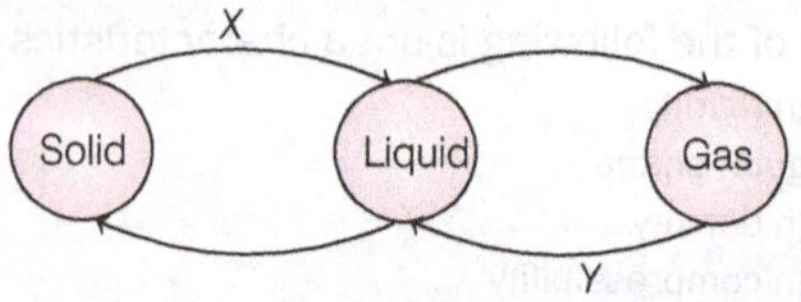

The diagram shows the change of state of H_2O. What is the process *X* called?

(iii) In the above diagram, what is the process *Y* called? Also, state the process of deposition.

Or

In which process particles move far from each other and vibrate strongly breaking the attractive force among them?

Constructed Response (Descriptive) Questions

Very Short Answer Type Questions

11 When a drop of blue ink is put in water, the blue colour spreads and the whole solution becomes blue. Explain the phenomenon in brief due to which this happens. **Competency Based Que.**

12 Out of dry and wet air which one is heavier? Give reason for your answer.

13 What happens when an inflated air balloon pricked with a pin? Name the property of the gaseous state exhibited by this observation.

14 Name two solid substances that can be converted to gas by sublimation.

15

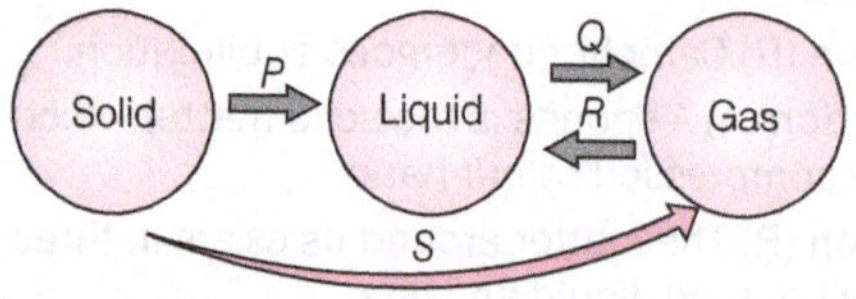

(i) Name the changes in the terms of process *P, Q, R* and S.

(ii) Which of the changes are exothermic and endothermic?

16 Explain what happens to the molecular motion and energy of 1 kg of water at 273 K when it is changed into ice at same temperature. How is the latent heat of fusion related to the energy exchange that takes place during this change of state? **Competency Based Que.**

Short Answer Type Questions

17 (i) Why do solids are generally denser than liquids and gases?

(ii) With the help of an example, explain how diffusion of gases in water is essential?

18 (i) How is high compressibility property of gas is useful to us?

(ii) The melting point of ice is 273.16 K. What does this mean? Explain in detail. **Competency Based Que.**

19 (i) Why are light and sound not considered as matter?

(ii) Rubber band is a solid, but it can change its shape. Why?

(iii) What happens to the rate of diffusion with temperature?

20 When ice at –10°C is slowly heated, temperature of ice gradually increases till 0°C, the temperature of the system remains constant when the ice changes into water and then further rises. Explain the observation.

Long Answer Type Questions

21 (i) For any substance, why does the temperature remain constant during the change of state?

(ii) Suggest a way to liquify atmospheric gases

(iii) Differentiate between liquid and gas on the basis of

(a) compressibility (b) rigidity

22 (i) Pressure and temperature determine the state of a substance. Explain this in detail.

(ii) Dry ice is compressed under high pressure. What happen to it when the pressure is released?

CHAPTER 02

Is Matter Around Us Pure?

In grocery shops, you may have notice the label of 'pure' written on many food items like oil, ghee, milk etc., which signify that they are pure.

But from scientific point of view, these substances are not pure because they are made up of more than one kind of particle or they are the mixture of different substances. e.g. Milk is a mixture of water, proteins, fat, etc.

The substances from which the mixture are formed are pure substances which are made up of single form of matter.

In last chapter we have already studied that matter can be classified as solid, liquid and gas on the basis of its physical state. However, on the basis of composition, matter can be classified in different ways.

Classification of Matter

On the basis of chemical composition matter can be classify as

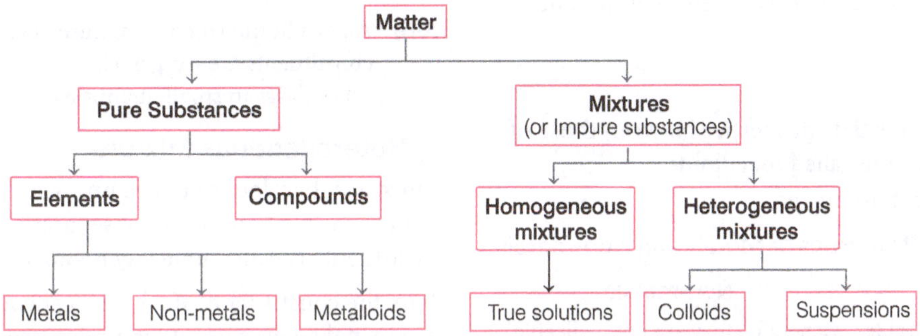

2.1 Pure Substances

A substance that consists of only a single type of constituent particles is called **pure substance**. It has fixed composition, e.g. gold, water etc. It cannot be separated into other kinds of matter by simple physical means.

Type of Pure Substances

Based upon the nature of the constituent particles, it is of two types, i.e. elements and compounds.

1. Elements

The term element was first used by **Robert Boyle** in 1661. According to **Antoine Laurent Lavoisier,** a French chemist, (1743-94), 'an element is a basic form of matter that contains only one kind of atoms and cannot be broken down into simpler substances by chemical reactions'. e.g. Copper, oxygen, iron, hydrogen etc.

Till november 118 elements have been discovered, out of these 92 are natural elements and others are man-made. Majority of elements are solid. 11 elements are in gaseous state at room temperature. Two elements i.e. mercury and bromine are liquid at room temperature. However, gallium and cesium become liquid slightly above room temperature (303 K).

Classification of Elements

On the basis of variation in properties, elements can be broadly classified as **metals, non-metals** and **metalloids.**

(i) Metals

Metals generally show following properties.

- They are malleable, i.e. can be hammered into thin sheets.
- They are ductile i.e. can be drawn into thin wires.
- They are lustrous (shine).
- They are generally silver-grey or yellow in colour.
- They are sonorous, i.e. make a ringing sound when hit.
- They conduct heat and electricity.
- e.g. Gold, silver, copper, mercury etc.

Note Mercury is the only metal that is liquid at room temperature.

(ii) Non-metals

Non-metals generally show following properties:

- They are poor conductors of heat and electricity.
- They display a variety of colours.
- They are not lustrous, sonorous or malleable.
- e.g. Hydrogen, oxygen, iodine, carbon (coal, coke), bromine, chlorine, etc.
- Bromine is the only non-metallic element that exists in liquid state at normal conditions of temperature and pressure.

(iii) Metalloids

Elements having intermediate properties between those of metals and non-metals are called metalloids.

e.g. Boron, silicon, germanium, etc.

Comparison among Properties of Metals and Non-metals

Metals	Non-metals
Generally they are malleable, strong, ductile and sonorous.	Generally, they are not malleable, strong, ductile and sonorous.
Generally, they are good conductors of heat and electricity.	Mostly, they are bad conductors of heat and electricity.
Generally, they are lustrous (shiny) and can be polished.	Generally, non-metals are non-lustrous (dull) and cannot be polished.
Generally, they are solids at room temperature.	Non-metals may be solids, liquids or gases at room temperature.

2. Compounds

A compound is a substance composed of two or more elements, chemically combined with one another in a fixed proportion. e.g. Water (H_2O), methane (CH_4), carbon dioxide (CO_2), ammonia (NH_3), sodium chloride (NaCl) etc.

2.2 Mixtures (Impure Substances)

A mixture is a substance in which two or more pure substances are mixed in any proportion without any chemical combination. e.g. Sea water, minerals, soil, air etc.

Dissolved sodium chloride can be separated from its solution in water by the physical process of evaporation. However, sodium chloride is itself a pure substance and cannot be separated by physical process into its chemical constituents.

Similarly, sugar is a substance which contains only one kind of pure matter and its composition is the same throughout.

Types of Mixtures

Depending upon the nature of the components that form a mixture, we have following two types of mixtures.

(i) Homogeneous Mixture

A mixture in which the constituents are uniformly distributed throughout, i.e. without any clear boundary of separation, is called **homogeneous mixture**. The composition of a homogeneous mixture is uniform throughout. Some of the examples of homogeneous mixtures are salt solution, sugar solution, air, soft drinks, petroleum, biogas, alloys etc.

Note Air is a homogeneous mixture of gas. Its two major constituents are oxygen (21%) and nitrogen (78%) and other gases in small quantities.

(ii) Heterogeneous Mixture

A mixture that does not have uniform composition, i.e. have visible boundaries of separation between its constituents is called **heterogeneous mixture.**

Here, the constituents of a heterogeneous mixture can be seen by naked eyes or under a microscope.

Some examples of heterogeneous mixtures are sugar and sand mixture, salt and sand mixture, polluted air, muddy water etc.

Comparison between Compounds and Mixtures

Compound	Mixture
Definite elements are present in a definite ratio.	Substances are mixed in any ratio.
Elements combine chemically to form a compound.	Chemical reaction does not take place during its formation.
Constituents lose their properties.	Constituents retain their properties.
Constituents can be separated by chemical or electrochemical reactions.	Constituents can be separated by simple physical methods.

Compound	Mixture
Considerable energy changes take place during the formation or decomposition of a compound.	Energy changes do not take place (or negligible) during the formation or decomposition of a mixture.
A compound is always homogeneous in nature.	A mixture may be homogeneous or heterogeneous in nature.

Try These 2.1

1. What does a substance called which has fixed composition?
2. Name one metal that is liquid at room temperature.
3. Why are soft drinks and soil not pure substances but mixtures?
4. What is the major constituent of air?
5. Give two examples of heterogeneous mixtures.
6. How is mixture of sand and salt a heterogeneous mixture?

2.3 Solution

A homogeneous mixture of two or more substances is called **solution**. A solution is sometimes also called a **true solution**. Lemonade, soda water, salt solution, sugar solution etc., all are the examples of solutions. In a solution, there is homogeneity at the particle level, i.e. the particles of dissolved substances are evenly distributed in the solution and are indistinguishable from one another.

Following are the two main components of a solution.

(i) **Solvent** (Dissolving phase) The component (usually present in larger amount) of the solution that dissolves the other component in it, is called the **solvent**.

(ii) **Solute** (Dissolved phase) The component (usually present in lesser quantity) of the solution that is dissolved in the solvent is called the **solute**.

Note Solutions are not always a liquid that contains either solid, liquid or gas dissolved in it. But it can be of solid (alloys) and gaseous (air) nature also.

Some common examples of solution are as follows:

- In sugar solution, sugar is the solute and water is the solvent.
- A solution of iodine in alcohol known as **tincture of iodine**, has iodine (solid) as the solute and alcohol (liquid) as the solvent.
- Aerated drinks like soda water etc., are gas in liquid solutions. i.e. having CO_2 (gas) as solute and water (liquid) as solvent.

Alloys

These are mixtures of two or more metals or a metal and a non-metal and cannot be separated into their components by physical methods. But still, an alloy is considered as a mixture because it shows the properties of its constituents and can have variable composition, e.g. brass is a mixture of approximately 30% zinc and 70% copper.

Properties of a Solution

Some important properties of a solution are as follows:

- A solution is a homogeneous mixture.
- The particles of a solution are smaller than 1 nm (10^{-9} m) in diameter. Therefore, they cannot be seen by naked eyes.
- Due to very small particles, they do not scatter a beam of light passing through the solution. So, the path of light is not visible in a solution.
- A solution is stable, i.e. the solute particles do not settle down when left undisturbed. The solute particles cannot be separated from the mixture by the process of filtration.

Concentration of a Solution

The concentration of a solution is the amount of solute mass or volume present in a given amount (mass or volume) of solution.

In a solution, the relative proportion of the solute and solvent can be varied. Depending upon the amount of solute present in a given amount of solvent, the solution can be classified as

(i) **Saturated solution** At any particular temperature, a solution that has dissolved as much solute as it is capable of dissolving is called saturated solution. In other words, when no more amount of solute can be dissolved in a solution at a given temperature, is called **saturated solution**. The amount of the solute present in the saturated solution at this temperature is called its **solubility**.

(ii) **Unsaturated solution** If the amount of solute contained in a solution is less than the saturation level, it is called an **unsaturated solution**.

Note Solution with higher solute concentration is called **concentrated solution** and those with low concentration is called **dilute solution**.

Expressing the Concentration of a Solution

The methods by which the concentration of a solution can be expressed are

- Mass by mass percentage of a solution
$$= \frac{\text{Mass of solute}}{\text{Mass of solution}} \times 100$$
- Mass by volume percentage of a solution
$$= \frac{\text{Mass of solute}}{\text{Volume of solution}} \times 100$$
- Volume by volume percentage of a solution
$$= \frac{\text{Volume of solute}}{\text{Volume of solution}} \times 100$$

Example 1. **A solution contains 50 g of common salt in 450 g of water. Calculate the concentration of the solution in terms of mass by mass percentage of solution.**

Sol. $\text{Concentration of solution} = \dfrac{\text{Mass of solute}}{\text{Mass of solution}} \times 100$

$\text{Mass of common salt (solute)} = 50\text{ g}$

$\text{Mass of water (solvent)} = 450\text{ g}$

$\text{Mass of solution} = 50 + 450 = 500\text{ g}$

$\text{Concentration of solution} = \dfrac{50}{500} \times 100 = 10\%$

Effect of Temperature on Solubility

Generally solubility of solids in liquids increases with increase in temperature and solubility of gases in liquids increases with decrease in temperature.

Try These 2.2

1. **What are the components of tincture of iodine?**
2. **What are the compositions of brass alloy?**
3. **Why path of light is not visible in a solution?**
4. **Calculate the mass of water and mass of glucose required to make 250 g of 40% solution of glucose.** **[Ans. 150 g, 100 g]**
5. **A solution of alcohol in water has been prepared by mixing 100 mL of alcohol in 300 mL of water. Calculate the volume percentage of the solution.** **[Ans. 25%]**
6. **What is the effect of temperature on solubility of solid in liquids?**

2.4 Suspension

A suspension is a heterogeneous mixture in which the solute particles do not dissolve, but remain suspended throughout the bulk of the medium, e.g. a mixture of chalk powder in water, a mixture of sand in water, smoke coming out of a chimney of a factory.

Properties of Suspension

Some important properties of suspension are as follows:

- Suspension is a heterogeneous mixture.
- Its particles can be seen by naked eyes.
- Its particles scatter a beam of light passing through it and make its path visible (Tyndall effect).
- It is unstable, i.e. the solute particles settle down when suspension is left undisturbed. They can be separated by the process of filtration. When the particles settle down, the suspension breaks and it does not scatter light any more.

Note The insoluble particles in a suspension are called **'suspended particles'**, whereas the solvent is referred to as **'medium'**.

2.5 Colloidal Solution

A colloid (or colloidal solution) is a mixture that is actually heterogeneous but appears to be homogeneous as the particles are uniformly spread throughout the solution, e.g. milk, shaving cream, cheese, etc. Colloidal solutions are also called **colloidal sols.**

- The components of a colloidal solution are the dispersed phase and the dispersion medium.
- The solute-like component or the dispersed particles in a colloid form is the dispersed phase and the component in which the dispersed phase is suspended is known as the dispersion medium.

Properties of a Colloid

Some important properties of a colloid are as follows:

- A colloid is a heterogeneous mixture.
- The size of particles of a colloid is too small to be individually seen by naked eyes.
- They are big enough to scatter a beam of light passing through it and make its path visible.
- They are quite stable. Particles do not settle down when a colloid is left undisturbed.
- Particles of colloid can pass through filter paper, therefore a colloid cannot be separated by filtration. However, they get separated by a special technique called **centrifugation.**

Tyndall Effect

The scattering of light by colloidal particles is known as Tyndall effect after the name of the scientist who discovered this effect. In a true solution, the solute particles are so small that they cannot scatter light falling on them. In a colloidal solution, the particles are big enough to scatter light. Tyndall effect can also be observed in the following situations.

(i) When a fine beam of light enters a room through a small hole (due to scattering of beam of light by the particles of dust and smoke in air).

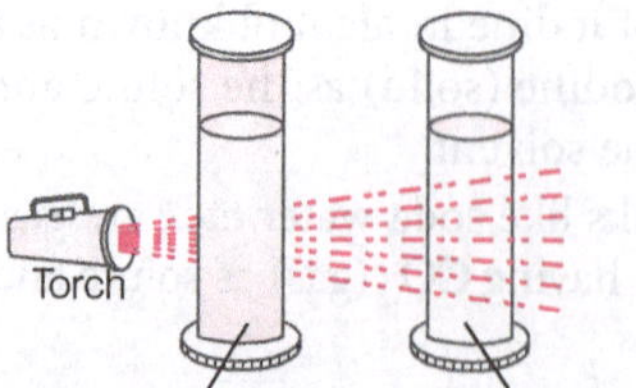

Demonstration of Tyndall effect

(ii) When sunlight passes through the canopy of a dense forest (as the mist containing tiny droplets of water scatter it).

Types of Colloids

Colloids are classified according to the state (solid, liquid or gas) of the dispersion medium and the dispersed phase.

Common Examples of Colloids

Type of colloid	Dispersed phase	Dispersion medium	Examples
Aerosol	Liquid	Gas	Fog, clouds, mist
Aerosol	Solid	Gas	Smoke, automobile exhaust
Foam	Gas	Liquid	Shaving cream
Emulsion	Liquid	Liquid	Milk, face cream
Sol	Solid	Liquid	Milk of magnesia, mud
Foam	Gas	Solid	Foam, rubber, sponge, pumice
Gel	Liquid	Solid	Jelly, cheese, butter
Solid sol	Solid	Solid	Milky glass, coloured gemstone

2.6 Physical and Chemical Changes

Compound is formed as a result of some chemical change while the mixing of the constituents in a mixture involves a physical change. Here, these two types of changes are discussed below.

Physical Changes

The properties that can be observed and specified like colour, hardness, rigidity, fluidity, density, melting point, boiling point etc., are physical properties.

The changes which occur without a change in composition and in chemical nature of the substance are called **physical changes.**

The interconversion of states is a physical change, e.g. change of water in ice is a physical change because chemically, ice and liquid water both are same. Although ice, water and water vapour all look different and display different physical properties but chemically they are same.

Chemical Changes

In chemical changes, one substance reacts with another substance to undergo a change in chemical composition. Chemical changes bring a change in the chemical properties of matter with the formation of a new substance.

A chemical change is also called a **chemical reaction**, e.g. both water and cooking oil are liquid, but their chemical characteristics are different. They differ in odour and inflammability.

Oil burns in air whereas, water extinguishes fire, i.e. it is the chemical property of oil that makes it different from water.

Note
- Burning is a chemical change.
- During burning of a candle, both physical and chemical changes takes place.

Comparison between Physical and Chemical Change

Physical Changes	Chemical Changes
No new chemical substance is formed in this change.	New substances are formed which have different chemical composition.
It is a temporary change.	It is a permanent change.
This change is easily reversible.	This change is usually irreversible.
The mass of a substance does not alter in this change.	The mass of a substance does alter in this change.
Generally, physical change is accompanied by very small or no energy changes.	Generally, chemical change is a accompanied by energy changes.

Try These 2.3

1. **Name the technique used to separate solute present in suspension.**
2. **What are the two major components of colloidal solution called?**
3. **Give a situation in which Tyndall effect is observed.**
4. **Write the dispersed phase and dispersion medium present in foam. Give an example.**
5. **Which type of colloid, a shaving cream is?**
6. **Why is change of water into ice a physical change?**
7. **Give an example in which physical and chemical changes take place together.**

Mind Map

IS MATTER AROUND US PURE?

Pure Substances
These substances have only single type of constituent particles and have fixed composition e.g. gold, water, etc.

Types

Compounds
It contains two or more atoms combined together in fixed proportion. e.g. water (H_2O).

Elements
It is a basic form of matter that cannot be broken down into simpler substances by chemical reactions. These contains only one kind of atoms. e.g. sodium, oxygen etc.

Metals
These are malleable, ductile, sonorous, conduct heat and electricity. e.g. gold, silver, etc. Mercury is the only metal that is liquid at room temperature.

Non-metals
These are neither malleable nor ductile and does not conduct heat and electricity. e.g. oxygen. Bromine is the only non-metallic element, that exists in liquid state at normal conditions of temperature and pressure.

Metalloids
These have properties intermediate of metals and non-metals. e.g. boron, silicon, germanium, etc.

Physical Change
The change in which only physical properties are affected. These are reversible in nature e.g. vaporisation of water.

Chemical Change
In these changes, chemical composition is changed and new substances are obtained. e.g. rusting of iron.

Mixtures
(Impure substances) These have two or more substances in any proportion. e.g. Sugar solution, milk, etc.

Types

Heterogeneous Mixtures
Their composition is not uniform throughout. e.g. water in oil, chalk powder in water etc.

Suspension
- A heterogeneous mixture in which the solute particles do not dissolve but remain suspended throughout the bulk of the medium. e.g. a mixture of sand in water.
- Can be seen by naked eye.
- Particles scatter a beam of light passing through a suspension.
- Solute particles can be separated by filtration.

Colloid solution/Colloid
- A mixture that is actually heterogeneous but appears to be homogeneous as the particles are uniformly spread throughout the solution. e.g. milk.
- Can not be seen by naked eye.
- Particle are small in size but big enough to scatter beam of light passing through the colloid.
- Can be separated by a special technique called centrifugation.

Type of Colloids on the basis of state

Type of Colloid	Dispersed Phase	Dispersion Medium	Example
Aerosol	Liquid	Gas	Fog,cloud,mist
Aerosol	Solid	Gas	Smoke, automobile,exhaust
Foam	Gas	Liquid	Shaving cream
Emulsion	Liquid	Liquid	Milk, face cream
Sol	Solid	Liquid	Milk of magnesia, mud
Foam	Gas	Solid	Foam,rubber,sponge,pumice
Gel	Liquid	Solid	Jelly,Cheese,Butter
Solid sol	Solid	Solid	Milky Glass,Coloured Gemstone

Tyndall Effect
The scattering of the beam of light by the dispersed phase particles present in a colloidal solution.

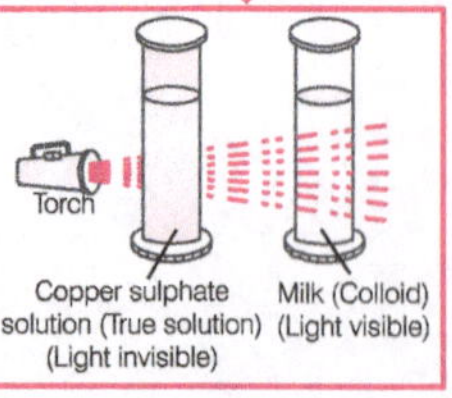

Homogeneous Mixtures
Composition of these mixtures is uniform throughout. e.g. salt and water

Solution
- A homogeneous mixture of two or more substances. e.g. soda water.
- Particles size smaller than 1 nm.
- Particles are of small size so cannot be seen by naked eye and do not scatter a beam of light passing through solution.
- Solute particle cannot be separated by filtration.

Components of solution
1. **Solvent**
   The component of the solution that dissolves the other component in it.
2. **Solute**
   The component of the solution that dissolves in the solvent.

Types

Solid Solution (Alloy)
These are mixtures of two or more metals and a non-metals that cannot be separated by physical method. e.g. Bronze is an alloy (solid solution) of copper and tin.

Liquid Solution
e.g. Sugar solution/mixture of sugar and water.

Gaseous solution
e.g. Air (mixture of various gases)

Types

1. **Saturated Solution**
   A solution in which no more amount of solute can be dissolved at a given temperature.
   Solubility
   The amount of solute (g) in 100g of water at a given temperature.
   (i) Solubility of solids in liquids increase in temperature and vice-versa.
   (ii) Solubility of gases in liquids increases with decrease in temperature and vice-versa.
2. **Unsaturated Solution**
   A solution in which the amount of solute is less than the saturation level, i.e. some more amount of solute can be dissolved at a given temperature.
3. **Dilute solution**
   A solution having lesser amount of solute relative to the amount of solvent.
4. **Concentrated solution**
   A solution having higher amount of solute.

Expressing the concentration of solution

Mass by Mass Percentage

$$= \frac{\text{Mass of solute}}{\text{Mass of solution}} \times 100$$

Mass by volume percentage

$$= \frac{\text{Mass of solute}}{\text{Volume of solution}} \times 100$$

Volume by volume percentage

$$= \frac{\text{Volume of solute}}{\text{Volume of solution}} \times 100$$

NCERT FOLDER

Complete Explanations of all NCERT's Questions

Intext Questions

Q.1 What is meant by a substance? **Page 15**

Sol. A substance is a pure form of matter consists of only a single type of constituent particle.
e.g. Hydrogen, oxygen, sulphur etc.

Q.2 List the points of differences between homogeneous and heterogeneous mixtures. **Page 15**

Or Differentiate between homogeneous and heterogeneous mixtures with examples. **Page 18**

Sol. The main points of differences between the homogeneous and heterogeneous mixtures are as follows:

Homogeneous Mixture	Heterogeneous Mixture
Its constituent particles are uniformly distributed all over the mixture.	Its constituent particles are not distributed uniformly.
There are no visible boundaries of separation.	There are distinct and visible boundaries of separation in most of the cases.
Its constituents cannot be easily separated. Special methods are required for this purpose.	Its constituents can be easily separated by simple methods.
e.g. Alloys, air, soft drinks, vinegar etc.	e.g. Mixture of sand and common salt, mixture of chalk powder and water etc.

Q.3 How are sol, solution and suspension different from each other? **Page 18**

Sol. The difference between true solution, sol and suspension are as follows:

Properties	True Solution	Sol or Colloidal Solution	Suspension
Nature	It is homogeneous.	It is heterogeneous (may appear homogeneous).	It is also heterogeneous.
Particle size	Less than 1 nm	Ranges between 1 nm to 100 nm	Greater than 100 nm
Tyndall effect	It doesn't show Tyndall effect.	It shows Tyndall effect.	It shows Tyndall effect.
Appearance	Transparent	Transparent or translucent	Translucent or opaque
Setting of particles	Particles don't settle at all.	Particles do not get settle in normal condition but on centrifugation they get settled.	Particles get settle down when suspension is left undisturbed.
Examples	Sugar solution, salt solution, etc.	Milk, cough syrup etc.	Sand in water, chalk in water, etc.

Q.4 To make a saturated solution, 36 g of sodium chloride is dissolved in 100 g of water at 293 K. Find its concentration at this temperature. **Page 18**

Sol. Mass of solute (NaCl) = 36 g

Mass of solvent (H_2O) = 100 g

Mass of solution = 36 + 100 = 136 g

Concentration (by mass) of the solution

$$= \frac{\text{Mass of solute}}{\text{Mass of solution}} \times 100$$

$$= \frac{36}{136} \times 100 = 26.47\%$$

Q.5 Classify the following as chemical or physical changes: **Page 19**

- cutting of trees,
- melting of butter in a pan,
- rusting of almirah,
- boiling of water to form steam,
- passing of electric current through water and the water breaking down into hydrogen and oxygen gases,
- dissolving common salt in water,
- making a fruit salad with raw fruits, and
- burning of paper and wood.

Sol. Physical changes

- cutting of trees,
- melting of butter in a pan,
- boiling of water to form steam,
- dissolving common salt in water, and
- making a fruit salad with raw fruits.

Chemical changes

- rusting of almirah,
- passing of electric current through water and breaking down of water into hydrogen and oxygen gases,
- burning of paper and wood.

Q.6 Try segregating the things around you as pure substances or mixtures. Page 19

Sol. **Pure substance** Sugar, common salt, water etc.

Mixture Air, wood, coal, milk, soap, soil etc.

Exercise

Q.1 Which separation techniques will you apply for the separation of the following?

(i) Sodium chloride from its solution in water.
(ii) Ammonium chloride from a mixture containing sodium chloride and ammonium chloride.
(iii) Small pieces of metal in the engine oil of a car.
(iv) Different pigments from an extract of flower petals.
(v) Butter from curd.
(vi) Oil from water.
(vii) Tea leaves from tea.
(viii) Iron pins from sand.
(ix) Wheat grains from husk.
(x) Fine mud particles suspended in water.

Sol. (i) Evaporation and crystallisation
(ii) Sublimation
(iii) Filtration
(iv) Chromatography
(v) Centrifugation
(vi) By using separating funnel
(vii) Filtration
(viii) Magnetic separation
(ix) Winnowing
(x) Loading and decantation

Loading Alum is added to muddy water so that the fine soil particles become heavy and settle down.

Q.2 Write the steps you would use for making tea. Use the words solution, solvent, solute, dissolve, soluble, insoluble, filtrate and residue.

Sol. **Method of preparation of tea**

(i) Take some water as **solvent** in a pan and heat it.
(ii) Add some sugar as **solute** and boil to **dissolve** the sugar completely to form **solution**.
(iii) Add tea leaves which are **insoluble** in the solution and boil it.
(iv) Now, add milk and boil again.
(v) Filter the mixture through the tea stainer and collect the **filtrate** or **soluble** substances, i.e. tea in a cup. The **insoluble** tea leaves left behind as **residue** in the strainer.

Q.3 Pragya tested the solubility of three different substances at different temperatures and collected the data as given below (results are given in the following table, as grams of substance dissolved in 100 g of water to form a saturated solution).

Substance Dissolved	Temperature (in K)				
	283	293	313	333	353
	Solubility				
Potassium nitrate	21	32	62	106	167
Sodium chloride	36	36	36	37	37
Potassium chloride	35	35	40	46	54
Ammonium chloride	24	37	41	55	66

(i) What mass of potassium nitrate would be needed to produce a saturated solution of potassium nitrate in 50 of water at 313 K?
(ii) Pragya makes a saturated solution of potassium chloride in water at 353 K and leaves the solution to cool at room temperature. What would she observe as the solution cools? Explain.
(iii) Find the solubility of each salt at 293 K. Which salt has the highest solubility at this temperature?
(iv) What is the effect of change of temperature on the solubility of a salt?

Sol. (i) At 313 K, solubility of potassium nitrate in 100 g of water = 62 g

$$\text{Solubility} = \frac{\text{Mass of solute}}{\text{Mass of solvent}} \times 100$$

$$\Rightarrow \text{Mass of solute} = \frac{\text{Solubility} \times \text{Mass of solvent}}{100}$$

$$\therefore \text{Mass of potassium nitrate} = \frac{62 \times 50\text{ g}}{100} = 31\text{ g}$$

Hence, 31g of potassium nitrate would be needed to produce a saturated solution of potassium nitrate in 50 g of water at 313 K.

(ii) The amount of potassium chloride that should be dissolved in water to make a saturated solution increases with temperature.
Thus, as the solution cools, some of the potassium chloride will precipitate out of the solution and form crystals.

(iii) The solubility of the salts at 293 K are:
Potassium nitrate = 32 g per 100 g water
Sodium chloride = 36 g per 100 g water
Potassium chloride = 35 g per 100 g water
Ammonium chloride = 37 g per 100 g water
Thus, ammonium chloride has the maximum solubility (37 g per 100 g of water) at 293 K.

(iv) The solubility of a solid (salt) decreases with fall in temperature, while it increases with rise in temperature.

Q.4 Explain the following giving examples :

(i) Saturated solution (ii) Pure substance

(iii) Colloid solution (iv) Suspension

Sol. (i) **Saturated solution** The solution in which no more solute can be dissolved in the same amount of solvent at a given temperature is called saturated solution, e.g. Adding table salt to water will result in a saturated solution when no more salt dissolves leaving some undissolved at the bottom.

(ii) **Pure substance** The substance which contains particles of only one kind of matter is called pure substance, e.g. Gold, water, clouds, etc.

(iii) **Colloid solution** Colloid is a heterogeneous mixture whose particles are bigger than that of solution but smaller than suspension, e.g. Milk, clouds, etc.

(iv) **Suspension** It is a heterogeneous mixture whose particles are larger in size and are visible with naked eye, e.g. chalk powder in water, mixture of sand and water etc.

Q.5 Classify each of the following as a homogeneous or heterogeneous mixture. Soda water, wood, air, soil, vinegar, filtered tea.

Sol. **Homogeneous mixtures** Air, soda water, vinegar, filtered tea.

Heterogeneous mixtures Wood, soil.

Q.6 How would you confirm that a colourless liquid given to you is pure water?

Sol. Take a given colourless liquid in a beaker and suspend a thermometer into it. Place beaker on a wire gauze and start heating with the help of burner.

Note down the temperature at which water begins to boil. If the given liquid boils at 100°C, the liquid will be a pure water as the boiling point of pure water is 100°C.

Q.7 Which of the following materials fall in the category of pure substance?

(i) Ice (ii) Milk

(iii) Iron (iv) Hydrochloric acid

(v) Calcium oxide (vi) Mercury

(vii) Brick (viii) Wood

(ix) Air

Sol. Ice, iron, hydrochloric acid, calcium oxide and mercury are pure substances as they either consist of only a single type of constituent particles or have a definite composition.

Q.8 Identify the solutions among the following mixtures.

(i) Soil (ii) Sea water

(iii) Air (iv) Coal

(v) Soda water

Sol. Sea water, air and soda water are the solutions among the given mixtures.

Note Sea water is also considered as heterogeneous solution.

Q.9 Which of the following will show Tyndall effect?

(i) Salt solution

(ii) Milk

(iii) Copper sulphate solution

(iv) Starch solution

Sol. Milk and starch solution being a colloid will show Tyndall effect, while salt solution and copper sulphate solution are true solutions that will not show Tyndall effect due to small size of their particles.

Q.10 Classify the following into elements, compounds and mixtures.

(i) Sodium (ii) Soil

(iii) Sugar solution (iv) Silver

(v) Calcium carbonate (vi) Tin

(vii) Silicon (viii) Coal

(ix) Air (x) Soap

(xi) Methane (xii) Carbon dioxide

(xiii) Blood

Sol.

Elements	Sodium, silver, tin, silicon
Compounds	Calcium carbonate, methane, carbon dioxide
Mixtures	Soil, sugar solution, coal, air, blood, soap

Q.11 Which of the following are chemical changes?

(i) Growth of a plant.

(ii) Rusting of iron.

(iii) Mixing of iron filings and sand.

(iv) Cooking of food.

(v) Digestion of food.

(vi) Freezing of water.

(vii) Burning of a candle.

Sol. Growth of a plant, rusting of iron, cooking of food, digestion of food and burning of a candle are the chemical changes.

Note Burning of a candle involves both physical and chemical changes.

To Study NCERT Activities

Scan the Code

REVIEW EXERCISE

Including Competency Based Questions

Competency Focused (Objective) Questions

Multiple Choice Questions

1 Which of the following is a pure substance?

(a) Air (b) Distilled water
(c) Steel (d) Brass

Sol. (*b*) Any substance that contains only one type of particles (e.g. molecules/atoms etc.) are said to be a pure substance. Thus, among the given options, distilled water is a pure substance.

2 In which solution, solvent is solid and the solute is gas.

(a) Copper dissolved in gold
(b) Camphor in nitrogen gas
(c) Solution of hydrogen in palladium
(d) All of the above

Sol. (*c*) Solution of hydrogen in palladium is an example of gas-solid solution in which hydrogen gas is dissolved in metal, palladium.

3 Which of the following property does not prove that water is a compound? **Competency Based Que.**

(a) Water is made up of two different elements (H and O) which chemically combined with one another in a fixed proportion.
(b) Water has fixed boiling point (b.p.).
(c) The constituents of water cannot be separated by simple physical methods.
(d) Distilled water and tap water have same taste and constituents.

Sol. (*d*) Distilled water and tap water have different taste and different constituents. Distilled water has pure H_2O molecules while tap water may contain others molecules also.

4 Two substances, *A* and *B* were made to react to form a third substance, A_2B according to the following reaction $2A + B \rightarrow A_2B$. Which of the following statements concerning this reaction is correct? **Competency Based Que.**

(a) The product A_2B shows the properties of substances *A* and *B*.
(b) The product will always have a fixed composition.
(c) The product so formed cannot be classified as a compound.
(d) The product so formed is an element.

Sol. (*b*) A_2B is a compound made up of two elements *A* and *B* in a fixed ratio. The properties of a compound (e.g., A_2B) are entirely different from those of its constituent elements (e.g., *A* and *B*). The composition of a compound is fixed.

5 Which of the following is not a property of non-metal?

(a) Sonorous (b) colourful
(c) poor conductor of heat (d) poor conductors of electricity

Sol. (*a*) Generally non-metals are not sonorous as they are brittle and break instead of vibrating when struck.

6 Brass is a solution of molten copper and

(a) solid zinc (b) molten zinc
(c) gaseous zinc (d) molten tin

Sol. (*b*) Brass is an alloy of molten copper and molten zinc.

7 An example of liquid metal and non-metal respectively is

(a) mercury and bromine (b) chlorine and gallium
(c) mercury and iodine (d) sulphur and gallium

Sol. (*a*) Mercury and bromine are the metal and non-metal, respectively which exist in liquid form.

8 Which of these is an alloy?

(a) Silver (b) Copper
(c) Bronze (d) Aluminium

Sol. (*c*) Silver, copper, and aluminium are the elements whereas bronze is an alloy of copper and tin.

9 Consider the lists of the properties of four substances. **Competency Based Que.**

	Is it shiny?	How does it conduct electricity?
Substance 1	yes	very good
Substance 2	no	very poor
Substance 3	yes	medium
Substance 4	no	poor

Which substance is most likely to be a metalloid?

(a) Substance 1 (b) Substance 2
(c) Substance 3 (d) Substance 4

Sol. (*c*) Substance 3 is most likely to be metalloid because it has intermediate qualities of metals and non-metals.

10 Which of the following property does not describe a compound?

(a) It is composed of two or more elements.

(b) It is a pure substances.

(c) It can't be separated into constituents by physical means.

(d) It is mixed in any proportions by mass.

Sol. (*d*) Compound is mixed in fixed proportion by mass.

11 The following are descriptions of three substances *A*, B and *C*.

A : A shiny, hard substance that is a good conductor of electricity and can be drawn into wires.

B : A liquid mixture of two immiscible liquids that requires a separating funnel for separation.

C : A homogeneous solid mixture of two or more metals.

Which of the following statement is correct?

(a) *A* is a non-metal and *C* is an alloy.

(b) *B* is a homogenous mixture and *A* is a metal.

(c) *A* is a metal and *B* is a heterogeneous mixture.

(d) *C* is a pure substance and *B* is a heterogeneous mixture.

Sol. (*c*) *A* is a metal according to given properties, *B* is a heterogeneous mixture as it consists of immiscible liquids and *C* is an alloy, which is a homogeneous mixture, not a pure substance.

12 The image shows two solutions.

What differentiates a homogeneous mixture from a heterogeneous mixture?

(a) Mixture 2 is homogeneous as it has two layers.

(b) Mixture 1 is homogeneous as its components is uniform throughout.

(c) Mixture 2 is heterogeneous as it has liquid components.

(d) Mixture 1 is heterogeneous as its components are not visible from the naked eye.

Sol. (*b*) Mixture 1 is homogeneous as its components is uniform throughout and thus has no separate layers.

13 During an activity, a student added 10 g iron filings and 10 g sulphur powder in a bowl. He brought a magnet over the bowl and noticed that iron filings were picked up by the magnet.

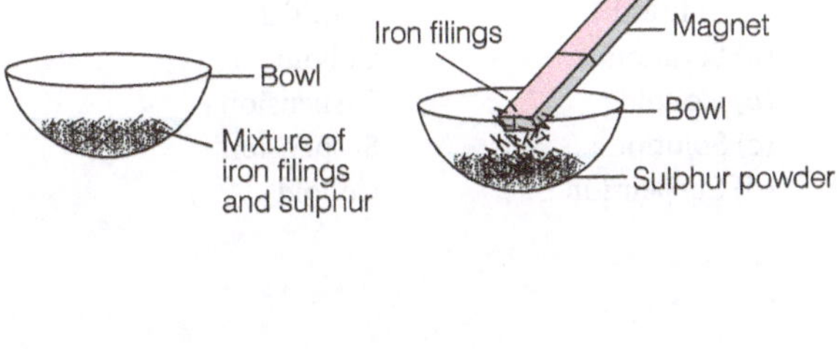

He put sulphur and iron filings back into the bowl and put it on heat. After sometime he brought the magnet over it again. This time, the iron filings were not attracted to the magnet.

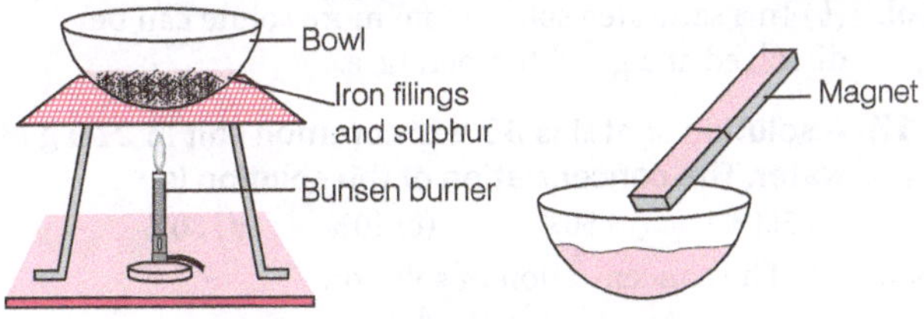

What can be inferred from the activity?

Competency Based Que.

(a) The contents in the bowl after heating can be classified as a mixture because they were not affected by the magnet.

(b) The contents in the bowl before heating can be classified as a mixture because they could be separated.

(c) The contents in the bowl before heating can be classified as a mixture because they appear different.

(d) The contents in the bowl after heating can be classified as a mixture because their properties changed after heating.

Sol. (*b*) Among the given statements (b) is correct about the activity.

When iron and sulphur are mixed they retain their original properties. Thus, they are classified, as mixture. Whereas, when iron and sulphur mixture is heated, a new compound is formed called iron sulphide which is black in colour.

14 What will be observed when a mixture of iodine and salt is heated in a China dish?

(a) No change in the China dish is observed.

(b) Salt is left behind in the China dish.

(c) Iodine is left behind in the China dish.

(d) The mixture starts melting.

Sol. (*b*) Iodine sublimes on heating and salt will be left behind in the China dish.

15 Which of the following is an example of solution?

(a) Soda water

(b) Unfiltered tea

(c) Sand and water

(d) Air

Sol. (*a*) Soda water is an example of gas in liquid solution and it is homogeneous also.

16 The tincture of iodine is made by dissolving

(a) iodine in potassium iodide.

(b) iodine in vaseline.

(c) iodine in water.

(d) iodine in alcohol.

Sol. (*d*) "Tincture of iodine" solution is made by dissolving 2-7% iodine into the alcohol. Iodine tincture can also be used as an antiseptic.

17 A solution in which no more solute can be dissolved at a given temperature is known as

(a) unsaturated solution (b) saturated solution
(c) diluted solution (d) true solution

Sol. (*b*) In a saturated solution no more solute can be dissolved at a given temperature.

18 A solution contains 30 g of common salt in 270 g of water. The concentration of the solution is

(a) 500% (b) 50% (c) 10% (d) 80%

Sol. (*c*) The concentration of solution

$$= \frac{\text{Mass of solute}}{\text{Mass of solution}} \times 100$$

Mass of common salt (solute) = 30 g
Mass of water = 270 g
Mass of solution = 30 + 270 = 300 g

$$\therefore \text{Concentration of solution} = \frac{30}{300} \times 100 = 10\%$$

19 The concentration of solution represents

(a) the total quantity of solutions.
(b) the quantity of the solvent present in a solution
(c) the quantity of the solute present in a solution
(d) the quantity of the impurities present in a solution.

Sol. (*c*) The concentration of a solution represents the amount of solute present in a solution.

20 A student made four solutions using different quantities of water and blue ink. The quantities are listed in the table. CBSE Question Bank

Solution	Volume of Ink (mL)	Volume of Water (mL)
1	25	200
2	10	100
3	15	50
4	50	250

Which solution has the least concentration with the lightest blue colour?

(a) Solution 4 (b) Solution 3
(c) Solution 2 (d) Solution 1

Sol. (*c*) Among the given solutions, solution 2 has the least concentration with lightest blue colour.

21 A student crushed a piece of chalk and mixed the chalk powder in 100 mL water. The water appeared white and cloudy. After sometime the particles settled at the bottom of the container. She claims that the mixture is a suspension. What justifies her claim? Competency Based Que.

(a) The particles of chalk form a separate layer.
(b) The particles of chalk are uniformly distributed in water.
(c) The particles of chalk are visible through the naked eye.
(d) The particles mix completely with water.

Sol. (*c*) The chalk particles are settled at the bottom of the container and are visible through the naked eye thus, it is a suspension.

22 A liquid is able to scatter a beam of light but it leaves no residue after passing through a filter paper. A liquid can be a

(a) true solution (b) suspension
(c) colloidal solution (d) concentrated solution

Sol. (*c*) Colloids can pass through ordinary filter paper and scatter a beam of light. Hence, the liquid is a colloidal solution.

23 Avinash listed some mixtures and classified them in various types.

Mixture	Components	Type of Mixture
W	Food colour + Water	Homogeneous
X	Sand + Water	Colloidal
Y	Milk + Sugar	Suspension
Z	Rice + Flour	Heterogeneous

Which mixtures are classified correctly?

(a) W and X (b) X and Y
(c) Y and Z (d) W and Z

Sol. (*d*) Mixture of food colour and water is homogeneous as it does not form any separate layer. Rice and flour is a heterogenous mixture as its components are not uniformly distributed.

24 Select the incorrect statement about colloids from the following options?

(a) Colloids are homogeneous.
(b) Colloids can scatter a beam of light passing through it.
(c) Colloids show Tyndall effect.
(d) Colloids are quite stable.

Sol. (*a*) Colloids are heterogeneous mixture. They are made up of two different phases, that are dispersed phase and dispersed medium.

25 Tina passes light beams through two liquid mixtures in separate glasses as shown in the picture.

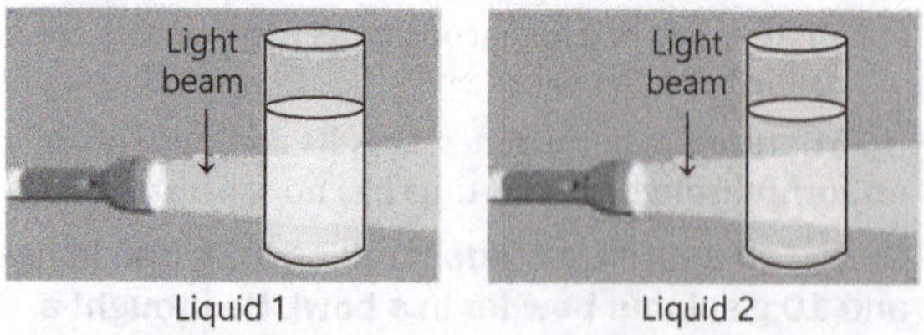

Based on the behaviour of the light beam what are liquids 1 and 2? Competency Based Que.

	Liquid 1	Liquid 2
(a)	Solution	Colloid
(b)	Colloid	Suspension
(c)	Solution	Suspension
(d)	Suspension	Colloid

Sol. (*b*) Liquid 1- Colloid and Liquid 2- Suspension
The particles in colloids and suspensions are large enough to cause the light beam to scatter, making it visible as it passes through the colloid or suspension. The scattering of light is more in case of colloid as compared to suspension. However, the colloid solution looks homogeneous but it is a heterogeneous mixture and it cannot be separated using filter paper. Whereas in suspension, solute particles are suspended in solution and can be filtered out.

26 Which of the following will not show Tyndall effect ?
(a) Smoke (b) Foam
(c) Jelly (d) Salt solution

Sol. (*d*) Salt solution will not show Tyndall effect as it is a true solution and particles of salt solution are very small (size < 1 nm). So, it cannot scatter a beam of light, hence do not show Tyndall effect.

27 Which of the following is not a physical change?
(a) Tearing of paper (b) Bending of iron rod
(c) Freezing water into ice (d) Curdling of milk

Sol. (*d*) Curdling of milk is a chemical change.

28 Which of these is common for all chemical changes? **Competency Based Que.**
(a) Change in shape
(b) Absorption of heat
(c) Increase in volume
(d) Formation of a new substance

Sol. (*d*) In chemical changes, a new substance gets formed.

29 Which of the following is a chemical change?
(a) Decaying of wood (b) Cutting of paper
(c) Sawing of wood
(d) Hammering of a nail into a piece of wood

Sol. (*a*) Decaying of wood is a chemical change, because in this process, the chemical composition of wood is changed and new substances are formed, which cannot be converted back into its original form.

30 Match column I with column II and select the correct option using the given codes.

Column I	Column II
A. Change in states of matter (solid to liquid).	(i) Physical change without composition change.
B. Combustion of methane.	(ii) Formation of carbon dioxide and water.
C. Mixing iron filing and sulphur without heating.	(iii) No new substance is formed.
D. Heating iron filings and sulphur together.	(iv) Formation of a new compound.

(a) A-(i), B-(ii), C-(iii), D-(iv)
(b) A-(i), B-(iii), C-(ii), D-(iv)
(c) A-(ii), B-(iii), C-(iv), D-(i)
(d) A-(ii), B-(i), C-(iii), D-(iv)

Sol. (*a*) The correct match is A-(i), B-(ii), C-(iii), D-(iv).

Assertion-Reason Questions

Direction (Ques 1-9) In each of the following questions, a statement of Assertion is given by the corresponding statement of Reason. Of the statements, mark the correct answer as

(a) Both Assertion and Reason are true and Reason is the correct explanation of Assertion.
(b) Both Assertion and Reason are true but Reason is not the correct explanation of Assertion.
(c) Assertion is true but Reason is false.
(d) Assertion is false, but Reason is true.

1 Assertion (A) Steel is the alloy.
Reason (R) Alloy are mixture of two or metals or metal and a non-metal and cannot be separated into their components by physical methods.

Sol. (*a*) Assertion and Reason both are true and Reason is the correct explanation for Assertion.

2 Assertion (A) A mixture of camphor and ammonium chloride cannot be separated by sublimation.
Reason (R) Camphor on heating sublimes, ammonium chloride does not.

Sol. (*c*) Both camphor and ammonium chloride sublime on heating.
Hence, Assertion is true but Reason is false.

3 Assertion (A) A solution of table salt in a glass of water is homogeneous.
Reason (R) A solution having different composition throughout is homogeneous.

Sol. (*c*) A solution having same composition throughout is homogeneous.
Hence, Assertion is true but Reason is false.

4 Assertion (A) The particles of a suspension can be seen by the naked eye.
Reason (R) Suspension is a homogeneous mixture.

Sol. (*c*) Suspension is heterogeneous mixture in which the solute particles do not dissolve but remain suspended throughout the liquid medium. Thus, these articles can be seen by the naked eye. Hence, Assertion is true but Reason is false.

5 Assertion (A) Colloidal particles do not show Tyndall effect.
Reason (R) Colloidal solutions are stable and colloidal particles do not settle down.

Sol. (*d*) Collodial particles show tyndall effect.
Hence, Assertion is false but Reason is true.

6 Assertion (A) True solutions exhibits Tyndall effect.

Reason (R) Particles are very small in size.

Sol. (*d*) True solutions do not exhibit Tyndall effect, since the particle size is very small in size.
Hence, Assertion is false but Reason is true.

7 Assertion (A) Tyndall effect can also be observed when a fine beam of light enters a room through a small hole.

Reason (R) Scattering of light by the particles of dust and smoke in the air cause a Tyndall effect.

Sol. (*a*) Both Assertion and Reason are correct, and reason is the correct explanation for assertion.

8 Assertion (A) Chemical changes bring a variation in chemical properties.

Reason (R) Chemical change is also known as chemical reaction.

Sol. (*b*) In chemical changes, one substance reacts with another and undergoes a chemical change which brings a variation in chemical properties.
Hence, both Assertion and Reason are true but Reason is not the correct explanation of Assertion.

Case Based/Source Based Questions

Direction (Ques 1-4) Answer the questions on the basis of your understanding of the following passage, table and related studied concepts.

1 Nikhil's father was suffering from high blood pressure and cardiac problems. Doctor suggested him to take low fat milk. Nikhil churned the milk and separated the butter (fat) from it and then he served that milk to his father.

(i) Name the technique by which Nikhil separated butter from milk.

(ii) Write any other application of that technique.

(iii) Write two properties of a colloid.

Or

Write two components of solution. Explain in brief.

Sol. (i) It is called centrifugation carried in a centrifugal machine. [1]

(ii) Washing machines that are used for washing dirty clothes are centrifugal machines. [1]

(iii) Two properties of colloids are as follows :

(a) Colloids are heterogeneous mixture.

(b) The size of particles of a colloid is too small to be individually seen by naked eyes. [2]

Or

Two components of solution are solute and solvent.
The component of the solution that is dissolved in the solvent is called the solute whereas, the component of the solution that dissolves the other component in it, is called the solvent. [2]

2 Pure substances are classified as elements or compounds. An element is a substance that contains only one type of atom. A compound is a substance composed of two or more different types of elements, chemically combined in a fixed proportion. The constitutents cannot be separated by simple physical methods.

However, these substances can be broken down into separate elements by chemical methods.

On the other hand, mixtures are different from pure substances. They are called impure substances. They have different characteristics than elements and compounds.

When, mixture forms, there is only a little or no energy change. Mixtures are further classified into homogeneous and heterogeneous mixture.

(i) Why is wood considered a mixture?

(ii) Common salt is a compound. Give reason.

(iii) Write two properties which prove that water is a compound.

Or

Write two differences between elements and compounds.

Sol. (i) Wood is a mixture because it contains compounds such as cellulose, lignin which are composed of elements like carbon, hydrogen and oxygen. [1]

(ii) Common salt, which is sodium chloride (NaCl) made up of two elements in fixed proportion is a compound. [1]

(iii) Two properties of water that proves that water is a compound are

(a) water is made up of two different elements.

(b) the constituents of water cannot be separated by simple physical methods. [2]

Or

Two differences between elements and compounds are

(a) Elements are pure substances while compounds are composed of two or more pure substances.

(b) Elements are composed of single atom while compounds are chemically combined in fixed proportions. [2]

3. **We know that dissolved sodium chloride can be separated from water by the physical process of evaporation. However, sodium chloride is itself a substance and cannot be separated by physical process into its chemical constituents. Similarly, sugar is a substance because it contains only one kind of pure matter and its composition is the same throughout. Soft drink and soil are not single substances. Whatever the source of a substance may be, it will always have the same characteristic properties. Therefore, we can say that a mixture contains more than one substance.**

(i) Which of the following is a mixture?
Salt, Air, Water, Alum, Sugar

(ii) Name any three mixtures found in nature.

(iii) (a) Give an example of one element, one compound and one mixture.

(b) Soil and soft drinks classified into which category?

Or Write any two characteristics of mixture.

Sol. (i) Air is a mixture as it is composed of different gases in any proportion. [1]

(ii) Milk, paint and glass are examples of mixtures found in nature. [1]

(iii) (a) Sulphur is an element, water is a compound, and air is a mixture.

(b) Soil and soft drinks are classified into mixtures because they doesn't have definite composition. [2]

Or The characteristic of mixture are:

- The mixture has no fixed composition.
- Components of mixtures can be separated by simple physical methods. [2]

4. **A group of students took an old shoe box and covered it with a black paper from all sides. They fixed a source of light (a torch) at one end of the box by making a hole in it and made another hole on the other side to view the light. They placed a milk sample contained in a tumbler in the box as shown in the figure below. They were amazed to see that milk taken in the tumbler was illuminated. They tried the same activity by taking a salt solution but found that light simply passed through it.**

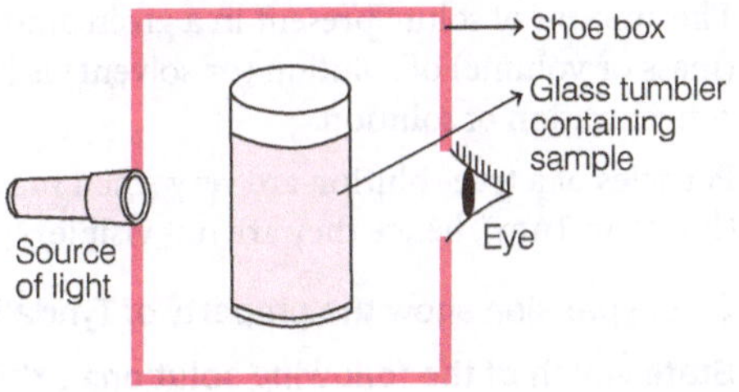

(i) Give one example of above phenomenon observed in our surroundings. [1]

(ii) Suggest two more solutions which could show the same effect as shown by the milk solution? [1]

(iii) Same results were not observed in a salt solution why? [1]

Or

Explain why the milk sample was illuminated? Name the phenomenon involved. [1]

Sol. (i) Tyndall effect is observed when sunlight passes through the canopy of a dense forest.

(ii) Soap solution and ink solution.

(iii) The Tyndall effects occurs when light is scattered by particles in a colloid or a suspension but salt solution is a true solution thus, tyndall effect is not observed in it.

Or

As milk solution is a colloidal solution and thus it would show Tyndall effect and gets illuminated. The phenomenon is known as Tyndall effect.

Constructed Response (Descriptive) Questions

Very Short Answer Type Questions

1. **(i) Is ice water homogeneous or heterogeneous substance? Is it pure or impure substance?**

(ii) Is fresh air free of dust particles and impurities of all other kind, a pure substance?

Sol. (i) Ice water is a heterogeneous substance because it has both a solid and liquid phase. It is a pure substance since ice is made up of water only. [1]

(ii) No, air is a mixture of gases and so, not a pure substance. [1]

2. **(i) The 'sea water' can be classified as a homogeneous as well as heterogeneous mixture. Comment.**

(ii) Write one property of suspension.

Sol. (i) Sea water is called homogeneous mixture as it contains dissolved salts in it. It may be called heterogeneous mixture as it contains various insoluble components too such as sand, microbes, shells made up of calcium carbonate and so many other things. [1]

(ii) Suspension is of heterogeneous nature. The solid particles represent one phase while the liquid in which these are present represents the other phase. [1]

3. (i) What is meant by concentration of a solution?

(ii) Why particles in a true solution cannot be seen with naked eyes?

Sol. (i) The amount of solute present in a given amount (mass or volume) of solution (or solvent) is known as concentration of solution. [1]

(ii) Particles of a true solution are very small in size (less than 1nm), hence they are not visible. [1]

4. (i) Do suspension show the property of Tyndall effect?

(ii) State which of the following solutions exhibit Tyndall effect?

Starch solution, sodium chloride solution, tincture of iodine, smoke. Competency Based Que.

Sol. (i) Yes, suspensions show the property of Tyndall effect because their particles are too large and they scatter the light. [1]

(ii) Starch solution and smoke. [1]

5. (i) What are the two component of solution. Also write the two common example of solution.

(ii) What are the favourable qualities given to gold when it is alloyed with copper or silver for the purpose of making ornaments?

Sol. (i) Solute and solvent are the two component of the solution.

Salt solution and a solution of iodine in alcohol i.e. tincture of iodine are two common examples of solution. [1]

(ii) When alloyed with copper or silver, the gold becomes harder and stronger and its brittleness decreases and become suitable for making ornaments. [1]

6. How will you justify that rusting of iron is a chemical change?

Sol. In a chemical change, new substance is formed and rust is totally different from iron. Iron is an element while rust is hydrated oxide of iron $(Fe_2O_3 \cdot xH_2O)$. Thus, formation of rust from iron is a chemical change. [2]

7. (i) Classify brass and diamond as element and mixture.

(ii) How is a chemical change differ from a physical change?

Sol. (i) Brass is a homogeneous mixture of copper and tin and diamond is an element. It is an allotropic form of carbon. [1]

(ii) In a chemical change, a new substance is formed as a result of chemical reaction. While in physical change, no new substance is formed. [1]

8. (i) Identify the heterogeneous mixture from the following.

Air, soda water, soap solution, brass

(ii) Write two components of a colloidal soltuion.

Sol. (i) Soap solution is a heterogeneous mixture while the rest are homogeneous mixture. [1]

(ii) The two components of a colloidal solution are dispersed phase and dispersion medium. [1]

9. 110 g of a solute are present in 550 g of solution. Calculate the concentration of solution.

Sol. Mass of solute = 110 g

Mass of solution = 550 g

$$\text{Concentration of solution} = \frac{\text{Mass of solute}}{\text{Mass of solution}} \times 100$$

$$= \frac{110}{550} \times 100 = 20\%$$ [2]

10. Smoke and fog both are aerosols. In what way are they different? Competency Based Que.

Sol. In smoke and fog, dispersion medium is same, i.e. air but they differ in dispersed phase. In smoke, solid carbon particle are dispersed in air while in fog, liquid water particles are dispersed in air. [2]

11. (i) Do mixture have definite chemical formula.

(ii) State any two properties of suspension.

Sol. (i) No, mixture does not have definite chemical formula. [1]

(ii) Suspension is a heterogeneous mixture having particle size greater than 100 nm. [1]

The particles of a suspension can be seen by the naked eye.

12. You are given two samples of water labelled as 'A' and 'B'. Sample 'A' boils at 100°C and sample 'B' boils at 102°C. Which sample of water will not freeze at 0°C? Comment Competency Based Que.

Sol. Sample 'B' will not freeze at 0°C because it is not pure. Water boils at 100°C and the freezing point of pure water is 0°C. [2]

13. Is it possible to distinguish particles of the solute from the solvent in solution? If yes or no, How?

Sol. No, it is not possible to distinguish the particles of the solute from the solvent in the solution. [1]

As a true solution is homogeneous in nature and solute and solvent molecules are very small in size. Thus, they cannot be distinguished even under a microscope. [1]

14. What is solid sol? Give example.

Sol. Solids in which dispersed phase and dispersion medium both are solids is called solid sol. [1]

Examples Gemstone, coloured glass, alloys etc. [1]

15. Zinc dissolves in hydrochloric acid with the evolution of hydrogen gas. Is it a physical or chemical change?

Sol. It is a chemical change because chemical reaction takes place between zinc and hydrochloric acid with the evolution of hydrogen gas and a compound zinc chloride is formed. [2]

Short Answer Type Questions

1 (i) Non-metals are usually poor conductors of heat and electricity. They are non-lustrous, non-sonorous, non-malleable and are coloured.

(a) Name a non-metal which is required for combustion.

(b) Name a non-metal that forms common salt with sodium.

(ii) Write two physical properties of metals.

Sol. (i) (a) Oxygen [½]

(b) Chlorine [½]

(ii) Two physical properties of metals are [2]

(a) Metals are malleable and ductile.

(b) They have shining surface known as lusture.

2 Classify the substances given below into elements and compounds.

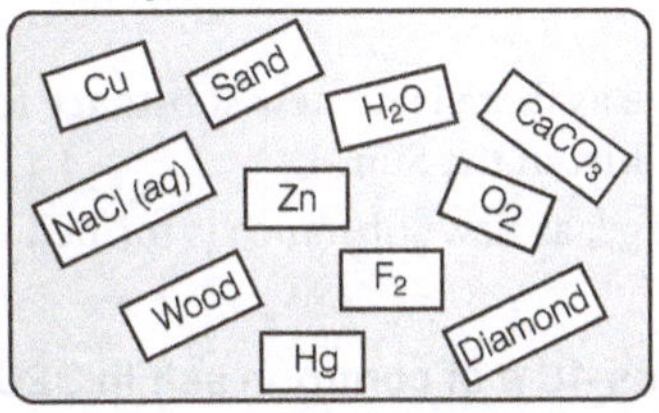

Competency Based Que.

Sol. The given substances are classified as follows.

Elements	Compounds
Cu	
O_2	H_2O
Zn	$CaCO_3$
F_2	NaCl(*aq*)
Hg	
Diamond (carbon)	

Wood and sand are neither an element nor a compound. They are mixtures. An element is made up of the same type of atoms and compound is a mixture of different elements but in a fixed ratio. O_2 and F_2 are molecular elements. [3]

3 (i) Which of the following are not compounds?

Chlorine gas, Potassium, Iron, Iron sulphide, Aluminium, Iodine, Carbon, Carbon monoxide and Sulphur powder. **NCERT Exemplar**

(ii) What is the difference between a pure substance and a mixture?

Sol. (i) (i) Chlorine gas (ii) Potassium

(iii) Iron (v) Aluminium

(vi) Iodine (vii) Carbon

(ix) Sulphur powder

Substances mentioned above are the elements, not compounds. Cl_2 gas is a molecular element. [1]

(ii) A pure substance is an element or compound that can not be separated into other kinds of matter by any physical means while a mixture is a physical combination of two or more pure substances. [2]

4 (i) Give the difference between mixture and compound.

(ii) Classify the following mixtures as homogeneous and heterogeneous.

(a) Tincture of iodine

(b) Smoke

(c) Brass

(d) Sugar solution

Sol. (i) Mixtures are substances that are formed by physically mixing two or more substances. Compounds are substances which can be formed by combining two or more elements in a fixed ratio. [2]

(ii) (a) Homogeneous (b) Heterogeneous

(c) Homogeneous (d) Homogeneous [1]

5 Tell whether each of the following properties describes a homogeneous mixture, a solution, a heterogeneous mixture, a compound or an element.

(i) A homogeneous liquid which leaves a solid residue on boiling.

(ii) A cloudy liquid which after sometime appears more cloudy towards the bottom.

(iii) A colourless liquid which boils at a definite temperature and can be decomposed into simpler substances. **Competency Based Que.**

Sol. (i) A solution (a solid like salt dissolved in water from which water evaporates on boiling, leaving a solid residue, salt). [1]

(ii) A heterogeneous mixture in which suspended particles start settling down at the bottom (muddy water). [1]

(iii) A compound as it can be decomposed into simpler substances. [1]

6 What would you observe when

(i) a saturated solution of potassium chloride prepared at 60°C is allowed to cool at room temperature?

(ii) an aqueous sugar solution is heated to dryness?

(iii) Sugar is added in a saturated sugar water solution?

Sol. (i) Crystals of potassium chloride are formed because solubility decreases with decrease in temperature. [1]

(ii) As water evaporates completely, sugar gets charred and turns black. [1]

(iii) No more sugar is dissolved in the saturated solution and will precipitate at the bottom. [1]

7 Why copper sulphate solution in water does not show Tyndall effect, but mixture of water and milk shows? **Competency Based Que.**

Sol. The solution of copper sulphate in water is a true solution. In a true solution, the solute particles are so small that they cannot scatter light falling on them.

Hence, copper sulphate solution in water does not show Tyndall effect. Mixture of water and milk is a colloid and in colloidal solution, the particles are big enough to scatter light. So, the mixture of water and milk shows Tyndall effect. [3]

8 Name the process associated with the following:

(i) A drop of ink placed on the surface of water contained in a glass spreads throughout the water.

(ii) Curdling of milk

(iii) Fine beam of light entering through a small hole in a dark room, illuminates the particles in its paths.

Sol. (i) Diffusion (ii) Chemical process

(iii) Tyndall effect [3]

9 Determine whether each of the following change is physical or chemical. Give reason for your answer.

(i) A balloon filled with hydrogen gas explodes upon contact with a spark.

(ii) Copper turns green on exposure to air and water.

(iii) A metal surface becomes dull because of continued abrasion.

Sol. (i) **Chemical change** Hydrogen gas burns to form water, a new substance. [1]

(ii) **Chemical change** Copper combines with oxygen of air and water to form copper oxide which has green colour. [1]

(iii) **Physical change** Some of the particles of metal from the surface are removed. As a result, only physical appearance changes. [1]

10 Can physical and chemical changes occur together? Explain it giving an example. **Competency Based Que.**

Sol. In some cases, physical and chemical changes occur together. One such example is burning of a candle. The solid wax present in the candle first changes into liquid state and then into the vapour state. Both these changes are physical changes. [1]

The wax vapours then combine with oxygen of the air to form a mixture of carbon dioxide and water. This involves a chemical change. [1]

The unburnt wax vapours again change first to the liquid state and finally to the solid state. This interconversion of states is a physical change. Thus, burning of a candle involves both physical and chemical changes. [1]

11 Calculate the mass of sodium sulphate required to prepare its 20% (mass per cent) solution in 100 g of water? **NCERT Exemplar**

Sol. Mass % of sodium sulphate solution = 20%

Mass of the solvent = 100 g

Let the mass of solute (sodium sulphate) = x g

Applying the formula,

$$\text{Mass \%} = \frac{\text{Mass of solute}}{\text{Mass of solution}} \times 100$$

$$20 = \frac{x \text{ g}}{(x + 100) \text{ g}} \times 100$$

$$\Rightarrow \quad 20(x+100) = 100x \quad \Rightarrow \quad 20x + 2000 = 100x$$

$$\Rightarrow \quad 100x - 20x = 2000 \quad \Rightarrow \quad 80x = 2000$$

$$\therefore \quad x = \frac{2000}{80} = 25 \text{ g}$$

Mass of sodium sulphate = 25 g [3]

12 Classify each of the following, as a physical or a chemical change. Give reasons.

(i) Drying of a shirt in the Sun.

(ii) Changing the colour of black tea on adding lemon juice to it.

Sol. (i) Physical change as there is no new substance formed in drying of a shirt in the Sun. [1½]

(ii) Chemical change, as new substance is formed in this process. [1½]

13 A solution contains 40 g of common salt in 320 g of water. Calculate the concentration in terms of mass by mass percentage of the solution.

Sol. Mass of solute (salt) = 40 g

Mass of solvent (water) = 320 g

Mass of solution = Mass of solute + Mass of solvent

$$= 40 \text{ g} + 320 \text{ g} = 360 \text{ g}$$

$$\text{Mass \% of solution} = \frac{\text{Mass of solute}}{\text{Mass of solution}} \times 100$$

$$= \frac{40}{360} \times 100 = 11.1\%$$

[3]

14 (i) Particles of colloidal solution' don't settle when left alone, but suspensions do. Explain.

(ii) What happens when hot saturated solution is allowed to cool? **Competency Based Que.**

Sol. (i) Colloidal particles are smaller in size. They remain in a state of *zig-zag* motion always. Thus they do not settles down. However, the particles in suspension are larger, so they settle down under the influence of gravity. [1½]

(ii) On cooling, the solubility of the saturated solution decreases and it starts forming crystals and settles down at the bottom of the container. [1½]

15 (i) State any one point of difference between mixture and compound.

(ii) Why are the mixtures called substances?

(iii) What are the types of colloids?

Sol. (i) Mixtures have variable composition while compounds have fixed composition. [1]

(ii) Mixtures are called substances because they are formed by mixing two or more substances with different proportions. [1]

(iii) Types of colloids are aerosol, emulsion, sol, gel, solid sol. [1]

16 Classify the following as physical or chemical properties.

(i) The composition of a sample of steel is 98% iron, 1.5% carbon and 0.5 % other elements.

(ii) Metallic sodium is soft enough to be cut with a knife.

(iii) Most metal oxides form alkalies on interacting with water.

Sol. (i) It is a physical property as no new compound is formed because steel is an alloy which is a homogeneous mixture of two or more metals or of metallic elements with non-metallic elements. [1]

(ii) It is a physical property because cutting with knife does not form new substance. [1]

(iii) It is a chemical property as new compound is being formed by the reaction of metal oxide and water.

$$\underset{\text{Metal oxide}}{M_2O(s)} + \underset{\text{Water}}{H_2O(l)} \longrightarrow \underset{\text{Metal hydroxide}}{2MOH(aq)}$$ [1]

Long Answer Type Questions

1 (i) What are elements?

(ii) What are the three main types of elements?

(iii) Identify the dispersed phase and dispersion medium in the following examples of colloids

(a) Fog

(b) Cheese

(c) Coloured gem stone

Sol. (i) An element consists of only one type of atoms. It is a basic form of matter that cannot be broken down into simpler substances further by chemical reactions. [1]

(ii) Metals, non-metals and metalloids. [1]

(iii) **Fog** Liquid (water drops) acts as a dispersed phase and gas (air) as the dispersion medium. [1]

Cheese Solid (fat) acts as the dispersed phase and water (liquid) as the dispersion medium. [1]

Coloured gem stone Solid acts as the dispersed phase as well as the dispersion medium. [1]

2 (i) Air is a mixture and not a compound. Explain.

(ii) Write a property of suspension.

(iii) Arrange the solids, liquids and gases in increasing order of the following properties of matter.

(a) Rigidity (b) Diffusion

Sol. (i) Air is a homogeneous mixture of different gases which can be separated by suitable methods. Therefore, it is a mixture and not a compound. [1½]

(ii) Suspension is a homogeneous in nature. The solid particles represents one phase while the liquid in which these are present, represents the other phase. [1½]

(iii) (a) **Rigidity** : Gases < Liquids < Solids

(b) **Diffusion** : Solids < Liquids < Gases [2]

3 (i) Pond water contains sand grains, clay particles, salt, pieces of paper and some air bubbles. Select from amongst these, an example each of a solvent, solute, colloid and suspension.

(ii) Give one example of each of the following:

Competency Based Que.

(a) A solution of gas in liquid

(b) A solution of two solids

(c) A solution of two gases

Sol. (i) Solvent–Water

Solute–Salt, pieces of paper, air bubbles

Colloid–Mixture of air bubbles and water

Suspension–

(a) Mixture of water and sand grains

(b) Mixture of water and clay particles [2]

(ii) (a) Aerated drinks, (b) Brass, (c) Air [3]

4 (i) What is meant by saying that non-metals are brittle? Give examples of non-metals.

(ii) What is the general name of the materials which contain atleast two pure substances and show the properties of their constituents?

(iii) What is the significant difference between a solution and an ordinary mixture?

Sol. (i) Non-metals are brittle and cannot be hammered into thin sheets. They will break into smaller pieces if hammered. e.g. Sulphur, phosphorus etc. [2]

(ii) Materials made up of two or more pure substances and showed the properties of their constituents are called mixtures. [1]

(iii) A mixture is a substance that consists of two or more elements or compounds in any proportion, which might be distinct or indistinct. On the other hand, a solution is an example of a homogeneous mixture, i.e. substances in the solution are entirely mixed and indistinguishable. [2]

5 (i) Identify two non-metals from the following elements:

Carbon, sodium, chlorine, neon, platinum

(ii) Identify dispersed phase and dispersion medium in foam and rubber.

(iii) Define solubility. How does solubility of a solid in water change with temperature?

Sol. (i) **Non-metals** Carbon, chlorine. [1]

(ii) Dispersed phase is gas and dispersion medium is solid. [1]

(iii) Solubility is the property of a solid, liquid or gaseous chemical substance called solute to dissolve in a solid, liquid or gaseous solvent to form a solution of the solute in the solvent.

The solubility increases with temperature. The increase in kinetic energy that comes with higher temperature allows the solvent molecules to more effectively break apart the solute particles that are held together by force between the particles. [3]

6 (i) Give reason for the following statements.

(a) Mixture does not have a fixed melting or fixed boiling point.

(b) Metals are good conductors of heat and electricity whereas non metals are not.

(ii) Write your observations when the following process-takes place.

(a) An aqueous solution of sugar is heated till it gets dried up.

(b) A saturated solution of KCl at 60 °C is allowed to cool at room temperature.

(iii) Mention one property in which colloids differs from suspension. **Competency Based Que.**

Sol. (i) (a) The mixtures does not have fixed melting or boiling point because it consists of different elements and they do not have fixed composition. [1]

(b) Metals are good conductors of heat and electricity because they have free electrons whereas non-metals are good conductors of heat and electricity because electrons are not free to move in non-metals. [1]

(ii) (a) Sugar remains as residue in form of solid mass.

(b) Crystals of KCl are formed. [2]

(iii) In suspension, residue is left on filter paper whereas in colloidal solution, particles pass through filter paper. [1]

7 During an experiment, the students were asked to prepare a 10% (mass/mass) solution of sugar in water. Ramesh dissolved 10 g of sugar in 100 g of water while Sarika prepared it by dissolving 10 g of sugar in water to make 100 g of the solution. **NCERT Exemplar**

(i) Are the two solutions of the same concentration?

(ii) Compare the mass % of the two solutions.

Sol. (i) No. [1]

(ii) Concentration of Ramesh's solution

$$\text{Mass \%} = \frac{\text{Mass of solute}}{\text{Mass of solution}} \times 100$$

$$= \frac{10\text{ g}}{(10+100)\text{g}} \times 100 = \frac{10}{110} \times 100 = \frac{100}{11}$$

$$= 9.09\% = 9.1\%$$

Concentration of Sarika's solution

$$\text{Mass \%} = \frac{10}{100} \times 100 = 10\%$$

The solution prepared by Ramesh has less percentage by mass than that of Sarika. [4]

8 Calculate the mass of sugarcane and water required to produce 250 g of solution with 25% concentration.

Sol. Let the mass of solute (sugarcane) be 'x'.

Mass of solution = 250 g

Therefore, concentration of solution

$$= \frac{\text{Mass of solute}}{\text{Volume of solution}} \times 100$$

$$25 = \frac{x}{250} \times 100$$

$$\therefore \quad x = 62.5\text{ g}$$ [2]

Also, the mass of water = Mass of solution − Mass of solute (sugar cane)

$$= 250\text{g} - 62.5\text{g}$$

$$= 187.5\text{ g}$$

Hence, the mass of sugarcane is 62.5g and mass of water is 187.5 g. [1]

ASSESSMENT EXERCISE

Competency Focused (Objective) Questions

Multiple Choice Questions

1 Select the homogeneous mixture from the following.
(a) Carbon dioxide gas dissolved in water.
(b) Air containing suspended particles.
(c) Soap bubbles formed by blowing air into soap solution.
(d) Water in milk.

2 Which of the following substance cannot be broken down by a chemical method?
(a) Ammonia (NH_3)
(b) Helium (He)
(c) Methane (CH_4)
(d) Water (H_2O)

3 Which of the following is a chemical change?
(a) Melting of iron metal.
(b) Rusting of iron.
(c) Bending of an iron rod.
(d) Drawing a wire of iron metal.

4 Fog is classified as
(a) emulsion (b) foam
(c) aerosol (d) sol

5 Which of the following substances shows tyndall effect?
(a) NaCl solution (b) Kerosene oil
(c) Milk (d) Cold drink

Assertion-Reason Questions

Direction (Q. Nos. 6-8) *In each of the following questions, a statement of Assertion is given by the corresponding statement of Reason. Of the statements, mark the correct answer as*

(a) Both Assertion and Reason are true and Reason is the correct explanation of Assertion.
(b) Both Assertion and Reason are true but Reason is not the correct explanation of Assertion.
(c) Assertion is true but Reason is false.
(d) Assertion is false and Reason is true.

6 Assertion (A) Milk of magnesia is an example of Aerosol.
Reason (R) Dispersed phase is solid and dispersion medium is liquid in case of sol.

7 Assertion (A) Tyndall effect is exhibited by a true solution.
Reason (R) Scattering of beam of light by the colloidal particles is known as Tyndall effect.

8 Assertion (A) A solution of table salt in a glass of water is homogeneous.
Reason (R) A solution having different composition throught is homogeneous.

Answers

1. (a) **2.** (b) **3.** (b) **4.** (c) **5.** (c)
6. (d) **7.** (d) **8.** (c)

Case Based/Source Based Questions

9 Ravi took some amount of substance *X* and add it into a transparent beaker containing water. He mixed the solution very well and then passed light through this solution by using a torch. The result observed by him is shown below.

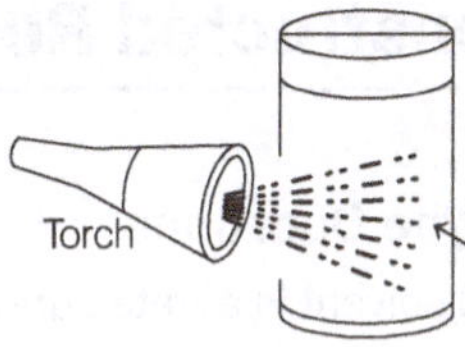

Ravi wants to show this experiment to his younger brother. He kept the solution for 10 minutes and calls his brother and further repeated the experiment, but results was different at this time. The path was not visible.

(i) What are the suspended particles and medium in this experiment?
(ii) What is the nature of solution obtained, when *X* is added to water?
(iii) What observation(s) was made when the light passed through the solution in this experiment?
Or What was the reason for change in result in the above experiment?

10 In chemistry, a mixture is made when two or more substances are combined, but they are not combined chemically. The components of a mixture can be easily separated. The physical and chemical properties of a mixture may vary depending on the relative concentrations of the substances contained within it. If a mixture is not uniform in composition, it is termed as heterogeneous mixture while a homogeneous mixture has uniform composition. A true solution is homogeneous and transparent mixture that can be completely filtered through filter paper. It remains stable on standing. A colloidal solution is heterogeneous and translucent mixture, that can be filtered completely through the filter paper. In colloidal solutions, solute particles do not easily settle down on standing. A suspension is heterogeneous mixture. The particles of a suspension are visible with the naked eyes. They settle down on standing and can be separated by filtration.

(i) Write two properties about the sand in water mixture. [1]

(ii) Three solutions *A*, *B* and *C* were filtered. Solution *A* passed through the filter paper and the filtrate was clear. Solution *B* passed through the filter paper and the solution was translucent. Solution *C* left residue on the filter paper while the filtrate was clear. What is the order of the relative size of solute particles in solutions *A*, *B* and *C*. [1]

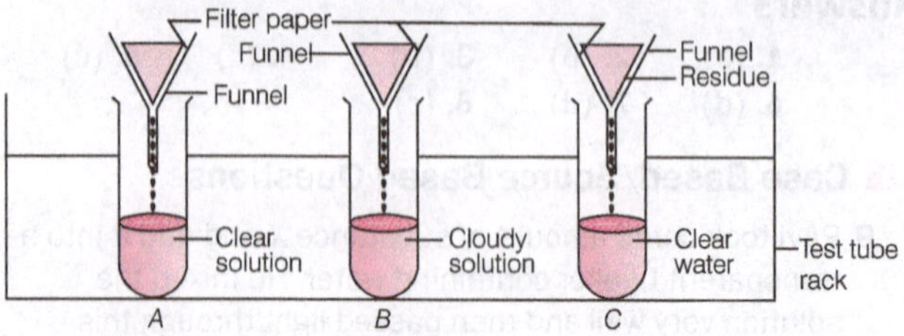

(iii) A student listed some common examples of colloids and classified them into various types.

	Example	Components	Type
A.	Fog	Solid + gas	Aerosol
B.	Shaving cream	Gas + liquid	Foam
C.	Jelly	Liquid + solid	Gel
D.	Milk	Liquid + liquid	Solid sol

Which colloids are classified correctly? Also explain how other are not classified correctly? [2]

Or A student added the substances given below to water kept in four separate beakers. He stirred the mixtures well and filtered each of them. In which case he would obtain a solid residue on the filter paper? Explain your answer. [2]

Constructed Response (Descriptive) Questions

Very Short Answer Type Questions

11 (i) What are solute and solvent in aerated drinks?

(ii) Name the two components of a colloid.

12 (i) What is the particle size of a colloidal solution?

(ii) Define the term colloidal solution.

13 (i) Differentiate between physical and chemical change.

(ii) 'All mixtures are homogeneous', comment upon this statement.

14 (i) A solution contains 16 g of urea in 120 g of the solution. What is mass by mass percentage of solution?

(ii) A solution contains 50 mL of alcohol mixed with 150 mL of water. Calculate the concentration of this solution.

15 (i) The solubility of potassium nitrate at 20°C is 32 g per 100 g of water. How much salt is required to prepare 66 g of its saturated solution?

(ii) How many litres of 15% (mass/volume) sugar solution would it take to get 75 g of sugar?

Competency Based Que.

Short Answer Type Questions

16 (i) What is the difference between a pure substance and a mixture? Give one example in each case.

(ii) List any two differences between mixtures and compounds.

17 (i) Define solubility. How does solubility of a solid in water changes with temperature?

(ii) Mention the three characteristics of a mixture.

18 What happens, when **Competency Based Que.**

(i) light is passed through a colloidal solution?

(ii) electricity is passed through a colloidal solution?

(iii) sugar solution is kept undisturbed.

19 Give one example of each of the following.

(i) Solution of a gas in liquid.

(ii) Solution of a liquid in solid.

(iii) Solution of a solid in solid.

Long Answer Type Questions

20 (i) Under which category of mixtures will you classify alloys and why?

(ii) A solution is always a liquid. Comment.

(iii) Can a solution be heterogeneous?

Competency Based Que.

21 (i) Explain why colloidal solutions particles don't get settle when left alone, but suspensions do.

(ii) What is the significant difference between a solution and an ordinary mixture?

22 (i) State one property in which a solution of sugar in water resembles of sugar and sand and one property in which it differ from it.

(ii) What would you observe when a colloidal solution of starch is passed through an ordinary filter paper?

(iii) Calculate the volume by volume percentage of a solution of 15 mL of alcohol in 60 mL of water.

CHAPTER 03

Atoms and Molecules

In the previous chapter, we learned about 'Matter'. An Indian philosopher Maharishi Kanad postulated that if we go on dividing matter, we shall get smaller and smaller particles. He named these tiniest particle, Parmanu.

Another Philosopher-Democritus and Leucippus suggested that if we go on dividing matter, a stage will come when particles obtained cannot be divided further. Democritus called these indivisible particles 'atoms'.

In the present chapter, we shall discuss about the various laws (which explains how atoms combine to form molecule), symbols and formulae of atoms and molecules and various ways of expressing their masses.

3.1 Laws of Chemical Combination

Whenever, the elements combine together to form a compound (or reactant react together to form the product), they do this according to certain laws. These laws are called laws of chemical combination.

Antoine L. Lavoisier laid the foundation of chemical sciences by establishing two important laws of chemical combination which are as follows

1. Law of Conservation of Mass

It states that, 'mass can neither be created nor destroyed during a chemical reaction.' This means that in any chemical reaction, the total mass of the reactants is equal to the total mass of the products and there is no change in mass during the chemical reaction.

Example 1. **If 4.0 g of sodium carbonate reacts with 10 g of hydrochloric acid, it results in the formation of 2.5 g of carbon dioxide and 11.5 g of sodium chloride solution. Show that these results are in accordance with the law of conservation of mass.**

Sol. $\underset{(4.0\text{ g})}{\text{Sodium carbonate}} + \underset{(10.0\text{ g})}{\text{Hydrochloric acid}} \longrightarrow \underset{(2.5\text{ g})}{\text{Carbon dioxide}} + \underset{(11.5\text{ g})}{\text{Sodium chloride}}$

Here, total mass of reactants $= 4.0 + 10 = 14\text{ g}$

Total mass of products $= 2.5 + 11.5 = 14\text{ g}$

Since, the reactants and products have the same mass, this means that there was no loss or gain of mass after the reaction. Hence, it proves the law of conservation of mass.

2. Law of Constant or Definite Proportions

This law was stated by Proust according to which 'in a chemical substance (or compound), the elements are always present in definite proportions (or ratio) by mass'.

e.g. In a compound such as water, the ratio of the mass of hydrogen to the mass of oxygen is always 1 : 8, whatever the source of water. Thus, if 9 g of water is decomposed, 1 g of hydrogen and 8 g of oxygen are always obtained.

Similarly, carbon dioxide (CO_2) always contains carbon and oxygen in the ratio of 3 : 8. If a sample of CO_2 contains 36 g of carbon, then it is compulsory that the sample has 96 g of oxygen.

This is calculated as $\frac{3}{8} = \frac{36}{x}$;

$$\therefore \quad x = \frac{36 \times 8}{3} = 96\text{ g}$$

Example 2. **Copper oxide was prepared by two different methods. In one case, 1.75 g of the metal gave 2.19 g of oxide. In the second case, 1.14 g of the metal gave 1.43 g of the oxide. Show that the given data illustrate the law of constant proportions.**

Sol. *Case* I Mass of copper = 1.75 g

And mass of copper oxide = 2.19 g

So, mass of oxygen = Mass of copper oxide − Mass of copper $= 2.19 - 1.75 = 0.44\text{ g}$

Now, in first sample of copper oxide compound.

Mass of copper : Mass of oxygen = 1.75 : 0.44

$$= \frac{1.75}{0.44} : 1 = 3.98 : 1 \approx 4 : 1$$

Case II Mass of copper = 1.14 g

And, mass of copper oxide = 1.43 g

So, mass of oxygen = Mass of copper oxide − Mass of copper

$$= 1.43 - 1.14 = 0.29 \text{ g}$$

Now, in second sample of copper oxide compound,

Mass of copper : Mass of oxygen = 1.14 : 0.29

$$= \frac{1.14}{0.29} : 1$$

$$= 3.93 : 1 \approx 4 : 1$$

From the above calculations we can see that the ratio (or proportion) of copper and oxygen elements in the two samples of copper oxide compound is the same, i.e. 4 : 1. So, the given data verify the law of constant proportions.

Explanation of Laws of Chemical Combination : Dalton's Atomic Theory

This theory provided an explanation for both the laws of chemical combination. According to this theory, all matter whether an element, a compound or a mixture is composed of small particles called **atoms.**

The main postulates of Dalton's atomic theory are as follows

- Every matter is made up of very small particles called atoms which participate in chemical reactions.
- Atoms are indivisible particles, which can neither be created nor be destroyed in a chemical reaction.
- Atoms of a given element are identical in mass as well as in chemical properties.
- Atoms of different elements have different masses and chemical properties.
- Atoms combine in the ratio of small whole numbers to form compounds.
- The relative number and kinds of atoms are constant in a given compound.

Try These 3.1

1. **If 100 g of calcium carbonate on heating produces 44 g of carbon dioxide, how much quicklime will be formed? Which law is followed for solving this problem?**
[Ans. 56 g; law of conservation of mass]
2. **In a given sample of ammonia, 9 g hydrogen and 42 g nitrogen are present. In another sample, 5 g hydrogen is present alongwith nitrogen. Calculate the amount of nitrogen in the second sample.** [Ans. 23.33 g]
3. **Which law states, that in a chemical compound, elements always combine in a fixed proportion?**
4. **What are 'atoms' according to Dalton's atomic theory?**
5. **20 g silver nitrate solution is added to 20 g of sodium chloride solution. What change in mass do you expect after the reaction and why?**

3.2 Atoms

These are the smallest particles of an element which may or may not have independent existence but take part in a chemical reaction. These are the building blocks of all matter.

The atoms of hydrogen, oxygen, nitrogen, etc., are not capable of independent existence whereas atoms of helium, neon etc., are capable of existing independently.

Size of Atoms

Atoms are very small and their radius is measured in **nanometres.** (1 m = 10^9 nm)

Hydrogen atom is the smallest atom and its radius is 0.1 nm.

Modern Day Symbols of Atoms of Different Elements

In chemistry, symbols are the representation of an element. It is simple to use the symbol of an element rather writing a whole word of an element. Dalton was the first scientist who introduced the symbols for representing elements in a very specific sense.

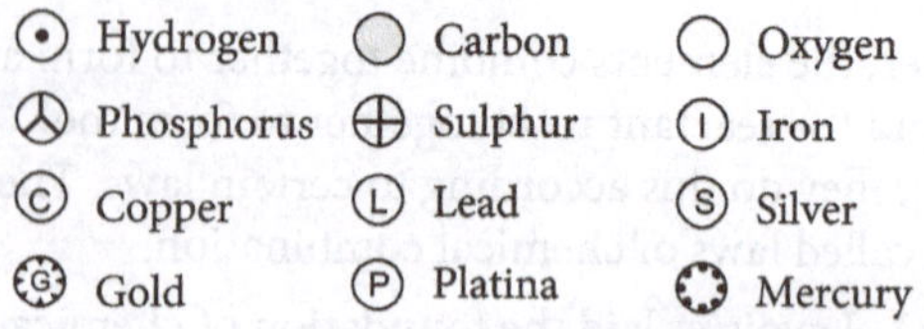

Symbols for some elements as proposed by Dalton

When he used a symbol for an element he also meant a definite quantity of that element, i.e. one atom of that element.

As Dalton's symbol for elements were difficult to draw and inconvenient to use, modern symbols for the elements were introduced by **J J Berzilius.** He suggested that the symbols of elements be made from one or two letters of the name of the element.

In the beginning, the names of elements were derived from the name of the place where they were found for the first time. e.g. copper from cyprus. Some names were taken from specific colours e.g. gold from english word meaning 'yellow'.

Now a days, IUPAC (International Union of Pure and Applied Chemistry) approves the names and symbols of the elements. The first letter of a symbol is always written in capital letter and the second letter in small letter.

e.g. Chlorine (Cl), zinc (Zn) and aluminium (Al).

Symbols of some elements have been taken from their names in different languages such as Latin, German, Greek etc.

e.g. Iron	—	Fe from *Ferrum* (Latin name)
Gold	—	Au from *Aurum* (Latin name)
Potassium	—	K from *Kalium* (Latin name)

Symbols for Some Elements

Element	Symbol	Element	Symbol	Element	Symbol
Aluminium	Al	Copper	Cu	Nitrogen	N
Argon	Ar	Fluorine	F	Oxygen	O
Barium	Ba	Gold	Au	Phosphorus	P
Boron	B	Hydrogen	H	Potassium	K
Bromine	Br	Iodine	I	Silicon	Si
Calcium	Ca	Iron	Fe	Silver	Ag
Carbon	C	Lead	Pb	Sodium	Na
Chlorine	Cl	Magnesium	Mg	Sulphur	S
Chromium	Cr	Mercury	Hg	Uranium	U
Cobalt	Co	Neon	Ne	Zinc	Zn

Atomic Mass

According to Dalton's, each element has a characteristic atomic mass. But determining the mass of an individual atom was a relatively difficult task due to its very small size. Hence, their relative atomic masses were determined by using the laws of chemical combinations and the compounds formed.

For this purpose, initially 1/16 of the mass of an atom of naturally occurring oxygen was taken as standard unit because of the following two reasons.

- Oxygen reacted with a large number of elements and formed compounds.
- This atomic mass unit gave masses of most of the elements as whole numbers.

However, in 1961 carbon 12 isotope was chosen as standard reference for measuring atomic masses universally.

Atomic Mass Unit

It is defined as the mass unit equal to exactly 1/12th of the mass of one atom of C-12 isotope. Earlier, it was abbreviated as **amu** but according to latest recommendations of IUPAC, it is now written as **'u'- unified mass.**

Relative Atomic Mass

It is defined as the number of times a given atom is heavier than 1/12th of mass of 1 atom of carbon-12 (C-12) or it is the average mass of the atom as compared to 1/12th the mass of one carbon-12 atom.

Atomic Masses of a few Elements

Element	Atomic Mass (u)
Hydrogen	1
Carbon	12
Nitrogen	14
Oxygen	16
Sodium	23
Magnesium	24
Sulphur	32
Chlorine	35.5
Calcium	40

Existence of Atoms

Atoms of most elements are not able to exist independently. Atoms form molecules and ions. These molecules or ions aggregate in large numbers to form the matter that we can see, feel or touch.

3.3 Molecules

The smallest particle of an element or compound which is capable of independent existence and shows all the properties of that substance is called a **molecule.**

In general, molecule is a group of two or more atoms that are chemically bonded together i.e. tightly held together by attractive forces. Atoms of the same element or of different elements can join together to form molecules.

Molecules can be divided into two categories.

1. Molecules of Elements

The molecules of an element contains same type of atoms. Molecules of many elements are made up of only one atom of that element. e.g. Noble gases like argon (Ar), helium (He) etc.

The molecules of most of the non-metals are made up of more than one atom.

e.g. A molecule of oxygen (O_2) consists of two atoms of oxygen, ozone (O_3) consists of three atoms of oxygen.

Atomicity

It is defined as the number of atoms present in a molecule. On the basis of atomicity, molecules can be classified as

(i) **Monoatomic molecules** They consist of only one atom.
e.g. He, Ne, Ar, Xe, Fe, Al etc.

(ii) **Diatomic molecules** They consist of two atoms.
e.g. $H_2, O_2, N_2, I_2, Br_2, Cl_2$ etc.

(iii) **Triatomic molecules** They consist of three atoms.
e.g. O_3 etc.

(iv) **Tetra-atomic molecules** They consist of four atoms.
e.g. P_4 etc.

(v) **Polyatomic molecules** They consist of more than four atoms.
e.g. S_8 (octa-atomic) etc.

2. Molecules of Compounds

Atoms of different elements join together in definite proportions to form molecules of compounds.

Molecules of Some Compounds

Compound	Combining Elements	Ratio by Mass
Water (H_2O)	Hydrogen and oxygen	1 : 8
Ammonia (NH_3)	Nitrogen and hydrogen	14 : 3
Carbon dioxide (CO_2)	Carbon and oxygen	3 : 8
Hydrogen sulphide (H_2S)	Hydrogen and sulphur	1 : 16
Sulphuric acid (H_2SO_4)	Hydrogen, sulphur and oxygen	1 : 16 : 32

Prediction of Number of Atoms from Mass Ratio

In order to predict the number of atoms from mass ratio, divide the given mass of each element by the atomic mass of the element and calculate the simplest ratio between the obtained moles, e.g. we know that mass ratio of nitrogen and hydrogen in ammonia molecule is 14 : 3.

The number of atoms of nitrogen and hydrogen present in the molecule of ammonia can be calculated as,

Element	Ratio by Mass (x)	Atomic Mass (y)	Mass Ratio/Atomic Mass (x/y)	Simplest Ratio
N	14	14	$\frac{14}{14}=1$	1
H	3	1	$\frac{3}{1}=3$	3

Thus, in ammonia molecule, one N and three H-atoms are present hence, the formula of ammonia is NH_3.

Try These 3.2

1. **Name any two elements whose symbols do not start with the same letter as that of the name of the element.**
2. **Why the symbols of few elements, like sodium, do not start with the initial letter of the name?**
3. **Write the correct symbol for each of the given elements.**
   (i) Sodium (So) (ii) Hydrogen (Hg)
   (iii) Copper (Co) (iv) Sulphur (s)
   (v) Calcium (CA)
4. **What is the difference between 2Cl and Cl_2? Which one of these two forms exists in nature? Also, give the atomic mass of this element.**
5. **An oxide of nitrogen is found to contain nitrogen and oxygen combined together in the ratio of 7 : 16 by mass. Derive the formula of the oxide and name it.**

3.4 Ions

Compounds composed of metals and non-metals contain charged species. These charged species are called ions. These are of two types, i.e. anions and cations.

Cations

The positively charged ions are known as cations, e.g. $Na^+, K^+, Ca^{2+}, Al^{3+}$ etc. These are formed when elements loses electrons. Usually, metals form cations.

Anions

The negatively charged ions are known as anions, e.g. $Cl^-, Br^-, O^{2-}, N^{3-}$ etc. These are formed when elements gain electrons. Usually, non-metals form anions.

Polyatomic Ions

A group of atoms carrying charge and act as a single entity are known as a polyatomic ions. It carries a fixed charge. e.g. NO_3^- (nitrate ion), CO_3^{2-} (carbonate ion) and SO_4^{2-} (sulphate ion) etc.

Some Ionic Compounds

Ionic Compounds	Constituting Elements	Ratio by Mass
Calcium oxide	Calcium and oxygen	5:2
Magnesium sulphide	Magnesium and sulphur	3:4
Sodium chloride	Sodium and chlorine	23:35.5

Note **Ionic compounds** are neutral compounds formed by cations and anions, e.g. sodium chloride or common salt (NaCl) consists of a positively charged sodium ion (Na^+, cation) and negatively charged chloride ion (Cl^-, anion).

3.5 Valency

The combining power (or capacity) of an element is called its **valency**. It can be used to find out how the atoms of an element will combine with the atom(s) of another element to form a chemical compound. The valency of an ion is equal to the charge on the ion.

Names, Symbols and Valency of Some Ions

Valency	Ion of metallic element	Symbol	Ion of non-metallic element	Symbol	Polyatomic ions	Symbol
1	Sodium	Na^+	Hydrogen	H^+	Ammonium	NH_4^+
	Potassium	K^+	Hydride	H^-	Hydroxide	OH^-
	Silver	Ag^+	Chloride	Cl^-	Nitrate	NO_3^-
	Copper (I)*	Cu^+	Bromide	Br^-	Hydrogen carbonate (bicarbonate)	HCO_3^-
			Iodide	I^-		
2	Magnesium	Mg^{2+}	Oxide	O^{2-}	Carbonate	CO_3^{2-}
	Calcium	Ca^{2+}	Sulphide	S^{2-}	Sulphite	SO_3^{2-}
	Zinc	Zn^{2+}			Sulphate	SO_4^{2-}
	Iron (II)*	Fe^{2+}				
	Copper (II)*	Cu^{2+}				
3	Aluminium	Al^{3+}	Nitride	N^{3-}	Phosphate	PO_4^{3-}
	Iron (III)*	Fe^{3+}	Phosphide	P^{3-}		

Note Some elements show more than one valency. Here, the Roman numeral written in brackets shows their valency.

3.6 Writing Chemical Formulae

The shortest way to represent a compound with the help of symbols and valency of elements is known as **chemical formula**. Chemical formula of a compound shows its constituent elements and the number of atoms of each combining element.
In ionic compounds, the charge on each ion is used to determine the chemical formula of a compound.

There are some rules for writing the chemical formula which are as follows

- The valencies or charges on the ion must be balanced.
- When a compound consists of a metal and a non-metal, the symbol of the metal is written first and on the left, whereas non-metal is written on the right. e.g. calcium oxide (CaO), sodium chloride (NaCl), iron sulphide (FeS), copper oxide (CuO) etc., where oxygen, chlorine, sulphur are non-metals and are written on the right, whereas calcium, sodium, iron and copper are metals and are written on left.
- When compound is formed with polyatomic ions, the ion is enclosed in a bracket before writing the number to indicate the ratio. e.g. $Ca(OH)_2$.
  In case if the number of polyatomic ion is one, the bracket is not required. e.g. NaOH.

Formulae of Simple Compounds

The simplest compounds made up of two different elements are called binary compounds.

Here, rules for writing the chemical formula for simple compounds are given as

- write the symbols of constituent elements and their charge.
- write the symbol of cation first followed by the symbol of anion.
- then criss-cross their charges or valencies to get the formula.
- the positive and negative charges must balance each other and the overall structure must be neutral.

e.g.

Hydrogen sulphide

Symbol H S
Charge +1 −2
Formula H_2S

Note When the subscript is number 1, then it does not need to write.

Carbon tetrachloride

Symbol C Cl
Charge +4 − 1
Formula CCl_4

Magnesium chloride

Symbol Mg Cl
Charge +2 −1
Formula $MgCl_2$

Calcium oxide

Symbol Ca O
Charge +2 −2
Formula Ca_2O_2 or CaO

Note When the valency of both elements are numerically equal, the subscripts are not written.

Aluminium oxide

Symbol Al O
Charge +3 −2
Formula Al_2O_3

Sodium nitrate

Symbol Na NO_3
Charge +1 −1
Formula $NaNO_3$

Potassium carbonate

Symbol	K	CO_3
Charge	+1	−2
Formula	K_2CO_3	

Sodium carbonate

Symbol	Na	CO_3
Charge	+1	−2
Formula	Na_2CO_3	

We use brackets when we have two or more of the same polyatomic ions in the formulae. e.g.

Aluminium hydroxide

Symbol	Al	OH
Charge	+3	−1
Formula	$Al(OH)_3$	

Ammonium sulphate

Symbol	NH_4	SO_4
Charge	+1	−2
Formula	$(NH_4)_2SO_4$	

All subscripts must be reduced to lowest term (except for molecule or covalent compound), e.g.

Tin (IV) oxide

Symbol	Sn	O
Charge	+4	−2
Formula	Sn_2O_4 or SnO_2	

3.7 Molecular Mass

The molecular mass of a substance is the sum of the atomic masses of all the atoms in a molecule of the substance. It is therefore, the relative mass of a molecule expressed in atomic mass units (u).

e.g. The relative molecular mass of water (H_2O) is 18 u, which can be calculated as,

atomic mass of hydrogen = 1 u

atomic mass of oxygen = 16 u

H_2O contains two hydrogen atoms and one oxygen atom. Therefore, molecular mass of water is

$= 2 \times 1 + 1 \times 16 = 18$ u

Example 3. **Calculate the molecular mass of the following substances.**

(i) Ammonia (ii) Hydrochloric acid

(iii) Phosphorus molecule (iv) Hydrogen molecule

(v) Oxygen molecule (vi) Sulphur dioxide

Sol. (i) Atomic mass of hydrogen = 1 u

Atomic mass of nitrogen = 14 u

So, the molecular mass of ammonia, which contains three atoms of hydrogen and one atom of nitrogen is

$= 1 \times 14 + 3 \times 1 = 17$ u

Similarly, we can calculate the molecular masses of given substances as

(ii) Molecular mass of hydrochloric acid (HCl)

$= 1 \times 1 + 1 \times 35.5 = 36.5$ u

(iii) Molecular mass of phosphorus molecule (P_4)

$= 4 \times 31 = 124$ u

(iv) Molecular mass of hydrogen molecule (H_2)

$= 2 \times 1 = 2$ u

(v) Molecular mass of oxygen molecule (O_2)

$= 2 \times 16 = 32$ u

(vi) Molecular mass of sulphur dioxide (SO_2)

$= 1 \times 32 + 2 \times 16 = 64$ u

Formula Unit Mass

It is the sum of the atomic masses of all atoms present in a formula unit of a compound. Formula unit mass is calculated in the same manner as we calculate the molecular mass.

The only difference is that, here the word formula unit is used for the substances whose constituent particles are ions.

e.g. Formula unit mass for sodium chloride (NaCl)

$= 1 \times 23 + 1 \times 35.5 = 58.5$ u

Try These 3.3

1. **How an ion is different from an atom? How cation is different from anion?**
2. **What is the role of valency in the combination of atoms?**
3. **Give symbol and valency of the following ions:**
   (i) Hydroxide ion (ii) Carbonate ion
4. **An element *X* forms $X_2(CO_3)_3$ type compound. What is the formula of its phosphate and chloride?**
5. **Write the formula of the following compounds: Magnesium sulphate, sodium bromide, calcium chloride, potassium nitrate and sodium phosphate.**

Mind Map

ATOMS AND MOLECULES

Dalton's Atomic Theory
Main postulates of this theory are as:
- Matter is made up of very small particles, called the atoms.
- Atoms are indivisible.
- Atoms of same element are identical in mass as well as in chemical properties.
- Atoms combine in the ratio of small whole numbers forming compounds.
- The relative number as well as kinds of atoms are constant in a

Law of Chemical Combination
Atoms combine together to give molecules in accordance to following laws, called the laws of chemical combination.

1. Law of Conservation of Mass
It was given by Antoine L. Lavoisier. This law states that, "mass can neither be created nor destroyed during a chemical

2. Law of Constant Proportions
It was given by Proust as "In a chemical substance the elements are always present in a definite proportions by

Atom
- It is the smallest particle of matter.
- It may or may not exist independently.
-

Symbols of Atoms
- These are short hand representation of the name of an element.
- Modern symbol were introduced by Berzilius.
- These are infact the first one or two letters of the element's name in English, Latin, Greek, German, etc.
- First letter of the symbol is always written in capital letter and second letter in a small letter. e.g. Iron (Fe from

Atomic Mass
Because of its very small size, it is a difficult task to determine the atomic mass of an individual atom, so term relative

Atomic Mass Unit (amu)
Now it is called 'u' (unified mass). It is defined as the mass of 1/12th of the

Relative Atomic Mass
It is defined as the number of times a given atom is heavier than 1/12th of mass

Ionic Compounds
These compounds are made up of cation and anion.

Polyatomic ions
It is a group of atoms carrying a charge and behaving like one entity
e.g. Cl^-, SO_4^{2-} O^{2-},

Ions
Atoms or group of atoms consist of charged species is known as ions.

Cation
- It is positively charged ion. In an electric field, it moves towards cathode.
- e.g. Na^+, Ca^{2+}, etc.

Anion
It is negatively charged ion.
- In an electric field, it moves towards anode.

e.g. Cl^-, Br^- O^{2-}, etc.

Monoatomic ions
An ion consisting of exactly one

Molecule
- Groups of two or more atoms chemically bonded together.
- Smallest particles of an element/compound that is capable of an independent existence

Chemical formula
The chemical formula of a compound is a symbolic representation of its composition.

Writing Chemical Formula
- Write the symbols and valencies (or charges) of constituent atoms.
- Write the symbol of cation before anion.
- Criss-cross the charges or valencies to get formula.
- The positive and negative charge must balance each other and the overall structure must be neutral.

e.g. Atom C Cl; Valency 4 1; CCl_4

Valency
- It is the combining power of an element.
- It is equal to charge in case

Molecules of Element
Contain only one type of atoms.

Molecules of compound
Contain two or more types of atoms.
e.g. methane (CH_4)

Atomicity
It shows the number of atoms present in a molecule.
e.g. H_2 is diatomic, O_3 is

Molecular Mass
It is the sum of atomic masses of all the atoms present in a

Formula Unit Mass
- It is the sum of atomic masses of all atoms present in a formula unit of a compound.
- It is the molar mass of ionic

NCERT FOLDER

Complete Explanations of all NCERT's Questions

Intext Questions

Q.1 In a reaction, 5.3 g of sodium carbonate reacted with 6 g of acetic acid. The products were 2.2 g of carbon dioxide, 0.9 g of water and 8.2 g of sodium acetate. Show that these observations are in agreement with the law of conservation of mass. **Page 27**

Sodium carbonate + Acetic acid $\longrightarrow$

Sodium acetate + Carbon dioxide + Water

Sol. Total mass of reactants = Mass of sodium carbonate + Mass of acetic acid

$= 5.3 + 6.0 = 11.3$ g

Total mass of products = Mass of sodium acetate + Mass of carbon dioxide + Mass of water

$= 8.2 + 2.2 + 0.9 = 11.3$ g

Since, the sum of masses of reactants is equal to the sum of masses of products, therefore the observation made is in agreement with the law of conservation of mass.

Q.2 Hydrogen and oxygen combine in the ratio of 1:8 by mass to form water. What mass of oxygen gas would be required to react completely with 3 g of hydrogen gas? **Page 28**

Sol. Since, H and O combine in the ratio of 1 : 8 by mass.

Therefore, $\frac{\text{Mass of H}}{\text{Mass of O}} = \frac{1}{8}$

Let the mass of oxygen required to react completely with 3 g of hydrogen gas be x.

$\therefore \quad \frac{3}{x} = \frac{1}{8}$ or $x = 24$ g

Therefore, 24 g of oxygen is required to react with 3 g of hydrogen to form water.

Q.3 Which postulate of Dalton's atomic theory is the result of the law of conservation of mass? **Page 28**

Sol. The postulate which is the result of law of conservation of mass is "atoms are indivisible particles, which can neither be created nor destroyed in a chemical reaction".

Q.4 Which postulate of Dalton's atomic theory can explain the law of definite proportions? **Page 28**

Sol. 'The relative number and kinds of atoms are constant in a given compound'. This postulate explains law of definite proportions.

Q.5 Define the atomic mass unit. **Page 30**

Sol. One atomic mass unit (u) is the mass unit equal to exactly 1/12th of the mass of one atom of C-12 isotope.

Q.6 Why is it not possible to see an atom with naked eyes? **Page 30**

Sol. Atoms are very small, they are smaller than anything we can imagine. More than millions of atoms when stacked would make a layer barely as thick as the sheet of paper. These are very small in radii and measured in terms of nanometers ($1 \text{nm} = 10^{-9}$m). Hence, it is not possible to see an atom with naked eyes.

Q.7 Write down the formulae of **Page 34**

(i) sodium oxide (ii) aluminium chloride

(iii) sodium sulphide (iv) magnesium hydroxide

Sol. (i) **Sodium oxide**

Symbol	Na	O
Charge	+1	−2
Formula	Na_2O	

(ii) **Aluminium chloride**

Symbol	Al	Cl
Charge	+3	−1
Formula	$AlCl_3$	

(iii) **Sodium sulphide**

Symbol	Na	S
Charge	+1	−2
Formula	Na_2S	

(iv) **Magnesium hydroxide**

Symbol	Mg	(OH)
Charge	+2	−1
Formula	$Mg(OH)_2$	

Q.8 Write down the names of compounds represented by the following formulae. **Page 34**

(i) $Al_2(SO_4)_3$ (ii) $CaCl_2$ (iii) K_2SO_4

(iv) KNO_3 (v) $CaCO_3$

Sol. (i) Aluminium sulphate [$Al_2(SO_4)_3$]

(ii) Calcium chloride ($CaCl_2$)

(iii) Potassium sulphate (K_2SO_4)

(iv) Potassium nitrate (KNO_3)

(v) Calcium carbonate ($CaCO_3$)

Q.9 What is meant by the term chemical formula ? **Page 34**

Sol. Chemical formula is the shortest way to represent a compound with the help of symbols and valency (charge) of elements.

e.g. Element Ca ⤫ Cl

Charge +2 −1

Formula $CaCl_2$

Q.10 How many atoms are present in a **Page 34**

(i) H_2S molecule and (ii) PO_4^{3-} ion ?

Sol. (i) In H_2S molecule, three atoms [i.e. 2 atoms of H and 1 atom of S] are present.

(ii) In PO_4^{3-} ion, five atoms [i.e. 1 atom of P and 4 atoms of O] are present.

Q.11 Calculate the molecular masses of **Page 35**

$H_2, O_2, Cl_2, CO_2, CH_4, C_2H_6, C_2H_4, NH_3, CH_3OH$

Sol. (i) Molecular mass of H_2 (hydrogen)

= Atomic mass of hydrogen × 2 = 1 × 2 = 2 u

(ii) Molecular mass of O_2 (oxygen)

= Atomic mass of oxygen × 2 = 16 × 2 = 32 u

(iii) Molecular mass of Cl_2 (chlorine)

= Atomic mass of chlorine × 2 = 35.5 × 2 = 71 u

(iv) Molecular mass of CO_2 (carbon dioxide)

= (Atomic mass of carbon × 1) + (Atomic mass of oxygen × 2)

= 12 × 1 + (16 × 2) = 12 + 32 = 44 u

(v) Molecular mass of CH_4 (methane)

= (Atomic mass of carbon × 1) +(Atomic mass of hydrogen × 4)

= 12 × 1 + (1 × 4) = 12 + 4 = 16 u

(vi) Molecular mass of C_2H_6 (ethane)

= (Atomic mass of carbon × 2) + (Atomic mass of hydrogen × 6)

= (12 × 2) + (1 × 6) = 24 + 6 = 30 u

(vii) Molecular mass of C_2H_4 (ethene)

= (Atomic mass of carbon × 2) + (Atomic mass of hydrogen × 4)

= (12 × 2) + (1 × 4) = 24 + 4 = 28 u

(viii) Molecular mass of NH_3 (ammonia)

= (Atomic mass of nitrogen × 1) + (Atomic mass of hydrogen × 3)

= (14 × 1) + (1 × 3) = 14 + 3 = 17 u

(ix) Molecular mass of CH_3OH (methanol or methyl alcohol) = (Atomic mass of carbon × 1)

+ (Atomic mass of hydrogen × 3)

+ (Atomic mass of oxygen × 1)

+ (Atomic mass of hydrogen × 1)

= (12 × 1) + (1 × 3) + (16 × 1) + (1 × 1)

= 12 + 3 + 16 + 1 = 32 u

Q.12 Calculate the formula unit masses of ZnO, Na_2O, K_2CO_3. **Page 35**

[Given, atomic masses of Zn = 65 u, Na = 23 u, K = 39 u, C = 12 u and O = 16 u]

Sol. (i) Formula unit mass of ZnO (zinc oxide)

= 65 + 16 = 81 u

(ii) Formula unit mass of Na_2O (sodium oxide)

= (23 × 2) + (16 × 1)

= 46 + 16 = 62 u

(iii) Formula unit mass of K_2CO_3 (potassium carbonate)

= (39 × 2) + (12 × 1) + (16 × 3)

= 78 + 12 + 48 = 138 u

Exercise

Q.1 A 0.24 g sample of compound of oxygen and boron was found by analysis to contain 0.096 g of boron and 0.144 g of oxygen. Calculate the percentage composition of the compound by weight.

Sol. Mass of the compound = 0.24 g

Mass of boron = 0.096 g

Mass of oxygen = 0.144 g

$$\text{Percentage of boron} = \frac{\text{Mass of boron}}{\text{Mass of the compound}} \times 100$$

$$= \frac{0.096\ g}{0.24\ g} \times 100 = 40\%$$

$$\text{Percentage of oxygen} = \frac{\text{Mass of oxygen}}{\text{Mass of the compound}} \times 100$$

$$= \frac{0.144\ g}{0.24\ g} \times 100 = 60\%$$

Alternative method

Percentage of oxygen = 100 − percentage of boron

= 100 − 40 = 60%

Q.2 When 3.0 g of carbon is burnt in 8.00 g oxygen, 11.00 g of carbon dioxide is produced. What mass of carbon dioxide will be formed when 3.00 g of carbon is burnt in 50.00 g of oxygen? Which law of chemical combination will govern your answer?

Sol. First we find the proportion of mass of carbon and oxygen in carbon dioxide.

In CO_2, C : O = 12 : 32 or 3 : 8

In other words, we can say that

∵ 12.00 g carbon reacts with oxygen = 32.00 g

∴ 3.00 g carbon will react with oxygen = 8 g

$$C + O_2 \longrightarrow CO_2$$

12 g 32 g 12+16×2 = 44 g

3 g 8 g 3+8 = 11 g

Therefore, 3.00 g of carbon will always react with 8.00 g of oxygen to form 11 g of carbon dioxide, even if a large amount (50.00 g) of oxygen is present.

This means when 3.00 g of carbon is burnt in 50.00 g of oxygen, only 8.00 g of oxygen will be used to produce 11.00 g of carbon dioxide.

The remaining 42.00 g of oxygen will remain as it is. This reaction will be governed by the law of constant proportions.

Q.3 What are polyatomic ions? Give examples.

Sol. A group of atoms carrying a charge and behaving like one entity are known as polyatomic ions.

e.g. Oxygen atom and hydrogen atom combine to form hydroxide ion (OH^-) and one C-atom and three O-atoms combine to form carbonate ion (CO_3^{2-}).

Q.4 Write the chemical formulae of the following:

(i) Magnesium chloride

(ii) Calcium oxide

(iii) Copper nitrate

(iv) Aluminium chloride

(v) Calcium carbonate

Sol. (i) $MgCl_2$ (ii) CaO

(iii) $Cu(NO_3)_2$ (iv) $AlCl_3$

(v) $CaCO_3$

Q.5 Give the names of the elements present in the following compounds:

(i) Quicklime

(ii) Hydrogen bromide

(iii) Baking powder

(iv) Potassium sulphate

Sol. (i) **Quicklime** (Calcium oxide) — CaO

Elements Calcium and oxygen

(ii) **Hydrogen bromide** — HBr

Elements Hydrogen and bromine

(iii) **Baking powder** (Sodium hydrogen carbonate) — $NaHCO_3$

Elements Sodium, hydrogen, carbon and oxygen

(iv) **Potassium sulphate** — K_2SO_4

Elements Potassium, sulphur and oxygen

Q.6 Calculate the molar mass of the following substances:

(i) Ethyne, C_2H_2

(ii) Sulphur molecule, S_8

(iii) Phosphorus molecule, P_4 (Atomic mass of phosphorus = 31)

(iv) Hydrochloric acid, HCl

(v) Nitric acid, HNO_3

Sol. (i) Molar mass of C_2H_2 = (2 × Atomic mass of C) + (2 × Atomic mass of H)

$= (2 \times 12) + (2 \times 1)$

$= 26$ u

(ii) Molar mass of S_8 = 8 × Atomic mass of S

$= 8 \times 32 = 256$ u

(iii) Molar mass of P_4 = 4 × Atomic mass of P

$= 4 \times 31 = 124$ u

(iv) Molar mass of HCl = (Atomic mass of H) + (Atomic mass of Cl)

$= 1 + 35.5$

$= 36.5$ u

(v) Molar mass of HNO_3 = (Atomic mass of H) + (Atomic mass of N) + (3 × Atomic mass of O)

$= 1 + 14 + (3 \times 16)$

$= 15 + 48 = 63$ u

To Study NCERT Activities Scan the Code

REVIEW EXERCISE

Including Competency Based Questions

Competency Focused (Objective) Questions

Multiple Choice Questions

1. If 12 g of C is burnt in the presence of 32 g of O_2, how much CO_2 will be formed ?

(a) 40 g CO_2 (b) 44 g CO_2
(c) 30 g CO_2 (d) 22 g CO_2

Sol. (*b*) CO_2 is formed by the following reaction :

$$\underset{12\text{ g}}{C} + \underset{32\text{ g}}{O_2} \longrightarrow CO_2$$

By the law of conservation of mass,

Mass of reactants = Mass of products

Mass of C+ Mass of O_2 = Mass of CO_2

$$12\text{ g} + 32\text{ g} = 44\text{ g}$$

Therefore, 44 g of CO_2 will be formed.

2. Which of the following statement is not true about an atom? **Competency Based Que.**

(a) Atoms are not able to exist independently.
(b) Atoms are the basic units from which molecules and ions are formed.
(c) Atoms are always neutral in nature.
(d) Atoms aggregate in large numbers to form the matter that we can see, feel or touch.

Sol. (*d*) Statement (d) is not true.

The corrected statement is written as : The molecules and ions aggregate together in large number to form the matter. We cannot see the individual molecules/ions with our eyes, only we can see the various substances which are a big collection of molecules/ions.

3. In a science project, Aditya has to make a chart, illustrating various elements and their atomicity. Aditya decided to show elements of different atomicity by different shapes.

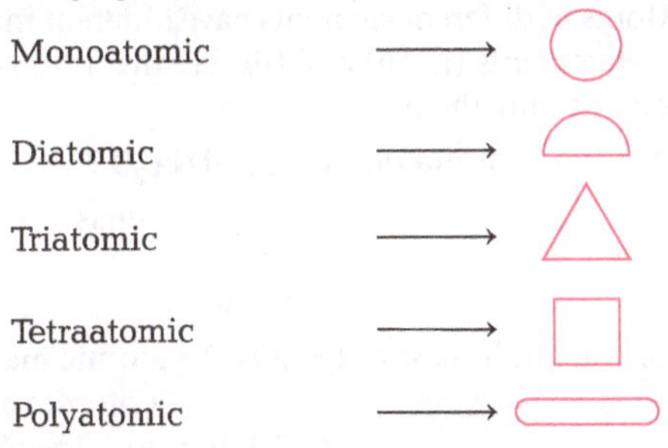

Pick the element which is shown incorrectly.

(a) Cl (b) Al
(c) C (d) S

Sol. (*c*) Carbon (C) is a tetraatomic element. Hence, it should be indicated as C.

4. Which of the following represent 1 amu ?

(a) Mass of hydrogen molecule.
(b) $\frac{1}{12}$th of mass of C-12 atom.
(c) Mass of O-16 atom.
(d) Mass of C-12 atom.

Sol. (*b*) 1 amu = $\frac{1}{12}$th of mass of C-12 atom.

5. Which of the following represents a correct chemical formula ? **NCERT Exemplar**

(a) CaCl (b) $BiPO_4$
(c) $NaSO_4$ (d) NaS

Sol. (*b*) $BiPO_4$, is the correct formula, its name is bismuth phosphate.

The correct chemical formula of remaining species are

$CaCl_2$—Calcium chloride

Na_2SO_4—Sodium sulphate

Na_2S—Sodium sulphide

6. The formula of chloride of a metal *M* is MCl_3, then the formula of the phosphate of metal *M* will be **Competency Based Que.**

(a) M_2PO_4
(b) MPO_4
(c) $M_2(PO_4)_3$
(d) M_3PO_4

Sol. (*b*) Valency of *M* is 3.

Symbol	*M*	$-PO_4$
Charge	+3	−3
Formula	MPO_4	

∴The formula of phosphate of metal *M* will be MPO_4.

7. A student makes two solutions using components as listed in the table.

Component	Mass of Components in Solution 1	Mass of Components in Solution 2
Sand	50 g	0 g
Water	100 g	200 g
Salt	60 g	50 g
Sugar	50 g	50 g

The students notices that sand settles at the bottom of the beaker in Solution 1. Which solution would be heavier? **Competency Based Que.**

(a) Solution 1, because sand is heavy.
(b) Solution 2, because it has more water.
(c) Solution 1, because it has more salt that disappears in water.
(d) Solution 2, because the total mass of components is greater.

Sol. (*d*) Mass of solution 1 = 50 g + 100 g + 60 g + 50 g = 260 g

Mass of solution 2 = 0 g + 200 g + 50 g + 50 g = 300 g

Therefore, solution 2 would be heavier.

8. Match Column I with Column II.

Column I		Column II
A. Relative atomic mass of oxygen	(i)	3
B. Valency of calcium	(ii)	2
C. Symbol of potassium	(iii)	16
D. Atomicity of ozone	(iv)	K

(a) A-(i), B-(iii), C-(ii), D-(iv)
(b) A-(i), B-(iv), C-(ii), D-(iii)
(c) A-(iii), B-(i), C-(iv), D-(ii)
(d) A-(iii), B-(ii), C-(iv), D-(i)

Sol. (*d*) The correct match is, A-(iii), B-(ii), C-(iv), D-(i).

9. Which type of an element is chlorine?

(a) Monoatomic (b) Diatomic
(c) Tetraatomic (d) Polyatomic

Sol. (*b*) Chlorine is a diatomic element represented as Cl_2.

10. What is the ratio by atomic mass of sulphur and oxygen in SO_2?

(a) 1 : 1 (b) 1 : 2 (c) 2 : 1 (d) 1 : 4

Sol. (*a*) Atomic mass of sulphur = 32

Atomic mass of oxygen = 32

Ratio = 32 : 32 = 1 : 1.

11. An element '*A*' has valency equal to 3. What will be its formula with carbonate ions?

(a) A_2CO_3 (b) ACO_3
(c) $A_2(CO_3)_3$ (d) $A(CO_3)_3$

Sol. (*c*) $A \times CO_3^{2-}$

Valency 3 2

Formula : $A_2(CO_3)_3$

12. The table list atomic masses and atomic numbers of three elements.

Elements	Atomic Radii (m)	Atomic Mass (amu)
Mg	12	24.305
Fe	26	55.845
O	8	16.0

A student studies that magnesium (Mg) and iron (Fe) react with oxygen (O) to form MgO and FeO. Although both compounds contain two atoms each of their molecular masses are different. What is the reason for the difference in their molecular masses?

CBSE Question Bank, Competency Based Que.

(a) Difference in the atomic mass of iron and magnesium.
(b) Difference in the number of iron and magnesium atoms.
(c) Different in the atomic number of iron and magnesium.
(d) Different in the number of O atoms in the two compounds.

Sol. (*a*) MgO and FeO, although both compounds contain two atoms but each have different molecular masses. This is because of the difference in the atomic mass of iron and magnesium as both compounds have oxygen in common. The atomic masses of Mg and Fe are 24 g and 55.8 g respectively.

$\therefore$ FeO > MgO

13. Consider the following statements.

(i) All matter is made up of atoms.
(ii) Atoms are tiny indivisible particles which can neither be created nor destroyed in a chemical reaction.
(iii) Atoms combine in small whole number ratios to form compounds.
(iv) Atoms of different elements can have the same mass.

Choose the statements which are the postulates of Dalton's atomic theory.

(a) Only (i) and (iv) (b) Only (ii) and (iii)
(c) (i), (ii) and (iv) (d) (i), (ii) and (iii)

Sol. (*d*) Atoms of different elements have different mass. Thus, statements (i), (ii) and (iii) are the postulates of Dalton's atomic theory.

14. What is the formula unit mass of Na_2O? **CBSE Question Bank**

(a) 20 u (b) 39 u
(c) 55 u (d) 62 u

Ans. (*d*) Formula unit mass of Na_2O = 2 × atomic mass of Na + atomic mass of O

= 2 × 23 + 16 = 46 + 16 = 62 u

15. What is the Latin name of sodium?

(a) Kalium (b) Plumbum
(c) Natrium (d) Niobium

Sol. (*c*) Latin name of sodium is natrium and it is represented as Na.

16. The most remarkable concept that Dalton's atomic theory proposed was that of the

(a) atomic weight (b) atomic mass
(c) molar mass (d) atomicity

Sol. (*b*) Atomic mass was the most remarkable concept proposed by Dalton's atomic theory.

17. Who coined the term 'Parmanu' for the smallest indivisible particles?

(a) Leucippus (b) L. Lavoisier
(c) Kanad (d) Dalton

Sol. (*c*) Maharishi Kanad was an Indian philosopher, postulated the smallest particles of matter and named it 'Parmanu'.

18. Percentage of calcium in calcium carbonate is

(a) 40 (b) 30
(c) 48 (d) 36

Sol. (*a*) Mass of calcium carbonate ($CaCO_3$) is 100.
Mass of calcium = 40
Percentage of calcium in calcium carbonate

$$= \frac{40}{100} \times 100 = 40\%$$

19. The table lists some compounds and their mass ratio.

Compound	Combining Elements	Ratio by Mass
Water (H_2O)	Hydrogen, oxygen	1:8
Carbon dioxide (CO_2)	Carbon, oxygen	3:4
Nitrogen dioxide (NO_2)	Nitrogen, Oxygen	7:16
Magnesium sulphide (MgS)	Magnesium, Sulphur	3:4

Which compound does NOT support the law of constant proportions? **CBSE Question Bank**

(a) H_2O (b) CO_2
(c) NO_2 (d) MgS

Ans. (*b*) The ratio of masses in carbon dioxide = 12 : 32 = 3 : 8
Therefore, among the given compounds, on the basis of ratio by mass, CO_2 does not support the law of constant proportions.

20. The formula of calcium phosphate is

(a) $Ca_3(PO_4)_2$ (b) $CaPO_4$
(c) $Ca(PO_4)_2$ (d) $Ca_2(PO_4)_3$

Sol. (*a*) Symbol Ca ↖↗ PO_4
Valency 2 ✕ 3
Formula : $Ca_3(PO_4)_2$

21. What can concluded from the result of the experiment?

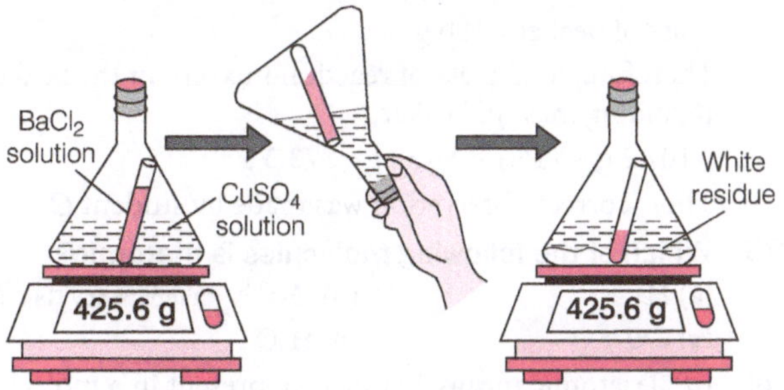

(a) Total mass of the chemicals remain the same.
(b) Total volume of the chemicals remain the same.
(c) State of matter of the chemicals remain the same.
(d) Composition of the chemicals remain the same.

Competency Based Que.

Sol. (*a*) According to the law of conservation of mass, the total mass of the products remains equal to the mass of the reactants during a chemical reaction.

22. The valency of hydrogen is 1 and that of sulphur is 2. The chemical formula of hydrogen sulphide is

(a) HS_2 (b) HSi_2 (c) H_2S (d) H_2Si

Sol. (*c*) Symbols H ↖↗ S
Valency 1 ✕ 2

Thus, the formula of hydrogen sulphide is H_2S.

23. Which of the following is correct pair of element and its symbol?

(a) Silicon - S (b) Aluminium - Am
(c) Iron - Fe (d) Tin - Ti

Sol. (*c*) Among the given pairs, the correct pair is iron - Fe
The corrected pairs of remaining elements and its symbols are given as :
Silicon - Si, Aluminium - Al and Tin - Sn

24. Four students *A*, *B*, *C* and *D* verified the law of conservation of mass in a chemical reaction of barium chloride and sodium sulphate. All of them took 107.2 g barium chloride solution and 116.1 g of sodium sulphate solution and mixed them in a beaker of mass 150 g. They reported their results as follows: **Competency Based Que.**

Students	Colour of Reaction Mixture after Mixing	Mass of reaction mixture in the Beaker Including Mass of Beaker
A	White precipitate	383.3 g
B	Brown precipitate	393.3 g
C	White precipitate	373.3 g
D	Brown precipitate	363.3 g

The correct observation is that of student

(a) *A* (b) *B* (c) *C* (d) *D*

Sol. (*c*) Mass of barium sulphate = 107.2 g
Mass of barium chloride = 116.1 g
Mass of beaker = 150 g
Therefore, total mass of reaction mixture in the beaker including mass of beaker.
= 107.2 g + 116.1 g + 150 g = 373.3 g.
Thus, correct observation was made by student C.

25. Which of the following molecules is triatomic? **Competency Based Que.**
(a) H_2 (b) C
(c) CO (d) H_2O

Sol. (*d*) Triatomic means 3 atoms are present in a molecule like H_2O.

Assertion-Reason Questions

Direction (Q.Nos. 1-10) In each of the following questions, a statement of Assertion is given by the corresponding statement of Reason. Of the statements, mark the correct answer as

(a) Both Assertion and Reason are correct and Reason is the correct explanation of Assertion.
(b) Both Assertion and Reason are correct but Reason is not the correct explanation of Assertion.
(c) Assertion is correct but Reason is incorrect.
(d) Assertion is incorrect but Reason is correct.

1. Assertion (A) Pure water obtained from different sources such as river, well, spring, sea, etc. always contains hydrogen and oxygen in the ratio of 1 : 8 by mass.
Reason (R) A chemical compound always contains elements combined in a fixed proportions by mass.

Sol. (*a*) The law of constant proportion states that in a chemical substance, the elements are always present in definite proportion by mass. So, pure water obtained from different sources such as river, well, spring, etc. contain H and O in the ratio 1 : 8. Hence, both Assertion and Reason are correct and Reason is the correct explanation of Assertion.

2. Assertion (A) Atomic mass of aluminium is 27.
Reason (R) An atom of aluminium is 27 times heavier than 1/12th of the mass of carbon-12 atom.

Sol. (*a*) Atomic mass of aluminium is 27. It shows how many times an atom of that element is heavier than 1/12th of the mass of C-12 atom. Hence, both Assertion and Reason are correct and Reason is the correct explanation of Assertion.

3. Assertion (A) On burning magnesium in oxygen, magnesium oxide is formed. The mass of magnesium oxide formed is equal to the total mass of magnesium and oxygen.
Reason (R) In a chemical substance, the elements are always present in a definite proportion.

Sol. (*b*) Mass of magnesium and oxygen is the same as magnesium oxide, because of the law of conservation of mass.
Hence, both Assertion and Reason are correct but Reason is not the correct explanation of Assertion.

4. Assertion (A) Magnesium ion and chloride ion combine to form a compound having chemical formula $MgCl_2$.
Reason (R) Magnesium ion and chloride ion contain +1 and −2 charges respectively.

Sol. (*c*) Assertion is correct but Reason is incorrect. The correct reason is as follows
Magnesium and chloride ions contain +2 and −1 charges respectively.

5. Assertion (A) Atoms always combine to form molecules and ions.
Reason (R) Atoms of most element are not able to exist independently.

Sol. (*a*) Both Assertion and Reason are true and Reason is the correct explanation of Assertion.

6. Assertion (A) Molecular weight of oxygen is 16 u.
Reason (R) Atomic weight of oxygen is 16 u.

Sol. (*d*) Molecular weight of oxygen $(O_2) = 16 \times 2 = 32$ u
Hence, Assertion is incorrect but reason is correct.

7. Assertion (A) The chemical formula of aluminium oxide is Al_2O_3.
Reason (R) The valency of aluminium is 2 and oxygen is 3.

Sol. (*c*) The chemical formula of aluminium oxide is
Symbol : Al O
Valency : 3 2
Formula : Al_2O_3
Thus, valency of aluminium is 3 and oxygen is 2.
Hence, Assertion is correct but Reason is incorrect.

8. Assertion (A) The correct symbol of gold is Au.
Reason (R) The latin name of gold is Kalium.

Sol. (*c*) Assertion is correct but Reason is incorrect. The latin name of gold is Aurum. Hence, its correct symbol is Au.

9. Assertion (A) Water molecules always contain hydrogen and oxygen in the ratio 1:8.
Reason (R) Water obeys law of constant proportions irrespective of method of preparation.

Sol. (*a*) Water molecules obey law of constant proportions as it always contain hydrogen and oxygen in the ratio 1:8. Hence, both Assertion and Reason are correct and reason is the correct explanation of assertion.

10. Assertion (A) Chlorine ion has negative charge.
Reason (R) Chlorine ion has less electron than a neutral atom.

Sol. (*c*) Chlorine ion has negative charge because it gains electron and has one more electron extra than neutral one. Hence, Assertion is correct but Reason is incorrect.

Case Based/Source Based Questions

Direction (Q. Nos. 1-4) Answer the questions on the basis of your understanding of the following passage and related studied concepts:

1. The molecular mass of a substance is the sum of the atomic masses of all the atoms in a molecule of the substance. It is therefore, the relative mass of a molecule expressed in atomic mass units (u). Depending upon the number of atoms of same or different elements present in the molecule, it can be monoatomic, diatomic, triatomic, tetra-atomic or polyatomic molecule.

(i) Calculate the ratio by mass of the combining elements in the compound : Methanol (CH_3OH).

(ii) What is the relative molecular mass of H_2O?

(iii) How many kinds of atoms are present in a molecule of copper carbonate ($CuCO_3$)?

Or

Explain polyatomic molecules with example.

Sol. (i) Methanol (CH_3OH) $\rightarrow C:H:O::12:4:16=3:1:4$.[1]

(ii) The relative molecular mass of water (H_2O)
$= 2\times1+1\times16=18$ u [1]

(iii) Copper carbonate ($CuCO_3$), contains three type of atoms, i.e. one copper atom, one carbon atom and three oxygen atoms. [2]

Or

Polyatomic molecules are compounds or elements that are made up of four or more atoms in a stable structure. S_8 has more than 4 atoms. Therefore, it is an example of polyatomic molecule (octa-atomic). [2]

2. Ravi was performing some experiments related to the laws of chemical combination in his science laboratory under the guidance of his chemistry teacher Mr. John. Mr. John gave him different samples of reacting species having different masses. Ravi performed the experiments and collected data as:

S. No.	Compounds	Reactant species	Masses of reactant species (in gram)
1.	H_2O	H	1
		O	16
2.	CO_2	C	12
		O	32
3.	NH_3	N	14
		H	3

(i) Calculate the mass of carbon dioxide gas formed.

(ii) Write a chemical reaction for the reaction between nitrogen and hydrogen.

(iii) In a given sample ammonia contains 3 g of hydrogen and 14 g of nitrogen. If another sample contains 5g of hydrogen then how much amount of nitrogen present in second sample?

Or

Name the two laws of chemical combination and state them.

Sol. (i) Mass of reactants = Mass of products

Mass of carbon dioxide

= Mass of carbon + Mass of oxygen

$= 12 + 32$ g $= 44$g [1]

(ii) The chemical reaction for the reaction between nitrogen and hydrogen is as follows

Nitrogen + Hydrogen $\longrightarrow$ Ammonia [1]

(iii) The ratio of mass of hydrogen and nitrogen $= 3:14$

If 5g of hydrogen, then nitrogen $= \dfrac{5\times14}{3}$

Mass of nitrogen = 23.3g [2]

Or

The two laws of chemical combination are as follows

- **Law of conservation of mass** This law states that matter can neither be created nor destroyed.
- **Law of definite proportions** It states that the proportion of elements by weight in a given compound will always remain exactly the same. [2]

3. In order to verify the law of conservation of mass, a student mixed 6.3 g of sodium carbonates and 15 g of ethanoic acid in a conical flask. After experiment, he weighed the flask again. The weight of the residue in the flask was only 18 g. He approached the teacher who guided him to carry the experiment in a closed flask with a cork. There was no difference in weight of the flask before and after the experiment.

(i) What was the mistake committed by the student?

(ii) Why did not the two weights match earlier ?

(iii) State and name the law of chemical combination which govern these experiments.

Or

What lesson was learnt by the student?

Sol. (i) The mistake committed by the student is that he carrying out the experiment in an open flask. [1]

(ii) Gas was evolved in the reaction escaped from the flask that's why, reactants and products weigh did not match. [1]

(iii) The given experiment is governed by the law of conservation of mass. In this, the total mass of the reactants is equal to the total mass of the products and there is no change in mass during chemical reactions. [2]

Or

The lesson was learnt by the student is that they should not do any unknown work by themselves. Always go to the teachers first, if there is any confusion and difficulty. [2]

4. Atoms and molecules are the building blocks of matter. An atom is the smallest unit of an element that retains its chemical properties, while a molecule is a group of two or more atoms held together by chemical bonds. Determining the mass of an individual atom was a relatively difficult task due to its very small size. Hence, their relative atomic masses was determined.

e.g.

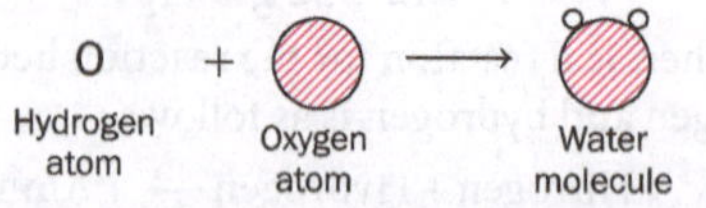

(i) What is a group of two or more atoms linked together by chemical bonds called?

(ii) What is an ion?

(iii) (a) Give one example of cation and anion.

(b) What is the atomic radius of hydrogen atom?

Or

(a) What is an atomic mass unit?

(b) Can atoms of all elements exist independently.

Sol. (i) Molecules are the group of two or more atoms held together by attractive forces known as chemical bonds. [1]

(ii) Charged atom is called an ion. The ion which is positively charged called cation or negatively charged called anion. [1]

(iii) (a) Cation = Na^+, anion = Cl^-. [1]

(b) Hydrogen atom is the smallest atom and its radius is 0.1 nm. [1]

Or

(a) The sum of the atomic masses of all the atoms in a molecule of the substance is expressed in atomic mass unit. [1]

(b) Atoms of most of the elements are not able to exist independently. Atoms form molecules and ions. These molecules or ions aggregate in large number to form the matter that we see, feel or touch. [1]

Constructed Response (Descriptive) Questions

Very Short Answer Type Questions

1. How did Berzilius assign symbols to the elements ?

Sol. Berzilius assigned symbols to the elements by taking first one or two letters of the element's name in english and in some cases the symbols have been taken from the names of elements in different languages such as Latin, German, Greek etc. [2]

2. Write one example of each

(i) tetra-atomic molecule

(ii) diatomic molecule

Sol. (i) Phosphorus (P_4) [1]

(ii) Nitrogen (N_2) [1]

3. (i) Is argon monoatomic or diatomic?

(ii) Give the difference between a cation and an anion.

Sol. (i) Argon (Ar) is monoatomic because its atom can exist independently. [1]

(ii) **Cation** It is the positively charged ion.

e.g. Na^+, K^+, Ca^{2+}, Mg^{2+} etc.

Anion It is the negatively charged ion.

e.g. Cl^-, Br^-, F^-, O^{2-}, N^{3-} etc. [1]

4. (i) Choose an ionic compound among S_8, $Cu(NO_3)_2$, P_4, H_2 and O_2?

(ii) What is the chemical formula of ammonium phosphate? Competency Based Que.

Sol. (i) $Cu(NO_3)_2$ is an ionic compound because it has Cu^{2+} and NO_3^- ions. [1]

(ii) $\underset{+1}{NH_4} \times \underset{-3}{PO_4} = (NH_4)_3PO_4$ [1]

5. (i) If an element *X* has its valence equal to 3, what will be its formula with carbonate ion?

(ii) Calculate the formula unit mass of $NaHCO_3$. [Atomic mass of Na = 23 u, H = 1 u, C = 12 u, O = 16 u] Competency Based Que.

Sol. (i) $\underset{+3}{X} \times \underset{-2}{CO_3} = X_2(CO_3)_3$ [1]

(ii) $NaHCO_3$ = (Atomic mass of Na) + (Atomic mass of H) + (Atomic mass of C) + (3 × Atomic mass of O) = (23 + 1 + 12 + 3 × 16) = 84 u [1]

6. (i) Calculate the molar mass of sugar ($C_{12}H_{22}O_{11}$). [Atomic mass of C = 12u, O = 16u, H = 1u]

(ii) The valency of an element *X* is 4. What is the formula of its oxide?

Sol. (i) $C_{12}H_{22}O_{11} = 12 \times 12 + 22 \times 1 + 11 \times 16$
$= 342$ u [1]

(ii) The formula of the oxide will be X_2O_4 or XO_2 [1]

7. List the elements present in

(i) Quick lime

(ii) Sodium hydrogen carbonate

Sol. (i) The chemical name of quicklime is calcium oxide, the elements present in it are calcium and oxygen. [1]

(ii) The chemical formula of sodium hydrogen carbonate is $NaHCO_3$.

The elements present in it are sodium, hydrogen, carbon and oxygen. [1]

8. (i) Name a non-metal which is tetra atomic.

(ii) What is atomicity? Give example.

Sol. (i) A non-metal phosphorus exists as tetratomic (P_4) molecule. [1]

(ii) The atomicity of an element is the number of atoms present in the one molecule of the element.

For example, atomicity of oxygen in $O_2 = 2$. [1]

9. (i) If the valency of carbon is 4 and that of sulphur is 2. What is the formula of the compound formed between carbon and sulphur atoms.

(ii) Determine the molecular mass of NH_4OH.

Competency Based Que.

Sol. (i) The formula of compound can be written by exchanging the valencies. Therefore, the formula is C_2S_4 or CS_2. [1]

(ii) Molecular mass of NH_4OH

$14 + 5 \times 1 + 16 = 35$ u. [1]

10. (i) How do atoms exist?

(ii) Give the chemical formula for ammonium sulphate.

Sol. (i) Atoms exist in the form of molecules or ions. [1]

(ii) Chemical formula of ammonium sulphate is $(NH_4)_2SO_4$. [1]

Short Answer Type Questions

1. (i) State the law of constant proportion with example.

(ii) In a compound carbon and oxygen react in a ratio 3 : 8 by mass to form carbon dioxide. What mass of oxygen is required to react completely with 9 g carbon?

Sol. (i) Law of constant proportion states that, "a pure chemical compound always consists of the same elements that are combined together in a fixed (or definite) proportion by mass". e.g. in a compound such as water, the ratio of the mass of hydrogen to the mass of oxygen is always 1 : 8, whatever the source of water. [1½]

(ii) Carbon : oxygen (by mass) = 3 : 8, i.e. 3 g of carbon requires 8 g of oxygen to form carbon dioxide.

∴ 9 g of carbon requires 24 g of oxygen to form carbon dioxide. [1½]

2. (a) What mass of silver nitrate will react with 5.85 g of sodium chloride to produce 14.35 g of silver chloride and 8.5 g of sodium nitrate?

(b) On which law is the above reaction based and state the law?

Sol. (a) Silver nitrate + Sodium chloride ⟶ Silver chloride + Sodium nitrate

(Sodium chloride: 5.85 g; Silver nitrate: x g; Silver chloride: 14.35 g; Sodium nitrate: 8.5 g)

Total mass of reactants = Total mass of products

$$x + 5.85 = 14.35 + 8.5$$

$$\Rightarrow x + 5.85 = 22.85$$

$$\Rightarrow x = 22.85 - 5.85$$

$$\Rightarrow x = 17 \text{ g}$$

Therefore, silver nitrate is 17 g. [2]

(b) It is based on law of conservation of mass which states that matter can neither be created nor destroyed in a chemical reaction. [1]

3. State three points of differences between an atom and a molecule.

Sol.

	Atom	Molecule
(i)	An atom is the smallest particle of an element that can take part in a chemical reaction.	A molecule is the smallest particle of an element or compound which has the properties of that element or compound.
(ii)	An atom may or may not exist independently.	A molecule is capable of independent existence.
(iii)	Examples : hydrogen (H), oxygen (O).	Examples: hydrogen molecule (H_2), oxygen molecule (O_2), water molecule (H_2O).

[3]

4 (i) An element Z forms an oxide with formula Z_2O_3. What is its valency?

(ii) Formula of the carbonate of a metal X is X_2CO_3. Write the formula of its chloride.

(iii) Name the element which is used as a reference for the atomic masses of the elements.

Competency Based Que.

Sol. (i) The valency of the metal Z in Z_2O_3 is +3. [1]

(ii) The valency of the metal X in X_2CO_3 is 1. Therefore, the formula of metal chloride is XCl. [1]

(iii) $\frac{1}{12}$ of the mass of carbon atom taken as 12 u and used as a reference for the atomic masses of the elements. [1]

5 Calcium carbonate decomposes on heating to form calcium oxide and carbon dioxide. When 10 g of calcium carbonate is decomposed completely then 5.6 g of calcium oxide is formed? Calculate the mass of carbon dioxide formed. Which law of chemical combination will you use in solving this problem? State the law. Competency Based Que.

Sol. The reaction occurs as follows:

$$CaCO_3 \xrightarrow{\Delta} CaO + CO_2$$

According to the law of conservation of mass,

Total mass of reactant(s) = Total mass of products(s)

$\Rightarrow$ $10\text{ g} = 5.6\text{ g} + \text{Mass of } CO_2$

$\Rightarrow$ $\text{Mass of } CO_2 = 10 - 5.6 = 4.4\text{ g}$

This problem is solved using law of conservation of mass according to which mass can neither be created nor destroyed during a chemical reaction. [3]

6 (i) State the atomicity of sulphur molecules.

(ii) Calculate the formula unit mass of $CaCl_2$.

Sol. (i) Atomicity of sulphur is 8 i.e. it is polyatomic molecules as it exists as S_8. [1]

(ii) Formula unit mass of $CaCl_2$

$= 1 \times (\text{atomic mass of Ca}) + (2 \times \text{atomic mass of Cl})$

$= (1 \times 40) + (2 \times 35.5) = 111\text{ u}$. [2]

7 (i) An element *X* has a valency of 2. Write the chemical formula for

(a) bromide of the element

(b) oxide of the element

(ii) Define formula unit mass of a substance.

Sol. (i) (a) Valency of $X = 2$

Valency of bromine = 1

$\therefore$ The formula of compound

X ⤫ Br

2 ⤫ 1

XBr_2

(b) Valency of $X = 2$

Valency of oxygen = 2

$\therefore$ The formula of compound

X ⤫ O

2 ⤫ 2

X_2O_2 or XO [2]

(ii) Formula unit mass is the sum of atomic masses of all atoms present in a formula unit of compound. It is calculated by adding the atomic masses of all the atoms present in one formula unit. [1]

8 (i) Give one point of difference between an atom and an ion.

(ii) Give one example each of a polyatomic cation and a polyatomic anion.

(iii) Write the chemical formula for the chloride of magnesium. Competency Based Que.

Sol. (i) An atom is always neutral that is it does not carry any charge, while an ion carries either positive charge or negative charge. [1]

(ii) Ammonium $[NH_4]^+$ ion is a polyatomic cation, while sulphate $[SO_4]^{2-}$ ion is a polyatomic anion. [1]

(iii) Chemical formula for the chloride of magnesium is $\begin{bmatrix} Mg & Cl \\ +2 & -1 \end{bmatrix}$ (criss-cross), $MgCl_2$. [1]

9 Write the chemical formulae of following compound, using criss-cross method.

(i) Magnesium bicarbonate

(ii) Barium nitrate

(iii) Potassium nitrate

Sol. (i) **Symbol** Mg ⤫ HCO_3

Charge +2 ⤫ −1

Formula $Mg(HCO_3)_2$ [1]

(ii) **Symbol** Ba ⤫ NO_3

Charge +2 ⤫ −1

Formula $Ba(NO_3)_2$ [1]

(iii) **Symbol** K ⤫ NO_3

Charge +1 ⤫ −1

Formula KNO_3 [1]

10 (i) What is the chemical symbol of the given elements?

(a) Gold

(b) Mercury

(ii) Find the ratio by mass of the combining elements in compound $CaCO_3$.

Sol. (i) Symbol of elements

(a) Gold : Au

(b) Mercury : Hg [1½]

(ii) The ratio of the mass of $CaCO_3$.

$= Ca : C : O$

$= 40 : 12 : (16 \times 3) = 40 : 12 : 48$

$= 10 : 3 : 12$

Hence, the ratio of the mass of $CaCO_3$ is 10 : 3 : 12. [1½]

11 Nitrogen and hydrogen atoms combine in the ratio 14 : 3 by mass to form ammonia molecule. Find the formula of ammonia molecule by calculating the molar ratio.
[Given atomic mass of N = 14 u and H = 1 u]

Sol. Number of nitrogen atom present in the molecule

$$=\frac{\text{Proportion by mass}}{\text{Atomic mass}}=\frac{14\text{ u}}{14\text{ u}}=1$$

Number of hydrogen atom present in the molecule

$$=\frac{\text{Proportion by mass}}{\text{Atomic mass}}=\frac{3\text{ u}}{1\text{ u}}=3$$

This means number of nitrogen and hydrogen atoms combine in ratio $=1:3$

Thus, the formula of molecule of ammonia is NH_3. [3]

12 Give the chemical formulae for the following compounds and compute the ratio by mass of the combining elements in each one of them.

(i) Ammonia (ii) Carbon monoxide
(iii) Hydrogen chloride (iv) Aluminium fluoride
(v) Magnesium sulphide

Competency Based Que.

Sol.

S.No.	Compound	Chemical Formula	Ratio by Mass of the Combining Elements
(i)	Ammonia	NH_3	$N:H=14:3$
(ii)	Carbon monoxide	CO	$C:O=12:16=3:4$
(iii)	Hydrogen chloride	HCl	$H:Cl=1:35.5$
(iv)	Aluminium fluoride	AlF_3	$Al:F=27:57=9:19$
(v)	Magnesium sulphide	MgS	$Mg:S=24:32=3:4$

[3]

13 I. An element $^{14}_{7}A$ exists as diatomic gas in nature which is relatively inert and forms 78% of earth's atmosphere.

(i) Identify the gas and write its molecular formula. Write the formulae of nitrite and nitrate ions.

(ii) Calculate the molecular mass of

(a) NH_4NO_3 and (b) HNO_3

[Given atomic masses N = 14 u, O = 16 u, H = 1 u]

II. Calculate the formula unit mass of Na_2SO_3. [Atomic mass of Na = 23 u, S = 32 u, O = 16u, H = 1 u and $N_A = 6.022\times 10^{23}\text{mol}^{-1}$]

Sol. I. (i) Nitrogen gas (N_2), nitrite ion (NO_2^-), nitrate ion (NO_3^-) [1]

(ii) (a) Molecular mass of NH_4NO_3
$=14+1\times 4+14+3\times 16=80$ u

(b) Molecular mass of $HNO_3=1+14+3\times 16=63$ u [1]

II. Formula unit mass of Na_2SO_3
$=2\times 23+32+3\times 16$
$=46+32+48=126$ u [1]

14 (i) 'SO_2 is an air pollutant released during burning of fossil fuels and from automobile exhaust'.

(a) Write the names of elements present in this gas.

(b) What are the valencies of sulphur in SO_2 and SO_3?

(ii) Define the term molecular mass.

(iii) Determine the molecular mass of $ZnSO_4$ [Atomic mass of Zn = 65 u, S = 32 u and O = 16 u].

Sol. (i) (a) Sulphur and oxygen

(b) Valency of sulphur in $SO_2=4$
Valency of sulphur in $SO_3=6$ [1]

(ii) **Molecular mass** It is the sum of the atomic masses of all the atoms present in a molecule of the substance. [1]

(iii) Molecular mass of $ZnSO_4=65+32+4\times 16=161$ u [1]

Long Answer Type Questions

1 (i) Illustrate the law of conservation of mass by giving an example.

(ii) Explain atomic mass unit.

(iii) How many atoms are present in

(a) MnO_2 molecule (b) CO molecule?

Sol. (i) According to the law of conservation of mass, mass can neither be created nor be destroyed in a chemical reaction. i.e. mass of reactants is equal to mass of products.

For example, on heating 100 g of calcium carbonate, we get reaction as follows :

$$\underset{100\text{ g}}{CaCO_3}\xrightarrow{\Delta}\underset{56\text{ g}}{CaO}+\underset{44\text{ g}}{CO_2}\uparrow$$

Mass of reactant (100 g) = Mass of product
(56 + 44) g = 100 g [2]

(ii) The unit of mass equivalent to the twelfth part of the mass of C-12 isotope of carbon is called atomic mass unit (amu) or unified mass (u). [1]

(iii) (a) In MnO_2 molecule, three atoms are present: one manganese atom and two oxygen atom. [1]

(b) In CO molecule, two atoms are present: one carbon atom and one oxygen atom. [1]

2 **(i) Which law states that, the sum of the masses of the reactants and products remains unchanged during a chemical reaction?**

(ii) What are polyatomic ions?

(iii) What is the formula unit mass of $Ca_3(PO_4)_2$?

(iv) What is the formula of sodium carbonate and ammonium sulphate?

(v) What is the ratio by mass in H_2S compound?

Competency Based Que.

Sol. (i) Law of conservation of mass states that during a chemical reaction the sum of the masses of the reactants and products remains unchanged. [1]

(ii) A group of atoms carrying a fixed charge on them is called polyatomic ions. [1]

(iii) $Ca_3(PO_4)_2 = 3 \times 40 + 2 \times 31 + 8 \times 16 = 310\,u$ [1]

(iv) Na_2CO_3; $(NH_4)_2SO_4$ [1]

(v) Mass of H = 1

Mass of sulphur = 32

In H_2S molecule, 2H : S

2 : 32

1 : 16

Therefore in H_2S molecule, combining elements are present in 1 : 16 ratio by mass. [1]

3 **(a) Write the molecular formulae of all the compounds that can be formed by the combination of following ions :**

Cu^{2+}, Na^+, Fe^{3+}, Cl^-, SO_4^{2-}, PO_4^{3-} **NCERT Exemplar**

(b) What is the molecular mass of PH_3 and sulphur dioxide?

Sol. **Compounds of Cu^{2+}**

(i) With $Cl^- \rightarrow Cu^{2+} \times Cl^{1-} = CuCl_2$

(ii) With $SO_4^{2-} \rightarrow Cu^{2+} \times SO_4^{2-} = CuSO_4$

(iii) With $PO_4^{3-} \rightarrow Cu^{2+} \times PO_4^{3-} = Cu_3(PO_4)_2$

Compounds of Na^+

(i) With $Cl^- \rightarrow Na^{1+} \times Cl^{1-} = NaCl$

(ii) With $SO_4^{2-} \rightarrow Na^{1+} \times SO_4^{2-} = Na_2SO_4$

(iii) With $PO_4^{3-} \rightarrow Na^{1+} \times PO_4^{3-} = Na_3PO_4$

Compounds of Fe^{3+}

(i) With $Cl^- \rightarrow Fe^{3+} \times Cl^{1-} = FeCl_3$

(ii) With $SO_4^{2-} \rightarrow Fe^{3+} \times SO_4^{2-} = Fe_2(SO_4)_3$

(iii) With $PO_4^{3-} \rightarrow Fe^{3+} \times PO_4^{3-} = FePO_4$ [3]

(b) Molecular mass of $PH_3 = 31 + 3 = 34$

Molecular mass of sulphur dioxide (SO_2)

$= 2 \times O + S \times 1$ [2]

$= 2 \times 16 + 32 = 64\,u$

4 **(i) Write the formulae for the following and calculate the molecular mass for each one of them :**

(a) Caustic potash **(b) Baking soda**

(c) Limestone **(d) Caustic soda**

(e) Ethanol **(f) Common salt**

(ii) How do atoms exist?

(iii) Define valency. What is the valency of magnesium?

Sol. (i) (a) KOH

Molecular mass of KOH $= 39 + 16 + 1 = 56\,u$

(b) $NaHCO_3$

Molecular mass of $NaHCO_3$

$= 23 + 1 + 12 + 3 \times 16 = 23 + 1 + 12 + 48 = 84\,u$

(c) $CaCO_3$

Molecular mass of $CaCO_3 = 40 + 12 + 3 \times 16 = 100\,u$

(d) NaOH

Molecular mass of NaOH $= 23 + 16 + 1 = 40\,u$

(e) C_2H_5OH

Molecular mass of C_2H_5OH or C_2H_6O

$= 2 \times 12 + 6 \times 1 + 16 = 24 + 6 + 16 = 46\,u$

(f) NaCl

Molecular mass of NaCl $= 23 + 35.5 = 58.5\,u$ [3]

(ii) Atoms of some elements are not able to exist independently, for such elements atoms form molecules and ions. In case of metals and inert gases, atom can exist independently. [1]

(iii) Valency is the combining capacity of an element. Valency of magnesium is 2. [1]

ASSESSMENT EXERCISE

Competency Focused (Objective) Questions

Multiple Type Questions

1 A sample of pure water, irrespective of its source, contain 11.1% hydrogen and 88.9% oxygen. The data supports
(a) law of multiple proportions
(b) law of reciprocal proportions
(c) law of constant proportions
(d) law of conservation of mass

2 In which of the following, the valency of each of the constituent elements is equal to the total number of atoms in one molecule of the compound? **Competency Based Que.**
(a) CH_4 (b) H_2S
(c) $MgCl_2$ (d) CaO

3 An element *X* is divalent and another element *Y* is tetravalent. The compound formed by these two elements will be
(a) XY (b) XY_2
(c) X_2Y (d) XY_4

4 Which of the following is a monoatomic element?
(a) Nitrogen (b) Hydrogen
(c) Helium (d) Oxygen

5 What is the ratio of mass between carbon and oxygen in carbon dioxide?
(a) 3 : 8 (b) 5 : 6
(c) 2 : 9 (d) 7 : 4

6 A student learns that aluminium forms compound with chlorine and oxygen. She records the valencies of the three elements. **Competency Based Que.**

Element	Valency
Aluminium	3 +
Chlorine	1 −
Oxygen	2 −

Which option gives the correct formula of aluminium oxide and aluminium chloride?
(a) Aluminium oxide: Al_2O_3; aluminium chloride: $AlCl_3$
(b) Aluminium oxide: $3AlO_2$; aluminium chloride: $3AlCl_2$
(c) Aluminium oxide: Al_3O_2; aluminium chloride: Al_3Cl_2
(d) Aluminium oxide: $3(AlO)_2$; aluminium chloride: $2(Al_3Cl)$

Assertion-Reason Questions

Direction (Q. Nos. 7-10) *In each of the following questions, a statement of Assertion is given by the corresponding statement of Reason. Of the statements, mark the correct answer as*
(a) Both Assertion and Reason are correct and Reason is the correct explanation of Assertion.
(b) Both Assertion and Reason are correct but Reason is not the correct explanation of Assertion.
(c) Assertion is correct but Reason is incorrect.
(d) Assertion is incorrect but Reason is incorrect.

7 **Assertion** (A) When 10 g of $CaCO_3$ is decomposed, 5.6 g of residue is left and 4.4 g of CO_2 escapes.
Reason (R) Law of conservation of mass is followed.

8 **Assertion** (A) In carbon dioxide the ratio of mass of carbon to the mass of oxygen is always 3 : 8.
Reason (R) According to law of constant proportion, the elements are always present in definite proportion by mass in a chemical substance.

9 **Assertion** (A) Ions are always positively charged.
Reason (R) Ions are formed by losing or gaining of electrons.

10 **Assertion** Atomicity of O_3 is 3.
Reason Atomicity is the combining power of an element with other atom.

Answers

1. (c)	**2.** (d)	**3.** (c)	**4.** (c)	**5.** (a)
6. (a)	**7.** (a)	**8.** (a)	**9.** (c)	**10.** (c)

Case Based/Source Based Questions

11 **Direction** (Q. Nos. i-iii) *Answer the questions on the basis of your understanding of the following passage and related studied concepts:*

The combining capacities of different elements are compared with that of hydrogen. The valency of hydrogen is taken as 1 and the valencies of all other elements are measured against this standard. An atom of calcium always combines with two atoms of hydrogen to form calcium hydride, a compound of calcium and hydrogen. Hence, the combining capacity or valency of calcium is twice that of hydrogen.

There are some elements which show different valencies in different compounds. Copper shows two valencies, one and two.

In the red oxide of copper, its valency is one, while in the black oxide, its valency is two. Similarly, iron shows valency two and three.

(i) The element *B* shows valencies of 4 and 6. Find formulae of its two oxides.

(ii) The formula of the sulphate of an element *X* is $X_2(SO_4)_3$. What is the formula of nitride of the element *X*?

(iii) What is meant by the term chemical formula? How is it related to valency of the element?

Or

The formula of oxide of an element *Z* is Z_2O_3. What is the valency of element *Z*?

Constructed Response (Descriptive) Questions

Very Short Answer Type Questions

12 In which form do atoms exist in aqueous solutions? Give example.

13 Give the symbols of the following elements.

(i) Aluminium (ii) Cobalt

(iii) Arsenic (iv) Radon

14 Write the ions present in (i) $Al_2(CO_3)_3$ (ii) $AlBr_3$

15 (i) An element has a valency of 3. Write the simplest formula for sulphide of the element.

(ii) Name the compound represented by formula K_2SO_4.

Competency Based Que.

16 (i) The formula of carbonate of a metal *M* is M_2CO_3. What is the formula for phosphate of *M*?

(ii) Give one point of difference between an atom and an ion.

Competency Based Que.

17 Write the chemical symbols of two elements.

(i) which are formed from the first letter of the element's name?

(ii) whose names have been taken from the names of the elements in Latin?

Short Answer Type Questions

18 Name any two monovalent cations, divalent cations and trivalent cations. Also name any one compound each one of them make.

19 The symbols of some of the ions are given below

Na^+, Mg^{2+}, H^+, CO_3^{2-}, Cl^-, S^{2-}

Using this information, find out the formulae of

(i) sodium carbonate (ii) magnesium chloride

(iii) hydrogen sulphide

20 In a chemical compound, calcium sulphate

(i) Identify the two ions.

(ii) Write the chemical formula of compound formed when positive ion is replaced by sodium ion.

(iii) Name the resulting compound.

21 (i) Name a greenhouse gas with molar mass 44 g mol^{-1} and is known to extinguish fire.

(ii) Name the elements present in this gas and write their valency.

(iii) Calculate the formula unit mass of Na_2CO_3.

[Given atomic mass of Na = 23 u, C = 12 u and O = 16 u]

22 An element *X* has a valency 1. **Competency Based Que.**

(i) Write the chemical formula of its phosphide.

(ii) Write the chemical formula of its chloride.

(iii) Is element *X* a metal or a non-metal?

Long Answer Type Questions

23 (i) State the two important laws of chemical combination. How Dalton's atomic theory explains the two Laws?

(ii) Write the chemical formulae of nitrates (NO_3^-) of Na^+, K^+, Al^{3+}, Mg^{2+}, Ca^{2+}, Zn^{2+}.

24 (i) What is the difference between 2H and H_2?

(ii) The valency of an element *X* is 4. Write the formula of its oxide.

(iii) Why are Dalton's symbols not used in chemistry?

Competency Based Que.

CHAPTER 04

Structure of the Atom

We have learnt that atoms and molecules are the fundamental building blocks of matter. The existence of different kinds of matter around us is due to different types of atoms and molecules present in them. Dalton assumed that atom is indivisible, i.e. it has no constituent particles. But, a series of experimental evidences revealed that some smaller particles, other than the atom, are also present which are called **sub-atomic particles**. These are electrons, protons and neutrons. The atoms of different elements differ in the number of electrons, protons and neutrons.

In this chapter, we will describe how electrons, protons and neutrons were discovered and the various models that have been proposed to explain how these particles are arranged within the atom.

4.1 Charged Particles in Matter

The particles that carry an electric charge are called **charged particles**. Generally, on rubbing two objects together, they become electrically charged. It means that some charged particles are present within the atom or atom is made up of some charged particles. Two such particles are electrons and protons.

Discovery of Electrons

The electron, was identified by **J. J. Thomson**. These are negatively charged particles and are denoted by symbol 'e^-'. Its charge is taken as −1. The mass of an electron is considered to be negligible.

Discovery of Protons

Before the identification of electron, **E. Goldstein** in 1886, discovered the presence of new radiations in a gas discharge and called them **canal rays** or **anode rays**.

These rays were positively charged radiations which are seen moving from anode towards the cathode in a specially designed discharge tube (with a porous cathode), when a high voltage is applied across the electrodes.

Porous cathode is used to provide the path for passing anode rays. It led to the discovery of another sub-atomic particle, the **proton**.

Protons are positively charged particles and are denoted by symbol 'p^+'. Its charge is taken as +1. The mass of proton is approximately 2000 times as that of the electron.

4.2 Structure of an Atom

According to **Dalton's atomic theory**, atom was indivisible and indestructible. The discovery of two fundamental particles (electrons and protons) inside the atom, led to the failure of this aspect of Dalton's theory. To know the arrangement of electrons and protons within an atom, many scientists proposed various atomic models.

These models are as follows

Thomson's Model of an Atom

J.J. Thomson was the first scientist to propose a model for the structure of an atom. Thomson's model of an atom was similar to Christmas pudding. The electrons in a sphere of positive charge, were like currants (dry fruits) in a spherical Christmas pudding.

It can also be compared to a watermelon, in which the positive charge in an atom is spread all over like the red edible part, while the electrons studded in the positively charged sphere, like the seeds in the watermelon.

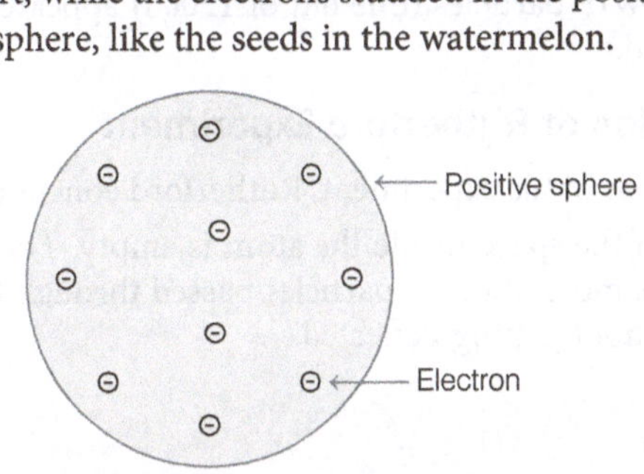

Thomson's model of an atom

Following are the postulates of this model.

- Electrons are embedded in the sphere of positive charge of an atom.
- The negative and positive charges are equal in magnitude. Therefore, the atom as a whole is electrically neutral.
- The mass of an atom is assumed to be uniformly distributed throughout the atom.

Limitations of Thomson's Model of an Atom

Some limitations of Thomson's model are as follows

- J.J. Thomson's model could not explain the experimental results of other scientists such as Rutherford, as there was no nucleus in the atomic model proposed by Thomson.
- It could not explain the stability of an atom, i.e. how positive and negative charges could remain, so close together.

Rutherford's Model of an Atom

Ernest Rutherford designed an experiment to know how the electrons are arranged within an atom. He bombarded fast moving α-particles having a considerable amount of energy on thin sheet of gold foil. These α-particles are double charged helium ions having a mass of 4 u.

He selected a gold foil because he wanted a layer as thin as possible. This gold foil was about 1000 atoms thick. It was expected by him that α-particles would be deflected by the sub-atomic particles in gold atoms. There will be small deflections as α-particles were much heavier than protons.

Observations of Rutherford Experiment

The following observations were made by Rutherford α-scattering experiment and gave totally unexpected results which are as follows

- Most of the fast moving α-particles passed straight through the gold foil.
- Some of the α-particles were deflected by the foil by small angles.
- Very few α-particles (one out of 12000) appeared to rebound.

Conclusion of Rutherford Experiment

On the basis of his experiment, Rutherford concluded that

- Most of the space inside the atom is empty. This is because most of the α-particles passed through the gold foil without getting deflected.
- Very few particles were deflected from their path. This indicate that the positive charge of the atom occupies very little space.
- A very small fraction of α-particles were deflected by $180°$ (i.e. they rebound). This indicate that all the positive charge and mass of gold atom were concentrated in a very small volume within the atom.

  From the data he also calculated that the radius of the nucleus is about 10^5 times less than the radius of the atom.

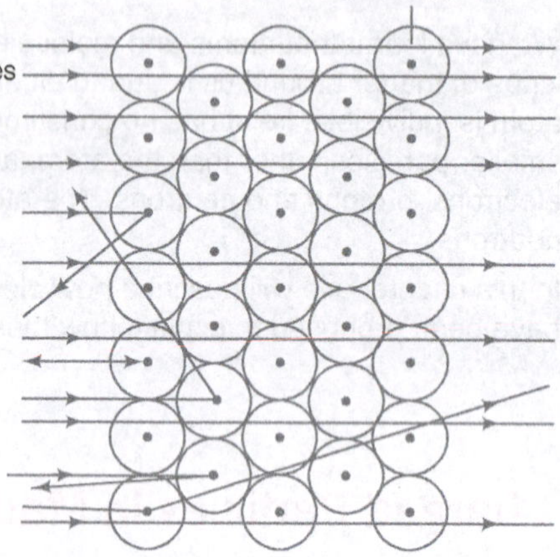

Scattering of α-particles by a gold foil

Rutherford's Nuclear Model of an Atom

On the basis of his experiment, Rutherford put forward the nuclear model of an atom, having the following features :

- There is a positively charged, highly dense centre in an atom, called **nucleus**. Nearly, the whole mass of the atom resides in the nucleus.
- The electrons revolve around the nucleus in circular paths.
- The size of the nucleus (10^{-15} m) is very small as compared to the size of the atom (10^{-10} m).

Note Rutherford suggested that his model of atom was similar to that of solar system. In the solar system, the different planets are revolving around the Sun. Similarly, in an atom the electrons are revolving around the nucleus. So, these electrons are also called **planetary electrons**.

Limitations of Rutherford's Model of an Atom

The limitations of Rutherford's model of an atom are

- To remain in a circular orbit, the electron would need to undergo acceleration. Consequently, it would radiate energy. Thus, the revolving electron would lose energy and finally fall into the nucleus. This would imply that matter would not exist, but this is not so. It means that atoms are quite stable.

Therefore, it could not explain the stability of an atom when charged electrons are moving under the attractive force of positively charged nucleus.

- Rutherford's model could not explain the distribution of electrons in the extra nuclear portion of the atom.

Bohr's Model of an Atom

To overcome the objections raised against Rutherford's model of the atom, **Neils Bohr** put forward the following postulates about the model of an atom.

- Atom consists of positively charged nucleus around which electrons revolve in **discrete orbits,** i.e. electrons revolve in certain permissible orbits and not just in any orbit.
- Each of these orbits are associated with certain value of energy. Hence, these orbits are called **energy shells** or **energy levels.** As the energy of an orbit is fixed (stationary), orbit is also called **stationary state.**
- Starting from nucleus, energy levels (orbits) are represented by numbers (1, 2, 3, 4 etc.) or by alphabets (*K*, *L*, *M*, *N* etc.).

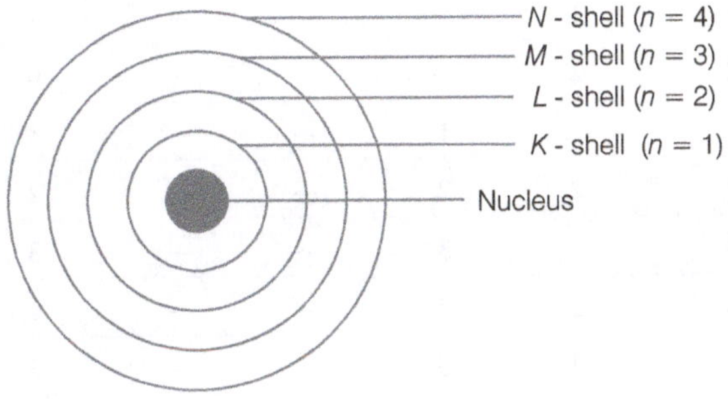

A few energy levels in an atom

- The electrons present in first energy level (E_1) have lowest energy. Energies increases on moving towards outer energy levels.
- Energy of an electron remains same as long as it remains in discrete orbit and it does not radiate energy while revolving.

Neutrons (*n*)

A neutron is another sub-atomic particle, discovered by **J. Chadwick** in 1932. It is represented by *n*. These are electrically neutral particles and are as heavy as protons. Neutrons are present in the nucleus of all atoms except hydrogen.

Try These 4.1

1. **When we rub two objects together they become electrically charged. Where did this electric charge came from?**
2. **What conclusion would be drawn by Rutherford when he observed that most of the fast moving α-particles passed straight through the gold foil?**
3. **What do you understand by the term 'discrete orbit'?**
4. **Why an orbit is also called as stationary state?.**
5. **Name the discoveror of electrons, protons and neutrons.**

4.3 Distribution of Electrons in Different Orbits (Shells)

The distribution of electrons into different orbits of an atom was suggested by **Bohr** and **Bury**. For writing the number of electrons in different energy levels or shells, some rules are followed. These are as follows

- The maximum number of electrons present in a shell is given by the formula $2n^2$, where, *n* is the orbit number or energy level, 1, 2, 3, ...

  Therefore, the maximum number of electrons in different shells are as follows

  – First orbit or *K*-shell $= 2 \times (1)^2 = 2$

  – Second orbit or *L*-shell $= 2 \times (2)^2 = 8$

  – Third orbit or *M*-shell $= 2 \times (3)^2 = 18$

  – Fourth orbit or *N*-shell $= 2 \times (4)^2 = 32$ and so on.

- The maximum number of electrons that can be accommodated in the outermost orbit is 8.
- Electrons are not accommodated in a given shell, unless the inner shells are filled (i.e. the shells are filled in a step-wise manner).

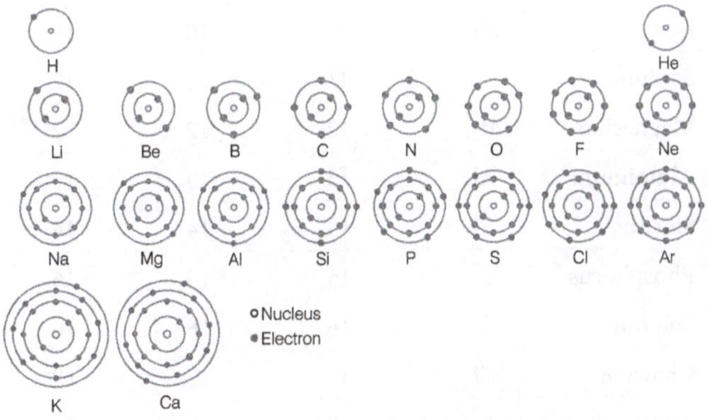

Schematic atomic structure of the first twenty elements

4.4 Valency

The electrons present in the outermost shell of an atom are known as the **valence electrons.** They govern the chemical properties of atoms. The atoms of elements having completely filled outermost shell means which has eight electrons show little chemical activity, i.e. they are highly stable. Such elements are called **inert elements.** It means, their combining capacity or valency is zero.

Of these inert elements, the helium atom has two electrons in its outermost shell and all other elements have atoms with eight electrons in the outermost shell.

It means, atom react with other atoms in order to attain fully-filled outermost shell.

An outermost shell, with eight electrons is called an **octet.** This is achieved by sharing, gaining or losing electrons. The number of electrons lost or gained or shared by an atom to become stable or to achieve an octet in the outermost shell is known as **valency of that element.**

In other words, **valency is the combining capacity of the atom of an element with the atom(s) of other element(s) in order to complete its octet.**

Hydrogen (H), lithium (Li), sodium (Na) and potassium (K) atoms contain one electron each in their outermost shell, therefore, each one of them can lose one electron to become stable. Hence, their valency is 1.

Similarly, all the inert elements, i.e. He, Ne, Ar etc., have completely filled outermost shells. Therefore, their valency is zero.

Note For metals, valency = Number of valence electrons and for non-metals, valency = 8 – number of valence electrons.

Composition of Atoms of the First Twenty Elements with Electron Distribution in Various Shells

Name of element	Symbol	Atomic number	Number of protons	Number of neutrons	Number of electrons	Distribution of electrons/Electronic configuration				Valency
						K	*L*	*M*	*N*	
Hydrogen	H	1	1	—	1	1	—	—	—	1
Helium	He	2	2	2	2	2	—	—	—	0
Lithium	Li	3	3	4	3	2	1	—	—	1
Beryllium	Be	4	4	5	4	2	2	—	—	2
Boron	B	5	5	6	5	2	3	—	—	3
Carbon	C	6	6	6	6	2	4	—	—	4
Nitrogen	N	7	7	7	7	2	5	—	—	3
Oxygen	O	8	8	8	8	2	6	—	—	2
Fluorine	F	9	9	10	9	2	7	—	—	1
Neon	Ne	10	10	10	10	2	8	—	—	0
Sodium	Na	11	11	12	11	2	8	1	—	1
Magnesium	Mg	12	12	12	12	2	8	2	—	2
Aluminium	Al	13	13	14	13	2	8	3	—	3
Silicon	Si	14	14	14	14	2	8	4	—	4
Phosphorus	P	15	15	16	15	2	8	5	—	3, 5
Sulphur	S	16	16	16	16	2	8	6	—	2
Chlorine	Cl	17	17	18	17	2	8	7	—	1
Argon	Ar	18	18	22	18	2	8	8	—	0
Potassium	K	19	19	20	19	2	8	8	1	1
Calcium	Ca	20	20	20	20	2	8	8	2	2

Try These 4.2

1. **What can be the maximum number of electrons in the outermost orbit?**
2. **Find out the number of electrons present in last shell of an atom having atomic number 15.** [Ans. 5]
3. **In an atom, first four shells (*K*, *L*, *M* and *N*) are completely filled. Then what is the total number of electrons in that atom?** [Ans. 36]
4. **Why helium and neon do not take part in chemical reactions?**
5. **How will you find out the valency of oxygen, fluorine and aluminium?**

4.5 Atomic Number and Mass Number

Atomic Number

It is defined as the number of protons present in the nucleus of an atom.

All the atoms of the same element have the same number of protons in their nuclei and hence, they have the same atomic number.

It is denoted by Z and written as a subscript to the left of the symbol.

$\therefore$ Atomic number = Number of protons

For example, atomic number of hydrogen is 1 ($Z = 1$) as there is only one proton present in the nucleus of its atom. Similarly, for carbon, $Z = 6$ as there are 6 protons present in the nucleus of its atom.

Mass Number

It is defined as the sum of number of protons and neutrons present in the nucleus of an atom. Protons and neutrons together are called as **nucleons**. Mass number is denoted by A.

$\therefore$ Mass number (A) = Number of protons + Number of neutrons.

For example, carbon has 6 protons and 6 neutrons, thus, its mass number is $6 + 6 = 12$ u.

Number of neutrons = Mass number – Atomic number

($\because$ Atomic number = Number of protons)

Mass number is written as a superscript to the left of the symbol. In the notation for an atom, the atomic number, mass number and symbol of the element are to be written as,

Mass number

Symbol of element or $^{A}_{Z}\boxed{X}$

Atomic number

e.g. Nitrogen is written as $^{14}_{7}N$.

Example 1. **An atom of an element *A* may be written as $^{24}_{12}A$.**

(i) What does the superscript 24 indicate?

(ii) What does the subscript 12 indicate?

(iii) What are the number of protons, neutrons and electrons in an atom A?

(iv) Write the symbol of ion formed by an atom of element A.

Sol. (i) 24 is the mass number of atom A.

(ii) 12 is the atomic number of atom A.

(iii) Number of protons = 12

Number of neutrons = Mass number – Atomic number
$= 24 - 12 = 12$

Number of electrons = 12

(iv) Electronic configuration of given atom = $\overset{K}{2}, \overset{L}{8}, \overset{M}{2}$.

It can lose two electrons (and attain stable configuration), therefore, symbol of its ion is A^{2+}.

4.6 Different Atomic Species

Isotopes

These are defined as the atoms of the same element, having same atomic number but different mass numbers. e.g. There are 3 isotopes of hydrogen atom, namely protium ($^{1}_{1}H$), deuterium ($^{2}_{1}H$ or D) and tritium ($^{3}_{1}H$ or T) and 2 isotopes of carbon, $^{12}_{6}C$, $^{14}_{6}C$.

In other words, it can be said that **isotopes have same number of protons but differ in the number of neutrons.** Many elements consist of a mixture of isotopes. Each isotope of an element is a pure substance.

The chemical properties of isotopes of an element are similar as they contain same number of valence electrons. They differ in their physical propeties because of having different atomic masses.

Average Atomic Mass

The mass of an atom of any natural element is taken as the average mass of all the naturally occurring atoms of that element.

If an element has no isotopes, the mass of its atom would be the same as the sum of masses of protons and neutrons in it. But if an element occurs in isotopic forms, then from the percentage of each isotopic form, the average mass is calculated as

Average atomic mass of an element =

$$\left[\left(\text{Atomic mass of isotope I} \times \frac{\text{Percentage of isotope I}}{100}\right) + \left(\text{Atomic mass of isotope II} \times \frac{\text{Percentage of isotope II}}{100}\right) + \cdots\right]$$

e.g. The two isotopic forms of chlorine atom with masses 35u and 37u occur in the ratio of 3 : 1. Therefore, the average atomic mass of chlorine atom, can be calculated as

$$= \left(35 \times \frac{75}{100} + 37 \times \frac{25}{100}\right) = \left(\frac{105}{4} + \frac{37}{4}\right) = \frac{142}{4} = 35.5 \text{ u}$$

Note The fractional atomic masses of elements are due to the existence of their isotopes having different masses.

Applications of Isotopes

Isotopes	Uses
• Uranium-235 (U-235)	Used as fuel for the production of electricity in nuclear reactions.
• Uranium-238 (U-238)	Used in determining the age of very old rocks and even the age of the Earth.
• Cobalt-60 (Co-60)	Used in the treatment of cancer.
• Carbon-14 (C-14)	Used in determining the age of old specimens of wood or old bones of living organisms.
• Iodine-131 (I-131)	Used in the treatment of goitre.

Isobars

Atoms of different elements with different atomic numbers but same mass number are known as **isobars.** In other words, **isobars are the atoms of different elements that have same number of nucleons (protons + neutrons) but differ in the number of protons.** e.g. $^{40}_{18}Ar$ and $^{40}_{20}Ca$ are isobars have same mass numbers, i.e. 40 but different atomic numbers, i.e. 18 and 20 for Ca.

Since, isobars have different atomic number as well as different electronic configuration. Thus, they also have different chemical properties.

Example 2. **Consider the following pairs,**

(i) $^{58}_{26}A$, $^{58}_{28}B$ (ii) $^{79}_{35}X$, $^{80}_{35}Y$

(a) Which of the above pairs are isotopes and isobars?

(b) What factors are responsible for the change in superscripts, 79, 80 (in case II), though the element is the same?

(c) Give the nuclear composition of $^{58}_{26}A$.

Sol. (a) **Isobars :** $^{58}_{26}A$ and $^{58}_{28}B$ **Isotopes :** $^{79}_{35}X$ and $^{80}_{35}Y$

(b) $^{79}_{35}X$ and $^{80}_{35}Y$ are a pair of isotopes. They have same number of protons but differ in the number of neutrons. Hence, their mass number differs from each other as mass number is the sum of number of protons and neutrons.

(c) Number of protons = 26, Number of electrons = 26

Number of neutrons = 58 − 26 = 32

Try These 4.3

1. **What are the number of protons, neutrons and electrons in $^{16}_{8}O$ and $^{40}_{18}Ar$? What are their atomic number and mass number?**
2. **The atomic number of Al and Cl are 13 and 17 respectively. What will be the number of electrons in Al^{3+} and Cl^{-}?** [**Ans.** 10 and 18]
3. **Lithium atom has an atomic mass of 6u and three protons in its nucleus. How many neutrons does it have?** [**Ans.** 3]
4. **Identify the isotopic pair(s) out of the following species ?**

   $_8C^{16}$, $_6C^{14}$, $_7N^{14}$, $_8O^{18}$, $_7N^{16}$
5. **Name the isotope used as a fuel in nuclear reactors.**

Mind Map

^A_ZX STRUCTURE OF ATOM
A=Mass number
X=Symbol of element
Z=Atomic number

Atomic Models
Explain the arrangement of sub-atomic particles within an atom.

Bohr's Model
- Main postulates of this model are:
- Electrons revolve around the nucleus in a circular orbit.
- Only certain special orbits called discrete orbits or energy levels of electrons are allowed inside the atom.
- While revolving in discrete orbits, the electrons do not radiate energy.
- Energy levels or shells are designated by K, L, M, N etc or the numbers, n = 1, 2, 3, 4 etc.

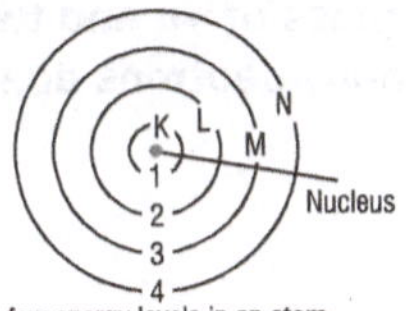

A few energy levels in an atom

Thomson's Model
It considered atom like Christmas pudding in which the electrons were embedded in a sphere of positive charge like currants in a spherical Christmas pudding.

Here, negative and positive charges balance each other, thus atom as a whole is electrically neutral.

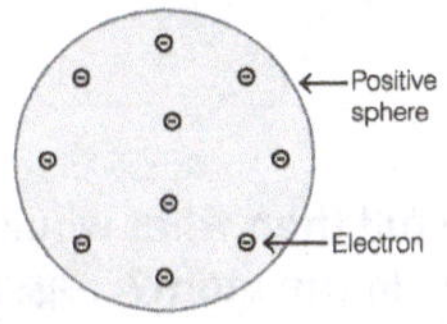

Limitations

It is failed to explain the results of α-particles scattering experiment of Rutherford.

Rutherford's Model
- On the basic of the α - particles scattering experiment, Rutherford stated that:
- There is a positively charged, highly densed centre in an atom, called the nucleus.
- The nucleus is very small as compared to the size of the atom.
- Nearly the whole mass of an atom resides in it.
- The electrons revolve around the nucleus in circular paths.

Limitations
- It is failed to explain the stability of atoms.

Characteristics of Atom
These are the properties by which an atom can be identified.

Atomic Number (Z)
- It is equal to the number of protons present in the nucleus of protons of an atom
- It is denoted by Z.

Mass Number (A)
- It is the sum of number of protons and neutrons present in the nucleus of an atom. $A = p + n$.

Different Type of Atomic Species

Isotopes
- The atoms of the same element, having same atomic number but different mass number. e.g. , $_1H^1$, $_1H^2$, $_1H^3$
- Their chemical properties are same due to same number of valence electrons.
- Their physical properties are different because of having different atomic masses.

Applications
- A uranium isotopes is used as a fuel.
- A cobalt isotopes is used in the treatment of cancer.
- An iodine isotope is used in the treatment of goitre.

Isobars
- Atoms of different elements with different atomic numbers but same mass number. e.g. $^{40}_{18}Ar$ and $^{40}_{20}Ca$
- Their chemical properties are different because of different atomic number.

Sub-Atomic Particles
These are the particles from which an atom is made.

- **Proton**
  It was discovered by E. Goldstein in 1886.
  It is represented as p^+ .
  These are the positively charged particles.
  Its mass was approximately 2000 times as that of the electron.
  It mass is taken as one unit and charge as +1.
- **Anode or Canal Rays** are the beam of protons but do not originate from anode.

Electron
- It was identified by J.J Thomson.
- It is represented as 'e^-'
- It is the negatively charged particle present in an atom.
- Its charge is taken as –1.
- The mass of an electron is considered to be negligible.

Neutrons
- These were discovered by J. Chadwick in 1932.
- In general, a neutron is represented as 'n'.
  These are electrically
- neutral particles.
  These are present inside the nucleus
- along with the protons.

Distribution of Electrons in Different Orbits
- Suggested by Bohr and Bury.
- These rules are:
- Maximum number of electrons present in a shell = $2n^2$ (Here, n = 1,2,3....)
- Outermost orbit can accommodate a maximum of 8 electrons.
- The shells are filled in a step-wise manner.

Valence Electrons
It is the number of electrons present in the outermost or valence shell of an atom.

Valency

It is the combining capacity of an element with the atom(s) of other element(s) in order to complete its octet.

NCERT FOLDER

Complete Explanations of all NCERT's Questions

Intext Questions

Q.1 What are canal rays? **Page 39**

Sol. Canal rays or anode rays are the positively charged rays which are seen moving from the anode towards cathode in a specially designed discharge tube, when a high voltage is applied across the electrodes.

Q.2 If an atom contains one electron and one proton, will it carry any charge or not? **Page 41**

Sol. An electron is a negatively charged particle, whereas a proton is a positively charged particle and the magnitude of their charges are equal. Therefore, an atom containing one electron and one proton will not carry any charge. Thus, it will be a neutral atom.

Q.3 On the basis of Thomson's model of an atom, explain how the atom is neutral as a whole? **Page 41**

Sol. According to Thomson model, an atom consists of a positively charged sphere and the electrons are embedded in it. As the negative and positive charges are equal in magnitude. So, the atom as a whole is electrically neutral.

Q.4 On the basis of Rutherford's model of an atom, which sub-atomic particle is present in the nucleus of an atom? **Page 41**

Sol. According to Rutherford's model of an atom, nucleus is positively charged, therefore, protons are present inside the nucleus of an atom.

Q.5 Draw a sketch of Bohr's model of an atom with three shells. **Page 41**

Sol. Three shells or orbits are presented by the letters *K*, *L*, *M* (or the numbers, $n = 1, 2, 3$)

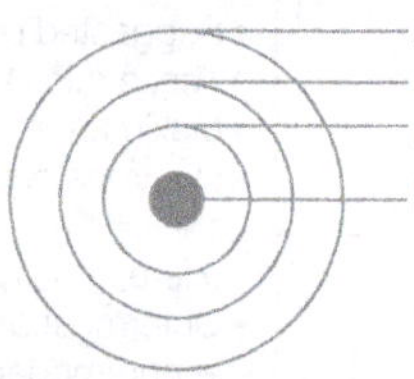

Q.6 What do you think would be the observation if the α-particle scattering experiment is carried out using a foil of a metal other than gold? **Page 41**

Or

Why did Rutherford select a gold foil in his α-rays scattering experiment? **NCERT Exemplar**

Sol. Rutherford used gold for the α-particle scattering experiment because gold is the most malleable metal; thus, can be made into a very thin foil, which is necessary for the experiment. More thick foils can be made by other metals like platinum and silver.As, the thickness of foil increases, the possibility of correctness of the experiment decreases. Hence, gold is preferred in this case.

Q.7 Name the three sub-atomic particles in an atom. **Page 41**

Sol. The three sub-atomic particles present in an atom are electrons, protons and neutrons.

Q.8 Helium atom has an atomic mass of 4u and two protons in its nucleus. How many neutrons does it have? **Page 41**

Sol. Atomic mass of helium = 4 u

Number of protons = 2

Let the number of neutrons = x

$\because$ Number of protons + Number of neutrons = Atomic mass

$\therefore \quad 2 + x = 4$

$\Rightarrow \quad x = 4 - 2 = 2$

Thus, the number of neutrons = 2.

Q.9 Write the distribution of electrons in carbon and sodium atoms. **Page 42**

Sol. Total number of electrons in a carbon atom is 6. The distribution of electrons in carbon atom is given by

1st orbit or *K*-shell = 2 electrons

2nd orbit or *L*-shell = 4 electrons

Total number of electrons in a sodium atom is 11. The distribution of electrons in sodium atom is given by

1st orbit or *K*-shell = 2 electrons

2nd orbit or *L*-shell = 8 electrons

3rd orbit or *M*-shell = 1 electron

Q.10 If *K* and *L*-shells of an atom are full then what would be the total number of electrons in the atom? **Page 42**

Sol. The maximum number of electrons that can occupy *K* and *L*-shells of an atom are 2 and 8 respectively. Therefore, the total number of electrons in the atom would be $(2 + 8) = 10$ electrons.

Q.11 How will you find the valency of chlorine, sulphur and magnesium? **Page 44**

Sol. Magnesium is a metal while chlorine and sulphur are non-metals.

Valency of a metal = Number of valence electrons (i.e. number of electrons present in the outermost shell)

Valency of a non-metal
= 8 − number of valence electrons

(i) $_{12}Mg = 2, 8, 2$; Valency of magnesium = 2

(ii) $_{16}S = 2, 8, 6$; Valency of sulphur = 8 − 6 = 2

(iii) $_{17}Cl = 2, 8, 7$; Valency of chlorine = 8 − 7 = 1

Q.12 If the number of electrons in an atom is 8 and the number of protons is also 8, then **Page 44**

(i) what is the atomic number of the atom? and

(ii) what is the charge on the atom?

Sol. (i) Atomic number = Number of protons = 8

(ii) The charge on the atom is zero because number of electrons and number of protons are equal.

Q.13 With the help of table given on page 72, find out the mass number of oxygen and sulphur atoms. **Page 44**

Sol. Mass number = Number of protons + Number of neutrons

∴ Mass number of oxygen = 8 + 8 = 16

and mass number of sulphur = 16 + 16 = 32

Q.14 For the symbol H, D and T, tabulate three sub-atomic particles found in each of them. **Page 45**

Sol.

Symbol	Protons	Neutrons	Electrons
^1_1H	1	0	1
^2_1D	1	1	1
^3_1T	1	2	1

Q.15 Write the electronic configuration of any one pair of isotopes and isobars. **Page 45**

Sol. Example of isotopes : $^{35}_{17}Cl$ and $^{37}_{17}Cl$

Electronic configuration of both the isotopes of chlorine is same as their atomic number is same. i.e.

$$\begin{matrix} & K & L & M \\ _{17}Cl = & 2, & 8, & 7 \end{matrix}$$

Example of isobars : $^{40}_{20}Ca$ and $^{40}_{18}Ar$.

Electronic configuration of both isobars would be different as both have different atomic numbers but have same mass number. i.e.

$$\begin{matrix} & K & L & M & N \\ _{20}Ca = & 2, & 8, & 8, & 2 \\ _{18}Ar = & 2, & 8, & 8 & \end{matrix}$$

Exercise

Q.1 Compare the properties of electrons, protons and neutrons.

Sol. Properties of electrons, protons and neutrons are as follows

Property	Electrons	Protons	Neutrons
Location	Outside the nucleus, i.e. they are present in orbits	Inside nucleus	Inside nucleus
Relative charge	−1	+1	Nil
Relative mass	1/2000 u	1 u	1 u

Q.2 What are the limitations of J.J. Thomson's model of the atom?

Sol. Limitations of J.J. Thomson's model of the atom are

(i) It could not explain the experimental results of other scientists such as Rutherford, as there is no nucleus in the atomic model was proposed by Thomson.

(ii) It does not have any experimental evidence in its support.

Q.3 What are the limitations of Rutherford's model of the atom?

Sol. Limitations of Rutherford's model of the atom are as follows

(i) It could not explain the stability of an atom when charged electrons are moving under the attractive force of positively charged nucleus.

(ii) The model could not explain as to how the electrons are distributed in the extra nuclear portion of an atom.

Q.4 Describe Bohr's model of the atom.

Sol. The main postulates of Bohr's model of an atom are as follows

(i) Electrons revolve around the nucleus in special orbits called **discrete orbits.**

(ii) These orbits are also called energy levels.

(iii) While revolving in discrete orbits, the electrons do not radiate energy.

(iv) These orbits are represented by the letters, *K, L, M, N* or the numbers $n = 1, 2, 3, 4$.

(v) The order of energy increases from *K* onwards. It means, $K < L < M < N$......

Q.5 Compare all the proposed models of an atom given in the chapter.

Sol.

Thomson's model	Rutherford's model	Bohr's model
Atoms consists of a positively charged sphere.	A positively charged centre in an atom called nucleus. All mass of an atom resides in the nucleus.	The positive charge in centre of an atom called nucleus.
Electrons are embedded in the sphere of positive charge.	Electrons revolve around the nucleus.	Electrons revolve in discrete orbits and do not radiate energy.
An atom is electrically neutral, as positive charge = negative charge	Size of nucleus is very small as compared to the size of an atom.	The orbits were termed as energy shells labelled as *K, L, M, N* or $n = 1, 2, 3, 4$.

Q.6 Summarise the rules for writing of distribution of electrons in various shells for the first eighteen elements.

Sol. Refer to text on Pg 71.

Q.7 Define valency by taking examples of silicon and oxygen.

Sol. The combining capacity of the atom of an element with the atom(s) of same or other element(s) in order to complete its octet is called the valency of that element. The valency of an element is determined by the number of valence electrons present in the atom of that element. If the number of valence electrons of the atom of an element is less than or equal to four then the valency of that element is equal to the number of valence electrons.

e.g. The atom of silicon has four valence electrons

[$\because$ atomic no. of silicon is 14, therefore its electronic configuration is $\begin{matrix} K & L & M \\ 2, & 8, & 4 \end{matrix}$].

Thus, the valency of silicon is four.

On the other hand, if the number of valence electrons of the atom of an element is greater than four, the valency of that element is obtained by subtracting the number of valence electrons from eight.

e.g. The atom of oxygen has six valence electrons. [Since, atomic no. of oxygen is 6, therefore, its electronic configuration is $\begin{matrix} K & L \\ 2, & 6 \end{matrix}$]. Thus, the valency of oxygen is two, $[8 - 6 = 2]$.

Q.8 Explain with examples.

(i) Atomic number (ii) Mass number

(iii) Isotopes (iv) Isobars

Give any two uses of isotopes.

Sol. (i) **Atomic number** The number of protons present in the nucleus of the atom of an element is called its atomic number.

Atomic number = Number of protons

e.g. Sodium atom has 11 protons. Thus, its atomic number is 11. It is represented as $_{11}Na$.

(ii) **Mass number** The sum of number of protons and neutrons (together called nucleons) present in the nucleus of an atom is called its mass number.

Mass number = Number of protons + number of neutrons

e.g. Sodium atom has 11 protons and 12 neutrons. Its mass number is 23. It is represented as ^{23}Na.

(iii) **Isotopes** Atoms of an element having same atomic number but different mass numbers are called isotopes of that element.

e.g. Hydrogen has 3 isotopes ^1_1H, ^2_1H and ^3_1H.

(iv) **Isobars** Atoms of different elements with different atomic numbers but same mass number are known as isobars.

e.g. $^{40}_{18}Ar$ and $^{40}_{20}Ca$ are isobars.

Uses of isotopes are

(i) An isotope of uranium (U-235) is used as a fuel for the production of electricity in nuclear reactors.

(ii) An isotope of cobalt (Co – 60) is used in the treatment of cancer.

Q.9 Na^+ has completely filled *K* and *L*-shells. Explain.

Sol. Electronic configuration of Na atom = $\begin{matrix} K & L & M \\ 2, & 8, & 1 \end{matrix}$.

When an atom loses one electron, it acquires a positive charge. Thus, when Na-atom lose one electron from its *M*-shell it gets converted into Na^+ ion.

Electronic configuration of Na^+(ion) = $\begin{matrix} K & L \\ 2, & 8 \end{matrix}$.

As the maximum capacity of *K*-shell to occupy electrons is 2 and that of *L*-shell is 8 electrons, so, Na^+ has completely filled *K* and *L*-shells.

Q.10 If bromine atom is available in the form of, say, two isotopes $^{79}_{35}Br$ (49.7%) and $^{81}_{35}Br$ (50.3%), calculate the average atomic mass of bromine atom.

Sol. Average atomic mass of an element is given as

$$= \left[\left(\text{Atomic mass of isotope I} \times \frac{\text{Percentage of isotope I}}{100}\right) + \left(\text{Atomic mass of isotope II} \times \frac{\text{Percentage of isotope II}}{100}\right)\right]$$

Average atomic mass of bromine

$$= \left[\left(79\text{u} \times \frac{49.7}{100}\right) + \left(81\text{u} \times \frac{50.3}{100}\right)\right]$$

$$= 39.263\text{u} + 40.743\text{u} = 80.006 \text{ u}.$$

Q.11 The average atomic mass of a sample of an element X is 16.2 u. What are the percentages of isotopes $^{16}_{8}X$ and $^{18}_{8}X$ in the sample?

Sol. Let, the percentage of $^{16}_{8}X = y\ \%$

Then, the percentage of $^{18}_{8}X = (100 - y)\ \%$ ...(i)

Average atomic mass of X = 16.2 u

According to the given data,

$$16 \times \frac{y}{100} + 18 \times \frac{(100-y)}{100} = 16.2 \quad ...(ii)$$

$$\frac{16y}{100} + \frac{1800 - 18y}{100} = 16.2$$

$$16y + 1800 - 18y = 1620$$

$$-2y = -1800 + 1620$$

$$\Rightarrow \quad y = \frac{180}{2} = 90\ \%$$

Placing the value of x in Eq. (i)

Percentage of $^{18}_{8}X = 100 - 90 = 10\%$

$\therefore$ Isotope $^{16}_{8}X = 90\%$, isotope $^{18}_{8}X = 10\%$

Q.12 If $Z = 3$, what would be the valency of the element? Also, name the element.

Sol. Electronic configuration of element, $(Z = 3) = \overset{K}{2}, \overset{L}{1}$

Valency of the element = Number of valence electrons = 1
Name of the element = Lithium (Li)

Q.13 Composition of the nuclei of two atomic species X and Y are given as under.

	X	Y
Protons	6	6
Neutrons	6	8

Give the mass numbers of X and Y. What is the relation between the two species?

Sol. Mass number = Number of protons + Number of neutrons

Mass number of $X = 6 + 6 = 12$

Mass number of $Y = 6 + 8 = 14$

To find the relation between X and Y.

Atomic number of X = Number of protons = 6

Atomic number of Y = Number of protons = 6

As the atomic numbers of both the elements X and Y are same (i.e. 6) but their mass number is different, so, X and Y are isotopes of the same element (carbon). Hence, X and Y are $^{12}_{6}C$ and $^{14}_{6}C$ respectively.

Q.14 For the following statements, write T for True and F for False.

(i) J.J. Thomson's proposed that the nucleus of an atom contains only nucleons.

(ii) A neutron is formed by an electron and a proton combining together. Therefore, it is neutral.

(iii) The mass of an electron is about $\frac{1}{2000}$ times that of proton.

(iv) An isotope of iodine is used for making tincture of iodine, which is used as a medicine.

Sol. (i) (F) Because in JJ Thomson's model, nucleus was not present.

(ii) (F) Neutron is a fundamental particle (a subatomic particle) of the atom of an element, thus cannot be made by combining an electron and a proton. It is neutral, as it carries no charge.

(iii) (T) Mass of an electron is $\frac{1}{1840}$ times, which is nearly about $\frac{1}{2000}$ times that of proton.

(iv) (F) Tincture of iodine is made by dissolving iodine in alcohol, not from the isotope of iodine.

Q.15 Rutherford's α-particle scattering experiment was responsible for the discovery of

(a) atomic nucleus
(b) electron
(c) proton
(d) neutron

Sol. (*a*) On the basis of his experiment, Rutherford predicted that the centre part of the atom is positively charged and is responsible for the mass of the atom. He called this portion as atomic nucleus.

Q.16 Isotopes of an element have

(a) the same physical properties.
(b) different chemical properties.
(c) different number of neutrons.
(d) different atomic numbers.

Sol. (*c*) Isotopes of an element have different physical properties, similar chemical properties, same atomic number but different mass numbers.

Hence, isotopes of an element have different number of neutrons.

Q.17 Number of valence electrons in Cl^- ion are

(a) 16 (b) 8
(c) 17 (d) 18

Sol. (*b*) Valence electrons are the electrons present in the outermost shell of an atom. Cl^- ion is formed when Cl atom gains an electron. The atomic number of Cl is 17, it has $17e^-$, when it gains one e^-, it becomes Cl^- ion and has $18e^-$.

Thus, electronic configuration of Cl atom and Cl^- ion are as follows

Cl (atom) = 2, 8 7; Valence electrons = 7
Cl^- (ion) = 2, 8, 8; Valence electrons = 8
Hence, Cl^- ion has 8 valence electrons.

Q.18 Which of the following is a correct electronic configuration of sodium?

(a) 2, 8 (b) 8, 2, 1
(c) 2, 1, 8 (d) 2, 8, 1

Sol. (*d*) The atomic number of sodium atom is 11, therefore, its electronic configuration is $\overset{K}{2}, \overset{L}{8}, \overset{M}{1}$.

Q.19 Complete the following table.

Atomic number	Mass number	Number of neutrons	Number of protons	Number of electrons	Name of the atomic species
9	—	10	—	—	—
16	32	—	—	—	Sulphur
—	24	—	12	—	—
—	2	—	1	—	—
—	1	0	1	0	—

Sol.

Atomic number	Mass number	Number of neutrons	Number of protons	Number of electrons	Name of the atomic species
9	19	10	9	9	Fluorine
16	32	16	16	16	Sulphur
12	24	12	12	12	Magnesium
1	2	1	1	1	Deuterium
1	1	0	1	0	Hydrogen ion

Explanation

(i) **Fluorine** ($^{19}_{9}F$) Given, atomic number = 9 and number of neutrons = 10

Mass number = Atomic number + Number of neutrons = 9 + 10 = 19

Number of protons = Atomic number
= Number of electrons = 9

(ii) **Sulphur** ($^{32}_{16}S$) Given, atomic number = 16

Number of protons = Number of electrons = 16

Number of neutrons
= Mass number − Atomic number
= 32 − 16 = 16.

(iii) **Magnesium** ($^{24}_{12}Mg$) Number of protons = 12

Atomic number = Number of protons = 12

Number of electrons = Number of protons = 12

Number of neutrons
= Mass number − atomic number = 24 − 12 = 12

(iv) **Deuterium** ($^{2}_{1}D$) Number of protons = 1 and Number of electrons = 1

∴ Atomic number = 1, Mass number = 2

Number of neutrons = 2 − 1 = 1

(v) **Hydrogen ion** ($_{1}H^{+}$) Mass number = 1

Number of protons = 1

Number of neutrons = 0

Number of electrons = 0

Atomic number = Number of protons = 1

Because number of electrons is zero, i.e. not equal to that of protons, so the species is hydrogen ion, not hydrogen atom.

To Study NCERT Activities
Scan the Code

REVIEW EXERCISE

Including Competency Based Questions

Competency Focused (Objective) Questions

Multiple Choice Questions

1 How the sub-atomic particles like proton is different from electron? Competency Based Que.

(a) An electron is much heavier than a proton.
(b) An electron carries more charge than a proton.
(c) A proton can be easily removed from the atom, but not an electron.
(d) A proton is positively charged, whereas an electron is negatively charged.

Sol. (*d*) Electrons and protons are sub atomic particles. Proton is different from electron because proton is positively charged whereas an electron is negatively charged.

2 What are the essential conditions for the production of anode rays?

(a) High voltage and low pressure
(b) High voltage and high pressure
(c) Low voltage and high pressure
(d) Low voltage and low pressure

Sol. (*a*) Anode rays are produced at high voltage and low pressure.

3

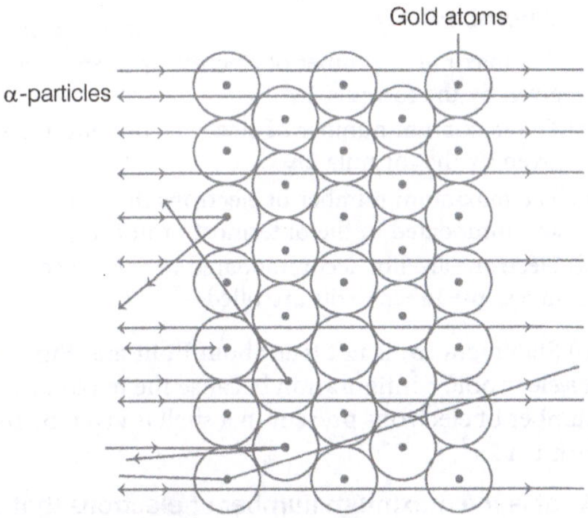

Which among the following statements about the given model of atom is correct?

(a) Considered the nucleus as positively charged.
(b) Established that the α-particles are four times as heavy as a hydrogen atom.
(c) Neutrons revolve around the nucleus of the atom.
(d) The given model of an atom represents Thomson's model.

Sol. (*d*) The given model of atom represents Rutherford's model. According to this model, a central positively charged nucleus is present in the atom and electrons revolve around it. This model is similar to solar system so also called planetary model.

4 Which of the following is true for Rutherford's model but not for Thomson's model of an atom? CBSE Question Bank

(a) An atom is electrically neutral.
(b) An atom contains many electrons.
(c) An atom has positive and negative parts.
(d) An atom contains a positively charged nucleus.

Sol. (*d*) According to Rutherford's model, an atom contains a positively charged nucleus. Around which the electrons revolve in well-defined circular orbit.

5 The alpha particle is also known as

(a) a sub-atomic particle.
(b) an unionised helium atom.
(c) a doubly-charged helium ion.
(d) a neutral particle.

Sol. (*c*) An alpha particle is a doubly-charged helium ion, i.e. He^{2+}.

6 Which of the following statements about the electron is not correct?

(a) It is a negatively charged particle.
(b) The mass of the electron is equal to the mass of the neutron.
(c) It is a basic constituent of cathode rays.
(d) It is a basic constituent of all atoms.

Sol. (*b*) Only statement (b) is incorrect. Its correct form is, The mass of an electron is much smaller that of mass of a neutron.

7 Which of the following formula is used to find the maximum number of electrons that can be accommodated in an orbit?

(a) $2n+2$ (b) $2(n+2)$
(c) $2n/n^2$ (d) $2n^2$

Sol. (*d*) The formula $2n^2$ is used to find the maximum number of electrons in an orbit, where n is the number of orbits.

8 Identify the Schematic atomic structure of Mg^{2+} ion from the figure where, *n* and *p* represent the number of neutrons and protons respectively.

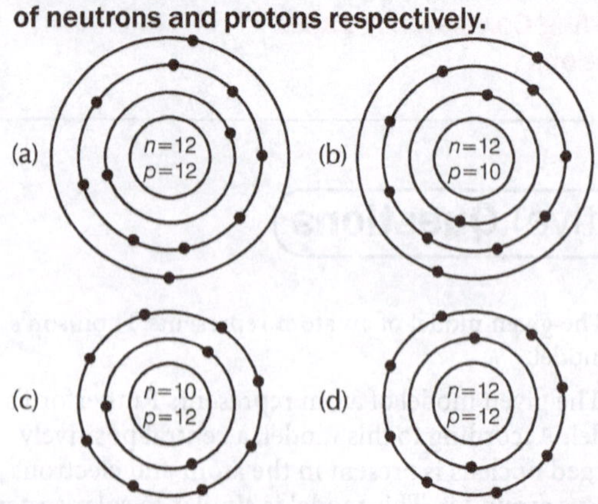

Competency Based Que.

Sol. (*d*) Electronic configuration $_{12}Mg$ atom $= \overset{K}{2}, \overset{L}{8}, \overset{M}{2}$ and that of Mg^{2+} ion $= \overset{K}{2}, \overset{L}{8}$

i.e. In *K*-shell = 2 electrons

In *L*-shell = 8 electrons

Now, number of protons in Mg atom $= 2 + 8 + 2 = 12$

Number of neutrons in Mg atom $= 24 - 12 = 12$

[as mass number of Mg atom = 24 and number of neutrons = mass number − number of protons]

Therefore, option (d) is the correct answer.

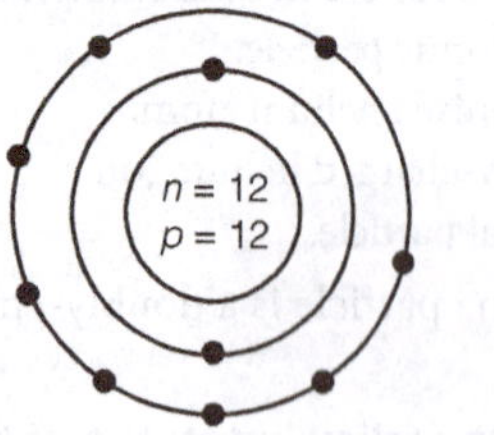

9 What can be the maximum number of electrons in *N* shell?

(a) 32 (b) 2 (c) 18 (d) 8

Sol. (*a*) For *N*-shell, $n = 4$

Thus, maximum number of electrons, it can hold is given by $2 \times 4^2 = 32$.

10 The electronic configuration of two elements *X* and *Y* are 2, 8, 8, 2 and 2, 8, 3. Identify the elements *X* and *Y* respectively.

(a) *X* is calcium and *Y* is aluminium.

(b) *X* is copper and *Y* is sodium.

(c) *X* is silver and *Y* is silicon.

(d) *X* is palladium and *Y* is zinc.

Sol. (*a*) The given electronic configuration contains 20 and 13 electrons respectively. Therefore, it is the electronic configuration of calcium and aluminium whose atomic numbers are 20 and 13.

11 Which among the following ion have 10 electrons?

(a) K^+ (b) Cl^-

(c) Ca^{2+} (d) Na^+

Sol. (*d*) (a) $K \rightarrow 19$ electrons

$K^+ \rightarrow 19 - 1 = 18$ electrons

(b) $Cl \rightarrow 17$ electrons

$Cl^- \rightarrow 17 + 1 = 18$ electrons

(c) $Ca \rightarrow 20$ electrons

$Ca^{2+} \rightarrow 20 - 2 = 18$ electrons

$Na \rightarrow 11$ electrons

$Na^+ \rightarrow 11 - 1 = 10$ electrons

12 Match Column I with Column II.

Column I		Column II
A. Maximum number of electrons in the *K*-shell.	(i)	$2n^2$
B. Electrons in the outermost shell of sodium.	(ii)	2
C. Maximum electrons in a shell.	(iii)	1
D. Number of electrons in Cl^- ion.	(iv)	18

(a) A-(ii), B-(iii), C-(i), D-(iv)

(b) A-(ii), B-(iv), C-(i), D-(iii)

(c) A-(iv), B-(i), C-(ii), D-(iii)

(d) A-(i), B-(ii), C-(iii), D-(iv)

Sol. (*a*) The correct match is, A-(ii), B-(iii), C-(i), D-(iv).

13 Which of the following is not true about Bohr and Bury's rule for electronic configuration, where *n* is the shell number?

CBSE Question Bank

(a) The maximum number of electrons present in a shell is given by the formula $2n^2$.

(b) The maximum number of electrons present in a shell is given by the formula $2n$.

(c) The maximum number of electrons that can be accommodated in the outermost orbit is 8.

(d) Electrons are not accommodated in a given shell, unless the inner shells are filled.

Sol. (*b*) Statement (b) is not true about Bohr and Bury's rule for electronic configuration because the maximum number of electrons present in a shell is given by the formula $2n^2$.

14 What is the maximum number of electrons that can be present in the first shell of an atom?

Competency Based Que.

(a) 1 (b) 2

(c) 4 (d) 8

Sol. (*b*) The maximum number of electrons that can be present in the first shell, i.e. *K* of atom is 2.

15 The symbol for sodium is $^{23}_{11}Na$. What can be concluded about sodium from the symbol? Competency Based Que.

(a) It contains 11 neutrons.
(b) It contains 12 protons.
(c) It contains 12 neutrons.
(d) It contains 34 electrons.

Sol. (*c*) Number of neutrons
$= \text{Mass number} - \text{Atomic number}$
$= 23 - 11 = 12$

16

Atoms	Mass number	Atomic number
A	40	20
B	7	3
C	14	7
D	16	8

Which of these atom contain 7 protons?

(a) *A* (b) *B* (c) *C* (d) *D*

Sol. (*c*) Proton count is equal to the atomic number of an element.
Hence, atom *C* contains 7 protons.

17 The atomic number of some elements is shown.

Elements	Atomic numbers
Beryllium (Be)	4
Oxygen (O)	8
Silicon (Si)	14
Chlorine (Cl)	17

Which elements have a valency of 2? Competency Based Que.

(a) Be and Si (b) Si and Cl
(c) Be and O (d) Cl and O

Sol. (*c*) The electronic configuration of the given elements are

Be = 2, 2 O = 2, 6
Si = 2, 8, 4 Cl = 2, 8, 7

Thus, among the given elements, Be and O have valency of 2.

18 The atomic number of an element is equal to

(a) number of neutrons
(b) number of electrons
(c) number of neutrons + number of protons
(d) number of protons

Sol. (*d*) The atomic number of an element is equal to number of protons.

19 The picture shows the arrangement of electrons in the shells of different atoms. Competency Based Que.

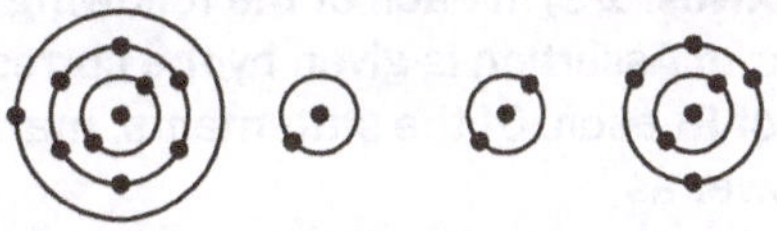

Which two atoms have the same valency?

(a) Atom 1 and atom 2 (b) Atom 2 and atom 3
(c) Atom 3 and atom 4 (d) Atom 4 and atom 1

Sol. (*a*) Valency of atom 1 and atom 2 is same, i.e. 1.

20 What will be the valency of an atom with 3 protons and 4 neutrons?

(a) 3 (b) 7 (c) 1 (d) 4

Sol. (*c*) An atom having 3 protons will have atomic number 3. Thus, its electronic configuration is 2, 1.
Hence, its valency will be 1.

21 What would be the valency of an element that is chemically inactive? Competency Based Que.

(a) 0 (b) 1 (c) 2 (d) 5

Sol. (*a*) Helium, neon, radon and argon etc. have zero valency because they have their outer shell completely filled and are chemically inactive.

22 Which of the following does not match the characteristics of an isotopes?

(a) Isotopes of some elements are radioactive.
(b) Isotopes are the atoms of different elements.
(c) They differ in number of neutrons.
(d) They have similar chemical properties.

Sol. (*b*) Since, isotopes are the atoms of same element. Thus, statement (b) is incorrect.

23 Which of the following atoms are isobars? Competency Based Que.

(a) $^{12}_{6}C$ and $^{14}_{6}C$ (b) $^{14}_{6}C$ and $^{40}_{18}Ar$
(c) $^{40}_{18}Ar$ and $^{40}_{20}Ca$ (d) $^{6}_{3}Li$ and $^{12}_{6}C$

Sol. (*c*) Atoms of different elements with different atomic numbers but same mass number are known as isobars. Thus, $^{40}_{18}Ar$ and $^{40}_{20}Ca$ are isobars having mass number 40.

24 Which radioactive element is used in the treatment of cancer?

(a) Iodine-131 (b) Uranium-234
(c) Plutonium-239 (d) Cobalt-60

Sol. (*d*) Cobalt-60 is a radioactive element which is used in the treatment of cancer.

25 Which isotopes is used in the nuclear power plants to generate electricity?

(a) Uranium-235 (b) Iodine-131
(c) Cobalt-60 (d) Uranium-238

Sol. (*a*) Uranium-235 is used in the nuclear power plants to generate electricity.

Assertion-Reason Questions

Direction (Q.Nos. 1-8) In each of the following questions, a statement of Assertion is given by the corresponding statement of Reason. Of the statements, mark the correct answer as

(a) Both Assertion and Reason are true and Reason is the correct explanation of Assertion.
(b) Both Assertion and Reason are true but Reason is not the correct explanation of Assertion.
(c) Assertion is true but Reason is false.
(d) Assertion is false and Reason is true.

1 Assertion (A) Atom is electrically neutral.
Reason (R) A neutral particle, i.e. neutron, is present in the nucleus of an atom.

Sol. (*b*) Because of the presence of equal number of protons and electrons, the atom is electrically neutral. Protons and neutrons collectively called as nucleons are present in the nucleus of the atom.
Hence, both Assertion and Reason are true but Reason is not the correct explanation of Assertion.

2 Assertion (A) The mass of the total number of protons and neutrons is a measure of the approximate mass of the atom.
Reason (R) The mass of an electron is negligible.

Sol. (*a*) Since, the mass of an electron is very less compared to that of a proton or neutron, it has little effect on the total mass of an atom.
Hence, Both Assertion and Reason are true and Reason is the correct explanation of Assertion.

3 Assertion (A) In Rutherford's gold foil experiment, very few α-particles are deflected back.
Reason (R) Nucleus present inside the atom is heavy.

Sol. (*b*) Nucleus present inside the atom is heavy. But in Rutherford's experiment, very few α-particles are deflected back because size of nucleus is very small in the atom.
Hence, both Assertion and Reason are true but Reason is not the correct explanation of Assertion.

4 Assertion (A) Electronic configuration of neon is 2, 8.
Reason (R) Atomic number of neon is 8.

Sol. (*c*) The atomic number of neon is 10. Therefore, its electronic configuration is

$$\begin{matrix} K & L \\ = 2, & 8 \end{matrix}$$

Hence, Assertion is true but Reason is false.

5 Assertion (A) Anions are larger in size than the parent atom.
Reason (R) In an anion, the number of protons in the nucleus is less than the number of electrons moving around it.

Sol. (*a*) Anion has more electrons than protons and it is formed when an atom gains one or more electrons. Therefore, anions are larger in size.
Hence, Both Assertion and Reason are true and Reason is the correct explanation of Assertion.

6 Assertion (A) The atomic masses of some elements are in fractions and not a whole numbers.
Reason (R) The fractional atomic masses of some elements are due to the existence of their isotopes having different masses.

Sol. (*a*) Both Assertion and Reason are true and Reason is the correct explanation of Assertion.

7 Assertion (A) The atoms of different elements having same mass number but different atomic numbers are known as isobars.
Reason (R) The sum of protons and neutrons, in the isobars is always different.

Sol. (*c*) Mass number = Number of protons + Number of neutrons.
It remains same in case of isobars.
Hence, Assertion is true but Reason is false.

8 Assertion (A) Isobars are identical in chemical properties.
Reason (R) Isobars have same mass number.

Sol. (*d*) Isobars are not identical in chemical properties because they have same mass number and different atomic numbers. Hence, Assertion is false but reason is true.

Case Based/Source Based Questions

Direction (Q.Nos. 1-4) Answer the questions on the basis of your understanding of the following passage and related studied concepts.

1 While carrying out the α-ray scattering experiments. Rutherford observed that a very few α-particles were deflected through very large angles and some even traversed back their original path. He was very surprised and stated "The result was almost incredible as if you fire a 15-inch cannon shell at a piece of paper and it comes back and hits you".

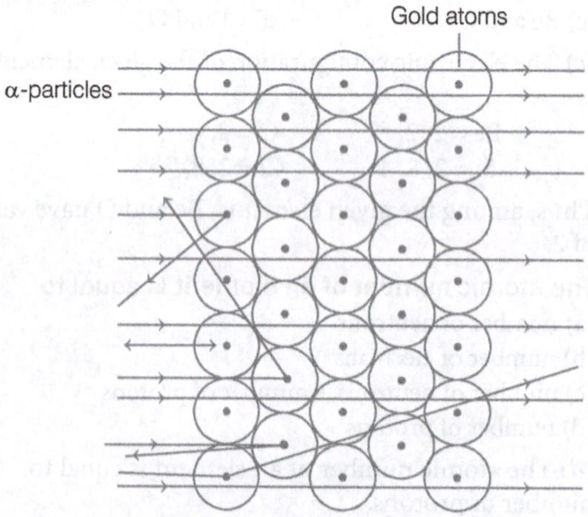

Scattering of α-particles by a gold foil

(i) Which charge is associated with α-particles?

(ii) Why did Rutherford chose gold foil for his experiment?

(iii) Why are a very few α particles deflected to very large angles and traversed back?

Or

What is the size of nucleus of the atom? Is nucleus charge always positive?

Sol. (i) α-particles are positively charged particles. [1]

(ii) Rutherford chose gold foil because gold foil has high malleability and can be converted into very thin foil. [1]

(iii) Rutherford's α-ray experiments led to the discovery of nucleus which is a small, heavy, rigid and positively charged part at the centre of the atom. As nucleus is very small in size, very few α-particles pass near to it or are deflected due to its positive charge. [2]

Or Radii of most of the atoms are of the order of 10^{-10} m and the radii of the nuclei are of the order of 10^{-5} m.

Therefore, nucleus is about $\frac{1}{10^5}$ times smaller than the atom. [1]

The nucleus of an atom is positively charged because it contains protons (+ ve) and neutrons (neutral). [1]

2 Atoms are all made from the same basic ingredients, the sub-atomic particles. (protons, neutrons and electrons).

The table given below gives the number of protons, neutrons and electrons in atoms or ions.

Particle	Number of protons	Number of electrons	Number of neutrons	Symbol or formula
A	9	9	10	${}^{19}_{9}F$
B	11	11	12	
C	18	18	22	
D	15	18	16	
E	13	10	14	

(i) Which atom in the table represents a cation?

(ii) Which atom in the table is an isotope of the atom with the composition 11*p*, 11 e^- and 14*n*? Give a reason for your choice.

(iii) Write the correct symbol or formula for *B, C, D* and *E*.

Or

If an element has 3 electrons in *M*-shell, what is its atomic number. Also calculate the neutrons if its mass number is 27.

Sol. (i) Particle *E* represents a cation because it has fewer electrons (10) than protons (13), resulting in a positive charge. [1]

(ii) *B*— is the isotope of the given atom as it has same number of protons but different number of neutrons. [1]

(iii) *B* is ${}^{23}_{11}Na$, *C* is ${}^{40}_{18}Ar$, *D* is ${}^{31}_{15}P^{3-}$ and *E* is ${}^{27}_{13}Al^{3+}$. [2]

Or Its *K* and *L*-shell are full so its atomic number

$$= 2 + 8 + 3 = 13$$

So, the atom is Al having atomic number 13.
Therefore, the number of neutrons in Al is [2]

$$= 27 - 13 = 14$$

3 Many elements consist of a mixture of isotopes. Each isotope of an element is a pure substance. The mass of an atom of any natural element is taken as the average mass of all the naturally occuring atoms of that element. If an element have no isotopes, then the mass of its atom would be same as the sum of protons and neutrons in it. But, if an element occurs in isotopic forms, then we have to know the percentage of each isotopic form and then average mass is calculated.

(i) Hydrogen has three isotopes : ${}^{1}_{1}H$, ${}^{2}_{1}H$, ${}^{3}_{1}H$. Why are these electrically neutral?

(ii) Why is that certain atoms are radioactive while many others are not?

(iii) The relative atomic mass of a sample of an element *X* is 17.4 u. Calculate percentage of isotopes ${}^{16}_{8}X$ and ${}^{18}_{8}X$ present in the sample.

Or Chlorine have two isotopes, ${}^{35}_{17}Cl$ and ${}^{37}_{17}Cl$. If the abundance of ${}^{17}_{35}Cl$ is 75% and ${}^{17}_{37}Cl$ is 25%, what is the average atomic mass of chlorine?

Sol. (i) Isotopes of hydrogen are electrically neutral because all these have only one electron and one proton. [1]

(ii) In certain atoms, the number of neutrons exceeds the number of protons and became unstable. [1]

(iii) Atomic masses of ${}^{16}_{8}X$ and ${}^{18}_{8}X$ are 16 and 18.

$$\left[16\,u \times \frac{A}{100} + 18\,u\frac{(100-A)}{100}\right] = 17.4\,u$$

$\therefore A = 30\%$ and $B = 70\%$ ($\because B = 100 - A$) [2]

Or Average mass of chlorine,

$$= \left[35\,u \times \frac{75}{100} + 37\,u \times \frac{25}{100}\right] = 35.5\,u$$ [2]

4 Isotopes are the atoms of the same element which have same atomic number but have different mass number. Isotopes differ with respect to the number of neutrons present in the nucleus. They have different physical properties but have identical chemical properties.

(i) Why do isotopes have identical chemical properties?

(ii) Give an example of any one pair of isotopes other than that of hydrogen.

(iii) Give the number of protons and neutrons present in the nuclei of the three isotopes of hydrogen.

Or

What are the two uses of isotopes?

Sol. (i) As the atomic number of isotopes is same, they have same number of electrons and thus, same electronic configuration. Hence, they have similar chemical properties. [1]

(ii) The two isotopes of carbon is $^{12}_{6}C$ and $^{14}_{6}C$. [1]

(iii) Hydrogen has three isotopes named protium, deuterium and tritium.

	Protium	Deuterium	Tritium
Number of protons	1	1	1
Number of neutrons	0	1	2

[2]

Or Isotopes are used for various purposes as

(i) An isotopes of cobalt-60 is used in the treatment of cancer. [1]

(ii) An isotope of iodine (I-131) is used in the treatment of goitre. [1]

Constructed Response (Descriptive) Questions

Very Short Answer Type Questions

1 (i) Which scientist concluded that size of nucleus is very small as compared to size of an atom?

(ii) Which subatomic particle is not present in a hydrogen atom?

Sol. (i) Ernest Rutherford's [1]

(ii) Neutron is not present in a H-atom. [1]

2 (i) Electrons attributes negative charge, protons attribute positive charge. An atom has both still it is neutral. Why?

(ii) What is the difference between atomic mass and average atomic mass? **Competency Based Que.**

Sol. (i) The positive and negative charges of protons and electrons are equal in magnitude. So, atom as a whole is electrically neutral. [1]

(ii) Atomic mass is the sum of mass of all the protons and neutrons. On the other hand, average atomic mass of an element is the mean mass of all of its isotopes and percentage of abundance. [1]

3 (i) Which observation of Rutherford's α-ray scattering experiment led to the fact that there is large empty space inside the atom?

(ii) Rutherford's model of atom was similar to that of solar system. Justify the statement. **Competency Based Que.**

Sol. (i) Most of α-particles passed through the gold foil without getting deflected and very few particles were deflected from their path, which led to the fact that most of the space is empty inside the atom. [1]

(ii) Rutherford's model was similar to that of solar system. Like the different planets are revolving around the Sun, in a similar way, the electrons are revolving around the nucleus in an atom. [1]

4 (i) What is the difference between Na and Na^+ in terms of number of electrons?

(ii) Consider the following few energy levels in an atom.

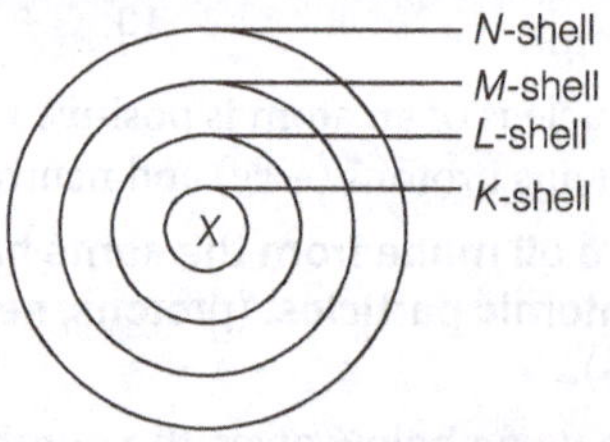

What does X represent in the atomic model? **Competency Based Que.**

Sol. The number of electrons in Na and Na^+ are different. It can be calculated as

(i) Number of electrons in Na = 11

Number of electrons in $Na^+ = 11 - 1 = 10$

[∵ In case of positive ion, number of electrons = Number of protons − Total positive charge] [1]

(ii) In atomic model, atom consists of positively charged nucleus around which electrons revolve in discrete orbits. Thus, X represent nucleus. [1]

5 In the atom of an element X, 6 electrons are present in the outermost shell. If it acquires noble gas configuration by accepting requisite number of electrons, then what would be the charge on the ion so formed? **NCERT Exemplar**

Sol. Element X has 6 electrons in the outermost shell. In order to acquire noble gas configuration, element X require 2 electrons. Therefore, when it gains electrons, it acquires negative charge, i.e. $-2 (X^{2-})$. [2]

6 Calculate the number of protons and neutrons present in the nucleus of an element *X* which is represented as $^{31}_{15}X$.

Sol. Atomic number, Z of $^{31}_{15}X = 15$

$\therefore$ Number of protons $= Z = 15$ [1]

Mass number, A of $^{31}_{15}X = 31$

$\therefore$ Number of neutrons $= A - Z = 31 - 15 = 16$ [1]

7 The picture shows the symbol for calcium : $^{40}_{20}Ca$

What does the number 20 represents for calcium?

Sol. In the notation for an atom, the atomic number, mass number and symbol of the element are to be written as

$^{\text{Mass number A}}_{\text{Atomic number Z}}X \longrightarrow$ Symbol of the element [1]

$\therefore$20 in the symbol, $^{40}_{20}Ca$, represents atomic number. [1]

8 (i) The atomic number of calcium and argon are 20 and 18 respectively but the mass number of both these elements is 40. What is the name given to such a pair of elements? **NCERT Exemplar**

(ii) What is the atomic number of the atom of an element *X*, which has 2 shells, *K* and *L* having 2 and 6 electrons respectively?

Sol. (i) Mass number of calcium $= 40$, i.e. $^{40}_{20}Ca$.

Mass number of argon $= 40$, i.e. $^{40}_{18}Ar$.

A pair of elements having same mass number but different atomic numbers is called isobars.

Thus, $^{40}_{20}Ca$ and $^{40}_{18}Ar$ are isobars. [1]

(ii) $K = 2$, $L = 6$

Total number of electrons $= 2 + 6 = 8$

$\because$ Atomic number $=$ Number of protons

$=$ Number of electrons in neutral atom

$\therefore$Atomic number $= 8$ [1]

9 (i) What are valence electrons?

(ii) Which electrons of an atom are involved in the chemical bond formation with other atoms?

Sol. (i) The electrons present in the outermost shell of an atom or ion are known as valence electrons. [1]

(ii) In a chemical bond formation, only valence electrons of an atom take part. [1]

10 (i) Why do elements like neon and argon have a zero valency?

(ii) Helium atom has 2 electrons in its valence shell but its valency is not 2. Give reason.

Sol. (i) Elements like argon and neon have 8 electrons in their valence shells. They do not have any tendency to combine with other elements. Hence, they have a valency equal to zero. [1]

(ii) Helium atom has 2 electrons in its valence shell and its duplet is complete. Hence, the valency is zero. [1]

11 (i) Write the correct representation of an element '*X*' which contains 15 electrons and 16 neutrons.

(ii) What will be the valency of an atom if it contains 3 protons and 4 neutrons?

Sol. (i) Elements '*X*' will have mass number $=$ number of electrons $+$ number of neutrons, i.e. $15 + 16 = 31$.

Hence, its correct representation will be $^{31}_{15}X$. [1]

(ii) An atom having 3 protons will have atomic number 3.

Thus, its electronic configuration will be 2, 1.

Therefore, its valency will be 1. [1]

12 Which of the two would be chemically more reactive: element *A* with atomic number 18 or element *D* with atomic number 16 and why?

Sol. Electronic configuration of $_{18}A = 2, 8, 8$

It would be chemically inert due to its complete octet.

On the other hand, electronic configuration of $_{16}D = 2, 8, 6$

To complete its octet, it will gain 2 electrons, therefore it will be more reactive. [2]

13 (i) Identify the pair of isotopes from the following:

$$^{16}_{8}X,\ ^{16}_{7}X,\ ^{17}_{8}X$$

(ii) Write one application of isotopes in the field of medical treatment.

Sol. (i) $^{16}_{8}X$ and $^{17}_{8}X$ are isotopes as they have same atomic number, but different mass number. [1]

(ii) An isotope of iodine (I-131) is used in the treatment of goitre. [1]

Short Answer Type Questions

1 In response to a question, a student stated that in an atom, the number of protons is greater than the number of neutrons, which in turn is greater than the number of electrons. Do you agree with the statement? Justify your answer. **NCERT Exemplar**

Sol. The given statement is incorrect.

According to this statement:

$$p > n > e^-$$

But actually, number of protons can never be greater than the number of neutrons (except protium). Number of neutrons can be equal to or greater than the number of protons because mass number is equal to double the atomic number or greater than double the atomic number.

Of course, number of neutrons can be greater than the number of electrons because number of electrons are equal to number of protons in the neutral atom. [3]

2 A student weighs 30 kg. Suppose his entire body is made up of electrons. How many electrons are there in his body? **Competency Based Que.**

Sol. Since, 9.1×10^{-31} kg is the mass of 1 electron.

$\therefore 1$ kg is the mass of $\dfrac{1}{(9.1 \times 10^{-31})}$ electrons

Thus, 30 kg is the mass of $\dfrac{30}{9.1 \times 10^{-31}}$ electrons

$= 3.30 \times 10^{31}$ electrons. [3]

3 Write the conclusions drawn by Rutherford when he observed the following.

(i) Most of the α-particles passing straight through the gold foil.

(ii) Some α-particles getting deflected from their path.

(iii) Very small fraction of α-particles getting deflected by 180°

Sol. (i) Most of the space inside the atom is empty. [1]

(ii) It indicates that the positive charge of the atom occupies a very little space. [1]

(iii) All the positive charge and mass of the atom were concentrated in a very small volume called nucleus. [1]

4 List down three different names given to the path in which electrons revolve around the nucleus. Also, explain why are they called so?

Sol. The three different names are

(i) **Discrete orbit** It is called so because electrons revolve in certain distinct path and not just in any orbit. [1]

(ii) **Energy level** (energy shell) The energy associated with different orbits (with which electron revolves) is distinct for each orbit, hence it is called so. [1]

(iii) **Stationary state** Since, the energy associated with an orbit is fixed. Hence, the electron revolving in a particular orbit have stationary energy. That's why, orbit is also called stationary state. [1]

5 (i) Write the name of an element whose atom has same number of sub-atomic particles. Draw the atomic structure of this atom.

(ii) Draw atomic structure of an atom with same number of electrons in *L* and *M*-shells. **Competency Based Que.**

Sol. (i) Name of element: Oxygen ($^{16}_{8}O$)

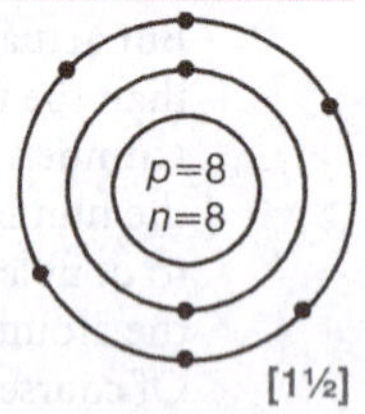

Atomic number (8) = $\overset{K}{2}, \overset{L}{6}$

Number of electrons = 8

Number of protons = 8

Number of neutrons = 16 − 8 = 8 [1½]

(ii) Name of element : Argon ($^{40}_{18}Ar$)

Atomic number (18) = $\overset{K}{2}, \overset{L}{8}, \overset{M}{8}$

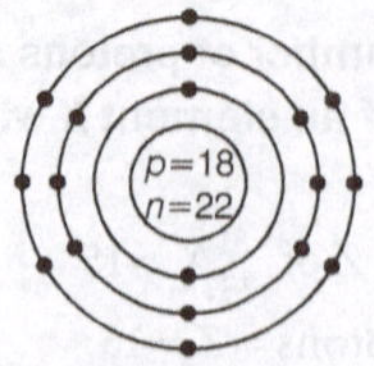

Number of electrons in *L*-shell = 8

Number of electrons in *M*-shell = 8 [1½]

6 (i) What will be the maximum number of electrons which can be filled in *Z*-shell of an imaginary atomic model?

(ii) Why is it almost impossible to find such an atom in nature?

Sol. (i) According to Bohr and Bury rule, the maximum number of electrons in *Z*-shell (16th shell, starting from *K*)

$= 2(16)^2 = 2 \times 16 \times 16 = 512$ [1]

(ii) Atom with greater number of electrons have greater number of protons and neutrons. Therefore, they have unstable nucleus which radiates energy or divide itself into smaller stable nucleus. Hence, elements with atomic number greater than 100 are rarely found in nature. [2]

7 Given below is the atomic structure of an atom of element $^{23}_{11}A$, according to Bohr's model of atom.

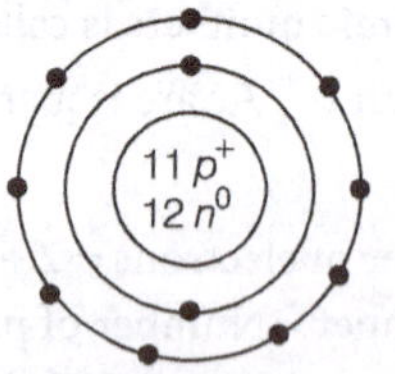

Analyse the figure and answer the following questions.

(i) What is wrong with this structure of atom?

(ii) Draw a correct representation of this atom.

(iii) Write the chemical formula of the chloride of this element.

Sol. (i) The element *A* is Na. It should has three shells *K*, *L* and *M* but here only 2 shells are given. Further, *L*-shell cannot have more than 8 electrons but here 9 electrons are shown. [1]

(ii) The correct representation is

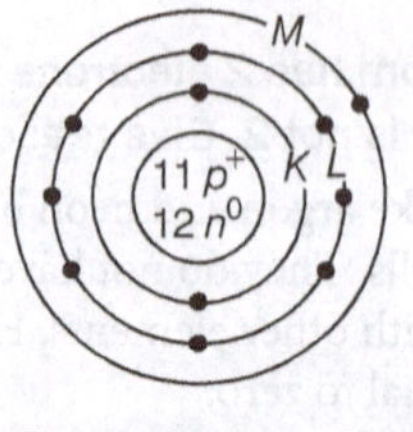

[1]

(iii) As Na has 1 valence electron, thus it has a valency of 1 and chlorine also has a valency of 1. Hence, the formula of its chloride is *A*Cl, i.e. NaCl. [1]

8 **Show diagramatically the electron distributions in a sodium atom and a sodium ion and also give their atomic number.** **NCERT Exemplar**

Sol. Atomic number of sodium $(Z) = 11$

Mass number of sodium $(A) = 23$

$\therefore$ Number of protons in the nucleus $= 11$

Number of neutrons in the nucleus $= 23 - 11 = 12$

Number of electrons $= 11$

$\therefore$ Electronic configuration of Na-atom $= \overset{K}{2}, \overset{L}{8}, \overset{M}{1}$

Na^+ ion is formed from sodium atom by loss of an electron (present in the outermost shell). Hence, its electronic configuration is $\overset{K}{2}, \overset{L}{8}$. However, number of protons and neutrons remain the same.

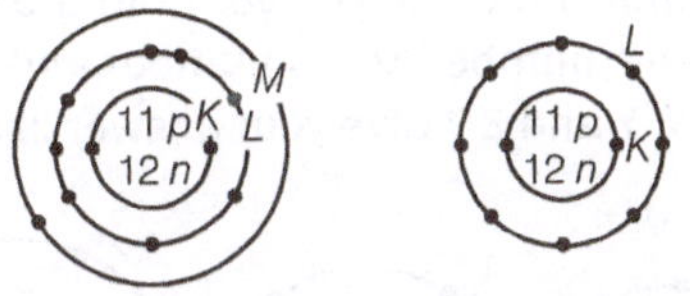

Sodium atom (Na) Sodium ion (Na^+)

9 (i) **Answer the following questions.**

(a) Name the scientist who proposed the model for the structure of an atom for the first time.

(b) Where is proton located in an atom?

(ii) An atom of an element has mass number 28 u and its atomic number is 14. How many neutrons does it have? Also, name the element.

Sol. (i) (a) JJ. Thomson was the first scientist to propose a model for the structure of an atom. [½]

(b) Proton is located in the nucleus of an atom. [½]

(ii) Number of neutrons

$=$ Mass number $-$ atomic number $= 28 - 14 = 14$

The element is silicon $({}^{28}_{14}Si)$. [2]

10 **Elements *A, B, C, D* and *E* have atomic numbers 4, 9, 13, 17 and 20 respectively.**

(i) Write their electronic distribution.

(ii) Determine their valency.

Sol. (i) The electronic distribution of elements *A, B, C, D* and *E* are given below:

	K	L	M	N
A (4)	2	2		
B (9)	2	7		
C (13)	2	8	3	
D (17)	2	8	7	
E (20)	2	8	8	2

[1½]

(ii) As valency of an element depends on the valence shell electrons thus, for the given elements valencies are $A = 2; B = 1; C = 3; D = 1; E = 2.$ [1½]

11 **Write the electronic configuration and valency of the following.**

(i) Chlorine (ii) Sodium (iii) Silicon

Sol. (i) Chlorine $({}_{17}Cl)$: $\overset{K}{2}, \overset{L}{8}, \overset{M}{7} \Rightarrow$ Valency $= 1$ [1]

(ii) Sodium $({}_{11}Na)$: $\overset{K}{2}, \overset{L}{8}, \overset{M}{1} \Rightarrow$ Valency $= 1$ [1]

(iii) Silicon $({}_{14}Si)$: $\overset{K}{2}, \overset{L}{8}, \overset{M}{4} \Rightarrow$ Valency $= 4$ [1]

12 **Atomic number of aluminium is 13 and mass number is 27. Calculate the number of electrons, protons and neutrons in its atom. Represent the ion of this element.**

Sol. Number of electrons $= 13$ [1/2]

Number of protons $= 13$ [1/2]

Number of neutrons $= 27 - 13 = 14$ [1/2]

Its electronic configuration is $\overset{K}{2}, \overset{L}{8}, \overset{M}{3}$ [1/2]

'Al' may lose 3 electrons easily to achieve completely filled outermost shell and hence, become stable, it acquires a positive charge of +3. Therefore, its ion is represented as Al^{3+}. [1]

13 **Find out the valency of atoms represented by the following figures.**

(i)

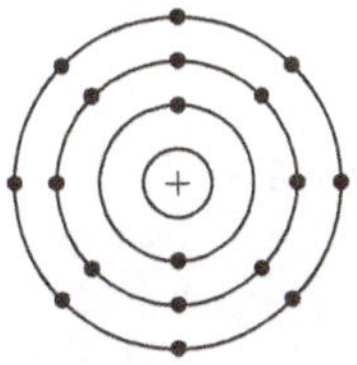

(ii)

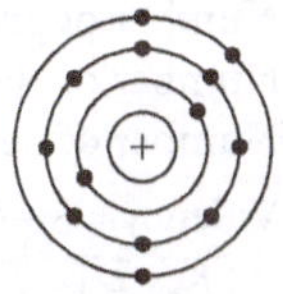

(iii)

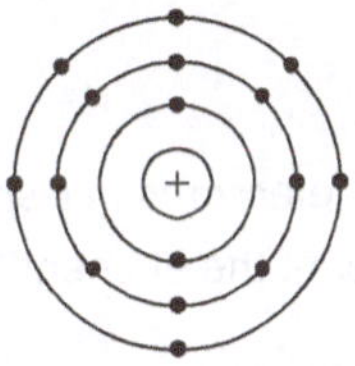

Sol. (i) Valency $= 0$ [$\because$ number of valence electrons $= 8$] [1]

(ii) Valency $= 3$ [$\because$ number of valence electrons $= 3$] [1]

(iii) Valency $= 2$ [$\because$ number of valence electrons $= 6$ and valency $= 8 - 6 = 2$] [1]

14 **The following data represents the distribution of electrons, protons and neutrons in atoms of four elements *A, B, C* and *D*.**

Element	Protons	Neutrons	Electrons
A	10	10	10
B	11	12	11
C	12	12	12
D	13	14	13

Solve the following questions.

(i) Write the electronic distribution of atoms of elements *A* and *D*.

(ii) Element *A* is an inert gas. Why?

(iii) What is the valency of element *C*?

Atomic number of *A* and *D* are 10 and 13 respectively. **Competency Based Que.**

Sol. (i) Electronic distribution of elements *A* and *D*.

$$\begin{matrix} & K & L & M \\ A = & 2, & 8 & \\ D = & 2, & 8, & 3 \end{matrix}$$ [1]

(ii) The number of electrons in the outermost shell of element *A* is 8. Since, the outermost shell of this element is complete and the element does not need to gain or lose electrons to complete its outermost shell. Hence, *A* is an inert gas. [1]

(iii) Electronic configuration of element *C* is 2, 8, 2. Thus, its valency is 2. [1]

15 You are given the atom of an element $^{16}_{8}X$. Find out the

(i) number of protons, electrons and neutrons in *X*.

(ii) valency of *X*.

(iii) chemical formula of the compound formed when *X* reacts with

(a) hydrogen (b) carbon

Sol. (i) Number of protons = 8

Number of electrons = 8

Number of neutrons = 16 − 8 = 8 [1]

(ii) Valency = 8 − 6 = 2 [1]

$$\because \begin{bmatrix} K & L \\ 2, & 6 \end{bmatrix}$$

(iii) (a) H_2X (b) CX_2 [1]

16 An atom of an element has 5 electrons in *L*-shell.

(i) What is the atomic number of the element?

(ii) State its valency.

(iii) Identify the element and write its name.

Sol. (i) Since, there are 5 electrons in *L*-shell and must have 2 electrons in *K*-shell. Thus, the element has a total of 7 electrons, which is equal to the number of protons, hence, the atomic number of the element is 7. [1]

(ii) As *L*-shell is outermost shell and it contains 5 electrons. Therefore, it has 5 valence electron. Thus, its valency is 3 [8 − 5 = 3]. [1]

(iii) Element having atomic number 7 is nitrogen (N). [1]

17 (i) An atom of an element has two electrons in the outermost *M*-shell. State

(a) electronic configuration and

(b) valency of this element.

(ii) What is the number of electrons in an atom whose *L*-shell is half-filled?

Sol. (i) (a) Atom of an element has two electrons in *M*-shell. Therefore, its electronic configuration = $\overset{K}{2}, \overset{L}{8}, \overset{M}{2}$

(b) Atomic number = 2 + 8 + 2 = 12 [1/2]

Its valency is 2, because there are 2 valence electrons, which it can lose easily to achieve stable outermost electronic configuration. [1/2]

(ii) As *L*-shell can hold maximum 8 electrons. Thus, *L*-shell has total 4 electrons in it, if it is half-filled.

∴ Total number of electrons = $\overset{K}{2}, \overset{L}{4} = 6$ electrons. [2]

18 What information do you get from the figure about the atomic number, mass number and valency of atoms X, Y and Z? Give your answer in a tabular form. **NCERT Exemplar**

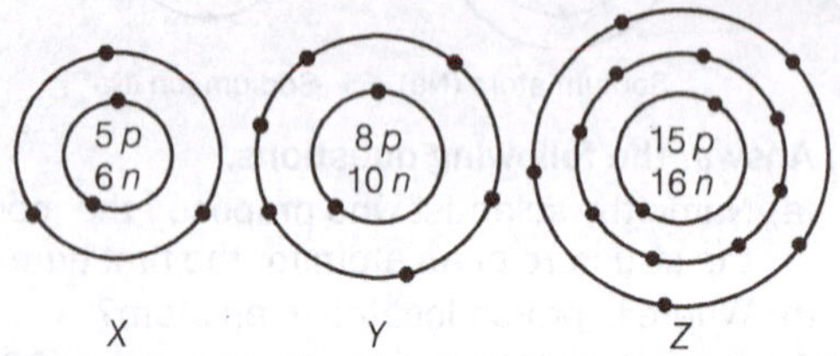

Sol. The information related to the figure is given in the tabulated form below.

Element	Atomic number (= no. of *p*)	Mass number {= no. of (*p* + *n*)}	Number of electrons (= no. of *p*)	Electronic configuration	Valency	
X	5	5 + 6 = 11	5	2, 3	3	[1]
Y	8	8 + 10 = 18	8	2, 6	2	[1]
Z	15	15+16 = 31	15	2, 8, 5	3, 5	[1]

19 (i) What is the mass number of an element whose atomic number is 17 and number of neutrons are 18?

(ii) What is the number of electrons in *M*-shell of atom of an element whose atomic number is 8?

(iii) Find the number of neutrons in an atom whose atomic number and mass number are 9 and 19 respectively.

Sol. (i) Atomic number = Number of protons = 17;

Mass number = Number of protons + Number of neutrons = 17 + 18 = 35 [1]

(ii) Electronic configuration of the element having atomic number 8.

$$\overset{K}{2}, \overset{L}{6}, \overset{M}{0}$$

Hence, there are zero electrons present in the *M*-shell. [1]

(iii) Atomic number = Number of protons = 9;
Number of neutrons
= Mass number − Number of protons
= 19 − 9 = 10 [1]

20 Two elements are represented as $_{17}X^{35}$ and $_{12}Y^{24}$.

(i) How many electrons element *X* needs to complete its outermost shell?

(ii) What is the number of neutrons present in atom of element '*Y*'?

(iii) Write the electronic configurations of *X* and *Y*.

Sol. (i) As there are 7 electrons in *M*-shell of its atom, which is the outermost shell (2, 8, 7).

Hence, it needs one electron to complete this shell. [1]

(ii) Element *Y* has mass number 24 and atomic number 12.

Number of neutrons = 24 − 12 = 12 [1]

(iii) Electronic configuration of *X* (atomic number = 17)

$= \overset{K}{2}, \overset{L}{8}, \overset{M}{7}$ [1/2]

Electronic configuration of *Y* (atomic number = 12)

$= \overset{K}{2}, \overset{L}{8}, \overset{M}{2}$ [1/2]

21 In the following table the mass numbers and the atomic numbers of certain elements are given.

Element	A	B	C	D	E
Mass no.	1	7	14	40	40
Atomic no.	1	3	7	18	20

(i) Select a pair of isobars from the above table.

(ii) What would be the valency of element *C* listed in the above table?

(ii) Which two sub-atomic particles are equal in number in a neutral atom? **Competency Based Que.**

Sol. (i) *D* and *E* have same mass number but different atomic numbers. Hence, they are a pair of isobars. [1]

(ii) Electronic configuration of *C* is 2(*K*), 5(*L*). Hence, its valency is three because it gains three electrons to attain stable electronic configuration.
[or valency can be find as, 8 − 5 = 3] [1]

(iii) For a neutral atom,
Number of electrons = Number of protons
Thus, electrons and protons are equal in numbers in a neutral atom. [1]

22 An ion M^{3-} contains 10 electrons and 7 neutrons. What is the atomic number and mass number of the element *M*? Name the element.

Sol. The number of protons in M^{3-} ion = 10 − 3 = 7
∴ The atomic number is 7.
Further, Mass number = Number of protons + Number of neutrons = 7 + 7 = 14
∴ The element is nitrogen. [3]

23 A metal (mass number = 40) having same number of protons and neutrons, combines with two chlorine atoms. Identify the element with which electronic configuration of this metal matches in combined state.

Sol. As, mass number = Number of protons + Number of neutrons

⇒ 40 = 2 × number of protons [1/2]

⇒ Number of protons = 20

Hence, the metal is calcium (Ca). [1]

Since, it combines with 2 Cl-atoms (total valency = 2)

Hence, it will acquire 2 positive charge, after losing 2 electrons. [1/2]

Electronic configuration of Ca^{2+} ion $= \overset{K}{2}, \overset{L}{8}, \overset{M}{8}$ [1/2]

This electronic configuration matches to that of argon (Ar). [1/2]

24 Study the data given below and answer the questions which follow:

Particle	Electrons	Protons	Neutrons
A	2	3	4
B	10	9	8
C	8	8	8
D	8	8	10

(i) Write the mass number and atomic number of particles *A*, *B*, *C*, *D*.

(ii) Which particles represent a pair of isotopes? Explain. **Competency Based Que.**

Sol. (i)

Particle	Atomic number	Mass number
A	3	3 + 4 = 7
B	9	9 + 8 = 17
C	8	8 + 8 = 16
D	8	8 + 10 = 18

[2]

(ii) Particles *C* and *D* represent a pair of isotopes as they have same number of protons, i.e. same atomic number but different mass numbers. [1]

25 The two isotopes of chlorine have mass number 35 and 37 and number of neutrons 18 and 20 respectively. Which one will have higher valency? Do they have same physical or chemical properties?

Sol. Number of protons in ^{35}Cl = 35 − 18 = 17
⇒ Number of electrons = Number of protons = 17
Similarly, number of protons in ^{37}Cl = 37 − 20 = 17
⇒ Number of electrons = Number of protons = 17
Since, both have same number of electrons (i.e. 17).
Hence, they will have same valency (i.e. 1).

Isotopes having same number of electrons show same chemical properties but may show some different physical properties. [3]

26 Sulphur dioxide (SO_2) is a colourless pungent smelling gas and is a major air pollutant.

(i) Write the electronic configuration of its constituent elements 'sulphur and oxygen' (Given, $^{32}_{16}S$, $^{16}_{8}O$).

(ii) Write the valency of sulphur and oxygen.

(iii) Are sulphur and oxygen isotopes of same element? Explain your answer.

Sol. (i) Electronic configuration of sulphur (S) : $\overset{K}{2}, \overset{L}{8}, \overset{M}{6}$

Electronic configuration of oxygen (O) : $\overset{K}{2}, \overset{L}{6}$ [1]

(ii) Valency of both sulphur and oxygen is 2, as they have the tendency to gain two electrons to achieve stable outer shell electronic configuration. [1]

(iii) Isotopes are the elements having the same atomic number but different mass numbers. Therefore, they are not isotopes as their atomic numbers are different. [1]

27 Two ions having 3 negative and 3 positive charges are found to have 7 and 14 neutrons respectively. If electronic configuration of these ions are similar to that of neon (Ne), then find the mass number of both the ions.

Sol. The electronic configuration of Ne = $\overset{K}{2}, \overset{L}{8}$

Atom, which forms ion similar to neon with 3 positive charges, will have electronic configuration as = $\overset{K}{2}, \overset{L}{5}$

Hence, the given atom is nitrogen.

Mass number = Number of protons + Number of neutrons

$= 7 + 7 = 14$ [1½]

Similarly, atom which forms ion similar to neon with 3 negative charges, will have electronic configuration as $= \overset{K}{2}, \overset{L}{8}, \overset{M}{3}$

Hence, the given atom is aluminium.

Mass number = Number of protons + Number of neutrons

$= 13 + 14 = 27$ [1½]

28 (i) What is the number of electrons in Cl^- ion (Cl=17)?

(ii) What is the electronic configuration of phosphorus (P = 15)?

(iii) Which isotope of uranium is used in nuclear fuel?

Sol. (i) Number of electrons in Cl^- ion = 17 + 1 (gained) = 18 electrons [because negative charge shows gain of electrons]. [1]

(ii) Atomic number of phosphorus = 15

Electronic configuration = $\overset{K}{2}, \overset{L}{8}, \overset{M}{5}$ [1]

(iii) Uranium-235 isotope is used in nuclear fuel. [1]

29 An element *M* forms the compound MH_3 when it reacts with hydrogen.

(i) Find the valency of element *M*.

(ii) Write the valency of chlorine and sulphur.

(iii) Name three isotopes of hydrogen.

Sol. (i) Valency of $M = 3$ because it combines with three atoms of hydrogen. [1]

(ii) Valency of chlorine, Cl (2, 8, 7) $= 8 - 7 = 1$

Valency of sulphur, S (2, 8, 6) $= 8 - 6 = 2$ [1]

(iii) Three isotopes of hydrogen are protium ^1_1H, deuterium ^2_1H and tritium ^3_1H. [1]

30 (i) Why do isotopes of an element show similar chemical properties?

(ii) How did Rutherford come to the conclusion that size of the nucleus is very small?

Sol. (i) Chemical properties depend on the electronic configuration of an atom. Since, isotopes of an element have same atomic number and number of electrons or more precisely same electronic configuration. Hence, isotopes of an element show similar chemical properties. [1½]

(ii) When Rutherford bombarded fast moving α-particles on gold foil he observed that few α-rays were deflected and very few α-rays re-bounded completely and most of the α-particles passed straight.

Then, he concluded that nearly all mass of an atom is concentrated within the positively charge nucleus which occupies very little space. [1½]

31 (i) Identify which of the following pairs are isotopes and which are isobars? Give reasons for your choice.

$$^{58}A_{26},\ ^{58}B_{28},\ ^{79}X_{35},\ ^{80}Y_{35}$$

(ii) Do isobars also have identical chemical properties like isotopes? State reason.

Sol. (i) *A* and *B* are isobars as they are atoms of different elements having the same mass number.

X and *Y* are isotopes as they are atoms of same element (same atomic number) having different mass numbers. [2]

(ii) No, isobars do not have identical chemical properties because they have different atomic numbers as well as electronic configurations. [1]

32 **On the basis of the number of protons, neutrons and electrons in the samples given below identify**

(i) the cation (ii) the pair of isobars, and

(iii) the pair of isotopes.

Sample	Protons	Neutrons	Electrons
A	17	18	16
B	18	19	18
C	17	20	17
D	17	17	17

Sol. (i) Sample *A* has more protons than the electrons, i.e. it has donated one electron and possessed positive charge. Hence, it is a cation. [1]

(ii) Sample *B* and *C* have same mass number (Mass number = Number of protons + number of neutrons = 37) but different atomic numbers (i.e. 18 and 17 respectively).

Hence, they are a pair of isobars. [1]

(iii) Samples *C* and *D* have same atomic number but different mass numbers. (i.e. 37 and 34). Hence, they are a pair of isotopes. [1]

Long Answer Type Questions

1. **(i) Which popular experiment is shown in the figure?**

(ii) List three observations of this experiment.

(iii) State conclusions drawn from each observation of this experiment.

(iv) State the model of the atom suggested on the basis of the experiment.

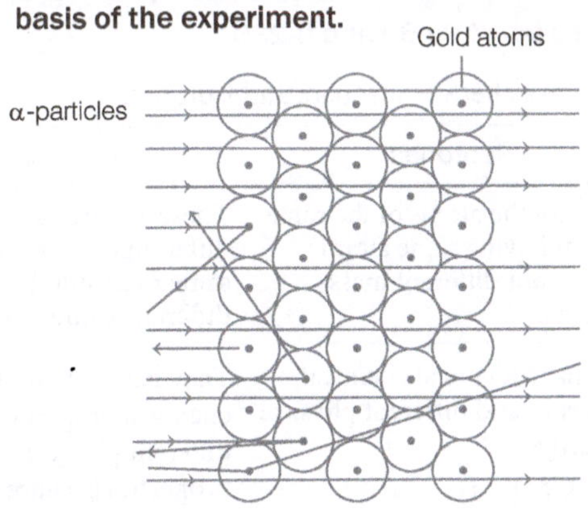

Sol. (i) This figure shows scattering of α-particles by a gold foil which is known as Rutherford's experiment or α-particle scattering experiment. [1/2]

(ii) Refer to text on Pg 70. [1½]

(iii) Refer to text on Pg 70. [1½]

(iv) **Rutherford's atomic model** Refer to text on Pg 70. [1½]

2 **(i) From Rutherford's α-particle scattering experiment, give the experimental evidence for deriving the conclusion that**

(a) most of the space inside the atom is empty.

(b) the nucleus of an atom is positively charged.

(ii) An element has mass number = 32 and atomic number = 16, find

(a) the number of neutrons in the atom of the element.

(b) the number of electrons in the outermost shell of the atom.

(iii) On the basis of Rutherford's model of an atom, which sub-atomic particle is present in the nucleus of an atom?

Sol. (i) (a) As most of the α-particles passed straight through the gold foil. [1]

(b) A few of the α-particles which are positively charged, deflected due to the positive charge of nucleus. [1]

(ii) (a) Number of neutrons

= Mass number − Atomic number

= 32 − 16 = 16 [1]

(b) The electronic configuration of the element will be as follows

$$\begin{matrix} K & L & M \\ 2, & 8, & 6 \end{matrix}$$

Hence, the number of electrons in the outermost shell is 6. [1]

(iii) According to Rutherford's model of an atom, positively charge protons are present in the nucleus of an atom. [1]

3 **(i) Describe Bohr's model of an atom. Draw a sketch of Bohr's model of an atom with three shells.**

(ii) What was the drawback of Rutherford's model of an atom?

Sol. (i) Refer to text on Pg 71. [2½]

(ii) Refer to text on Pg 70 and 71. [2½]

4 **(i) What is an octet? How do elements attain an octet?**

(ii) Make a schematic atomic structure of magnesium and phosphorus.

[Given number of protons of magnesium = 12 and that of phosphorus = 15]

Sol. (i) An outermost shell, which has eight electrons is said to possess an octet.

Elements attain their octet by sharing, gaining or losing electrons. [2]

(ii) Atomic number of magnesium = 12

Distribution of electrons $_{12}Mg = \begin{matrix} K & L & M \\ 2, & 8, & 2 \end{matrix}$

Atomic structure of Mg

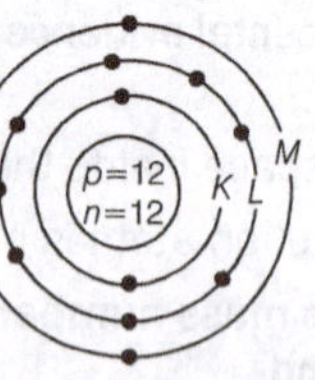

[1½]

Atomic number of phosphorus = 15

Distribution of electrons $_{15}P = \overset{K}{2}, \overset{L}{8}, \overset{M}{5}$

Atomic structure of P

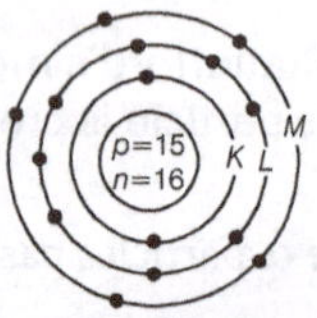

[1½]

5 (i) An element *X* has an atomic number = 12 and mass number = 26. Draw a diagram showing the distribution of electrons in the orbits and the nuclear composition of the neutral atom of the element. What is the valency of the element and why?

(ii) If this element *X* combines with another element *Y* whose electronic configuration is 2, 8, 7. What will be the formula of the compound thus formed? State how did you arrive at this formula.

Competency Based Que.

Sol. (i) Atomic number of atom $X = 12$

Mass number = 26

Electronic configuration = 2, 8, 2

Atomic structure of *X*

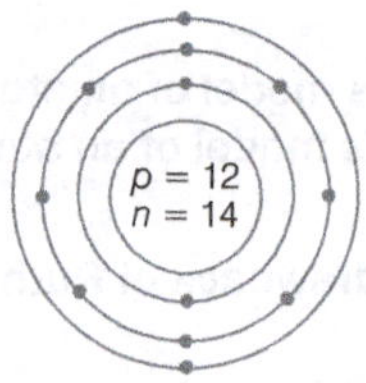

Nuclear composition

Number of protons = 12

Number of neutrons = 26 − 12 = 14

Valency of this element is 2 as it can donate 2 electrons easily to complete its octet and become stable. [3]

(ii) Valency of the element *Y* with electronic configuration 2, 8, 7 would be 1, i.e. it can gain 1 electron to become stable.

When it combines with the element *X* of valency 2, the compound formed will be XY_2.

Element	*X*	*Y*
Valency	2	1

Formula of the compound will be XY_2. [2]

6 Number of electrons, protons and neutrons in chemical species *A*, *B*, *C* and *D* is given below.

Chemical species	Electrons	Protons	Neutrons
A	2	3	4
B	10	9	8
C	8	8	8
D	8	8	10

Now answer the following questions using given data in the table.

Competency Based Que.

(i) What is the mass number of *A* and *B*?

(ii) What is the atomic number of *B*?

(iii) Which two chemical species represent a pair of isotopes and why?

(iv) What is the valency of element *C*?

Also justify your answers.

Sol. (i) Mass number = Number of protons + number of neutrons

Mass number of $A = 3 + 4 = 7$

Mass number of $B = 9 + 8 = 17$ [1]

(ii) Atomic number of B = Number of protons = 9 [1]

(iii) *C* and *D* are isotopes as they have same atomic number but different mass numbers. [1]

(iv) Electronic configuration of $C : \overset{K}{2}, \overset{L}{6}$

It needs two electrons to complete its octet. Hence, its valency is 2. [2]

7 (i) Write two differences between isotopes and isobars.

(ii) Write uses of Co-60 and U-235.

Sol. (i) Differences between isobars and isotopes:

Isotopes	Isobars
These are the atoms of the same element having same atomic number but different mass numbers.	These are the atoms of the different elements having same mass number but different atomic numbers.
They have identical chemical properties and different physical properties. e.g. ^1_1H, ^2_1H, ^3_1H	They have different chemical properties and different physical properties because these are the atoms of different elements. e.g. $^{40}_{18}Ar$ and $^{40}_{20}Ca$

[3]

(ii) Isotope of cobalt (Co-60) is used in the treatment of cancer and isotope of uranium (U-235) is used as a fuel in nuclear reactor. [2]

ASSESSMENT EXERCISE

Competency Focused (Objective) Questions

Multiple Choice Questions

1. Which of the following model describes the structure of an atom proposed by Thomson?

Competency Based Que.

(a) 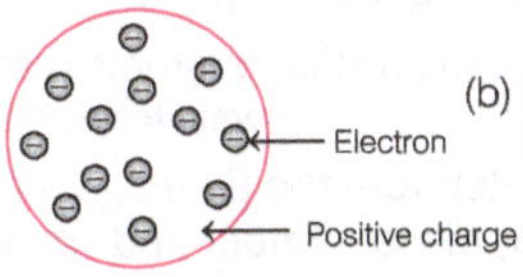

(b) 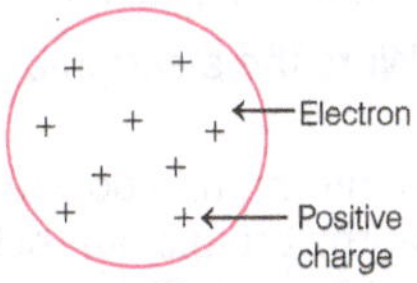

(c) 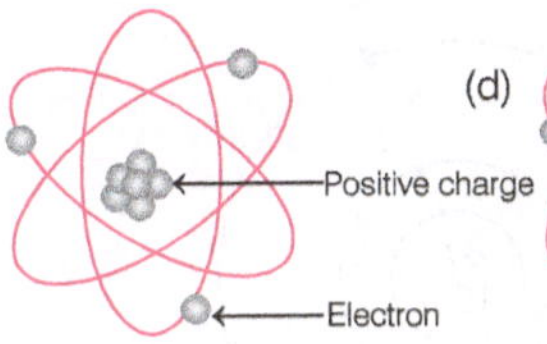

(d) 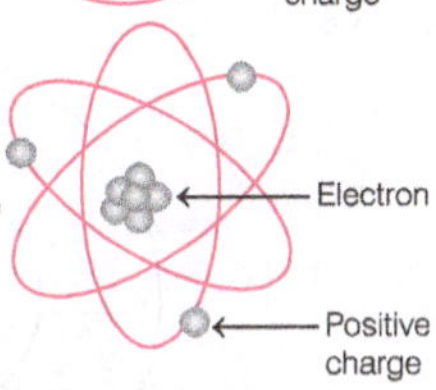

2. The ion of an atom has 2 negative charges. Mass number of the atom is 16 and the number of neutrons are 8. What is the number of electrons in the ion?

Competency Based Que.

(a) 6 (b) 7
(c) 8 (d) 10

3. How many neutrons are present in the nucleus of hydrogen atom?

(a) 1 (b) 2
(c) 3 (d) 0

4. Which of the following correctly represent the electronic distribution in the Mg atom ?

(a) 2, 8, 1 (b) 2, 8, 2
(c) 1, 8, 2 (d) 8, 2, 2

5. Which of the following is an accurate illustration of a nitrogen atom?

(a) 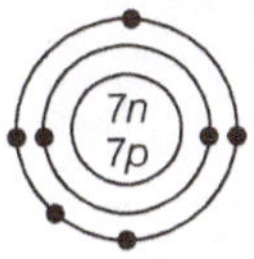

(b) 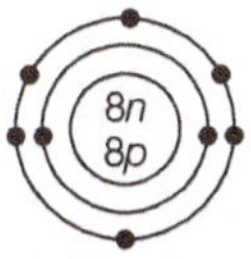

(c) 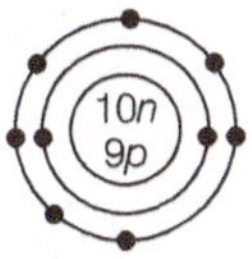

(d) 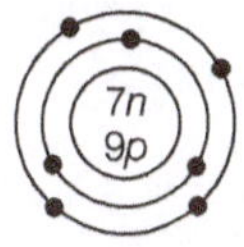

6. The number of electrons in an element X is 15 and the number of neutrons is 16. Which of the following is the correct representation of the element?

(a) $^{31}_{15}X$ (b) $^{31}_{16}X$ (c) $^{16}_{15}X$ (d) $^{15}_{16}X$

Assertion-Reason Questions

Direction (Q. Nos. 7-9) *In each of the following questions, a statement of Assertion is given by the corresponding statement of Reason. Of the statements, mark the correct answer as*

(a) Both Assertion and Reason are true and Reason is the correct explanation of Assertion.
(b) Both Assertion and Reason are true but Reason is not the correct explanation of Assertion.
(c) Assertion is true but Reason is false.
(d) Assertion is false but Reason is true.

7. Assertion (A) Bohr's orbits are called stationary orbits.

Reason (R) Electrons remain stationary in these orbits for sometime.

8. Assertion (A) According to Bohr's model, the orbits of an atom are also called energy levels.

Reason (R) Orbits are associated with definite value of energy.

9. Assertion (A) The valency of an atom of fluorine is 7.

Reason (R) The number of electrons present in the outermost shell of fluorine atom is 7.

Answers

1. (a) **2.** (d) **3.** (d) **4.** (b) **5.** (a)
6. (a) **7.** (c) **8.** (a) **9.** (d)

Case Based/Source Based Questions

Direction [Q. (i)-(iii)] *Answer the questions on the basis of your understanding of the following passage and related studied concepts:*

10. The maximum number of the electrons which are permitted to be assigned to an energy shell of an atom is called the electron capacity of that shell. The distribution of electrons in different orbits or shell is governed by a scheme known as Bohr-Bury scheme.

According to this scheme, the maximum number of electrons that can be present in any shell is given by the formula $2n^2$ where, n is the number of energy level.

The maximum number of electrons that can be accommodated in the outermost shell is 8.

Electrons are filled in the shells in a stepwise manner in increasing order of energy of the energy shell.

(i) What is the maximum electron capacity of N-shell?

(ii) Which of the following have same valency $A(2, 8, 2)$, $B(2, 8, 4)$, $C(2, 6)$, $D(2, 8)$?

(iii) What are the postulates of Bohr's model of an atom?

Or Why do He, Ne and Ar have zero valency?

Constructed Response (Descriptive) Questions

Very Short Answer Type Questions

11. (i) How is the mass of electron, proton and neutron related?

(ii) What is meant by the term valence electrons?

12. (i) Does the nucleus contain neutrons also?

(ii) An element *X* has 3 electrons in its *M*-shell. What is its atomic number?

13. (i) Give the number of neutrons in an atom of the element $^{107}_{47}Ag$.

(ii) What are nucleons?

14. If an atom of an element has atomic number = 15 and mass number = 31, find the number of protons, electrons, neutrons in its atoms.

15. How are the following pairs of atoms related?

$_8X^{16}$, $_8X^{17}$, $_{18}Y^{40}$, $_{20}Z^{40}$

Competency Based Que.

Short Answer Type Questions

16. Describe the essential properties of the atomic nucleus. Compare these with the properties of electron.

17. The electronic configurations of some elements are given below. Name the elements.

(i) 2, 8, 5 (ii) 2, 8, 8, 2 (iii) 2, 8, 1

18. An atom *X* has 4 protons and 5 neutrons with electronic configuration 2, 2.

Give information about its

(i) atomic number

(ii) mass number

(iii) valency

19. The number of neutrons and protons present in the nuclei of two atomic species *A* and *B* are given below.

Atomic species	*A*	*B*
Protons	8	8
Neutrons	8	10

(i) Write the mass numbers of *A* and *B*.

(ii) What is the relation between two species?

(iii) Write the electronic configuration of atoms *A* and *B*.

Competency Based Que.

20. What information do you get from the figure given below about the atomic number, mass number and valency of atom *X*?

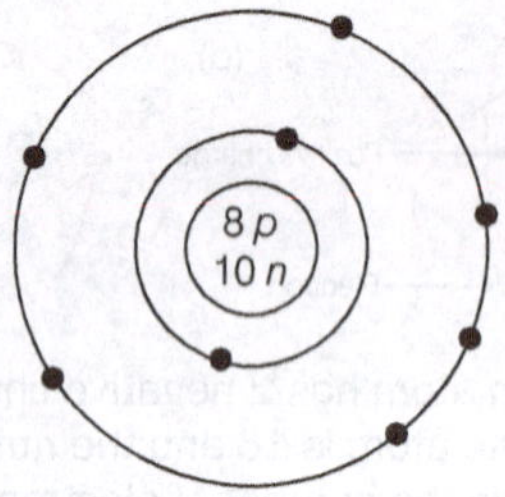

Long Answer Type Questions

21. (i) How did discovery of protons take place?

(ii) What is meant by the term average atomic mass? Give its formula.

22. (i) What are inert elements? Why are they called so?

(ii) What is the valency of these elements and why?

(iii) How many electrons can be accommodated in a *M* and *N*-shell?

CHAPTER 05

The Fundamental Unit of Life

All organisms including plants and animals are composed of cells. They are the smallest unit of life that exists independently or in a group to perform all the basic functions of life. Therefore, cell is known as **the basic fundamental, structural** and **functional unit of living organisms.**

5.1 Discovery of Cell

Robert Hooke (in 1665), examined a thin slice of cork under the self designed primitive microscope. He observed that cork consists of small box-like structures resembling honeycomb. He called these boxes as **cells.** The term 'cell' has been derived from a Latin word *cellula* which means 'a little room'.

Major Landmarks Related to Cell Discovery

Scientists	Years	Work
Robert Hooke	1665	Discovered cells for first time in a cork slice with the help of a primitive microscope.
Leeuwenhoek	1674	Discovered free-living cells in pond water using an improved microscope.
Robert Brown	1831	Discovered the nucleus in the cell.
Schleiden (1838) and Schwann (1839)	1838-1839	Presented cell theory, which states that all plants and animals are composed of cells and that the cells are the basic unit of life.
Purkinje	1839	Coined the term 'protoplasm' for the fluid substance of the cell.
Virchow	1855	Expanded the cell theory by suggesting that all cells arise from pre-existing cells.

The invention of magnifying lenses made the discovery of single-celled microscopic organisms possible.

Microscopes

- These are high resolution instruments that are used for observing the fine details of very minute things, e.g. cells. With the help of a microscope, the size of a small cell can be magnified upto 300-1500 times.
  The microscope, which is often used in schools is **compound microscope.** It uses sunlight or bulb for illumination of objects to be seen, so it is called as **light microscope.**
- An electron microscope is used to observe complex internal structures of the cell.

Cellular Composition in Different Organisms

On the basis of the number of cells present, organisms are classified as unicellular and multicellular.

Organisms

Unicellular organisms
- Made up of a single cell.
- All life processes like digestion, respiration, etc., are performed by a single cell only.
- For example, *Amoeba*, *Chlamydomonas*, *Paramecium*, bacteria, etc.

Multicellular organisms
- Made up of many cells that are grouped together in a single body.
- All cells are specialised to perform different functions.
- For example, plants, animals and some fungi.

Each multicellular organism starts its life as a single cell (i.e. zygote) that divides to form many cells.

Division of Labour

Each living cell performs certain basic functions that are the characteristic of all living forms.

To perform these functions, there is a **division of labour in multicellular organisms** which means that different parts of the human body perform different functions. For example, heart is made to pump blood, stomach to digest food, kidney to filter blood, etc.

Division of labour is also seen within a single cell. Each cell has certain specific components within it known as **cell organelles.**

These organelles perform a specific function, e.g. making new material in the cell, clearing waste material, etc. All these organelles together constitute the cell.

Thus, a cell is able to live and perform all its functions because of these cell organelles.

Shape and Size of Cells

The shape and size of cells are related to the specific functions they perform.

- Some cells have fixed shape (e.g. most plant and animal cells), while some cells like WBCs and *Amoeba* keep changing their shapes.
- Fix shaped cells may be of various types such as elliptical (e.g. fat cell), spherical (e.g. ovum), spindle-shaped (e.g. smooth muscle cell), thread-like (e.g. sperm), round and biconcave (e.g. RBC), elongated (e.g. nerve cell), etc.

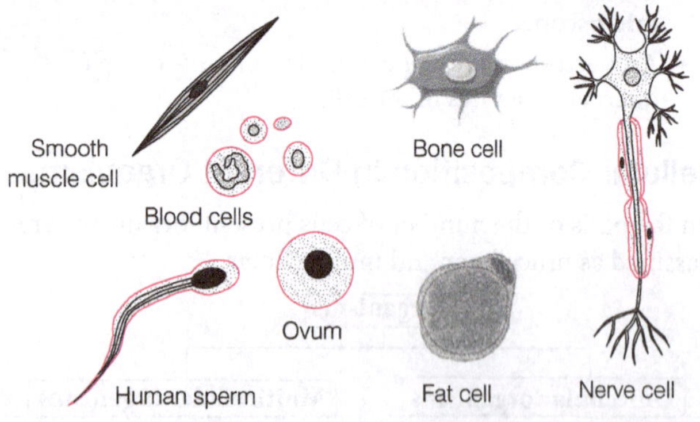

Various cells from the human body

- The size of cell varies significantly from the smallest cell of mycoplasma (0.1-0.5 µm) to the largest egg cell of the ostrich (18 cm). Longest cells of human body are the nerve cells, which may reach up to a length of 90 cm (motor neurons).

Try These 5.1

1. **Name the scientist who observed small box-like structures resembling honeycomb.**
2. **Two scientists described that all animals and plants are composed of cells. Name the scientists.**
3. **Name a unicellular organism that keeps on changing its shape.**
4. **Identify the term use to describe the specialisation of different cells, tissues and organs in the human body to perform specific function?**
5. **Name the longest cell present in multicellular organisms.**

5.2 Structural Organisation of a Cell

The microscopic studies revealed that almost every cell possesses three basic features in common, i.e.

(i) **Plasma membrane** Outer covering of all cells. Plant cell also contains cell wall.

(ii) **Nucleus** Control centre of the cell.

(iii) **Cytoplasm** Contains cell organelles.

Due to the presence of these features, all activities inside the cell and interactions of the cell with its environment are possible.

Plasma Membrane or Cell Membrane

This is the outermost living, thin and delicate covering of a cell that separates the contents of the cell from its external environment.

The structure of the plasma membrane can only be observed through an electron microscope. The plasma membrane is made up of organic molecules called **lipids** and **proteins** which provides flexibility to it.

Functions of Plasma Membrane

Important functions of plasma membrane are as follows

(i) It allows the movement of selective materials in and out of the cell. The cell membrane therefore, acts as a **selectively permeable membrane.**

(ii) It helps to maintain the shape of the cell.

(iii) It acts as a mechanical barrier and protects the internal contents of the cell.

(iv) The flexibility of a cell membrane enables the cell to engulf food and other materials from its external environment. This process is called **endocytosis**. For example, *Amoeba* acquires its food through this process, with the help of finger-like projections called **pseudopodia**.

Transport of Substances Across the Cell Membrane

Transport of substances across the cell membrane occurs by the process of diffusion and osmosis.
These process are discussed below

1. Transport of Substance Across the Membrane by Diffusion

The spontaneous movement of a substance (i.e. solid, liquid or gas) from a region of its higher concentration to a region of its lower concentration is called **diffusion.**

For example,

(i) Some substances like CO_2 (cellular waste, which needs to be excreted out) accumulates in higher concentration inside the cell. In the cell's external environment, the concentration of CO_2 is low as compared to that inside the cell. Due to this difference in the concentration, CO_2 moves out of the cell by the process of diffusion.

(ii) Similarly, O_2 enters the cell by the process of diffusion, when the level or concentration of O_2 inside the cell decreases.

Significance

The process of diffusion plays an important role in exchange of gases and water between the cells as well as the cell and its external environment.

Note Diffusion is faster in gases than in liquids and solids.

2. Transport of Substance Across the Membrane by Osmosis

The process of osmosis involves the movement of water molecules from the region of its higher concentration towards the region of its lower concentration through a semipermeable membrane.

For example,

(i) Unicellular freshwater organisms and most plant cells tend to gain water through osmosis.

(ii) Plant roots absorb water by the process of osmosis.

The movement of water across the plasma membrane is affected by the amount of substance dissolved in water.

The process of osmosis can be seen in a cell placed in solution of different concentrations such as hypotonic, isotonic and hypertonic.

(i) **Hypotonic solution** The medium or solution surrounding the cell has a higher water concentration as compared to that inside of the cell.

A cell placed in hypotonic solution gains water and swells up *via* **endosmosis**. This happens because the water molecules are free to pass across the cell membrane in both directions, but more water enters the cell than that leaving it.

(ii) **Isotonic solution** The medium or solution surrounding the cell has exactly the same concentration of water as that present inside the cell.

A cell placed in isotonic solution remains same in size. This is because there is no net movement of water, i.e. the amount of water going in is same as the amount of water coming out.

(iii) **Hypertonic solution** The medium or solution surrounding the cell has a lower concentration of water than the cell.

A cell placed in hypertonic solution shrinks *via* **exosmosis.** This is because in this case also the water crosses the cell membrane in both directions, but more water leaves the cell then enters it.

Cell Wall

It is a rigid, non-living covering that lies outside the plasma membrane in all plant, bacterial and fungal cells. The cell wall is absent in animal cells. When compared to cell membrane, the cell wall is freely permeable in nature.

Cell wall is mainly composed of cellulose, a complex carbohydrate that provides structural strength to the plants.

Functions of Cell Wall

Different functions of cell wall are as follows

(i) It provides definite shape to the cell.

(ii) It permits the cells of plants, fungi and bacteria to withstand very dilute or hypotonic external media without bursting.

In hypotonic medium, the cells tend to take up water by osmosis.

The cell swells up building pressure against the cell wall. The wall exerts an equal pressure against the swollen cell.

Because of the presence of cell wall, these cells can withstand much greater changes in the surrounding medium than animal cells.

(iii) It protects the cell by providing structural and mechanical strength.

Plasmolysis

It is the process of shrinkage of contents of the living cell along with the plasma membrane away from the cell wall.

Plasmolysis occurs due to exosmosis or when a plant cell is placed in a hypertonic solution.

Try These 5.2

1. Name three basic features commonly present in cell due to which all activities inside the cell and its interactions with its environment are made possible.
2. Which substances are responsible for the presence of flexibility in the outermost living, thin covering of the cell?
3. Give the name of the process through which *Amoeba* acquires its food.
4. Name the process through which CO_2 is transported out of cells.
5. What happens when raisins are kept in water? Name the process involved.

Nucleus

A nucleus is a spherical or oval structure present inside the cell. It is popularly called as the **brain of cell**.

Structure of Nucleus

Nucleus is differentiated into the following parts

(i) **Nuclear membrane** It is the outer, double-layered covering that has numerous pores called **nuclear pores** that allow the transfer of materials from inside the nucleus to the cytoplasm.

(ii) **Nucleoplasm** It is a gel-like substance enclosed by a nuclear membrane. It contains nucleolus and chromatin material.

(iii) **Nucleolus** It is a more or less round, structure found inside the nucleus. It does not have a covering or membranes. It is known as the **factory of ribosomes.**

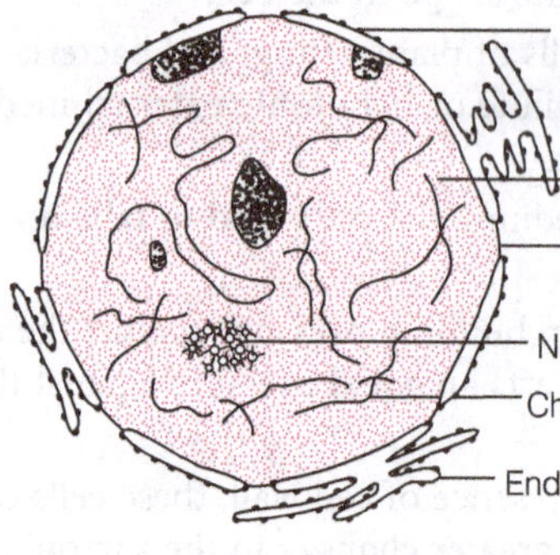

Eukaryotic nucleus

(iv) **Chromatin** It is an entangled network of long, thread-like structures. It condenses to form chromosomes during cell division. These chromosomes appear as rod-shaped structures and are visible only when the cell is about to divide. They contain information for the inheritance of characters or features from parents to next generation in the form of **DNA** (Deoxyribonucleic Acid) molecules. Chromosomes are composed of two components, (i.e. DNA and protein).

The DNA molecules contain information necessary for constructing and organising cells. The functional segments of DNA are called **genes.**

Functions of Nucleus

Nucleus performs the following important functions

(i) Nucleus plays essential role in cellular reproduction. In this process, a cell divides to form two new cells.

(ii) It determines the cell development and maturity by directing the chemical activities of the cell.

(iii) It helps in the transmission of hereditary traits from parents to offsprings.

(iv) It controls all metabolic activities of the cell.

Prokaryotic and Eukaryotic Cell

On the basis of complexity of cell structure and the absence or presence of true nucleus, cells can be classified into following two types

Prokaryotic Cells

(Gr. *Pro*-Primitive or primary; *karyos*-nucleus)

These cells contain primitive, unorganised nucleus which is not bounded by any membrane. In some organisms like bacteria, the nuclear region of the cell is poorly defined because of the absence of nuclear membrane.

The nuclear region in these organisms contains only nucleic acids. Such an undefined nuclear region is called **nucleoid**. Organisms whose cells lack a nuclear membrane are called **prokaryotes.**

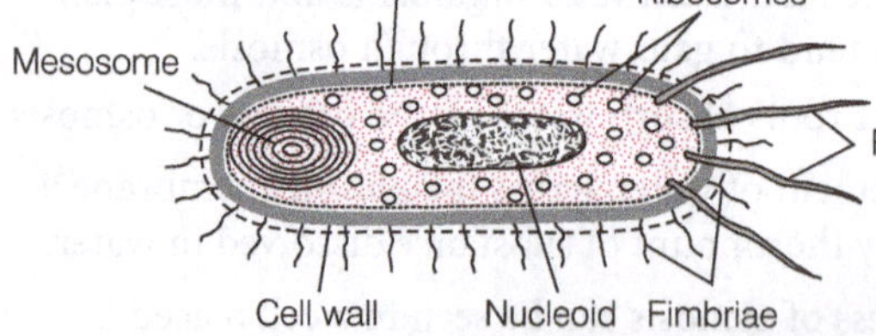

Prokaryotic cell

The prokaryotes also lack most of the cytoplasmic organelles. Many of the functions of such organelles are thus performed by the poorly developed parts of cytoplasm.

For example, the chlorophyll in photosynthetic prokaryotic bacteria is associated with membranous vesicles (bag-like structures) or lamellar structures but not with plastids. This is because plastids are not observed in prokaryotic bacteria as in photosynthetic eukaryotic plant cells.

Eukaryotic Cells

(Gr. *Eu*-Advanced; *karyos*-nucleus)

The cells which possess a well-defined membrane-bound nucleus are called eukaryotic cells.

Along with nucleus these cells also possess membrane-bound organelles such as mitochondria, chloroplasts, etc.

The eukaryotic cells are further categorised into plant and animal cells. These are also different from each other in many ways.

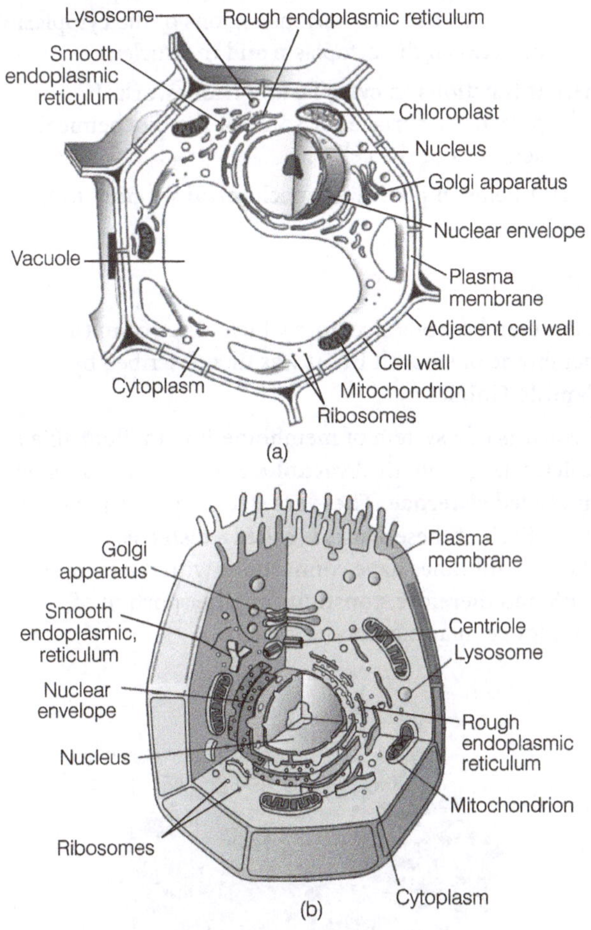

(a) Plant cell, (b) Animal cell

Differences between Prokaryotic and Eukaryotic Cells

Features	Prokaryotic cells	Eukaryotic cells
Size	Generally small (1-10 μm).	Generally large (5-100 μm).
Nuclear Region	Poorly developed, nuclear membrane absent and is called as nucleoid.	Well-defined, surrounded by nuclear membrane.
Chromosome	Single	More than one
Nucleolus	Absent	Present
Membrane-bound Cell Organelles	Absent	Present, e.g. mitochondria, plastids, endoplasmic reticulum, etc.
Centriole	Absent	Present in animal cells.
Organisms	Found in bacteria, blue-green algae, etc.	Found in fungi, plants and animals.
Cell Division	Takes place by binary fission and budding.	Takes place by mitotic and meiotic cell division.

Cytoplasm

It is the fluid content present inside the plasma membrane. It contains many specialised cell organelles, each of which performs a specific function for the cell.

Functions of Cytoplasm

It perform the following functions

(i) It helps in the exchange of material between cell organelles.

(ii) It acts as a storehouse of vital molecules such as amino acid, glucose, vitamin, iron, etc.

(iii) It acts as the site for certain metabolic pathways.

Try These 5.3

1. **Which cell organelle controls most of the activities of the cell?**
2. **Which structure of nucleus maintains continuity with cytoplasm?**
3. **Where are the functional segments of DNA located?**
4. **Give the name of the structure also known as the factory of ribosomes.**
5. **Which term is often used for the genetic material that lies in direct contact with the cytoplasm?**

5.3 Cell Organelles

These are microscopic, membrane-bound structures that perform specific functions for the cell.

Large and complex cells need a lot of chemical activities to support their complicated structure and function. To keep these activities separated from each other, these cells use membrane-bound structures. This is one of the main characteristic feature that differentiates eukaryotic cells from prokaryotic cells.

Some of these organelles are visible only with the help of an electron microscope.

Endoplasmic Reticulum (ER)

It is a large network of membrane-bound tubes and sheets extending from outer nuclear membrane into the cytoplasm. The ER looks like long tubules or round or oblong bags (vesicles). It occurs in three different forms, such as cisternae, vesicles and tubules.

The membrane of endoplasmic reticulum is similar in structure to the plasma membrane.

Types of Endoplasmic Reticulum

Depending upon the nature of its membrane, ER is divided into main two types

(i) **Rough Endoplasmic Reticulum** (RER) It contains ribosomal particles on its surfaces due to which its surface appears rough. RER is mainly formed of cisternae.

(ii) **Smooth Endoplasmic Reticulum** (SER) Its surface is smooth due to the absence of ribosomes. It is formed of vesicles and tubules.

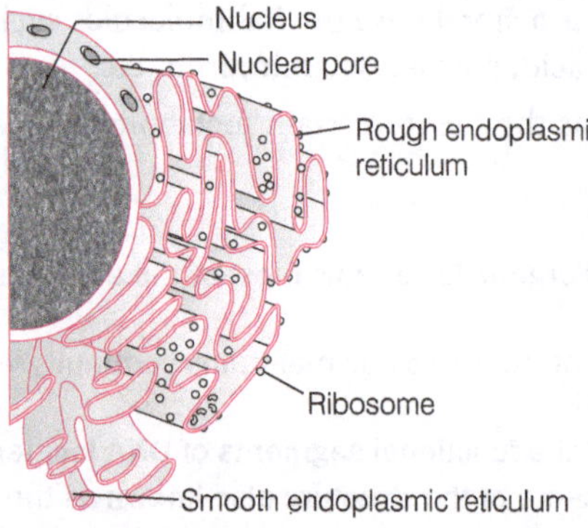

Ultrastructure of endoplasmic reticulum

Functions

Various functions of endoplasmic reticulum are as follows

(i) Ribosomes present in all active cells act as sites for protein synthesis. The proteins manufactured here are transported throughout the cell using the ER (**Endoplasmic Reticulum).**

(ii) The SER helps in the manufacture of fat molecules, or lipids, important for cell function.

(iii) Some of these proteins and lipid molecules helps in building cell membrane and other cell components. This process is called **membrane biogenesis.**

(iv) Some other proteins and lipids synthesised by ER function as enzymes and hormones.

(v) SER plays a crucial role in **detoxification** of poisons and drugs in the liver cells of vertebrates (or group of animals).

(vi) Although, the ER varies greatly in appearance in different cells, the ER forms a network system, providing channels for proteins. It transports materials between various regions of the cytoplasm or between the cytoplasm and the nucleus.

(vii) It functions as **cytoplasmic framework.** It provides a surface for some of the biochemical activities of the cell.

(viii) It helps in providing **mechanical support** to the cells.

Golgi Apparatus

It is a membranous structure which arises from the membrane of smooth ER. It was first described by **Camillo Golgi.**

It consists of a system of membrane-bound, fluid-filled **vesicles**, large spherical **vacuoles** and smooth, flattened sacs called **cisternae.** These are stacked parallel to each other. Each of these stacks is called a **cisterns.**
These membranes have connections with the membranes of ER and therefore, constitute another portion of a complex cellular membrane system.

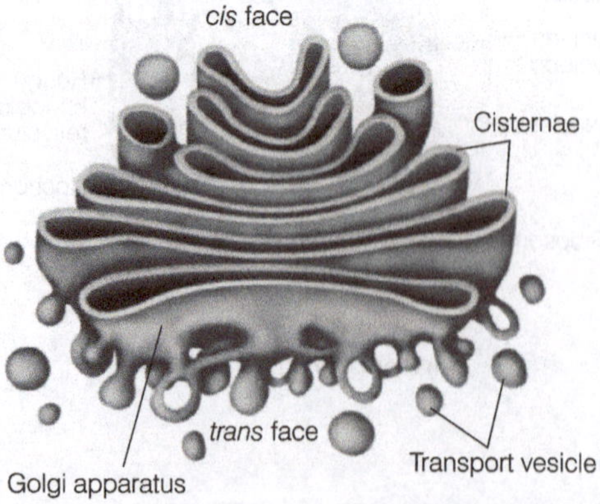

Ultrastructure of Golgi apparatus

Functions

The Golgi apparatus performs following functions

(i) It stores, modifies and packs products in vesicles. The material that is synthesised near Endoplasmic Reticulum (ER) is packaged and dispatched to various parts of the cell through Golgi apparatus.

(ii) In some cases, it also forms complex sugars from simple sugars.

(iii) It is also involved in the formation of **lysosomes**.

Black Reaction by Camillo Golgi

- The scientist, who described Golgi apparatus known as **Camillo Golgi** was born in the year 1843 at Corteno near Brescia. Most of his investigations were concerned with the nervous system. His greatest work was a revolutionary method of staining individual nerve and cell structures. This method is called **'black reaction'**.
- It uses a weak solution of silver nitrate to trace the most the delicate ramification of cells. Golgi received the highest honours and awards in the recognition of this work.
- He shared the Nobel Prize in 1906 with Santiago Ramón y Cajal for their work on the structure of nervous system.

Lysosomes

These are membrane-bound sacs filled with digestive enzymes which are made by rough endoplasmic reticulum. These enzymes are capable of breaking down all organic materials. Lysosomes are present in all animal cells except mammalian RBCs.

Functions

The important functions of lysosomes are given below.

(i) These are a kind of waste disposal system of the cell, thus help to keep the cell clean by digesting old and worn-out cell organelles.

(ii) They also protect the cells from infections. The foreign materials entering the cell, such as bacteria, end up in the lysosomes and get destroyed.

(iii) During the disturbance in the cellular metabolism, e.g. when the cell gets damaged, lysosomes may burst and the enzymes digest their own cell. Therefore, lysosomes are also known as the **suicidal bags of the cell**.

Mitochondria

It is small rod-like or spherical structure present in the cytoplasm.

It is a **double membrane** bounded cell organelle. The outer membrane is porous, while the inner membrane is deeply folded into finger-like projections called **cristae**. These folds help to increase the surface area for ATP generating chemical reactions.

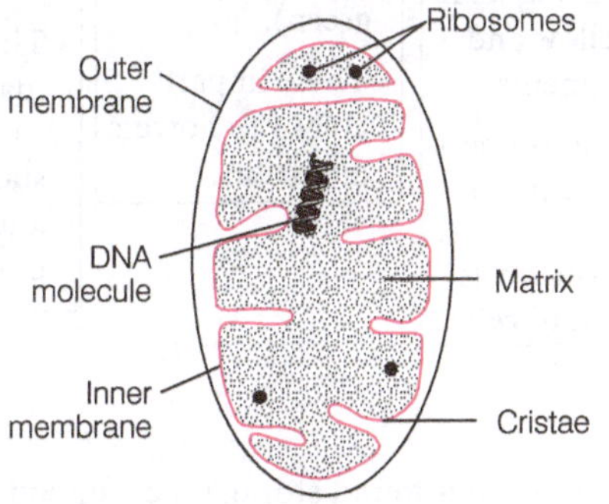

An ultrastructure of mitochondria

Functions

It perform following functions

(i) Mitochondria helps to generate energy for various chemical activities in the cells. It is therefore known as the **powerhouse of the cell.** It releases energy required by the cell in the form of ATP (Adenosine Triphosphate).

This ATP is known as **energy currency** of the cell. The ATP released by mitochondria is used by the body for making new chemical compounds and for other mechanical work.

(ii) Mitochondria are strange organelles in the sense that they have their own DNA and ribosomes. Hence, they are able to make some of their own proteins.

Plastids

These are oval or discoidal double membrane-bound organelle that are found only in plant cells.

The internal organisation of plastids contains numerous membrane layers embedded in a material called **stroma**. These are similar to mitochondria in external structure. Like mitochondria, plastids also contain their own DNA and ribosomes.

Types of Plastids

They are of three types

Plastids

Chloroplasts	Chromoplasts	Leucoplasts
• These are coloured plastids that contain chlorophyll (a green pigment) along with various yellow and orange pigments. • These are important for photosynthesis in plants. Therefore, these are known as **the kitchen of cells.**	• These are coloured plastids that contain all pigments (except green). • These impart colour to flowers and fruits.	• These are white or colourless plastids. • They store materials such as starch, oils and protein granules.

Vacuoles

These are membrane-bound storage sacs for solid or liquid contents.

In plant cells, the vacuoles are full of fluid known as **cell sap** and the membrane that surrounds the vacuole is known as **tonoplast.** It is a watery substance containing amino acids, minerals, proteins, sugars, etc.

Vacuoles are small-sized in animal cells, but in plant cells they are large-sized. The central vacuoles of some plants may occupy 50-90% of the total cell volume.

Functions

The functions of vacuoles are as follows

(i) Vacuoles provide turgidity and rigidity to cells in plants.

(ii) Many substances like amino acids, sugars, organic acids and proteins are stored in vacuoles.

(iii) In *Amoeba*, consumed food items are stored in food vacuoles.

(iv) In some unicellular organisms, vacuoles also play an important role in expelling excess water and some wastes from the cell.

5.4 Cell Division

It is the process of formation of new cells from the pre-existing cells. Cell division is of two types

1. Mitosis or Mitotic Cell Division

The process of cell division by which most of the cells divide for growth is called **mitosis.** The dividing cells are called mother cells which form two identical daughter cells.

Each daughter cell has the same number of chromosomes as that of mother cell.

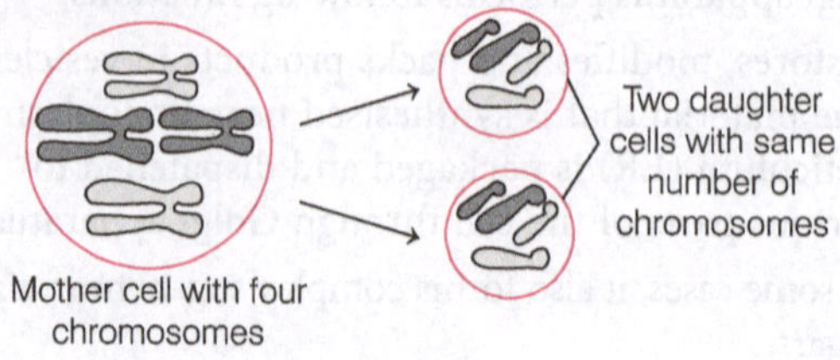

Mitosis

Significance of Mitosis

(i) It helps in growth and repair of tissues in organisms.

(ii) It helps to replace old, dead and injured cells.

2. Meiosis or Meiotic Cell Division

The process of cell division by which specific cells of reproductive organs or tissues in animals and plants divide to form gametes is called **meiosis.**

When a cell divides by meiosis, it produces four new cells instead of just two.

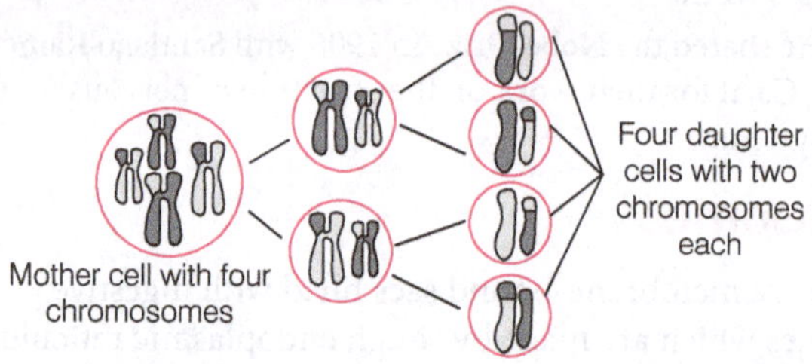

Meiosis

The process of meiosis occurs in two stages, i.e. meiosis-I and meiosis-II. In meiosis-I, the germ cells divide into two daughter cells which have only half number of chromosomes in comparison to mother germ cells. In contrast to meiosis-I, meiosis-II resembles mitosis.

Significance of Meiosis

(i) It results in the formation of gametes which after fertilisation give rise to offsprings.

(ii) It maintains the diploid number of chromosomes in the offspring.

Try These 5.4

1. **Name the organelle that serves as a channel for transport of materials between cytoplasm and brain of the cell.**
2. **Which organelle is involved in the formation of suicidal bags.**
3. **Two organelles other than nucleus contain their own DNA and protein, name them.**
4. **Give name of the plastid that imparts colour to flowers and fruits.**
5. **What term is given to the membrane of the storage sacs?**

Mind Map

Cell Division
Formation of new cell from pre-existing cell.

Mitosis
Cells divide for growth and give rise to two identical daughter cells.

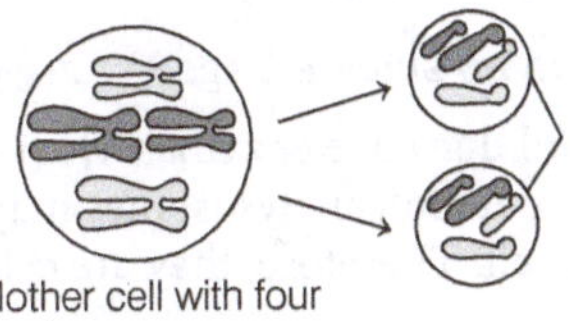

Meiosis
Reproductive cell divide to form gametes and give rise to four daughter cells.

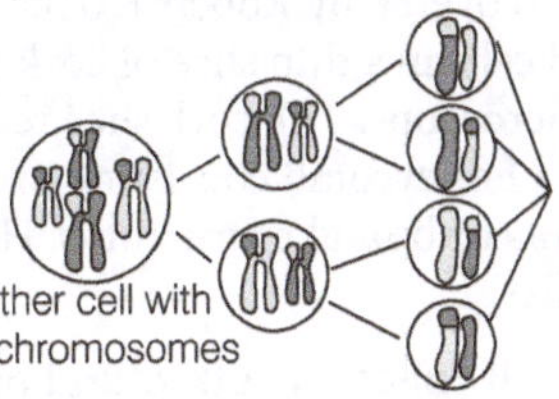

Cell
Cell is the basic structural and functional unit of all living organisms.

Multicellular Organisms
Many cells grouped together acquiring different functions in the body to form various body parts, e.g. plants, animals.

Unicellular Organisms
A single-cell constitute the whole organism, e.g. *Amoeba*, *Chlamydomonas*, bacteria.

Prokaryotic Cell
It does not consist nuclear envelope and membrane bound organelle, e.g. bacteria, cyanobacteria.

Eukaryotic Cell
Nucleus is well-defined and has DNA in it, e.g. plant, animal.

Types of eukaryotic cell

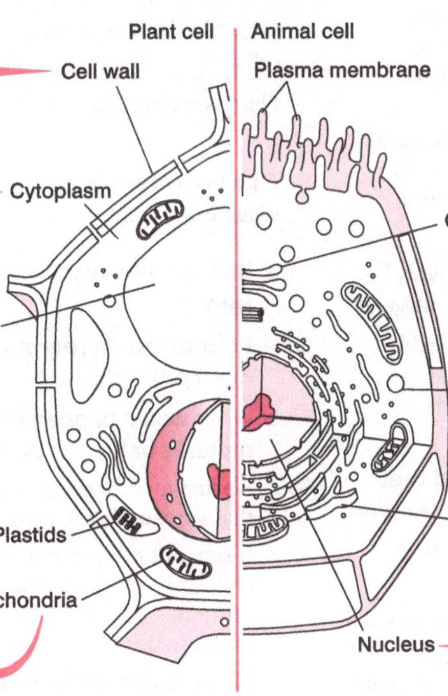

Cell wall: It is found only in the plant cell. It is tough, flexible, but fairly rigid outer covering lining the outside of plasma membrane.

Cytoplasm: It is the fluid content inside the plasma membrane. It also contains many specialised cell organelles. It helps in exchange of material between cells

Vacuoles: These are storage sacs for solid and liquid contents. They are small sized in animal cell and large sized in plant cell.

Plastids: These are found only in plant cell. They are chromoplast, chloroplast and leucoplast.

Mitochondria: It is known as the **powerhouse of the cell**. It releases energy required by the cell in the form of ATP.

Plasma membrane: It is the outermost covering of the cell that is composed of proteins and lipid. It permits the entry and exit of some materials.

Golgi apparatus: It consists of a system of membrane-bound vesicles called cisternae. It helps in the formation of lysosomes.

Lysosomes: These are called as **suicidal bags of a cell.** It forms the waste disposal system of a cell.

ER: It is a large network of membrane bound tubules and sheet. ER is the side of lipid and proteins formation.

Nucleus: It is popularly called as **brain of the cells**. It controls all the functions of a cell. It plays the important role in cellular reproduction in which a cell divides to form new daughter cell.

NCERT FOLDER

Complete Explanations of all NCERT's Questions

Intext Questions

Q.1 Who discovered cells and how? Page 51

Sol. Cells were discovered by Robert Hooke in 1665. He observed cells in a thin slice of cork with the help of a primitive microscope. The cork slice resembled the structure of a honeycomb consisting of many small compartments or box-like structures. Hooke called these boxes as cells.

Q.2 Why is the cell called the structural and functional unit of life? Page 51

Sol. All living organisms are made up of cells which perform various functions essential for the survival of the organisms, e.g. respiration, digestion, excretion, etc. Thus, cell is the functional unit of life.

In unicellular organisms, a single cell carries out all the functions, while in multicellular organisms, group of cells carry out different functions. Thus, cell is the structural and functional unit of all living organisms.

Q.3 How do substances like CO_2 and water move in and out of the cell? Discuss. Page 53

Sol. CO_2 and other gases move in and out of the cell by the process of diffusion. When the concentration of carbon dioxide is more inside the cell compared to outside, CO_2 diffuses out of the cell. If CO_2 concentration inside the cell is less, CO_2 moves inside the cell from outside.

The water moves in and out of the cell by the process of osmosis. Thus, osmosis is the diffusion of water from a region of its high concentration to low concentration through a selectively permeable membrane.

Q.4 Why is the plasma membrane called a selectively permeable membrane? Page 53

Sol. The plasma membrane is called a selectively permeable membrane because it allows the entry and exit of some selected materials through the cells. It also prevents movement of unwanted materials into the cell.

Q.5 Can you name two organelles we have studied that contain their own genetic material? Page 57

Sol. Mitochondria and plastids are the two cell organelles that contains their own genetic material.

Q.6 If the organisation of a cell is destroyed due to some physical or chemical influence, what will happen? Page 57

Sol. Living cells are capable of performing certain basic functions due to the presence of cell organelles present. If these are destroyed then cell will not be able to work properly and will die after some time.

Q.7 Why are lysosomes known as suicide bags? Page 57

Sol. Lysosomes contain powerful digestive enzymes. During the disturbance in cellular metabolism, lysosomes may burst and digest their own cell. Therefore, they are called suicide bags of the cell.

Q.8 Where are proteins synthesised inside the cell?

Sol. Ribosomes are the sites of protein synthesis inside the cell. Page 57

Exercise

Q.1 Make a comparison and write down ways, in which plant cells are different from animal cells.

Sol. Comparison of plant cells and animal cells are as follows

Plant cells	Animal cells
Cell wall is present outside the plasma membrane.	Cell wall is absent.
Generally regular in shape.	Generally irregular in shape.
Larger in size than animal cells.	Smaller in size than plant cells.
Plastids are present.	Plastids are absent in all except *Euglena*.
A permanent and large vacuole is present.	Vacuoles are many, small and temporary.

Q.2 How is a prokaryotic cell different from a eukaryotic cell?

Sol. Refer to text on page no. 101 (Prokaryotic and Eukaryotic cell).

Q.3 What would happen if the plasma membrane ruptures or breaks down?

Sol. Plasma membrane is selectively permeable membrane that surrounds the cells.

It separates the contents of the cells from its external environment. If plasma membrane ruptures, the unwanted material will be able to enter the cell and useful material will leak out of the the cell.

This will disrupt the metabolic activities of the cell and may ultimately lead to the death of the cell.

Q.4 What would happen to the life of a cell if there was no Golgi apparatus?

Sol. Effects of the absence of Golgi apparatus on life of a cell are as follows

(i) The packaging and dispatching of different types of proteins to various targets inside and outside the cell will be affected.

(ii) The products of a cell cannot be stored and modified.

(iii) It will also affect the lysosome formation. This will cause accumulation of worn out and dead cell organelles within the cell, which may cause cell death.

Q.5 Which organelle is known as the powerhouse of the cell? Why?

Sol. Mitochondria are called powerhouse of the cell because it generates energy in the form of ATP (Adenosine Triphosphate). This energy is used by body for making new chemical compounds and for performing other works.

Q.6 Where do the lipids and proteins constituting the cell membrane get synthesised?

Sol. The synthesis of lipids occurs in Smooth Endoplasmic Reticulum (SER). The proteins are synthesised in the ribosomes, which are attached to the Rough Endoplasmic Reticulum (RER). These lipids and proteins aid in the formation of a membrane.

Q.7 How does *Amoeba* obtain its food?

Sol. *Amoeba* obtains its food through endocytosis. It is the process of ingestion of food through the plasma membrane. This occurs due to the flexibility of plasma membrane, which enables the *Amoeba* to engulf food and other materials from the surroundings.

Q.8 What is osmosis?

Sol. Refer to text on page no. 99.

Q.9 Carry out the following osmosis experiment. Take four peeled potato halves and scoop each one out to make potato cups. One of these potato cups should be made from a boiled potato. Put each potato cup in a trough containing water. Now,

- **keep cup *A* empty.**
- **put one teaspoon sugar in cup *B*.**
- **put one teaspoon salt in cup *C*.**
- **put one teaspoon sugar in the boiled potato cup *D*.**

Keep them for two hours. Then observe the four potato cups and answer the following.

(i) Explain, why water gathers in the hollowed portions of *B* and *C*.

(ii) Why is potato *A* necessary for this experiment?

(iii) Explain why water does not gather in the hollowed out portions of *A* and *D*.

Sol. (i) The water gathers in the hollowed portion of *B* and *C* due to the process of osmosis. This happens because the concentration of solute (sugar in cup *B* and salt in cup *C*) is higher inside the cup than water. Hence, water flows from a region of its higher concentration to the region of lower concentration.

(ii) Potato *A* acts as reference of control for the experiment, which helps in comparing the results with the other two cups, i.e. *B* and *C*.

(iii) Water does not gather in the hollowed out portion of *A* and *D* because of the following reasons

(a) Hollow portion of potato *A* is empty and there is no concentration difference between the inside and outside of the cell. Hence, no osmosis occurs.

(b) The hollowed portion of potato *D* contains sugar, but the potato cup is boiled due to which the osmosis could not occur as the semipermeable membrane is destroyed by boiling.

Q.10 Which type of cell division is required for growth and repair of body and which type is involved in the formation of gametes?

Sol. The mitotic cell division is required for growth and repair of the body. The meiotic cell division is involved in the formation of gametes.

To Study NCERT Activities
Scan the Code

REVIEW EXERCISE

Including Competency Based Questions

Competency Focused (Objective) Questions

Multiple Choice Questions

1 Choose the name of the scientist who coined the term 'protoplasm' in a cell.

(a) Purkinje
(b) Robert Hooke
(c) Virchow
(d) Robert Brown

Sol. (a) Purkinje in 1839 coined the term 'protoplasm' for the fluid substance of the cell.

2 Choose the incorrect statement from the following options. **Competency Based Que.**

(a) All cells arise from pre-existing cells only
(b) Rudolf Virchow proposed the cell theory
(c) Nucleus was discovered by Robert Brown in 1831
(d) The nucleus and cytoplasm of a living cell, altogether form the protoplasm

Sol. (b) The cell theory was proposed by Schleiden (1838) and Schwann (1839), postulating that all the plants and animals are composed of cells and that the cell is the basic unit of life. In 1855, Rudolf Virchow modified the cell theory with his postulate, *'Omnis cellula-e-cellula'*, which means, a new cell is derived from a pre-existing cell only.

3 Which scientist discovered free-living cells in pond water?

(a) Robert Hooke
(b) Purkinje
(c) Leeuwenhoek
(d) Robert Brown

Sol. (c) Free-living cells in pond water were discovered by Leeuwenhoek in 1674, using an improved microscope.

4 Which pair of cells keeps changing their shapes?

(a) Fat and bone cells
(b) WBCs and RBCs
(c) Sperm cells and ovum
(d) *Amoeba* and WBCs

Sol. (d) *Amoeba* and WBCs keep changing their shapes.

5 The flexibility of plasma membrane can be contributed to the presence of

(a) proteins (b) lipids
(c) nucleic acids (d) Both (a) and (b)

Sol. (d) Presence of lipids and proteins provides flexibility to the plasma membrane. This helps the cell in engulfing food and other materials from external environment.

6 Select the odd one out. **Competency Based Que.**

(a) The movement of water across a semipermeable membrane is affected by the amount of substances dissolved in it
(b) Membrane are made up of organic molecules like proteins and lipids
(c) Molecules soluble in organic solvents can easily pass through the membrane
(d) Plasma membrane contain chitin sugar in plants

Sol. (d) Plasma membrane is a selectively permeable membrane that is made up of a lipid bilayer and proteins. It is present inside the cell wall in plant cells. Chitin is present in the cell wall of fungi and algae.

7 *Amoeba* acquires its food through a process, termed **NCERT Exemplar**

(a) exocytosis
(b) endocytosis
(c) plasmolysis
(d) Both exocytosis and endocytosis

Sol. (b) *Amoeba* acquires its food through a process termed as endocytosis. In this, it engulfs the food and other materials from external environment with the help of finger-like projections called pseudopodia.

8 What property of the plasma membrane helps *Amoeba* to acquire food? **Competency Based Que.**

(a) It is flexible
(b) It is selectively permeable
(c) It is made up of proteins and lipids
(d) It allows diffusion of some substances across it

Sol. (a) The property of the plasma membrane that helps *Amoeba* acquire food is flexibiity of the membrane.

9 **Refer to the given figure which represents the parts labelled as *A*, *B* and C that shows a process called '*X*' in the cell. Select the correct option regarding '*X*'.** **Competency Based Que.**

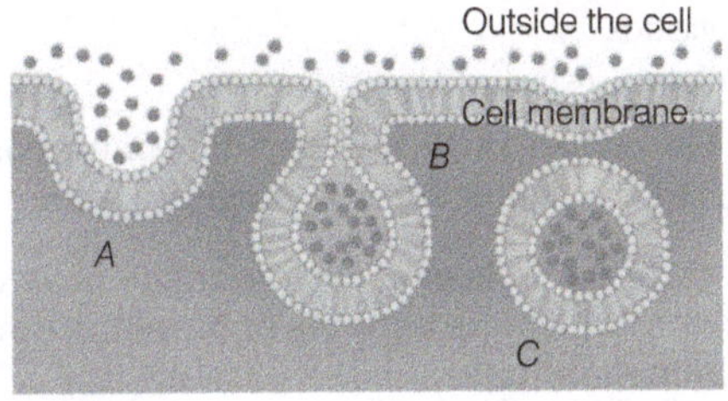

(a) Endocytosis (b) Exocytosis
(c) Osmosis (d) Diffusion

Sol. (a) In above figure, process '*X*' represents endocytosis. In this process, materials can be brought into the cell by invagination and formation of a vesicle.

10 **Following are a few definitions of osmosis. Read carefully and select the correct definition.** **NCERT Exemplar**

(a) Movement of water molecules from a region of higher concentration to a region of lower concentration through a semipermeable membrane
(b) Movement of solvent molecules from its higher concentration to lower concentration
(c) Movement of solvent molecules from higher concentration to lower concentration of solution through a permeable membrane
(d) Movement of solute molecules from lower concentration to higher concentration of solution through a semipermeable membrane

Sol. (a) The correct definition of osmosis is the movement of water molecules from a region of higher concentration to a region of lower concentration through a semipermeable membrane.

11 **A cell will swell up if the**

(a) concentration of water molecules in the cell is higher than the concentration of water molecules in the surrounding medium
(b) concentration of water molecules in surrounding medium is higher than the concentration of water molecules in the cell
(c) concentration of water molecules is same in the cell and in the surrounding medium
(d) concentration of water molecules does not matter

Sol. (b) Osmosis is a spontaneous process where movement of water molecules occurs from a region of its higher concentration to a region of lower concentration through a selectively permeable membrane.

When movement of the solvent takes place from outside to inside of the cell (inward movement), the process is called endosmosis. It occurs in hypotonic solution and causes swelling of the cell.

12 **The cell wall of which out of these is not made up of cellulose?** **NCERT Exemplar**

(a) Bacteria (b) *Hydrilla* (c) Mango tree (d) Cactus

Sol. (a) Plant cells, in addition to the plasma membrane, have another rigid outer covering called the cell wall. Bacteria is not a plant therefore, its cell wall is not made up of cellulose. Rather it is made up of peptidoglycan.

13 **Which of the following option is correct description about plasmolysis?**

(a) Breakdown (lysis) of plasma membrane in hypotonic medium
(b) Shrinkage of cytoplasm in hypertonic medium
(c) Shrinkage of nucleoplasm
(d) None of the above

Sol. (b) Plasmolysis in a plant cell is a shrinkage of cytoplasm in hypertonic medium.

14 **The undefined nuclear region of prokaryotes are also known as** **NCERT Exemplar**

(a) nucleus (b) nucleolus
(c) nucleic acid (d) nucleoid

Sol. (d) The undefined nuclear region of prokaryotes is also known as nucleoid. It is in direct contact with the cytoplasm as it does not have a nuclear membrane.

15 **Which of these properties qualifies *Amoeba* as eukaryotes?** **Competency Based Que.**

(a) It is unicellular
(b) It needs food for energy
(c) It has a membrane bound nucleus
(d) It is surrounded by a plasma membrane

Sol. (c) *Amoeba* has a membrane bound nucleus. This property among the above given properties qualifies *Amoeba* as eukaryotes.

16 **The table below describes some of the organelles visible in a cell under a microscope. Identify the type of living organism to which the cell belongs.** **Diksha**

Cell organelles	Descriptions
Cell wall	Present
Vacuole	Large
Centriole	Not visible
Nucleus	Present

(a) It is the cell of an animal
(b) It is the cell of a plant
(c) It is the cell of a bacterium
(d) It is the cell of a virus

Sol. (b) From the information given in the table above we can say that the type of living organism to which this cell belongs is plant because a plant cell bears a cell wall and a large central vacuole. Also, the centrioles are not visible.

17 Which of the following is the function of cytoplasm present in the cell?

(a) It plays a central role in cellular reproduction
(b) It helps transport material into the cell
(c) It is involved in the formation of lysosomes
(d) It holds the organelles of the cell in place

Sol. (d) The cytoplasm is the fluid content found inside the plasma membrane. It holds the cell organelles of the cell in place.

18 Which one of the following cellular functions is performed by endoplasmic reticulum ? **CBSE Question Bank**

(a) Production of hydrolytic enzymes
(b) Supply of energy to cell
(c) Formation of lysosomes
(d) Production of vacuoles

Sol. (a) Rough Endoplasmic Reticulum (RER) helps in the production of the digestive or hydrolytic enzymes (proteins).

19 Which of these options are not a function of ribosomes? **NCERT Exemplar**

I. It helps in manufacture of protein molecules.
II. It helps in manufacture of enzymes.
III. It helps in manufacture of hormones.
IV. It helps in manufacture of starch molecules.

(a) I and II (b) II and III (c) III and IV (d) IV and I

Sol. (c) Ribosomes are dense, spherical and granular particles which remains free in the matrix or remain attached to endoplasmic reticulum. They are not bound by the membrane and are present in both prokaryotic and eukaryotic cells. They play important role in synthesis of proteins. All enzymes are proteins, but all hormones are not proteins.

20 The proteins and lipids, essential for the building of the cell membrane are manufactured by

(a) rough endoplasmic reticulum and smooth endoplasmic reticulum
(b) Golgi apparatus
(c) plasma membrane
(d) mitochondria

Sol. (a) The proteins and lipids, essential for the building of the cell membrane are manufactured by rough endoplasmic reticulum and smooth endoplasmic reticulum, respectively. This process is known as membrane biogenesis.

21 Which cell organelle plays a crucial role in detoxifying many poisons and drugs in a cell? **NCERT Exemplar**

(a) Golgi apparatus (b) Lysosomes
(c) Smooth endoplasmic reticulum (d) Vacuoles

Sol. (c) Smooth endoplasmic reticulum plays a crucial role in detoxifying many poisons and drugs in a cell.

22 The cell organelle involved in forming complex sugars from simple sugars are **NCERT Exemplar**

(a) endoplasmic reticulum
(b) ribosomes
(c) plastids
(d) Golgi apparatus

Sol. (d) The cell organelle involved in forming complex sugars from simple sugar is Golgi apparatus.

23 Which of the following cell organelle have digestive enzyme, which are capable of breaking down all organic materials?

(a) Endoplasmic reticulum (b) Golgi apparatus
(c) Lysosome (d) Mitochondria

Sol. (c) Lysosomes have digestive enzymes, which are capable of breaking down all organic materials.

24 Organelle other than nucleus, containing DNA is **NCERT Exemplar**

(a) endoplasmic reticulum (b) Golgi apparatus
(c) mitochondria (d) lysosome

Sol. (c) Organelle other than nucleus, containing DNA is mitochondria. It contains its own DNA and ribosomes hence, is able to make some of its own proteins.

25 Refer to the given Venn diagram. **Competency Based Que.**

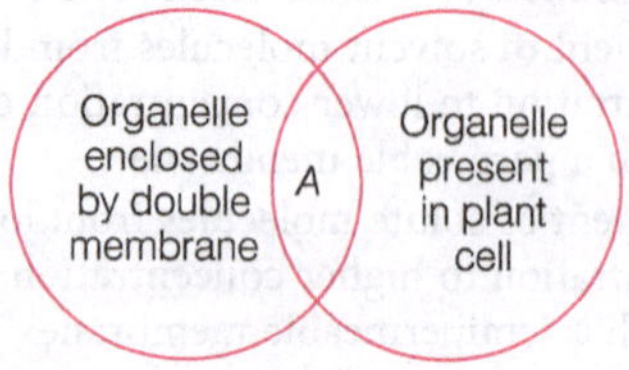

Select the correct option regarding organelle *A*.

(a) Organelle *A* could be the smallest organelle which is absent in mature mammalian RBCs
(b) Organelle *A* has outer membrane infolded into finger-like processes called cristae which bear oxysomes
(c) Organelle *A* is a semi-autonomous organelle, often referred to as kitchen of cells
(d) All of the above

Sol. (c) Chloroplasts are called semi-autonomous organelle and contains green colour pigment called chlorophyll which helps the cell to prepare their own food by the process of photosynthesis. This is is why chloroplast is known as the kitchen of the cell.

Also, chloroplast is enclosed by a double membrane.

26 Which of the following are covered by a single membrane?

(a) Mitochondria (b) Vacuole
(c) Nucleus (d) Plastid

Sol. (b) Only vacuoles are covered by a single membrane.

27 **Which out of the following is not a function of vacuole?** **NCERT Exemplar**

(a) Storage
(b) Providing turgidity and rigidity to the cell
(c) Waste excretion
(d) Locomotion

Sol. (d) Vacuoles are the storage sacs which provide turgidity and rigidity to the cell and help in waste excretion. They do not play any role in locomotion.

28 **Select the incorrect statement regarding mitosis.** **Competency Based Que.**

(a) It helps in growth and repairing of tissues
(b) It helps to replace old, dead and injured cells
(c) The mother cell forms two identical daughter cells
(d) It occurs in two stages

Sol. (d) The incorrect statement regarding mitosis is that it occurs in two stages. Mitosis is a single stage division while, meiotic cell division occurs in two stages, i.e. meiosis-I and meiosis-II.

29 **Choose the location in plant where the meiotic cell division takes place.**

(a) Leaves and stem (b) Stem and branches
(c) In anther and ovary (d) None of these

Sol. (c) The meiotic cell division occurs in anthers and ovary to form pollen grain (male gamete) and egg cell female gamete.

Assertion–Reason Questions

Direction (Q.Nos. 1-5) ***In each of the following questions, a statement of Assertion (A) is given by the corresponding statement of Reason (R). Of the statements, mark the correct answer as***

(a) Both A and R are true and R is the correct explanation of A
(b) Both A and R are true, but R is not the correct explanation of A
(c) A is true, but R is false
(d) A is false, but R is true

1 **Assertion** (A) Rudolf Virchow proposed cell theory.
Reason (R) Cell theory states that all plants and animals are composed of cells.

Sol. (d) A is false, but R is true. A can be corrected as 'All plant and animals are composed of cells'. This statement was presented as cell theory by Schleiden and Schwann (1838-39). Rudolf Virchow modified and expanded this earlier theory by suggesting that 'all cells arise from pre-existing cells'.

2 **Assertion** (A) Chromosomes are constituted by DNA and proteins.
Reason (R) These are thread-like structures present in nucleus.

Sol. (b) Both A and R are true, but R is not the correct explanation of A.
Chromosomes are the structures made up of DNA and proteins (i.e. histones). These are thread- like structures present in nucleus of the cell and contain genetic information that is transferred from parents to next generation.

3 **Assertion** (A) Prokaryotic cells are primitive and larger than eukaryotic cells.
Reason (R) Prokaryotic cells lack cytoplasmic organelles.

Sol. (d) A is false, but R is true. A can be corrected as Prokaryotic cells are smaller in size as compared to eukaryotic cells. These cells also lack cytoplasmic membrane bound organelles. Thus, most functions are performed by poorly developed parts of cytoplasm.

4 **Assertion** (A) Golgi bodies store, modify and pack products in vesicles.
Reason (R) They are involved in the formation of lysosomes.

Sol. (b) A and R are true, but R is not the correct explanation of A.
Golgi bodies store, modify and pack products (proteins) in vesicles, which are distributed to various parts of the cell. The Golgi bodies are also involved in the formation of lysosomes (waste disposal system of the cell).

5 **Assertion** (A) Mitochondria are known as the powerhouse of a cell.
Reason (R) Mitochondria generate energy (as ATP) for various cellular activities.

Sol. (a) Both A and R are true and R is the correct explanation of A.
Mitochondria are the sites of cellular respiration. They help to generate energy required by the cell in the form of ATP which gets utilised in cellular functions. That is why mitochondria are also known as powerhouse of the cell.

Case Based/Source Based Questions

1 ***Read the following passage and answer the questions that follows***

In a school laboratory, Ram is examining a slide under a microscope. He observes the two distinct structures as follows.

Structure *A* – It is a spherical entity having well defined membrane.

Structure *B* –Thread like fibres that are present inside the structure *A*.

Based on the above observations, answer the questions that follows.

(i) Identify the structures *A* and *B*.

Sol. *A*–Nucleus, *B*–Chromatin fibres. [1]

(ii) State any two functions of structure *A*.

Sol. (a) It controls all metabolic activities of the cell.

(b) It helps in the transmission of hereditary traits from parents to offspring. [1]

(iii) Is structure *B* present in the prokaryotic cells?

Sol. No, chromatin fibres are not present in prokaryotic cell. [1]

(iv) Structure *B* get condensed to form *X* during cell division. Identify *X*.

Sol. *X* represents chromosomes. [1]

2 ***Read the following case carefully and answer the questions that follows***

Sania conducts an experiment to know how plant cells lose or gain water through osmosis.

She cuts out 5 cm long potato strips. She puts three potato strips in each of the following beakers.

Beaker 1 containing only water.

Beaker 2 containing 1% salt solution.

Beaker 3 containing 2% salt solution.

Sania leaves the potato strips in the beaker for 5 hours.

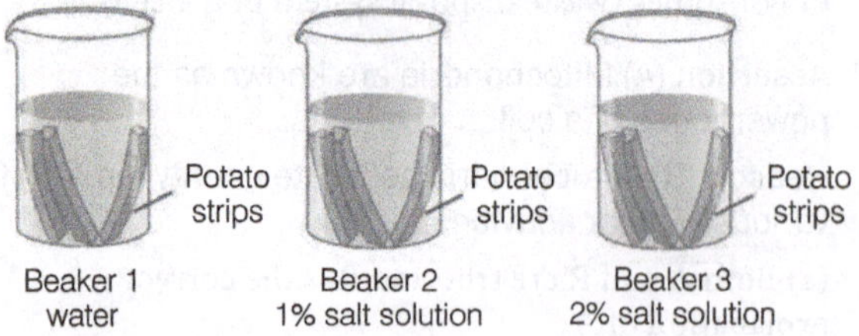

She records the length of the potato strips in each beaker after 5 hours.

	Length of the potato strip before placing in the beaker (cm)	Length of the potato strip after 5 hours in the beaker (cm)
Beaker 1 water	5.0	5.3
	5.0	5.2
	5.0	5.2
Beaker 2 1% salt solution	5.0	5.0
	5.0	5.0
	5.0	4.9
Beaker 3 2% salt solution	5.0	4.8
	5.0	4.9
	5.0	4.7

(i) What can Sania conclude from her experiment?

Sol. Water molecules move out of the cell based on the amount of salt present in the solution. [1]

(ii) In which beaker was the concentration of water molecules inside and outside the potato cells likely to be the same? Explain your answer.

Sol. In beaker 2, the concentration of water molecules inside and outside the potato cells is likely to be the same. This can be inferred because the lengths of the potato strips are almost the same in this beaker. [2]

(iii) Why did Sania placed three potato strips in each beaker?

Sol. Sania placed three potato strips in each beaker to reduce errors in the measurement and confirm the results of the experiment. [1]

Constructed Response (Descriptive) Questions

Very Short Answer Type Questions

1 The unicellular organisms are made up of single cell that performs all life processes. Name any two such organisms.

Sol. *Paramecium* and *Chlamydomonas* are the two unicellular organisms.

2 It is often suggested that a cell can vary in size from smaller to larger. Give the name of the smallest and longest cell you know. NCERT Exemplar

Sol. The smallest known cell is mycoplasma (0.1-0.5 μm) and the longest cell is a nerve cell (90 cm).

3 What does the process called in which diffusion takes place through a semipermeable membrane? Give an example of this process.

Sol. Osmosis takes place through a semipermeable membrane, e.g. unicellular freshwater organisms and most plant cells tend to gain water through osmosis.

4 Think what will happen if the already swollen raisin is kept in salt solution. Competency Based Que.

Sol. In the already swollen raisin, the water flows out from the raisin and goes into the solution medium. Consequently, causing shrinkage in the size of a raisin.

5 Name and explain the process by which unicellular freshwater organisms and most plant cells tend to gain water.

Sol. The process by which unicellular freshwater organisms and most plant cells tend to gain water is endosmosis. It is the process in which water moves into the cell from the surrounding medium.

6 State two major functions of cellulose in plant cell.

Sol. (i) The plant cell wall is mainly composed of cellulose. It is a complex substance, which provides structural strength to plants.

(ii) It helps the plant to maintain its shape.

7 Which cell organelle controls most of the activities of the cell? NCERT Exemplar

Sol. Nucleus, also known as the brain of the cell and controls most of the activities of the cell.

8 What is DNA? Where is it present?

Sol. DNA is Deoxyribonucleic Acid. It is the genetic map of an organism, present in nucleus. [1+1]

9 In which form DNA is present in a cell when it is
(i) dividing? (ii) not dividing?

Sol. (i) Chromosomes [1]

(ii) Part of chromatin material. [1]

10 Name the cell organelle which is known as the factory of ribosomes. Where it is present?

Sol. Nucleolus is called factory of ribosomes. It is present in the nucleus.

11 State two important functions of the nucleus of the cell.

Sol. (i) Nucleus is the control centre of a cell. [1]

(ii) It consists of cell's DNA (genetic information) in the form of genes, which carries hereditary characters from one generation to another. [1]

12 What does the figure depict? Label *X*, *Y* and *Z*. Competency Based Que.

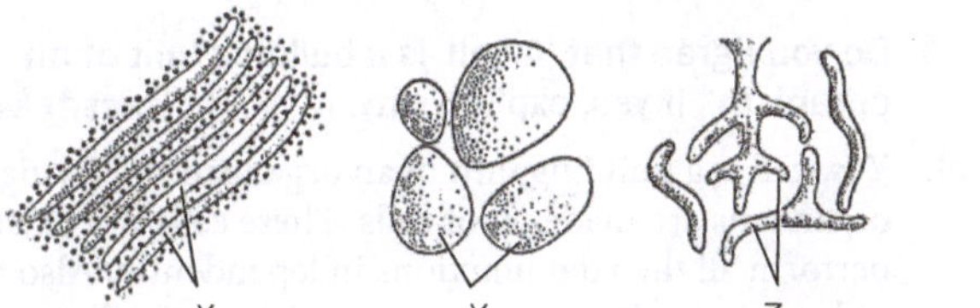

Sol. The above figure depicts various parts of endoplasmic recticulum. *X* represents cisternae, *Y* represents vesicles, whereas *Z* represents tubules.

13 Name any two cells that lack lysosomes.

Sol. Bacterial cells and mammalian RBCs (Red Blood Corpuscles) are the type of animal cell that lack lysosomes.

14 Which cell organelle in the animal cell is able to prepare its own protein?

Sol. The cell organelle called mitochondria has the ability to prepare its own proteins because of the presence of DNA and ribosomes.

15 What is known as the energy currency of the cell? Name the organelle involved in its production.

Sol. **Adenosine Triphosphate** (ATP) is considered by biologists to be the energy currency of cell. Mitochondria is involved in the production of ATP.

16 Which features allows the possibility of activities and interaction inside the cell from its external environment? Competency Based Que.

Sol. Plasma membrane, nucleus and cytoplasm.

17 Explain the following terms.
(i) Tonoplast (ii) Leucoplasts

Sol. (i) **Tonoplast** It is the membrane that surrounds the vacuole. [1]

(ii) **Leucoplasts** These are white or colourless plastids. They store oils, starch, etc. [1]

18 Mitotic cell division can be observed in which part of the organisms? How many cells are formed during mitosis?

Sol. Mitosis occurs in somatic cells of the organisms. Two identically similar daughter cells are produced during mitosis.

19 Name the process by which gametes are formed in sexually reproducing organisms? Write the significance of this process.

Sol. Gametes are formed by meiotic cell division in sexually reproducing organisms.

Significance of meiosis It maintains the diploid number of chromosomes in the offspring.

Short Answer Type Questions

1 Do you agree that 'A cell is a building unit of an organism'. If yes, explain why. NCERT Exemplar

Sol. Yes, cell is a building unit of an organism. All living organisms are made up of cells. These cells can exist and perform all the vital functions independently. Also these cells are organised into tissues, which are further organised to form organ and organ systems.

2 What are the consequences of the following conditions? Competency Based Que.

(i) Cell having higher water concentration than surrounding medium.

(ii) A cell having lower water concentration than a surrounding medium.

(iii) A cell having equal concentration to its surrounding medium.

Sol. (i) A cell having higher water concentration than surrounding medium will undergo exosmosis and will lose water. [1]

(ii) A cell having lower water concentration than surrounding medium will undergo endosmosis and absorb water from outside. [1]

(iii) A cell having equal concentration to its surrounding medium will neither gain nor lose water to the external medium. [1]

3 A person takes concentrated solution of salt, after some time, he starts vomiting. What is the phenomenon responsible for such situation? Explain. Competency Based Que.

Sol. When a person takes concentrated solution of salt, he starts vomiting after some time. This happens because the concentrated salt solution is hypertonic by nature which causes exosmosis. Thus, leading to irritation and dehydration in the alimentary canal and thereby results in vomiting.

4 If cells of onion peel and RBC are separately kept in hypotonic solution, what among the following will take place? Explain the reason for your answer. NCERT Exemplar

(a) Both the cells will swell

(b) RBC will burst easily while cells of onion peel will resist the bursting to some extent

(c) Both (a) and (b) are correct

(d) RBC and onion peel cells will behave similarly

Sol. (c) If the cells of onion peel and RBC are separately kept in hypotonic solution, RBC will burst easily, while cells of onion peel will resist the bursting to some extent. This is because when kept in hypotonic solution, water or solvent will enter the cells, due to endosmosis. The presence of cell wall in onion peel will permit it to withstand hypotonic conditions without bursting. Whereas in RBC the movement of water will lead to bursting of the cell because it does not have a rigid cell wall.

5 (i) Explain how do cell walls permit the cells of fungi to withstand very dilute external media without bursting.

(ii) Why does the skin of your fingers shrink when you wash clothes for a long time? NCERT Exemplar

Sol. (i) Fungi withstands very dilute or hypotonic external media without bursting because of their cell walls. In such media, the cells swell by taking up water through osmosis and hence building up pressure against the cell wall. The wall exerts an equal pressure against the swollen cell, thus preventing it from bursting. [1½]

(ii) The solution of soaps and detergents are hypertonic as compared to the osmotic concentration of our skin. Therefore, washing of clothes results in exosmosis in skin cells that come in contact with the soap solution. Due to this reason, the skin of the fingers shrinks, while washing clothes for a long time. [1½]

6 If you are provided with some vegetables to cook, you generally add salt into the vegetables during cooking process. After adding salt, vegetables release water. What mechanism is responsible for this? Competency Based Que.

Sol. If we are provided with some vegetables to cook, we generally add salt into the vegetables during cooking process.

After adding salt vegetables releases water due to the process of exosmosis. This is because when the salt is added a hypertonic medium is created leading to the movement of water from the vegetables to outside.

7 **State in brief, what happens when**

(i) **Dry apricots are left for some time in pure water and later transferred to sugar solution.**

(ii) ***Rheo* leaves are boiled in water first and then a drop of sugar syrup is poured on it.**

(iii) **Golgi apparatus are removed from the cell.** **NCERT Exemplar**

Sol. (i) Dry apricots will swell up due to endosmosis when placed in pure water. On being transferred to sugar solution, they shrink due to exosmosis. [1]

(ii) Cells of *Rheo* leaves are killed due to boiling, so they will not undergo plasmolysis. [1]

(iii) Formation of lysosome and secretory vesicles will stop. [1]

8 **State three differences between plasma membrane and cell wall.**

Sol. Differences between plasma membrane and cell wall are as follows

Plasma membrane	Cell wall
It provides support and shape to the cell.	It gives strength and rigidity to the plant cell.
It is semipermeable in nature allowing the entry of selected molecules into the cell.	It is completely permeable in nature.
It is elastic, living and thin.	It is rigid, non-living and thick.

[1×3]

9 **Explain in detail what do you know about the structure of nucleus?**

Sol. Refer to text on page no. 100.

10 **What are chromosomes made up of ? How are chromatin, chromatid and chromosomes related to each other?** **NCERT Exemplar**

Sol. Chromosomes are the structures made up of both DNA and protein. Chromatin is a thread-like structure that condenses to form chromosome. During the cell division, chromosomes are thick rod-like in appearance that consist of two similar halves called chromatids that are attached to each other through centromere.

11 **What do you mean by the following terms?**

(i) Protoplasm (ii) Cytoplasm (iii) Nucleoplasm

Sol. (i) **Protoplasm** It is the living substance present in the cell containing both cytoplasm and nucleoplasm. [1]

(ii) **Cytoplasm** It is a part of protoplasm filled within the space between the nuclear membrane and cell membrane. It is homogenous in nature containing water, amino acids, oxygen, etc. [1]

(iii) **Nucleoplasm** It is a transparent, semi-fluid substance filled within the space between nuclear membrane and nucleolus. It consists of nucleic acids, proteins, lipids and minerals. [1]

12 **Differentiate between Rough Endoplasmic Reticulum (RER) and Smooth Endoplasmic Reticulum (SER). How endoplasmic reticulum is important for membrane biosynthesis?** **NCERT Exemplar**

Sol. Differences between RER and SER are as follows

Rough Endoplasmic Reticulum (RER)	Smooth Endoplasmic Reticulum (SER)
In RER, ribosomes are attached to the surface.	In SER, ribosomes are not attached to the surface.
It helps in protein synthesis.	It helps in lipid synthesis.
It is formed of tubules and is situated near the nucleus.	It is formed of cisternae and is situated near the plasma membrane. [1]

Importance of ER in membrane biosynthesis are as follows

(i) RER synthesises proteins, which are passed on to Golgi apparatus.

(ii) The SER helps in the manufacturing of fats and lipids, which along with protein help in building of cell membrane.

(iii) It also helps in transporting proteins to various places. [2]

13 **Describe the phenomenon of membrane biogenesis. Give one function of ER.**

Sol. Ribosomes attached to the surface of RER are the sites of protein synthesis. The smooth endoplasmic reticulum helps in the manufacture of lipid or fat molecules, important for cell function. Some of these lipids and proteins manufactured in RER help in building the cell membrane. This process is known as membrane biogenesis. [2]

ER also functions as a cytoplasmic framework providing surface for some of the biochemical activities of the cells. [1]

14 **Name the organelle of the cell, which is involved in the formation of lysosomes. Write its functions in the cell.**

Sol. Golgi apparatus is the organelle involved in the formation of lysosomes. [1]

Functions of Golgi apparatus are as follows

(i) It helps in the storage, modification and packaging of products in vesicles.

(ii) It helps to make complex sugars from simple sugars.

(iii) The material synthesised near the ER is packaged and dispatched to various targets inside and outside the cell through Golgi apparatus. [2]

15 Name the organelle of the cell, which has membrane-bound sac filled with powerful digestive enzymes. Write any four common functions it performs inside the cell.

Sol. Lysosome is the membrane-bound sac filled with powerful digestive enzymes.

For functions of lysosomes, refer to text on page no. 103.

16 (i) Why lysosomes are known as 'scavengers of the cell'? **NCERT Exemplar**

(ii) Lysosomes are self-destructive. True/ False. Give reason.

Sol. (i) Lysosomes are also called 'scavengers of the cell' because they have ability to remove dead and worn out cells by digesting them and act as a kind of waste disposal system of a cell. [1½]

(ii) Lysosomes are self-destructive. This is true as during breakdown of cell structure, lysosomes may burst and the enzymes contained in it may eat up their own cells. [1½]

17 How many membranes are present in mitochondria ? Give the characteristic features of these membranes. What is the advantage of such features?

Sol. Mitochondria is a double membranous structure. The outer membrane is porous in nature, while the inner membrane is deeply folded and is selectively permeable. [1]

The porous membrane helps in getting oxygen and food, while the folds create a large surface area for ATP generating chemical reactions. [1]

18 Name a cell organelle found only in a plant cell and mention its various types along with their functions and location.

Sol. Plastids are found in plant cells only. [½]

Types of plastids are as follows

Name of the plastids	Pigment present	Functions	Locations
Chloroplast	Green (called chlorophyll)	Involved in the photosynthesis of food.	Leaves
Chromoplast	Any colour other than green.	Impart attractive colours to flowers and fruits.	Coloured parts of plant.
Leucoplast	No pigment (colourless)	Stores starch, oils and protein granules.	Underground/ storage parts of plant.

[2½]

19 Give the differences between leucoplasts and chromoplasts.

Sol. Differences between leucoplasts and chromoplasts are as follows

Leucoplasts	Chromoplasts
These are white or colourless plastids.	These are coloured plastids that contain many pigments (except green).
They store materials such as starch, oils and protein granules.	They impart colour to the flower and fruits.

20 Write the name of different plant parts in which chloroplast, chromoplast and leucoplast are present. **NCERT Exemplar**

Sol. Refer to Sol. of Q. 18.

21 State reason for the following. **Competency Based Que.**

(i) Mitochondria is known as the powerhouse of the cell.

(ii) Plastids are able to make their own protein.

(iii) Plant cell shrinks when kept in hypertonic solution.

Sol. (i) Oxidation of food takes place in mitochondria, that results in the release of energy in the form of ATP. This energy helps in various chemical activities needed for life. Hence, mitochondria is known as powerhouse of the cell. [1]

(ii) Plastids have their own DNA and ribosomes. Therefore, they are able to make their own proteins. [1]

(iii) Hypertonic solution has lower concentration of water than the cell. When a plant cell is kept in it, water present in the cell leaves the cell due to exosmosis. Therefore, cell shrinks. [1]

22 Why does plant cell possesses large-sized vacuoles? **NCERT Exemplar**

Sol. Plant cell possesses large-sized vacuole because

(i) It stores salt, sugar, amino acid, organic acid and some proteins. [1]

(ii) The vacuole contains cell sap and helps in maintaining turgidity of cell. [1]

(iii) They store some metabolic byproducts or end products of plant metabolism. [1]

23 Name the organelles, which show analogy written as under.

(i) Transporting channels of the cell.

(ii) Powerhouse of the cell.

(iii) Packaging and dispatching unit of the cell.

(iv) Digestive bag of cell.

(v) Storage sac of the cell.

(vi) Control room of the cell. **NCERT Exemplar**

Sol. (i) Endoplasmic reticulum (ii) Mitochondria

(iii) Golgi apparatus (iv) Lysosome

(v) Vacuole (vi) Nucleus [½ ×6]

24 Differentiate between the mitosis and meiosis.

Sol. Differences between mitosis and meiosis are as follows

Mitosis	Meiosis
It occurs in somatic cells of body of the organisms.	It occurs in germ cells of the body of organisms.
Two daughter cells are formed.	Four daughter cells are formed.
The number of chromosome remains same in daughter cells as found in mother cell.	The number of chromosomes is reduced to half in daughter cells in comparison to mother cells.
It is helpful in growth, repair of body of organisms.	It is helpful in sexual reproduction by forming male and female gametes.

Long Answer Type Questions

1 Describe an activity to demonstrate endosmosis and exosmosis. Draw the diagram also.

Sol. Activity to show endosmosis and exosmosis is as follows

Put dried raisins in plain water and leave them for some time. Then place them into a concentrated solution of salt.

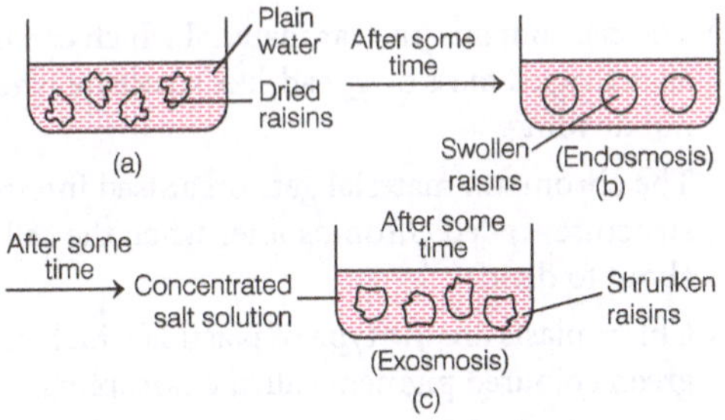

[2]

Observation

(i) When dried raisins are placed in plain water, raisins swell up due to osmotic entry of water into raisins. Plain water is hypotonic medium for raisins. Thus, endosmosis occurs.

(ii) When swollen raisins are transferred to a concentrated solution, raisins shrink. Concentrated solution is a hypertonic medium for swollen raisins. Thus, exosmosis occurs. [3]

2 Draw a well labelled diagram of an eukaryotic nucleus. How is it different from nucleoid? **NCERT Exemplar**

Sol.

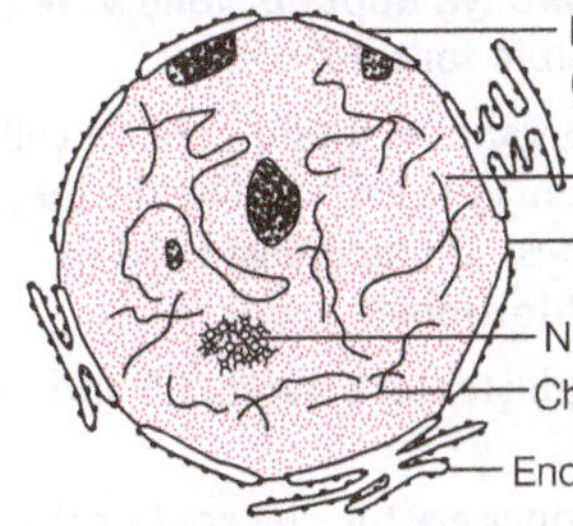

[2]

Differences between nucleus and nucleoid are as follows

Nucleus	Nucleoid
Bounded by a nuclear membrane.	Not bounded by nuclear membrane.
Present in eukaryotes.	Present in prokaryotes.
Have nucleolus and nucleoplasm.	Does not possess nucleolus and nucleoplasm.

3 Illustrate only a plant cell as seen under electron microscope. How is it different from animal cell? **NCERT Exemplar**

Sol. For the diagram of a plant cell refer to fig. on page no. 101.

For the solution, refer to exercise solution 1 on page 106.

4 (i) Draw a neat labelled diagram of animal cell. **NCERT Exemplar**

(ii) Name the structures, which helps in

(a) energy production.

(b) exchange of materials between cytoplasm and nucleoplasm.

(c) lipid synthesis.

Sol. (i) For the diagram of an animal cell. Refer to the fig. on page no. 101. [2]

(ii) (a) Mitochondria

(b) Nuclear pore

(c) Smooth endoplasmic reticulum [3]

5 Why are mitochondria called powerhouse of the cell? Give three similarities and one difference between mitochondria and plastid. **Competency Based Que.**

Sol. Refer to Sol. 5 on page no. 107. [1]

Three similarities between mitochondria and plastids are as follows

(i) Both have their own DNA and ribosomes.

(ii) Both have similar external structures.

(iii) Both have more than one membrane layer. [2]

One major difference between mitochondria and plastids is that mitochondria are present in both plant and animal cells, whereas plastids are found in plant cells only. [2]

6 Grass looks green, papaya appears yellow. Which cell organelle is responsible for this?

Sol. **Plastids** are the cell organelles found in plant cells only. On the basis of pigments present in plastids, they are divided into three types; (i) **leucoplasts** and (ii) **chromoplasts**, (iii) **chloroplast**

The colourless **leucoplasts** store starch, oil and protein granules.

The most important ones are the chloroplast that contains a pigment called **chlorophyll.** These are responsible for the manufacturing of food by photosynthesis. **Chromoplasts** contains non-green pigments, which are responsible for the characteristic colours of fruits and flowers, e.g. anthocyanin.

7 Given below statements have underlined words which may be incorrect. Rewrite these words and state one function for each of them other than those (if) given.

(i) The fundamental organisational unit of life is an organ.

(ii) The cell wall is an active part of the cell and is selectively permeable.

(iii) The presence of plasma membrane enables the cells of plants and fungi to exist in hypotonic media without bursting.

(iv) The Golgi body functions both as a passageway for intracellular transport and as a manufacturing surface.

(v) Leucoplasts contain carotenoids and their primary function is to provide colours to flowers and fruits.

Competency Based Que.

Sol. (i) **A Cell**

It perform many important physiological functions in living organisms that is essential for life.

(ii) **Plasma membrane**

It acts as a mechanical barrier, preventing the leakage of cellular contents to the outside environment.

(iii) **Cell wall**

It helps in the interaction among plant cells through cytoplasmic channels.

(iv) **Endoplasmic reticulum**

It functions as a cytoplasmic framework providing surface for some biochemical activities of the cell.

(v) **Chromoplasts**

They impart colour to the parts of plants like flowers and fruits. [1×5]

8 Write the main functions of atleast ten cell components.

Sol. (i) **Plasma membrane** It acts as a semipermeable membrane and allows only selective substances to pass through it.

(ii) **Chromosomes** To carry hereditary characters of an organism from one generation to another.

(iii) **Lysosomes** Breakdown of unwanted macromolecules is the main function of these organelles.

(iv) **Ribosomes** These help in protein synthesis.

(v) **Nucleus** Control centre of the cell. It contains cellular DNA (genetic information) in the form of genes.

(vi) **Mitochondria** The main function of mitochondria in aerobic cells is the production of energy by synthesis of ATP.

(vii) **Nucleolus** It is known as the factory of ribosomes which are required for protein synthesis.

(viii) **Cell wall** It provides protection and rigidity to the plant cell.

(ix) **Chloroplasts** These are the sites of photosynthesis within plant cells.

(x) **Endoplasmic reticulum** These serve as channels for the transport of materials. [½ ×10]

9 How are the following related to each other?

(i) Chromatin network and chromosomes

(ii) Chloroplast and chlorophyll

(iii) Genes and DNA

Sol. (i) The cell contains nuclear material which can be seen as entangled mass of thread-like structure when it is not dividing.

The chromatin material gets organised into rod-like structures called chromosomes when the cell is about to divide. [2]

(ii) Chloroplasts are the type of plastids which contain green coloured pigment called chlorophyll. [1]

(iii) Genes are the functional segments of DNA (present on DNA) which control a specific trait by making specific protein. [2]

10 Discuss in detail the importance of mitotic and meiotic cell division.

Sol. Refer to text on page no. 104.

ASSESSMENT EXERCISE

Competency Focused (Objective) Questions

Multiple Choice Questions

1. Which of the following statement is correct about history of cell?
   (a) Rudolf Virchow discovered cell first time
   (b) Robert Brown discovered living cell
   (c) Leeuwenhoek first discovered living cell in pond water
   (d) Schleiden discovered protoplasm

2. Which of the following organelle controls all the metabolic activities of cell and if it is removed the protoplasm dries up?
   (a) Mitochondria
   (b) Endoplasmic reticulum
   (c) Nucleus
   (d) Plastid

3. In the absence of endoplasmic reticulum, which of the following option does not occur in the cell? **Competency Based Que.**
   (a) Membrane biosynthesis
   (b) ATP generation
   (c) Packaging of materials
   (d) Photosynthesis

4. The given below cell organelle involved in forming complex sugars from simple sugars are

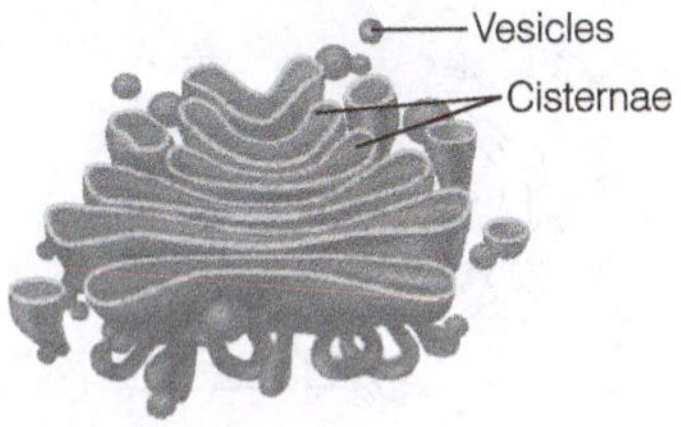

   (a) endoplasmic reticulum
   (b) ribosomes
   (c) plastids
   (d) Golgi apparatus

5. The best material for the study of mitosis in laboratory is
   (a) anther (b) root tip
   (c) leaf tip (d) ovary

Assertion-Reason Questions

Direction (Q.Nos. 6-9) *In each of the following questions, a statement of Assertion (A) is given by the corresponding statement of Reason (R). Of the statements, mark the correct answer as*

(a) Both A and R are true and R is the correct explanation of A
(b) Both A and R are true, but R is not the correct explanation of A
(c) A is true, but R is false
(d) A is false, but R is true

6. **Assertion** (A) Robert Brown discovered nucleus.
   Reason (R) Nucleoplasm and cytoplasm of a living cell together form the protoplasm.

7. **Assertion** (A) Lysosomes are often called as 'suicidal bags' of a cell.
   Reason (R) Lysosomes contain hydrolytic enzymes capable of digesting cellular waste.

8. **Assertion** (A) Chromoplasts are coloured plastids.
   Reason (R) Chromoplasts helps in pollination and dispersal of seeds.

9. **Assertion** (A) Vacuoles are large sized in plant cell, but small sized in animal cell.
   Reason (R) In plant cell, vacuoles are full of fluid from inside.

Case Based/Source Based Questions

Direction (Q. Nos. 10-13) *Answer the questions on the basis of your understanding of the following passage and related studied concepts:*

Meiosis is a type of cell division where the number of chromosomes becomes half in the daughter nuclei compared to the parental nuclei. It involves two successive cell divisions, i.e. meiosis-I and II. Meiosis-I is often called as reductional division while II is called as equational division.

10. How is meiosis different from mitotic cell division?
11. How can meiosis cell division help in the process of reproduction?
12. Do you think meiosis cell division contributes to evolutionary process ?
13. Mitosis or meiosis, which cell division helps in maintaining the specific chromosome number of each species across generations in sexually reproducing organisms?

Answers

1. (c) **2.** (c) **3.** (a) **4.** (d) **5.** (b) **6.** (b)
7. (a) **8.** (b) **9.** (b)

Constructed Response (Descriptive) Questions

Very Short Answer Type Questions

14. From where does the new cells arise?

15. Which complex substance primarily composes the plant cell wall contributing to its structural strength and rigdity?

16. In which form is the DNA present in a cell, when the cell is not dividing? **Competency Based Que.**

17. What would happen to the life of a cell, if there are no vacuoles?

Short Answer Type Questions

18. Name the fluid content of a cell. Write its function(s).

19. Why is it said that 'a cell without nucleus is without any future'?

20. Identify the cells (a and b) below and write three differences between the two. **Competency Based Que.**

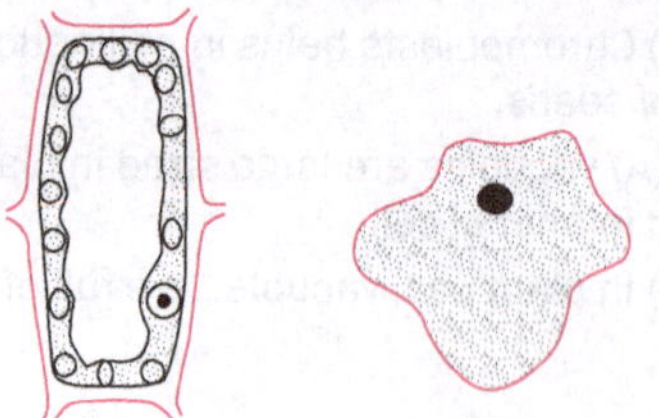

(a) (b)

21. Identify the figure and label its parts *A*, *B* and *C*. **Competency Based Que.**

22. Write the function of leucoplast and chromoplast.

23. How is bacterial cell different from onion peel? **NCERT Exemplar**

24. What is endocytosis? Why is endocytosis found in animals only?

25. We eat food composed of all the nutrients like carbohydrates, proteins, fat, minerals and water. After digestion, these are absorbed in the form of glucose, amino acids, fatty acids, glycerol, etc. What mechanisms are involved in absorption of digested food and water? **Competency Based Que.**

26. How do vacuoles perform differently in plant cell and a unicellular organism like *Amoeba*?

Long Answer Type Questions

27. Study the figure given below and answer the questions that follows **Competency Based Que.**

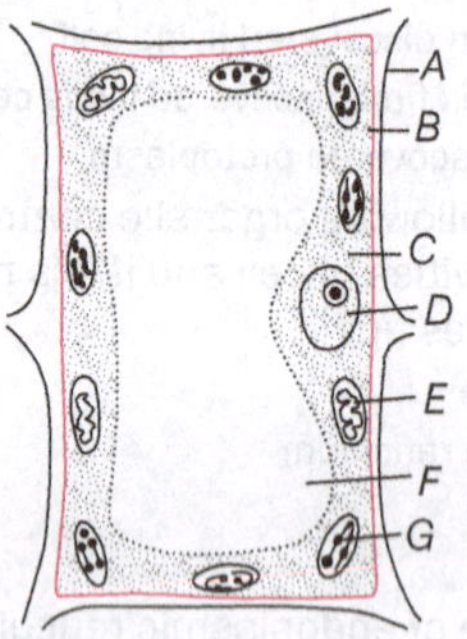

(i) Identify the figure.

(ii) Label the parts *A*-*G*.

(iii) Is it a plant cell or an animal cell? Give reason in support of your answer.

(iv) State the functions of the parts *A, D, E* and *G*.

28. Study the figure given below of an animal cell and answer the following questions.

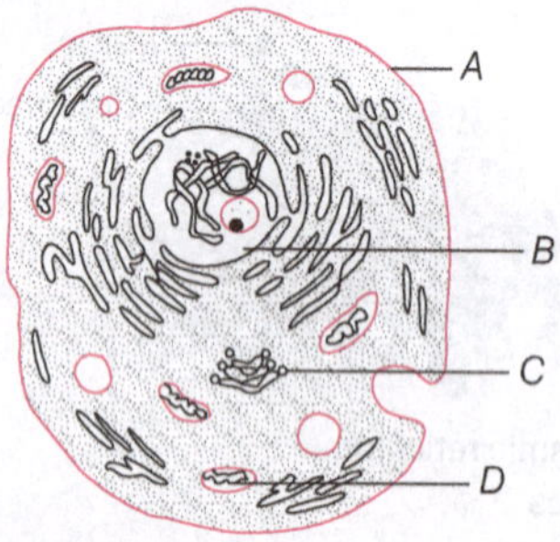

(i) Label the parts *A*-*D*.

(ii) Name a structure in this cell which is not found in plant cells.

(iii) What is the function of part *B* in the physiological activity of the cell?

(iv) Write one function of cell organelle labelled as *D*.

29. Discuss the importance of meiotic cell division.

CHAPTER 06(a)

Plant Tissues

All living organisms are made up of **cells**. Unicellular organisms perform all the functions, such as digestion, respiration, excretion, reproduction, etc., by a single cell, e.g. *Amoeba*.
However, multicellular organisms have several cells, which are grouped together to form **tissues**. These tissues further gets specialised to carry out different functions.

6(a).1 Tissues

A group of cells with similar structure performing the same function and having a common origin are called **tissues**. The structural and functional organisations are different in both plants and animals, i.e. plants remain stationary or fixed, while animals move around in search of food, mates and shelter as per their needs. They consume more energy as compared to plants.

Most of tissues are living in nature. Thus, each of them possesses different feeding methods and are differently adapted.

Based on these habits, the tissues in plants and animals are strikingly different. So, tissues are further classified as **plant tissue** and **animal tissue**.

6(a).2 Plant Tissues

On the basis of dividing capacity, plant tissues can be classified into two fundamental types as follows

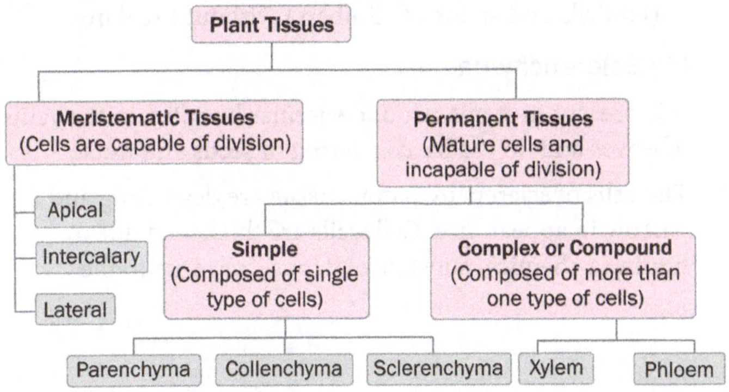

1. Meristematic Tissue

The tissues in which cells always divide and give rise to new cells are called meristematic tissues. The growth in plants occurs only in those regions where meristematic tissues are present, e.g. root and shoot tip.

Hence, meristematic tissue is also called **dividing tissue** due to its actively dividing property.
Characteristics of meristematic tissue are as follows

(i) Cells of this tissue are very active.

(ii) They have dense cytoplasm and thin cellulosic walls.

(iii) They have prominent nuclei.

(iv) Cells of this tissue lack vacuoles.

The characteristics of meristematic tissue changes once they grow and become differentiated as component of other tissues.

Types of Meristematic Tissue

On the basis of region where they are present in plant, meristematic tissues are of following types

(i) **Apical meristem** It is present at the growing tips of stems and roots. It is helpful in increasing the length of the stems and the roots.

(ii) **Intercalary meristem** It is present at the base of the leaves or internodes (on either side of the node). It helps in the longitudinal growth (elongation) of plants.

(iii) **Lateral meristem** (Cambium) It is present on the lateral sides of stems and roots. It helps in increasing the girth of the stem and the root.

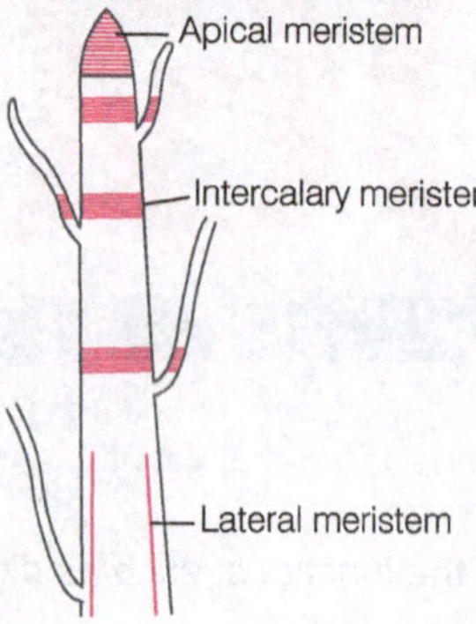

Location of meristematic tissues in plant body

2. Permanent Tissue

These tissues are formed from the cells of meristematic tissue when they loose their ability to divide. This process of taking up a permanent shape, size and function is called **differentiation**.

As a result of differentiation, the meristematic tissues tend to form different types of permanent tissues. These are as follows

I. Simple Permanent Tissue

It is made up of only one type of cells, i.e. the cells forming these tissues are similar in structure and function. These are mainly found beneath the epidermis. The simple permanent tissue can be either supportive or protective in function. This tissue is further classified into three types, which are as follows

(i) Parenchyma

It is the most common simple permanent tissue. These are present in the soft parts of the plant like leaves, roots, fruits, flowers, etc.

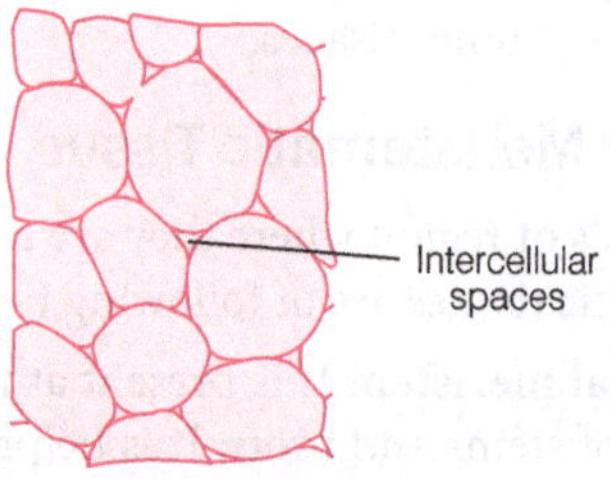

Parenchyma tissue

It consists of simple living cells with little or no specialisation and thin cell walls. The cells are usually loosely packed with large spaces between them (intercellular spaces).

It performs the following functions

- Parenchyma serves as a food storage tissue.
- In some situations, parenchyma cell contains chlorophyll and performs photosynthesis. Such type of tissue is called **chlorenchyma.**
- In aquatic plants, large air cavities are present in parenchyma cells in order to give buoyancy to plants, which help them to float. Such type of parenchyma tissue is called **aerenchyma.**
- Parenchyma of stems and roots also stores nutrients and water.

(ii) Collenchyma

These tissues are generally found in leaf stalks below the epidermis. Cells of this tissue are living, elongated and irregularly thickened at the corners. These have very little intercellular spaces.

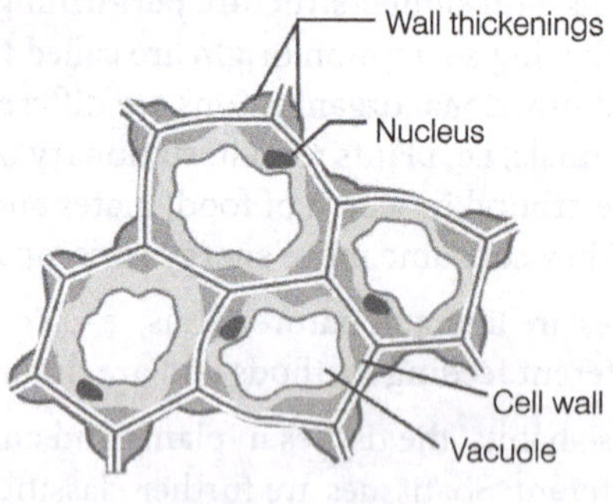

Collenchyma tissue

It performs the following functions

- Collenchyma provides mechanical support and flexibility to plants.
- It also allows easy bending in various parts of a plant (tendrils and stems of climbers) without breaking.

(iii) Sclerenchyma

It is present in stems, around vascular bundles, in the veins of leaves and in the hard covering of seeds and nuts.

The cells of sclerenchymatous tissue are dead, long and narrow in appearance. Cell walls are thickened due to **lignin** (a chemical substance) deposition. Due to the presence of thick walls, there is no internal space between the cells.

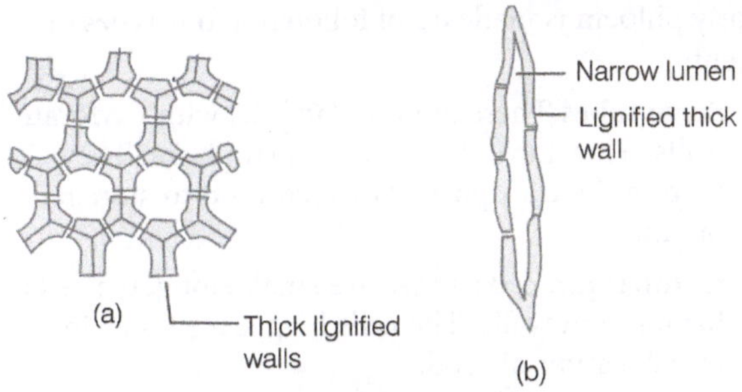

Sclerenchyma; (a) Transverse section, (b) Longitudinal section

It performs the following functions

- It provides mechanical strength to the plant parts.
- It makes the plant hard and stiff. For example, husk of coconut is made up of sclerenchymatous tissue.

Protective Permanent Tissues

These tissues cover the surface of roots, stems and leaves. They mainly include epidermis and cork.

(i) Epidermis

It forms the outermost layer of plant body and is made by single layer of cells. Cells of epidermal tissue form a continuous layer. They have no intercellular spaces. Most epidermal cells are relatively flat. Their outer wall and side walls are thicker than the inner wall.
Epidermal cells of leaf, bear small pores known as **stomata**. These are enclosed by two kidney-shaped cells called **guard cells**.

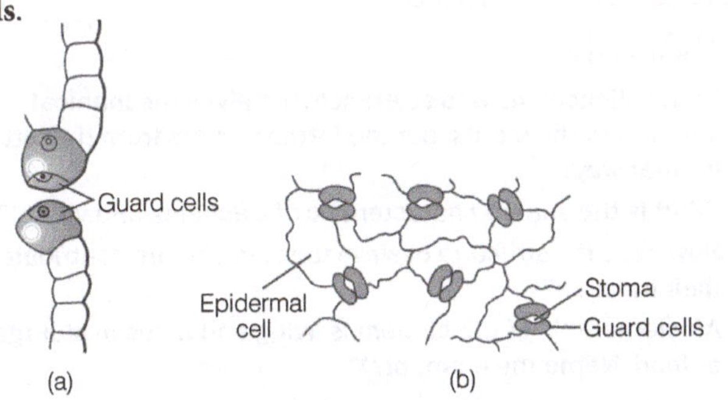

Guard cells and epidermal cells : (a) Lateral view, (b) Surface view

It performs the following functions

- On the aerial parts of the plant, epidermal cells often secrete a waxy, water-resistant layer on the outer surface. This aids in protection against mechanical injury and invasion by parasitic fungi.
- In some plants like desert plants, epidermis has thick waxy coating of cutin (a substance that has a water proof quality) in order to minimise the water loss.
- Epidermal cells of root bear long hair-like parts that greatly increase the total absorptive surface area.
- Stomata helps in gaseous exchange and in the process of transpiration (i.e. loss of water in the form of water vapour).

(ii) Cork

It is the strip of secondary meristem, located in the cortex, forming a layer of cell which constitute the cork.

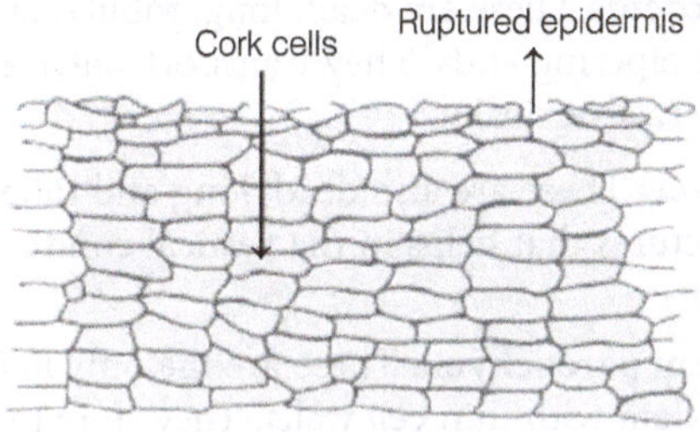

Protective tissue

Cells of cork are dead, compactly arranged and have no intercellular spaces.

It possess a substance called **suberin** in the walls to makes them impervious to gases and water. It also protects the plant from mechanical injury.

Try These 6(a).1

1. **Name the tissue which contains cells that are capable of division.**
2. **Tissue 'Y' is located near nodes and is responsible for longitudinal growth in the absence of tissue 'X'. Identify the 'X' and 'Y'.**
3. **Tissue 'X' is accountable for the increase in girth of roots and shoots. Identify 'X'.**
4. **A special type of parenchyma is found in lotus. Name it.**
5. **Simple permanent tissue 'X' provides mechanical support to plants. In which plant parts this tissue 'X' is commonly found?**

II. Complex Permanent Tissue

These tissue are made up of more than one type of cells. All these cells present in a tissue coordinate to perform a common function.

There are two types of complex permanent tissue, i.e. xylem and phloem.

Both of them are **conducting tissues** and constitute to form a **vascular bundle**. This is a distinctive feature of complex plants. It has made possible their survival in the terrestrial environment.

(i) Xylem

It is a type of conducting tissue responsible for the transport of water and minerals from roots to other parts of the plant.

Xylem consists of four different types of elements, which are as follows

(a) **Tracheids** These are dead, long, tubular structures with tapering ends. They transport water and minerals vertically.

(b) **Vessels** These are also dead, long and tube-like structures that helps in the vertical conduction of water.

(c) **Xylem parenchyma** These are the only living cells of xylem with thin cell walls. They store food and help in the sideways conduction of water.

(d) **Xylem fibres** They have elongated dead cells with tapering end and thick cell walls. These are mainly supportive in function.

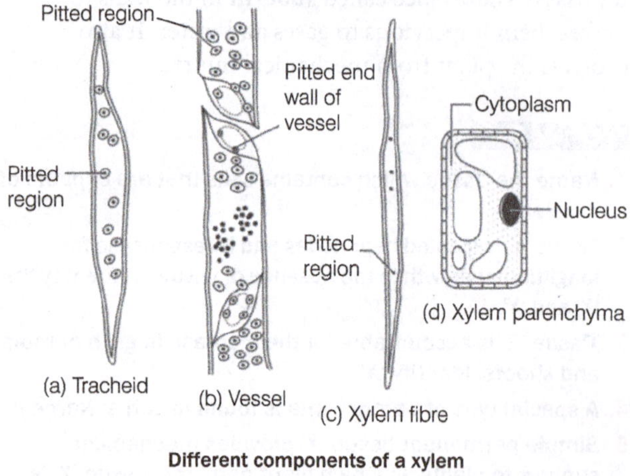

Different components of a xylem

(ii) Phloem

It transports food from leaves to other parts of the plant. Majorly phloem is made up of following four types of elements

(a) **Sieve tubes** These are tubular cells with perforated walls. They have thin layer of cytoplasm. They help in the transport of formed food to storage organs.

(b) **Companion cells** These are small elongated cells having thin walls. The cells help sieve tubes in translocation of food.

(c) **Phloem fibres** These are dead, thick walled sclerenchyma cells which provide mechanical strength to the tissue.

(d) **Phloem parenchyma** These are dead, thin-walled cells which help in storage of food.

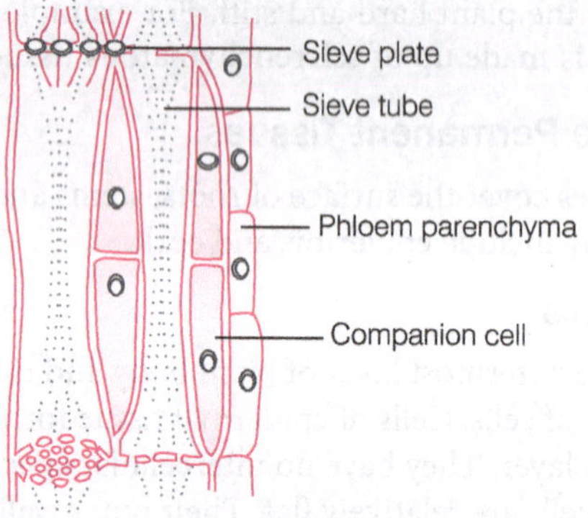

Section of phloem

All phloem cells are living except phloem fibres. In hilly areas, certain plants have sieve cells in place of sieve tubes. Sieve cells lacks sieve plates.

Try These 6(a).2

1. **Both collenchyma and sclerenchyma gives mechanical strength to the plants, but the former differs from the latter in what way?**
2. **What is the shared characteristic of tracheids and vessel?**
3. **How does the structure of sieve tubes in phloem contribute to their function?**
4. **An element '*X*' of the phloem is living and helps in storage of food. Name the element '*X*'.**

Mind Map

Tissues

A group of cells that are similar in structure and work together to achieve a particular function forms a tissue.

Plant Tissues

Plant tissues are classified based on their structure and function and they mainly provide support, transport and facilitate growth to plant.

Meristematic Tissues

The tissues whose cells divide actively throughout the life. They are found in the growing regions of plant like root and shoot tip.These tissues are living and bring about an increase in length and girth of the plant.

Permanent Tissues

These tissues do not divide. They take up permanent shape, size and function. These are formed from meristematic tissue when they loose the ability to divide.

Types of Meristematic Tissues

1. **Apical Meristem** Present at growing tips of stems and roots.
2. **Intercalary Meristem** Present at base of the leaves or internodes on twigs.
3. **Lateral Meristem** Present on the lateral sides of stems and roots.

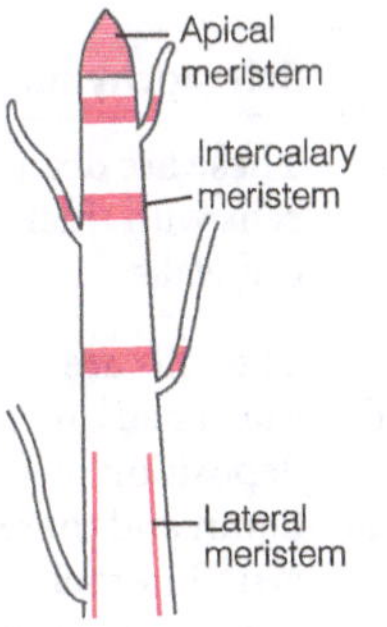

Simple Permanent Tissues

These are made up of only one type of cell.

1. **Parenchyma** Simplest form of tissue with little specialisation. These provide support to plants and also store food.
2. **Collenchyma** Cells are living, elongated and irregularly thickened at the corners, generally found in leaf stocks below the epidermis. These provide mechanical support and elasticity in plants.
3. **Sclerenchyma** Present in stems around vascular bundles in the veins of leaves and in the hard covering of seeds and nuts. These provide strength and enables them to bear various stresses.

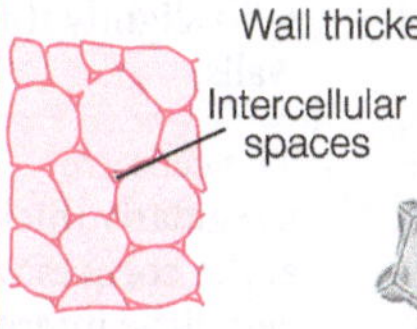

Parenchyma

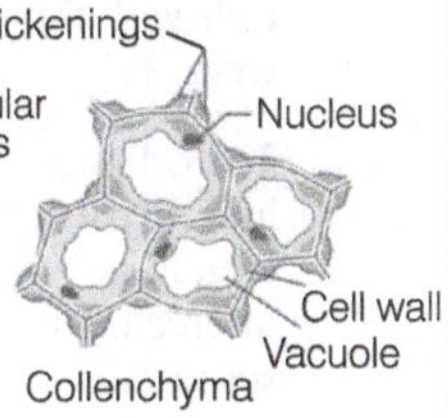

Collenchyma

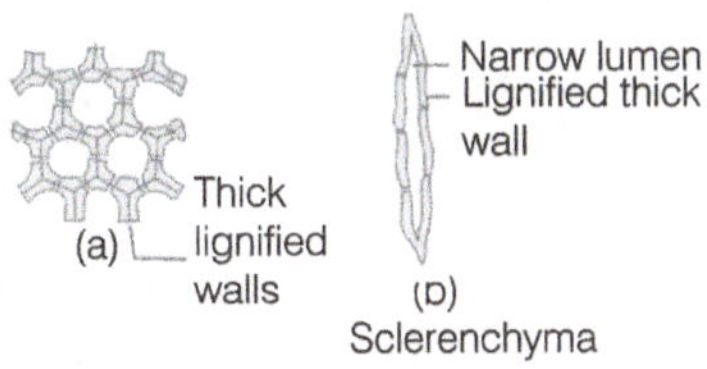

Sclerenchyma

Complex Permanent Tissues

They are made up of more than one type of cells.

1. **Xylem** A vascular and mechanical conducting tissue, known as wood. Responsible for transport of water and minerals from roots to other parts.
2. **Phloem** A vascular tissue also known as bast, responsible for transport of food from leaves to other parts of the plant.

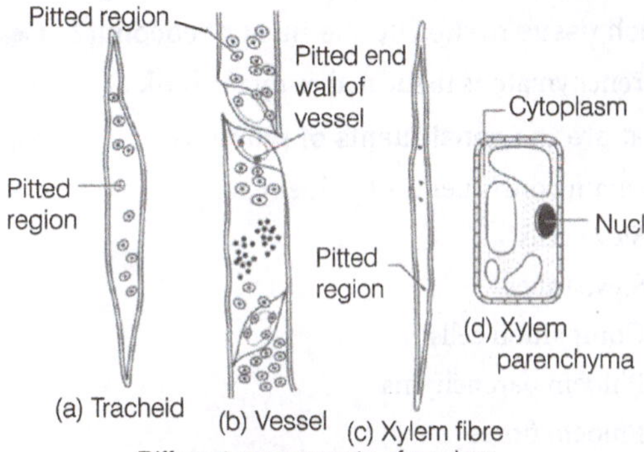

Different components of a xylem

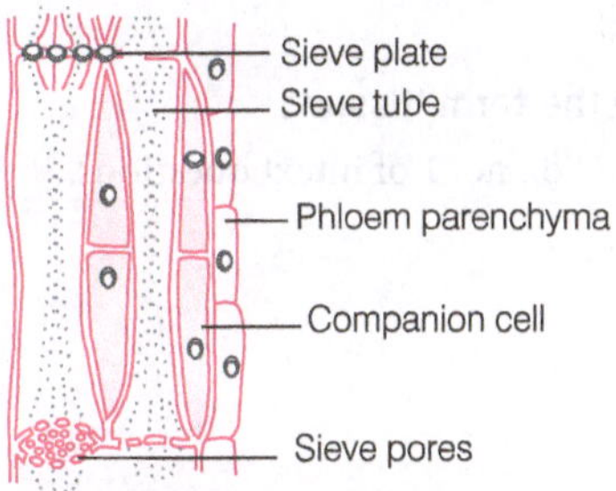

Section of phloem

NCERT FOLDER

Complete Explanations of all NCERT's Questions

Intext Questions

Q.1 What is a tissue? Page 61

Sol. The group of cells that are similar in structure and/or work together to perform a common function is called tissue, e.g. blood, muscle.

Q.2 What is the utility of tissues in multicellular organisms? Page 61

Sol. Multicellular organisms show division of labour because a particular function is carried out by a cluster of cells (tissue) at a definite place in the body. The tissue is arranged and designed so as to give the highest possible efficiency of function.

Q.3 Where is apical meristem found? Page 65

Sol. Apical meristem is found in growing tips of stems and roots of plants.

Q.4 Name the types of simple tissue. Page 65

Sol. The three main types of simple tissues in plants are

(i) Parenchyma
(ii) Collenchyma
(iii) Sclerenchyma

Q.5 Which tissue makes up the husk of coconut? Page 65

Sol. Sclerenchymatous tissue makes up the husk of coconut.

Q.6 What are the constituents of phloem? Page 65

Sol. The main constituents of phloem are

(i) Sieve cells
(ii) Sieve tubes
(iii) Companion cells
(iv) Phloem parenchyma
(v) Phloem fibres

Exercise

Q.1 Define the term 'tissue'.

Sol. Refer to Sol. no. 1 of intext questions.

Q.2 How many types of elements together make up the xylem tissue? Name them.

Sol. Four elements make up the xylem tissue which includes

(i) tracheids
(ii) vessels
(iii) xylem parenchyma
(iv) xylem fibres

Q.3 How are simple tissues different from complex tissues in plants?

Sol. Differences between simple tissues and complex tissues are as follows

Simple tissue	Complex tissue
These are made up of only one type of cells.	These are made up of more than one type of cells.
These are mainly responsible for storage and mechanical support.	These are mainly responsible for transportation.
e.g. parenchyma, collenchyma.	e.g. xylem, phloem.

Q.4 Differentiate between parenchyma, collenchyma and sclerenchyma on the basis of their cell wall.

Sol. Differences between parenchyma, collenchyma and sclerenchyma are as follows

Parenchyma	Collenchyma	Sclerenchyma
These are living cells with thin walls.	These are living cells with slightly thick walls.	These are dead cells with thick cell walls.
The cells are loosely packed with large intercellular spaces.	The cells are irregularly thickened at the corners with very little intercellular spaces.	The cells are thickened due to deposition of lignin and there is no internal space inside the cell.

Q.5 What are the functions of the stomata?

Sol. The main functions of stomata are

(i) They help in exchange of gases (CO_2 and O_2) with atmosphere.

(ii) They help in transpiration (loss of water in the form of water vapour).

Q.6 Name the following.

Tissue that transports food in plants.

Sol. Phloem

Q.7 Identify the type of tissue in following: Bark of tree, vascular bundle.

Sol. **Bark of tree** Cork

Vascular bundle Complex permanent tissue (xylem and phloem).

Q.8 Name the regions in which parenchyma tissue is present.

Sol. Parenchyma tissue is mainly found in soft parts of the plant such as roots, stem and leaves.

Q.9 What is the role of epidermis in plants?

Sol. In old plants, epidermal layer becomes thick and forms cork. The cells of cork contain a chemical called suberin in their walls, which makes them impervious to gases and water.

Q.10 How does the cork act as a protective tissue?

Sol. The cells of cork are dead and compactly arranged without any intercellular spaces. They also have a chemical called suberin in their walls, which makes cork impervious to gases and water. Thus, it protects underlying tissue from mechanical injury.

Q.11 Complete the table.

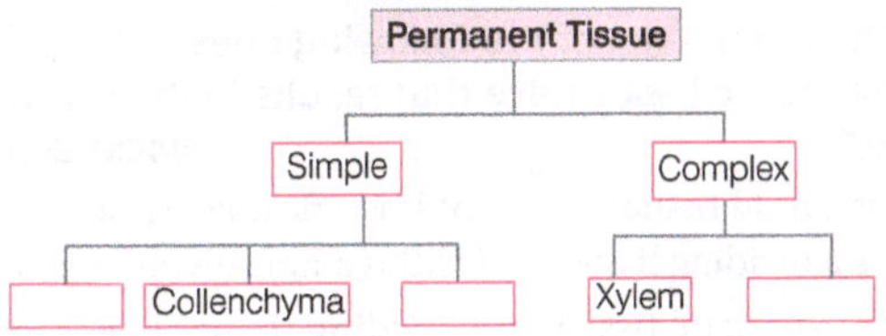

Sol.

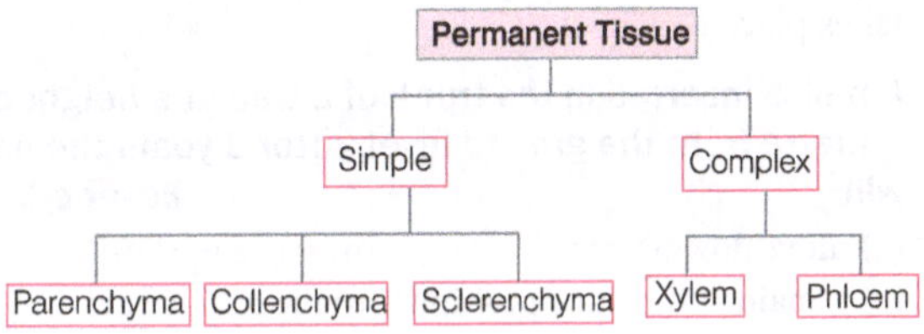

To Study NCERT Activities

Scan the Code

REVIEW EXERCISE

Including Competency Based Questions

Competency Focused (Objective) Questions

Multiple Choice Questions

1 Which property out of the following does meristematic tissue have that results in the growth of plants? NCERT Exemplar

(a) It is a dead tissue (b) It is a flexible tissue
(c) It is a dividing tissue (d) It is a non-dividing tissue

Sol. (c) Meristematic tissues are dividing tissues hence, all the regions where they are present, the growth of plants takes place.

2 A nail is inserted in the trunk of a tree at a height of 1 metre from the ground level. After 3 years the nail will NCERT Exemplar

(a) move downwards (b) move upwards
(c) remain at the same position (d) move sideways

Sol. (c) Apical meristem is present at the growing tips of stem and root. Therefore, longitudinal growth in the stem always takes place at the top. Hence, there will be no change in position of nail inserted in the trunk of tree.

3 If the tip of sugarcane plant is removed from the field, even then it keeps on growing in length. It is due to the presence of Competency Based Que.

(a) cambium (b) apical meristem
(c) lateral meristem (d) intercalary meristem

Sol. (d) Intercalary meristems are present in the stems at the base of nodes. So, even if the tip of sugarcane (which possess apical meristem) is removed it still can grow with the help of intercalary meristem.

4 Girth of stem increases due to

(a) apical meristem (b) lateral meristem
(c) intercalary meristem (d) vertical meristem

Sol. (b) The girth of stem or root increases due to the lateral meristem (cambium).

5 A permanent slide shows thin walled isodiametric cells with a large vacuole. This slide contains NCERT Exemplar

(a) parenchyma cells (b) aerenchyma cells
(c) collenchyma cells (d) nerve cells

Sol. (a) Parenchyma is the most common, simple, permanent tissue that have relatively unspecialised cells with thin cell walls, the cells are isodiametric and has a large vacuole. Also, they are usually loosely packed, thus has large space between them.

6 The cells of tissue *X* are elongated and irregularly thickened at the corners. Identify *X* out of the following options.

(a) Collenchyma (b) Sclerenchyma
(c) Parenchyma (d) Chlorenchyma

Sol. (a) Collenchyma is a mechanical tissue in young dicotyledonous stems that provides mechanical support and flexibility to plant organs. It allows easy bending in various parts of a plant mainly young growing stem without breaking them.

7 In desert plants, the rate of water loss gets reduced due to the presence of NCERT Exemplar

(a) cuticle (b) stomata (c) lignin (d) suberin

Sol. (a) Cuticle is a protective layer covering the young shoots and other aerial parts of plant. It contains lipids and has water proof quality. This minimises the effects of heat and reduces the loss of water.

8 Survival of plants in terrestrial environment has been made possible by the presence of Competency Based Que.

(a) intercalary meristem (b) conducting tissue
(c) apical meristem (d) parenchymatous tissue

Sol. (b) Survival of plants in the terrestrial environment has been made possible by the presence of conducting tissues like xylem and phloem.
Xylem conducts water from roots to all the parts of the plant and phloem transports food and other nutrients from leaves to other parts of plant.

9 Choose the cell out of the following that does not have perforated cell wall.

(a) Tracheids (b) Companion cells
(c) Sieve tubes (d) Vessels

Sol. (a) Tracheids are elongated hollow cells which do not have perforated cell wall. These are water conducting cells found in xylem.

10 A long tree has several branches. The tissue that helps in the sideways conduction of water in the branches is NCERT Exemplar

(a) collenchyma (b) xylem parenchyma
(c) parenchyma (d) xylem vessels

Sol. (b) Xylem parenchyma helps in sideways conduction of water. It also helps in storage of food.

11 **Refer to the given figure and select the correct statement regarding *X*, *Y* and *Z*.**

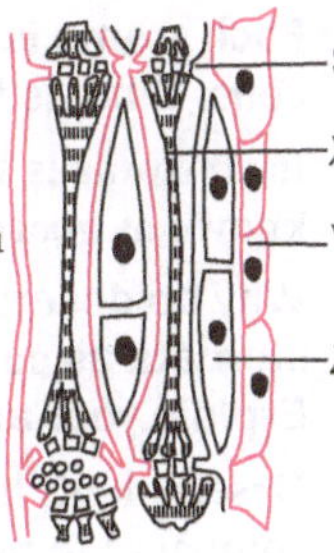

(a) *X* is involved in the conduction of organic food

(b) *Y* cells are made up of dead cells and provide mechanical support to *X*

(c) *Z* is made up of non-living cells and is involved in transportation of water

(d) None of the above

Sol. (a) *X* is to be identified as sieve tube that is responsible for conduction of organic food from leaves to other parts of the plant.

12 **Which of the following cells do not lose their nucleus at maturity?**

(a) Companion cells (b) Red blood cells

(c) Vessel (d) Sieve tube cells

Sol. (a) Companion cells do not lose their nucleus at maturity. The activity of sieve tube is controlled by the nucleus of companion cells.

Assertion-Reason Questions

Direction (Q. Nos. 1-5) ***In each of the following questions, a statement of Assertion (A) is given by the corresponding statement of Reason (R). Of the statements, mark the correct answer as***

(a) Both A and R are true and R is the correct explanation of A

(b) Both A and R are true, but R is not the correct explanation of A

(c) A is true, but R is false

(d) A is false, but R is true

1 **Assertion** (A) Apical meristems are present along the side of various organs in plants.

Reason (R) These help in the growth of plants.

Sol. (d) A is false, but R is true. A can be corrected as

Apical meristem is present at the growing tips of stem and roots.

2 **Assertion** (A) Cork is a protective tissue present in plants.

Reason (R) It aids in protection against water loss, mechanical injury and microbial infestation.

Sol. (a) Both A and R are true and R is the correct explanation of A.

3 **Assertion** (A) Lateral meristem adds thickness to plants.

Reason (R) It is found in between the vascular bundles.

Sol. (c) A is true, but R is false. R can be corrected as

Lateral meristem are found on the lateral sides of stems and roots.

4 **Assertion** (A) Meristematic tissues constitutes the major part of a plant body.

Reason (R) Meristematic tissues after differentiation give rise to permarent tissues.

Sol. (a) Both A and R are true and R is the correct explanation of A.

5 **Assertion** (A) Most of the plant tissues are dead.

Reason (R) The plants are sedentary in nature, thus the dead cells provide mechanical strength in comparison to live ones and need low maintenance.

Sol. (a) Both A and R are true and R is the correct explanation of A.

Case Based/Source Based Questions

1 ***Read the following case carefully and answer the questions that follows***

Apical meristem is a type of tissue that help plants to grow in length.

Tina took two identical potted plants and cut the shoot tip of one of them.

She observed if the two plants grew in height after a week.

(i) **What was Tina trying to find out about shoot tips through her experiment?**

Sol. Tina was trying to confirm the presence of apical meristem at the shoot tip. [1]

(ii) **Which of these conditions would have made Tina's experiment invalid?**

Circle 'Yes' or 'No' to mark your responses.

	Would this have made the experiment invalid?	Yes or No
(a)	Keeping one plant in sunlight and the other in a dark room	Yes/No
(b)	Watering both the plants equally	Yes/No
(c)	Adding manure to the soil of plant 1 only	Yes/No

Sol. (a) Yes (b) No (c) Yes [2]

(iii) **Why do cells of apical meristem lack vacuoles?**

Sol. The cells of apical meristem lack vacuoles because they are actively dividing cells. [1]

2 ***Read the following case carefully and answer the questions that follows***

Stomata are minute openings found in the epidermis of plant leaves.
Each stoma allows carbon dioxide, oxygen and water vapour to diffuse in and out of a plant's internal tissues. **Competency Based Que.**

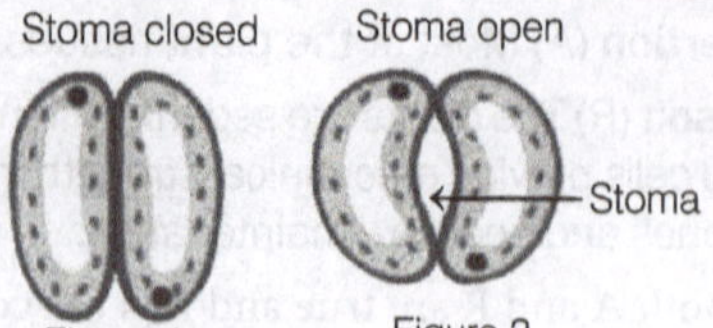

Figure 1 Figure 2

(i) Each stoma is surrounded by pair of elongated cells. What is this pair of cells known as?

Sol. Each stoma is surrounded by pair of elongated cells known as guard cells. [1]

(ii) Why do desert plants have smaller and fewer stomata as compared to rainforest plants? Explain your answer.

Sol. Desert plants have smaller and fewer stomata as compared to rainforest plants due to scarcity of water in the deserts. Smaller and fewer stomata help desert plants to minimise the loss of water. [3]

Constructed Response (Descriptive) Questions

Very Short Answer Type Questions

1 Which process in meristematic tissue converts it to permanent tissue?

Sol. Differentiation is the process by which meristematic tissue takes up a permanent shape, size and function.

2 Water hyacinth floats on water surface. Explain. **NCERT Exemplar**

Sol. Aerenchyma present in the water hyacinth provides buoyancy to it. Thus, helps it floating on water surface.

3 Which structure protects the plant body against the invasion of parasites? **Competency Based Que.**

Sol. The epidermis of plants has thick cuticle and waxy substances to prevent the invasion of parasites.

4 Identify the following. **Competency Based Que.**

(i) Living component of xylem.

(ii) Dead element of phloem.

Sol. (i) Xylem parenchyma consists of living cells having thin cell walls. [1]

(ii) Phloem fibres are the dead elements of phloem. [1]

5 Which type of conducting tissues conduct water and minerals vertically?

Sol. Tracheids and vessels of xylem are the two conducting tissues, which conduct water and minerals vertically. [1 + 1]

Short Answer Type Questions

1 Draw a diagrammatic labelled sketch of stem tip to show the location of meristematic tissue. Mention the functions of different types of meristematic tissue.

Sol. Refer to fig. 'Location of meristematic tissues in plant body' on page no. 121 and 122. [1]

Functions of meristematic tissue are

(i) **Apical meristem** It increases the length of stem and root.

(ii) **Lateral meristem** It increases the girth of stem and root.

(iii) **Intercalary meristem** It increases longitudinal growth of plant. [2]

2 Explain the basic criteria for classification of permanent tissue in plants.

Sol. The following points form the basic criteria for classification of permanent tissue in plants

(i) Whether the tissue is made up of one type of cell (simple) or more than one type of cells (complex). [1]

(ii) Whether the function is supportive (parenchyma), protective (epidermis) or conducting (xylem and phloem). [1]

(iii) Whether the cell wall is thick or thin. [1]

3 (i) A plant tissue is observed under a microscope, as shown in the figure below. Identify the tissue.

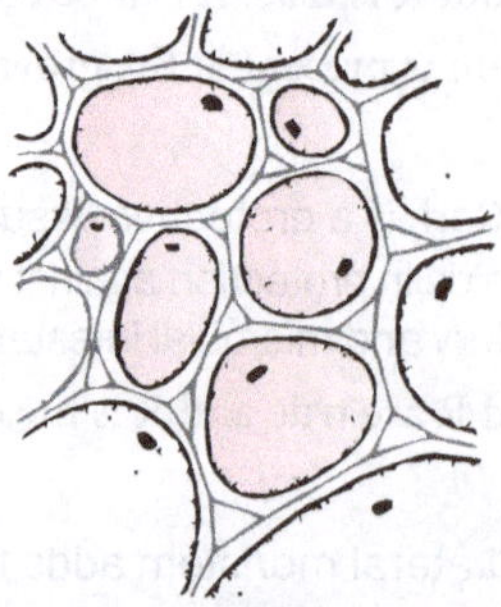

(ii) State the characteristic features of these cells.

(iii) Name parts of the plant, where such cells are present. **Competency Based Que.**

Sol. (i) The tissue given in the figure is parenchyma. [1]

(ii) It consists of thin-walled unspecialised cells, which are loosely packed, i.e. have intercellular spaces. Each cell has a prominent nucleus. [1]

(iii) It is mainly found in soft parts of the plant such as root stem and leaves. [1]

4 List any three characteristics of parenchyma.

Sol. Major characteristics of parenchyma are as follows

(i) The cells of parenchyma are living and possess the power of division. [1]

(ii) The cells are loosely packed with large intercellular spaces between them. [1]

(iii) It serves as a packing tissue to fill the spaces between other tissues and maintains the shape of plant. [1]

5 (i) Identify the tissue given in the following figure.

(ii) Mention the characteristic features of the cells.

(iii) Specify the function of this tissue.

Competency Based Que.

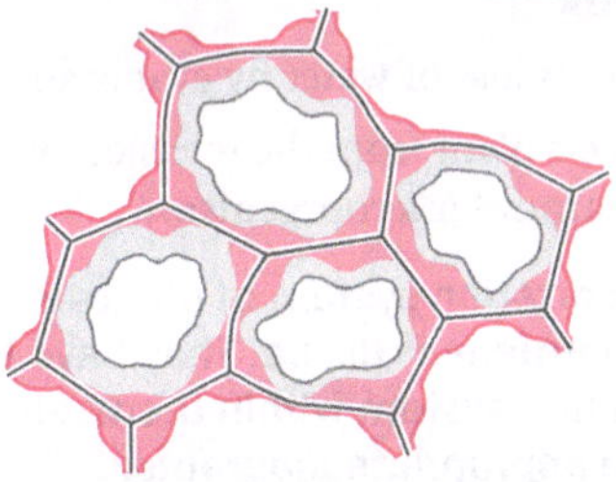

Sol. (i) The tissue given in the figure is collenchyma. [1]

(ii) The cells of collenchyma are living, elongated, thickened at the corners and have very little intercellular space. [1]

(iii) It provides flexibility to plants. [1]

6 Name the tissue responsible for the flexibility in plants. How would you differentiate it from other permanent tissues?

Sol. Collenchyma tissue is responsible for providing flexibility in plants. [1]

Differences between collenchyma tissue and other permanent tissues (parenchyma and sclerenchyma) are as follows

Parenchyma	Collenchyma	Sclerenchyma
These are formed of living cells.	These are formed of living cells.	They are composed of dead cells.
Cell wall is very thin.	Cell wall has irregular thickenings.	Cell wall is uniformly thick due to the deposition of lignin.
It provides turgidity to plant.	It provides mechanical strength as well as flexibility to plant.	It provides mechanical strength to plant.

[2]

7 Answer the following **Competency Based Que.**

(i) How is the epidermis of the plants living in very dry habitats adapted?

(ii) Write the functions of guard cells of stomata in the leaf.

(iii) Epidermal cells help in the absorption of water and nutrients from soil. How?

Sol. (i) The epidermis of the plants living in very dry habitats have a thick waxy coating of waterproof cutin over it. This prevents the loss of water. [1]

(ii) They help in exchange of gases with atmosphere, due to opening and closing of stomatal pore. [1]

(iii) Epidermal cells in roots bear long hair-like outgrowth, i.e. root hairs that greatly increase the total absorptive surface area and help in increased absorption of water and nutrients from soil. [1]

8 Describe three functions of protective tissue in plants.

Sol. Two types of protective tissue present in plants are epidermis and cork. The three common functions of these protective tissues are

(i) Cork protects plants from invasion of parasitic microorganisms. [1]

(ii) The cuticle of epidermis checks the excessive evaporation of water. [1]

(iii) Epidermis allows transpiration and gaseous exchange through stomata. [1]

9 Name the different components of xylem and draw a living component? **NCERT Exemplar**

Sol. Xylem consists of xylem fibre, xylem parenchyma, tracheids and vessels. The only living component of xylem is xylem parenchyma.

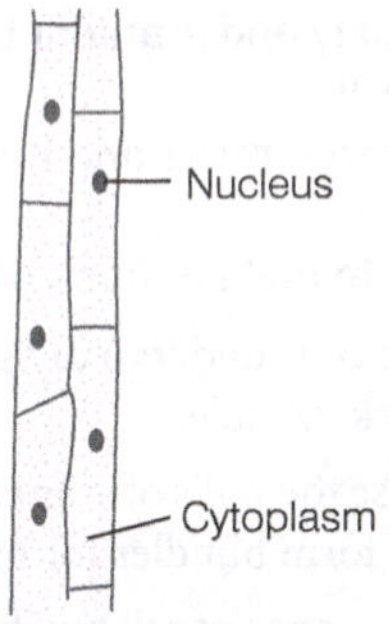

Xylem parenchyma

10 List the constituents of phloem. What will happen if the phloem at the base of a branch is removed?

Competency Based Que.

Sol. Major constituents of phloem include sieve cells, sieve tubes, companion cells, phloem fibres and phloem parenchyma. [1]

If the phloem at the base of branch is removed, then lower area of the branch will not receive food from the leaves. But the plant will not die, as it will continue to receive food from other branches as food can move through phloem in both the directions. [2]

11 **Give the name of the following**

(i) Tissue concerned with the conduction of food materials.

(ii) Tissue capable of cell division.

(iii) Multiple pores present in epidermis of leaf.

Sol. (i) Complex tissue (phloem) [1]

(ii) Meristematic tissue [1]

(iii) Stomata (Singular stoma) [1]

12 **Give one function of each of the following**

(i) Stomata

(ii) Tracheids

(iii) Sieve tubes

Sol. (i) **Stomata** These help in the gaseous exchange between the plant and atmosphere. Transpiration also takes place through stomata. [1]

(ii) **Tracheids** These are present in xylem and help in the transport of water and minerals vertically. [1]

(iii) **Sieve tubes** These are present in phloem and are responsible for the transport of formed food to the storage organs. [1]

Long Answer Type Questions

1 **Give reasons for the following.** **Competency Based Que.**

(i) Meristematic cells have prominent nucleus and dense cytoplasm, but they lack vacuole.

(ii) Intercellular spaces are absent in sclerenchymatous tissue.

(iii) We get crunchy and granular feeling, when we chew pear fruit.

(iv) Branches of tree move and bend freely in high wind velocity.

(v) It is difficult to pull out husk of coconut.

Sol. (i) Meristematic cells undergo division and do not store food, thus lack vacuole.

(ii) This is because the walls of sclerenchymatous tissue are lignified and form bundles for mechanical functions.

(iii) Due to the presence of sclerenchymatous tissue (stone cell) or sclereids, we get a crunchy feeling, when we chew pear fruit.

(iv) The presence of collenchyma tissue provides flexibility to the branches of tree.

(v) Husk of coconut is made up of sclerenchymatous fibres, which are closely packed. [1×5]

2 **List the characteristics of cork. How is it formed? Mention its role.** **NCERT Exemplar**

Sol. The common characteristics of a cork are

(i) It is the outer protective tissue of older stem.

(ii) Cells possess a chemical substance suberin in their walls.

(iii) The mature cork becomes dead and filled with tannin and resin.

(iv) The cells are arranged compactly without intercellular spaces. [2]

Formation of Cork

As plant grows older, the outer protective tissue undergoes certain changes. A strip of secondary meristem replaces the epidermis of stem.

Cells on the outside are cut-off from this epidermal layer. This forms several layer thick cork or bark with no intercellular spaces. [2]

Role of Cork

(i) It prevents loss of water by evaporation.

(ii) It protects plant from the invasion of parasites and other harmful microorganisms. [½ ×2]

3 **The transportation system of plants is composed of complex permanent tissue. They have their transportation system within themselves. Justify in detail with appropriate diagrams.**

Sol. Refer to text on page no 123-124.

4 **Explain the significance of the following**

(i) Hair-like structures on epidermal cells.

(ii) Epidermis has a thick waxy coating of cutin in desert plants.

(iii) Small pores in epidermis of leaf.

(iv) Numerous layers of epidermis in cactus.

(v) Presence of a chemical suberin in cork cells.

Sol. (i) Hair-like structures called root hairs on epidermal cells increase the total absorptive surface area and help in absorption of water and nutrients.

(ii) Cutin has a waterproof quality and helps in preventing water loss due to transpiration. It also protects plants from entry of pathogens, etc.

(iii) Stomata help in gaseous exchange and transpiration process.

(iv) Numerous layers of epidermis in cactus prevent water loss.

(v) Suberin makes cork cells impervious to gases and water. [1×5]

ASSESSMENT EXERCISE

Competency Focused (Objective) Questions

Multiple Choice Questions

1 Meristematic tissues are classified as apical, lateral and intercalary on the basis of which out of these?

(a) Shape (b) Dividing capacity
(c) Location (d) Size

2 The living simple tissue that provides support to the growing parts of a plant is

(a) sclerenchyma (b) collenchyma
(c) parenchyma (d) fibres

3 Which of the following is not a part of epidermal tissue system?

(a) Companion cells (b) Guard cells
(c) Root hairs (d) Stomata

4 Find out incorrect sentence. **Competency Based Que.**

(a) Parenchymatous tissues have intercellular spaces
(b) Collenchymatous tissues are irregularly thickened at corners
(c) Apical and intercalary meristems are permanent tissues
(d) Meristematic tissues, in its early stage, lack vacuoles

5 Aerenchyma in the aquatic plants provides

(a) mechanical strength to plants
(b) extra space for photosynthesis and storage of food
(c) flexibility to plants
(d) buoyancy to hydrophobic plants

Assertion-Reason Questions

Direction (Q. Nos. 6-7) *In each of the following questions, a statement of Assertion (A) is given by the corresponding statement of Reason (R). Of the statements, mark the correct answer as*

(a) Both A and R are true and R is the correct explanation of A
(b) Both A and R are true, but R is not the correct explanation of A
(c) A is true, but R is false
(d) A is false, but R is true

6 **Assertion** (A) Specialisation in cells are advantageous for the organisms.

Reason (R) It decreases the efficiency of an organism.

7 **Assertion** (A) Plants like grape vines are climbers with high percentage of bending capacity.

Reason (R) Flexibility in such plants is due to collenchyma.

Answers

1. (c) **2.** (b) **3.** (a) **4.** (c) **5.** (d)
6. (c) **7.** (a)

Case Based/Source Based Questions

Direction (Q. Nos. 8-11) *Answer the questions on the basis of your understanding of the following paragraph and related studied concepts.*

Simple permanent tissues are the type of tissues that are made up on only one type of cells. These are mainly found beneath the epidermis.

8 What are the different types of simple permanent tissues found in a plant?

9 Identify the below given figure and label the parts marked as *A*, *B*, *C*, and *D*.

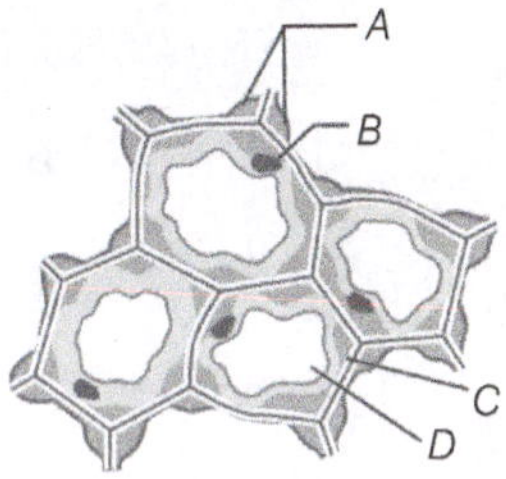

10 State the importance of sclerenchyma in plants.

11 The cell walls of selerenchyma tissue are thickened. Give the name of a chemical substance responsible for this.

Constructed Response (Descriptive) Questions

Very Short Answer Type Questions

12 Give one similarity between permanent and meristematic tissues.

13 Name a component of phloem that stores food.

Short Answer Type Questions

14 Bark of a tree is impervious to gases and water. Give reasons. **Competency Based Que.**

15 Where are companion cells located in plants? Mention their functions.

Long Answer Type Questions

16 (i) You can very easily bend the stem of a plant without breaking it. Name the tissue in the plant, which makes it possible. Where is it located? State any two characteristics of the cells of this tissue.

(ii) Draw a labelled diagram of the transverse section of this tissue.

17 (i) Identify the structures marked below as *A*, *B* and *C*.

(ii) Complete the labelling of each structure.

(iii) Write the function of each structure.

Competency Based Que.

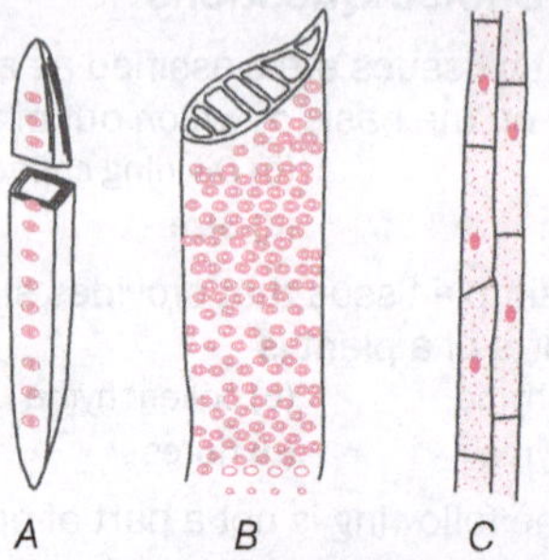

18 Name the tissue and write characteristic feature of following.

(i) Has prominent middle lamella.

(ii) Transports water and minerals in plants.

CHAPTER 06(b)

Animal Tissues

A group of similar cells, performing the same function and having a common origin are called tissues. The term tissue was given by **Bichat**.

The structural and functional organisations are different in both plants and animals, i.e. plants remain stationary, while animals move as per their needs. Thus, each of them possesses different feeding methods and are differently adapted. Based on these habits, the tissues in plants and animals are strikingly different.

Types of Animal Tissues

On the basis of the different functions they perform, animal tissues are classified into four basic types. These are as follows

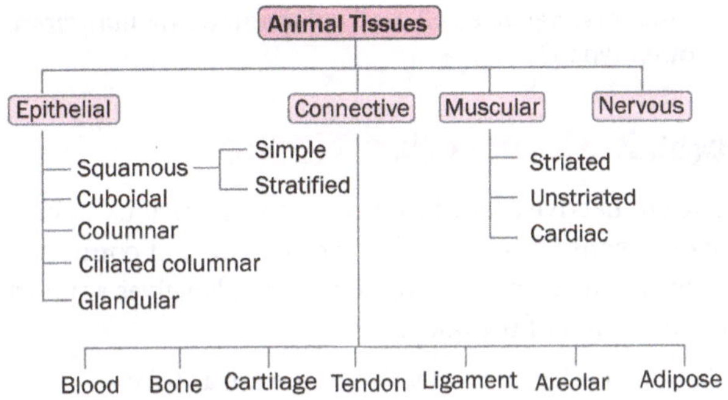

6(b).1 Epithelial Tissue

It is the covering or protective tissue of the animal body. This tissue covers most organs and cavities within the body. It also forms a barrier to keep different body systems separated from each other.

Important characteristics of epithelial tissue are as follows

- In this tissue, cells are tightly packed and form a continuous sheet.
- There is almost no intercellular space between them.
- They have a very small amount of cementing material between them.
- The epithelium is separated from underlying tissue by an extracellular fibrous basement membrane.
- The skin, lining of mouth, lining of blood vessels, alveoli and kidney tubules, all are made up of epithelial tissue.

On the basis of shape of the cells and their arrangement, epithelial tissues are further classified as follows

(i) Squamous Epithelium

Squamous (*Squama* means scale) is made up of simple flat kind of cells. It is further categorised into two types

(a) Simple Squamous Epithelium

- It is single-layered and closely fitted epithelium. The cells are very thin and flat and appear as tiles over the floor.
- It forms a delicate lining of blood vessels and lung alveoli, where substance transport occurs through a selectively permeable membrane.
- It also covers the oesophagus and the lining of mouth and the blood vessels.

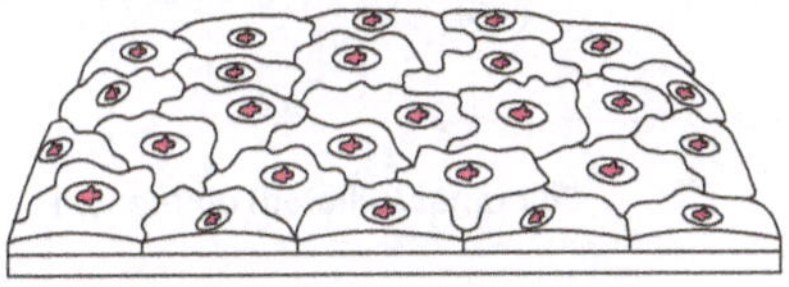

Simple squamous epithelium

(b) Stratified Squamous Epithelium

- Cells are arranged in the pattern of layers to prevent wear and tear.

- It is found in the outer side of skin as it is highly resistant to mechanical injury.

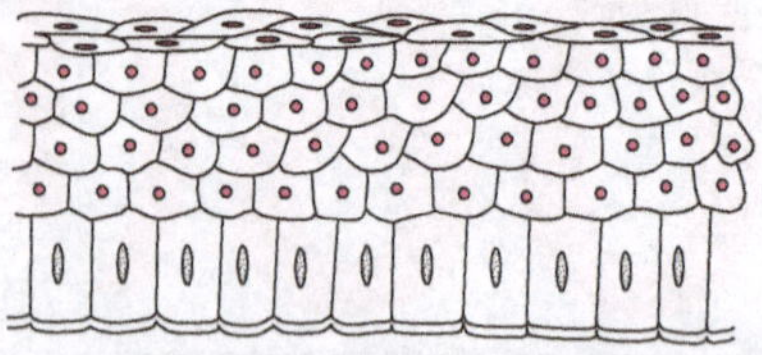

Stratified squamous epithelium

(ii) Cuboidal Epithelium

- It is made up of cube-shaped cells.
- It forms the lining of kidney tubules and the ducts of salivary glands, where it provides mechanical support.

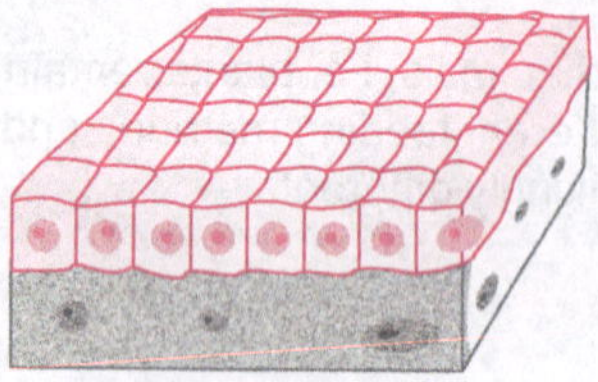

Cuboidal epithelium

(iii) Columnar Epithelium

- Columnar (columnar means pillar-like) epithelium is made up of tall, pillar-like cells.
- It usually lines the surfaces where absorption and secretion occurs. For example, inner lining of intestine.
- It facilitates the movement across epithelial barrier.

(iv) Ciliated Columnar Epithelium

- When columnar epithelial cells posses cilia (hair-like projections) on its outer surface, it is called ciliated columnar epithelium.
- It is found in the respiratory tract and also in the lining of oviducts, sperm ducts, etc.
- The cilia have the ability to move. Their movement pushes substances like mucus forward to clear it.

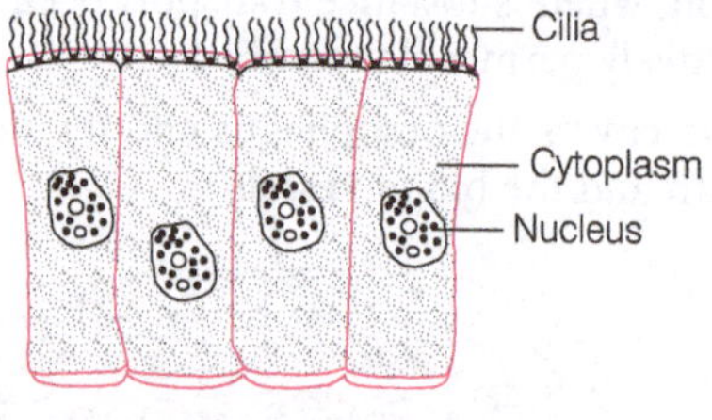

Columnar (Ciliated) epithelium

(v) Glandular Epithelium

- It is a modified columnar epithelium. Its cells are modified to secrete chemical substances at the epithelial surface.
- Sometimes, portion of the epithelial tissue folds inwards. As a result the formation of a multicellular gland occurs.

Functions of Epithelial Tissue

It performs following important functions

(i) It protects the underlying cells from drying, injury, infections and from the harmful effects of chemicals.

(ii) It plays a vital role in regulating the exchange of materials between the body and the external environment and also between different body parts.

(iii) It helps in absorption of water and nutrients and in diffusion of gases.

(iv) It helps in the elimination of waste products from the body.

Try These 6(b).1

1. **Name the structure which separates epithelium from underlying tissue.**
2. **In what areas of the body does simple squamous epithelium serves a protective function?**
3. **What type of epithelium is found in areas where absorption and secretion takes place?**
4. **The tissue '*X*' found in the respiratory tract facilitates the forward movement of mucus for effective clearance. What is the name of tissue '*X*'?**
5. **What distinguishes ciliated columnar epithelium from other types?**

6(b).2 Connective Tissue

The connective tissue binds or connects various tissue and body organs with each other. For example, it connects two or more bones, muscles to bones and also gives support to various parts of the body.

Characteristics of connective tissue are as follows

- The cells of connective tissue are loosely packed.
- These cells are living and are found embedded in an intercellular matrix that may either be jelly-like fluid, dense or rigid in nature.
- The nature of matrix differs in concordance with the function of the particular connective tissue.

Various types of connective tissues are as follows

(i) Blood

It is a fluid connective tissue that links different parts of the body. It contains fluid (liquid) matrix called **plasma** in which **RBCs** (Red Blood Corpuscles), **WBCs** (White Blood Corpuscles) and **platelets** are suspended.

Plasma also contains proteins, salts and hormones.

Blood flow transports nutrients, gases, digested food, waste material, hormones and vitamins to various tissues of the body. It also conducts heat and regulates body temperature.

The properties shown by different blood cells in the body are as follows

- **RBCs** help in transport of respiratory gases, oxygen and carbon dioxide with the help of haemoglobin to and from the various parts of our body. The average lifespan of RBCs is about 120 days.
- **WBCs** help to fight with diseases by producing antibodies.
- **Blood platelets** help in the clotting of blood.

Different types of blood cells are shown below

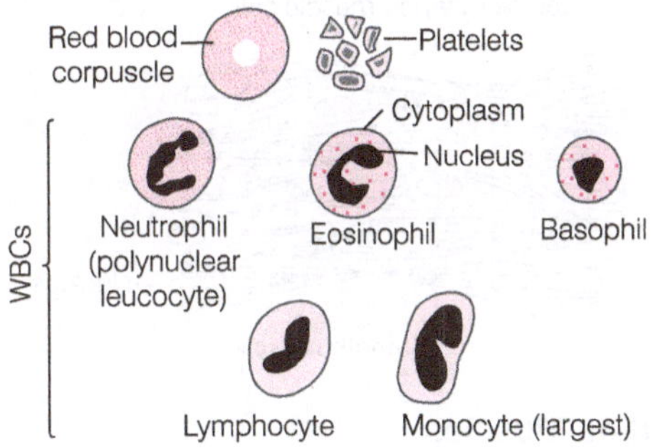

Different types of blood cells

(ii) Bone

It is another example of a connective tissue. It is a very strong and non-flexible tissue. Bone cells are embedded in a hard matrix that is composed of calcium and phosphorus compounds. It forms the framework that supports the body. It also anchors the muscles and supports the main organs.

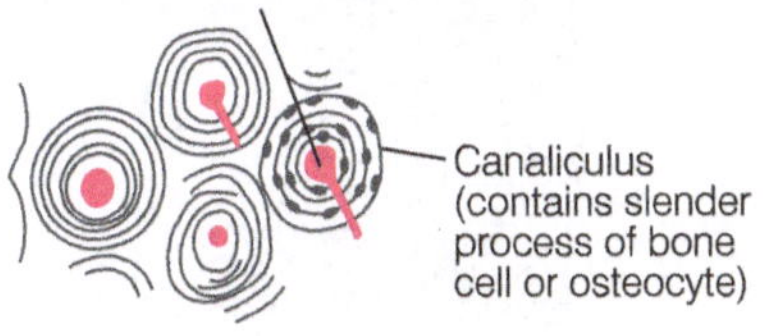

Compact bone

(iii) Ligaments

Two bones can be connected to each other by another type of connective tissue called **ligament**. A ligament is very elastic and has considerable strength. It contains very little matrix.

Ligaments strengthen the joints and permit normal movement. Their overstretching may lead to sprain.

(iv) Tendons

These are strong and inelastic structures, which join skeletal muscles to bones. These are composed of white fibrous tissues with limited flexibility, but has great strength.

(v) Cartilage

It is a specialised connective tissue having widely spaced cells. It has a solid matrix which is composed of proteins and sugars.

It is present in nose, ear, trachea and larynx. Cartilage provides smoothness to the bone surfaces at the joints. It also provides support and flexibility to body parts.

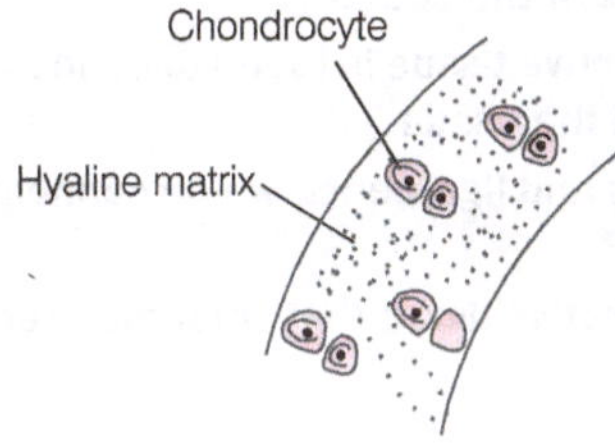

Hyaline cartilage

(vi) Areolar Tissue

It is a supporting and packing tissue found between the organs lying in the body cavity. It is located between skin and muscles, around blood vessels and nerves and in the bone marrow. It fills the space inside the organs, supports internal organs and helps in the repair of tissues.

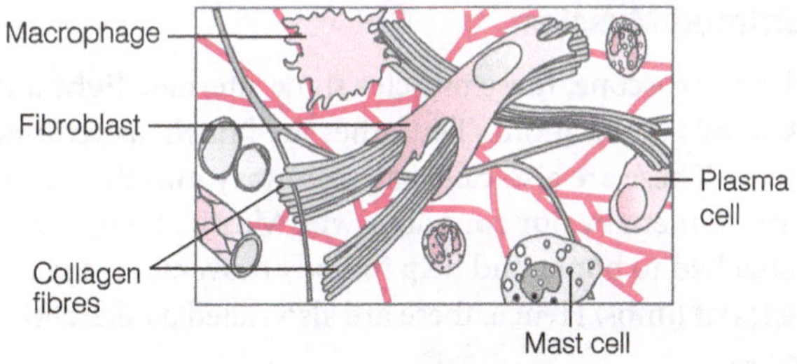

Areolar tissue

(vii) Adipose Tissue

It is located below the skin and between the internal organs.

It serves as a fat reservoir. Thus, cells of this tissue are filled with fat globules. It acts as an insulator due to the storage of fats.

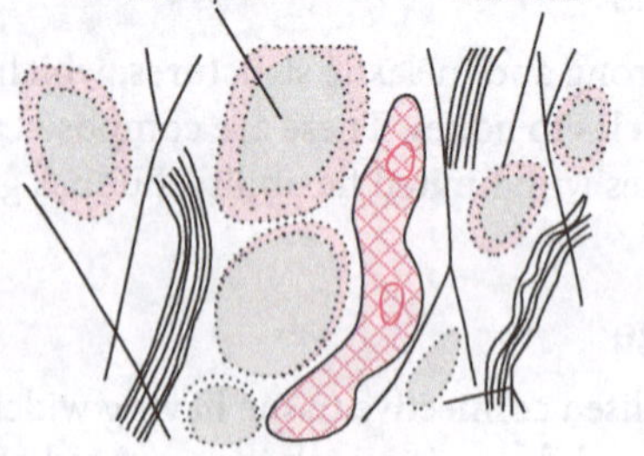

Adipose tissue

Try These 6(b).2

1. **What comprises the fluid matrix of blood ?**
2. **Which connective tissue attaches the muscles and supports the main organs of the body?**
3. **A type of connective tissue is found to connect two bones in our body. Name the tissue.**
4. **Among tendons and ligaments, which connective tissue has more flexibility?**
5. **Name the connective tissue that smoothens bone surfaces at joints.**

6(b).3 Muscular Tissue

It consists of elongated cells, called **muscle fibres.** This tissue is mainly responsible for the movement in our body. It contains special type of proteins called **contractile proteins,** which causes movement of muscles by contraction and relaxation.

Different types of muscular tissues are given below

(i) Striated Muscles

Under microscope, these muscles show alternate **light** and **dark bands** or striations. Thus, they are known as **striated muscles.** These are also called as **voluntary muscles** as we can move them by our conscious will. Mostly, these muscles are attached to bones and help in body movement, e.g. muscles of limbs. Hence, these are also called as **skeletal muscles.**

The cells of such muscles are long, cylindrical, unbranched and multinucleated (having many nuclei).

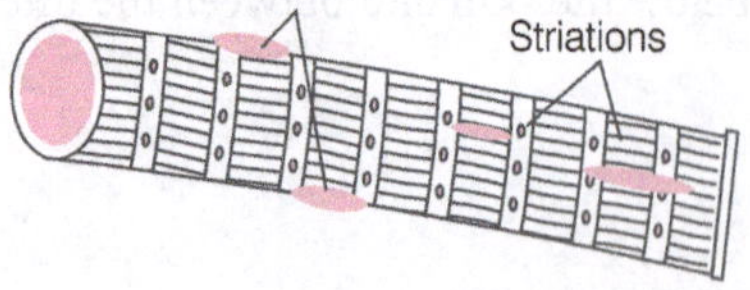

Striated muscle

(ii) Smooth Muscles

These muscles do not show any dark or light band. Hence, these are also called **unstriated muscles.**

These muscles are also called **involuntary muscles** as they do not show movement as per our will.

The movement of food in the alimentary canal, contraction and relaxation of blood vessels are involuntary movements.

Smooth muscles are found in the iris of eye, in ureters, in bronchi of the lungs, etc.

The cells constituting these muscles are long with pointed ends (spindle-shaped) and uninucleate (single nucleus).

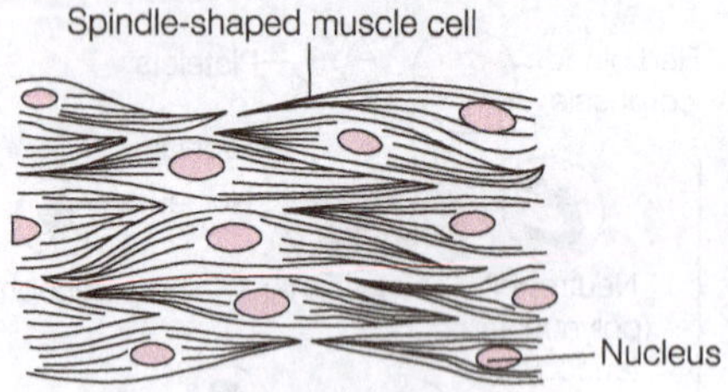

Smooth muscle

(iii) Cardiac Muscles

These are involuntary muscles present only in our **heart.** These muscles perform rhythmic contraction and relaxation throughout the life. The cells constituting cardiac muscles are cylindrical, uninucleate and branched. Cardiac muscles have stripes of light and dark bands.

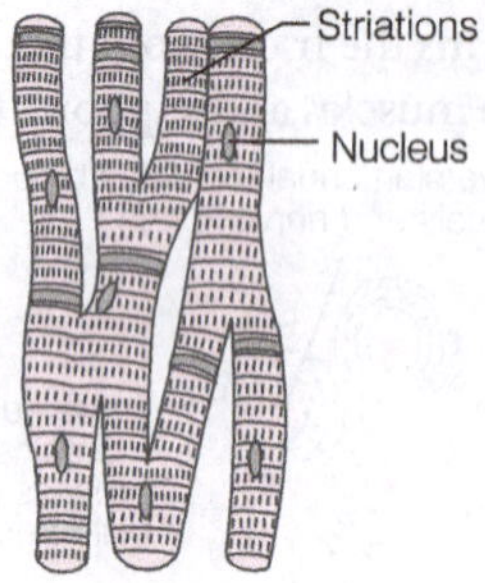

Cardiac muscle

6(b).4 Nervous Tissue

The tissue that receives stimulus and transmits it from one part of the tissue to other are called nervous tissues.The cells that constitute nervous tissue are called **nerve cells** or **neurons.**

These are highly specialised for receiving stimulus and then transmitting it very rapidly from one place to another within the body itself. Brain, spinal cord and nerves are composed of nervous tissue.

An individual nerve cell or a neuron may be upto a metre long and is composed of three major parts, i.e.,

(i) **Cell body** It consists of cytoplasm and nucleus.

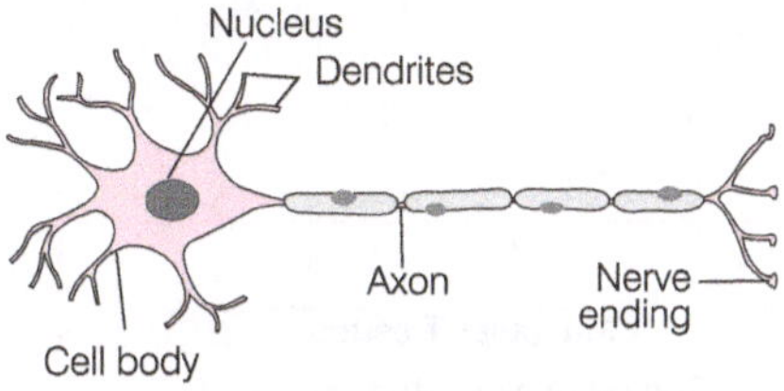

Neuron : Unit of nervous tissue

(ii) **Axon** It is a single, long conducting fibre extending from cell body. It transmits impulses away from the cell body.

(iii) **Dendrites** These are short branched fibres of the neuron, which receive nerve impulses.

Many nerve fibres bound together by connective tissue are made up of a nerve. The signal that passes along the nerve fibre is called **nerve impulse**. It allows us to move our muscles according to our will. Combination of nerve and muscle tissue in animals is of fundamental importance as it causes rapid movement in response to stimuli.

Differences between Plant Tissues and Animal Tissues

Plant tissues	Animal tissues
In plants, dead supportive tissues are more abundant as compared to living tissues.	In multicellular animals, living tissues are more common as compared to dead tissues.
They require less maintenance energy as they are autotrophic and can make their own food.	They require more maintenance energy as they are heterotrophic and have to move in search of food.
There is a differentiation of tissues into meristematic and permanent tissues, which are localised in certain regions of plant based on their dividing capacity.	Such differentiation is absent in animals as their growth is uniform.
Due to activity of meristematic tissue, plants continue to grow throughout their life.	Animals do not show growth after reaching maturity. Reparative growth is however present.
Organisation of plant tissues is simple.	Organisation of animal tissues is complex with the development of more specialised and localised organs and organ systems.
Tissue organisation is meant for stationary habit of plants.	Tissue organisation is targeted towards high mobility of animals.

Try These 6(b).3

1. **Name the special type of proteins that are responsible for contraction and relaxation of muscles.**
2. **Which muscle fibre has long cylindrical, unbranched and multinucleated cells?**
3. **Name the type of muscles that allow movement of excretory fluid in our body.**
4. **Which muscles perform rhythmic contraction and relaxation throughout the life?**
5. **Name the part of neuron that are involved in the transmission of nerve impulses.**

Mind Map

Animal Tissues

Epithelial Tissues
It is the covering or protective tissue, which are tightly packed. They are present in skin, lining of mouth. etc.

1. **Squamous Epithelium** Simple, flat kind of epithelium forms a delicate lining of skin.
   It is further divided into two types as simple squamous epithelium and stratified squamous epithelium.
2. **Cuboidal Epithelium** Cube shaped cells have rounded nuclei, forms lining of the kidney tubules and ducts of salivary glands providing mechanical support.
3. **Columnar Epithelium** Tall, pillar like cells have elongated nuclei. Usually found in inner lining of intestine, where absorption and secretion occurs.
4. **Ciliated Columnar Epithelium** Cells have cilia, hair like projections found on the outer surface of epithelial cells.
5. **Glandular Epithelium** Epithelium acquire additional specialisation known as gland cells, can secrete substances at the epithelial surface.

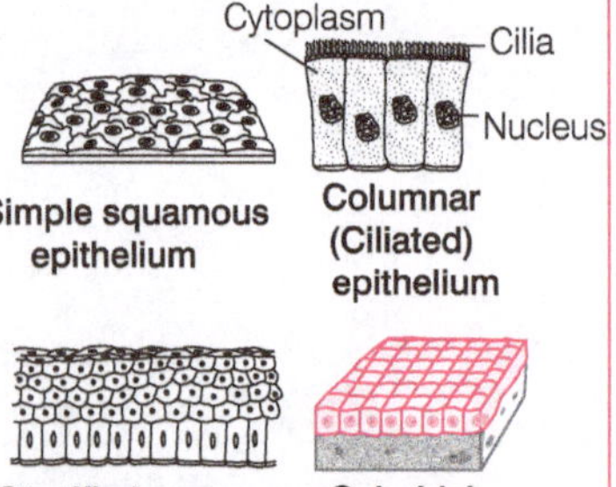

Simple squamous epithelium | **Columnar (Ciliated) epithelium** | **Stratified squamous epithelium** | **Cuboidal epithelium**

Connective Tissues
They connect various body organs.

1. **Blood** A liquid that links different parts of the body.
2. **Bone** Forms the framework that supports the body.
3. **Tendon** Joins skeletal muscles to bones.
4. **Ligament** It connects two bones together.
5. **Cartilage** Provides smoothness to the bone surfaces at the joints.

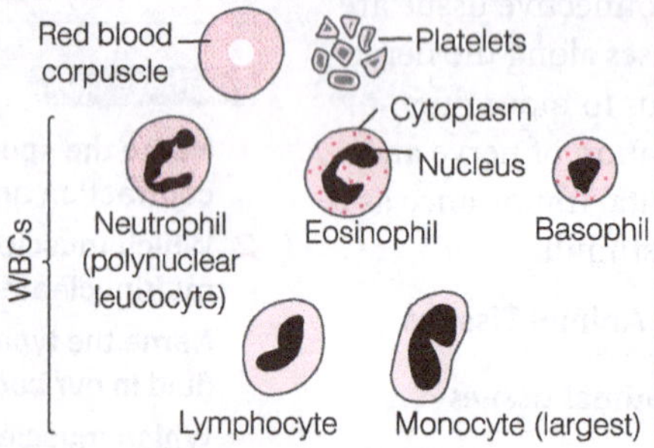

Different types of blood cells

Compact bone

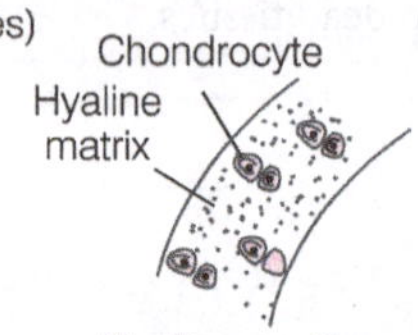

Hyaline cartilage

Muscular Tissues
Consist of elongated cells and responsible for movement.

1. **Striated Muscles** Mostly attached to bones and helps in body movement.
2. **Smooth Muscles** Mostly involved in the involuntary movement in the body.
3. **Cardiac Muscles** Present in heart, shows rhythmic contraction and relaxation throughout life.

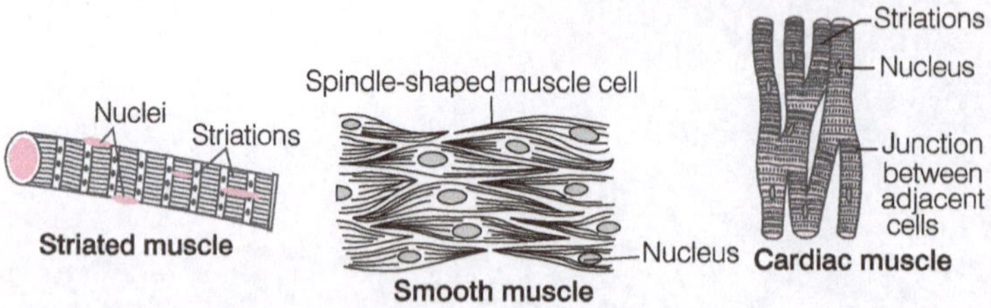

Striated muscle | **Smooth muscle** | **Cardiac muscle**

Nervous Tissues
These enables body to respond against stimulus. They transmit stimuli from one place to another within body, e.g. in vital organs.

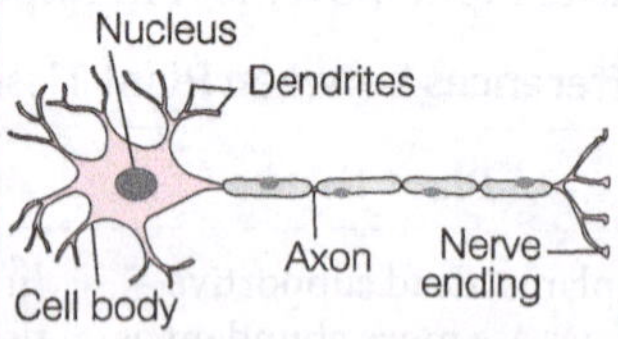

NCERT FOLDER

Complete Explanations of all NCERT's Questions

Intext Questions

Q.1 Name the tissue responsible for movement in our body. **Page 69**

Sol. Muscular tissue is responsible for movement in our body.

Q.2 What does a neuron look like? **Page 69**

Sol. A neuron, possesses a cell body with a nucleus and cytoplasm, from which long thin hair-like parts called dendrites arise. And a single long part called the axon.

Q.3 Give three features of cardiac muscles. **Page 69**

Sol. Three features of cardiac muscles are listed below

(i) These are involuntary muscles.

(ii) Cells of these muscles are cylindrical, branched and uninucleate.

(iii) These muscles shows rhythmic contraction and relaxation throughout the life.

Q.4 What are the functions of areolar tissue? **Page 69**

Sol. Functions of areolar tissue are as follows

(i) It fills the space inside the organs and supports internal organs.

(ii) It helps in the repair of the tissues.

Exercise

Q.1 Diagrammatically show the difference between the three types of muscle fibres.

Sol. The difference between the three types of muscles fibres are given below.

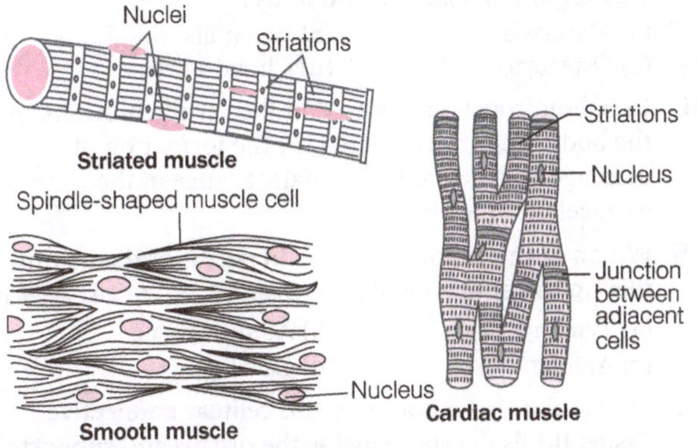

Q.2 What is the specific function of cardiac muscle?

Sol. Cardiac muscles contract and relax rhythmically throughout the life.

Q.3 Differentiate between striated, smooth and cardiac muscles on the basis of their structure and site/ location in the body.

Sol. The differences between striated, smooth and cardiac muscles are as follows

Types	Striated muscles	Smooth muscles	Cardiac muscles
Structures	These are made up of long, cylindrical, unbranched and multinucleate cells.	These muscles are made up of long, uninucleate cells with pointed ends.	These are made up of cylindrical, branched and uninucleate cells.
	These show alternate light and dark striations.	These do not show striations.	These muscles show faint striations.
Site/ Locatioos	These are located in limbs and are mostly attached to the bones to help in body movement.	These are mostly present in walls of alimentary canal, blood vessels, ureters, bronchi of the lungs and in the iris of eyes.	These are present only in the walls of heart.

Q.4 Draw a labelled diagram of a neuron.

Sol. Refer to fig. on page no. 139.

Q.5 Name the following.

(i) Tissue that forms the inner lining of the mouth.

(ii) Tissue that connects muscle to bone in humans.

(iii) Tissue that stores fat in our body.

(iv) Connective tissue with a fluid matrix.

(v) Tissue present in the brain.

Sol. (i) Simple squamous epithelium

(ii) Tendons

(iii) Adipose tissue

(iv) Blood

(v) Nervous tissue.

Q.6 Identify the type of tissue in following: Skin, bone, lining of kidney tubule.

Sol. **Skin** Stratified squamous epithelium

Bone Connective tissue

Lining of kidney tubule Cuboidal epithelium

REVIEW EXERCISE

Including Competency Based Questions

Competency Focused (Objective) Questions

Multiple Choice Questions

1 Choose the wrong statement. Competency Based Que.

(a) The nature of matrix differs according to the function of the tissue

(b) Fats are stored below the skin and in between the internal organs

(c) Epithelial tissues have intercellular spaces between them

(d) Cells of striated muscles are multinucleate and unbranched

Sol. (c) Statement given in option (c) is incorrect. In the epithelial tissues, cells are tightly packaged and form a continuous sheet. There is almost no intercellular space between them. Rest other statements are correct.

2 Lining of kidney tubules is made up of

(a) stratified columnar epithelium

(b) simple cuboidal epithelium

(c) stratified squamous epithelium

(d) simple columnar epithelium

Sol. (b) Lining of kidney tubules and ducts of salivary glands are made up of cuboidal epithelium (cube-shaped cells having round nuclei). It provides mechanical support and also helps in absorption, excretion and secretion.

3 Choose the correctly matched pair.

(a) Inner lining of salivary ducts– Ciliated epithelium

(b) Moist surface of buccal cavity– Glandular epithelium

(c) Tubular parts of nephrons– Cuboidal epithelium

(d) Inner surface of bronchioles– Squamous epithelium

Sol. (c) Cuboidal epithelium is present in the tubular parts of nephron. These cells often form microvilli to increase the absorptive surface area of cell.

4 Intestine absorb the digested food materials. What type of epithelial cells are responsible for this? Competency Based Que.

(a) Stratified squamous epithelium

(b) Columnar epithelium

(c) Spindle fibres

(d) Cuboidal epithelium

Sol. (b) Columnar epithelium is found in the inner lining of intestine. It is responsible for the absorption of digested food materials in intestine.

5 Bone matrix is rich in

(a) fluoride and calcium

(b) calcium and phosphorus

(c) calcium and potassium

(d) phosphorus and potassium

Sol. (b) Bone is very strong and non-flexible tissue. Its cells are embedded in a hard matrix that is composed of calcium and phosphorus compounds.

6 A person met with an accident in which two long bones of hand were dislocated. Which among the following may be the possible reason? Competency Based Que.

(a) Tendon break
(b) Break of skeletal muscle
(c) Ligament break
(d) Areolar tissue break

Sol. (c) Ligaments connect the two bones. Therefore, breakage of ligament causes the dislocation of bones.

7 Select the incorrect sentence. NCERT Exemplar

(a) Blood has matrix containing proteins, salts and hormones

(b) Two bones are connected with ligament

(c) Tendons are non-fibrous tissue and fragile

(d) Cartilage is a form of connective tissue

Sol. (c) A tendon is a white fibrous tissue which has great strength, but limited flexibility. They join skeletal muscles to bones.

8 Which of the following cells is found in the cartilaginous tissue of the body?

(a) Mast cells
(b) Basophils
(c) Osteocytes
(d) Chondrocytes

Sol. (d) Chondrocytes are found in the cartilaginous tissue of the body. They are essential for the formation of cartilage matrix and in the maintenance of the extracellular matrix.

9 Which of the following helps in repair of tissue and fills up the space inside the organ? NCERT Exemplar

(a) Tendon
(b) Adipose tissue
(c) Areolar
(d) Cartilage

Sol. (c) Areolar tissue is a loose and cellular connective tissue. It fills the space inside the organs and supports internal organs. It also helps in the repair of tissues.

10 While doing work and running, you move your organs like hands, legs, etc. Which among the following is correct? **NCERT Exemplar**

(a) Smooth muscles contract and pull the ligament to move the bones
(b) Smooth muscles contract and pull the tendon to move the bones
(c) Skeletal muscles contract and pull the ligament to move the bones
(d) Skeletal muscles contract and pull the tendon to move the bones

Sol. (d) While doing work and running, skeletal muscles contract and pull the tendon (which connects muscles to bones) to move the bone.

11 The muscular tissue which function throughout the life continuously without fatigue is **NCERT Exemplar**

(a) skeletal muscle (b) cardiac muscle
(c) smooth muscle (d) voluntary muscle

Sol. (b) Cardiac muscles functions throughout the life continuously without fatigue. These muscles perform rhythmic contraction and relaxation.

12 Which muscles act involuntarily?

(i) Striated muscles
(ii) Smooth muscles
(iii) Cardiac muscles
(iv) Skeletal muscles

(a) (i) and (ii) (b) (ii) and (iii)
(c) (iii) and (iv) (d) (i) and (iv)

Sol. (b) Smooth muscles and cardiac muscles act involuntarily. The muscles which we cannot move as per our will are called involuntary muscles.

13 Nervous tissue is not found in

(a) brain (b) spinal cord (c) tendons (d) nerves

Sol. (c) Brain, spinal cord and nerves are composed of nervous tissue. It is not found in tendons.

Assertion-Reason Questions

Direction (Q. Nos. 1-5) ***In each of the following questions, a statement of Assertion (A) is given by the corresponding statement of Reason (R). Of the statements, mark the correct answer as***

(a) Both A and R are true and R is the correct explanation of A
(b) Both A and R are true, but R is not the correct explanation of A
(c) A is true, but R is false
(d) A is false, but R is true

1 Assertion (A) Blood is a fluid connective tissue.
Reason (R) It is a motile connective tissue which connects all the tissues and organs with each other.

Sol. (a) Both A and R are true and R is the correct explanation of A.

2 Assertion (A) The movements of alimentary canal, iris of the eye and bronchi of lungs are not under our will.
Reason (R) These are controlled by voluntary muscles.

Sol. (c) A is true, but R is false. R can be corrected as

These are controlled by involuntary muscles. These muscles are not under our control, e.g. alimentary canal, iris of the eye and bronchi of lungs.

3 Assertion (A) Ciliated epithelium helps in the movement of particles.
Reason (R) Cilia present on epithelium have the ability to move.

Sol. (a) Both A and R are true and R is the correct explanation of A.

4 Assertion (A) Two bones are connected to one another by a type of connective tissue.
Reason (R) Tendon is a type of loose connective tissue that joins two bones together.

Sol. (c) A is true, but R is false. R can be corrected as

A ligament is a connective tissue that connects two bones together to form a joint.

5 Assertion (A) Axon and dendrites are special features of neurons.
Reason (R) They help in the rapid conduction of nerve impulses.

Sol. (a) Both A and R are true and R is the correct explanation of A.

Case Based/Source Based Question

1 In the given image, a girl is performing a classical dance move. This activity requires strength, coordination and flexibility. Observe the image carefully and answer the following questions.

(i) Which muscles are primarily involved in supporting this activity?

Sol. The skeletal muscles (voluntary muscles) are primarily involved in this activity, as they control the movement of the limbs, balance and posture required for dance. [1]

(ii) What is the structural characteristic of these muscles?

Sol. Voluntary muscles are striated (striped) in appearance and are composed of long cylindrical fibres with multiple nuclei. [1]

(iii) Name two functions of these muscles in daily activities.

Sol. Voluntary muscles help in locomotion (e.g. walking, running) and performing skilled movements (e.g. writing, dancing). [2]

Constructed Response (Descriptive) Questions

Very Short Answer Type Questions

1 Stratified squamous epithelium is abundantly found in the outer side of skin. What is the advantage of this arrangement in living body?

Sol. Stratified squamous epithelium is multilayered, thus capable of preventing the wear and tear occurring in living body.

2 Which body cell provides resistance against infection and how?

Sol. WBCs provide resistance against infection by producing antibodies in the body.

3 Blood, bone, ligaments, cartilages, etc., are all types of connective tissue present in the body with different nature of matrix. Why? **Competency Based Que.**

Sol. The nature of matrix of different connective tissues differs in concordance with their specific function, e.g. blood transports nutrient, gases, etc., hence it is a fluid tissue. Where as bone forms the frame work that supports the body, hence it has hard matrix.

4 Name the connective tissue, which provides smoothness to the bone surfaces at the joints. Where it is present in the body?

Sol. Cartilage provides smoothness to the bone surfaces at the joints. It is present the in nose, ear and trachea.

5 What is the prominent function of adipose tissue?

Sol. It serves as a fat reservoir, keeps visceral organs in position and acts as an insulator.

6 Differentiate the following activities on the basis of voluntary (V) or involuntary (IV) muscles.

I. Jumping of frog. **NCERT Exemplar**

II. Pumping of the heart.

III. Writing with hand.

IV. Movement of chocolate in your intestine.

Sol. I. V II. IV

III. V IV. IV [½ × 4]

7 Name the following

(i) Multinucleate muscle.

(ii) Muscle with intercalated discs.

Sol. (i) Skeletal muscle. (ii) Cardiac muscle. [1 + 1]

8 What will happen if the cardiac muscles stop performing the rhythmic contraction and relaxation in living body? **Competency Based Que.**

Sol. The heart will stop beating and the organism will die.

9 Given below *A* and *B* are animal tissues. Identify them and write one function of each.

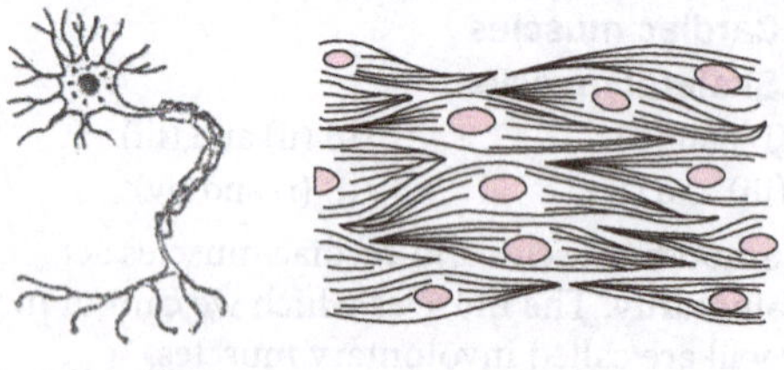

(A) (B)

Sol. *A*–Neuron (Nervous tissue)

B–Unstriated muscles (Muscular tissue)

Function

A–It receives stimulus and transmits it from one part of the body to other part of body. [1]

B–It is responsible for the movement in our body. For example, movement of food in alimentary canal. [1]

Short Answer Type Questions

1 Which is the protective tissue that is present in the animal body? State its two functions.

Sol. The protective tissue present in animal body is epithelial tissue. [1]

Its major functions are as follows

(i) It protects underlying cells from drying, injury and infections. [1]

(ii) It helps in elimination of waste products from the body. [1]

2 Name the type of epithelium present in respiratory tract. What is its specialisation?

Sol. Ciliated columnar epithelium is present in respiratory tract of human. It has specialised hair-like projections called cilia which help in the movement of substances and mucus in the forward direction.

3 Give three differences between epithelial tissue and connective tissue.

Sol. Differences between epithelial and connective tissues are as follows

Epithelial tissue	Connective tissue
It is the covering tissue and protects body from infections, injury, etc.	It is connective tissue as it connects various body organs.
Cells are tightly packed.	Cells are loosely packed.
Cells contain very little or no intercellular matrix.	Space between cells is filled with matrix (solid or fluid).

[1×3]

4 Mention three different types of blood cells with their functions. Draw diagrams also.

Sol. Three different types of blood cells with their function are as follows

(i) **Red Blood Cells** (RBCs) It contains haemoglobin, help in the transportation of gases, nutrients, hormones, etc. [1]

(ii) **White Blood Cells** (WBCs) Integral part of immune system, help in fighting diseases by producing antibodies and engulfing the germs and pathogens. [1]

(iii) **Platelets** Help in the clotting of blood.

For diagram, refer to page no. 137. [1]

5 What happens, when Competency Based Que.

(i) formation of cork in older stem does not occur.

(ii) apical meristem is damaged in plants.

(iii) blood platelets are removed from blood.

Sol. (i) If the formation of cork does not occur in older stems, then the outer tissue will rupture due to the increase in girth and plant will get infected by the diseases. [1]

(ii) If apical meristem get damaged in plants, the growth of plant will not occur. [1]

(iii) Blood clotting will not occur at the site of injury. The bleeding will continue and a significant loss of blood may lead to death. [1]

6 Give the differences between tendon and ligament.

Sol. The differences between tendon and ligament are as follows

Tendon	Ligament
It is strong and non-flexible in nature.	It is elastic and flexible in nature.
It joins muscles to bones.	It joins two bones.

7 State the functions of skeletal connective tissue.

Sol. The functions of skeletal connective tissue are as follows

(i) It gives definite shape to the body. [1]

(ii) It protects the vital organs of the body, e.g. brain. [1]

(iii) It provides a surface for the attachment of muscles to increase their efficiency. [1]

8 Animals of colder regions and fishes of cold water have thicker layer of subcutaneous fat. Describe why. Competency Based Que.

Sol. Animals of colder regions and fishes of cold water have thicker layer of subcutaneous fat because fat acts as an insulator and prevents the loss of heat from their body during cold climatic conditions. Thus, it helps in maintaining the temperature of the body.

9 Write a note about structure and significance of striated muscles with diagram. Competency Based Que.

Sol. Cells of striated muscles are long, cylindrical, unbranched and multinucleate, e.g. muscle of limbs. They show alternate light and dark bands or striations (when stained appropriately). The structure of striated muscles is shown below

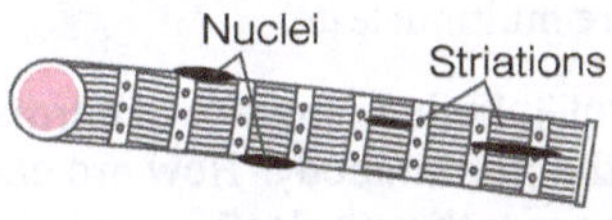

Striated muscle [2]

Striated muscles are voluntary muscles, i.e. we can move these muscles according to our conscious will. These are mostly attached to bones and help in body movement. [1]

10 Draw a labelled diagram of unstriated muscle tissue and mention its occurrence, features and functions.

Sol. The diagram of unstriated muscle tissue (Refer to fig. on page no. 138).

Occurrence These tissues are found in the walls of alimentary canal, urinary bladder, oesophagus, iris of eye and bronchi, etc. [1]

Features

(i) They are unbranched and non-striated.

(ii) Cells are long, thin and spindle-shaped.

(iii) Each cell has a single central nucleus. [1]

Functions

(i) They produce contractions in the wall of alimentary canal and help to push the food down.

(ii) They carry out the movement in urinary bladder and gall bladder. [1]

11 Name the kinds of muscles found in your limbs and lungs. How do they differ from each other structurally and functionally?

Sol. (i) The striated muscles are found in our limbs.

Structure Cells are long and cylindrical in shape, presence of dark and light bands, multinucleate and unbranched.

Function Responsible for voluntary movements. [1½]

(ii) The smooth or non-striated muscles are found in our lungs.

Structure Cells are spindle-shaped, absence of striation, uninucleate and unbranched.

Function Responsible for involuntary movements. [1½]

12 Which type of muscle, smooth or striated is found in the iris of eye? Why are smooth muscles called involuntary muscles? In what way they are different from striated muscles with respect to number of nuclei?

Sol. Smooth muscles are found in the iris of eye. These muscles do not work according to our will. So, they are known as involuntary muscles.

Smooth muscles are uninucleate, whereas striated muscles are multinucleate. [1×3]

13 Draw a well-labelled diagram of cardiac muscle found in the human body. How are cardiac muscles similar to smooth muscles?

Sol. Refer to text on page no. 138.

14 What are neurons? Where are they found in the body? What function do they perform in the body of an organism?

Sol. Neurons are the structural and functional units of nervous system. These are found in brain, spinal cord and nerves. [1]

Functions

(i) They coordinate various body parts during any body function.

(ii) They control all the activities of the body.

(iii) They transmit message in the form of nerve impulses. [2]

15 Differentiate between axon and dendrite.

Sol. Differences between axon and dendrite are as follows

Axon	Dendrite
It carries impulses away from the cell body.	It carries impulses towards the cell body.
It is long and may or may not be branched.	It is short and always branched.

16 Write functions of the following.

(i) Areolar connective tissues

(ii) Neurons

(iii) Adipose connective tissues

Sol. (i) **Areolar connective tissues**

These tissues fill the space inside the organs and supports internal organs of the body. They also help in repair of tissues. [1]

(ii) **Neurons**

These are the fundamental cells of nervous tissue. They are highly specialised for being stimulated and then transmitting the stimulus very rapidly from one place to another within the body. [1]

(iii) **Adipose connective tissues**

These are fat storing tissue found below the skin between internal organs. The cells of this tissue are filled with fat globules. Due to storage of fats, these act as an insulators. [1]

17 Give one function of each of the following.

(i) Contractile proteins in muscles

(ii) Cardiac muscle fibres

Sol. (i) **Contractile proteins in muscles** These proteins contract and relax to cause movement in the body parts. [1½]

(ii) **Cardiac muscle fibres** These help in rhythmic contraction and relaxation of heart throughout the life. [1½]

Long Answer Type Questions

1 Describe the structure and function of different types of epithelial tissues. Draw diagram of each epithelial tissue.

Sol. Refer to text on page no. 135 and 136.

2 (i) What will happen if cells are not properly organised in tissue?

(ii) Under certain circumstances squamous epithelium is known as stratified squamous epithelium. Justify.

(iii) Draw the diagram of simple squamous and stratified epithelium. Competency Based Que.

Ans (i) Different organisms whether unicellular or multicellular need to perform many functions in the body such as respiration, digestion, locomotion.

In multicellular organisms, cells present in a group and specialised for one particular function form a tissue.

Some tissues help in growth, while others in locomotion and some in body movement. So, if cells are not organised in the tissues, then these process will become disorganised. There will be no coordination in the functioning of the cells and body. [2]

(ii) When simple squamous epithelium is arranged in a pattern of multilayers to prevent wear and tear, the epithelium is called stratified squamous epithelium, e.g. skin. [1]

(iii) Refer to text on page no. 135 and 136. [2]

3 Differentiate between bone and cartilage with respect to structure, function and location.

Sol. Differences between bone and cartilage are as follows

Point of differences	Bone	Cartilage
Structure	It is strong and non-flexible tissue, whose cells are embedded in a hard matrix, which is composed of calcium and phosphorus compounds.	It is soft and flexible tissue, whose solid matrix is composed of proteins and sugars. It also has widely spaced cells.
Function	It forms the framework that supports the body. It anchors the muscles that support the main organs of the body.	It smoothens bone surfaces at joints.
Location	It is present in skeletal system of vertebrates.	It is present in nose, ear, trachea and larynx.

4 (i) Describe adipose tissue with the help of diagram.

(ii) How is adipose tissue different from blood tissue?

Sol. (i) Refer to text on page nos. 137 and 138. [3]

(ii) Differences between adipose and blood tissue are as follows

Adipose tissue	Blood tissue
It is a loose connective tissue.	It is a fluid connective tissue.
The matrix contains fibres.	The matrix does not contain fibres.
It stores and metabolises fats.	It helps in the transport of substances and respiratory gases.

[2]

5 Differentiate between various types of muscular tissues. Draw appropriate diagrams.

Sol. Refer to text on page no. 138.

6 'We can control some of the actions of our body, but some are not in our control'. Comment on this statement. Competency Based Que.

Sol. Some of the actions like moving our limbs, fingers, neck, etc., can be controlled by our will. We can move these parts of our body whenever we want to, but some actions of our body like contraction and relaxation of heart, blinking of eye, etc., are not under our will, i.e. we cannot stop functioning of heart, if we want to do so.

The actions, which can be manipulated by our wishes are known as voluntary actions. The muscles, which can perform voluntary actions are voluntary muscles. These muscles are also called skeletal muscles or striated muscles.

These muscles are mostly attached to bones and help in body movement. Their cells are long, cylindrical, unbranched and multinucleate (having many nuclei). The actions, which are not under our control are known as involuntary actions.

These actions are performed by smooth muscles or involuntary muscles. Their cells are long with pointed ends (spindle-shaped) and uninucleate (single nucleus). Striated and smooth muscles (Refer to fig. on page no. 138).

7 Define nervous tissue. Describe the structure of a typical neuron and also draw a well-labelled diagram of it. Write the functions of nervous tissue.

Sol. Refer to text, 'Nervous tissue' on page no. 138 and 139.

8 Write differences between plant tissue and animal tissue.

Sol. Refer to text 'differences between plant tissues and animal tissues' on page no. 139.

ASSESSMENT EXERCISE

Competency Focused (Objective) Questions

Multiple Choice Questions

1 The number of nuclei present in striped muscle fibre is/are
(a) one
(b) many
(c) two
(d) None of the above

2 Which structure of neuron is responsible for transfer of impulse to muscles? **Competency Based Que.**
(a) Dendrites (b) Nerve endings
(c) Cell body (d) Cytoplasm

3 Choose the incorrect statement regarding connective tissue. **Competency Based Que.**
(a) Cells are loosely packed
(b) Cells are living in nature
(c) Connects various tissues and organs with each other
(d) Helps in the absorption of water and minerals.

4 The inner lining of intestine has which of the following
(a) cuboidal epithelium
(b) columnar epithelium
(c) glandular epithelium
(d) simple squamous epithelium

Assertion-Reason Questions

Direction (Q. No. 5-7) *In each of the following questions, a statement of Assertion (A) is given by the corresponding statement of Reason (R). Of the statements, mark the correct answer as*
(a) Both A and R are true and R is the correct explanation of A
(b) Both A and R are true, but R is not the correct explanation of A
(c) A is true, but R is false
(d) A is false, but R is true

5 **Assertion** (A) Connective tissues are protective tissue.
Reason (R) Materials are exchanged at the surface across the epithelial tissue.

6 **Assertion** (A) Bones and cartilage are rigid connective tissues.
Reason (R) Blood is a fluid connective tissue.

7 **Assertion** (A) Adipose tissue is found around the blood vessels.
Reason (R) The adipose tissue also acts as an insulator.

Answers

1. (b) **2.** (b) **3.** (d) **4.** (b)
5. (d) **6.** (b) **7.** (d)

Case Based/Source Based Questions

Direction (Q. Nos. 8-11) *Answer the questions on the basis of your understanding of the following paragraph and related studied concepts.*

The cells that produce the bone are called *A*. Once bone cells are mature and embedded within the matrix, they are known as osteocytes. Dense bone has a very regular structure, composed of repeating units called Haversian system. Each Haversian system has concentric rings of hard material enclosing the bone cells. Haversian canals running through the bone contain blood vessels and nerves.

8 Identify the structure *A* in the given paragraph.

9 Name the substance secreted by structure *A* that forms the rigid bone.

10 Why is a bone classified as connective tissue?

11 Bone is a strong and non-flexible tissue. What would be the advantage of these properties for bone functions?

Constructed Response (Descriptive) Questions

Very Short Answer Type Questions

12 What is the function of thin, hair-like projections present on the columnar epithelium?

13 Which part of neuron receives and transmits impulses?

Short Answer Type Questions

14 Name the tissue, which helps in transportation of oxygen that we inhale to various parts of the body. Write the composition of this tissue.

15 Mention the location of the following tissues. **Competency Based Que.**

(i) Tendon

(ii) Areolar tissues

(iii) Cuboidal epithelium

16 The functional combination of nerve and muscle tissue is fundamental to most animals. Comment. **Competency Based Que.**

Long Answer Type Questions

17 (i) Identify *A*, *B*, *C* and *D*.

(ii) Write the functions of *A*, *B*, *C* and *D*.

(iii) Write the difference between *A* and *D*.

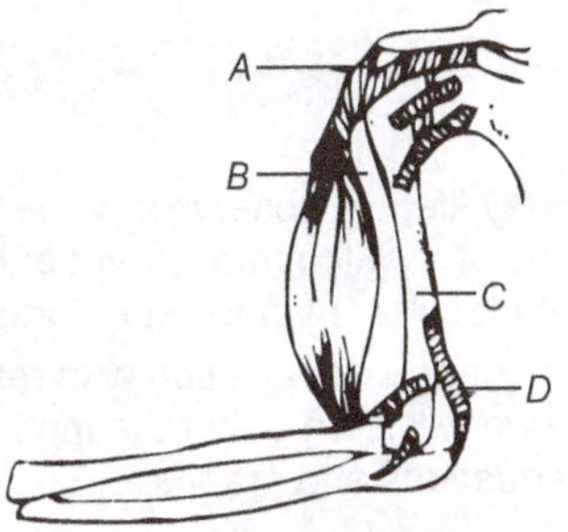

18 Write important functional differences between striated and smooth muscle tissues. Draw a labelled diagram of the muscle tissue that shows rhythmic contraction and relaxation throughout the life. **Competency Based Que.**

19 Name the tissue and write characteristic feature of following.

(i) Connects bone to bone in humans.

(ii) Forms inner lining of alveoli.

CHAPTER 07

Motion

In everyday life, we observe several types of motions like vehicles moving on a road, flying birds, movement of needles of a watch, movement of blades of a fan, circulation of blood through veins and arteries, etc. Atoms, molecules, planets, stars and galaxies are all in motion.

If a body changes its position with respect to time and its surroundings, it is said to be in motion. In this chapter, we will learn about the motion of objects along a straight line and represent such motions through simple equations and graphs.

7.1 Various Terms Related to Motion

Position

The location of an object with respect to a particular point is known as the **position** of the object. The particular point about which the position of the object is defined is called **reference point** or **origin**.

Scalar and Vector Quantities

- A physical quantity which has only magnitude, i.e. number is called **scalar quantity**. e.g. mass, time, distance, speed, etc.
- A physical quantity which has magnitude as well as direction is called **vector quantity**. e.g. weight, displacement, velocity, etc.

Distance

The distance travelled by a moving body is the actual length of the path covered by it, irrespective of the direction in which the body travels.

It is a **scalar quantity**. Its SI unit is **metre**.

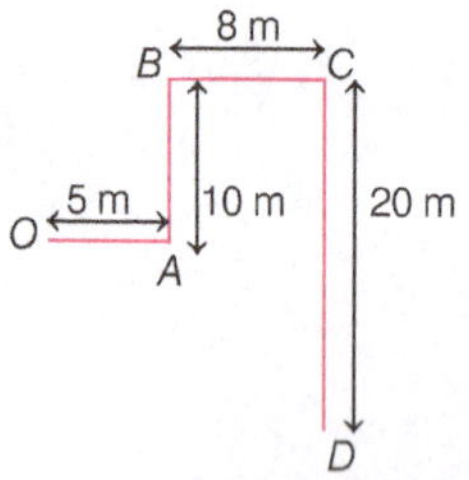

e.g. Consider the motion of an object moving along a straight path. Let the object start its motion from point *O* and move through point *A*, *B*, *C* and reach upto point *D*.

Then, total distance covered to the object = actual length upto *D* of the path travelled

$= OA + AB + BC + CD$

$= 5\text{ m} + 10\text{ m} + 8\text{ m} + 20\text{ m} = 43\text{ m}$

Displacement

The displacement of an object is equal to the length of the shortest path measured in the direction from the initial position to the final position of the object.

It is a **vector quantity**. Its SI unit is **metre** (m).

Suppose an object starts to move from point *O* and reaches to point *B*, passing through *A*.

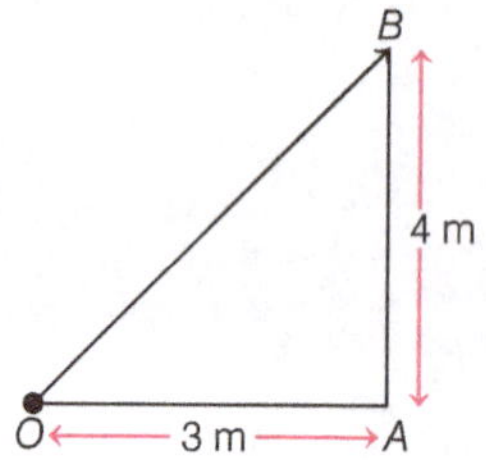

Here, initial position of the object is *O* and final position is *B*. So, displacement of the object

= length of the shortest path between initial position (*O*) and final position (*B*)

$= OB = \sqrt{OA^2 + AB^2}$ [from Pythagoras theorem]

$= \sqrt{(3)^2 + (4)^2}$

$= \sqrt{9 + 16}$

$= \sqrt{25} = 5\text{ m}$

But, distance in this case = length of actual path

$= OA + AB$

$= 3\text{ m} + 4\text{ m} = 7\text{ m}$

Distance *versus* Displacement

(i) Displacement of a moving object can never be greater than the distance travelled by it.

$\therefore$ Displacement $\leq$ Distance

$$\Rightarrow \frac{\text{Displacement}}{\text{Distance}} \leq 1$$

i.e. Ratio of displacement and distance is always less than or equal to 1.

(ii) If a body moves along a straight line (only in one direction), then distance and displacement will be equal.

(iii) Displacement of the object can be positive, negative or zero but distance cannot be negative or zero.

Example 1. **A Jogger jogs along one length and breadth of a rectangular park. If the dimensions of park are 150 m × 120 m, then find the distance travelled and displacement of the Jogger.**

Sol. According to question, the Jogger starts from point *A* and after covering one breadth and one length reaches at point *C*.

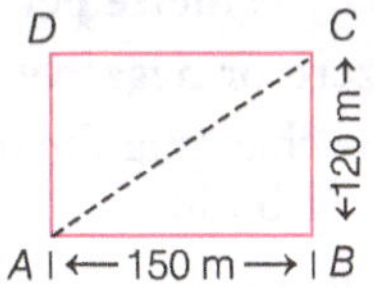

Length, $AB = l = 150$ m,

Breadth, $BC = b = 120$ m

Distance travelled, $s = ?$

Displacement of the Jogger $= ?$

Distance, $s =$ Length of the total path covered

$= AB + BC = 150 + 120 = 270$ m

Displacement = Minimum distance between initial and final position $= AC$

From Pythagoras theorem, $AC = \sqrt{(AB)^2 + (BC)^2}$

i.e. Displacement $= \sqrt{(150)^2 + (120)^2} = 30\sqrt{41}$ m

Thus, the Jogger travels a distance of 270 m and his displacement is $30\sqrt{41}$ m.

Example 2. **A body moves in a circular path of radius 20 cm. If it completes two and half revolution along the circular path, then find distance and displacement of the body.**

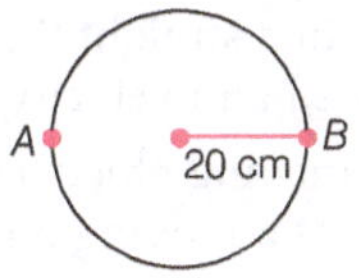

Sol. According to question, body moves in a circular path of radius 20 cm. So, during one complete revolution the distance (s) moved by the body is equal to the circumference of the circular path, i.e. $2\pi r$.

where, $r =$ radius of circular path

So, for two and half revolution, body covers two complete revolutions, i.e. $2 \times 2\pi r$ distance and half revolution,

i.e. $\frac{2\pi r}{2} = \pi r$

Total distance (s) covered by the body

$= (2 \times 2\pi r) + \pi r = 5\pi r$

$= 5 \times 3.14 \times 20$ $\quad [\because \pi = 3.14]$

$= 314$ cm

Now, as we know displacement (d) is the straight line distance between initial and final position of the body. So, after two and half revolution, total displacement (d) of the body will be $2r$, i.e. displacement $(d) = 2 \times 20 = 40$ cm.

Try These 7.1

1. **Fill in the blank**
   Displacement is a .... quantity.
2. **What is the displacement of a satellite when it makes a complete round along its circular path?**
3. **Suppose a ball is thrown vertically upwards from a position *P* above the ground. It rises to the highest point *Q* and returns to the same point *P*. What is the net displacement and distance travelled by the ball?**
4. **What is the numerical ratio of displacement to distance for a moving object?**
5. **If a body is moving only in one direction, then displacement and distance will be**

7.2 Uniform and Non-Uniform Motion

Uniform Motion A body is said to have a uniform motion, if it travels equal distances in equal intervals of time. The distance travelled by an object in uniform motion increases **linearly.**

e.g. A car moving along a straight line path, covers equal distances in equal intervals of time, it is said to be in uniform motion.

Non-uniform Motion A body is said to have a non-uniform motion, if it travels unequal distances in equal intervals of time.

e.g. A car moving through a crowded market has non-uniform motion.

7.3 Rate of Motion

The ratio of distance travelled by an object to the time taken is called rate of motion. The various terms required to measure the rate of motion are as given below

Speed

Speed of an object is defined as the distance travelled by it per unit time.

$$\text{Speed of an object } (v) = \frac{\text{Distance}(s)}{\text{Time}(t)}$$

- Speed is a **scalar quantity**.
- The SI unit of speed is **metre per second** (m/s).
- The other units of speed is **centimetre per second** (cms^{-1}) and **kilometre per hour** (kmh^{-1}).
- The speed may be positive or zero but never negative.

Speed can be classified as

(i) **Uniform speed** If a moving body does not change its speed during motion, then the speed of the body is said to be uniform, i.e. constant speed.

(ii) **Non-uniform speed** If a moving body changes its speed during motion, then the speed of the body is said to be non-uniform, i.e. variable speed.

(iii) **Average speed** It is defined as the ratio of the total distance travelled by a body to the total time taken. It is expressed as

$$\text{Average speed} = \frac{\text{Total distance travelled}}{\text{Total time taken}}$$

$$v_{av} = \frac{s_1 + s_2 + s_3 + \ldots}{t_1 + t_2 + t_3 + \ldots}$$

Note **Instantaneous speed** The speed of an object at any particular instant of time or at a particular point of its path is called the instantaneous speed of the object.

Example 3. **The odometer of a bike reads 1600 km at the start of the trip and 2000 km at the end of the trip. If the bike took 16 h, calculate the average speed of the bike in km/h and m/s.**

Sol. Distance covered by bike, $s = 2000\text{ km} - 1600\text{ km} = 400\text{ km}$

Time taken, $t = 16$ h

$\therefore$ Average speed, $v_{av} = \frac{s}{t} = \frac{400}{16} = 25$ km/h

$v_{av} = 25 \times \frac{5}{18}$

$= 6.9$ m/s

Therefore, the average speed of the bike is 6.9 m/s.

Example 4. **An object travels 14 m in 4 s and then another 16 m in 2 s. What is the average speed of an object?**

Sol. According to question,

First distance, $s_1 = 14$ m

Second distance, $s_2 = 16$ m, Time, $t_1 = 4$ s, $t_2 = 2$ s

$$\therefore \text{Average speed} = \frac{\text{Total distance}}{\text{Total time}}$$

$$= \frac{s_1 + s_2}{t_1 + t_2} = \frac{14 + 16}{4 + 2} = \frac{30}{6} = 5 \text{ m/s}$$

Therefore, the average speed of an object is 5 m/s.

Speed with Direction : Velocity

Velocity of an object is defined as the displacement of the object per unit time. i.e. velocity is the speed of an object moving in a definite direction.

It is expressed as

$$\text{Velocity of an object } (v) = \frac{\text{Displacement}(d)}{\text{Time } (t)}$$

- It is a **vector quantity.**
- The SI unit of velocity is **metre per second** (m/s).
- It can be **positive, zero** or **negative.**
- It can be changed by changing the object's speed, direction of motion or both.

Velocity can be classified as

(i) **Uniform velocity** If an object does not change, its velocity during motion without changing direction, then its velocity is known as uniform velocity, i.e. constant velocity.

(ii) **Non-uniform velocity** If an object changes its velocity during motion, then its velocity is known as non-uniform velocity, i.e. variable velocity.

(iii) **Average velocity** It is defined as the ratio of total displacement of the object to the total time taken.

It is expressed as $v_{av} = \frac{\text{Total displacement}}{\text{Total time taken}}$

If the velocity of an object changes at a uniform rate, then average velocity,

$$(v_{av}) = \frac{\text{Initial velocity } (u) + \text{ Final velocity } (v)}{2}$$

- Speedometer is a device which is used to measure instantaneous speed of a moving body.
- If a body is moving in a straight line, then the magnitude of its speed and velocity will be equal.
- Average speed of a moving object can never be zero but the average velocity of a moving object can be zero.

Note **Instantaneous velocity** The velocity of an object at a particular instant of time or at a particular point of its path is called its instantaneous velocity.

Example 5. **Rajeev went from Delhi to Chandigarh and returned to Delhi on his motorbike. The odometer of that read 4200 km at the start of trip and 4460 km at the end of his trip. If Rajeev took 4 h 20 min to complete his trip, then find the average speed and average velocity in km/h as well as in m/s.**

Sol. As we know that, the total distance covered,

s = final reading of odometer − initial reading of odometer

$= (4460 - 4200)$ km $= 260$ km

Total time taken, $t = 4$ h 20 min $= 4.33$ h

$$\therefore \text{Average speed} = \frac{\text{Total distance covered } (s)}{\text{Total time taken } (t)}$$

$$= \frac{260 \text{ km}}{4.33 \text{ h}} = 60 \text{ km/h} = \frac{60 \times 5}{18} = 16.67 \text{ m/s}$$

$$\therefore \text{Average velocity} = \frac{\text{Total displacement}(d)}{\text{Total time taken}(t)}$$

$$= \frac{0}{4.33} = 0 \text{ m/s or } 0 \text{ km/h}$$

Average speed of Rajeev is 16.67 m/s and average velocity is 0.

Rate of Change of Velocity : Acceleration

Acceleration is defined as the rate of change of velocity with respect to time.

Mathematically, it is expressed as

$$\text{Acceleration } (a) = \frac{\text{Change in velocity } (\Delta v)}{\text{Change in time } (\Delta t)}$$

If in a given time interval t, the velocity of a body changes from u to v, then acceleration a is expressed as

$$a = \frac{\text{Final velocity}(v) - \text{Initial velocity}(u)}{\text{Time interval}(t)}$$

or $$a = \frac{v - u}{t}$$

This kind of motion is known as **accelerated motion.**

- The SI unit of acceleration is m/s^2.
- It is a **vector quantity.**
- The acceleration is taken to be **positive**, if it is in the direction of velocity, **negative** if it is opposite to the direction of velocity and **zero** when a body is moving with a constant velocity.
- If velocity of an object decreases with time, then it is said to have **negative acceleration.** Negative acceleration is also called **deceleration** or **retardation.**

Acceleration can be classified as

(i) **Uniform acceleration** If an object travels in a straight line and its velocity increases or decreases by equal amounts in equal intervals of time, then the object is said to be in a uniform acceleration.

e.g.

(a) The motion of a freely falling body.

(b) The motion of a ball rolling down on an inclined plane.

(ii) **Non-uniform acceleration** If velocity of an object increases or decreases by unequal amounts in equal intervals of time, then the object is said to be in a non-uniform acceleration.

e.g. (a) The movement of a car on a crowded city road.

(b) The motion of the train leaving or entering the platform.

Example 6. **Starting from a stationary position, a car attains a velocity of 5 m/s in 20 s. Then, the driver of the car applies a brake such that the velocity of the car comes down to 3 m/s in the next 6 s. Calculate the acceleration of the car in both the cases.**

Sol. ***Case* I** Initial velocity of the car, $u = 0$

[∵ it starts from stationary position]

Final velocity, $v = 5$ m/s, Time taken, $t = 20$ s

$$\therefore \text{Acceleration, } a = \frac{\text{Change in velocity}}{\text{Time}}$$

$$= \frac{\text{Final velocity} - \text{Initial velocity}}{\text{Time}}$$

$$= \frac{v-u}{t} = \frac{5-0}{20}$$

$$= 0.25 \text{ m/s}^2$$

***Case* II** Initial velocity, $u = 5$ m/s

Final velocity, $v = 3$ m/s, Time taken, $t = 6$ s

$$\therefore \text{Acceleration, } a = \frac{v-u}{t} = \frac{3-5}{6} = -0.33 \text{ m/s}^2$$

Thus, the acceleration in both the cases are 0.25 m/s^2 and -0.33 m/s^2.

Try These 7.2

1 **Raman leaves his house at 8 : 30 am for his school. The school is 2 km away and classes starts at 9 : 00 am. If he walks at a speed of 3 km/h for first kilometre, at what speed should he walk the second kilometre to reach just in time?** [Ans. 6 km/h]

2 **An object travels 10 m in 2 s and then another 16 m in 2 s. What is the average speed of the object?** [Ans. 6.5 m/s]

3 **Which of the two can be zero under certain conditions : average speed of a moving body or average velocity of a moving body?**

4 **Suppose Rahul is enjoying a ride on a merry-go-round which is moving with a constant speed of 10 ms^{-1}. Which type of motion it is?**

7.4 Graphical Representation of Motion

In order to describe the motion of an object, we can use line graphs. In this case, line graphs show dependence of one physical quantity, such as distance or velocity, on another quantity, such as time.

Note For graphical description of a motion, it is convenient to take time along X-axis as it is an independent variable, whereas distance, speed or velocity is taken along Y-axis as they are dependent variable.

Types of Graph

There are two main types of graph which we will be studying as given below.

1. Distance-Time Graph

The change in the position of an object with time can be represented on the distance-time graph by adopting a convenient scale of choice.

To draw a distance-time graph, time is plotted along X-axis and distance of the body is plotted along Y-axis. In this case, the slope of the distance-time graph is equal to the speed of the object. If the distance-time graph is a straight line parallel to time axis, it means the object is at rest.

Distance-time graphs under various conditions are explained below

(i) Distance-Time Graph for Uniform Motion

If an object travels equal distances in equal intervals of time, then it moves with uniform speed. This shows that the distance travelled by the object is directly proportional to the time.

For uniform speed, a graph of distance travelled against time is a straight line as shown in figure given below

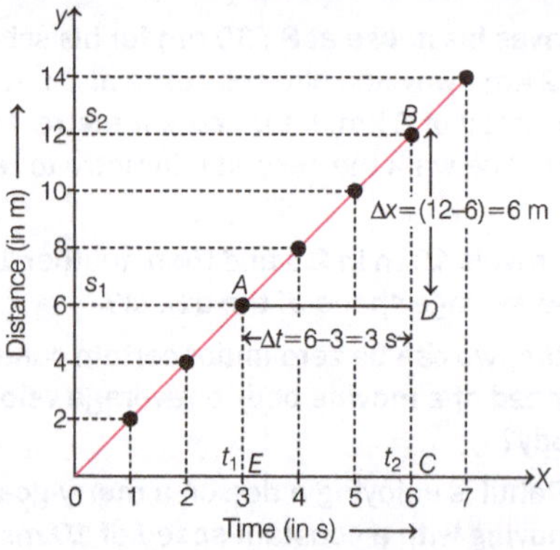

Distance-time graph for uniform motion

Interpretation

From the graph, it is clear that in equal interval of time, i.e. 1s, the object covers equal distance 2 m, so the motion is uniform and graph is a straight line.

Calculation of speed To calculate the speed of the object from a distance-time graph, choose any two points say A and B on the straight line. From points A and B, draw perpendiculars AE and BC respectively, on time axis. Now, draw a perpendicular AD on BC.

The distance travelled by the object from point A to B is given by

$$\Delta x = BC - CD = s_2 - s_1$$

Time taken by the object to cover this distance

$$= \Delta t = t_2 - t_1$$

$\therefore$ Speed, $\quad v = \Delta x/\Delta t = (s_2 - s_1)/(t_2 - t_1)$

i.e. $\quad \Delta x/\Delta t =$ Slope of distance-time graph.

(ii) Distance-Time Graph for Non-uniform Motion

If a body travels unequal distances in equal intervals of time, then the motion of the body is known as non-uniform motion.

Non-uniform motion is of two types such as

(a) When the speed of the body increases with passage of time, then the distance-time graph will be a curve with positive slope as shown below

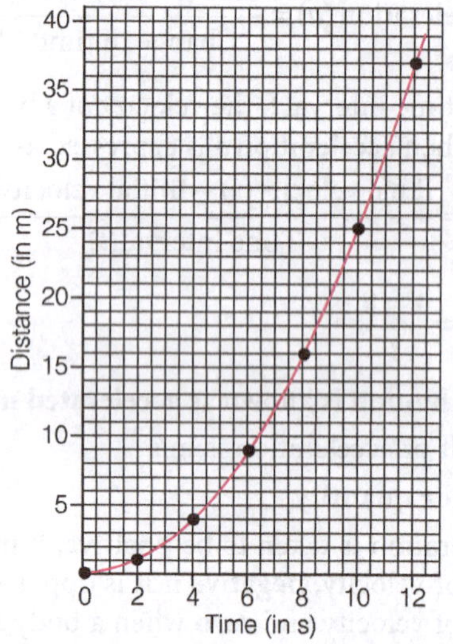

Distance-time graph for non-uniform motion

Interpretation

From the graph, it is clear that in equal intervals of time of two seconds, the body is covering unequal distances and this distance goes on increasing. That means, with the passage of time, the body is covering more and more distance in equal time, i.e. the speed of the body is increasing.

(b) When the speed of the body decreases with passage of time, then the distance-time graph will be a curve with negative slope as shown below

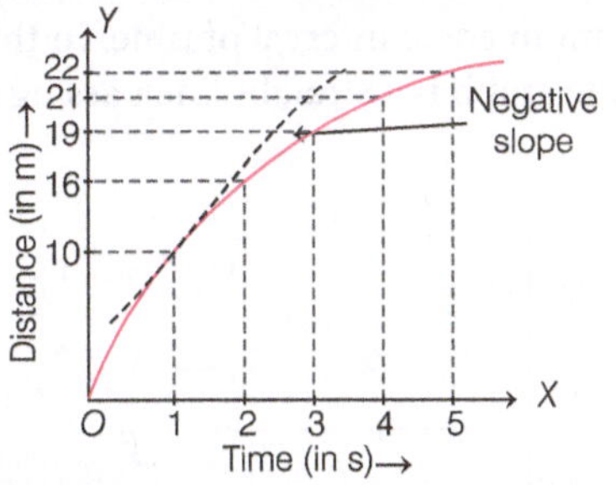

Distance-time graph for non-uniform motion

Interpretation

From the graph, it is clear that in equal intervals of time of one second, the body is covering unequal distances and this distance goes on decreasing. That means, with the time, the body is covering lesser and lesser distance in equal time, i.e. the speed of the body is decreasing.

Example 7. **The graph shows below the positions of a body at different times. Calculate the speed of the body as it moves from (i) *A* to *B*, (ii) *B* to *C* and (iii) *C* to *D*.**

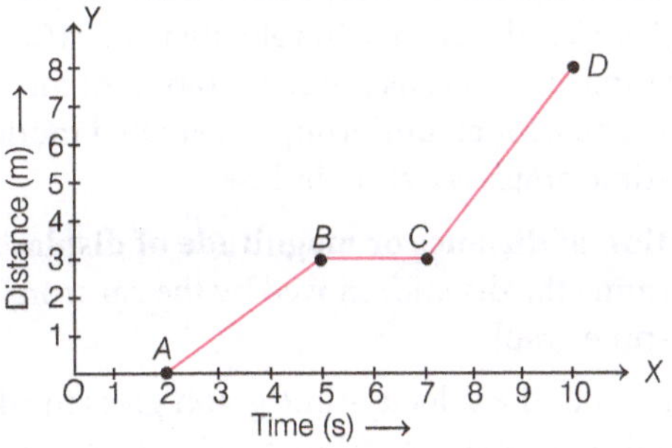

Sol.

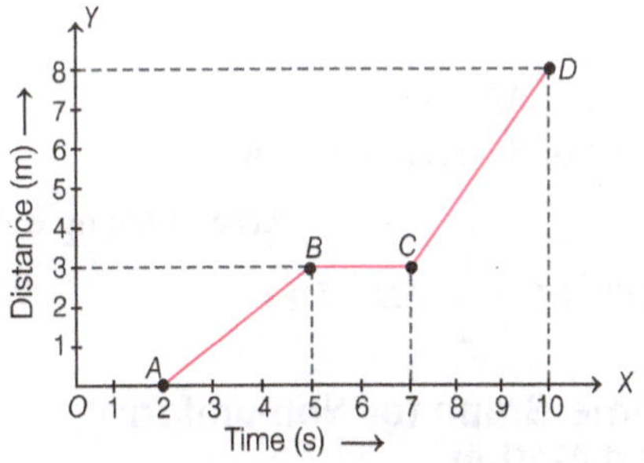

(i) For the motion from point *A* to *B*,

time taken, $t = 5 - 2 = 3$ s

Distance covered $= 3 - 0 = 3$ m

∴ Speed during the motion from point *A* to *B*

$$= \frac{\text{Distance}}{\text{Time}} = \frac{3}{3} = 1 \text{ m/s}$$

(ii) For the motion from point *B* to *C*,

time taken, $t = 7 - 5 = 2$ s

Distance covered $= 3 - 3 = 0$ m

[∵ body does not change its position from point *B* to *C*]

∴ Speed during the motion from point *B* to *C*

$$= \frac{\text{Distance}}{\text{Time}}$$

$$= \frac{0}{2} = 0 \text{ m/s} = 0$$

(*iii*) For the motion from point *C* to *D*,

time taken, $t = 10 - 7 = 3$ s

Distance covered $= 8 - 3 = 5$ m

∴ Speed during the motion from point *C* to *D*

$$= \frac{\text{Distance}}{\text{Time}} = \frac{5}{3} \text{ m/s}$$

Example 8. **The following table gives the data about motion of a car**

Time (h)	11:00	11:30	12:00	12:30	1:00
Distance (km)	0	20	30	65	100

Plot the graph and answer the following questions

(i) Find the speed of the car between 12:00 h and 12:30 h.

(ii) What is the average speed of the car?

(iii) Is the car's motion is an example of uniform motion? Justify.

Sol. According to given data about motion of a car, graph of distance-time will be plotted as

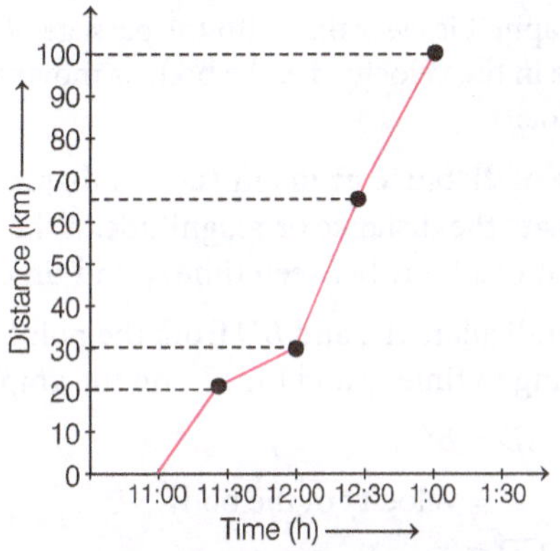

(i) Speed of the car between 12:00 h and 12:30 h is given by

$$v = \frac{65 - 30}{\frac{30}{60}} = \frac{35}{\left(\frac{1}{2}\right)} = 70 \text{ km/h}$$

(ii) Average speed, $v_{av} = \frac{100}{2} = 50$ km/h

(iii) No, because the car covered unequal distances in equal intervals of time.

2. Velocity-Time Graph

Velocity-time graph shows how the velocity of a body changes with passage of time. The slope of velocity-time graph gives the acceleration.

To draw velocity-time graph, velocity of the body is plotted along Y-axis and the time taken by the body is plotted along X-axis.

The area under velocity-time graph gives displacement. Velocity-time graphs under various conditions are explained as below

(i) Velocity-Time Graph for a Body Moving with Constant Velocity

When a body moves with constant velocity, i.e. its motion is uniform, then its velocity does not change with time.

The graph will be a straight line parallel to the time axis.

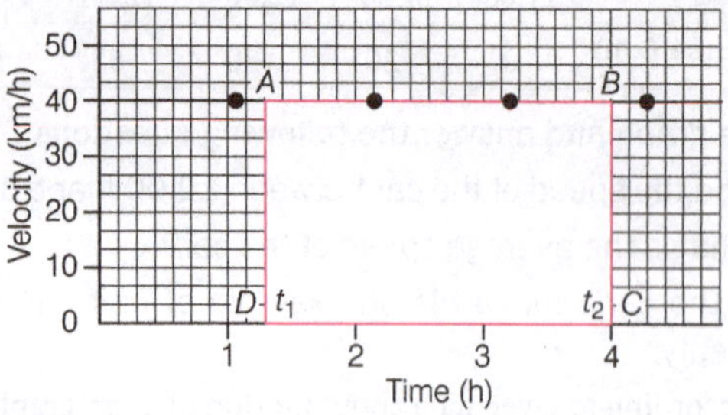

Interpretation

From the graph, it is clear that with the passage of time, there is no change in the velocity, i.e. the body is moving with constant velocity.

Calculation of distance or magnitude of displacement

Let us calculate the distance or magnitude of the displacement of a body between time t_1 and time t_2.

Draw perpendiculars AC and BD from the points corresponding to time t_1 and time t_2 on the graph.

Now, $AD = BC$

$= \text{velocity of the body}$

$CD = (t_2 - t_1)$

$= \text{time interval}$

Thus, $AD \times CD = \text{area of rectangle } ABCD$

Also, $AD \times CD = \text{velocity} \times \text{time}$

$= \text{distance or magnitude of displacement}$

Thus, magnitude of displacement

$= \text{area under velocity-time graph}$

(ii) Velocity-Time Graph for Uniformly Accelerated Motion

In uniformly accelerated motion, the velocity changes by equal amount in equal interval of time. In this case, the velocity-time graph is a straight line passing through the origin.

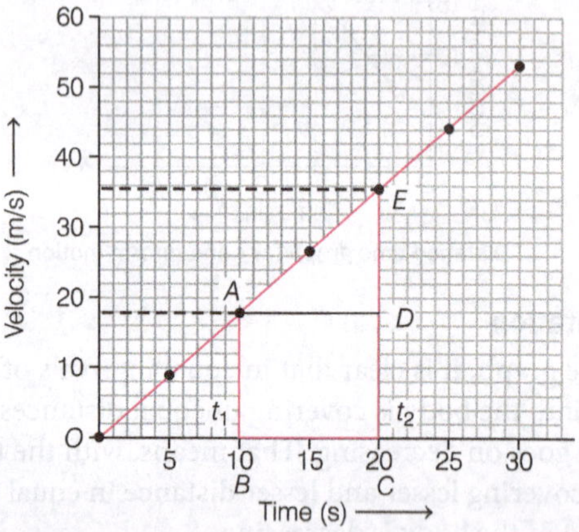

Interpretation

The nature of the graph shows that velocity changes by equal amounts in equal intervals of time. In equal interval of time, i.e. 10 s, the change in velocity is 18 m/s, which remains same, that means the acceleration of the body is constant. Thus, for all uniformly accelerated motion, the velocity-time graph is a straight line.

Calculation of distance or magnitude of displacement

To determine the distance moved by the car from its velocity-time graph.

The area under the velocity-time graph gives the distance (magnitude of displacement) moved by the car in a given interval of time.

Therefore, $S = \text{Area of } ABCDE$

$= \text{Area of the rectangle } ABCD + \text{Area of triangle } ADE$

$$= AB \times BC + \frac{1}{2}(AD \times DE)$$

(iii) Velocity-Time Graph for Non-uniformly Accelerated Motion

In non-uniformly accelerated motion, velocity-time graphs can have any shape.

If the velocity changes non-uniformly, the velocity-time graph is a curve having increasing or decreasing slope.

Velocity-time graph for non-uniformly accelerated motion is given below

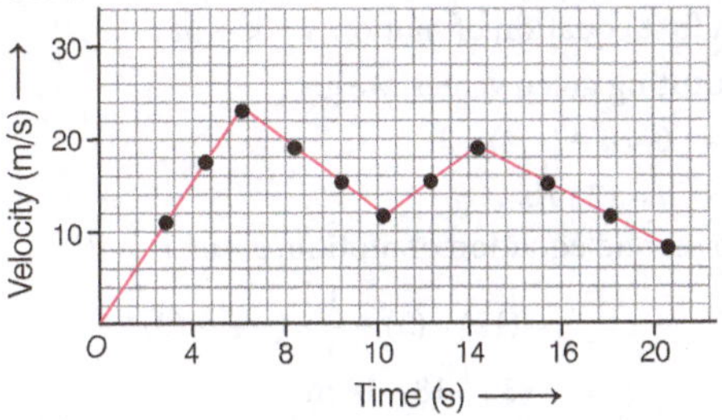

It shows that the velocity of a body (or object) varies non-uniformly with time.

Example 9. **The velocity-time graph of an ascending passenger lift is shown in figure below.**

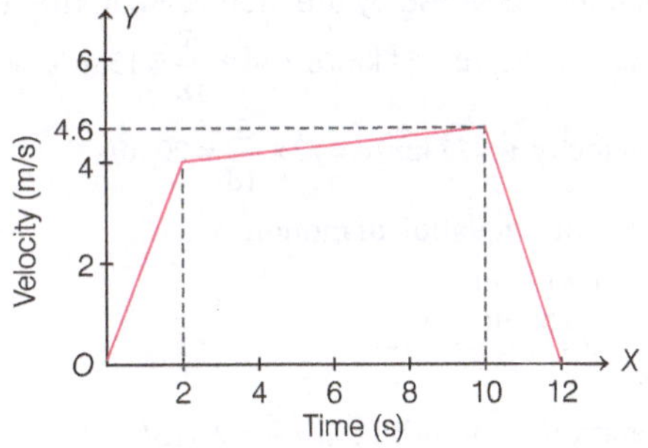

What is the acceleration of the lift

(i) during the first two seconds?

(ii) between 2nd and 10th second?

(iii) during the last two seconds?

Sol. (i) ***Case* I** From given graph, we have

Change in velocity, $\Delta v = 4 - 0 = 4 \text{ m/s}$,

Time, $\Delta t = 2 - 0 = 2 \text{ s}, a_1 = ?$

$\therefore$ Acceleration, $a_1 = \frac{\Delta v}{\Delta t} = \frac{4}{2} = 2 \text{ m/s}^2$

(ii) ***Case* II** Change in velocity, $\Delta v = 4.6 - 4$

$= 0.6 \text{ m/s}$,

Time, $\Delta t = 10 - 2 = 8 \text{ s}, a_2 = ?$

$\because$ Acceleration, $a_2 = \frac{\Delta v}{\Delta t} = \frac{0.6}{8} = 0.075 \text{ m/s}^2$

(iii) ***Case* III** Change in velocity, $\Delta v = 0 - 4.6$

$= -4.6 \text{ m/s}$,

Time, $\Delta t = 12 - 10 = 2 \text{ s}, a_3 = ?$

$\therefore$ Acceleration, $a_3 = \frac{\Delta v}{\Delta t} = \frac{-4.6}{2} = -2.3 \text{ m/s}^2$

Negative sign shows retardation.

Example 10. **A body moves with a velocity of 2 m/s for 5 s, then its velocity increases uniformly to 10 m/s in next 5 s. There after, its velocity begins to decrease at a uniform rate until it comes to rest after 5 s.**

(i) Plot a velocity-time graph for the motion of the body.

(ii) From the graph, find the total distance covered by the body after 2 s and 12 s.

Sol. (i) Velocity-time graph for the motion of the body is

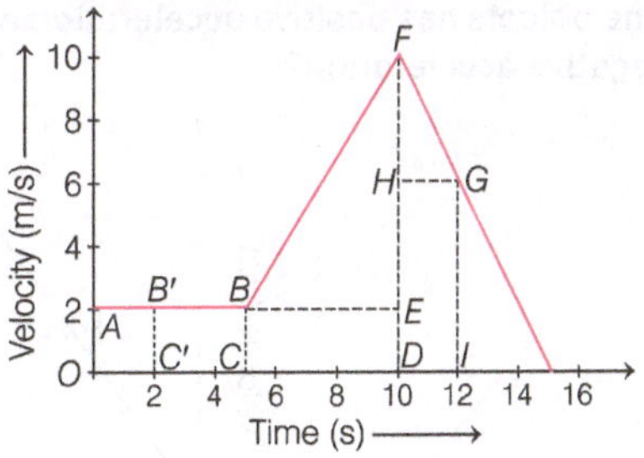

(ii) As we know, the distance moved by the body after 2 s

$= \text{Area } OAB'C' = 2 \times 2 = 4 \text{ m}$

Again distance covered by the body after 12 s

$= \text{Area } OAED + \text{Area of } \Delta BEF$

$+ \text{Area of } DHGI + \text{Area of } \Delta FHG$

$= 2 \times 10 + \frac{1}{2} \times 5 \times 8 + 6 \times 2 + \frac{1}{2} \times 2 \times 4$

$= 20 + 20 + 12 + 4 = 56 \text{ m}$

Try These 7.3

1 **If the distance-time graph of a particle is parallel to time axis, then how much is the velocity of the particle?**

2 **The time-distance graph of cyclist is shown in the figure below**

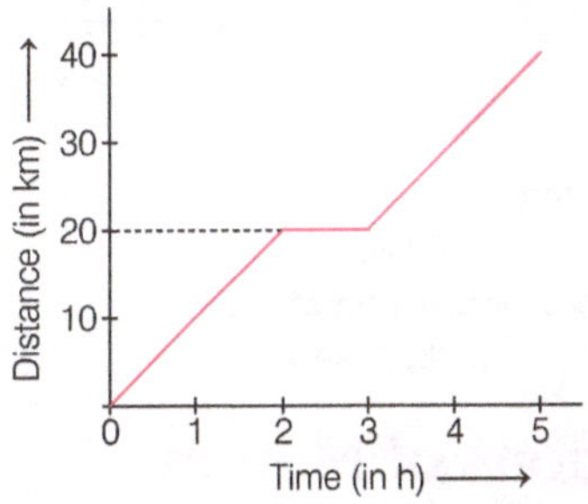

From the graph, find out average speed in the whole journey. [**Ans.** 8 km/h]

3 **Give one similarity and one dissimilarity between the two graphs:**

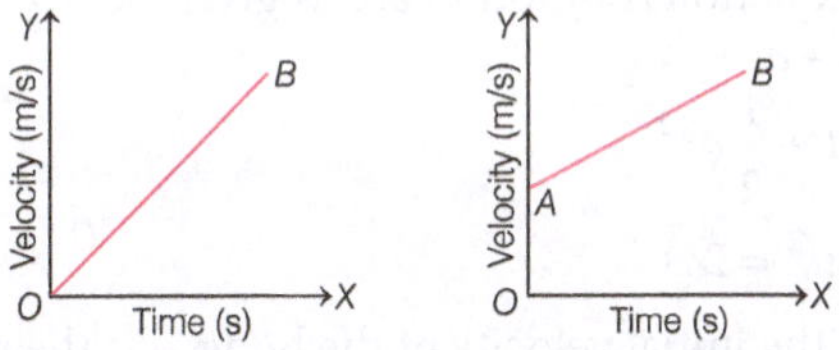

4 **The value of acceleration in the following graph is ....**

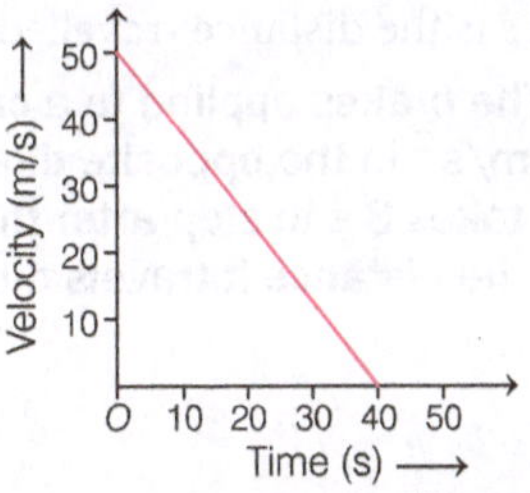

[**Ans.** -1.25 m/s^2, negative sign for retardation]

5 **Given graphs represent the motion of two objects *P* and *Q*. Which of the objects has positive acceleration and which one has negative acceleration?**

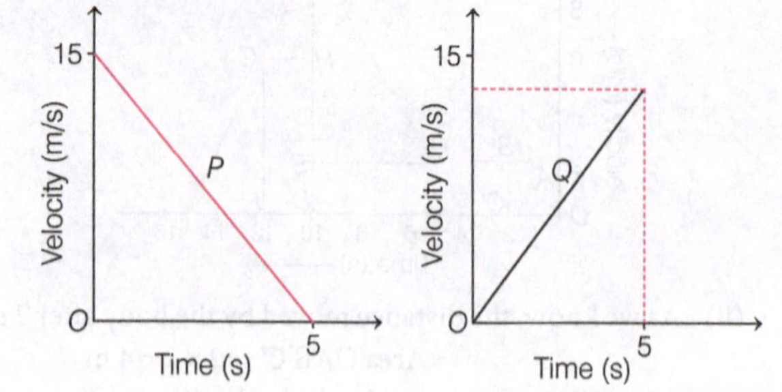

6 **Velocity-time graphs of two objects *P* and *Q* are as given below**

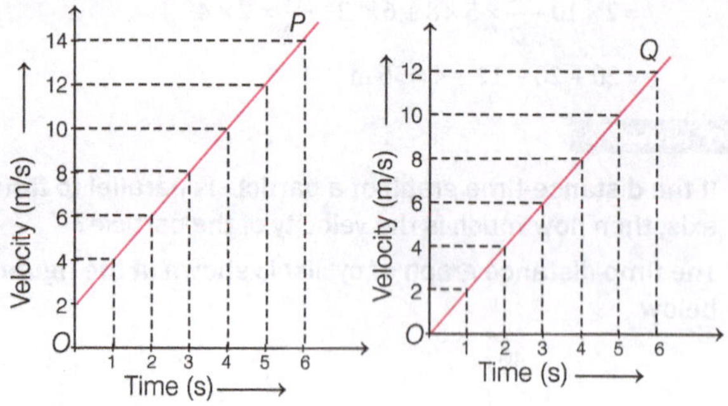

(i) Object *Q* starts from rest.

(a) True (b) False

(ii) Object *Q* has more velocity after 5 s.

(a) True (b) False

7.5 Equations of Motion

Relation between velocity of the body, acceleration of the body and the distance travelled by the body in a particular time interval is known as equation of motion.

The three equations of motion are as given below

1. $v = u + at$
2. $s = ut + \frac{1}{2}at^2$
3. $v^2 - u^2 = 2as$

where, u is the initial velocity of the body, a is the uniform acceleration of the body, v is the final velocity of the body after t second and s is the distance travelled in this time.

Example 11. **The brakes applied to a car produces an acceleration of 4 m/s^2 in the opposite direction to the motion. If the car takes 3 s to stop after the application of brakes, calculate the distance it travels during this time.**

Sol. Given, final velocity, $v = 0$, Time, $t = 3$ s,

Acceleration, $a = -4\ m/s^2$

From first equation of motion, $v = u + at$

Substituting given values, we get

$$0 = u + (-4) \times 3$$

$$\Rightarrow \quad u = 12\ m/s$$

From second equation of motion, $s = ut + \frac{1}{2}at^2$

$$= (12) \times (3) + \frac{1}{2} \times (-4) \times (3)^2$$

$$= 36 - 18 = 18\ m$$

Thus, car covers the distance during time, $t = 3$ s is 18 m.

Example 12. **A motorbike accelerates uniformly from 54 km/h to 72 km/h in 2 s. Calculate**

(i) the acceleration and

(ii) the distance covered by the motorbike in that time.

Sol. (*i*) Initial velocity, $u = 54\ km/h = 54 \times \frac{5}{18} = 15\ m/s$

Final velocity, $v = 72\ km/h = 72 \times \frac{5}{18} = 20\ m/s$

From the first equation of motion,

$$v = u + at$$

$$a = \frac{v - u}{t} = \frac{20 - 15}{2}$$

Acceleration of motorbike, $a = \frac{5}{2} = 2.5\ m/s^2$

(*ii*) The distance covered by the motorbike

$$s = ut + \frac{1}{2}at^2 = 15 \times 2 + \frac{1}{2} \times (2.5) \times (2)^2$$

$$= 30 + 5 = 35\ m$$

The acceleration of the motorbike is 2.5 m/s^2 and the distance covered is 35 m.

Example 13. **A train starting from rest attains a velocity of 90 km/h in 3 min. Assuming that the acceleration is uniform, find**

(i) the acceleration and

(ii) the distance travelled by the train for attaining this velocity.

Sol. Given, final velocity, $v = 90\ km/h = 90 \times 5/18 = 25\ m/s$

Initial velocity, $u = 0$, Time, $t = 3\ min = 3 \times 60 = 180$ s

(i) Acceleration, $a = ?$

$a = (v - u)/t$ [from first equation of motion]

$a = (25 - 0)/180 = 5/36\ m/s^2$

(ii) From the third equation of motion,

$$v^2 = u^2 + 2as$$

$$v^2 = 0 + 2as \qquad [\because u = 0]$$

$$\text{Distance, } s = \frac{v^2}{2a} = \frac{(25)^2}{2 \times 5/36} = 2250\ m$$

7.6 Uniform Circular Motion

If an object moves in a circular path with uniform speed, then its motion is called uniform circular motion.

- When an object moves along a circular path, its direction of motion keeps changing continuously. The velocity changes due to continuous change in direction and thus motion along a circular path is said to be accelerated.
- When a body takes one round of a circular path, then it travels a distance equal to its circumference which is $2\pi r$, where r is the radius of the circular path.
- Then, speed of the body moving in a circular path, $v = 2\pi r/t$, where t is the time taken for one round of circular path and π is constant having value 22/7.

Some of the examples of uniform circular motion are as follows

(i) A piece of stone tied to a thread and rotated in a circle with a uniform speed.

(ii) The motion of blades of an electric fan around the axle.

(iii) The motion of the moon and the earth.

(iv) A satellite in a circular orbit around the earth.

(v) A car moves on a circular path with constant speed.

Example 14. **The minute hand of a wall clock is 10 cm long. Find its displacement and the distance covered from 10:00 am to 10:30 am.**

Sol. Given, length of the minute hand, $l = 10$ cm

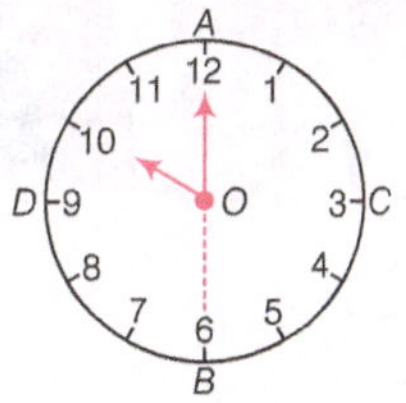

$\therefore$ Displacement from 10:00 am to 10:30 am is given by diameter $= AOB = 2l = 20$ cm

Total distance covered by the minute hand

$$= ACB = \pi l$$

$$= \frac{22}{7} \times 10 \text{ cm} = \frac{220}{7} = 31.43 \text{ cm}$$

The displacement of the minute hand is 20 cm and distance is 31.43 cm.

Try These 7.4

1 **A body is moving with a velocity of 10 m/s. If it starts accelerating with the rate of 2.5 m/s^2. Find out its velocity after 10 s.** [Ans. 35 m/s]

2 **Fill in the blank**

If a car travels 50 m distance in 4 s with a acceleration of 5 m/s^2, then its initial speed is .... m/s. [Ans. 2.5]

3 **A cyclist is moving with a speed of 14 m/s. He starts accelerating with a rate of 6 m/s^2 and acquires the speed of 18 m/s. Calculate, what distance did he move in acquiring that speed?** [Ans. 10.67 m]

4 **If the acceleration of the particle is constant in magnitude but not in direction, then what type of path does the particle follow?**

Mind Map

MOTION

If a body changes its position with respect to time and its surroundings, its is said to be in motion. Motion and rest are always relative but never absolute.

Types of Motion

- **Uniform Motion** The object travels equal distance in equal interval of time.
- **Non-uniform Motion** The object travels unequal distances in equal intervals of time.

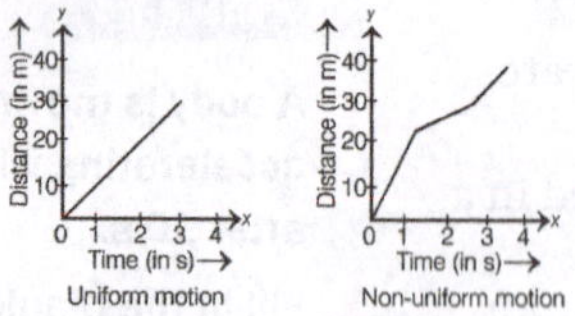

Equations of Motion

Relations between velocity, acceleration and the distance covered by the body in particular time interval.

(i) $v = u + at$

(ii) $s = ut + \frac{1}{2}at^2$

(iii) $v^2 - u^2 = 2as$

Rate of Motion

Rate of Distance

- **Speed** Distance travelled by an object in unit time. $v = \frac{s}{t}$

– Its SI unit is m/s.
– It is a scalar quantity.
– It is always positive.

Types of Speed

- **Uniform Speed** If a body does not change its speed during motion. It is also known as **constant speed**.
- **Non-uniform Speed** If a body changes its speed during motion. It is also known as **variable speed**.
- **Average Speed** It is the ratio of total distance travelled by an object to the total time taken.

$$v_{av} = \frac{s_1 + s_2 + \ldots}{t_1 + t_2 + \ldots}$$

- **Instantaneous Speed** The speed of an object at any particular instant of time during its motion.

Rate of Displacement

- **Velocity** The displacement of the body per unit time. $v = \frac{d}{t}$

– Its SI unit is m/s.
– It is a vector quantity.
– It can be positive, negative or zero.

Types of velocity

- **Uniform Velocity** If an object does not change its velocity during motion. It is known as uniform or **constant velocity**.
- **Non-uniform Velocity** If an object changes its velocity during motion. It is known as non-uniform or **variable velocity**.
- **Average Velocity** It is the ratio of total displacement of the object to the total time taken.

$$v_{av} = \frac{\text{Total displacement}}{\text{Total time}}$$

Rate of Change of Velocity

- **Acceleration** It is defined as the rate of change of velocity with respect to time.

$$a = \frac{\Delta v}{\Delta t} = \frac{v - u}{t}$$

– Its SI unit is m/s^2.
– It is a vector quantity.
– It is taken as positive, if it is in direction of velocity, negative if it is in opposite direction of velocity and zero when it is moving with constant velocity.
– Negative acceleration is called as **deceleration or retardation.**

Types of Acceleration

- **Uniform Acceleration** If an object travels in a straight line and its velocity increases or decreases by equal amounts in equal intervals of time.
- **Non-uniform Acceleration** If an object travels with unequal changes in velocity in equal intervals of time.

Various Terms Related To Motion

- **Position** The location of an object with respect to a particular point is known as position.
- **Origin** The particular point about which the position of the object is defined **called** origin.
- **Scalar Quantity** Physical quantities which have only magnitude. e.g. Mass, Time, etc.
- **Vector Quantity** Physical quantities which have both magnitude as well as direction. e.g. Displacement, Velocity, etc.
- **Distance** The actual length of the path covered by a moving body in particular direction.

– Its SI unit is metre.
– It is a scalar quantity.

- **Displacement** The shortest possible distance from the initial and the final positions of the body.

– Its SI unit is metre.
– It is a vector quantity.

Uniform Circular Motion

– When a body moves in a circular path with uniform speed.
– It changes its direction continuously.
– Speed of the body moving in a circular path $v = \frac{2\pi r}{t}$
– e.g. a piece of stone tied to a thread and rotated
– in a circle with uniform speed.
A car is moving on a circular path with constant speed.

Graphical Representation of Motion

– It is the diagrammatical representation of position of an object.
– Independent variable always taken along *X*-axis
– Dependent variable always taken along *Y*-axis.

Types of Graph

There are mainly two type of graphs

(i) Distance-time graph

– Change in the position of an object with time can be represented on the distance-time graph by adopting a convenient scale of choice.

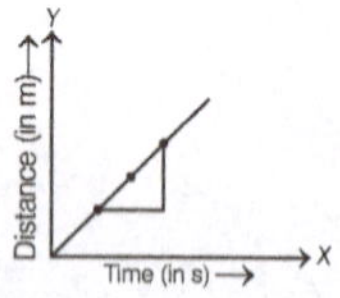

– To draw distance-time graph, time is plotted along *X*-axis and distance of the body is plotted along *Y*-axis.

(ii) Velocity-time graph

– It shows how the velocity of a body changes with passage of time.

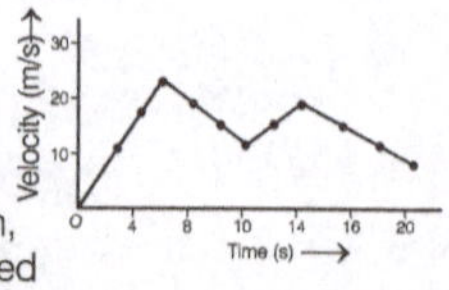

– To draw velocity-time graph, velocity of the body is plotted along *Y*-axis and the time taken by the body is plotted along *X*- axis.

NCERT FOLDER

Complete Explanations of all NCERT's Questions

Intext Questions

Q.1 An object has moved through a distance. Can it have zero displacement? If yes, support your answer with an example. Page 74

Sol. Yes, the displacement can be zero even, if the object has moved through a distance, e.g. a boy starts from his home to market and comes back. He has covered a distance but his displacement is zero.

Q.2 A farmer moves along the boundary of a square field of side 10 m in 40 s. What will be the magnitude of displacement of the farmer at the end of 2 min 20 s from his initial position? Page 74

Sol. Farmer takes 40 s to move along the boundary of the square field of side 10 m, i.e. after 40 s farmer is again at his initial position, so his displacement is zero.

Time given = 2 min 20 s = (2 × 60 + 20) s = 140 s

Displacement of farmer after 2 min 20 s, i.e. after 140 s

= Displacement after (3 × 40 + 20) s

= 0 + displacement after 20 s

[∵ after each 40 s displacement is zero]

Farmer completes one round in 40 s, so he will complete 1/2 round in 20 s, i.e. after 20 s final position of farmer is C.

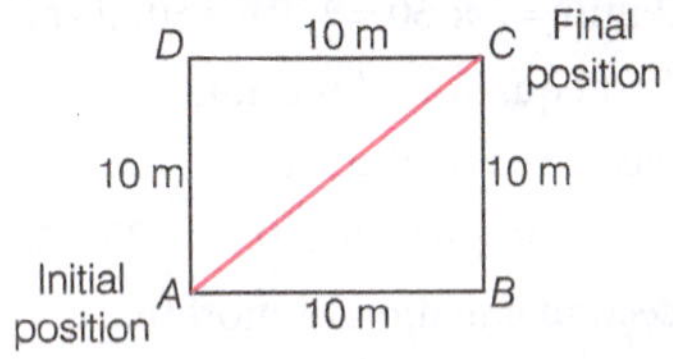

Displacement of farmer,

$$AC = \sqrt{AB^2 + BC^2}$$

$$= \sqrt{10^2 + 10^2} = 10\sqrt{2} = 10 \times 1.414$$

$$= 14.14 \text{ m}$$

Q.3 Which of the following is true for displacement?

(i) It cannot be zero.

(ii) Its magnitude is greater than the distance travelled by the object. Page 74

Sol. (i) The displacement can be zero, so the first statement is false.

(ii) The magnitude of displacement can never be greater than the distance travelled by the object. So, the second statement is also false.

Q.4 Distinguish between speed and velocity. Page 76

Sol. Difference between speed and velocity are as given below

Speed	Velocity
Distance travelled per unit time.	Displacement per unit time.
It is a scalar quantity.	It is a vector quantity.
Speed is always positive.	Velocity can be negative, positive or zero.

Q.5 Under what condition(s) is the magnitude of average velocity of an object equal to its average speed? Page 76

Sol. When the object travels in one direction along a straight line path, then its average velocity will be equal to average speed.

Q.6 What does the odometer of an automobile measure? Page 76

Sol. It measures the distance travelled by an automobile.

Q.7 What does the path of an object look like when it is in a uniform motion? Page 76

Sol. An object having uniform motion has a straight line path.

Q.8 During an experiment, a signal from a spaceship reached the ground station in five minutes. What was the distance of the spaceship from the ground station? The signal travels at the speed of light, i.e. 3×10^8 m/s. Page 76

Sol. Given, speed of signal $= 3 \times 10^8$ m/s

Time taken by the signal in reaching the earth

$= 5 \text{ min} = 5 \times 60 = 300 \text{ s}$

Distance of spaceship from ground station

= Distance travelled by the signal in 5 min

$= \text{Speed} \times \text{Time} = 3 \times 10^8 \times 300 = 9 \times 10^{10}$ m

Q.9 When will you say a body is in (i) uniform acceleration? (ii) non-uniform acceleration? Page 77

Sol. (i) A body is in uniform acceleration, if it travels in a straight path when its velocity increases or decreases by equal amount in equal time intervals.

(ii) A body is in non-uniform acceleration, if it travels in a straight path when its velocity increases or decreases by unequal amount in equal time intervals.

Q.10 A bus decreases its speed from 80 km/h to 60 km/h in 5 s. Find the acceleration of the bus. Page 77

Sol. Given, initial speed of the bus,

$$u = 80 \text{ km/h} = 80 \times \frac{5}{18} = 22.22 \text{ m/s}$$

Final speed of the bus,

$$v = 60 \text{ km/h} = 60 \times \frac{5}{18} = 16.67 \text{ m/s}$$

Time taken to decrease the speed, $t = 5$ s

$\therefore$ Acceleration of the bus, $a = \frac{v - u}{t}$

[$\because$ first equation of motion]

$$= \frac{16.67 - 22.22}{5} = -1.11 \text{ m/s}^2$$

The negative sign of acceleration indicates that the velocity of the bus is decreasing, i.e. the bus retards.

Q.11 A train starting from a railway station and moving with uniform acceleration attains a speed of 40 km/h in 10 min. Find its acceleration. Page 77

Sol. Initial velocity of train, $u = 0$

Final velocity of train, $v = 40 \text{ km/h} = 40 \times \frac{5}{18}$

$$= 11.11 \text{ m/s}$$

Time taken, $t = 10 \text{ min} = 10 \times 60 = 600$ s

$$\therefore \text{Acceleration}, \ a = \frac{v - u}{t} = \frac{11.11 - 0}{600} = 0.0185 \text{ m/s}^2$$

$$= 1.85 \times 10^{-2} \text{ m/s}^2$$

Hence, acceleration of the train is $= 1.85 \times 10^{-2}$ m/s^2.

Q.12 What is the nature of distance-time graphs for uniform and non-uniform motion of an object? Page 81

Sol. The distance-time graph for uniform motion of an object is a straight line.

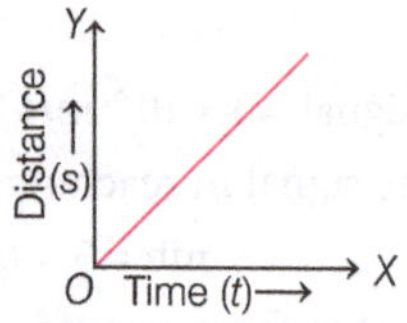

Uniform motion

The distance-time graph for non-uniform motion of an object is a curved line.

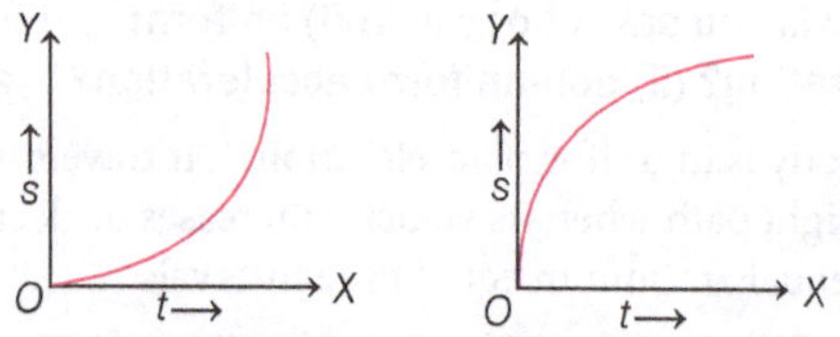

(Speed increases) (Speed decreases)

Non-uniform motion

Q.13 What can you say about the motion of an object whose distance-time graph is a straight line parallel to the time axis? Page 81

Sol. When an object is at rest, then its distance-time graph is a straight line parallel to the time axis. Thus, it indicates that with a change in time, there is no change in the position of the object, i.e. the object is at rest.

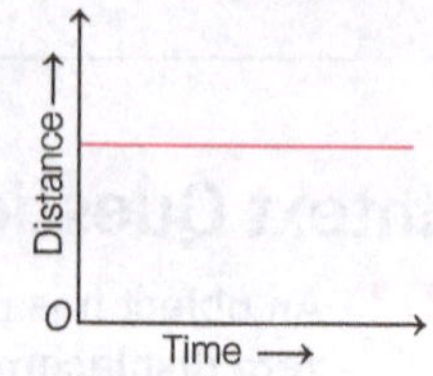

Q.14 What can you say about the motion of an object, if its speed-time graph is a straight line parallel to time axis? Page 81

Sol. A straight line parallel to the time axis in a speed-time graph indicates that a change in time, there is no change in the speed of the object. This indicates the speed of the object is constant.

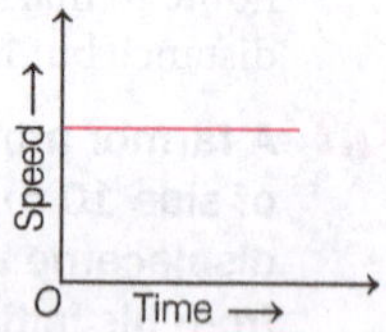

Q.15 What is the quantity which is measured by the area occupied below the velocity-time graph? Page 81

Sol. The displacement is measured by the area occupied below the velocity-time graph.

Q.16 A bus starting from rest moves with a uniform acceleration of 0.1 m/s^2 for 2 min. Find

(i) the speed acquired. Page 82

(ii) the distance travelled.

Sol. Given, acceleration, $a = 0.1$ m/s^2

Time, $t = 2 \text{ min} = 2 \times 60 = 120$ s, initial speed, $u = 0$

(i) From first equation of motion,

speed acquired by the bus,

$$v = u + at = 0 + 0.1 \times 120 = 12 \text{ m/s}$$

(ii) From second equation of motion,

distance travelled, $s = ut + \frac{1}{2}at^2$

$$= 0 \times 120 + \frac{1}{2} \times 0.1 \times 120 \times 120$$

$$= 0.1 \times 60 \times 120 = 720 \text{ m}$$

The distance travelled by the bus is 720 m.

Q.17 A train is travelling at a speed of 90 km/h. Brakes are applied, so as to produce a uniform acceleration of -0.5 m/s^2. Find how far the train will go before it is brought to rest? Page 82

Sol. Given, initial speed, $u = 90 \text{ km/h} = 90 \times \frac{5}{18} = 25$ m/s

Acceleration, $a = -0.5$ m/s^2

Train brought to rest, so final speed, $v = 0$

From third equation of motion, $v^2 = u^2 + 2as$

$$\Rightarrow \quad 0 = (25)^2 - 2 \times 0.5 \times s$$

$$0 = 625 - s \Rightarrow s = 625 \text{ m}$$

The train will travel a distance of 625 m before it is brought to rest.

Q.18 **A trolley while going down an inclined plane has an acceleration of 2 cm/s^2. What will be its velocity 3 s after the start?** **Page 82**

Sol. Given, initial velocity of trolley, $u = 0$

Acceleration, $a = 2 \text{ cm/s}^2 = 0.02 \text{ m/s}^2$,

Time taken, $t = 3$ s

From first equation of motion,

$$v = u + at = 0 + 0.02 \times 3 = 0.06 \text{ m/s}$$

Hence, the velocity of the trolley after 3 s of start is 0.06 m/s.

Q.19 **A racing car has a uniform acceleration of 4 m/s^2. What distance will it cover in 10 s after the start?** **Page 83**

Sol. Given, acceleration, $a = 4 \text{ m/s}^2$

Time taken, $t = 10$ s,

Initial velocity of the racing car, $u = 0$

From second equation of motion,

$$s = ut + \frac{1}{2} at^2 = 0 + \frac{1}{2} \times 4 \times (10)^2 = 200 \text{ m}$$

The distance travelled by the racing car in 10 s is 200 m.

Q.20 **A stone is thrown in a vertically upward direction with a velocity of 5 m/s. If the acceleration of the stone during its motion is 10 m/s^2 in the downward direction, then what will be the height attained by the stone and what time will it take to reach there?** **Page 83**

Sol. Given, initial velocity, $u = 5$ m/s,

Acceleration, $a = -10 \text{ m/s}^2$,

[negative sign is due to downward direction]

Final velocity, $v = 0$

[at maximum height velocity is zero]

Height attained, $s = ?$

Time taken, $t = ?$

(i) From third equation of motion,

$$v^2 = u^2 + 2as$$

$$0 = (5)^2 + 2 \times (-10) \times s$$

$$s = \frac{25}{20} = 1.25 \text{ m}$$

Height attained by the stone is 1.25 m.

(ii) From first equation of motion,

$$v = u + at$$

$$0 = 5 + (-10)\, t$$

$$t = \frac{5}{10} = 0.5 \text{ s}$$

The time taken by the stone to reach at the top will be 0.5 s.

Exercise Questions

Q.1 **An athlete completes one round of a circular track of diameter 200 m in 40 s. What will be the distance covered and the displacement at the end of 2 min 20 s?**

Sol. According to the question,

diameter of the circular track = 200 m

Hence, radius, $r = 100$ m

In 40 s, an athlete completes 1 round.

In 140 s, an athlete completes $\frac{140}{40} = 3\frac{1}{2}$ rounds.

Hence, the distance covered by the athlete

$$= 3 \times 2\pi r + \frac{1}{2} \times 2\pi r$$

$$= 3 \times 2 \times \frac{22}{7} \times 100 + \frac{1}{2} \times 2 \times \frac{22}{7} \times 100 = 2200 \text{ m}$$

Displacement = Shortest path between the initial position and the final position $= 2r = 2 \times 100 = 200$ m

Q.2 **Joseph jogs from one end A to the other end B of a straight 300 m road in 2 min 30 s and then turns around and jogs 100 m back to point C in another 1 min. What are Joseph's average speeds and velocities in jogging**

(i) from A to B and (ii) from A to C?

Sol. Joseph jogs from one end A to other end B of a straight 300 m road in 2 min 30 s and then turns around and jogs 100 m back to point C in another 1 min, as shown in figure

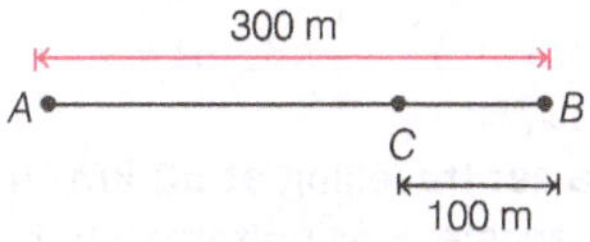

(i) From A to B, Joseph covers distance = 300 m

Time = 2 min 30 s = 2 × 60 + 30

= 120 + 30 = 150 s

Hence, average speed $= \frac{\text{Total distance}}{\text{Total time}} = \frac{300}{150} = 2$ m/s

$\therefore$ Average velocity $= \frac{\text{Total displacement}}{\text{Total time}} = \frac{300}{150} = 2$ m/s

As in both cases, distance covered and direction are same.

(ii) From A to C, Joseph covers distance = 400 m

Time = 150 + 60 = 210 s

Hence, average speed $= \frac{400}{210} = 1.9$ m/s

Displacement = 200 m

Time = 150 + 60 = 210 s

Hence, average velocity $= \frac{200}{210} = 0.952$ m/s

Q.3 Abdul, while driving to school, computes the average speed for his trip to be 20 km/h. On his return trip along the same route, there is less traffic and the average speed is 30 km/h. What is the average speed for Abdul's trip?

Sol. Let the distance covered by Abdul while driving to school $= x$

While going $v_1 = 20 = \dfrac{x}{t_1}$

[where, t_1 = time taken to cover distance x]

While returning $v_2 = 30 = \dfrac{x}{t_2}$

[where, t_2 = time taken to cover distance x while returning]

Hence, $t_1 = \dfrac{x}{20}$, $t_2 = \dfrac{x}{30}$

$$\therefore \text{Average speed} = \frac{\text{Total distance}}{\text{Total time}} = \frac{2x}{\frac{x}{20}+\frac{x}{30}} = \frac{2x}{\frac{5x}{60}}$$

$$= \frac{2x \times 60}{5x} = 24 \text{ km/h}$$

Q.4 A motorboat starting from rest on a lake accelerates in a straight line at a constant rate of 3 m/s^2 for 8 s. How far does the boat travel during this time?

Sol. The motorboat starts from rest, so initial velocity, $u = 0$

Time taken, $t = 8$ s, Acceleration, $a = 3$ m/s^2

$\therefore$Distance covered during the given time,

$$s = ut + \frac{1}{2}at^2 \quad \text{[from second equation of motion]}$$

$$= 0 \times 8 + \frac{1}{2} \times 3 \times (8)^2 = \frac{1}{2} \times 3 \times 64 = 96 \text{ m}$$

Q.5 A driver of a car travelling at 52 km/h applies the brakes and accelerates uniformly in the opposite direction. The car stops in 5 s. Another driver going at 3 km/h in another car applies his brakes slowly and stops in 10 s. On the same graph paper, plot the speed *versus* time graphs for the two cars. Which of the two cars travelled farther after the brakes were applied?

Sol. $\therefore$ Initial speed of car, $A = 52 \text{ km/h} = 52 \times \dfrac{5}{18} = 14.44$ m/s

The car stops in 5 s, i.e. final speed of car, $v = 0$, time, $t = 5$ s. For speed-time graph of car A,

Speed (s)	14.44 m/s	0
Time (t)	0	5

Initial speed of car $B = 3 \text{ km/h} = 3 \times \dfrac{5}{18} = 0.83$ m/s

The car stops in 10 s, i.e. final speed of car, $v = 0$, time, $t = 10$ s.

For speed-time graph of car B,

Speed (s)	0.83 m/s	0
Time (t)	0	10 s

The speed-time graph of both cars A and B is shown as below

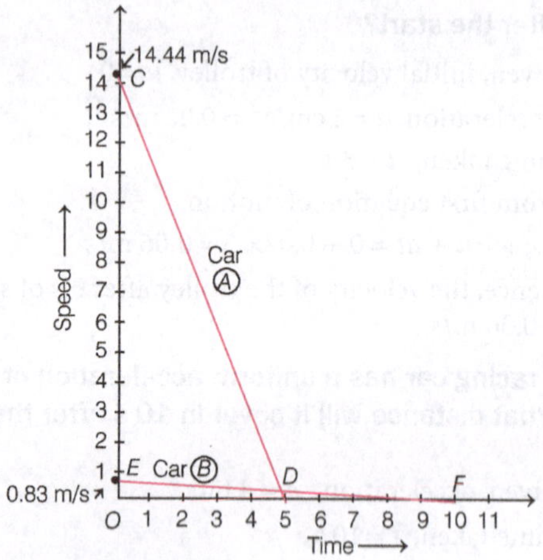

Distance travelled by car A = Area of ΔOCD

$$= \frac{1}{2} OC \times OD = \frac{1}{2} \times 14.44 \times 5 = 36.1 \text{ m}$$

Distance travelled by car B = Area of ΔOEF

$$= \frac{1}{2} OE \times EF = \frac{1}{2} \times 0.83 \times 10 = 4.15 \text{ m}$$

Thus, the car A travelled farther than car B after the brakes are applied.

Q.6 Figure shows the distance-time graph of three objects *A*, *B* and *C*. Study the graph and answer the following questions

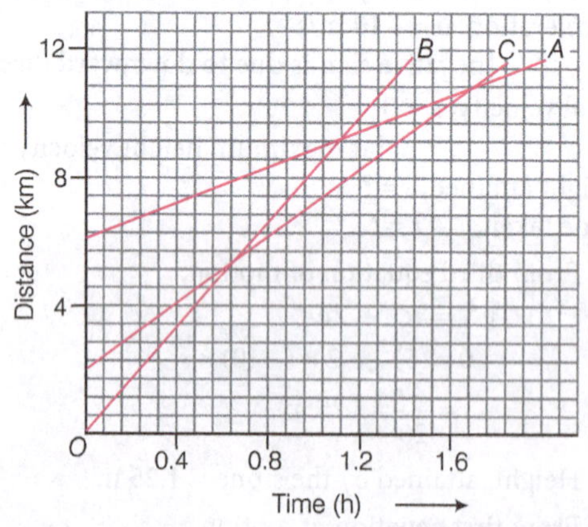

(i) Which of the three is travelling the fastest?

(ii) Are all three ever at same point on the road?

(iii) How far has C travelled when B passes A?

(iv) How far has B travelled by the time it passes C?

Sol.

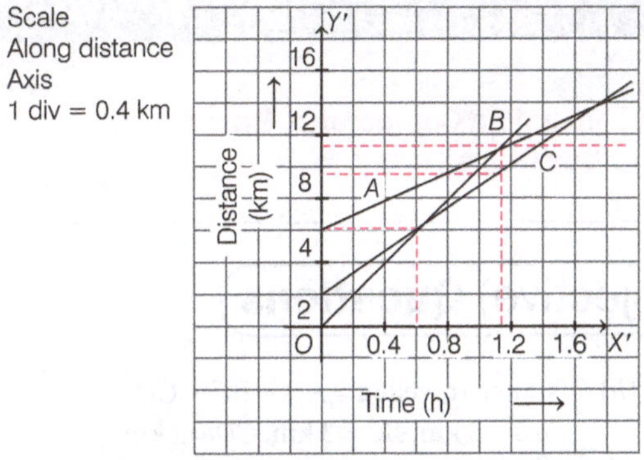

(i) The object for which slope of distance-time graph is maximum will have maximum speed, i.e. it will travel the fastest. Here, for object *B*, slope is maximum, so it is travelling the fastest.

(ii) All the three objects will be at the same point on the road, if the speed-time graphs intersect each other at any point. Here, all the three graphs do not intersect each other, so these three will never be at the same point on the road.

(iii) When *B* passes *A*, then distance travelled by

$$C = 9.6 - 2 = 7.6 \text{ km}$$

(iv) Distance travelled by *B* when it passes $C = 6$ km.

Q.7 A ball is gently dropped from a height of 20 m. If its velocity increases uniformly at the rate of 10 m/s², then with what velocity will it strike the ground? After what time will it strike the ground?

Sol. Initial velocity of the ball, $u = 0$

Acceleration, $a = 10 \text{ m/s}^2$

Distance, $s = 20$ m

From the equation of motion, $v^2 - u^2 = 2as$

$$v^2 - 0 = 2 \times 10 \times 20$$

$$v^2 = 400 \quad \Rightarrow \quad v = 20 \text{ m/s}$$

Again, from the first equation of motion

$$v = u + at \Rightarrow 20 = 0 + 10 \times t \Rightarrow t = 2 \text{ s}$$

After time $t = 2$s, it will strike the ground.

Q.8 The speed-time graph for a car is shown in the below figure

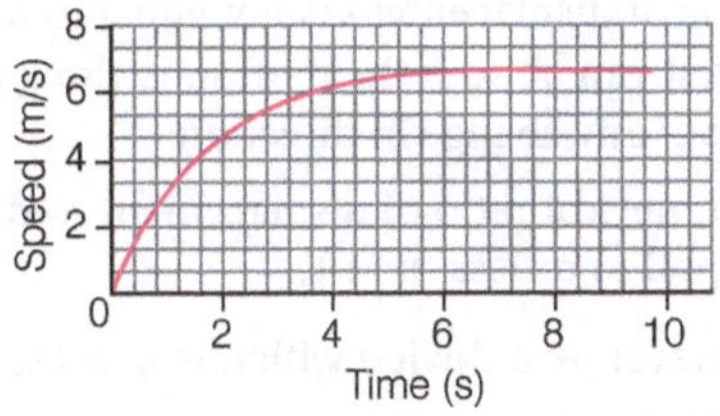

(i) Find how far does the car travel in the first 4 s? Shade the area on the graph that represents the distance travelled by the car during the period.

(ii) Which part of the graph represents uniform motion of the car?

Sol. The area under the slope of the speed-time graph gives the distance travelled by an object.

(i) We will calculate the distance represented by 1 square of the graph. This can be done as follows.

If 5 square on *X*-axis = 2 s,
1 square on *X*-axis = 2/5 s,

3 square on *Y*-axis = 2 m/s,
1 square on *Y*-axis = 2/3 m/s

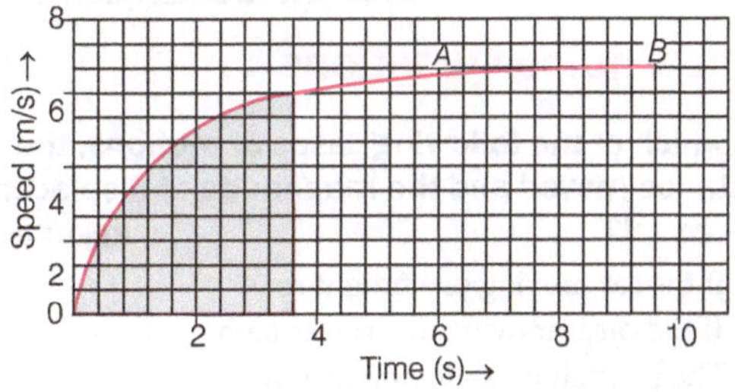

So, area of 1 square on graph $= \frac{2}{5} \times \frac{2}{3} = \frac{4}{15}$ m

1 square represents distance $= \frac{4}{15}$ m

Since, approximately 62 squares come under the area of slope for the time of 4 s.

So, distance travelled in 4 s $= \frac{4}{15} \times 62 = 16.53$ m

(ii) For uniform motion, the speed-time graph is a straight line parallel to the time axis. So, the straight part of the curve parallel to the time axis represents the uniform motion of the car.

Q.9 State which of the following situations are possible and give an example for each.

(i) An object with a constant acceleration but with zero velocity.

(ii) An object moving in a certain direction with an acceleration in the perpendicular direction.

Sol. (i) When an object is thrown vertically upward, then at highest point its velocity is zero but it has constant acceleration 9.8 m/s² (acceleration due to gravity).

(ii) An aeroplane flies in horizontal direction but the acceleration due to gravity acts on it in vertically downward direction, i.e. along the direction perpendicular to the direction of motion.

Q.10 An artificial satellite is moving in a circular orbit of radius 42250 km. Calculate its speed, if it takes 24 h to revolve around the earth.

Sol. $d = 2\pi r = 2 \times \frac{22}{7} \times 42250 = 265571.43$ km

$\therefore$ Speed of satellite $= \frac{\text{Distance}}{\text{Time}} = \frac{265571.43}{24} = 11065.48$ km/h

To Study NCERT Activities
Scan the Code

REVIEW EXERCISE

Including Competency Based Questions

Competency Focused (Objective) Questions

Multiple Choice Questions

1 In which of the following cases of motions, the distance moved and the magnitude of displacement are equal? **NCERT Exemplar**

(a) If the car moving on straight road
(b) If the car is moving in circular path
(c) The pendulum is moving to and fro
(d) The earth is revolving around the sun

Sol. (*a*) If the car is moving on a straight road, then the distance moved and the magnitude of displacement both are equal.

2 The sound of thunder is heard approximately 6 s after the flash of lightning is seen. If speed of sound in air is 346 m/s, then distance of point of lightning is

(a) 1200 m (b) 2076 m
(c) 3460 m (d) 965 m

Sol. (*b*) $\Rightarrow$ Distance = Speed × Time

$\Rightarrow$ Distance $= 346 \times 6 = 2076$ m

3 In 10 min a car whose speed is 35 km/h, travels a distance of

(a) 6 km (b) 3.5 km
(c) 14 km (d) 28 km

Sol. (*a*) Speed = 35 km/h

$$= 35 \times \left(\frac{5}{18}\right) = 9.72 \text{ m/s}$$

Time = 10 min

$= (10 \times 60) = 600$ s

Distance = Speed × Time

$= 9.72 \times 600$

$= 5832 \text{ m} = 5.832 \text{ km}$

$= 6$ km (approx)

4 A car travels 5 km towards north, then turns right and travels 3 km further, the car again turns right and travel 1 km and comes to rest. What is the distance travelled and displacement of the car? **Competency Based Que.**

(a) Distance: 5 km and Displacement: 9 km
(b) Distance: 9 km and Displacement: 5 km
(c) Distance: 9 km and Displacement: 7 km
(d) Distance: 7 km and Displacement: 9 km

Sol. (*b*) Distance travelled $= AB + BC + CD$

$AB = 5$ km, $BC = 3$ km, $CD = 1$ km

Distance travelled $= 5 + 3 + 1 = 9$ km

Displacement $= AD$

$AD^2 = AE^2 + ED^2$ (By using Pythagorous theorem)

$AE = AB - BE$

$AB = 5$ km

$BE = CD = 1$ km

$AE = 5 - 1 = 4$ km

$ED = BC = 3$ km

$AD^2 = 4^2 + 3^2$

$AD^2 = 16 + 9$

$AD^2 = 25$

Taking square root on both sides, $AD = 5$ km

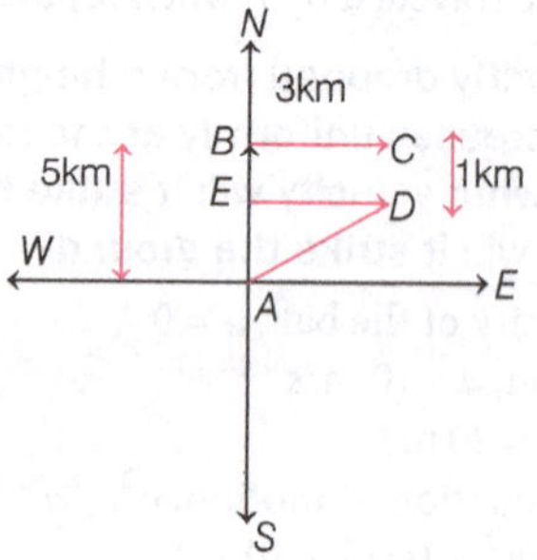

5 The numerical ratio of displacement and distance for a moving object is **NCERT Exemplar**

(a) always less than 1 (b) always equal to 1
(c) always more than 1 (d) equal or less than 1

Sol. (*d*) Displacement of an object can be less than or equal to the distance covered by the object, because the magnitude of displacement is not equal to distance. However, it can be so if the motion is along a straight line without any change in direction.

So, the numerical ratio of displacement to distance is always equal to or less than 1.

6 Speedometer is a device which is used to measure

(a) average speed
(b) average acceleration
(c) instantaneous speed
(d) instantaneous acceleration

Sol. (*c*) Speedometer is used to measure instantaneous speed.

7 **A car travels 3 km of distance in 10 min to reach the destination. On the return journey, the car travels the same distance in 15 min. What is the average speed of car in entire journey?** **CBSE Question Bank**

(a) 5 m/s (b) 4 m/s
(c) 6 m/s (d) 3 m/s

Sol. (*b*) Total distance travelled by the car $= 3 + 3 = 6$ km

i.e. 6000 m

Total time taken for the whole joining

$$= 10 + 15 = 25 \text{ min}$$

i.e. 1500 s [1 min = 60 s]

$$\therefore \text{Average speed} = \frac{\text{Total distance}}{\text{Total time}} = \frac{6000}{1500} = 4 \text{ m/s}$$

8 **A car moves towards South with a speed of 20 ms^{-1}. It changes its direction to East and moves with speed of 20 ms^{-1}. What is its velocity now?** **Competency Based Que.**

(a) 20 ms^{-1} South-East (b) $20\sqrt{2}$ ms^{-1} South-East
(c) 10 ms^{-1} South-East (d) 40 ms^{-1} South-East

Sol. (*b*) A car moves towards South with speed 20 ms^{-1}, then it changes its direction to East with speed 20 ms^{-1} as shown in figure below

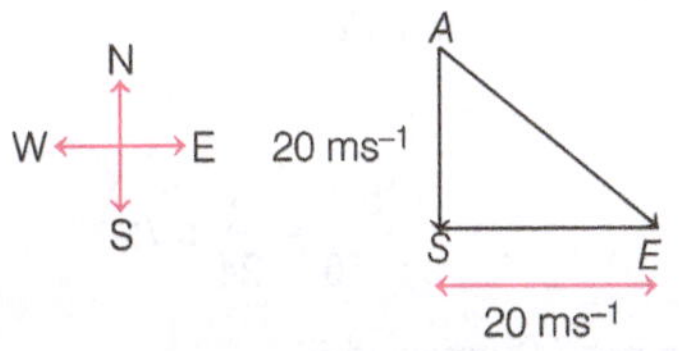

$AE = ?$

Now, $AE^2 = AS^2 + SE^2$

$$AE = \sqrt{AS^2 + SE^2}$$

$$= \sqrt{(20)^2 + (20)^2} = 20\sqrt{2}$$

$AE = 20\sqrt{2}$ m/s, South-East

Thus, its velocity is $20\sqrt{2}$ m/s South-East.

9 **A car travels on a straight road with a velocity of 30 km/h in first one hour and in the next one hour it changes its velocity to 40 km/h. What is the average velocity of the car?**

(a) 5 km/h (b) 10 km/h
(c) 35 km/h (d) 60 km/h

Sol. (*c*) Given, $v_1 = 30$ km/h

$v_2 = 40$ km/h

$$\text{Average velocity} = \frac{v_1 + v_2}{2}$$

$$= \frac{30 + 40}{2}$$

$$= \frac{70}{2} = 35 \text{ km/h}$$

10 **A person rides a motorbike at the speed of 30 m/s. The person applies the brake and the velocity of motorbike comes down to 20 m/s in 3 s. What is the magnitude of acceleration of motorbike?** **CBSE Question Bank**

(a) -3.3 m/s^2 (b) 6.6 m/s^2
(c) 10 m/s^2 (d) -6.6 m/s^2

Sol. (*a*) $\text{Acceleration} = \dfrac{\text{Final velocity} - \text{Initial velocity}}{\text{Time taken}}$

$$a = \frac{20 - 30}{3} \Rightarrow a = -3.3 \text{ m/s}^2$$

11 **If velocity of an object decreases with time, then it is called**

(a) retardation (b) deceleration
(c) negative acceleration (d) All of these

Sol. (*d*) When velocity of an object decreases with time, then it is said to be retardation, deceleration or negative acceleration.

12 **Four cars *A*, *B*, *C* and *D* are moving on a levelled road. Their distance *versus* time graphs are shown in figure. Choose the correct statement.** **Competency Based Que.**

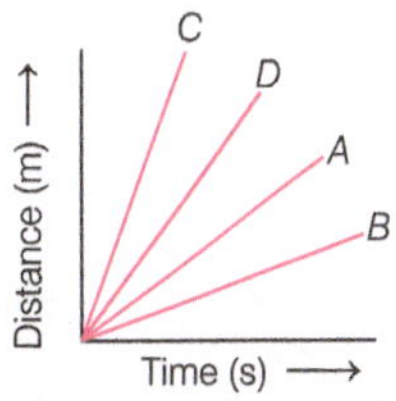

(a) Car *A* is faster than car *D* (b) Car *B* is the slowest
(c) Car *D* is faster than car *C* (d) Car *C* is the slowest

Sol. (*b*) The slope of distance-time graph represents the speed. From the given graph, it is clear that the slope of distance-time graph for car *B* is less than all other cars. So, the slope is minimum for car *B*. Hence, car *B* is the slowest.

13 **Which of the following figures represents uniform motion of a moving object correctly?** **Competency Based Que.**

(a)
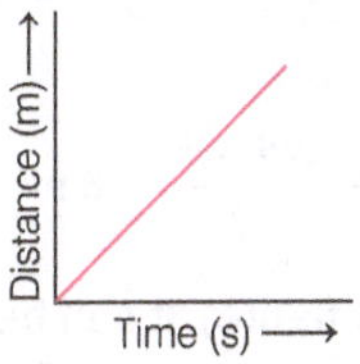

(b)
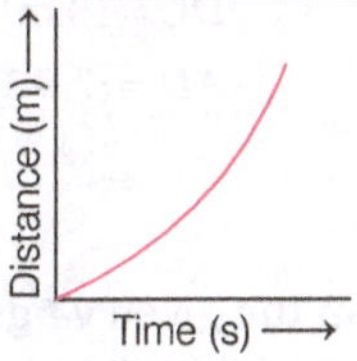

(c)
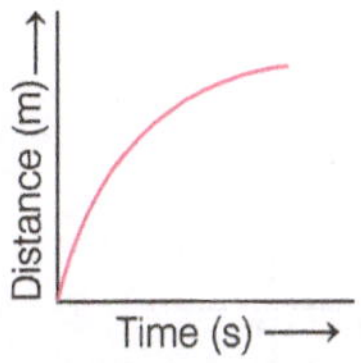

(d)
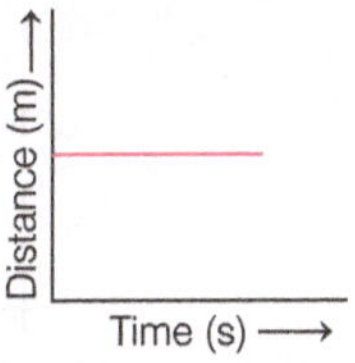

Sol. (*a*) For uniform motion, the distance-time graph is a straight line (because in uniform motion object covers equal distances in equal intervals of time).

14 Velocity-time graph for a moving object is found to be curved line, then its acceleration is

(a) constant (b) variable
(c) zero (d) None of these

Sol. (*b*) Since, velocity-time graph for a moving object is curved line, this means that object is moving with non-uniformly accelerated motion, therefore body is moving with variable acceleration.

15 Slope of a velocity-time graph gives **NCERT Exemplar**

(a) the distance (b) the displacement
(c) the acceleration (d) the speed

Sol. (*c*) Slope of velocity-time graph gives acceleration.

Because slope of the curve $= \frac{\text{Velocity}}{\text{Time}} = \frac{v}{t}$

where, $\frac{v}{t}$ = acceleration.

16 In the following figure of velocity-time graph for the motion of the body, the total distance covered by the body from 3 s to 7 s is **Competency Based Que.**

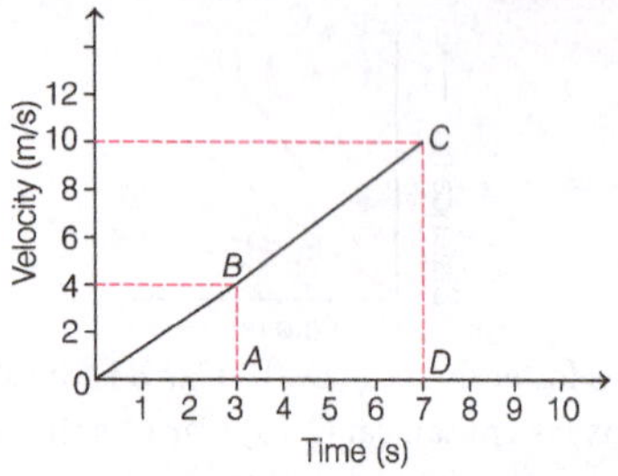

(a) 28 m (b) 56 m (c) 14 m (d) 35 m

Sol. (*a*) Total distance moved by the body from 3 s to 7 s

$= \text{Area of shape } ABCD = \frac{(AB + DC) \times AD}{2}$

From given graph, we have

$AB = 4 \text{ m/s}$

$DC = 10 \text{ m/s}$

$AD = (7 - 3) = 4 \text{ s}$

$= \frac{(4 + 10)(7 - 3)}{2} = \frac{14 \times 4}{2} = 28 \text{ m}$

17 From the given *v-t* graph (see figure), it can be inferred that the object is **NCERT Exemplar**

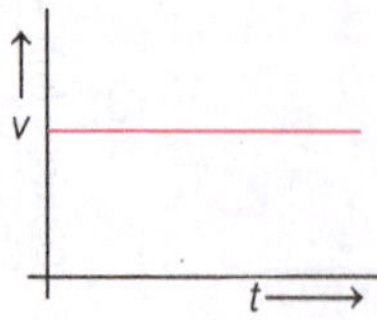

(a) in uniform motion
(b) at rest
(c) in non-uniform motion
(d) moving with uniform acceleration

Sol. (*a*) In the given graph we find that the velocity is constant throughout, hence the object represented in *v-t* graph is said to be in uniform motion.

18 Area under a *v-t* graph represents a physical quantity which has the unit **NCERT Exemplar**

(a) m^2 (b) m
(c) m^3 (d) ms^{-1}

Sol. (*b*) Area under velocity-time graph represents Velocity × Time = Distance, which has the unit as metre (m).

19 A train starting from rest attains a velocity of 90 km/h in 2 min, then the distance travelled by the train for attaining this velocity is

(a) 1.5 km (b) 2 km (c) 2.5 km (d) 1.2 km

Sol. (*a*) Given, initial velocity, $u = 0$

Final velocity, $v = 90 \text{ km/h} = 90 \times \frac{5}{18} = 25 \text{ m/s}$

Time, $t = 2 \text{ min} = 2 \times 60 = 120 \text{ s}$

From the equation of motion,

$$v = u + at$$

$$\Rightarrow \quad a = \frac{v}{t} \qquad [\because u = 0]$$

$$= \frac{25}{2 \times 60} = \frac{5}{24} \text{ m/s}^2$$

Distance (s) covered is

$$s = ut + \frac{1}{2}at^2 = 0 + \frac{1}{2} \times \frac{5}{24} \times (120)^2$$

$$= \frac{1}{2} \times \frac{5}{24} \times 120 \times 120$$

$$= 1500 \text{ m} = 1.5 \text{ km}$$

20 If the displacement of an object is proportional to square of time, then the object moves with **NCERT Exemplar**

(a) uniform velocity (b) uniform acceleration
(c) increasing acceleration (d) decreasing acceleration

Sol. (*b*) Let object starts from rest *i.e.,* initial velocity (u) = 0 and an acceleration (a) in time (t).

From second equation of motion,

$$s = ut + \frac{1}{2}at^2$$

Then, $s = 0 \times t + \frac{1}{2}at^2 \Rightarrow s = \frac{1}{2}at^2$

$s \propto t^2$, if a = constant

Thus, displacement (s) of an object is proportional to square of time t, then the object moves with constant or uniform acceleration.

21 **A body is thrown vertically upward with velocity *u*, the greatest height *h* to which it will rise is** NCERT Exemplar

(a) $\frac{u}{g}$ (b) $\frac{u^2}{2g}$

(c) $\frac{u^2}{g}$ (d) $\frac{u}{2g}$

Sol. (*b*) Initial velocity $= u$

Final velocity at height $h, v = 0$

Equation of motion $= v^2 - u^2 = 2gh$

$\Rightarrow \qquad h = \frac{u^2}{2g} \qquad$ (as $a = -g$)

22 **A body moving along a straight line at 10 m/s undergoes an acceleration of 2 m/s². After 2 s, its speed will be**

(a) –8 m/s (b) 12 m/s

(c) 14 m/s (d) 16 m/s

Sol. (*c*) $u = 10$ m/s

$a = 2$ m/s^2

$v = u + at = 10 + 2 \times 2 = 10 + 4 = 14$ m/s

23 **A particle is moving in a circular path of radius *r*. The displacement after half a circle would be** NCERT Exemplar

(a) zero (b) πr

(c) $2r$ (d) $2\pi r$

Sol. (*c*) Given, after half the circle, the particle will reach the diametrically opposite point *i.e.*, from point *A* to point *B* as shown in figure below. We know displacement is shortest path between initial and final point.

$\therefore$ Displacement after half circle $= AB = OA + OB$

$= r + r = 2r \qquad [\because$ Given, OA and $OB = r]$

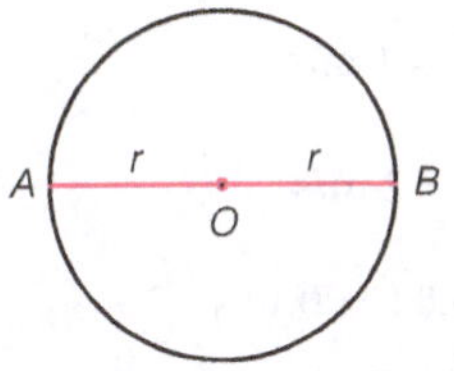

Hence, the displacement after half circle is $2r$.

24 **Suppose a boy is enjoying a ride on a merry-go-round which is moving with a constant speed of 10 ms⁻¹. It implies that the boy is** NCERT Exemplar

(a) at rest

(b) moving with no acceleration

(c) in accelerated motion

(d) moving with uniform velocity

Sol. (*c*) In merry-go-round, the speed is constant but velocity is not constant, because its direction goes on changing i.e. there is acceleration in the motion.

25 **Match Column A with Column B and select the correct option using the given codes.**

Column A	Column B
1. Uniform motion	A. Rate of change of velocity
2. Acceleration	B. Covers equal distances in equal intervals of time
3. Distance–time graph of uniform motion	C. Straight line
4. Velocity	D. Displacement per unit time

(a) 1-B, 2-A, 3-C, 4-D (b) 1-A, 2-B, 3-D, 4-C

(c) 1-B, 2-A, 3-C, 4-D (d) 1-C, 2-B, 3-D, 4-A

Sol. (*a*) 1-B, 2-A, 3-C, 4-D

Assertion–Reason Questions

Direction (Q.Nos. 1-8) ***In each of the following questions, a statement of Assertion is given by the corresponding statement of Reason. Of the given statements, mark the correct answer as***

(a) If both Assertion and Reason are true and Reason is the correct explanation of Assertion.

(b) If both Assertion and Reason are true but Reason is not the correct explanation of Assertion.

(c) If Assertion is true but Reason is false.

(d) If Assertion is false but Reason is true.

1 **Assertion** (A) Displacement of body may be zero, when distance travelled by it is not zero.

Reason (R) The displacement is the longer distance between initial and final positions.

Sol. (*c*) The shortest distance between two points is called displacement. Displacement may be positive, negative or zero, while distance is always positive. Hence, Assertion is true but Reason is false.

2 **Assertion** (A) The displacement of an object can be either positive, negative or zero.

Reason (R) Displacement has both the magnitude and direction.

Sol. (*a*) Both Assertion and Reason are true and Reason is the correct explanation of Assertion.
Displacement may be positive, negative or zero as displacement is a vector quantity.

3 **Assertion** (A) Speedometer is a device used to measure instantaneous speed.

Reason (R) Speedometer is used for measuring various speeds in each time interval.

Sol. (*c*) Speedometer is a device used to measure instantaneous speed. Hence, Assertion is true but Reason is false.

4 **Assertion** (A) Motion with uniform velocity is always along a straight line path.

Reason (R) In such a motion, speed is the magnitude of the velocity and is equal to the instantaneous velocity.

Sol. (*a*) Both Assertion and Reason are true and Reason is the correct explanation of Assertion.
Uniform velocity means that speed and direction remains unchanged.

5 **Assertion** (A) Acceleration of a moving body is always positive.

Reason (R) Acceleration of a moving body is the rate of change in velocity with respect to time.

Sol. (*d*) Assertion is false because acceleration may be positive, negative or zero.
Hence, Assertion is false but Reason is true.

6 **Assertion** (A) A body can have acceleration even its speed is constant.

Reason (R) In uniform circular motion, speed of body is constant but its velocity continuously changes.

Sol. (*a*) In uniform circular motion, speed of body remains same while its velocity continuously changes due to change in its direction at each point. Hence, body moves with acceleration. Therefore, Assertion and Reason both are true and Reason is the correct explanation of Assertion.

7 **Assertion** (A) Acceleration and displacement are in the opposite direction during retardation.

Reason (R) Acceleration is given as the change in velocity per unit time.

Sol. (*a*) Acceleration is defined as the rate of change of velocity with respect to time and negative acceleration is called retardation. Displacement is length of the shortest path measured in direction from initial position to final position of the object. Both Assertion and Reason are true and Reason is the correct explanation of Assertion.

8 **Assertion** (A) The graph between two physical quantities *P* and *Q* is straight line, when *P*/*Q* is constant.

Reason (R) The straight line graph means that *P* is proportional to *Q* or *P* is equal to constant multiplied by *Q*.

Sol. (*a*) Both Assertion and Reason are true and Reason is the correct explanation of Assertion.
Equation of straight line, $y = mx$

$$P = mQ$$

$$\frac{P}{Q} = \text{constant}$$

Therefore, $P \propto Q$ or $P = mQ$
So, option (a) is correct.

Case Based/Source Based Questions

Direction (Q.Nos. 1-4) ***Answer the questions on the basis of your understanding of the following passage and related studied concepts***

1. Imagine a car with a leaky engine that drips oil at a regular rate of 50 drops per second. As the car travels through town, it would leave a trace of oil on the street that would reveal information about the motion of the car. The trace of the oil in four different situations are shown. (The positions are given in centimeters.)

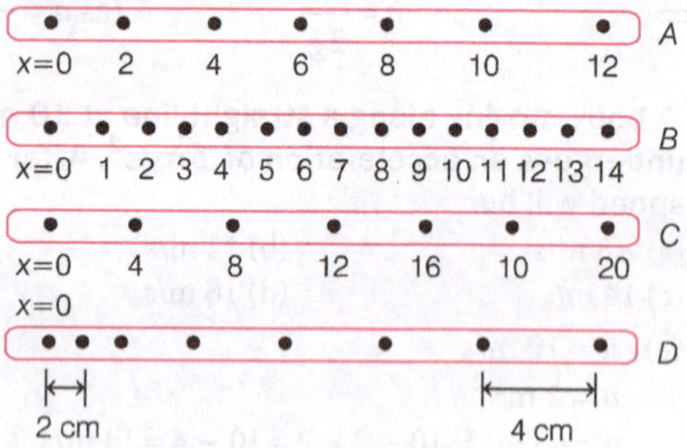

(i) Identify the type of motion by the car in situations *A*, *B*, *C* and *D*. [1]

(ii) What is the ratio of speed of the car in situations *A*, *B* and *C*. [1]

(a) 1:2:4 (b) 2:1:4
(c) 4:2:1 (d) 2:4:1

(iii) What is the acceleration of the car in situation *D*? [2]

Sol. (i) *A*, *B* and *C* show uniform motion.
D shows non-uniform/uniform accelerated motion.

(ii) (b) 2:1:4

(iii) Time between each drop = 1/50 = 0.02 s

$$u = \frac{0.02}{0.02} = 1 \text{ m/s}$$

$$v = \frac{0.04}{0.02} = 2 \text{ m/s}$$

$$t = 7 \times 0.02 = 0.14 \text{ s}$$

$$a = \frac{v-u}{t} = 7.14 \text{ m/s}^2$$

2. Distance travelled by a train and time taken by it is shown in the following table

Time	Distance (in km)
10:00 am	0
10:30 am	25
10:40 am	28
11:00 am	40
11:15 am	42
11:30 am	50

(i) Plot distance-time graph. [1]

(ii) When is the train travelling at the highest speed? [1]

(iii) What is the average speed of the train? [1]

(iv) At what distance does the train slow down? [1]

Sol. (i) Distance-time graph is shown as

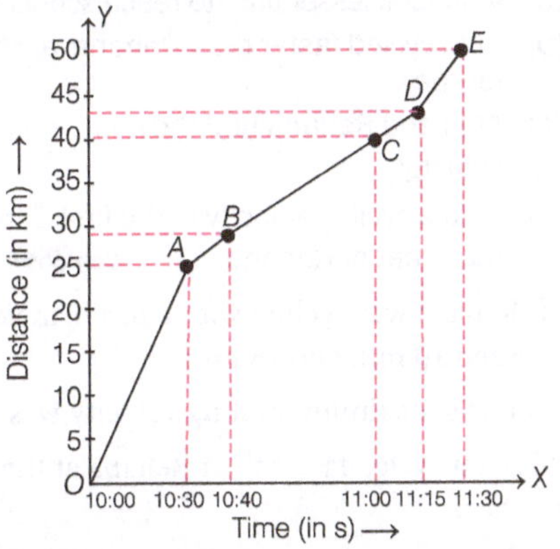

(ii) We know that, speed = slope of distance-time graph. The greater the slope, greater is the speed. From the graph, it is clear that slope of distance-time graph is maximum between 10:00 am to 10:30 am, so the train was travelling at the highest speed during this interval of time.

(iii) Here, Average speed $= \dfrac{\text{Total distance travelled}}{\text{Total time taken}}$

From the given table, total distance travelled = 50 km

Total time taken 10:00 am to 11:30 am = 1 h 30 min

$$= 1\frac{1}{2}\text{ h} = \frac{3}{2}\text{ h}$$

Now, average speed $= \dfrac{50\text{ km}}{3/2\text{ h}} = \dfrac{100}{3} = 33.33\text{ km/h}$

(iv) The part *CD* of the graph has minimum slope, so the train had minimum speed between 11:00 am and 11:15 am. Thus, the train had slowed down between 40 km and 42 km.

3. The graph below shows the positions of a body at different time intervals, while travelling from his home to school in the morning. Based on the given graph, answer the following questions.

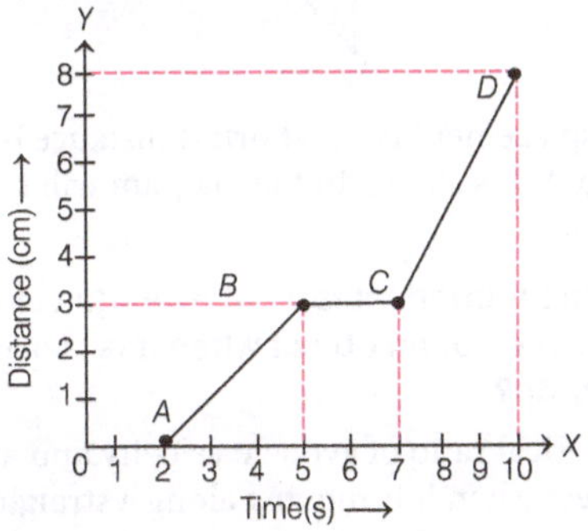

(a) Calculate the speed of the body as it moves from

(i) *A* to *B* (ii) *B* to *C*

(b) Find the time interval during which speed is maximum.

(c) Calculate

(i) The total distance covered.

(ii) The distance covered between *B* and *C*

Or (c) Is the motion of the body during time interval from *A* to *D* is uniform?

Sol. (a) (i) For the motion from point *A* to *B*

Time taken, $t = 5 - 2 = 3$ s

Distance covered $= 3 - 0 = 3$ m

∴ Speed will be during point *A* to *B*

$$= \frac{\text{Distance}}{\text{Time}} = \frac{3}{3} = 1\text{ m/s}$$

(ii) Similarly, for the motion from point *B* to *C*

Time taken $= 7 - 5 = 2$ s

Distance covered $= 3 - 3 = 0$ m

∴ Speed $= \dfrac{\text{Distance}}{\text{Time}} = \dfrac{0}{2} = 0\text{ m/s} = 0$

(b) Speed in the interval *C* to *D*,

Time taken = 3 s

Distance covered $= 8 - 3 = 5$ m

∴ Speed will be during point *C* to *D*

$$= \frac{\text{Distance}}{\text{Time}} = \frac{5}{3} = 1.66\text{ m/s}$$

Speed is maximum from point *C* to *D*.

(c) (i) Total distance covered

$= AB + BC + CD$

$= 3 + 0 + 5 = 8$ m

(ii) Body does not change its position from *B* to *C*. So, distance covered is zero.

Or (c) No, boy is moving with different speed at different time interval.

4. Rehana and Anju stay at different places but study in the same school.
The velocity-time graph shows how Rehana and Anju bicycled from house to school.

Velocity-time graph of Rehana's cycling

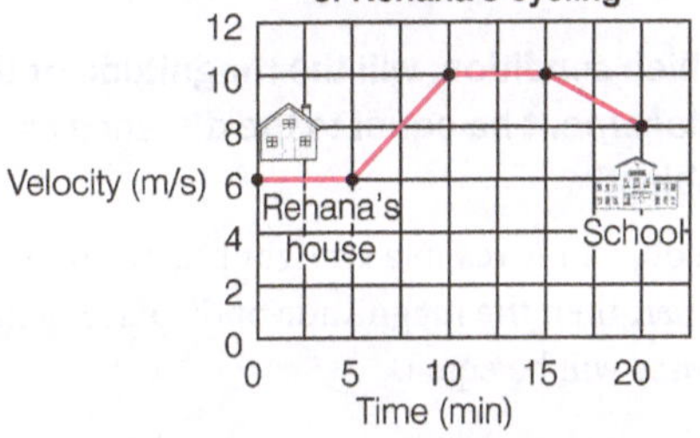

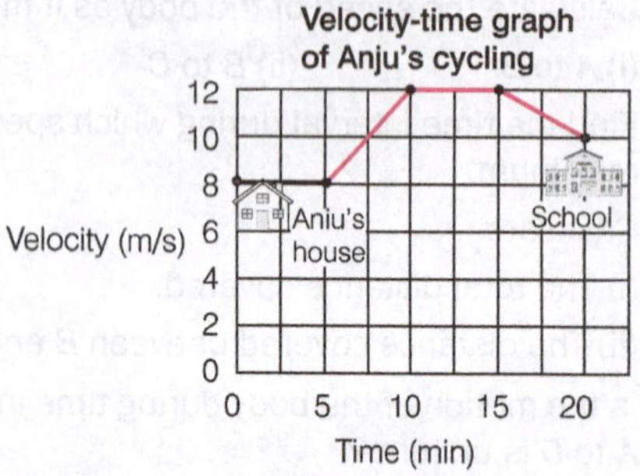

(i) Which statement can be concluded from Rehana's cycling graph? [2]
(a) Rehana was at rest during the first 5 min.
(b) Rehana cycled the fastest between 5 min and 10 min.
(c) Rehana cycled with uniform acceleration between 15 min and 20 min.
(d) Rehana was cycling with a uniform velocity between 10 min and 15 min.

(ii) What was Rehana's maximum cycling velocity? [1]

(iii) What can be concluded by comparing the velocity-time graphs of Rehana and Anju? [1]
(a) Anju took lesser time to reach school than Rehana.
(b) Anju cycled faster than Rehana at the start of the journey.
(c) Anju and Rehana had the same maximum cycling velocity.
(d) Anju's cycling velocity in the first 5 min was lesser than that of Rehana. **Competency Based Que.**

Sol. (i) (*d*) Rehana was cycling with a uniform velocity between 10 min and 15 min.
(ii) Rehana's maximum cycling velocity was 10 km/h.
(iii) (*b*) Anju cycled faster than Rehana at the start of the journey.

Constructed Response (Descriptive) Questions

Very Short Answer Type Questions

1 Is it possible that the train in which you are sitting appears to move while it is at rest?

Sol. Yes, if other train is moving in adjacent line to the train we are sitting, then it seems that our train is moving in opposite direction.

2 Can an object be at rest as well in motion at the same time?

Sol. Yes, an object may be at rest related to one reference point and at the same time, it may be in motion related to another reference point.

3 If the displacement of a body is zero, is it necessary that the distance covered by it is also zero?

Sol. No, when the body comes back to the same position after travelling a distance its displacement is zero but it has travelled some distance. So, the distance travelled by it is non zero.

4 In which condition, will the magnitude of the displacement be equal to the distance travelled by an object?

Sol. If an object moves in a straight line from one point to another, then the magnitude of displacement and distance will be equal.

5 A man leaves his house at 6 : 30 am for a morning walk and returns at 7 :15 am. Find the displacement in this time.

Sol. Displacement is zero. As his initial point and final point are the same. Thus, there is no change in his position and the displacement is zero.

6 A honey bee travels from *A* to *B* and then moves from *B* to *C* (as shown in the diagram). Show resultant displacement in the diagram. **Competency Based Que.**

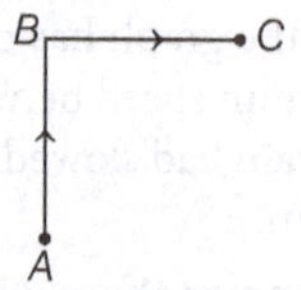

Sol.

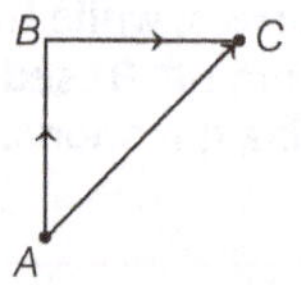

Since, displacement is the shortest distance between two points, so *AC* as shown in the diagram will be the resultant displacement.

7 What is the numerical ratio of average velocity to average speed of an object when it is moving along a straight path?

Sol. The numerical ratio of average velocity and average speed of an object when it is moving along a straight path is 1 : 1.

8 The distance-time graph for motion of Ram and Shyam is shown below.

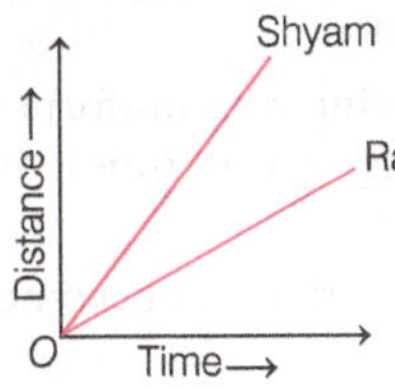

Which of them has greater acceleration? Justify your answer. **Competency Based Que.**

Sol. Both Ram and Shyam have zero acceleration as they are moving with constant velocity. Since, distance-time graph is a straight line.

9 What are the characteristics of distance-time graph for an object moving with a non-uniform speed?

Sol. The characteristics of distance-time graph for an object moving with a non-uniform speed is

(i) The graph is not a straight line. It forms a curve, as the object's speed is changing.

(ii) The slope of the tangent to the curve at any point represents the instantaneous speed.

10 Study the given velocity-time graph of two bodies *M* and *N* and answer the following questions.

(i) Which body starts from rest and which body has some initial velocity? [1]

(ii) Which body is having lesser acceleration? [1]

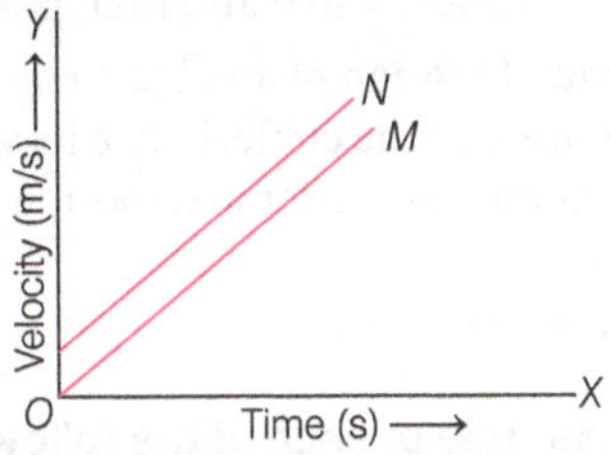

Sol. (i) Body M starts from rest, as $t = 0, v = 0$ but body N has some initial velocity as $v \neq 0$.

(ii) Acceleration is lesser for body M. Because acceleration is the slope of velocity-time graph, which is lesser for body M.

11 Is the motion of a body uniform or accelerated, if it goes round the sun with constant speed in a circular orbit?

Sol. In this case, the motion of a body is accelerated as its velocity changes due to the change in direction. Then, the motion will be accelerated motion.

12 Two particles are moving with constant speed *v*. Such that, they are always at constant distance *d* apart and their velocities are equal and opposite. After how much time, will they return to their initial positions? **Competency Based Que.**

Sol. The two particles moving with constant speed are always at a constant distane d, they must be at the two ends of diameter of a circular path as shown in figure.

Each particle will return to its initial position after completing the circular path i.e., $2\pi r = \pi d$.

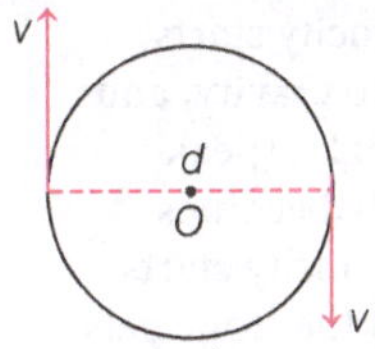

$$\text{Time} = \frac{\text{Distance}}{\text{Speed}} = \frac{\pi d}{v}$$

Short Answer Type Questions

1 Express average velocity when the velocity of a body changes at a non-uniform rate and a uniform rate.

Sol. When the velocity of a body changes at a non-uniform rate, then its average velocity is calculated by dividing the net displacement covered with the total time taken.

i.e. $$\text{Average velocity} = \frac{\text{Net displacement}}{\text{Total time taken}}$$

In case, the velocity of a body changes at a uniform rate, the average velocity is given by the arithmetic mean of initial velocity and final velocity for a given period of time, i.e.

$$\text{Average velocity} = \frac{\text{Initial velocity} + \text{Final velocity}}{2}$$

2 The velocity-time graph (see figure) shows the motion of a cyclist. Find,

(i) its acceleration, (ii) its velocity and

(iii) the distance covered by the cyclist in 15 s. **NCERT Exemplar**

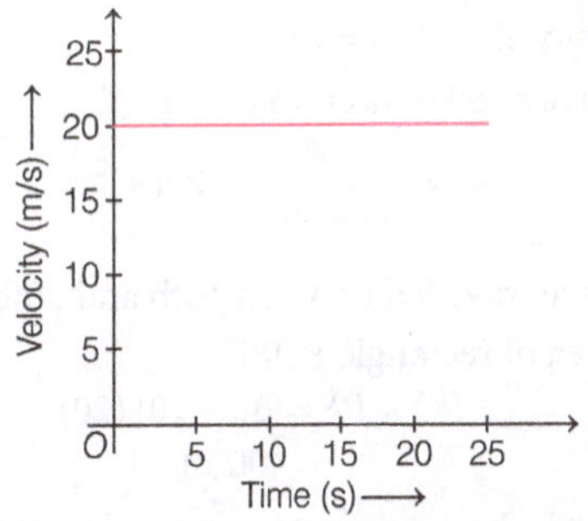

Sol. (i) From the given graph, it is clear that velocity is not changing with time, i.e. acceleration is zero.

(ii) Again from the graph, we can see that there is no change in the velocity with time, so velocity is after 15 s will remain same as 20 m/s.

(iii) Distance covered in 15 s = Velocity × Time

$= 20 \times 15 = 300$ m

3 Draw a velocity-time graph of a stone thrown vertically upwards and then coming downwards after attaining the maximum height. **Competency Based Que.**

Sol. When a stone is thrown vertically upward as positive direction, its velocity starts decreasing due to gravity, and at maximum height, (peak point) its velocity becomes zero. Then, its velocity starts increasing when the stone gets downward from the peak point and becomes maximum while reaching the ground.

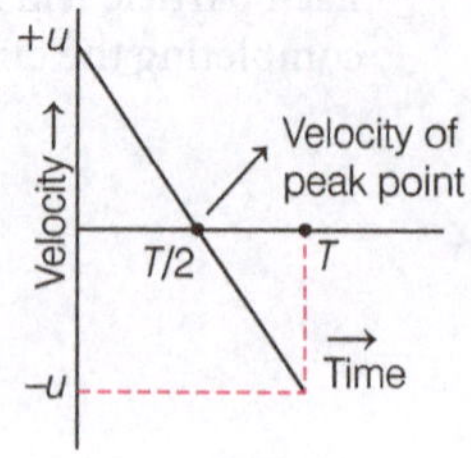

4 The velocity-time graph of a body is shown below

(i) State the kind of motion represented by *OP* and *PQ*. [½]

(ii) Find the velocity of the body after 30 s and 40 s. [½]

(iii) What is the negative acceleration of the body? [1]

(iv) Find the distance travelled between 10th and 30th s. [1]

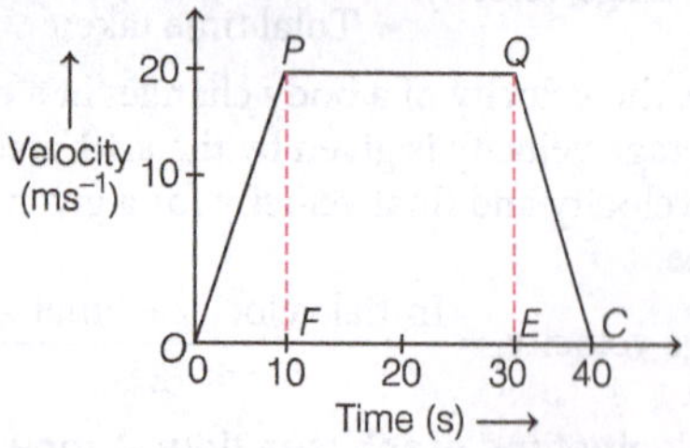

Competency Based Que.

Sol. (i) *OP* represents uniform acceleration,

PQ represents constant velocity.

(ii) Velocity after 30 s $= 20\ \text{ms}^{-1}$

Velocity after 40 s = zero.

(iii) Negative acceleration = Slope of *QC*

$$= \frac{0-20}{40-30} = -2\ \text{ms}^{-2}$$

(iv) Distance travelled between 10th and 30th s are

$\Rightarrow$ Area of rectangle *PQEF*

$$\Rightarrow \quad PQ \times PF = (30-10)\,(20)$$

$$= 400\ \text{m}$$

5 How will the equations of motion for an object moving with a uniform velocity change? **NCERT Exemplar**

Sol. We know that, the equations of uniformly accelerated motion are

(i) $v = u + at$

(ii) $s = ut + \frac{1}{2}at^2$

(iii) $v^2 = u^2 + 2as$

where, u = initial velocity, v = final velocity,

a = acceleration, t = time

and s = distance

For an object moving with uniform velocity (velocity which is not changing with time), then acceleration $a = 0$.

So, equations of motion will become (putting $a = 0$ in above equations)

(i) $v = u$ (ii) $s = ut$

(iii) $v^2 = u^2$

6 An object is moving with a uniform speed in a circle of radius *r*. Calculate the distance and displacement,

(i) when it completes half the circle, [1]

(ii) when it completes full circle, [1]

(iii) what type of motion does the object possess? [1]

Sol. (i) When an object completes half the circle, then the distance travelled by an object

$$= \frac{1}{2} \times \text{circumference of a circle}$$

$$= \frac{1}{2} \times 2\pi r = \pi r$$

$\therefore$ Displacement of an object $= 2r$

(ii) When an object completes full circle, then

distance travelled by an object $= 2\pi r$

Displacement travelled by an object $= 0$

[since, initial and final positions are same]

(iii) Direction of motion of an object changes continuously in the circle, hence its velocity changes and its motion is accelerated motion.

Long Answer Type Questions

1 Give one example of each of the following situations

(i) Uniformly accelerated motion. [1]

(ii) Motion with uniform retardation. [1]

(iii) Accelerated motion with uniform magnitude of velocity. [1]

(iv) Motion in a direction with acceleration in perpendicular direction. [1]

(v) Motion in which *v-t* graph is a horizontal line parallel to *X*-axis. [1]

Sol. (i) Object dropped down from a height towards the surface of the earth.

(ii) Object thrown up with a velocity, retards uniformly.

(iii) Uniform circular motion, say planetary motion.

(iv) A bullet fired horizontally from a rifle, has acceleration in downward direction (due to gravity).

(v) A car moving with uniform velocity along a straight line.

2 Deduce the following equations of motion.

(i) $s = ut + (1/2)\,at^2$ [2½]

(ii) $v^2 = u^2 + 2as$ [2½]

Sol. (i) Consider a body which starts with initial velocity u and due to uniform acceleration a, its final velocity becomes v after time t. Then, its average velocity is given by

$$= \frac{\text{initial velocity} + \text{final velocity}}{2} = \frac{u+v}{2}$$

$\therefore$ The distance covered by the body in time t is given by distance, s = average velocity × time

or $$s = \frac{u+v}{2} \times t$$

$\Rightarrow$ $$s = \frac{u+(u+at)}{2} \times t \quad [\because v = u + at]$$

$\therefore$ $$s = \frac{2\,ut + at^2}{2}$$

or $$s = ut + \frac{1}{2}at^2$$

(ii) From second equation of motion,

$$s = ut + \frac{1}{2}at^2 \quad \text{...(i)}$$

Also, $$a = \frac{v-u}{t} \Rightarrow t = \frac{v-u}{a}$$

Substituting the value of t in Eq. (i), we get

$$s = u\left(\frac{v-u}{a}\right) + \frac{1}{2}a\left(\frac{v-u}{a}\right)^2$$

or $$s = \frac{uv - u^2}{a} + \frac{v^2 + u^2 - 2\,uv}{2a}$$

$$[\because (a-b)^2 = a^2 + b^2 - 2ab]$$

or $$2\,as = 2\,uv - 2\,u^2 + v^2 + u^2 - 2\,uv$$

or $v^2 - u^2 = 2as$

or $$v^2 = u^2 + 2as$$

Numerical Questions

1 A boy is moving 3 m North, then 4 m East and finally 6 m South. Calculate the distance travelled and the displacement.

Sol. As shown in the figure, the boy starts from O and moves 3 m North (= OA), 4 m East (= AB) and 6 m South (= BC)

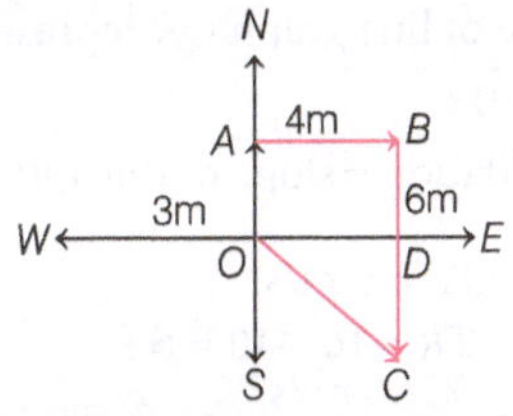

Distance travelled = $OA + AB + BC$
$= 3\text{ m} + 4\text{ m} + 6\text{ m} = 13\text{ m}$

Displacement = OC,

where, $OC = |OC|$
$$= \sqrt{OD^2 + DC^2}$$
$$= \sqrt{AB^2 + (BC - BD)^2}$$
$$= \sqrt{4^2 + (6-3)^2} = 5\text{ m}$$

2 Ram in his cycle goes one round a circular track of diameter 105 m in 5 min. Calculate his speed.

Sol. Here,

Diameter = 105 m

Radius $= \frac{105}{2}$ m

Time taken, $t = 5\text{ min} = 5 \times 60\text{ s} = 300\text{ s}$

As, $$v = \frac{2\pi r}{t}$$

$$v = 2 \times \frac{22}{7} \times \frac{105}{2 \times 300} = 1.1\text{ m/s}$$

3 A railway track is 500 m long. A 100 m long train crosses the track at a speed of 30 m/s. Find the time taken by train to cross it.

Sol. Total length of path covered by train = 500 m + 100 m = 600 m

Speed of train = 30 m/s

Time taken by train to cover the bridge

$$= \frac{\text{Distance}}{\text{Speed}} \Rightarrow \frac{600}{30} = 20\text{ s}$$

4 A bike acquires a velocity of 36 km/h in 10 s just after the start. It takes 20 s to stop. Find the acceleration and retardation in these cases?

Sol. **Case I** Initial velocity, $u = 0$

Final velocity, $v = \frac{36\text{ km}}{h} = \frac{36 \times 1000\text{ m}}{60 \times 60\text{ s}}$
$= 10\text{ m/s}$

Time taken, $t = 10$ s, $a = ?$

As, $$a = \frac{v-u}{t},$$

$$a = \frac{10-0}{10} = 1\text{ m/s}^2$$

Case II Here, $u = 36\text{ km/h} = 10\text{ m/s}$

As the bike stops $v = 0$, $t = 20$ s, $a = ?$

As, $$a = \frac{v-u}{t},$$

$$a = \frac{0-10}{20} = -0.5\text{ m/s}^2$$

5 **An object is sliding down an inclined plane. The velocity changes at constant rate from 10 cm/s to 15 cm/s in 2 s. What is its acceleration ?**

Competency Based Que.

Sol. Here, $v = 15$ cm/s, $u = 10$ cm/s, $t = 2$ s

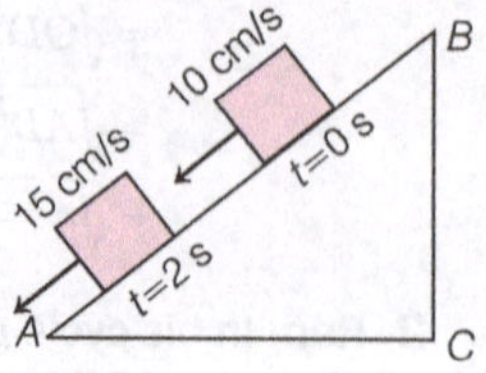

$$a = \frac{v - u}{t}$$

$$a = \frac{15 - 10}{2} \text{ cm/s}^2$$

$$a = 2.5 \text{ cm/s}^2$$

6 **A car moves with a speed of 30 km/h for half an hour, 25 km/h for one hour and 40 km/h for two hours. Calculate average speed of the car.**

Sol. Time taken to travel, $t_1 = 0.5$ h, $t_2 = 1$ h, $t_3 = 2$ h

$\therefore$ Total time, $t = t_1 + t_2 + t_3$

$= 0.5 + 1 + 2 = 3.5$ h

Speeds, $v_1 = 30$ km/h, $v_2 = 25$ km/h, $v_3 = 40$ km/h

$\therefore$ Distances, $s_1 = v_1 t_1 = 30 \times 0.5 = 15$ km

$s_2 = v_2 t_2 = 25 \times 1 = 25$ km

and $s_3 = v_3 t_3 = 40 \times 2 = 80$ km

$\therefore$ Total distance, $s = s_1 + s_2 + s_3$

$= 15 + 25 + 80 = 120$ km

$$\text{Average speed} = \frac{\text{Total distance}}{\text{Total time}}$$

$$= \frac{s}{t} = \frac{120}{3.5} = 34.3 \text{ km/h}$$

7 **The velocity-time graph for motion of two bodies P and Q is shown. Read the graph carefully and answer the following questions**

Competency Based Que.

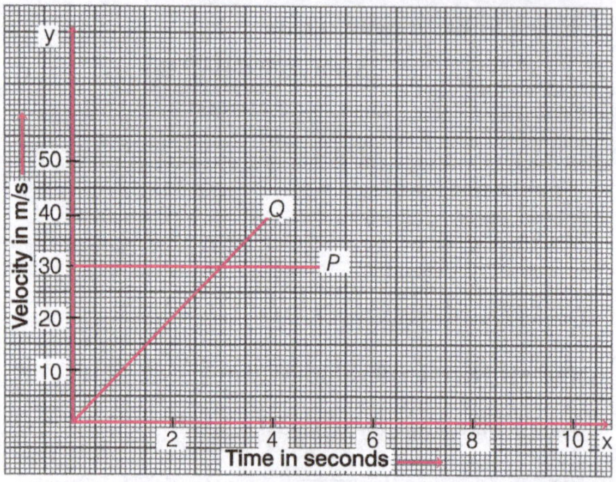

(i) Which of the two bodies has a lower velocity at time (a) $t = 2$ s (b) $t = 4$ s? [1]

(ii) Which of the two bodies has (a) constant velocity (b) increasing velocity? [1]

(iii) At what time is the velocity of the two bodies same? [1]

(iv) What are the velocities of P and Q at time $t = 2$ s? [1]

(v) What is the change in the velocity of body Q in an interval of 4 s? [1]

Sol. (i) At $t = 2$ s, $v_Q < v_P$

At $t = 4$ s, $v_P < v_Q$

(ii) $P \rightarrow$ constant velocity

$Q \rightarrow$ increasing velocity

(iii) At $t = 3$ s

(iv) When $t = 2$ s, $v_Q = 20$ m/s, $v_P = 30$ m/s

(v) $\frac{dv}{dt} = \frac{40 - 0}{4} = 10 \text{ m/s}^2$

8 **Study the speed-time graph of a body given here and answer the following questions**

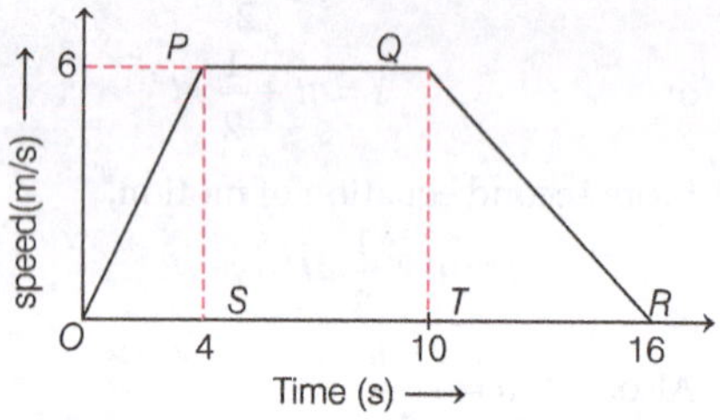

(i) What type of motion is represented by PQ? [1]

(ii) What type of motion is represented OP? [1]

(iii) What type of motion is represented QR? [1]

(iv) Calculate the retardation of the body? [1]

(v) Find the distance travelled by the body from P to Q. [1]

Sol. (i) PQ represents straight line graph between speed and time, which is parallel to the time axis so, PQ represents uniform speed. There is no acceleration from P to Q.

(ii) OP is a straight line graph between speed and time and it is sloping upwards from O to P. Therefore, the graph OP represents uniform acceleration.

(iii) QR is a straight line graph between speed and time which is sloping downwards from Q to R. Therefore, QR represents uniform retardation or negative acceleration.

(iv) The slope of line graph QR represents the retardation of the body.

So, retardation = slope of line $QR = \frac{QT}{TR}$

We have $QT = 6$ m/s,

$TR = 16 - 10 = 6$ s

$$\text{Retardation} = \frac{6 \text{ m/s}}{6 \text{ s}} = 1 \text{ m/s}^2$$

(v) Distance travelled from P to Q = Area under the line PQ and the time axis

= Area of rectangle $SPQT = SP \times ST$

Here, $SP = 6$ m/s

and $ST = 10 - 4 = 6$ s

$\therefore$ Distance travelled from P to $Q = 6 \times 6 = 36$ m

9 Two stones are thrown vertically upwards simultaneously with their initial velocities u_1 and u_2, respectively.

Prove that the heights reached by them would be in the ratio of $u_1^2 : u_2^2$. Assume upward acceleration is $-g$ and downward acceleration is $+g$. Competency Based Que.

Sol. According to the question,

	Stone 1	Stone 2
Initial velocity	u_1	u_2
Acceleration	$-g$	$-g$
Final velocity	$v_1 = 0$	$v_2 = 0$
Height	h_1	h_2

From third equation of motion,

For first stone,

$$v_1^2 = u_1^2 + 2gh_1 \text{ and}$$

For second stone,

$$v_2^2 = u_2^2 + 2gh_2$$

or $$h_1 = \frac{-u_1^2}{-2g} = \frac{u_1^2}{2g}$$

and $$h_2 = \frac{-u_2^2}{-2g} = \frac{u_2^2}{2g}$$

$$\because \quad h_1 : h_2 = \frac{\frac{u_1^2}{2g}}{\frac{u_2^2}{2g}} = u_1^2 : u_2^2$$

Ratio of heights reached by two stone

$$\frac{h_1}{h_2} = \frac{u_1^2}{u_2^2}$$

$$h_1 : h_2 = u_1^2 : u_2^2$$

10 An object is dropped from rest at a height of 150 m and simultaneously another object is dropped from rest at a height of 100 m. What is the difference in their heights after 2 s, if both the objects drop with same acceleration? How does the difference in heights vary with time? NCERT Exemplar

Sol. Acceleration for both $= g = 10$ m/s^2

For first

$$s = \frac{1}{2}gt^2$$

$$= \frac{1}{2} \times 10 \times (2)^2 = 20 \text{ m}$$

For second

$$s = \frac{1}{2}gt^2$$

$$= \frac{1}{2} \times 10 \times (2)^2 = 20 \text{ m}$$

Height of

1st $= (150 - 20) = 130$ m

2nd $= (100 - 20) = 80$ m

Difference of height $= (130 - 80)$ m

$= 50$ m

The difference of height of both will remain the same until the second body reaches the ground.

11 An electron moving with a velocity of 5×10^4 ms^{-1} enters into a uniform electric field and acquired uniform acceleration 10^4ms^{-2} in the direction of the initial motion. NCERT Exemplar

(i) Calculate the time in which the electron would acquire a velocity double of its initial velocity.

(ii) How much distance an electron would cover in this time?

Sol. Here, initial velocity of the electron $u = 5 \times 10^4$ ms^{-1}

Acceleration, $a = 10^4$ ms^{-2}

(i) $v = 2u$

$= 2 \times 5 \times 10^4$ ms^{-1}

$= 10 \times 10^4$ ms^{-1}

To find t, use $v = at + u$

or $$t = \frac{v - u}{a}$$

$$= \left(\frac{10 \times 10^4 - 5 \times 10^4}{10^4}\right)$$

$$= \frac{5 \times 10^4}{10^4} = 5 \text{ s}$$

(ii) Using $s = ut + \frac{1}{2}at^2$

$$= (5 \times 10^4) \times 5 + \frac{1}{2} \times 10^4 \times (5)^2$$

$$= 25 \times 10^4 + \frac{25}{2} \times 10^4$$

$$= 25 \times 10^4 + 12.5 \times 10^4$$

$$= 37.5 \times 10^4 \text{ m}$$

12 A bus accelerates uniformly from 90 km/h to 108 km/h in 5 s. Calculate

(i) acceleration in m/s²

(ii) distance covered by the bus (in m) during this interval.

Sol. Given, $u = 90$ km/h

or $90 \times \frac{5}{18} = 25$ m/s

$v = 108$ km/h or $108 \times \frac{5}{18} = 30$ m/s

$t = 5$ s

(i) $a = \frac{v - u}{t} = \frac{30 - 25}{5}$

$= \frac{5}{5} = 1 \text{ m/s}^2$

(ii) $s = \frac{v^2 - u^2}{2a}$

$= \frac{(30)^2 - (25)^2}{2 \times 1} = \frac{900 - 625}{2}$

$= \frac{275}{2} = 137.5$ m

13 A ball is gently dropped from a height of 20 m. If its velocity increases uniformly at the rate of 10 ms⁻², with what velocity will it strike the ground? After what time, will it strike the ground?

Sol. Initial velocity of ball, $u = 0$

Height, $h = 20$ m, Acceleration, $a = 10 \text{ ms}^{-2}$,

Final velocity, v = ?, Time, t = ?

We know that,

$v^2 = u^2 + 2as$

$s = h$

$v^2 = 0 + 2 \times 10 \times 20 = 400$ m/s

$v^2 = 400$ m/s

or final velocity, $v = 20 \text{ ms}^{-1}$

$v = u + at$

$20 = 0 + 10 \times t$

$t = \frac{20}{10}$

$t = 2$ s

14 Brakes applied to a car produce an acceleration of 6 m/s² in opposite direction to motion. If the car takes 2 s to stop after application of brakes, then calculate the distance it travels during this time.

Sol. Given, final velocity, $v = 0$,

[since, car stops after applying the brakes]

Acceleration, $a = -6 \text{ m/s}^2$, Time, $t = 2$ s

From first equation of motion, $v = u + at$

or $u = v - at = 0 - (-6)(2) = 12$ m/s

From the second equation of motion,

$s = ut + \frac{1}{2}at^2 = (12)(2) + \frac{1}{2}(-6)(2)^2 = 12$ m

Distance travelled in 2 s is 12 m.

15 A train accelerates uniformly from 36 km/h to 72 km/h in 20 s. Find the distance travelled.

Sol. Given, initial velocity, $u = 36 \text{ km/h} = 36 \times \frac{5}{18} = 10$ m/s

Final velocity, $v = 72 \text{ km/h} = 72 \times \frac{5}{18} = 20$ m/s

Time, $t = 20$ s

From first equation of motion,

$a = \frac{v - u}{t} = \frac{20 - 10}{20} = 0.5 \text{ m/s}^2$

From third equation of motion, $s = \frac{v^2 - u^2}{2a}$

$= \frac{(20)^2 - (10)^2}{2 \times 0.5} = 300$ m

Thus, distance travelled by train = 300 m

16 The speedometer readings of a car are shown below. Find the acceleration of the car and its displacement.

Competency Based Que.

Time	Speedometer
9:25 am	36 km/h
9:45 am	72 km/h

Sol. Initial velocity, $u = 36 \text{ km/h} = 36 \times \frac{5}{18} = 10$ m/s

Final velocity, $v = 72 \text{ km/h} = 72 \times \frac{5}{18} = 20$ m/s

$t = 9:45 - 9:25 = 20 \text{ min} = 20 \times 60 = 1200$ s

From first equation of motion,

$a = \frac{v - u}{t} = \frac{20 - 10}{1200} = \frac{10}{1200} = \frac{1}{120} \text{ m/s}^2$

From third equation of motion,

$s = \frac{v^2 - u^2}{2a} = \frac{(20)^2 - (10)^2}{2 \times \frac{1}{120}} = \frac{400 - 100}{1/60}$

$= 300 \times 60 = 18000 \text{ m} = 18$ km

17 A car starts from rest and moves along the X-axis with constant acceleration 5 m/s² for 8 s. If it then continues with constant velocity, then what distance will the car cover in 12 s, since it started from rest?

NCERT Exemplar

Sol. Given, the car starts from rest, so its initial velocity, $u = 0$

Acceleration, $a = 5 \text{ m/s}^2$ and time, $t = 8$ s

From first equation of motion, $v = u + at$

$v = 0 + 5 \times 8 = 40$ m/s

So, final velocity v is 40 m/s.

Again, from second equation of motion,

$$s = ut + \frac{1}{2}at^2$$

$$s = 0 \times 8 + \frac{1}{2} \times 5 \times (8)^2$$

$$= \frac{1}{2} \times 5 \times 64$$

$$s = 5 \times 32 = 160 \text{ m}$$

So, the distance covered in 8 s is 160 m.

Given, total time, $t = 12$ s

After 8 s, the car continues with constant velocity, i.e. the car will move with a velocity of 40 m/s.

The distance covered in the last 4 s $= 40 \times 4 = 160$ m

[$\because$ distance = velocity × time]

We have used the direct formula because after 8 s, car is moving with constant velocity, i.e. zero acceleration.

$\therefore$ Total distance travelled in 12 s

$$= 160 + 160$$

$$= 320 \text{ m}$$

18 On a 100 km track, a train travels the first 30 km at a uniform speed of 30 km/h. How fast must the train travel the next 70 km, so as to average 40 km/h for the entire trip?

Sol. Given, total distance, $s = 100$ km

A train travels the first 30 km at a uniform speed of 30 km/h.

$$\text{Time, } t_1 = \frac{\text{Distance}}{\text{Speed}} = \frac{30 \text{ km}}{30 \text{ km/h}}$$

Let speed of train is x for next 70 km.

$$\text{Similarly, time, } t_2 = \frac{70 \text{ km}}{x}$$

$$\text{Total time, } \quad t = t_1 + t_2 = \frac{30 \text{ km}}{30 \text{ km/h}} + \frac{70 \text{ km}}{x}$$

$$t = 1 + \frac{70}{x} = \left(\frac{x+70}{x}\right)\text{h} \quad \ldots\text{(i)}$$

Now, average speed, $v = \frac{s}{t} = 40$ km/h ...(ii) (Given)

According to question, $\dfrac{100}{\dfrac{x+70}{x}} = 40$

$$\Rightarrow \quad 10 = 4\left(\frac{x+70}{x}\right)$$

$$\Rightarrow \quad 10x = 4x + 280$$

$$\Rightarrow \quad 6x = 280$$

$$\Rightarrow \quad x = 46.67 \text{ km/h}$$

Speed for next 70 km to maintain an average of 40 km/h is 46.67 km/h.

19 An insect moves along a circular path of radius 10 cm with a constant speed. It takes 1 min to move from a point on the path to the diametrically opposite point.

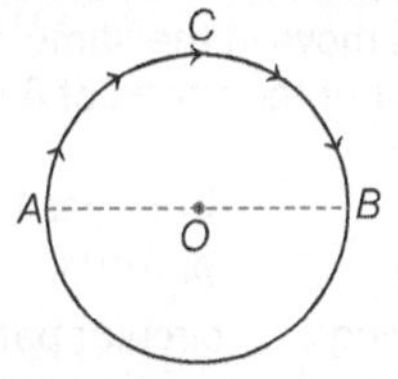

Find

(i) the distance covered,

(ii) the speed,

(iii) the displacement and

(iv) the average velocity.

Sol. Suppose the insect was at A initially and it moves along ACB to reach the diametrically opposite point B in 1 min.

(i) $\therefore$ The distance moved in 1 min $= \pi r$

$$= 3.14 \times 10 = 31.4 \text{ cm}$$

(ii) $\therefore$ Speed $= \dfrac{\text{Distance}}{\text{Time}} = \dfrac{31.4}{1} = 31.4$ cm/min

(iii) $\therefore$ Displacement, $AB = 2r = 2 \times 10 = 20$ cm

(iv) $\therefore$ Average velocity,

$$v_{av} = \frac{\text{Displacement}}{\text{Time}} = \frac{20 \text{ cm}}{1 \text{ min}}$$

$$= 20 \text{ cm/min}$$

ASSESSMENT EXERCISE

Competency Focused (Objective) Questions

Multiple Type Questions

1 A bridge is 400 m long. A 150 m long train crosses the bridge at a speed of 50 m/s. Time taken by the train to cross it.

(a) 5 s (b) 8 s
(c) 6 s (d) 11 s

2 When two bodies moves uniformly towards each other, then they cross each other at the speed of 10 m/s. If both the bodies move in the same direction, then they cross each other at the speed of 6 m/s. The speed of both bodies are

(a) 8 m/s, 2 m/s (b) 8 m/s, 4 m/s
(c) 6 m/s, 2 m/s (d) 6 m/s, 4 m/s

3 If a body is moving on a circular path of radius 21 cm with velocity of 2 m/s, then time taken by the body to complete half revolution is

(a) 11 s (b) 22 s
(c) 44 s (d) 33 s

4 From the given *v-t* graph (see figure), it can be inferred that the object is

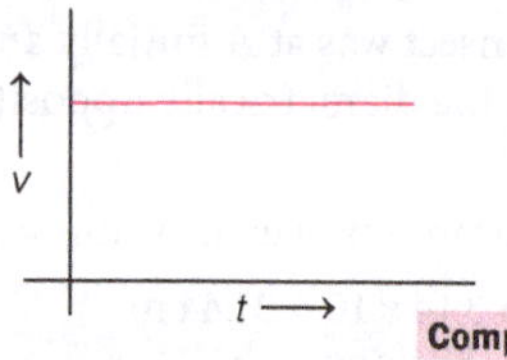

Competency Based Que.

(a) in uniform motion
(b) at rest
(c) in non-uniform motion
(d) moving with uniform acceleration

5 Suppose a boy is enjoying a ride on a merry-go-round which is moving with a constant speed of 10 ms^{-1}. It implies that the boy is **NCERT Exemplar**

(a) at rest
(b) moving with no acceleration
(c) in accelerated motion
(d) moving with uniform velocity

Assertion–Reason Questions

Direction (Q.Nos. 6-8) In each of the following questions, a statement of Assertion is given by the corresponding statement of Reason. Of the statements, mark the correct answer as

(a) If both Assertion and Reason are true and Reason is the correct explanation of Assertion.
(b) If both Assertion and Reason are true but Reason is not the correct explanation of Assertion.
(c) If Assertion is true but Reason is false.
(d) If Assertion is false but Reason is true.

6 Assertion (A) Distance travelled by a body may be positive, negative or zero.

Reason (R) Shortest distance travelled by the body between two points is called displacement.

7 Assertion (A) Acceleration of a body can be calculated from velocity-time graph.

Reason (A) Area of velocity-time graph gives displacement of an body.

8 Assertion (A) A body performing uniform circular motion with constant speed may have acceleration.

Reason (R) When speed of a body remains constant, then its acceleration is always zero.

Case Based/Source Based Question

Direction (Q.No 9) *Answer the questions on the basis of your understanding of the following passage and related studied concepts*

9 Shikhaj and Sharman went from Delhi to Mathura through Yamuna - Expressway. Shikhaj started the car and accelerated, so highly that the car was running at 108 km/h within 10 s. Sharman stopped him from doing so and told him that overspeeding on road was a straight invitation to life staking situation Though, Shikhaj wanted the adventure of speeding but he was convinced by Sharman. When they return from Mathura, the odometer of their car reads 1600 km at the start of the trip and 2000 km at the end of trip. The car takes 10 h to cover this distance.

(i) Name the measuring device used by tracking the speed of car.
(ii) Find the ratio of average velocity to average speed of an object when it is moving along a straight path.
(iii) What is the acceleration of the car?
(iv) What advice is given by Sharman to Shikhaj regarding overspeeding on road?
(v) What will be their average speed when they return from Mathura to Delhi?

Answers

1. (d)	**2.** (a)	**3.** (d)	**4.** (a)
5. (c)	**6.** (d)	**7.** (d)	**8.** (c)

Constructed Response (Descriptive) Questions

Very Short Answer Type Questions

10 If the acceleration of the particle is constant in magnitude but not in direction, then what type of path does the particle follow? **Competency Based Que.**

11 What does the path of an object look like when it is in uniform motion? **Competency Based Que.**

12 The velocity of a body increases by 10 m/s in every one second. What physical quantity does the body represent and what is its magnitude?

13 Area under the velocity-time graph line is 40 m. What physical quantity does this area represent?

14 Does the motion of second's hand of a watch represent uniform velocity or uniform speed?

Short Answer Type Questions

15 How can you calculate the following?

(i) Speed from distance-time graph.

(ii) Acceleration from velocity-time graph.

(iii) Displacement from velocity-time graph.

16 Given below is the velocity-time graph for the motion of the car. What does the nature of the graph show? Also, find the acceleration of the car. **Competency Based Que.**

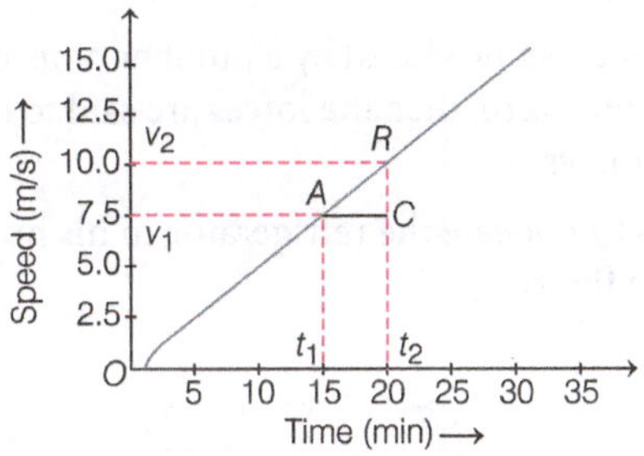

[**Ans.** 0.5 m/s^2]

17 (i) If the velocity-time graph of an object is parallel to X-axis, then what does it mean? Can it be parallel to Y-axis?

(ii) What type of motion is represented by each one of the following graphs?

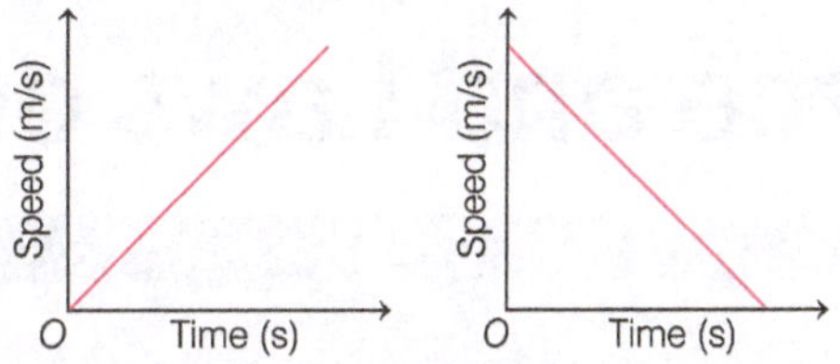

(iii) A bus increases its speed from 36 km/h to 54 km/h in 10 s. Find its acceleration. [**Ans.** 0.5 m/s^2]

Long Answer Type Questions

18 An object starting from rest travels 20 m in first 2 s and 160 m in next 4 s. What will be the velocity after 7 s from the start? [**Ans.** 70 m/s]

19 Obtain a relation for the distance travelled by an object moving with a uniform acceleration in the interval between 4th and 5th seconds. [**Ans.** $u + 9\frac{a}{2}$]

20 Study the velocity-time graph and calculate **Competency Based Que.**

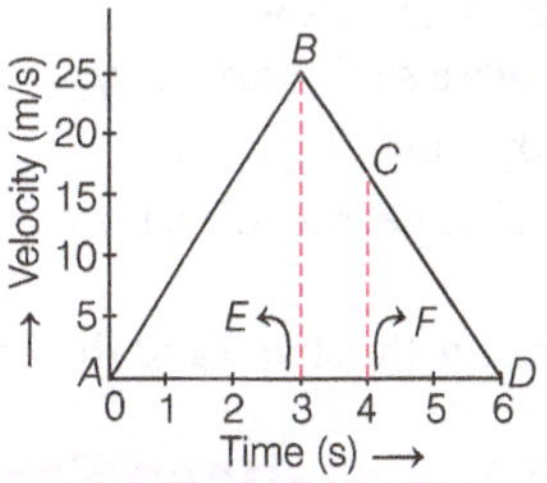

(i) the acceleration from A to B. [**Ans.** 8.33 m/s^2]

(ii) the acceleration from B to C. [**Ans.** – 8 m/s^2]

(iii) the distance covered in the region ABE. [**Ans.** 37.5 m]

(iv) the average velocity from C to D. [**Ans.** – 8.5 m/s]

(v) the distance covered in the region BCFE. [**Ans.** 21 m]

21 A body starts to slide over a horizontal surface with an initial velocity of 0.5 m/s. Due to friction, its velocity decreases at the rate 0.105 m/s^2. How much time will it take for the body to stop? [**Ans.** 4.8 s]

CHAPTER 08

Force and Laws of Motion

In our everyday life, we observe that some efforts are required to put a stationary object into motion or to stop a moving object. We ordinarily experience this as a muscular effort and say that we must push, hit or pull an object to change its state of motion. The concept of force is based on this push, hit or pull.

Further, in this chapter, we will learn about different types of forces and Newton's laws of motion.

8.1 Force

A push or pull acting on a body is known as force. Force cannot be seen but it can be judged only by the effects which it produces in various bodies around us. Many effects of force are as given below

(i) A force can move a stationary body.
(ii) A force can stop a moving body.
(iii) A force can change the direction and speed of a moving body.
(iv) A force can change the shape and the size of a body.

Balanced and Unbalanced Forces

Forces are of two types, as given below

Balanced Forces

When the net effect produced by a number of forces acting on a body is zero, then the forces are said to be balanced forces.

Balanced forces can only bring a change in the shape of the body.

A block of wood is placed on a horizontal surface and two strings *A* and *B* are connected to it as shown in figure. The block is in a state of rest.

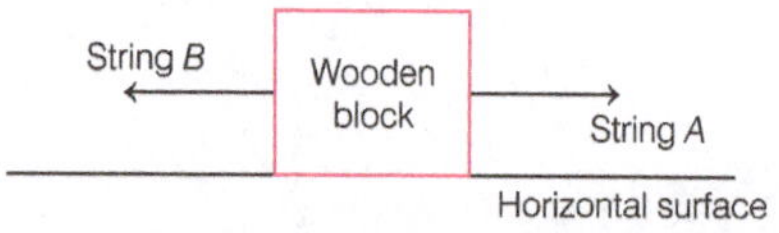

Balanced forces

If we pull *A* and *B* strings with equal magnitude of forces, then the block does not change its state of rest. Such type of forces are known as balanced forces.

Balanced forces do not change

(i) The state of rest
(ii) The state of motion

e.g. In a game of tug of war, when both the teams apply similar forces from both sides, rope does not move either side, i.e. resultant force is zero. Hence, it is a balanced force.

Unbalanced Forces

When the net effect produced by a number of forces acting on a body is non-zero, then the forces are said to be unbalanced forces.

A boy wants to relocate the refrigerator in his house as shown in the figure.

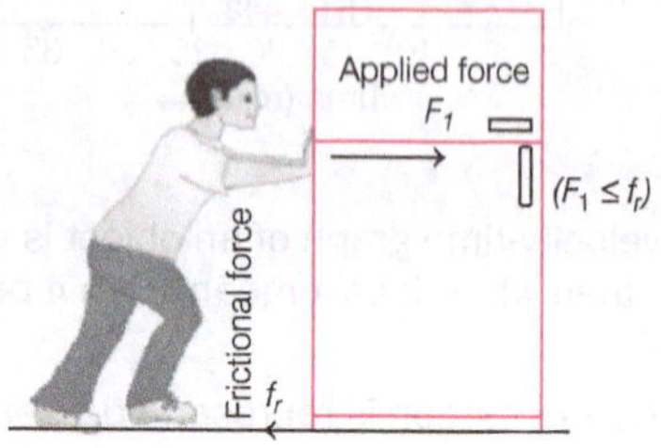

He pushes the refrigerator with a small force, the refrigerator does not move due to frictional force acting **in a direction opposite to the applied force.**

This frictional force arises between two surfaces in contact, i.e. between bottom of refrigerator and floor's rough surface. It balances the pushing force and therefore refrigerator does not move.

If he pushes the refrigerator harder, then the pushing force becomes more than the friction and due to this, the refrigerator starts moving **in the direction of push** as shown in the figure.

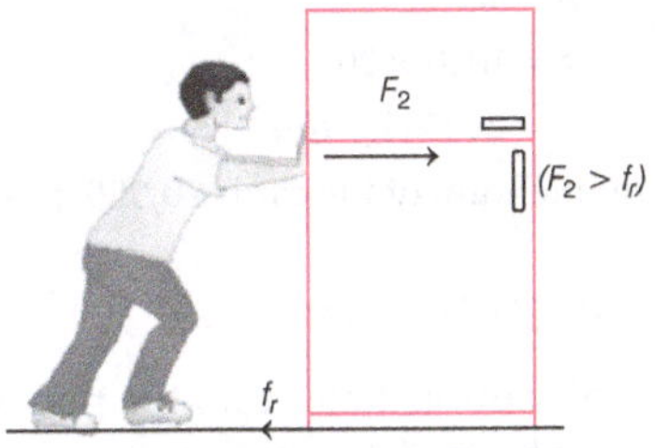

In the above example, there is an unbalanced force which causes motion in the refrigerator. **The unbalanced forces cause a change in the state of rest or in uniform motion of a body.**

e.g. In a tug of war, when one of the teams suddenly releases the rope, then an unbalanced force acts on the other team, due to which they fall backward.

If an unbalanced force is applied on a moving object, there will be a change either in its speed or in the direction of its motion. Thus, to accelerate the motion of an object, an unbalanced force is required.

An object maintains its motion under the continuous application of an unbalanced force. e.g. We have to pedal again and again, to keep the bicycle in motion.

Resultant Force

The resultant force of a number of forces acting on a body is a single force which produces the same effect as produced by all the individual forces taken together.

Case I When two forces acting in same direction then the resultant force is the net force.

Case II When two forces acting in opposite directions

(a) If the two forces are equal in magnitude, then the resultant force will be zero because the opposite forces cancel each other out.

(b) If the two forces are not equal in magnitude, then the resultant force will be in the same direction as the force with the larger magnitude and will have magnitude equal to the difference between the magnitudes of the two forces.

8.2 Newton's Laws of Motion

Newton studied the ideas of Galileo regarding the motion of an object. He formulated three fundamental laws that govern the motion of objects.

These three laws are known as Newton's laws of motion, which are as given below

Newton's First Law of Motion

It states that **an object will continue to remain in its state of rest or of uniform motion along a straight line path unless an external force acts on it.** This means, all objects resist of change in their state.

The state of any object can be changed by applying external forces only.

(i) A person standing in a bus falls backward when the bus starts moving suddenly. This happens because the person and bus both are in rest while the person is not moving. As the bus starts moving, the legs of the person start moving along with bus, but rest of the portion of his body has tendency to remain in rest. Because of this, person falls backward if he is not alert.

(ii) A person standing in a moving bus falls forward, if driver applies brakes suddenly.

Inertia

The natural tendency of an object to resist a change in their state of rest or uniform motion along a straight line is called inertia of the object.

It is the inherent property of all the objects. Newton's first law of motion is also known as the law of inertia.

Inertia of an object is measured by its mass. It is directly proportional to the mass. It means that inertia increases with increase in mass and decreases with decrease in mass. A heavy object will have more inertia than lighter one.

Types of Inertia

Inertia is divided into three types as given below

1. **Inertia of rest** The tendency of a body to resist (oppose) any change in its state of rest is known as inertia of rest.

   e.g.

   (i) When a bus suddenly starts moving forward, then the passengers in the bus fall backward.

   (ii) The carpet is beaten with a stick to remove the dust particles.

   (iii) When a tree is vigorously shaken, then some of the leaves fall from the tree.

2. **Inertia of motion** The tendency of a body to resist (oppose) any change in its state of uniform motion is known as inertia of motion.

e.g.

(i) The passengers fall forward when a fast moving bus stops suddenly.

(ii) A person falls forward while getting down from a moving bus or train.

(iii) A luggage is usually tied with a rope on the roof of a bus.

3. **Inertia of direction** The tendency of a body to oppose any change in its direction of motion is known as inertia of direction.

e.g.

(i) When a fast moving bus takes a turn on the curved road, then passengers fall away from the centre of the curved road.

(ii) The sparks produced during sharpening of a knife against a grinding wheel leave tangentially to its rim.

(iii) A stone tied to string is whirling in a horizontal circle. If the string breaks, then the stone flies away tangentially.

Try These 8.1

1. **State any one change that a force brings about on a body.**
2. **What kind of force is involved when you open house door?**
3. **How does inertia of direction affect a vehicle when going around a curve?**
4. **State True or False for the following statement.**
   (i) **The blades of an electric fan continue to rotate for some time after the current is switched OFF due to inertia of motion.**
   (ii) **When a tree is vigorously shaken, then some of the leaves fall from the tree.**

Momentum

Momentum measures the quantity of motion possessed by a body. It was introduced by Newton.

It is defined as the product of mass and velocity of the body. Besides magnitude, momentum also has a direction. At any instant, its direction is the same as the direction of the velocity.

If a body of mass m moves with a velocity v, then momentum p is given by $p = mv$

The **SI unit of momentum** is kg-m/s.

Note If a body is at rest, its velocity, $v = 0$ and so momentum $p = 0$.

Example 1. **A car of mass 1000 kg is moving with a velocity of 72 km/h. Find its momentum.**

Given, mass, $m = 1000$ kg

Velocity, $v = 72 \text{ km/h} = 72 \times \frac{5}{18} = 20 \text{ m/s}$

Momentum, $p = ?$

$\therefore$ Momentum = Mass $\times$ Velocity

or $p = mv$

$p = 1000 \times 20$

$= 20000$ kg-m/s

Thus, the momentum of the car is 20,000 kg-m/s.

Newton's Second Law of Motion

The second law of motion states that the rate of change of momentum of an object is directly proportional to the applied external force and takes place in the direction in which external force acts.

Mathematical Formulation of Second Law of Motion

If a body of mass m moving at initial velocity u accelerates uniformly with an acceleration a for time t, so that its final velocity changes to v, then

Initial momentum, $p_1 = mu$

Final momentum, $p_2 = mv$

$\therefore$ Change in momentum $= p_2 - p_1 = mv - mu = m(v - u)$

According to the second law of motion,

$$\text{Force} \propto \frac{\text{Change in momentum}}{\text{Time}}$$

$$\Rightarrow \quad F \propto \frac{p_2 - p_1}{t} \Rightarrow F \propto \frac{m(v-u)}{t}$$

$$\Rightarrow \quad F \propto ma \qquad \left[\because \frac{v-u}{t} = a\right]$$

$$\therefore \quad F = kma$$

The quantity k is a **constant of proportionality.**

One unit of force is defined as the amount that produces an acceleration of 1 m/s^2 in an object of 1 kg mass.

i.e. 1 unit of force $= k \times 1 \text{ kg} \times 1 \text{ m/s}^2 \Rightarrow k = 1$

Thus, the force can be written as $F = ma$

The **SI unit of force is newton,** which is denoted by the symbol N and it is equivalent to kg-m/s^2.

Note
- When the applied force F is zero, then the acceleration a is also zero and the body remains in its state of rest or of uniform motion.
- 1 dyne $= \frac{1}{10^5}$ N $= 10^{-5}$ N

Applications of Newton's Second Law of Motion

The following applications are based on Newton's second law of motion

(i) A cricket player (or fielder) moves his hands backward while catching a fast cricket ball.

(ii) During athletics meet, athletes doing high jump and long jump land on foam or a heap of sand to decrease the force on the body for comfortable landing.

Newton's First Law from Mathematical Expression of Second Law

It can be stated from mathematical expression of second law of motion.

As we know, $F = ma$

$$\Rightarrow \quad F = \frac{m(v-u)}{t} \qquad \left[\because a = \frac{(v-u)}{t}\right]$$

$$\Rightarrow \quad Ft = mv - mu$$

From this equation, if $F = 0$, then $v = u$ for any value of time. This means that, in the absence of an external force, the object will continue moving with uniform velocity u throughout the time t and if u is zero, then v will also be zero, i.e. the **object will remain at rest.**

Example 2. **Force acts on an object of mass 4 kg and changes its velocity from 10 m/s to 20 m/s in 5 s. Find the magnitude of force.**

Given, mass of an object, $m = 4$ kg

Initial velocity, $u = 10$ m/s

Final velocity, $v = 20$ m/s

Time taken, $t = 5$ s

We know that, Newton's first equation of motion,

$$v = u + at \text{ or } a = \frac{v-u}{t}$$

$$\therefore \quad a = \frac{20-10}{5} = \frac{10}{5} = 2 \text{ m/s}^2$$

$\therefore$ Magnitude of force = Mass × Acceleration

$$\Rightarrow \quad F = ma = 4 \text{ kg} \times 2 \text{ m/s}^2 = 8 \text{ N}$$

Hence, magnitude of force is 8 N.

Example 3. **A force of 50 N acts on a stationary body of mass 10 kg for 2 s. Find the acceleration produced in the body and velocity attained by it.**

Initial velocity, $u = 0$ [since, the body is stationary]

Force $(F) = 50$ N, mass $(m) = 10$ kg, time $(t) = 2$ s

Final velocity, $v = ?$, acceleration, $a = ?$

$$\therefore \text{ Acceleration, } a = \frac{F}{m} \qquad [\because F = ma]$$

$$a = \frac{50}{10} = 5 \text{ m/s}^2$$

$$\text{Final velocity, } v = \frac{Ft}{m} + u \qquad [\because Ft = m(v-u)]$$

$$\therefore \quad v = \frac{50 \times 2}{10} + 0 = 10 \text{ m/s}$$

Thus, the acceleration produced in the body is 5 m/s^2 and velocity attained by it is 10 m/s.

Example 4. **A bullet train is moving with a velocity of 180 km/h and it takes 5 s to stop after the brakes are applied. Find the force exerted by the brakes on the wheel of train if its mass with the wagon is 2000 kg.**

Given, initial velocity, $u = 180 \text{ km/h} = 180 \times \frac{5}{18} = 50$ m/s

Final velocity, $v = 0$,

Time, $t = 5$ s, mass, $m = 2000$ kg

As, acceleration is given by $a = \frac{(v-u)}{t}$

$$\Rightarrow \quad a = -\frac{u}{t} = \frac{-50}{5} = -10 \text{ m/s}$$

Now, force exerted by the brakes on the wheel is given by Newton's second law, $F = ma = 2000 \times (-10) = -20000$ N

Negative sign shows that the direction of force is opposite to motion of the body.

Example 5. **A force of 6 N gives a mass m_1 an acceleration of 18 m/s^2 and a mass m_2 an acceleration of 24 m/s^2. What acceleration would it give if both the masses were tied together?**

Given, force $F = 6$ N

Acceleration of mass m_1 $(a_1) = 18$ m/s^2

Acceleration of mass m_2 $(a_2) = 24$ m/s^2

Acceleration produced when both masses are tied together, $a = ?$

From Newton's second law of motion,

$$m_1 = \frac{F}{a_1} = \frac{6}{18} = \frac{1}{3} \text{ kg}$$

$$m_2 = \frac{F}{a_2} = \frac{6}{24} = \frac{1}{4} \text{ kg}$$

$$\text{Total mass, } m = m_1 + m_2 = \frac{1}{3} + \frac{1}{4}$$

$$m = \frac{4+3}{12} = \frac{7}{12} \text{ kg}$$

Acceleration produced in combined mass, $a = \frac{F}{m}$

$$a = \frac{12 \times 6}{7}$$

$$= 10.28 \text{ m/s}^2$$

Example 6. **The velocity-time graph of a ball of mass 30 g moving along a straight line on a long table is given below. How much force does the table exert on the ball to bring it to rest?**

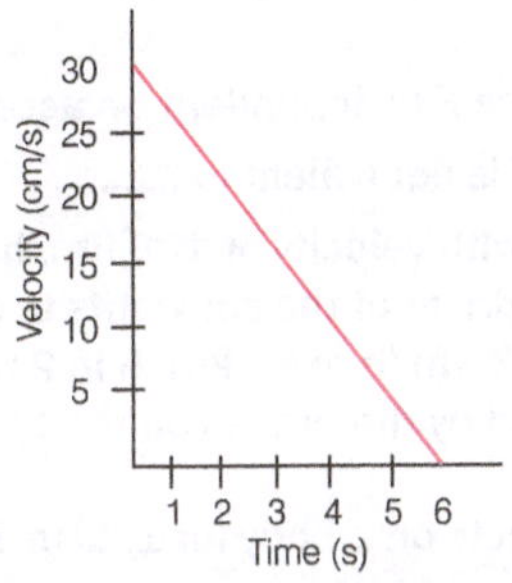

The initial velocity of the ball, $u = 30$ cm/s

Final velocity, $v = 0$

Time, $t = 6$ s

Acceleration, $a = \frac{v-u}{t} = \frac{(0-30)}{6}$

$a = -5 \text{ cm/s}^2 = -0.05 \text{ m/s}^2$

The force exerted on the ball,

$F = ma = \left(\frac{30}{1000}\right) \times (-0.05)$

$= -1.5 \times 10^{-3}$ N

The negative sign shows that frictional force exerted by the table is opposite to the direction of motion of the ball.

Impulse

It is termed as the **total impact of force acting for time *t*.** This is equal to the change in momentum of the body. In other words, **impulse is defined as the product of force and a small time in which force act.**

According to Newton's second law, $F = ma$

$$F = \frac{m(v-u)}{t} \qquad \left[\because a = \frac{v-u}{t}\right]$$

$$\Rightarrow \quad F = \frac{mv - mu}{t} \quad \Rightarrow \quad Ft = mv - mu$$

Impulse, $I = Ft = p_2 - p_1$

or Impulse = Change in momentum

The SI unit of impulse is N-s or kg-m/s.

Example 7. **If a force of 1000 N is applied over a vehicle of 500 kg, then for how much time the velocity of the vehicle will increase from 2 m/s to 10 m/s. Also, find the impulse.**

Given, $F = 1000$ N, mass, $m = 500$ kg

Final velocity, $v = 10$ m/s

Initial velocity, $u = 2$ m/s

$$F = \frac{m(v-u)}{t} \Rightarrow t = \frac{m(v-u)}{F} = \frac{500 \times (10-2)}{1000} = 4\text{s}$$

$\therefore$ Impulse, $I = Ft = 1000 \times 4 = 4000$ N-s

Thus, the time required by the vehicle is 4s and its impulse is 4000 N-s.

Try These 8.2

1 **Is it true that force *F* is dependent on acceleration?**

2 **SI unit of force *F* is equivalent to ....** [Ans. 1 kg-m/s^2]

3 **A car is moving with velocity of 108 km/h. Mass of the car is 300 kg. If driver of the car wants to change its velocity from 108 km/h to 90 km/h in 2 min, what force should be applied by the brakes on the tyres?** [Ans. – 12.5 N]

4 **A force of 50 N acts on a body for 1/10 s. Find the change in the momentum of the body.** [Ans. 5 kg-m/s]

Newton's Third Law of Motion

It states that, whenever an object exerts a force on another object, then the second object exerts an equal and opposite force on the first object. These pair of opposing forces are also known as **action and reaction forces.**

These action and reaction forces are equal in magnitude and opposite in direction. These forces may not produce accelerations of equal magnitudes. This is because each force acts on a different object, that may have a different mass.

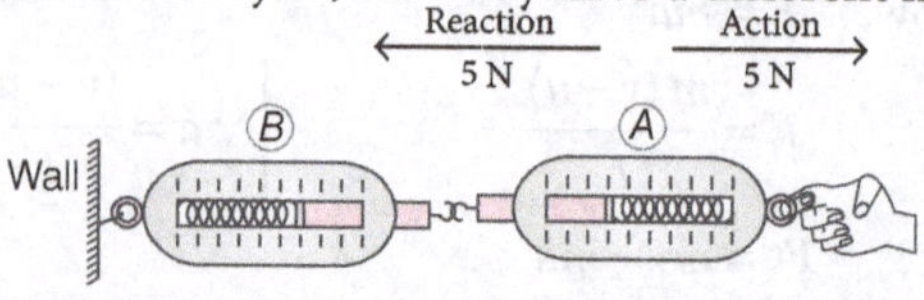

Spring balance action and reaction forces are equal and opposite

Applications of Newton's Third Law of Motion

(i) **Collision of two persons** When two persons walking or running in opposite direction collide with each other, then both feel hurt, because they apply force on each other. Two opposing forces are in action and reaction pair.

(ii) **Walking of a person** A person is able to walk because of the Newton's third law of motion. During walking, a person pushes the ground in backward direction and in the reaction, the ground also pushes the person with equal magnitude of force but in opposite direction. This enables him to move in forward direction against the push.

(iii) **Recoil of gun** When bullet is fired from a gun, then the bullet also pushes the gun in opposite direction with equal magnitude of force. Since, the gun has a greater mass than bullet, acceleration of the gun is much less than the acceleration of the bullet.

(iv) **Propulsion of a boat in forward direction** Sailor pushes water with oar in backward direction resulting water to push the oar in forward direction. Consequently, the boat is pushed in forward direction. Force applied by oar and water are of equal magnitude but in opposite directions.

(v) **Rocket propulsion** The propulsion of rocket is based on the principle of **action and reaction.** The rapid burning of fuel produces hot gases which rush out from the nozzle at the rear end at a very high speed. The equal and opposite reaction force moves the rocket upward at a great speed.

Try These 8.3

1 **Walking on a road can be described by which law?**

2 **Which statement is true?**

Statement I Action and reaction forces are unequal in magnitude and opposite in direction.

Statement II Action and reaction forces are equal in magnitude and same in direction.

Mind Map

FORCE AND LAWS OF MOTION

Force

- Any change which causes pull, hit or push on a body.
- Its SI unit is newton (N).
- It is a vector quantity.

$$F = ma$$

Effects on body

- Change in position.
- Change in state of rest or motion.
- Change in speed, direction or shape.

Types of Forces

- **Balanced force** When the net effect produced by a number of forces on a body is zero.

- **Unbalanced force** When the net effect produced by a number of forces on a body is non-zero.

Newton's First Law of Motion

- An object will continue to remain in its state of rest or in uniform motion along a straight line path unless an external force acts on it.
- It is also known as **law of inertia.**

Inertia

- The tendency of a body to oppose or resist any change in its state of rest or uniform motion.
- Mass is measure of inertia.
- Larger the mass greater is the inertia.

Types of Inertia

- **Inertia at rest** The tendency of a body to oppose any change in its state of rest. e.g. When the card is flicked with the finger, the coin placed over it falls into the tumbler due to inertia of rest.

- **Inertia of motion** The tendency of a body to oppose any change in its state of uniform motion.
  e.g. The passengers fall forward when a fast moving bus stops suddenly.

- **Inertia of direction** The tendency of a body to oppose any change in its direction of motion.
  e.g. A stone tied to string flies away tangentially, when string breaks at the time of whirling.

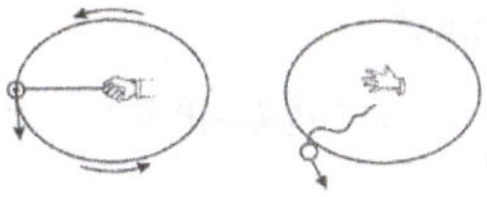

Newton's Third Law of Motion

- To every action there is an equal and opposite reaction.

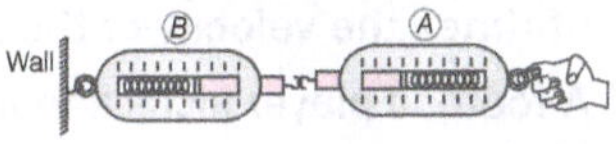

Applications

- When two persons walking or running in opposite directions collide with each other, then both feel hurt, because they apply force to each other.
- When bullet is fired from a gun, then the bullet also pushes the gun in opposite direction with equal magnitude of force.

Newton's Second Law of Motion

- The rate of change of momentum of an object is proportional to the applied unbalanced force in the direction of force.

$$F ? \frac{m(v-u)}{t}$$

$$F = ma$$

Applications

- A cricket player moves his hands backward while catching a fast cricket ball.
  Athelets doing high jump land on a foam to decrease the force on the body.
-

Momentum

- The product of mass and velocity of a body.

$$p = mv$$

- Its SI unit is kg-m/s.
- It is a vector quantity.

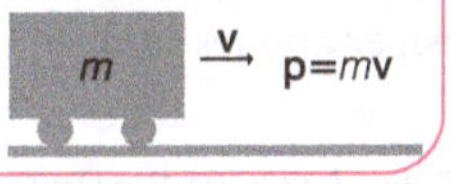

Impulse

- Change in linear momentum of the body when a large force acts on a body for short interval of time.

$$I = Ft$$

- Its SI unit is N-s or kg-m/s.
- It is a vector quantity.

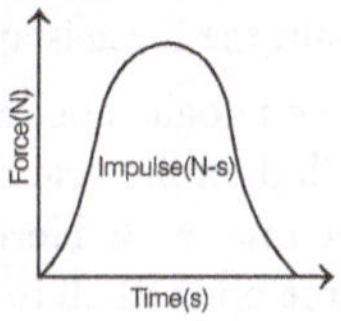

NCERT FOLDER

Complete Explanations of all NCERT's Questions

Intext Questions

Q.1 Which of the following has more inertia? Page 91

(i) A rubber ball and a stone of same size

(ii) A bicycle and a train

(iii) A five-rupees coin and a one-rupee coin

Give reasons for your answer.

Inertia of an object is proportional to its mass.

(i) A stone of same size as that of rubber ball will have greater mass, so the stone will have more inertia.

(ii) A train has much greater mass than that of a bicycle, so the train will have more inertia.

(iii) A five-rupees coin has more mass than a one-rupee coin, so five-rupees coin will have greater inertia.

Q.2 In the following example, try to identify the number of times the velocity of the ball changes.

A football player kicks a football to another player of his team who kicks the football towards the goal. The goalkeeper of opposite team collects the ball and kicks it towards a player of his own team.

Also, identify the agent supplying the force in each case. Page 91

There are a number of times at which the direction and magnitude of velocity of the ball changes, which are as given below

Whenever a force will be applied on the ball, then the velocity of the ball will change.

(i) When first player kicks the ball towards another player of his team, then the velocity of ball will change, because first player applies some force on the ball.

(ii) When another player kicks the ball towards the goal, then the velocity of ball will change, because here again the force is applied on the ball.

(iii) When goalkeeper of the opposite team collects the ball, then the velocity of ball will be changed, it becomes zero. Here, the goalkeeper applies some force on the ball to stop.

(iv) When the goalkeeper kicks the ball towards his own team, then the velocity of the ball changes, because goalkeeper applies some force on the ball.

Q.3 Explain, why some of the leaves may get detached from a tree, if we vigorously shake its branch? Page 91

Leaves have inertia of rest. When the branch is shaken, they tend to remain in same state and get detached when the position of branch changes.

Q.4 Why do you fall in the forward direction when a moving bus brakes to a stop and fall backwards when it accelerates from rest? Page 91

When the moving bus applies brakes to a stop, then our body has inertia of motion, that opposes a change in its state. However, the lower portion of our body which is in contact with bus comes to rest. But the upper part still remains in motion. Hence, to balance our body, we fall forward. When the bus accelerates from rest, then our body has inertia of rest, which opposes a change in its state. However, the lower portion of our body starts moving with the bus. Hence, we fall backwards.

Exercise Questions

Q.1 An object experiences a net zero external unbalanced force. Is it possible for the object to be travelling with a non-zero velocity? If yes, state the conditions that must be placed on the magnitude and direction of the velocity. If no, provide a reason.

As per the Newton's first law of motion, no force is needed to move an object which is already moving with a constant (non-zero) velocity. So, when an object experiences a net zero external unbalanced force, then it can move with a non-zero velocity. When external force is zero, then velocity of an object remains same both in magnitude and direction.

Q.2 When a carpet is beaten with a stick, dust comes out of it. Explain.

When a carpet is beaten with a stick, then the fibres of the carpet attain the state of motion while the dust particles remain at rest due to inertia of rest and hence, dust particles get detached.

Q.3 Why is it advised to tie any luggage kept on the roof of a bus with a rope?

When the bus stops suddenly, it comes in the state of rest but the luggage remains in the state of motion. So, due to inertia of motion, the luggage moves forward and may fall down from the roof of the bus. If the bus starts suddenly, it comes in the state of motion but luggage remains in the state of rest. Due to inertia of rest, the luggage does not move in the forward direction and may fall down.

So, it is advised to tie the luggage kept on the roof of the bus with a rope.

Q.4 A batsman hits a cricket ball which then rolls on a level ground. After covering a short distance, the ball comes to rest. Why does the ball slows down to stop?

(a) The batsman did not hit the ball hard enough

(b) Velocity is proportional to the force exerted on the ball

(c) There is a force on the ball opposing the motion

(d) There is no unbalanced force on the ball, so the ball would want to come to rest.

(*c*) The ball slows down to stop because the force of friction acting between the ground and the ball acts as an external force which opposes the motion of the ball.

Q.5 A truck starts from rest and rolls down a hill with a constant acceleration. It travels a distance of 400 m in 20 s. Find its acceleration and the force acting on it, if its mass is 7 tonne.
(1 tonne = 1000 kg)

The truck starts from rest, so initial velocity, $u = 0$.

Distance, $s = 400$ m, Time, $t = 20$ s

Mass, $m = 7$ tonne $= 7 \times 1000 = 7000$ kg

From Newton's second law of motion, $s = ut + \frac{1}{2}at^2$

$$\Rightarrow \quad 400 = 0 \times 20 + \frac{1}{2} \times a \times (20)^2$$

$$\Rightarrow \quad 400 = 200\,a \Rightarrow a = 2\text{ m/s}^2$$

From Newton's second law of motion, force acting on the truck,

$$F = ma = 7000 \times 2 = 14000 = 1.4 \times 10^4\text{ N}$$

Thus, acceleration of truck is 2 m/s^2 and force acting on it is 1.4×10^4 N.

Q.6 A stone of size 1 kg is thrown with a velocity of 20 m/s across the frozen surface of a lake and comes to rest after travelling a distance of 50 m. What is the force of friction between the stone and the ice?

Given, mass of stone, $m = 1$ kg, initial velocity, $u = 20$ m/s

Final velocity, $v = 0$ [since, stone comes to rest]

Distance covered, $s = 50$ m

From Newton's third law of motion, $v^2 = u^2 + 2as$

$$(0)^2 = (20)^2 + 2a\,(50)$$

$$\Rightarrow \quad 100\,a = -400 \Rightarrow a = -4\text{ m/s}^2$$

Here, negative sign shows that there is a retardation in the motion of stone.

Force of friction between stone and ice

= Force required to stop the stone

$= ma = 1 \times (-4) = -4$ N

Q.7 A 8000 kg engine pulls a train of 5 wagons, each of 2000 kg along a horizontal track. If the engine exerts a force of 40000 N and the track offers a friction force of 5000 N, then calculate

(i) the net accelerating force and

(ii) the acceleration of the train.

(i) Net accelerating force = Force exerted by engine − Frictional force

[Here, frictional force is subtracted because it opposes the motion]

$= 40000 - 5000 = 35000 = 3.5 \times 10^4$ N

(ii) From Newton's second law of motion, accelerating force (F) = mass of the train (m) × acceleration of train (a)

$$\Rightarrow \quad a = \frac{F}{m}$$

Mass of train = 5 × Mass of one wagon

= 5 × 2000 = 10000 kg

$$\therefore \text{ Acceleration} = \frac{35000}{10000} = 3.5\text{ m/s}^2$$

Q.8 An automobile vehicle has a mass of 1500 kg. What must be the force between the vehicle and road, if the vehicle is to be stopped with a negative acceleration of 1.7 m/s^2 ?

Given, mass, $m = 1500$ kg, acceleration, $a = -1.7\text{m/s}^2$

From Newton's second law of motion,

$$F = ma = 1500 \times (-1.7) = -2550\text{ N}$$

Q.9 What is the momentum of an object of mass *m* moving with a velocity *v*?

(a) m^2v^2 (b) mv^2 (c) $\frac{1}{2}mv^2$ (d) mv

(*d*) The momentum of an object of mass m moving with a velocity v is given by, $p = mv$.

Q.10 Using a horizontal force of 200 N, we intend to move a wooden cabinet across a floor at a constant velocity. What is the friction force that will be exerted on the cabinet?

The cabinet will move across the floor with constant velocity, if there is no net external force applied on it. Here, a horizontal force of 200 N is applied on the cabinet, so for the net force to be zero, an external force of 200 N should be applied on the cabinet in opposite direction.

Thus, the frictional force = 200 N

[frictional force always acts in the direction opposite to the direction of motion]

Q.11 According to the third law of motion when we push on an object, the object pushes back on us with an equal and opposite force. If the object is a massive truck parked along the roadside, it will probably not move. A student justifies this by answering that the two opposite and equal forces cancel each other. Comment on this logic and explain why the truck does not move.

The logic given by the student is not correct, because two equal and opposite forces cancel each other only in the case, if they act on the same body. Action and reaction forces always act on two different bodies, so they cannot cancel each other.

When a massive truck is pushed, then the truck may not move because the force applied is not sufficient to overcome the force produced by friction acting opposite to applied force to move the truck.

Q.12 A hockey ball of mass 200 g travelling at 10 ms^{-1} is struck by a hockey stick, so as to return it along its orginal path with a velocity at 5 ms^{-1}. Calculate the magnitude of change of momentum occurred in the motion of the hockey ball by the force applied by the hockey stick.

Given, mass of hockey ball, $m_1 = 200 \text{ g} = 0.2 \text{ kg}$

Initial velocity, $v_1 = 10$ m/s

So, initial momentum $= m_1 v_1 = 0.2 \times 10$
$= 2$ kg-m/s

Now, mass of hockey ball, $m_2 = 200$ g
$= 0.2$ kg

Final velocity, $v_2 = -5$ m/s
(as the ball is going in reverse direction)

So, final momentum $= m_2 \times v_2 = 0.2 \times (-5)$
$= -1$ kg-m/s

Now, change in momentum = final momentum − initial momentum
$= -1 - 2 = -3$ kg-m/s

Therefore, the change in momentum of the hockey ball is 3 kg-m/s.

Q.13 A bullet of mass 10 g travelling horizontally with a velocity of 150 m/s strikes a stationary wooden block and comes to rest in 0.03 s. Calculate the distance of penetration of the bullet into the block. Also, calculate the magnitude of the force exerted by the wooden block on the bullet.

Given, mass of bullet,

$$m = 10 \text{ g} = \frac{10}{1000} \text{ kg} = 0.01 \text{ kg}$$

Initial velocity, $u = 150$ m/s

Final velocity, $v = 0$ [since, bullet comes to rest]

Time, $t = 0.03$ s

We know that,

$$v = u + at$$
$$0 = 150 + a \times 0.03$$
$$\Rightarrow \quad a = \frac{-150}{0.03}$$
$$= -5000 \text{ m/s}^2$$

Distance covered by the bullet before coming to rest is given by $v^2 = u^2 + 2as$

$$0 = (150)^2 + 2(-5000)\, s$$
$$\Rightarrow \quad s = \frac{(150)^2}{10000} = 2.25 \text{ m}$$

Magnitude of the force applied by the bullet on the block,

$$F = ma = 0.01 \times -5000 = -50 \text{ N}$$

Q.14 An object of mass 1 kg travelling in a straight line with a velocity of 10 ms^{-1} collides with, and sticks to a stationary wooden block of mass 5 kg, then they both move off together in the same straight line. Calculate the total momentum just before the impact and just after the impact. Also, calculate the velocity of the combined object.

Given, mass of objects, $m = 1$ kg

Velocity, $u_1 = 10$ m/s

Mass of wooden block, $M = 5$ kg

From the perspective of momentum conservation,

Initial momentum = Final momentum

$$\Rightarrow \quad mu_1 + mu_2 = (m + M)v$$
$$\Rightarrow \quad 1 \times 10 + 5 \times 0 = (1 + 5)v$$
$$\Rightarrow \quad v = \frac{5}{3} \text{ ms}^{-1}$$

Hence, the velocity of both is $v = \frac{5}{3} \text{ ms}^{-1}$.

The total momentum just before and after the collision is 10 kg-m/s.

Q.15 An object of mass 100 kg is accelerated uniformly from a velocity of 5 m/s to 8 m/s in 6 s.
(i) Calculate the initial and final momentum of the object.
(ii) Also, find the magnitude of the force exerted on the object.

Given, mass of the object, $m = 100$ kg

Initial velocity, $u = 5$ m/s

Final velocity, $v = 8$ m/s

Time, $t = 6$ s

(i) ∴ Initial momentum $= mu$
$= 100 \times 5 = 500$ kg - m/s

and final momentum = mv

$= 100 \times 8 = 800$ kg-m / s

(ii) From Newton's second law, force exerted on the object = rate of change of momentum

$$= \frac{\text{Change in momentum}}{\text{Time}}$$

$$= \frac{\text{Final momentum} - \text{Initial momentum}}{\text{Time}}$$

$$= \frac{800 - 500}{6} = \frac{300}{6} = 50 \text{ N}$$

Q.16 How much momentum will a dumb-bell of mass 10 kg transfer to the floor, if it falls from a height of 80 cm? Take, its downward acceleration to be 10 m/s^2.

Given, mass of dumb-bell, $m = 10$ kg

Initial velocity, $u = 0$ [because it falls from rest]

Distance covered, $s = 80$ cm $= 0.8$ m

Acceleration, $a = 10$ m/s^2

From Newton's third law of motion, $v^2 = u^2 + 2as$

$$v^2 = 0 + 2 \times 10 \times 0.8 = 16 \Rightarrow v = \sqrt{16} = 4 \text{ m/s}$$

Momentum of dumb-bell just before it touches the floor is given by $p = mv = 10 \times 4 = 40$ kg-m/s

When the dumb-bell touches the floor, then its velocity becomes zero and hence the momentum. Thus, the total momentum of the dumb-bell is transferred to the floor.

So, the momentum transferred to the floor is 40 kg-m/s.

Q.17 The following is the distance-time table of an object in motion

Time (in s)	**Distance** (in m)
0	0
1	1
2	8
3	27
4	64
5	125
6	216
7	343

(i) What conclusion can you draw about the acceleration? Is it constant, increasing and decreasing or zero?

(ii) What do you infer about the force acting on the object?

(i) Here, initial velocity, $u = 0$

We know that, $s = ut + \frac{1}{2}at^2 = \frac{1}{2}at^2$ $[\because u = 0]$

We get, $a = \frac{2s}{t^2}$

Time (in s)	**Distance** (in m)	$a = 2s/t^2$
0	0	0
1	1	2
2	8	4
3	27	6
4	64	8
5	125	10
6	216	12
7	343	14

Thus, acceleration is increasing.

(ii) Since, acceleration is increasing, so net unbalanced force is acting on the object.

Q.18 Two persons manage to push a motorcar of mass 1200 kg at a uniform velocity along a level road. The same motorcar can be pushed by three persons to produce an acceleration of 0.2 m/s^2.
With what force does each person push the motorcar? (Assume that all persons push the motorcar with the same muscular effort)

Given, mass of motorcar, $m = 1200$ kg

Acceleration produced, $a = 0.2$ m/s^2

$\therefore$ Force applied on the car by three persons,

$$F = ma = 1200 \times 0.2 = 240 \text{ N}$$

Force applied on the car by one person $= \frac{240}{3} = 80$ N

Each person push the motorcar with a force of 80 N.

Q.19 A hammer of mass 500 g moving at 50 m/s strikes a nail. The nail stops the hammer in a very short time of 0.01 s. What is the force of the nail on the hammer?

Given, mass of the hammer = 500 g = 0.5 kg

Initial velocity of hammer, $u = 50$ m/s

Final velocity of hammer, $v = 0$

[because the hammer stops]

Time, $t = 0.01$ s

According to Newton's second law of motion, force of the nail on the hammer

= rate of change of momentum of hammer

$$= \frac{mv - mu}{t}$$

$$= \frac{0.5 \times 0 - 0.5 \times 50}{0.01}$$

$$= -\frac{25}{0.01} = -2500 \text{ N}$$

The force of the nail on the hammer is equal and opposite to that of hammer on nail.

Q.20 A motorcar of mass 1200 kg is moving along a straight line with a uniform velocity of 90 km/h. Its velocity is slowed down to 18 km/h in 4 s by an unbalanced external force. Calculate the acceleration and change in momentum. Also, calculate the magnitude of the force required.

Given, mass, $m = 1200$ kg

Initial velocity, $u = 90$ km/h

$$= 90 \times \frac{5}{18} = 25 \text{ m/s}$$

Final velocity, $v = 18$ km/h

$$= 18 \times \frac{5}{18} = 5 \text{ m/s}$$

Time, $t = 4$ s

(i) $\therefore$ Acceleration, $a = \frac{v - u}{t} = \frac{5 - 25}{4}$

$$= -\frac{20}{4} = -5 \text{ m/s}^2$$

[here, negative sign indicates that the velocity decreases]

(ii) $\therefore$ Change in momentum

= Final momentum − Initial momentum

$= mv - mu = m(v - u) = 1200\,(5 - 25)$

$= 1200 \times (-20)$

$= -24000$ kg-m/s

(iii) $\therefore$ Magnitude of the force required

= Rate of change of momentum

$$= \frac{\text{Change in momentum}}{\text{Time}}$$

$$= \frac{-24000}{4} = -6000 \text{ N}$$

To Study NCERT Activities Scan the Code

REVIEW EXERCISE

Including Competency Based Questions

Competency Focused (Objective) Questions

Multiple Choice Questions

1 A water tanker filled upto $\frac{2}{3}$ of its height is moving with a uniform speed. On sudden application of the brake, the water in the tank would Competency Based Que.

(a) move backward (b) move forward
(c) be unaffected (d) rise upwards

Sol. (*b*) On the sudden application of brake, the tanker will come in the state of rest but the water remains in the state of motion, so the water will move forward.

2 Which of the following statement is not correct for an object moving along a straight path in accelerated motion? NCERT Exemplar

(a) Its speed keep changing.
(b) Its velocity always changes.
(c) It always goes away from the earth.
(d) A force is always acting on it.

Sol. (*c*) For an object moving along a straight path in an accelerated motion, it is not necessary that it always goes away from the earth.

3 An object of mass 2 kg is sliding with a constant velocity of 4 ms^{-1} on a frictionless horizontal table. The force required to keep the object moving with the same velocity is NCERT Exemplar

(a) 32N (b) 0 N
(c) 2 N (d) 8 N

Sol. (*b*) An object is sliding with a constant velocity on a frictionless horizontal table, the object will move at constant velocity without any resistance in the state of uniform motion. Force required will be 0 N.

4 A bullock cart carrying a block of wood moves on a rough road with frictional force *F* with constant speed 4 m/s. The cart can be kept moving with constant speed by applying a force of Competency Based Que.

(a) 2 F (b) $\frac{F}{2}$
(c) F (d) 0

Sol. (*c*) An external force of equal magnitude as frictional force would be required to keep the cart moving with constant speed and the direction of external force will be in opposite direction to frictional force.

5 Luggages at the top of a bus are tied using a string to avoid the effect of

(a) impulse (b) inertia
(c) force (d) None of these

Sol. (*b*) Due to inertia of motion, body resists any change in its state of uniform motion.

If not tied and driver applies brakes, luggage will drop from the top of bus.

6 What can be the cause of bringing a car in state of constant velocity?

(a) Impulse (b) External force
(c) Inertia (d) Momentum

Sol. (*b*) An external force is required to change the state of rest/uniform motion of an object.

7 Two blocks of masses $\frac{M}{2}$ and $\frac{M}{3}$ are shown in the figure, a force of 20 N is applied to right and blocks starts to move with an acceleration $2 m/s^2$. The value of *M* will be Competency Based Que.

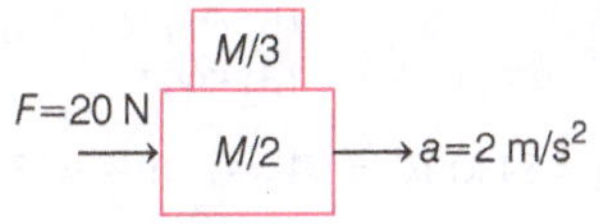

(a) 10 (b) 14 (c) 12 (d) 16

Sol. (*c*) From second law of motion

$$F = Ma$$

Given, $F = 20\text{N}, \ a = 2\text{m/s}^2$

$$20 = M \times 2$$
$$M = 10 \text{ kg}$$
$$M = \frac{M}{3} + \frac{M}{2} = \frac{5M}{6} = 10$$
$$M = \frac{60}{5} = 12 \text{ kg}$$

Option (c) is correct.

8 Two forces F_1 and F_2 are acting on a body as shown in the figure, then acceleration in the body is Competency Based Que.

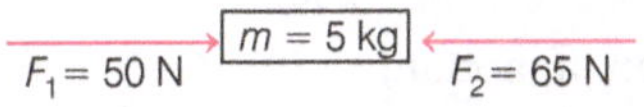

(a) 23 m/s^2 (b) 3 m/s^2 (c) 2 m/s^2 (d) 22 m/s^2

Sol. (*b*) Resultant force on a body,

$$F = F_2 - F_1 = 65 - 50 = 15\text{ N}$$

By Newton's second law of motion,

$$F = ma \Rightarrow 15 = 5a \Rightarrow a = 3\text{ m/s}^2$$

9 A bullet of 20 g strikes a sand bag at a speed of 200 m/s and gets embedded after travelling 2 cm, then the resistive force exerted by sand on the bullet is

(a) 2×10^3 N

(b) 2×10^4 N

(c) 2×10^6 N

(d) 2×10^5 N

Sol. (*b*) Given, $u = 200$ m/s, $v = 0$, $s = 0.02$ m and $m = 20\text{ g} = 20 \times 10^{-3}$ kg

From third equation of motion,

$$v^2 = u^2 + 2as \Rightarrow a = \frac{v^2 - u^2}{2s}$$

$$= \frac{(0)^2 - (200)^2}{2 \times 0.02} = -10^6\text{ m/s}^2$$

Negative sign indicates retardation.

$\therefore$ Resistive force, $F = ma = 20 \times 10^{-3} \times 10^6$

$$= 2 \times 10^4\text{ N}$$

10 A truck moving with a speed of 54 km/h. Truck driver applied brakes suddenly and brings the truck to rest in 5 s, then the average retarding force on truck, if mass of the truck and driver is 400 kg, will be

(a) 1200 N (b) 600 N

(c) 800 N (d) 500 N

Sol. (*a*) Given, $u = 54\text{ km/h} = 54 \times \frac{5}{18}\text{ m/s} = 15\text{ m/s}$,

$v = 0$ and $t = 5$ s

$\therefore$ Retardation, $a = \frac{v - u}{t} = \frac{0 - 15}{5} = -3\text{ m/s}^2$

Negative sign shows retardation.

Average retarding force, $F = ma = 400 \times 3 = 1200$ N

11 A bus of mass 500 kg is moving with a velocity of 5 m/s and is acted upon by a forward force of 500 N due to engine and retarding force of 200 N due to friction velocity of bus after 20 s will be

(a) 15 m/s (b) 17 m/s

(c) 19 m/s (d) 21 m/s

Sol. (*b*) Given, $m = 500$ kg, $u = 5$ m/s and $t = 20$ s

Resultant force, $F = 500 - 200 = 300$ N

$\therefore$ Acceleration, $a = \frac{F}{m} = \frac{300}{500} = 0.6\text{ m/s}^2$

By equation of motion,

$$v = u + at = 5 + 0.6 \times 20 = 17\text{ m/s}$$

12 A force acts on a body of mass 5 kg and changes its velocity from 8 m/s to 12 m/s in 4 s, then magnitude of force is

(a) 8 N (b) 4 N (c) 5 N (d) 6 N

Sol. (*c*) According to Newton's second law of motion,

Force = Rate of change in momentum

$$F = \frac{m(v-u)}{t} = \frac{5(12-8)}{4} = 5\text{ N}$$

13 Which of the following statements is not correct? **Competency Based Que.**

(a) Momentum is a vector quantity.

(b) Magnitude of force *F* is a scalar quantity.

(c) Inertia of direction is to resist any change in state of uniform motion.

(d) Frictional force can be larger/smaller than external force.

Sol. (*c*) Inertia of direction is to resist any change in its direction of motion.

14 Impulse is equal to

(a) rate of change in momentum

(b) rate of change in force

(c) change in reaction force

(d) change in momentum

Sol. (*d*) Impulse, $I = F \times \Delta t = \frac{\Delta p}{\Delta t} \cdot \Delta t = \Delta p$

= Change in momentum

15 Two billiard balls *A* and *B*, each of mass 50 g and moving in opposite directions with speed of 5 ms^{-1} each, collide and rebound with the same speed. If the collision lasts for 10^{-3} s, which of the following statements are true? **Competency Based Que.**

(a) The impulse imparted to each ball is 0.25 kg-ms^{-1} and the force on each ball is 250 N.

(b) The impulse imparted to each ball is 0.25 kg-ms^{-1} and the force exerted on each ball is 25×10^{-5} N.

(c) The impulse imparted to each ball is 0.5 N-s.

(d) The impulse and the force on each ball are different in magnitude and acts in same direction.

Sol. (*c*) $m_A = m_B = 50\text{ g} = 50 \times 10^{-3}$ kg

$$v_A = -v_B = 5\text{ ms}^{-1}$$

Impulse imparted to each ball on collision

= Change in momentum of each ball

$= 2m_A v_A = 2m_B v_B$

$= 2 \times 50 \times 10^{-3} \times 5 = 0.5$ N-s

$$\text{Force} = \frac{\text{Impulse}}{\text{Time}} = \frac{\text{Change in momentum}}{10^{-3}} = \frac{0.5}{10^{-3}} = 500\text{ N}$$

As direction of change of momentum of *A* is opposite to that of *B*, so the impulse and the force on each ball are equal in magnitude and opposite in direction.

16 **A goalkeeper in a game of football pulls his hands backwards after holding the ball shot at the goal. This enables the goalkeeper to** **Competency Based Que.**

(a) exert larger force on the ball.
(b) reduce the force exerted by the ball on hands.
(c) increase the rate of change of momentum.
(d) decrease the rate of change of momentum.

Sol. (*d*) From Newton's second law of motion.

$$F = Ma = M\frac{(v-u)}{t}$$

The goalkeeper pulls his hands backwards to increase the time of catching, to decrease the force and rate of change of momentum also.

17 **According to the third law of motion, action and reaction** **NCERT Exemplar**

(a) always act on the same body.
(b) always act on different bodies in opposite directions.
(c) have same magnitude and directions.
(d) act on either body at normal to each other.

Sol. (*b*) According to third law of motion,

Action and reaction forces are equal in magnitude and opposite in direction. They always act on different objects.

18 **A man pushes a block of wood (w_1) to the left which is attached to another block (w_2). If the man is pushing with enough force such that the blocks accelerate to the left, what can be concluded about the magnitudes of the forces on the blocks?** **Competency Based Que.**

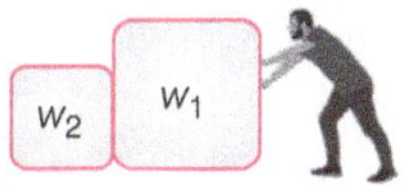

$(M_{w_1} > M_{w_2})$

(a) The force on block 2 exerted by block 1 is smaller in magnitude than the force on w_1 exerted by w_2.
(b) The force on w_2 exerted by w_1 is larger in magnitude than the force on w_1 exerted by w_2.
(c) The force on w_2 exerted by w_1 is not dependent on the size of the block (w_1) and *vice-versa*.
(d) The force on w_2 exerted by w_1 can be large/small depending on the size of the acceleration.

Sol. (*c*) According to Newton's third law of motion, force on w_2 exerted by w_1 and *vice-versa* will be equal in magnitude and opposite in direction, acting on different blocks in the two cases.

19 **Consider two spring balances hooked as shown in the figure below. We pull them in opposite directions. If the reading shown by *A* is 1.5 N, the reading shown by *B* will be** **Competency Based Que.**

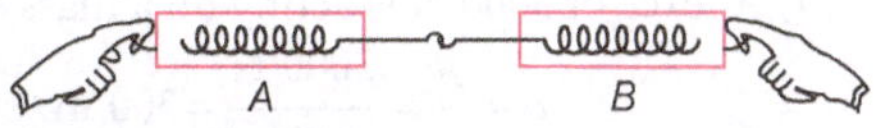

(a) 1.5 N (b) 2.5 N (c) 3.0 N (d) zero

Sol. (*a*) According to Newton's third law, every action has equal and opposite reaction. Hence, force (action) exerted by *A* on *B* and force exerted by *B* on *A* reaction are equal and reading shown by *B* will be 1.5 N in both the spring balance.

20 **Rocket propulsion phenomena can be described by which Newton's law of motion?**

(a) First law of motion (b) Second law of motion
(c) Third law of motion (d) None of the above

Sol. (*c*) Rocket propulsion is based on the principle of action and reaction pair of forces.

Assertion-Reason Questions

Direction (Q.Nos. 1-5) ***In each of the following questions, a statement of Assertion is given by the corresponding statement of Reason. Of the statements, mark the correct answer as***

(a) If both Assertion and Reason are true and Reason is the correct explanation of Assertion.
(b) If both Assertion and Reason are true but Reason is not the correct explanation of Assertion.
(c) If Assertion is true but Reason is false.
(d) If Assertion is false but Reason is true.

1 **Assertion** (A) If a balanced force is applied on a table, it will move.

Reason (R) Balanced force doesn't change the state of rest or uniform motion.

Sol. (*d*) When a unbalanced force is applied on table, then it will move. Balanced force can change the shape of object only.

2 **Assertion** (A) To keep moving with uniform velocity, a cycle has to be pedaled continuously.

Reason (R) To balance the force of friction due to ground on cycle, an external force in the form of pedaling is applied.

Sol. (*a*) If pedalling of cycle is stopped, cycle will stop after sometime due to friction acting in the opposite direction of motion.

3 **Assertion** (A) 1 kg book has more inertia than that of 1 kg cotton.

Reason (R) Inertia depends upon the mass.

Sol. (*d*) Both the 1 kg book and 1 kg of cotton will have same inertia as it depends upon the mass.

4 **Assertion** (A) Road accidents occurring due to high speeds are much worse than accidents due to low speeds of vehicles.

Reason (R) Momentum of high speed vehicles is more than that of low speed vehicles.

Sol. (*a*) Road accidents due to high speeds are much worse than accidents due to low speeds of vehicles. This is because the momentum of high speed vehicles is more than that of the low speed vehicles, as momentum is the product of mass and velocity.

5 **Assertion** (A) If two persons walking or running in opposite direction collide with each other, then both feel hurt.

Reason (R) To every action, there is an equal and opposite reaction.

Sol. (*a*) According to Newton's third law of motion, every action has an equal and opposite reaction, but always act on two different bodies.

Therefore, both persons feel hurt after collision.

Case Based/Source Based Questions

Direction (Q.Nos. 1-3) ***Answer the questions on the basis of your understanding of the following passage and related studied concepts***

1 **A man pushes four boxes of different mass.**

The table shows the acceleration produced for each box during the push.

Mass of the box (kg)	Acceleration produced (m/s^2)
10	200
20	100
40	50
80	25

(i) What amount of force does the man exert on each box? Show the calculation. [2]

(ii) Is the force acting on each box unbalanced? Explain your answer. [1]

(iii) Which of these represent a balanced force? [1]

(a) A boy sitting on a chair.

(b) An object sinking in water.

(c) An apple falling from a tree.

(d) A magnet attracting an iron nail.

Sol. (i) Force is given by $F = ma$

where m = mass of the box (in kg)

and a = acceleration of box (in m/s^2).

$$F_1 = 10 \times 200 = 2000 \text{ N}$$
$$F_2 = 20 \times 100 = 2000 \text{ N}$$
$$F_3 = 40 \times 50 = 2000 \text{ N}$$
$$F_4 = 80 \times 25 = 2000 \text{ N}$$

Same amount of force on each box.

(ii) Initially the box is at rest and acceleration is produced in each box during the push, which is caused by only unbalanced force. To keep it moving, unbalanced force must be applied continuously.

(iii) (*a*) Total force acting on a boy sitting on a chair sums up to zero. Gravitational force acting downwards balances normal force of chair acting upwards.

2 **A football and a tennis ball fall freely on a marble floor from a height of 5 m.**

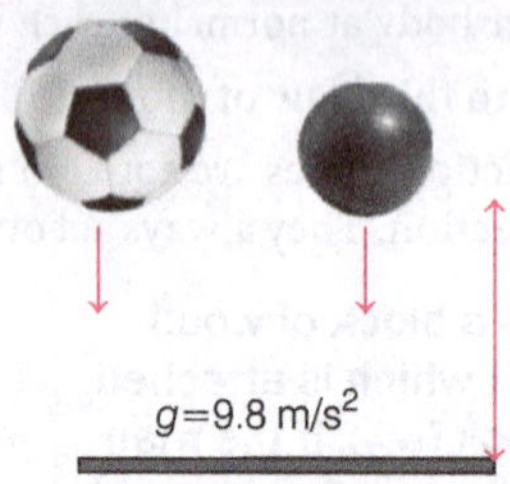

(i) Will the football and the tennis ball hit the floor with the same momentum? Explain your answer. [1]

(ii) Both balls bounced back after hitting the floor. What caused the balls to bounce back? [1]

(iii) Will the balls reach a height of 5 m or less than 5 m after bouncing back? Explain your answer. [1]

(iv) Which of these will produce the maximum acceleration? [1]

(a) A force of 1000 N acting on a mass of 10 kg.

(b) A force of 1000 N acting on a mass of 5 kg.

(c) A force of 3000 N acting on a mass of 30 kg.

(d) A force of 3000 N acting on a mass of 10 kg.

Sol. (i) No, momentum depends on mass proportionally.

(ii) Reaction force caused the balls to bounce back after hitting the floor.

(iii) Yes, balls reaches a height of less than 5 m after bouncing back because some energy will be lost due to friction.

(iv) (*d*) A force of 3000 N is acting on a mass of 10 kg,

$$a = \frac{F}{m} = \frac{3000 \text{ N}}{10\text{kg}} = 300 \text{ m/s}^2$$

3 **During a collision, two bodies interact and exert force on each other.**

According to Newton's second law, the rate of change in momentum of the body is directly proportional to the force acting on it and the change takes place in the direction of the applied force.

Mathematically,

$$\mathbf{F}_{\text{net}} = \frac{\Delta \mathbf{p}}{\Delta t}$$

where, change in momentum is also known as Impulse.

According to Newton's third law, when two bodies collide with each other, they exert equal and opposite forces on each other.

$$\mathbf{F}_A = -\mathbf{F}_B$$

(i) Consider collision of a tennis ball in different cases depending on different physical properties of the ball and the wall.

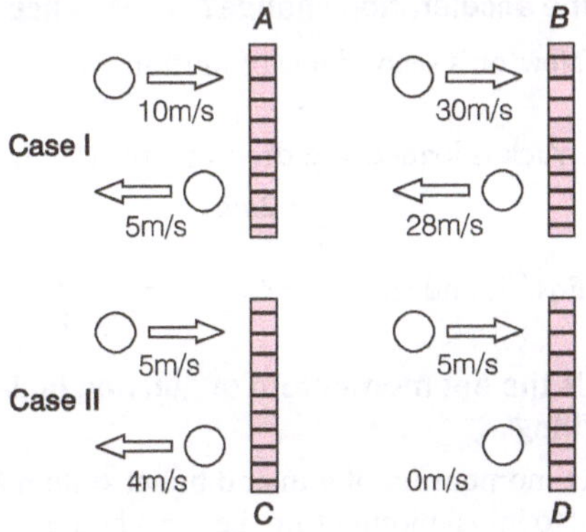

Which collision under the two cases has the greater Impulse? [1]

	I	II
(a)	A	C
(b)	A	D
(c)	B	C
(d)	B	D

(ii) In an accident, two cars can either collide and bounce off each other on collision or collide, crumple up and travel together with the same speed after the collision. Which would be more damaging? Justify your answer. [2]

(iii) Draw the force acting on cars versus time for the above two situations. [1]

Sol. (i) (*c*)

(ii) Bouncing off after a collision will be more dangerous. The momentum change will be larger in less time, hence greater force will be exerted. The crumpling up of cars is the safest type of automobile collision.

(iii) (a) When the two cars collide and bounce off.

(b) When they crumple up and move together.

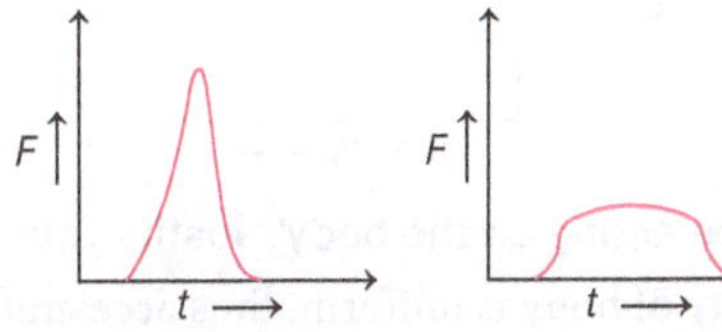

(i) (ii)

Constructed Response (Descriptive) Questions

Very Short Answer Type Questions

1 **A book of weight 10 N is kept on a smooth horizontal table. The force exerted by the table on the book will be of magnitude.**

Sol. The resultant force on the book must be zero as the book is at rest on table. Gravitational force of 10 N is acting downward. The table must exert force of 10 N in upward direction to make the resultant force zero.

2 **What do you mean by resultant force?**

Sol. When two or more forces act on a body simultaneously, then the single force which produces the same effect as produced by all the other forces acting together is known as the resultant force.

3 **Using a horizontal force of 200 N, we intend to move a wooden cabinet across a floor at a constant velocity. What is the frictional force that will be exerted on the cabinet?** **Competency Based Que.**

Sol. To move the wooden cabinet with constant velocity, total external force on the cabinet must be zero. Along with horizontal force, only frictional force is acting in opposite direction.

So, frictional force will be 200 N.

4 **In the interstellar space, an astronaut gets separated out of his small spaceship accelerating at constant rate of 150 m/s^2. What is the acceleration of the astronaut the instant after he is outside the spaceship?** **Competency Based Que.**

Sol. At the instant of separation, his velocity remains same as that spaceship due to inertia of motion. Due to negligible gravitational of small mass of spaceship and there are no stars nearby.

So, astronaut experiences no force, i.e. acceleration will be zero.

5 While riding on the bicycle, if we stop pedalling, why does the bicycle begin to slow down?

Sol. The bicycle begins to slow down because of the frictional force acting opposite to the direction of motion. We have to start pedalling again and again to keep it moving.

6 There are three solids made up of aluminium, steel and wood, of the same shape and same volume. Which of them would have highest inertia? **Competency Based Que.**

Sol. As the steel has the largest density among wood and aluminium of same shape and volume and inertia is proportional to mass, so steel would have highest inertia.

7 Velocity-time graph of a moving particle of mass 1 kg is shown in figure.

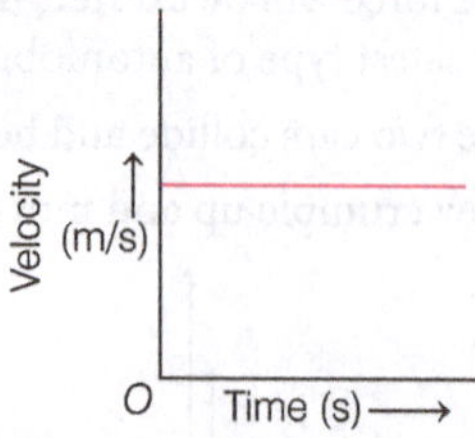

Is any force acting on the body? Justify your answer.

Sol. The velocity of body is uniform, thus acceleration is zero. Hence, no unbalanced force acts on the body.

8 Name the agent which is the cause of change in momentum in a body with time and write the mathematical relation for it.

Sol. Force is the agent which is the cause of change in momentum in a body with time.

Mathematical relation, $F \propto \dfrac{(p_2 - p_1)}{t}$

$$\Rightarrow \quad F = k\frac{\Delta p}{\Delta t}$$

$$\Rightarrow \quad F = km\frac{\Delta v}{\Delta t}$$

$$\Rightarrow \quad F = kma \qquad \left(\text{where, } \frac{\Delta v}{\Delta t} = a \text{ and } k = 1\right)$$

9 A passenger in a moving train tosses a coin which falls behind him. From this incident, what can you predict about the motion of train? **NCERT Exemplar**

Sol. If the coin falls behind the passenger, that means the train is accelerated. When the coin is tossed, then it has same velocity as that of train but when, it is in air so, its velocity becomes less than that of train (because the train is accelerated), so it falls behind the passenger.

10 Derive Newton's first law of motion from the mathematical expression of the second law of motion.

Sol. From Newton's second law of motion, $F = ma$

$$F = m\frac{(v-u)}{t}$$

$$Ft = m(v-u)$$

If $\quad F = 0, u = v$ for any time t.

i.e. Body will continue to move forever with uniform velocity u throughout time t.

and if $u = 0,\ v = 0$

i.e. Body will remain at rest.

Newton's first law of motion states that body will remain in its state (rest/uniform motion) unless external force is applied on it.

11 A truck of mass *M* is moved under a force *F*. If the truck is then loaded with an object equal to the mass of the truck and the driving force is halved, then how does the acceleration change? **NCERT Exemplar**

Sol. From Newton's second law of motion,

$$F = ma_1 \qquad \ldots \text{(i)}$$

When truck is loaded and driving force is halved.

$$\frac{F}{2} = 2ma_2 \qquad \ldots \text{(ii)}$$

From Eqs. (i) and (ii), $a_1 = 4a_2 \Rightarrow a_2 = \dfrac{a_1}{4}$

12 What is the net momentum of gun and bullet system after firing?

Sol. The net momentum of gun and bullet system after firing is equal to initial momentum, i.e. zero because no external force is acting.

Short Answer Type Questions

1 Identify the type of force acting in the case given below by observing the *v*-*t* graphs.

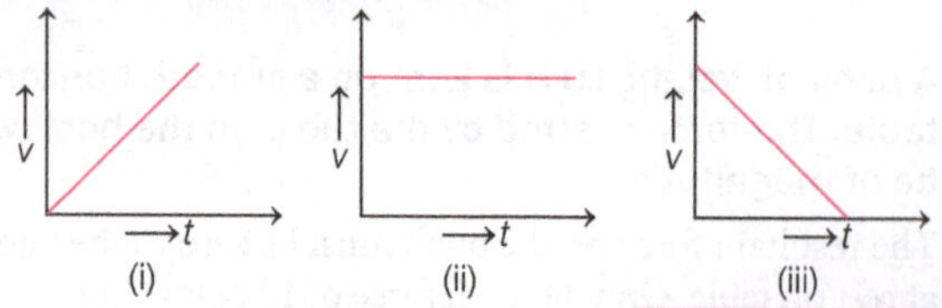

Competency Based Que.

Sol. (i) Unbalanced force / External force

Acceleration of the object is constant, that means some force is acting on the object to keep moving it. Therefore, resultant force is non-zero.

(ii) Balanced force

Acceleration of the object is zero, i.e. it is moving with constant velocity. External forces sum up to zero, that means forces are balanced. So, resultant force is zero.

(iii) Frictional force

Velocity of the object decreases to 0 from v, i.e., it comes to rest after sometime t. Friction is the cause which opposes the motion.

2 State the type of inertia that acts on a passenger while standing still in a moving bus.

(i) When bus takes a turn on curved road, passenger feels an outward force. [1]

(ii) Passenger suddenly moves in forward direction. [1]

(iii) Passenger suddenly moves in backward direction. [1]

Sol. (i) Inertia of direction, i.e. resists any change in direction of moving bus.

(ii) Inertia of motion, i.e. resists change in state of uniform motion.

(iii) Inertia of rest, i.e. resists change in the state of rest.

3 Glasswares are wrapped in straw during their transportation. Justify giving reason.

Sol. During transportation, the glasswares may break, if they collide with each other in the event of jerks. When they are wrapped in straw, then the force of jerk is transmitted to them through the pieces of straw in a longer period of time. Thus, the change in momentum of the glasswares takes place in a longer period of time. Therefore, a very small force is experienced by them in the event of jerks and they do not break.

4 What would happen, if a fielder stops the fast moving ball suddenly? Justify your answer. **Competency Based Que.**

Sol. When a fielder stops a fast moving ball suddenly, the force exerted by the fielder's hand causes the ball to decelerate. The high velocity of the ball decreases to zero in a short time. It means that in a short time, there is a large change in momentum of the ball.

Therefore, to stop the fast moving ball, the fielder have to apply a large force and in the process he may hurt his palm.

5 A bullet fired against a glass pane makes a hole in it and the glass pane is not cracked. But on the other hand, when a stone strikes the same glass pane, then it gets smashed. Why is it so? **Competency Based Que.**

Sol. When the bullet strikes the glass pane, then the part of the glass pane which comes in contact with the bullet immediately shares the large velocity of bullet and makes a hole, while the remaining part of the glass remains at rest and is therefore not smashed due to inertia of rest.

But when a slow moving stone strikes the same glass pane, then the various parts of the glass pane gets enough time to share the velocity of the stone and the glass is smashed, its inertia gets disturbed.

6 If a bird collides with the windshield of a fast moving aeroplane, which experiences an impact force with larger magnitude?

Sol. According to Newton's third law, the bird and the aeroplane experience forces that are equal in magnitude and opposite in direction. As the bird has small mass, Newton's second law concludes that bird will have large acceleration. The large mass of plane doesn't affect any change in motion of the plane.

i.e. Change in velocity will be large, hence the impact force on bird will be large.

7 By observing the diagram below, answer the following questions in brief.

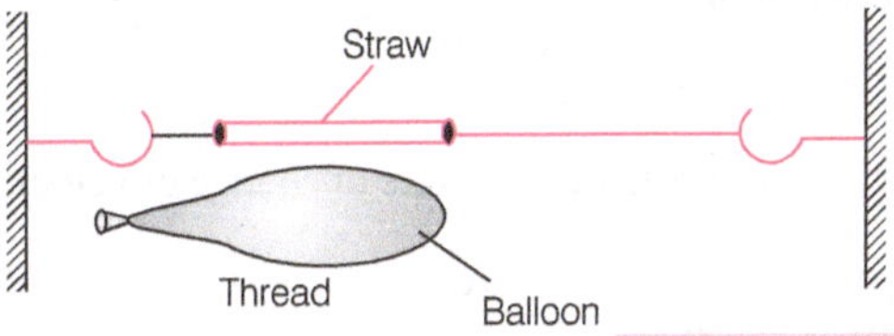

Competency Based Que.

(i) When the thread tied to balloon's neck is removed, then in which direction does the balloon move? [1]

(ii) Which Newton's law of motion is applicable here? [1]

(iii) What conclusion can be drawn from this activity? [1]

Sol. (i) When tied thread is removed, air filled inside the balloon escapes and balloon moves from left to right.

(ii) Newton's third law of motion can best describe the above situation.

(iii) Pair of action and reaction forces are equal and opposite in direction.

8 Look at the diagram below and answer the following questions **Competency Based Que.**

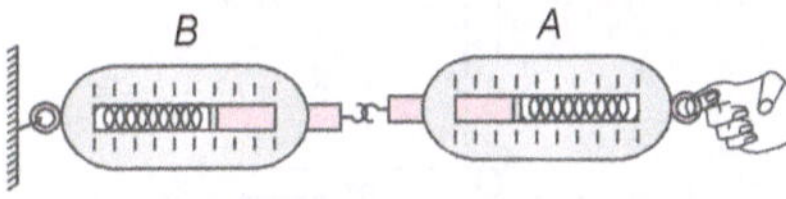

(i) When a force is applied through the free end of the spring balance A, then the reading on the spring balance A is 15 g-wt. What will be the measure of the reading shown by spring balance B? [1]

(ii) Write reasons for your answer. [1]

(iii) Name the forces which balance A exerts on balance B and balance B exerts on balance A. [1]

Sol. (i) 15 g-wt

(ii) From Newton's third law, the force exerted by B on A and the force exerted by A on B are equal.

(iii) The balance A exerts the force of reaction on balance B, whereas balance B exerts the action force on balance A.

Long Answer Type Questions

1 What is momentum? Write its SI unit. Interpret force in terms of momentum. Represent the following graphically [3] **NCERT Exemplar**

(i) momentum *versus* velocity when mass is fixed. [1]

(ii) momentum *versus* mass when velocity is constant. [1]

Sol. **Momentum** The quantity of motion possessed by a moving body is known as momentum of the body. It is the product of mass and velocity of the body.

Momentum, $p = mv$. Its SI unit is kg-m/s.

Force applied on an object of mass m moving with acceleration a,

$$F = ma = m\frac{\Delta v}{\Delta t}$$

$$[\because \text{acceleration} = \text{rate of change of velocity} = \frac{\Delta v}{\Delta t}]$$

$$= \frac{\Delta p}{\Delta t}$$

$\therefore$ Force applied on an object is equal to the rate of change of momentum of the object.

(i) Momentum *versus* velocity graph when mass is fixed,

$$p = mv$$

If m is fixed, then $p \propto v$

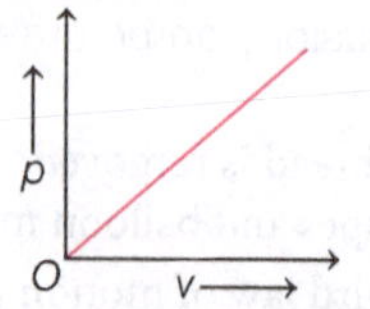

$\therefore$Momentum *versus* velocity graph will be a straight line passing through the origin (if $v = 0$, then $p = 0$).

(ii) Momentum *versus* mass graph when velocity is constant, $p = mv$.

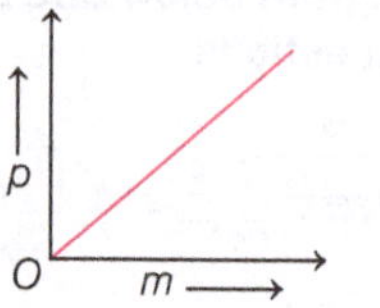

If velocity is constant, then $p \propto m$.

So, the momentum *versus* mass graph will be a straight line passing through the origin (if $m = 0$, then $p = 0$).

2 (i) **What will you observe in the diagram given below, if the card is given a sharp horizontal flick with a finger?** [3]

(ii) **A karate player can break a pile of tiles with a single blow of her hand. Explain it.** [2] **Competency Based Que.**

Sol. (i) This phenomenon can be explained by Newton's first law of motion which states an object will remain in the state of rest/motion unless an external force act upon it.

When the card is given a sharp horizontal flick with finger, the card underneath the coin shoots away. The coin due to its inertia of rest, tends to remain in the state of rest. Thus, the coin falls vertically into the glass.

(ii) In a very short span of time, the large momentum of fast moving hand of karate player is reduced to zero. This action of player applies a very large force on the pile of tiles which is enough to break with a single blow of hand.

Numerical Questions

1 (i) **What is the relation between SI unit of force and weight of 1 kg mass?** [1]

(ii) **You are applying force on the weighing balance pan by pressing against it and the pointer points to 150 g. What will be the magnitude of force in Newton exerted by you ($a = 9.8\,m/s^2$)** [1]

Sol. (i) $F = ma$

$m = 1$ kg $\Rightarrow$ $a = 9.8$ m/s^2

$F = 9.8$ N

1 kg weight = 9.8 N.

(ii) $F = m \times a$ where $m = 150$ g, $a = 9.8$ m/s^2

$$F = \left(\frac{150}{1000}\right)(9.8) = 1.47 \text{ N}$$

2 If F and F' are balanced forces, then what will be the magnitude of F_2? **Competency Based Que.**

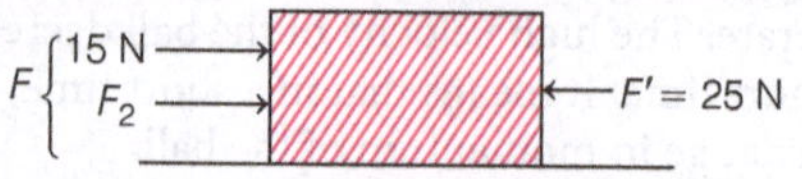

Sol. As per question, F and F' are balanced forces.

So, $F = F' \Rightarrow 15 + F_2 = 25$ N

$\therefore$ $F_2 = 10$ N

3 A wooden box of mass 6 kg is dropped from a height of 30 m. Calculate the initial momentum and the momentum just before it strikes the ground. (Take, $g = 9.8\,m/s^2$)

Sol. Initial velocity, $u = 0$ m/s

Then, initial momentum will be $p_i = 6 \times 0 = 0$ kg-m/s

Let us consider the velocity just before striking the ground be v m/s.

From third equation of motion,

$$v^2 = u^2 + 2gh \Rightarrow v^2 = 0^2 + 2 \times 9.8 \times 30$$

$$v^2 = 588 \Rightarrow v = \sqrt{588} = 24.24 \text{ m/s}$$

Momentum just before striking the ground

$$p_f = 6 \times 24.24 = 145.49 \approx 145.5 \text{ kg-m/s.}$$

4 **A girl throws a stone of mass 0.2 kg vertically upwards with a velocity of 15 m/s. What will be the initial momentum? What would be its momentum at the highest point of its reach?**

Sol. Given, mass of stone, $m = 0.2$ kg

Initial velocity, $u = 15$ m/s

Initial momentum, $p_1 = mu = 0.2 \times 15 = 3$ kg-m/s

When the stone reaches the highest point,

Velocity of the ball will be zero, i.e. $v = 0$

Momentum, $p_2 = mv = 0.2 \times 0 = 0$ kg-m/s

5 (i) A force P acting on a body A of mass 4 kg produces an acceleration of 6 m/s^2 . An another force Q action on body B of mass 9 kg produces an acceleration of 4 m/s^2. Find the ratio of forces P and Q. [1½]

(ii) If the two forces X and Y are acting on a body as shown below. Find the resultant acceleration is produced in which direction. [1½]

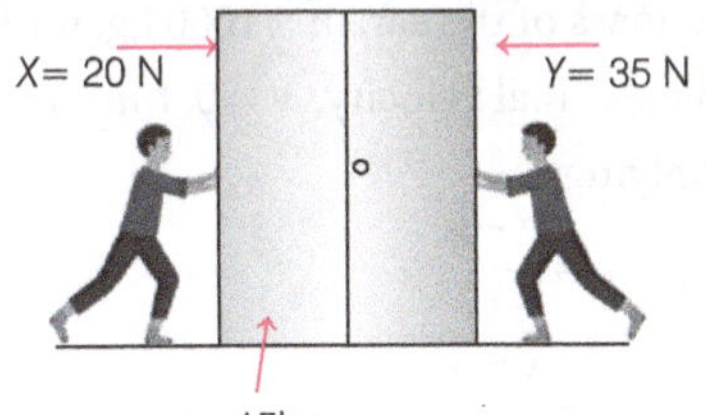

Sol. (i) From Newton's second law of motion, $F = ma$

Here, $P = m_1 a_1 = 4 \times 6 = 24$ N

$Q = m_2 a_2 = 9 \times 4 = 36$ N

Ratio of forces P and Q will be

$$\frac{P}{Q} = \frac{24}{36} = \frac{2}{3}$$

$$\frac{P}{Q} = 2:3$$

(ii) Here, mass, $m = 15$ kg

Forces, $X = 20$ N and $Y = 35$ N

Resultant force, $F = Y - X = (35 - 20)$ N $= 15$ N

and $F = ma$

$$a = \frac{F}{m} = \frac{15}{15} = 1 \text{ m/s}^2$$

Body will move in left direction with acceleration 1 m/s^2.

6 **A bullet of mass 4 g when fired with a velocity of 50 m/s can enter a wall upto a depth of 10 cm. How much will be the average resistance offered by the wall?**

Sol. Given, mass of the bullet, $m = 4\text{g} = 4 \times 10^{-3}$ kg

Initial velocity, $u = 50$ m/s, depth, $s = 10 \text{ cm} = \frac{1}{10}$ m

Final velocity, $v = 0$, force, $F = ?$

We know that,

$$\Rightarrow \quad v^2 - u^2 = 2as$$

$$\Rightarrow \quad 0 - (50)^2 = 2\,a \times \frac{1}{10}$$

$$\Rightarrow \quad -2500 = \frac{a}{5} \Rightarrow a = -12500 \text{ m/s}^2$$

$\therefore$ Force, $F = ma = 4 \times 10^{-3} \times (-12500)$

$= -50$ N

Thus, the average resistance offered is 50 N.

Negative sign indicates that the force is acting opposite to the motion.

7 **Velocity *versus* time graph of a ball of mass 50 g rolling on a concrete floor is shown in figure. Calculate the acceleration and frictional force of the floor on the ball.** **Competency Based Que.**

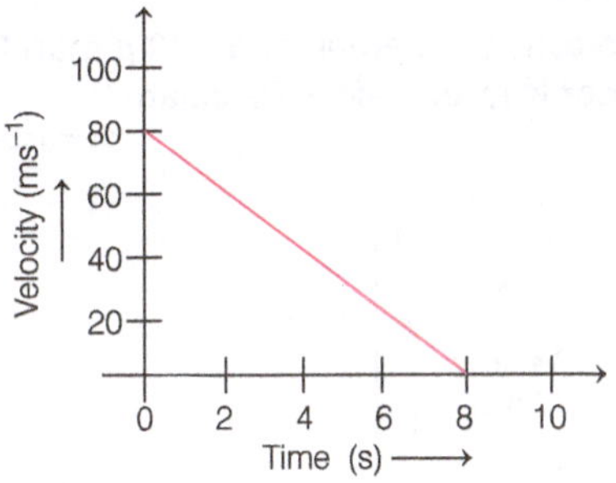

Sol. From the graph,

$u = 80$ m/s

$v = 0$ m/s

$t = 8$s

Acceleration, $a = \frac{v - u}{t} = \frac{0 - 80}{8} = -10 \text{ m/s}^2$

Frictional force, $F = ma$

$= [50 \times 10^{-3} \text{ kg}] \times (-10 \text{ m/s}^2)$

$= 0.5$ N

8 **Using second law of motion, derive the relation between force and acceleration. A bullet of 10 g strikes a sand bag at a speed of 10^3 m/s and gets embedded after travelling 5 cm. Calculate** **NCERT Exemplar**

(i) the resistive force exerted by sand on the bullet. [3]

(ii) the time taken by bullet to come to rest. [2]

Sol. Refer to text on page 184 (Newton's second law of motion).

Given, $m = 10 \text{ g} = 0.01$ kg, $u = 10^3$ m/s, $v = 0$,

$s = 5 \text{ cm} = 0.05$ m, $t = ?$, $a = ?$, $F = ?$

(i) From third equation of motion,

$$a = \frac{v^2 - u^2}{2s} = \frac{0 - (10^3)^2}{2 \times 0.05}$$

$$= -10^7 \text{ m/s}^2$$

$\therefore$ Force applied by the bullet,

$$F = ma = 0.01 \times (-10^7)$$
$$= -10^5 \text{ N}$$

[negative sign shows that force is against the direction of motion]

The resistive force exerted by the sand on the bullet is 10^5 N.

(ii) Time taken by bullet to come to rest,

$$t = \frac{v-u}{a}$$
$$= \frac{0-10^3}{-10^7} = 10^{-4} \text{s}$$

9 **(i) Which law provides the formula for measuring force and then law which gives the definition of force?** [2]

(ii) Velocity-time graph of a 100 g marble rolling on floor is given below. Calculate

Competency Based Que.

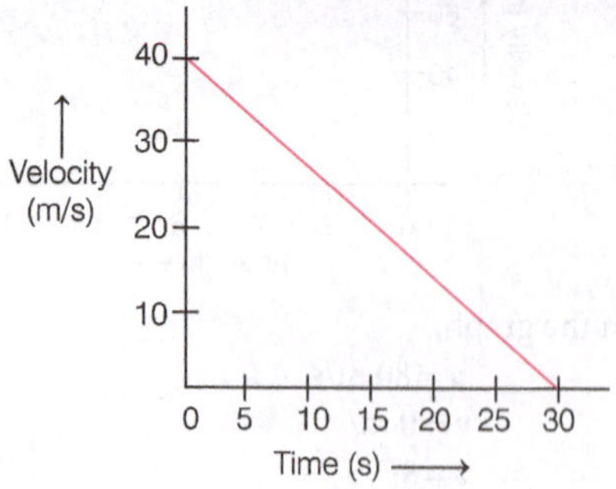

(a) time in which it stops. [1]
(b) negative acceleration produced in it. [1]
(c) positive force acting on the marble. [1]

Sol. (i) Newton's second law of motion provides the formula for measuring force and gives the definition of force. Rate of change of momentum is equal to the force.

i.e. $F = ma$

where, m is the mass of body

and a is the acceleration in the body,

(ii) From graph,

(a) $t = 30$ s

(b) $a = \frac{0-40}{30} = -1.33 \text{ m/s}^2$

(c) $F = ma = \frac{100}{1000} \times (-1.33) = -0.133$ N

$|F| = 0.133$ N

10 **The speed-time graph of a car is given. The car weighs 1000 kg.**

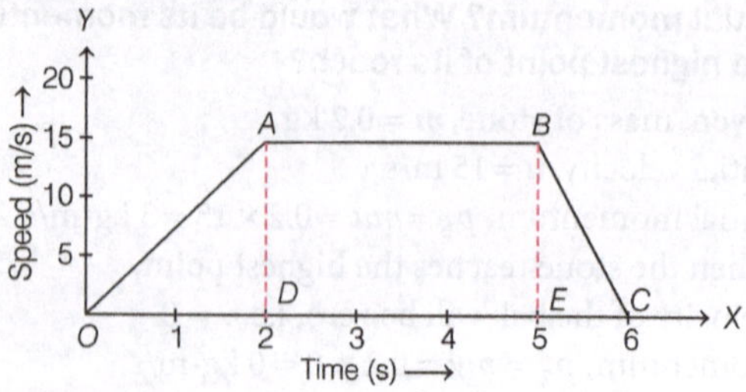

(i) What is the distance travelled by the car in first 2s? [1]

(ii) What is the braking force applied at the end of 5 s to bring the car to stop within one second? [2]

Sol. (i) Distance travelled by the car in first 2 s = Area of

$$\Delta OAD = \frac{1}{2} \times 2 \times 15 = 15\text{m}$$

(ii) Braking force, $F = m \times a$

Given, mass of the car, $m = 1000$ kg, initial velocity, $u = 15$ m/s, final velocity, $v = 0$, time, $t = 1$ s

On applying,

$$a = \frac{v-u}{t}$$

$$\Rightarrow \quad a = \frac{0-15}{1}$$
$$= -15 \text{ m/s}^2$$

$$\therefore \quad F = m\,a = 1000 \times (-15) = -15000 \text{ N}$$

11 **The velocity-time graph of a ball moving on the surface of floor is as shown in figure. Calculate the force acting on the ball, if mass of the ball is 100 g.**

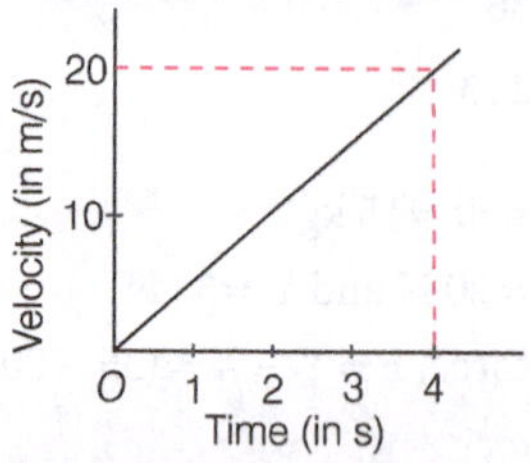

Sol. The velocity-time graph shows that the velocity of the ball at $t = 0$ is zero, so initial velocity of the ball, $u = 0$.

Velocity of the ball at $t = 4$ s is 20 m/s

i.e. Final velocity, $v = 20$ m/s, time, $t = 4$ s

$\therefore$ Acceleration of the ball,

$$a = \frac{v-u}{t} = \frac{20 \text{ m/s} - 0}{4 \text{ s}} = 5 \text{ m/s}^2$$

Also, mass of the ball, $m = 100 \text{ g} = \frac{100}{1000} \text{ kg} = \frac{1}{10} \text{ kg}$

$\therefore$ Force acting on the ball, $F = ma$

$$= \frac{1}{10} \text{ kg} \times 5 \text{ m/s}^2$$

$$= 0.5 \text{ kg-m/s}^2 = 0.5 \text{ N} \quad [\because 1 \text{ kg-m/s}^2 = 1 \text{ N}]$$

12 A constant force of friction of 50 N is acting on a body of mass 200 kg moving initially with a speed of 15 m/s. How long does the body take to stop? What distance will it cover before coming to rest?

Sol. Given, $F = -50$ N, $m = 200$ kg, $u = 15$ m/s

Acceleration of the body is obtained from $F = ma$

or $$a = \frac{F}{m} = \frac{-50}{200}$$

$$= -0.25 \text{ m/s}^2$$

We know that,

$$v = u + at$$

$$\Rightarrow \quad t = \left(\frac{v - u}{a}\right)$$

$$= \left(\frac{0 - 15}{-0.25}\right) = 60 \text{s}$$

Also, distance travelled is obtained from

$$s = ut + \frac{1}{2}at^2$$

$$= 15 \times 60 + 1/2 \times (-0.25) \times (60)^2$$

$$= 450 \text{ m}$$

13 For how much time should a force of 200 N acts on an object having mass 5 kg, so as to increase its velocity from 50 m/s to 100 m/s and impact of force within time interval?

Sol. Given, force, $F = 200$ N, mass of an object, $m = 5$ kg

Initial velocity, $u = 50$ m/s

Final velocity, $v = 100$ m/s

From Newton's second law of motion, we get

$$F = ma = m\left(\frac{v - u}{t}\right) \quad \left[\because a = \frac{v - u}{t}\right]$$

$$200 = 5\left(\frac{100 - 50}{t}\right)$$

$$\therefore \quad t = 5\left(\frac{100 - 50}{200}\right) = 1.25 \text{ s}$$

Thus, the time taken is 1.25 s.

Impact of force, $I = F \times t = 200 \times 1.25 = 250$ N-s

14 The motion of a body of mass 5 kg is shown in the velocity-time graph.

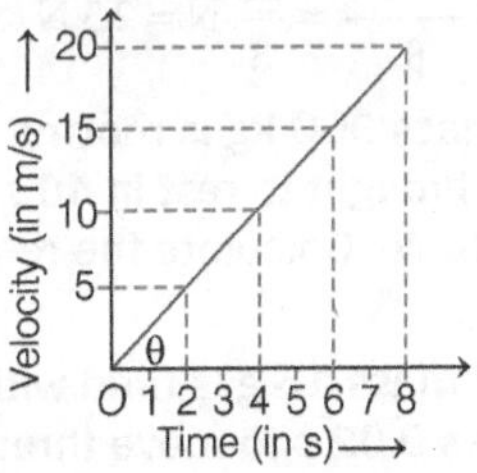

Find the following from the graph.

(i) Its acceleration. [1]

(ii) The force acting on the body. [1]

(iii) The change in momentum of body in 2 s after start. [1]

Sol. (i) Acceleration = Slope of the line of velocity-time graph

$$a = \frac{v_2 - v_1}{t - t_1} = \frac{5 - 0}{2 - 0} = \frac{5}{2} = 2.5 \text{ m/s}^2$$

(ii) The force acting on the body is given by

$$F = ma = 5 \times 2.5 = 12.5 \text{ N}$$

(iii) $\therefore$ Change in momentum $= mv - mu$

$$[\because u = 0 \text{ and } v = 5 \text{ m/s}]$$

$$= 5 \times 5 - 5 \times 0 = 25 \text{ kg-m/s}$$

15 (i) **Find the force required to impart a car a velocity of 50 m/s in 20 s. The mass of the car is 2000 kg.** [2]

(ii) **An object of mass 5 kg is accelerated uniformly from a velocity of 4 m/s to 8 m/s in 8 s. Calculate the initial and final momentum of the object. Also, find the magnitude of the force exerted on the object.** [3]

Sol. (i) Given, $u = 0$ m/s, $v = 50$ m/s, $t = 20$ s.

Mass, $m = 2000$ kg, $F = ?$ (to find)

As $F = ma$

$$\Rightarrow \quad F = m\left(\frac{v - u}{t}\right) = 2000\left(\frac{50 - 0}{20}\right) = 5000 \text{ N}$$

Hence, force required by the car is 5000 N.

(ii) Given, mass, $m = 5$ kg, initial velocity, $u = 4$ m/s

Final velocity, $v = 8$ m/s, time, $t = 8$ s

$\therefore$ Initial momentum, $p_1 = mu = 5 \times 4 = 20$ kg-m/s

and final momentum, $p_2 = mv = 5 \times 8 = 40$ kg-m/s

Now, force $= \frac{\Delta p}{t} = \frac{p_2 - p_1}{t}$

$$= \frac{40 - 20}{8} = \frac{20}{8} \text{ N} = 2.5 \text{ N}$$

16 **(i) A bus of mass 900 kg is moving at a speed of 30 m/s is brought to rest in 40 s by a constant retarding force. Calculate the retarding force (in N).** [2½]

(ii) A bullet of mass 15 g is fired with a rifle. The bullet takes 0.02 s to move through the barrel and leaves with a velocity of 300 m/s. Find the force (in N) exerted on the bullet by rifle. [2½]

Sol. (i) Here, mass, $m = 900$ kg

$u = 30$ m/s, $v = 0$ (bus comes to rest finally)

$t = 40$ s

Acceleration of the bus,

$$a = \frac{v - u}{t} = \frac{0 - 30}{40}$$

$$= -0.75 \text{ m/s}^2$$

Now, force,

$$F = ma = 900 \times (-0.75) = -675 \text{ N}$$

Negative sign indicates that the force is retarding.

(ii) Here, mass of bullet, $m = 15$ g

Time, $t = 0.02$ s

$v = 300$ m/s, $u = 0$ m/s

If force exerted on the bullet by the rifle is F.

$$F = m\left(\frac{v - u}{t}\right)$$

$$\Rightarrow \quad F = ma$$

$$a = \frac{v - u}{t} = \frac{300}{0.02} = 15 \times 10^3 \text{ m/s}^2$$

$$F = \frac{15}{1000} \times 15 \times 10^3 = 225 \text{ N}$$

17 **Derive the unit of force using the second law of motion. A force of 5 N produces an acceleration of 8 m/s² on a mass m_1 and an acceleration of 24 m/s² on a mass m_2. What acceleration would the same provide, if both masses were tied together?**

NCERT Exemplar

Sol. Refer to text on page 184 (Newton's second law of motion).

Given, $F_1 = 5$ N, $a_1 = 8$ m/s², $m_1 = ?$

$F_2 = 5$ N, $a_2 = 24$ m/s², $m_2 = ?$

From $F = ma$, $5 = m_1 \times 8$

$$\Rightarrow \quad m_1 = \frac{5}{8} \text{ kg}$$

Similarly, $5 = m_2 \times 24$

$$\Rightarrow \quad m_2 = \frac{5}{24} \text{ kg}$$

$$\therefore \quad m_1 + m_2 = \frac{5}{8} + \frac{5}{24}$$

$$= \frac{15 + 5}{24} = \frac{20}{24} = \frac{5}{6}$$

Acceleration produced by the same force provided, if both the masses are tied together,

$$a = \frac{F}{(m_1 + m_2)}$$

$$= \frac{5}{5/6} = 6 \text{ m/s}^2$$

ASSESSMENT EXERCISE

Competency Focused (Objective) Questions

Multiple Type Questions

1 The inertia of an object tends to cause the object **NCERT Exemplar**

(a) to increase its speed
(b) to decrease its speed
(c) to resist any change in its state of motion
(d) to decelerate due to friction

2 Trolleys *X* and *Y* are joined with stretched spring. Trolley *X* has twice the mass of trolley *Y*.

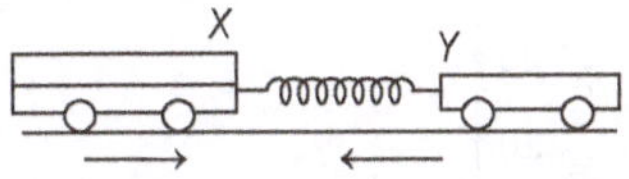

When the trolleys are released, the acceleration of *X* is $2\ m/s^2$ to the right. What is the initial acceleration of trolley *Y* to the left? **Competency Based Que.**

(a) $1\ m/s^2$
(b) $2\ m/s^2$
(c) $3\ m/s^2$
(d) $4\ m/s^2$

3 The resultant force acting on a body is zero, then a

(a) body is in unequilibrium
(b) body is in equilibrium
(c) body moves with constant acceleration
(d) body moves with retardation

4 An object of mass 2 kg is sliding with a constant velocity of $4\ ms^{-1}$ on a frictionless horizontal table. The force required to keep the object moving with the same velocity is

(a) 32 N (b) 0 N
(c) 2 N (d) 8 N

5 The image shows the forces acting on a block. The length of the arrow shows the strength of the force and the direction of the arrow shows the direction of application of the force.

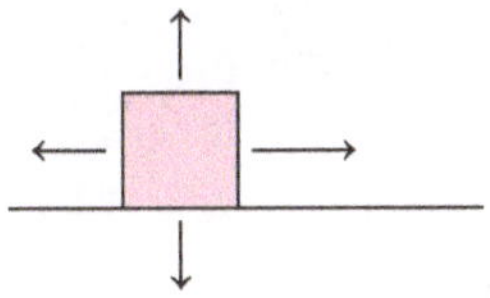

What is the direction of the resultant force? **Competency Based Que.**

(a) Downwards
(b) Upwards
(c) Towards left
(d) Towards right

Assertion-Reason Questions

Direction (Q.Nos. 6-8) *In each of the following questions, a statement of Assertion is given by the corresponding statement of Reason. Of the statements, mark the correct answer as*

(a) If both Assertion and Reason are true and Reason is the correct explanation of Assertion.
(b) If both Assertion and Reason are true but Reason is not the correct explanation of Assertion.
(c) If Assertion is true but Reason is false.
(d) If Assertion is false but Reason is true.

6 **Assertion** (A) Rate of change of momentum of a body is equal to resultant force applied on the body.

Reason (R) Change in momentum is equal to impulse.

7 **Assertion** (A) Newton's third law of motion apply to a system where bodies do not actually touch each other.

Reason (A) Action and reaction forces act on only first body.

8 **Assertion** (A) We should wear a seat belt while driving a car.

Reason (R) Seat belts prevents us from falling forward due to inertia, when sudden brakes are applied.

Answers

1. (c) **2.** (d) **3.** (b) **4.** (b) **5.** (d) **6.** (b) **7.** (c) **8.** (a)

Case Based/Source Based Question

Direction (Q.No. 9) *Answer the questions on the basis of your understanding of the following passage and related studied concepts.*

9 Make a pile of carrom coins. Now, hit the bottom coin hard with a striker. If you do it well, the lowest coin will move away but the rest of the pile will remain at the original position. The lowest coin moves because of the force exerted by the striker on it. However, the rest of the pile remains at its place due to inertia of rest. As the lowest coin moves very fast, any force exerted by it on the coins above it is for a very short time, which is not able to move the upper coins in the horizontal direction.

(i) What is the motion of the coin hit by the striker?
(ii) Why does the rest of pile remain at the original position?
(iii) State the factor, which is responsible for not able to move the upper coin.
(iv) What will happen, when you hit the bottom coin hard with a striker?

Constructed Response (Descriptive) Questions

Very Short Answer Type Questions

10 Two similar vehicles are moving with the same velocity on the road such that one of them is loaded and the other one is empty. Which of the two vehicles will require larger force to stop it? Give reasons. **Competency Based Que.**

11 Name two effects a force can bring about other than moving or stopping a body.

12 A body *P* has mass 2 m and velocity 5 *v*. Another body *Q* has mass 8 m and velocity 1.25*v*. Which of the *P* and *Q* has more momentum?

13 A body of mass 20 kg moves with an acceleration of 2 m/s^2. Calculate change in momentum.

Short Answer Type Questions

14 When Shyam is trying to push a heavy stone, mention various forces acting on the stone and explain them.

15 A bus starts from the stop and take 50 s to get the speed of 10 m/s. If the mass of the bus along with passengers is 10000 kg, then calculate the force applied by the engine of bus to push the bus at the speed of 10 m/s. **[Ans.** 2000 N]

16 A force of 5 N produces an acceleration of 8 m/s^2 in mass m_1 and an acceleration of 24 m/s^2 in mass m_2. What acceleration would it give if both the masses are tied together?

17 The velocity-time graph of a ball moving on the surface of a floor is shown in the figure. Find the force acting on the ball, if the mass of the ball is 50 g. **Competency Based Que.**

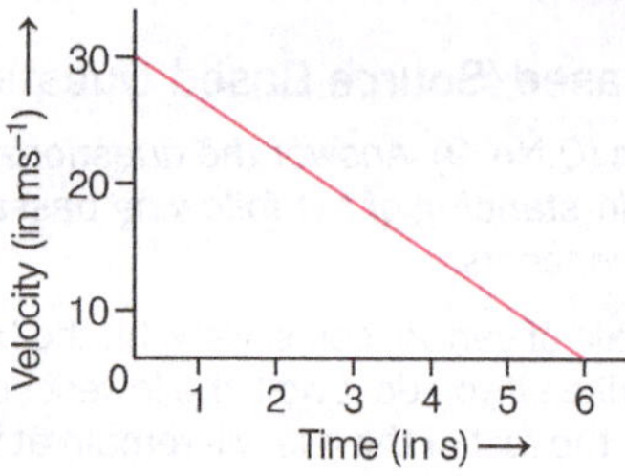

18 State the action and reaction in the following.

(i) Moving rocket

(ii) Firing of a bullet from a gun

(iii) A person walking on the floor

Long Answer Type Questions

19 (i) State the law that provides the formula for measuring force and the law which provides the definition of force.

(ii) Velocity-time graph of a 50 g marble rolling on floor is given below. Find

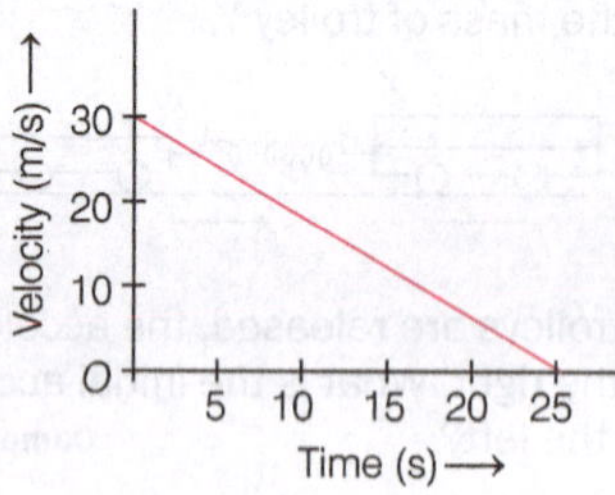

(a) time in which it stops.

(b) negative acceleration produced on it.

(c) positive force acting on the marble.

[Ans. (a) 25s (b) −12 m/s^2 (c) 0.06 N

Competency Based Que.

20 (i) Explain, why is it difficult to walk on sand?

(ii) Why is the recoil of a heavy gun, on firing, not so strong as that of a light gun using the same cartridge?

(iii) A constant force acts on an object of 5 kg for a period of 2 s. It increases the velocity of an object from 3 m/s to 7 m/s.

(a) Find the magnitude of the applied force.

(b) Now, if the force was applied for a period of 5 s, then what would be the final velocity of the object? **[Ans.** (a) 10 N (b) 13 m/s]

Topics to be Assessed Formatively

Law of Conservation of Momentum

Law of conservation of momentum is a result of Newton's third law of motion. According to this law, the total momentum of a system of objects remains conserved before and after their interaction or collision provided that there is no external unbalanced force acting on them.

Consider a system of objects of masses m_A and m_B moving with initial velocities u_A and u_B respectively, (where, $u_A > u_B$) in the same direction. After collision, the bodies move with velocities v_A and v_B, respectively. The collision lasts for time t.

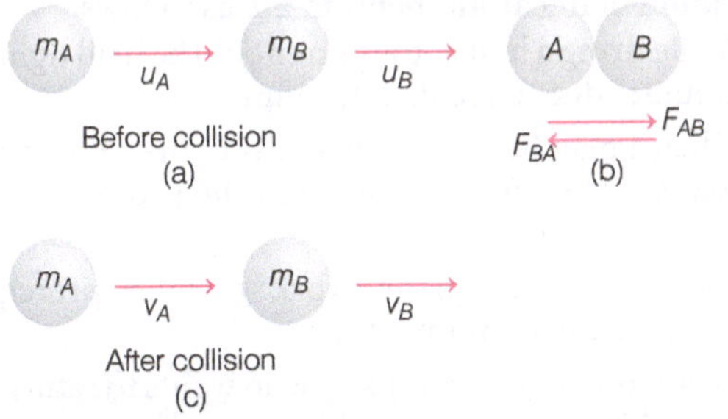

Conservation of momentum in collision of two balls

Total initial momentum of the system is given by

$$= m_A u_A + m_B u_B$$

Total final momentum of the system is given by

$$= m_A v_A + m_B v_B$$

To prove $m_A u_A + m_B u_B = m_A v_A + m_B v_B$

Proof From Newton's third law of motion, force exerted by m_A on $m_B = -$ (force exerted by m_B on m_A)

From Newton's second law,

Force, $F = ma$,

$$m_B\left(\frac{v_B - u_B}{t}\right) = -m_A\left(\frac{v_A - u_A}{t}\right)$$

$$\left[\because \text{ acceleration, } a = \frac{\text{final velocity} - \text{initial velocity}}{\text{time taken}}\right]$$

$$\Rightarrow \quad \frac{m_B v_B - m_B u_B}{t} = \frac{-m_A v_A + m_A u_A}{t}$$

$$\Rightarrow \quad m_B v_B - m_B u_B = -m_A v_A + m_A u_A$$

or $m_A v_A + m_B v_B = m_A u_A + m_B u_B$

where, $(m_A u_A + m_B u_B)$ is the total momentum of two objects before collision and $(m_A v_A + m_B v_B)$ is their total momentum after collision. Thus, the total momentum of two objects is unchanged or conserved before and after the collision. **Hence proved.**

Example 1. Find the recoil velocity of a gun having mass equal to 5 kg, if a bullet of 25 g acquires the velocity of 500 m/s after firing from the gun.

Sol. Given, mass of bullet, $m_B = 25 \text{ g} = 0.025 \text{ kg}$

Velocity of bullet before firing, $u_B = 0$

Velocity of bullet after firing, $v_B = 500 \text{ m/s}$

Mass of gun, $m_G = 5 \text{ kg}$

Velocity of gun before firing, $u_G = 0$

Velocity of gun after firing, $v_G = ?$

From the law of conservation of momentum, total momentum before firing = total momentum after firing

$$m_B u_B + m_G u_G = m_B v_B + m_G v_G$$

$$0.025 \times 0 + 5 \times 0 = 0.025 \times 500 + 5 \times v_G$$

$$v_G = -2.5 \text{ m/s}$$

Thus, recoil velocity of gun is equal to 2.5 m/s. Here, negative sign shows that gun moves in the opposite direction of bullet.

Example 2. A bullet of mass 20 g is horizontally fired with a velocity 150 ms^{-1} from a pistol of mass 2 kg. What is the recoil velocity of the pistol?

Sol. Given, mass of bullet, $m_1 = 20 \text{ g} (= 0.02 \text{ kg})$ and the mass of the pistol, $m_2 = 2 \text{ kg}$

Initial velocities of the bullet (u_1) and pistol $(u_2) = 0$,

Final velocity of the bullet, $v_1 = +150 \text{ m s}^{-1}$.

Let v be the recoil velocity of the pistol. Total momenta of the pistol and bullet before the fire, when the gun is at rest

$= (2 + 0.02) \text{ kg} \times 0 \text{ ms}^{-1} = 0 \text{ kg ms}^{-1}$

Total momenta of the pistol and bullet after it is fired

$= 0.02 \text{ kg} \times (+150 \text{ m s}^{-1}) + 2 \text{ kg} \times v \text{ ms}^{-1} = (3 + 2v) \text{ kg ms}^{-1}$

According to the law of conservation of momentum,

Total momenta after the fire

= Total momenta before the fire

$3 + 2v = 0 \Rightarrow v = -1.5 \text{ ms}^{-1}$

Negative sign indicates that the direction in which the pistol would recoil is opposite to that of bullet, that is right to left.

Example 3. A girl of mass 40 kg jumps with a horizontal velocity of 5ms^{-1} onto a stationary cart with frictionless wheels. The mass of the cart is 3 kg. What is her velocity as the cart starts moving? Assuming that

there is no external unbalanced force working in the horizontal direction?

Sol. The total momenta of the girl and cart before the interaction

$$=40\times5+3\times0=200 \text{ kg-m/s}$$

Total momenta after the interaction

$$=(40+3)v=43v \text{ kg-m/s}$$

According to the law of conservation of momentum, the total momentum is conserved during the interaction.

$$43v=200 \Rightarrow v=4.65 \text{ m/s}$$

The girl on cart would move with a velocity of 4.65 m/s in the direction in which the girl jumped.

Example 4. Two bodies as shown in the figure collide with each other and join thereafter, with what velocity will they move after combining together?

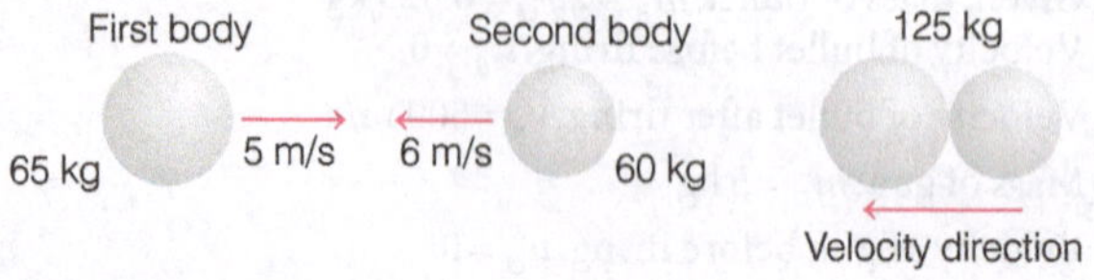

Sol. Given, $m_1=65$ kg, $m_2=60$ kg

$u_1=+5$ m/s positive direction

$u_2=-6$ m/s negative direction, $v=?$

Total momentum of two bodies before collision

$$=m_1u_1+m_2u_2=65\times5+60\times(-6)=-35 \text{ kg-m/s}$$

If v is the velocity of two combined bodies.

After collision, the total momentum will be $=m_1v_1+m_2v_2$

$$=(m_1+m_2)v \qquad [\because v_1=v_2=v]$$

$$=(65+60)\text{ kg}\times v \text{ m/s}=125v \text{ kg-m/s}$$

$\therefore$ According to the law of conservation of momentum,

$$m_1u_1+m_2u_2=m_1v_1+m_2v_2 \Rightarrow -35=125v$$

$$\therefore \qquad v=\frac{-35}{125}=-0.28 \text{ m/s}$$

So, two bodies will move with velocity 0.26 m/s in the direction of the second body.

Example 5. Two hockey players of opposite teams, while trying to hit a hockey ball on the ground collide and immediately become entangled. One has a mass of 60 kg and was moving with a velocity 5.0 ms^{-1} from left to right while the other has a mass of 55 kg and was moving faster with a velocity 6.0 ms^{-1} towards the first player. In which direction and with what velocity will they move after they become entangled? Assume that the frictional force acting between the feet of the two players and ground is negligible.

Sol. If v is the velocity of the two entangled players after the collision, the total momentum then

$$= (m_1+m_2)\times v$$

$$= (60+55) \text{ kg}\times v \text{ ms}^{-1}$$

$$= 115\times v \text{ kg ms}^{-1}.$$

Let the first player be moving from left to right. If m and u represent the mass and initial velocity of the two players, respectively.

Then, $m_1 = 60$ kg, $u_1 = +5 \text{ ms}^{-1}$ and

$m_2 = 55$ kg, $u_2 = -6 \text{ ms}^{-1}$

The total momentum of the two players before the collision

$$= 60 \text{ kg}\times(+5 \text{ ms}^{-1}) + 55 \text{ kg}\times(-6 \text{ ms}^{-1})$$

$$= -30 \text{ kg ms}^{-1}$$

Equating the momenta of the system before and after collision, in accordance with the law of conservation of momentum, we get

$$v = -30/115 = -0.26 \text{ ms}^{-1}$$

Thus, the two entangled players would move with velocity 0.26 ms^{-1} from right to left, i.e., in the direction the second player was moving before the collision.

Applications of the Law of Conservation of Momentum

Some practical applications based on the law of conservation of linear momentum are as follows

(*i*) While firing a bullet, the gun should be held tight to the shoulder due to recoil of the gun.

(*ii*) When a man jumps out of a boat to the shore, then the boat slightly moves away from the shore to conserve the momentum.

(*iii*) Rocket and jet plane work on the principle of conservation of momentum.

(*iv*) An astronaut in open space, who wants to return to the spaceship, throws some object in a direction opposite to the direction of motion of the spaceship.

Conservation Laws

All conservation laws such as conservation of momentum, energy, angular momentum and charge, etc, are considered to be fundamental laws in physics. These are based on observations and experiments. It is important to remember that a conservation law cannot be proved. It can be verified or disproved by experiments.

An experiment whose result is in conformity with the law verifies or substantiates the law, it does not prove the law. On the other hand, a single experiment whose result goes against the law is enough to disprove it.

The law of conservation of momentum has been deduced from large number of observations and experiments. This law was formulated nearly three centuries ago. It is interesting to note that not a single situation has been realised so far, which contradicts this law. Several experiences of everyday life can be explained on the basis of the law of conservation of momentum.

Solved Questions

Q.1 If action is always equal to the reaction, then explain how a horse can pull a cart?

Ans. The horse pushes the ground in the backward direction. The ground exerts a reaction force on horse and cart system to push them forward. When the reaction force exceeds the force of friction between the wheels of cart and the ground, then the cart is pushed forward.

Q.2 Explain, why is it difficult for a fireman to hold a hose-pipe, which ejects large amount of water with a high velocity?

Ans. A fireman finds it difficult to hold a hose-pipe which is ejecting large amount of water at high velocity. Because the stream of water rushing out of the pipe in the forward direction exerts a large force on the pipe. Due to the reaction of the forward force, a force is applied on the pipe in backward direction. Therefore, the fireman struggles to keep the hose-pipe in rest.

Q.3 From a rifle of mass 4 kg, a bullet of mass 50 g is fired with an initial velocity of 35 m/s. Calculate the initial recoil velocity of the rifle.

Ans. Given, mass of gun, $M = 4$ kg

Mass of bullet, $m = 50 \text{ g} = 50 \times 10^{-3}$ kg

Initial velocity of bullet, $u = 35$ m/s

Let recoil velocity of the gun be v m/s.

Before firing the bullet both gun and bullet were at rest, so total momentum of gun and bullet is zero.

After firing, momentum of bullet $= mu$

Momentum of gun $= Mv$

Total momentum of bullet and gun after firing

$$= mu + Mv$$

Since, there is no external force applied on the system.

So, total momentum after firing = total momentum before firing

$$mu + Mv = 0$$

$$Mv = -mu$$

$$\Rightarrow \quad v = -\frac{mu}{M} = \frac{50 \times 10^{-3} \times 35}{4}$$

$$= -0.44 \text{ m/s}$$

Here, negative sign shows that the recoil velocity of the gun is in the direction opposite to the velocity of the bullet.

Q.4 Two objects of masses 100 g and 200 g are moving along the same line and direction with velocities of 2 m/s and 1 m/s, respectively. They collide and after collision, the first object moves at a velocity of 1.67 m/s. Determine the velocity of the second object.

Sol. $m_1 = 100 \text{ g} = \frac{100}{1000} = 0.1$ kg $\quad [\because 1 \text{ kg} = 1000 \text{ g}]$

$$m_2 = 200 \text{ g} = \frac{200}{1000} = 0.2 \text{ kg},$$

Before collision,

$$u_1 = 2 \text{ m/s},$$
$$u_2 = 1 \text{ m/s}$$

After collision,

$$m_1 = 100 \text{ g} = 0.1 \text{ kg},$$
$$m_2 = 200 \text{ g} = 0.2 \text{ kg},$$
$$v_1 = 1.67 \text{ m/s}$$

Let velocity of second object after collision be v_2 m/s.

Since, there is no external force on the system.

$\therefore$ Total momentum before collision

= Total momentum after collision

$$m_1u_1 + m_2u_2 = m_1v_1 + m_2v_2$$

$$\Rightarrow \quad 0.1 \times 2 + 0.2 \times 1 = 0.1 \times 1.67 + 0.2 \times v_2$$

$$\Rightarrow \quad 0.2 + 0.2 = 0.167 + 0.2v_2$$

$$\Rightarrow \quad 0.2v_2 = 0.4 - 0.167$$

$$\Rightarrow \quad 0.2v_2 = 0.233$$

$$\therefore \quad v_2 = \frac{0.233}{0.2} = 1.16 \text{ m/s}$$

Practice Questions

Q.1 Pieces of bursting cracker fall in all possible directions.

Q.2 A tennis ball of mass 0.11 kg travelling at 40 m/s hits a wall head on and bounces off, returning along the same path at 30 m/s.

(i) Calculate the change in velocity of the ball

(ii) Calculate the change in momentum of that ball including the units in your answer.

Q.3 A truck of mass 500 kg moving at 4 m/s collides with another truck of mass 1500 kg moving in same direction at 2 m/s. What is their common velocity just after collision, if they move off together?

CHAPTER 09

Gravitation

It has been observed that an object dropped from a height falls towards the earth. Newton generalised this idea and said that not only the earth but every object in the universe attracts every other object. This force of attraction between two objects is called the **force of gravitation** or **gravitational force**.

In this chapter, we shall learn about gravitation and universal law of gravitation and we shall also study about how the weight of a body varies from place to place and the conditions for objects to float in liquids.

9.1 Gravitation

It is defined as the force of attraction between any two bodies in the universe. The earth attracts (or pulls) all objects lying on or near its surface towards its centre.

The force with which the earth pulls the objects towards its centre is called the **gravitational force of the earth** or **gravity of the earth.**

Universal Law of Gravitation

According to this law, **the attractive force between any two bodies in the universe is directly proportional to the product of their masses and inversely proportional to the square of distance between them.**

It was given by **Isaac Newton.**

The direction of the force is along the line joining the centres of two objects.

Consider two bodies A and B having masses m_1 and m_2, whose centres are at a distance d from each other.

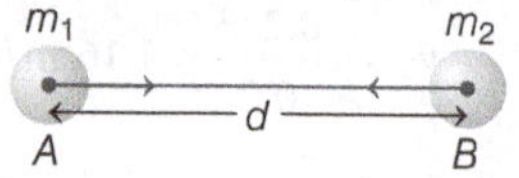

The gravitational force between two bodies is directed along the line joining their centres

Then, the force between two bodies is directly proportional to the product of their masses, i.e.

$$F \propto m_1 m_2 \quad \ldots(i)$$

and the force between two bodies is inversely proportional to the square of the distance between them, i.e.

$$F \propto \frac{1}{d^2} \quad \ldots(ii)$$

Combining Eqs. (i) and (ii), we get

$$F \propto \frac{m_1 m_2}{d^2} \quad \text{or} \quad F = G\frac{m_1 m_2}{d^2}$$

where, $G = 6.67 \times 10^{-11}$ N-m^2/kg^2 is called the **universal gravitational constant.**

Isaac Newton was born in Woolsthorpe near Grantham, England in 1642. In 1665, he observed an apple falling on the ground which prompted Newton to explore the possibility of connecting gravity with the force that kept the moon in its orbit. This led him to the universal law of gravitation.

Its value does not depend on the medium between the two bodies and the masses of the bodies or the distance between them.

Suppose the masses of two bodies are 1 kg each and the distance d between them is 1 m, then

$$F = G \qquad [\because m_1 = m_2 = 1 \text{ kg and } d = 1 \text{ m}]$$

Hence, **the universal gravitational constant is defined as the gravitational force between two bodies of unit masses separated by a unit distance from each other and placed anywhere in space.**

- The SI unit of G is N-m^2 kg^2.
- The value of G was found out by Henry Cavendish (1731-1810) by using a sensitive balance.

Note
- According to third law of motion, an object like apple does not attract the earth because the mass of an apple is negligibly small compared to that of the earth.
- Universal law of gravitation is universal in the sense that it is applicable to all bodies, whether the bodies are big or small whether they are terrestrial.

- F is inversely proportional to the square of d means that, if d gets bigger by a factor of 6, then F becomes $\frac{1}{36}$ times smaller.

Importance of Universal Law of Gravitation

The universal law of gravitation successfully explained several phenomena given as below

(i) The force that binds us to the earth.
(ii) The motion of the moon around the earth.
(iii) The motion of planets around the sun.
(iv) The occurrence of tides is due to the gravitational force of attraction of moon.
(v) The flow of water in rivers is also due to gravitational force of the earth on water.

Motion of Moon Around Earth and Centripetal Force

The force that keeps a body moving along the circular path acting towards the centre is called **centripetal** (centre seeking) **force**. This force is responsible for changing the direction and velocity of an object.
The motion of the moon around the earth is due to the centripetal force. The centripetal force is provided by the gravitational force of attraction of the earth.
If there were no such force, then the moon would pursue a uniform straight line motion.

Note A straight line that meets the circle at one and only one point is called a tangent to the circle. In figure, ABC represents the tangent to circle.

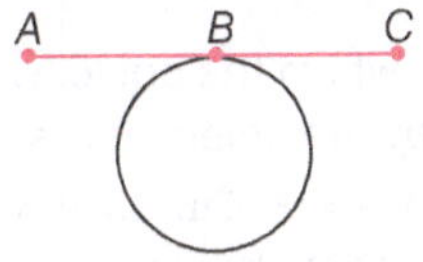

Example 1. **Find the gravitational force between earth and an object of 2 kg mass placed on its surface. (Given, mass of the earth = 6×10^{24} kg and radius of the earth = 6.4×10^{6} m)**

Sol. Given, mass of the earth, $m_e = 6\times10^{24}$ kg
Mass of an object, $m_o = 2$ kg
Radius of the earth, $R = 6.4\times10^{6}$ m
Gravitational force, $F = ?$

$$\therefore \quad F = G\frac{m_e m_o}{R^2} \quad \text{[by universal law of gravitation]}$$

$$\therefore \quad F = \frac{6.67\times10^{-11}\times6\times10^{24}\times2}{(6.4\times10^{6})^2} = 19.5 \text{ N}$$

Example 2. **The mass of the mars is 6.39×10^{23} kg and that of the jupiter is 1.89×10^{27} kg. If the distance between mars and jupiter is 7.49×10^{5} m, calculate the force exerted by the jupiter on the mars. ($G = 6.7\times10^{-11}$ Nm^2 kg^{-2})**

Sol. Given, the mass of the mars, $M_m = 6.39\times10^{23}$ kg
The mass of the jupiter,
$M_j = 1.89\times10^{27}$ kg
The distance between the mars and jupiter,
$$d = 7.49\times10^{5} \text{ m}$$
Gravitational constant, $G = 6.7\times10^{-11}$ Nm^2/kg^2
The force exerted by the jupiter on the mars,

$$F = G\frac{M_m\times M_j}{d^2}$$
$$= \frac{6.7\times10^{-11}\times6.39\times10^{23}\times1.89\times10^{27}}{(7.49\times10^{5})^2}$$
$$= 1.44\times10^{29} \text{ N}$$

Thus, the force exerted by the jupiter on the mars is 1.44×10^{29} N.

Try These 9.1

1 **What is the force of gravity between the earth and mass of 20 kg placed on its surface?** [Ans. 196 N]

2 **If the distance between masses of two objects is increased by five times, by what factor would the mass of one of them have to be changed to maintain the same gravitational force? Would there be an increase or a decrease in the same?**

3 **Find the gravitational force of attraction between a body of unit mass and the moon. (Mass of the moon = 7.4×10^{22} kg, radius of the moon = 1.74×10^{6} m and $G = 6.67\times10^{-11}$ Nm^2/kg^2)** [Ans. 1.63 N]

4 **Name the source of centripetal force that the moon requires to revolve around the earth.**

9.2 Free Fall

When objects fall towards the earth under the influence of earth's gravitational force alone, then these objects are called freely falling objects and such motion is called free fall.

Acceleration due to Gravity (g)

Whenever an object falls towards the earth, an acceleration is involved. This acceleration is due to the earth's gravitational pull and is called acceleration due to gravity.

- It is denoted by g.
- The SI unit of g is the same as that of acceleration, i.e. m/s^2.

Let mass of the earth be M and an object falling freely towards it be m. The distance between centres of the earth and the object is R.
From Newton's law of gravitation,

$$F = \frac{GMm}{R^2} \quad \text{...(i)}$$

Also, from second law of motion, force exerted on an object,

$$F = ma$$

Since, $a = g$ (i.e. acceleration due to gravity)

$$F = mg \quad \ldots(ii)$$

Equating RHS of Eqs. (i) and (ii), we get

$$mg = \frac{GMm}{R^2} \quad or \quad g = \frac{GM}{R^2}$$

From the formula, it is clear that, acceleration due to gravity does not depend on the mass of a falling object. It depends only on the mass of the earth or celestial bodies.

- As distance of an object from the centre of the celestial body increases, the value of g decreases.
- Earth is flattened at poles, thus radius of the earth is less at poles than at equator. Hence, the value of g is less at equator than at poles.

Calculation the Value of *g*

To calculate the value of g, we should put the values of G, M and R in above formula, i.e. $g = GM/R^2$.

$\because$ Mass of the earth, $M = 6 \times 10^{24}$ kg

Radius of the earth, $R = 6.4 \times 10^6$ m

Universal gravitational constant,

$$G = 6.67 \times 10^{-11} \text{N-m}^2/\text{kg}^2$$

$$g = \frac{GM}{R^2} = \frac{6.67 \times 10^{-11} \times 6 \times 10^{24}}{(6.4 \times 10^6)^2}$$

$$g = 9.8 \text{ m/s}^2$$

Equations of Motion for Free Fall

The three equations of motion which we have derived earlier are for bodies under uniform acceleration.

In case of motion of bodies under free fall, there is a uniform acceleration, i.e. acceleration due to gravity (g) acting downward.

So, the previous three equations of motion can be applied for the motion of bodies under free fall as follows

General equations of motion	Equations for body under free fall	
$v = u + at$	$v = u + gt$	$[\because a = g]$
$s = ut + \frac{1}{2}at^2$	$h = ut + \frac{1}{2}gt^2$	$[\because a = g]$
$v^2 = u^2 + 2as$	$v^2 = u^2 + 2gh$	$[\because a = g]$

where, h is the height from which the object falls, t is the time of fall, u is the initial velocity and v is the final velocity when the body accelerates at g.

In solving numerical problems, we should remember the following points

(i) If an object falls vertically downwards, then acceleration due to gravity is taken as **positive**, since its velocity increases while falling.

(ii) If an object is thrown vertically upwards, then acceleration due to gravity is taken as **negative**, since its velocity decreases as it moves upward.

Example 3. **A car falls off a ledge and drops to the ground in 0.6 s. The value of g is 10 m/s² (for simplifying the calculation).**

(i) What is its speed on striking the ground?

(ii) What is its average speed during the 0.6 s?

(iii) How high is the ledge from the ground?

Sol. Given, initial velocity, $u = 0$

Acceleration due to gravity, $g = 10 \text{ m/s}^2$

Time, $t = 0.6$ s

(i) Speed, $v = u + gt$

$$v = 0 + 10 \times 0.6$$

$$v = 6 \text{ m/s}$$

(ii) Average speed $= \frac{u+v}{2} = \left(\frac{0+6}{2}\right) = 3.0$ m/s

(iii) Distance travelled, $h = ut + \frac{1}{2}gt^2$

$$h = 0 + \frac{1}{2}gt^2$$

$$h = \frac{1}{2} \times 10 \times (0.6)^2 = 5 \times 0.36 = 1.80 \text{ m}$$

Example 4. **An object is thrown vertically upwards and rises to a height of 13.07 m. Calculate**

(i) the velocity with which the object was thrown upwards.

(ii) the time taken by the object to reach the highest point.

Sol. Distance travelled, $h = 13.07$m, final velocity, $v = 0$

Acceleration due to gravity, $g = -9.8 \text{ m/s}^2$ (upward motion)

(i) $v^2 = u^2 + 2gh \Rightarrow 0 = u^2 + 2 \times (-9.8) \times 13.07$

$$u^2 = 256 \Rightarrow u = 16 \text{ m/s}$$

(ii) $v = u + at \Rightarrow 0 = 16 - 9.8 \times t \Rightarrow t = 1.63$ s

Example 5. **A ball is thrown vertically upwards with a velocity of 25 m/s. If g is 10 m/s², then calculate**

(i) height it reaches and (ii) time taken to return back.

Sol. Given, initial velocity, $u = 25$ m/s, final velocity, $v = 0$

If a body is thrown upwards, then its velocity becomes zero at the highest point, where it reaches.

Acceleration due to gravity, $g = -10 \text{ m/s}^2$

(i) $\therefore$ Height, $h = \frac{v^2 - u^2}{2g} = \frac{0 - (25)^2}{2(-10)} = \frac{-625}{-20} = 31.25$ m

(ii) $\therefore$ Time, $t = \frac{v-u}{g} = \frac{0-25}{-10} = 2.5$ s

Time taken to return back,

$$T = \text{Time of ascent} + \text{Time of descent} = 2t$$

Time taken to return back, $T = 2 \times 2.5 = 5$ s

Try These 9.2

1 **Suppose a planet exists whose mass and radius both are half that of the earth. The acceleration due to gravity on the surface of this planet will be double. Justify.**

2 **Find the acceleration due to gravity on the surface of Jupiter using the data given below (Mass of Jupiter, $M = 1.9 \times 10^{27}$ kg, radius of jupiter, $R = 7 \times 10^{7}$ m)** [Ans. 25.879 m/s^2]

3 **A body drops down a tower and reaches the ground in 0.6s. If $g = 10$ m/s^2, then find the height of the tower.** [Ans. 1.8 m]

9.3 Mass

It is the total content of the body which measures the inertia of a body. In other words, mass is the quantity of matter contained in a body. It is a **scalar quantity** and its SI unit is **kilogram.**

Irrespective of the position of the body in the universe, mass always remains constant everywhere. The mass of the body cannot be zero.

Note The centre of mass of a body may be defined as the point at which whole mass of the body may be assumed or concentrated.

9.4 Weight

The weight of an object is the force with which it is attracted towards the earth. It is denoted by w.

We know that,

$$F = m \times a$$

i.e.

$$F = m \times g \quad \text{...(i)}$$

The force of attraction of the earth on an object is known as the weight of the object.

Substituting the same in Eq. (i), we get

Weight of an object, $w = mg$

where, m = mass and g = acceleration due to gravity.

or

$$w = \frac{GMm}{R^2}$$

Here, M = mass of the earth and R = radius of the earth.

Important points regarding weight are as follow

(i) Weight is a **vector quantity**, it acts in vertically downward direction and its SI unit is **newton** (N). Weight of 1 kg mass is 9.8 N (i.e. 1 kg-wt = 9.8 N).

(ii) Weight of an object is not constant, it changes from place to place.

(iii) In the space, where $g = 0$, weight of an object is zero.

(iv) At the centre of the earth, weight becomes zero. This is due to the fact that on going down to the earth value of g decreases and at the centre of the earth, $g = 0$.

(v) The value of g is constant at a given place. Therefore, at that place, the weight of an object is directly proportional to the mass.

It is due to this reason, we can use the weight of an object as a measure of its mass at that place.

(vi) Spring balance is used to measure the weight of a body and pan balance is used to measure the mass of a body.

(vii) It is a point in an object where the distribution of weight is equal in all directions.

(viii) The state when object does not weigh anything is called **weightlessness.**

Weight of an Object on the Moon

The weight of an object on the moon is the force with which the moon attracts the object.

The moon exerts lesser force of attraction on objects than that of earth because the mass of moon is less than that of the earth.

Let the mass of an object be m and its weight on the moon be w_m. Suppose the mass of the moon is M_m and its radius be R_m. According to universal law of gravitation, the weight of an object on the moon will be

$$w_m = G\frac{M_m \times m}{R_m^2} \quad \text{...(i)}$$

Let the weight of the same object on the earth be w_e, mass of the earth be M_e and the radius of the earth be R_e.

$$w_e = \frac{GM_e m}{R_e^2} \quad \text{...(ii)}$$

From Eqs. (i) and (ii), we have

$$\frac{w_m}{w_e} = \frac{\frac{GM_m m}{R_m^2}}{\frac{GM_e m}{R_e^2}} = \frac{M_m}{M_e} \times \frac{R_e^2}{R_m^2}$$

Now, $M_m = 5.98 \times 10^{24}$ kg, $M_e = 7.36 \times 10^{22}$ kg

$R_m = 1.74 \times 10^6$, $R_e = 6.37 \times 10^6$

$$\therefore \quad \frac{w_m}{w_e} = \frac{5.98 \times 10^{24}}{7.36 \times 10^{22}} \times \frac{(6.37 \times 10^6)^2}{(1.74 \times 10^6)^2} \approx \frac{1}{6}$$

Thus, **the weight of an object on the moon is one-sixth of its weight on the earth.**

Example 6. **Mass of an object is 12 kg. Calculate**

(i) its weight on the earth.

(ii) its weight on the moon.

Sol. Given, mass of an object, $m = 12$ kg

(i) Acceleration due to gravity on earth, $g_e = 9.8\ m/s^2$

Weight on the earth, $w_e = mg_e = 12 \times 9.8 = 117.6$ N

(ii) Acceleration due to gravity on moon, $g_m = \frac{g_e}{6}$

$$g_m = \frac{9.8}{6}\ m/s^2$$

Weight on the moon, $w_m = mg_m = 12 \times \frac{9.8}{6} = 9.8 \times 2 = 19.6$ N

Example 7. **A man weighs 600 N on the earth. What is his mass, if g is 10 m/s²? On the moon, his weight would be 100 N. What is the acceleration due to gravity on the moon?**

Sol. Given, weight of man on the earth, $w_e = 600$ N

Acceleration due to gravity on the earth, $g_e = 10\ m/s^2$

Weight of man on the moon, $w_m = 100$ N

Acceleration due to gravity on the moon, $g_m = ?$

As we know, mass of the man, $m = \frac{w_e}{g_e} = \frac{600}{10} = 60$ kg

$$\Rightarrow \quad g_e = \frac{w_e}{m}$$

Similarly, for the moon, $g_m = \frac{w_m}{m}$

$$g_m = \frac{100}{60} = 1.66\ m/s^2$$

Thus, acceleration due to gravity on the moon is $1.66\ m/s^2$, i.e. $g_m = \frac{g_e}{6}$.

Example 8. **A particle weighs 120 N on the surface of the earth. At what height above the earth's surface will its weight be 30 N? (Radius of the earth = 6400 km)**

Sol. Given, weight of particle on the surface of earth, $w = 120$ N

Weight of particle at height h above the earth's surface,

$$w_1 = 30 \text{ N}$$

The weight of a particle on the surface of the earth,

$$w = mg = \frac{GMm}{R^2} \qquad \left[\because g = \frac{GM}{R^2}\right]$$

Let w_1 be the weight of a particle at height h above the earth's surface.

$$\text{So,} \quad \frac{w}{w_1} = \frac{G\frac{M}{R^2}}{G\frac{M}{(R+h)^2}} = \frac{(R+h)^2}{R^2}$$

Substituting given values, we get

$$\Rightarrow \quad \frac{120}{30} = \left(\frac{R+h}{R}\right)^2 \Rightarrow 4 = \left(\frac{R+h}{R}\right)^2 \Rightarrow 2 = \frac{R+h}{R}$$

$$\Rightarrow \quad 2R = R + h \Rightarrow R = h$$

$\therefore$ Height of the particle, h = Radius of the earth = 6400 km

Try These 9.3

1. **Fill in the blank.**
   A body of mass 10 kg is taken to the centre of the earth. Its weight will be ....
2. **What will the weight of an object of mass 175 kg at the centre of the earth?**
3. **Mitali weighs 750 N on the earth. On the planet mars, the force of gravity is 38% of that of the earth. How much will Mitali weight on the mars?** [Ans. 285 N]
4. **Weight of a girl on the earth's surface is 66 N. Find out her weight on the moon.** [Ans. 11 N]

9.5 Thrust and Pressure

Thrust is the force acting on an object perpendicular to its surface. The effect of thrust depends on the area on which it acts.

The unit of thrust is the same as that of force, i.e. the SI unit of thrust is **newton** (N). It is a **vector quantity.**

Pressure is the force acting perpendicularly on a unit area of an object.

$$\text{Pressure } (p) = \frac{\text{Force}(F)}{\text{Area }(A)} = \frac{\text{Thrust}}{\text{Area}}$$

The SI unit of pressure is **Nm^{-2}**, which is also called **pascal** (Pa) named after the scientist **Blaise Pascal.** It is a **scalar quantity.**

$$1 \text{ Pa} = 1 \text{ Nm}^{-2}$$

From the formula of pressure, it is clear that the same force can produce different pressures depending on the area over which it acts.

A force acting on a smaller area exerts a large pressure while the same force acting on a larger area exerts a small pressure. This is the reason why a nail has a pointed tip, knives have sharp edges and buildings have wide foundations.

Example 9. **Force of 200 N is applied to an object of area 4 m². Find the pressure.**

Sol. Given, force, $F = 200$ N, area, $A = 4\ m^2$

$$\text{Now, Pressure, } p = \frac{\text{Force}(F)}{\text{Area }(A)} = \frac{200}{4} = 50 \text{ Nm}^{-2}$$

Example 10. **A woman is wearing sharp-heeled sandal (stilettos). If the mass of woman is 60 kg and the area of one heel is 1 cm², find out the pressure exerted on the ground, when the woman stands on just one heel. (Take, g = 10ms⁻²)**

Sol. In the given case, the force will be the weight of woman which is given by $m \times g$ (where, m is the mass of woman and g is the acceleration due to gravity).

$\therefore$ Force, $F = m \times g$ (weight of woman)

$= 60 \times 10$ [given, mass of woman, $m = 60$ kg]

$= 600$ N

and area, $A = 1\text{ cm}^2 = \dfrac{1}{10000}\text{ m}^2$

$\therefore$ Pressure, $p = \dfrac{\text{Force}(F)}{\text{Area}(A)} = \dfrac{600 \times 10000}{1}$

$= 6000000\text{ Nm}^{-2}$ or 6000000 Pa

Thus, the pressure exerted by the woman (of 60 kg) standing on only one heel of area 1 cm^2 is 6000000 Nm^{-2}.

Example 11. A block of wood is kept on a table top. The mass of wooden block is 6 kg and its dimensions are 50 cm × 30 cm × 20 cm.

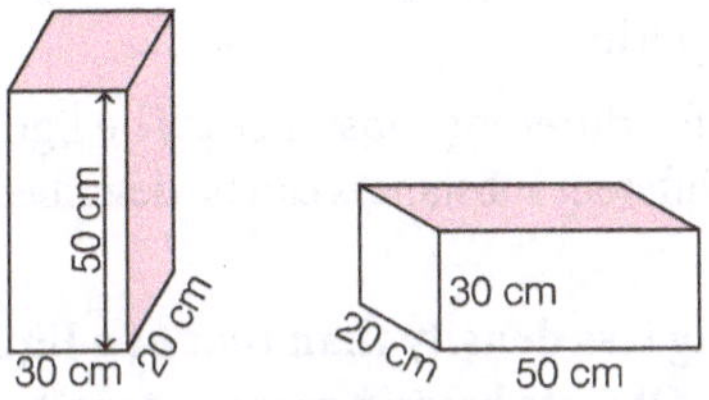

Find the pressure exerted by the wooden block on the table top, if it is made to lie on the table top with its sides of dimensions

(i) 30 cm × 20 cm (ii) 50 cm × 30 cm

Sol. Given, the mass of the wooden block = 6 kg

Dimensions = 50 cm × 30 cm × 20 cm

Thrust, $F = mg = 6 \times 9.8 = 58.8$ N

(i) Area of a side = Length × Breadth

Area, $A = 30 \times 20 = 600\text{ cm}^2 = 0.06\text{ m}^2$

Pressure, $p_1 = \dfrac{F}{A} = \dfrac{58.8}{0.06} = 980\text{ N/m}^2$

(ii) When the block lies on its side of dimensions 50 cm × 30 cm, it exerts the same thrust.

Area = Length × Breadth

$A = 50 \times 30 = 1500\text{ cm}^2 = 0.15\text{ m}^2$

Pressure, $p_2 = \dfrac{F}{A} = \dfrac{58.8}{0.15} = 392\text{ N/m}^2$

Some Daily Life Applications of Pressure

- The handles of bags, suitcases, etc., are made broad, so that less pressure is exerted on the hand.
- Buildings are provided with broad foundations, so that the pressure exerted on the ground becomes less.
- Railway tracks are laid on cement or iron sleepers, so that the pressure exerted by train could spread over the larger area and thus pressure decreases.
- Pins, needles and nails are provided with sharp pointed ends to reduce the area and hence, to increase the pressure.
- Cutting tools have sharp edges to reduce the area, so that with lesser force, more pressure could be exerted.
- Pressure on ground is more when a man is walking than when he is standing because in case of walking, the effective area is less.
- Depression is much more when a man stands on the cushion than when he lies down on it because in standing case, area is lesser than in case of lying.
- The tractors have broad tyres to create less pressure on the ground, so that tyres do not sink into comparatively soft ground in the field.

9.6 Pressure in Fluids

All liquids and gases are together called **fluids.** Water and air are two most common fluids. Solids exert pressure on a surface due to their weight.

Fluids also have weight, therefore fluids also exert pressure on the base and walls of the container in which they are enclosed. Fluids exert pressure in all directions.

Buoyancy

The tendency of a liquid to exert an upward force on an object immersed in it is called **buoyancy.** Gases also exhibit this property of buoyancy.

Buoyant force is an upward force which acts on an object when it is immersed in a liquid. It is also called **upthrust.**

It is the buoyant force due to which a heavy object seems to be lighter in water. As we lower an object into a liquid, the liquid underneath it provides an upward force.

e.g. A piece of cork is held below the surface of water. When we apply a force by our thumb, the cork immediately rises to the surface. This is due to the fact that every liquid exerts an upward force on the objects immersed in it.

Note
- An object seems lighter when immersed in liquid. This reduced weight of an object in liquid is called **apparent weight** of an object.
- The pressure exerted by a liquid increases with depth and acts in all directions.

Factors Affecting Buoyant Force

The magnitude of buoyant force depends on the following factors

(i) Density of the Fluid

The liquid having higher density exerts more upward buoyant force on an object than another liquid of lower density.

This is the reason why it is easier to swim in sea water in comparison to normal water. The sea water has higher density and hence, exerts a greater buoyant force on the swimmer than the fresh water having lower density.

(ii) Volume of Object Immersed in the Liquid

As the volume of solid object immersed inside the liquid increases, the upward buoyant force also increases. The magnitude of buoyant force acting on a solid object does not depend on the nature of the solid object. It depends only on its volume.

e.g. When two balls made of different metals having different weights but equal volume are fully immersed in a liquid, they will experience an equal upward buoyant force as both the balls displace equal amount of the liquid due to their equal volumes.

Floating or Sinking of Objects in Liquid

When an object is immersed in a liquid, then following two forces act on it

- **Weight** of the object which acts in **downward direction**, i.e. it tends to pull down the object.
- **Buoyant force** (upthrust) which acts in **upward direction**, i.e. it tends to push up the object.

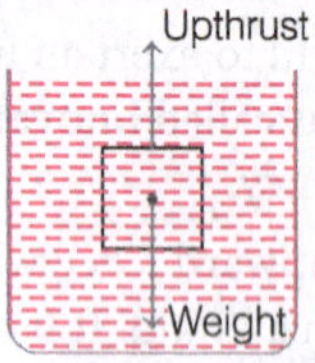

Whether an object will float or sink in a liquid, depends on the relative magnitudes of these two forces which act on the object in opposite directions.

There are three conditions of floating and sinking of objects as given below

(i) If the buoyant force or upthrust exerted by the liquid is less than the weight of the object, the **object will sink** in the liquid.

(ii) If the buoyant force is equal to the weight of the object, the **object will float** in the liquid.

(iii) If the buoyant force is more than the weight of the object, the **object will rise** in the liquid and then float.

Try These 9.4

1 **A force of 150 N acts on a surface of area 15 cm^2. Calculate thrust and pressure.** [Ans. Thrust = 150 N and pressure = 100000 Pa]

2 **What pressure is exerted by a force of 50000 N acting on 2.5 m^2?** [Ans. 20000 Pa]

3 **Name the forces acting on an object while immersed in a liquid.**

9.7 Density

The density of a substance is defined as mass per unit volume.

$$\text{Density} = \frac{\text{Mass of the substance}}{\text{Volume of the substance}} \quad \text{or} \quad \rho = \frac{m}{V}$$

- The SI unit of density is **kilogram per metre cube** (kg/m^3).
- It is a **scalar quantity**.

The density of a substance under specified conditions always remains same, hence the density of a substance is one of its characteristic properties. It can help us to determine its purity.

It is different for different substances. The lightness and the heaviness of different substances can be described by using the word density.

Objects having less density than that of a liquid, will float on the liquid. Objects having greater density than that of liquid, will sink in the liquid. The density decreases with increase in temperature.

The object having density equal to that of liquid will float on the liquid in such a way that it is totally submerged in the liquid and no part of it remains above the surface of the liquid.

Example 12. A sealed can of mass 700 g has a volume of 500 cm^3. Will this can sink in water? (Density of water is 1 g cm^{-3})

Sol. Given, mass of can, $m = 700$ g

Volume of can, $V = 500 \text{ cm}^3$

$\therefore$ Density of can, $\rho = \frac{m}{V} = \frac{700}{500}$

$= 1.4 \text{ g cm}^{-3}$

Since, density of the can is greater than the density of water, so the can will sink in water.

9.8 Archimedes' Principle

It states that, "when an object is fully or partially immersed in a liquid, it experiences a buoyant force or upthrust, which is equal to the weight of liquid displaced by the object", i.e.

Buoyant force or upthrust acting on an object
= Weight of liquid displaced by the object

According to this principle, "an object will float in a liquid, if the weight of object is equal to the weight of liquid displaced by it". This is called **law of floatation.**

Even gases like air, exert an upward force or buoyant force on the objects placed in them. It is buoyant force or upthrust which makes a balloon rise in air.

Applications of Archimedes' Principle

Archimedes' principle is used in

- designing ships and submarines.
- lactometer (a device used to determine the purity of milk).
- hydrometer (a device used for determining the density of liquid).

How does a Boat Float in Water?

A boat floats on water due to upward force called buoyant force (or upthrust) which is caused by the pressure of water pushing up the bottom of the boat.

When boat is gradually lowered into water, it displaces more and more water. Hence, buoyant force on it also increases. When this buoyant force becomes just enough to support the weight of boat, the boat stops sinking down in water.

Now, according to Archimedes' principle, "buoyant force is equal to the weight of liquid displaced by the boat." Hence, during the floating of the boat, the weight of water displaced by the submerged part of the boat is equal to the weight of the boat.

Example 13. **If an iron object is immersed in water, it displaces 8 kg of water. How much is the buoyant force acting on the iron object in newton? (Take, $g = 10 ms^{-2}$)**

Sol. According to Archimedes' principle, "the buoyant force acting on this iron object will be equal to the weight of water displaced by this iron object."

We know that, weight,

$$w = m \times g \quad \ldots(i)$$

Given, mass of water, $m = 8$ kg

Acceleration due to gravity,

$$g = 10 \text{ ms}^{-2}$$

On putting values in Eq. (i), we get

$$w = 8 \times 10 = 80 \text{ N}$$

Since, the weight of water displaced by the iron object is 80 N, therefore the buoyant force acting on the iron object (due to water) will also be 80 N.

Try These 9.5

1. **The volume of a 350 g sealed tin is 200 cubic cm. Find the density of the tin in g/cc. Also, find the density in SI unit.** [**Ans.** 1.75 g/cm^3/1750 kg/m^3]
2. **A dining room has dimensions 50 m × 15 m × 3.5 m. Calculate the mass of air in the hall. (Density of air $= 1.30 \text{ kg/m}^3$)** [**Ans.** 3412.5 kg]

Mind Map

ATOMS AND MOLECULES

Dalton's Atomic Theory

Main postulates of this theory are as:

- Matter is made up of very small particles, called the atoms.
- Atoms are indivisible.
- Atoms of same element are identical in mass as well as in chemical properties.
- Atoms combine in the ratio of small whole numbers forming compounds.
- The relative number as well as kinds of atoms are constant in a

Law of Chemical Combination

Atoms combine together to give molecules in accordance to following laws, called the laws of chemical combination.

1. Law of Conservation of Mass

It was given by Antoine L. Lavoisier. This law states that, "mass can neither be created nor destroyed during a chemical

2. Law of Constant Proportions

It was given by Proust as "In a chemical substance the elements are always present in a definite proportions by

Atom

- It is the smallest particle of matter.
- It may or may not exist independently.
-

Symbols of Atoms

- These are short hand representation of the name of an element.
- Modern symbol were introduced by Berzilius.
- These are infact the first one or two letters of the element's name in English, Latin, Greek, German, etc.
- First letter of the symbol is always written in capital letter and second letter in a small letter. e.g. Iron (Fe from

Atomic Mass

Because of its very small size, it is a difficult task to determine the atomic mass of an individual atom, so term relative

Atomic Mass Unit (amu)

Now it is called 'u' (unified mass). It is defined as the mass of 1/12th of the

Relative Atomic Mass

It is defined as the number of times a given atom is heavier than 1/12th of mass

Ionic Compounds

These compounds are made up of cation and anion.

Polyatomic ions

It is a group of atoms carrying a charge and behaving like one entity

e.g. Cl^-, SO_4^{2-} O^{2-},

Ions

Atoms or group of atoms consist of charged species is known as ions.

Cation

- It is positively charged ion.
- In an electric field, it moves towards cathode.
- e.g. Na^+, Ca^{2+}, etc.

Anion

- It is negatively charged ion.
- In an electric field, it moves towards anode.
- e.g. Cl^-, Br^- O^{2-}, etc.

Monoatomic ions

An ion consisting of exactly one

Chemical formula

The chemical formula of a compound is a symbolic representation of its composition.

Writing Chemical Formula

- Write the symbols and valencies (or charges) of constituent atoms.
- Write the symbol of cation before anion.
- Criss-cross the charges or valencies to get formula.
- The positive and negative charge must balance each other and the overall structure must be neutral.

e.g. Atom C, Cl; Valency 4, 1 → CCl_4

Valency

- It is the combining power of an element.
- It is equal to charge in case

Molecule

- Groups of two or more atoms chemically bonded together.
- Smallest particles of an element/compound that is capable of an independent existence

Molecules of Element

Contain only one type of atoms.

Molecules of compound

Contain two or more types of atoms. e.g. methane (CH_4)

Atomicity

It shows the number of atoms present in a molecule. e.g. H_2 is diatomic, O_3 is

Molecular Mass

It is the sum of atomic masses of all the atoms present in a

Formula Unit Mass

- It is the sum of atomic masses of all atoms present in a formula unit of a compound.
- It is the molar mass of ionic

NCERT FOLDER

Complete Explanations of all NCERT's Questions

Intext Questions

Q.1 State the universal law of gravitation. **Page 102**

Sol. The universal law of gravitation states that, "the force of attraction between any two objects is directly proportional to the product of their masses and inversely proportional to the square of the distance between them".

This law is applicable on any two objects anywhere in the universe.

Q.2 Write the formula for magnitude of gravitational force between the earth and an object on the surface of the earth. **Page 102**

Sol. The formula for magnitude of gravitational force between the earth and an object on the surface of the earth is given by $F = G\frac{Mm}{R^2}$

where, M = mass of the earth,

m = mass of an object,

G = gravitational constant

$= 6.67 \times 10^{-11}$ N-m^2/kg^2

and R = distance between centres of the earth and an object.

Q.3 What do you mean by free fall? **Page 104**

Sol. The falling of a body from a height towards the earth under the gravitational force of the earth is called free fall. Hence, the motion of a particle falling down or going up under the action of gravity means the body is under free fall.

Q.4 What do you mean by acceleration due to gravity? **Page 104**

Sol. Acceleration of a body during free fall towards a celestial body is called acceleration due to gravity. Its value is 9.8 m/s^2.

For objects on or near the surface of the earth,

$$mg = G\frac{M \times m}{R^2}$$

where, g = acceleration due to gravity,

M = mass of the earth,

m = mass of an object

and R = radius of the earth.

Hence, $g = \frac{GM}{R^2}$.

Q.5 What are the difference between the mass of an object and its weight? **Page 106**

Sol. Difference between the mass of an object and its weight are as below

Mass	Weight
Quantity of matter contained in an object.	Force with which an object is attracted towards centre of the earth due to gravity.
Constant everywhere.	Changes from place to place.
It is a scalar quantity.	It is a vector quantity.
Its SI unit is kg.	Its SI unit is N.
Mass is never zero.	Weight is zero at the centre of the earth or free space.

Q.6 Why is the weight of an object on the moon (1/6)th its weight on the earth? **Page 106**

Sol. Weight of an object, $w = mg$

where, m = mass of an object and g = acceleration due to gravity.

The mass of an object m remains constant at all the places. Acceleration due to gravity changes from place to place. So, we can say that the weight of an object depends on the acceleration due to gravity.

On the moon, the acceleration due to gravity is (1/6)th that of the earth, this is the reason why the weight of an object on the moon is (1/6)th its weight on the earth.

Q.7 Why is it difficult to hold a school bag having a strap made of thin and strong string? **Page 109**

Sol. It is difficult to hold a school bag having a strap made of a thin and strong string because the area under the strap is small. Hence, large pressure is exerted by the strap on the fingers or shoulders. Due to the large pressure, the strap tends to cut the skin and hence pain is caused.

Q.8 What do you mean by buoyancy? **Page 109**

Sol. The upward force exerted by a liquid on any object immersed in liquid is called buoyancy or upthrust.

Q.9 Why does an object float or sink when placed on the surface of water? **Page 109**

Sol. When an object is placed on the surface of water, two forces act on the object

(i) The weight of the object, acting vertically downwards.

(ii) The upthrust of the water, acting vertically upwards.

The object will float on the surface of water, if the upthrust is greater than the weight of the object. The object will sink, if the weight of the object is more than the upthrust of the water.

Q.10 You find your mass to be 42 kg on a weighing machine. Is your mass more or less than 42 kg? **Page 110**

Sol. Mass is more than 42 kg. As the buoyant force due to air is acting on us, the reading of weighing machine will be less than the actual mass of a person.

Q.11 You have a bag of cotton and an iron bar, each indicating a mass of 100 kg when measured on a weighing machine. In reality, one is heavier than other. Can you say which one is heavier and why? **Page 110**

Sol. Cotton bag is heavier as the buoyant force acting on the cotton bag is more as its surface area is more than that of the iron piece.

Exercise Questions

Q.1 How does the force of gravitation between two objects change when distance between them is reduced to half?

Sol. Force of gravitation between two objects is given by

$$F = G\frac{m_1 m_2}{r^2}$$

If distance is reduced to half, i.e. $r' = r/2$, then new force of gravitation,

$$F' = \frac{Gm_1 m_2}{r'^2} = \frac{Gm_1 m_2}{(r/2)^2} = 4\times\frac{Gm_1 m_2}{r^2} = 4F$$

i.e. The force of gravitation becomes 4 times of the original value.

Q.2 Gravitational force acts on all objects in proportion to their masses. Why a heavy object does not fall faster than a light object?

Sol. Acceleration due to gravity (g) is independent of mass of the falling object and is equal for all objects at a point. So, a heavy object falls with same acceleration as light object.

Q.3 What is the magnitude of the gravitational force between the earth and a 1 kg object on its surface? (Take, mass of the earth is 6×10^{24} kg and radius of the earth is 6.4×10^6 m)

Sol. Gravitational force between the earth and an object is given by $F = \frac{GMm}{R^2}$.

where, G = gravitational constant $= 6.67\times10^{-11}\text{N-m}^2/\text{kg}^2$,

M = mass of the earth $= 6\times10^{24}$ kg,

R = radius of the earth $= 6.4\times10^6$ m

and m = mass of an object = 1 kg

$$\therefore \quad F = \frac{6.67\times10^{-11}\times6\times10^{24}\times1}{(6.4\times10^6)^2}$$

$$= 9.77 \approx 9.8 \text{ N}$$

Thus, magnitude of gravitational force between the earth and 1 kg object is 9.8 N.

Q.4 The earth and the moon are attracted to each other by gravitational force. Does the earth attract the moon with a force that is greater than or smaller than or equal to the force with which the moon attracts the earth? Why?

Sol. When two objects attract each other, then gravitational force of attraction applied by first object on the second object is same as the force applied by the second object on the first object. So, both earth and moon attract each other by the same gravitational force of attraction.

Q.5 If the moon attracts the earth, then why does the earth not move towards the moon?

Sol. The earth does not move towards the moon inspite of the attraction by the moon because the mass of earth is much greater than mass of moon and for a given force, acceleration is inversely proportional to mass of the object.

Q.6 What happens to the force between two objects, if
(i) the mass of one object is doubled?
(ii) the distance between the objects is doubled and tripled?
(iii) the masses of both objects are doubled?

Sol. Force of attraction between two objects is given by

$$F = \frac{Gm_1 m_2}{r^2} \quad \text{...(i)}$$

where, m_1 and m_2 = masses of the objects,

r = distance between the objects

and G = gravitational constant.

(i) If mass of one object is doubled $(m_1 = 2m_1)$, then the new force,

$$F' = \frac{G(2m_1)m_2}{r^2} = 2\times\frac{Gm_1 m_2}{r^2} = 2F$$

i.e. Force becomes double.

(ii) If the distance between the objects is doubled $(r)^2 = (2r)^2$, then the new force,

$$F' = \frac{Gm_1 m_2}{(2r)^2} = \frac{Gm_1 m_2}{4r^2} = \frac{1}{4}\cdot\frac{Gm_1 m_2}{r^2} = \frac{F}{4} \quad \text{[from Eq. (i)]}$$

i.e. Force becomes one-fourth.

If the distance between the objects is tripled, then new force,

$$F' = \frac{Gm_1m_2}{(3r)^2} = \frac{Gm_1m_2}{9r^2} = \frac{1}{9}\left(\frac{Gm_1m_2}{r^2}\right) = \frac{F}{9}$$

[from Eq. (i)]

i.e. Force becomes one-ninth.

(iii) If masses of both objects are doubled, then new force,

$$F' = \frac{G(2m_1)(2m_2)}{r^2} = 4 \times \frac{Gm_1m_2}{r^2} = 4F \text{ [from Eq. (i)]}$$

i.e. Force becomes four times.

Q.7 What is the importance of universal law of gravitation?

Sol. The universal law of gravitation successfully explained several phenomena given as below

(i) The force that binds us to the earth.

(ii) The motion of the moon around the earth.

(iii) The motion of planets around the sun.

(iv) The tides due to the moon and the sun.

(v) The flow of water in rivers is also due to gravitational force of the earth on water.

Q.8 What is the acceleration of free fall?

Sol. The acceleration of free fall is the acceleration produced in the motion of an object when it falls freely towards the earth. It is also called acceleration due to gravity. Its value on the earth surface is 9.8 m/s^2.

Q.9 What do we call gravitational force between the earth and an object?

Sol. The gravitational force between the earth and an object is called force of gravity or gravity.

Q.10 Amit buys few grams of gold at the poles as per the instruction of one of his friends. He hands over the same when he meets him at the equator. Will the friend agree with the weight of gold bought? If not, why?
[Hint The value of g is greater at the poles than at equator]

Sol. No, his friend will not agree with the weight of gold.

$$w = mg \quad \text{...(i)}$$

$$w = \frac{GMm}{R^2} \quad \text{...(ii)}$$

From Eqs. (i) and (ii), we get

$$mg = \frac{GMm}{R^2}$$

$$g \propto \frac{1}{(\text{Distance of an object from centre of the earth})^2}$$

or $$g \propto \frac{1}{R^2}$$

The value of g is greater at poles than at the equator. Therefore, gold at equator weighs less than that at poles. Thus, Amit's friend will not agree with the weight of the gold bought.

Q.11 Why does a sheet of paper fall slower than one that is crumpled into a ball?

Sol. The sheet of paper falls slower than one that is crumpled into a ball because in first case, the area of the sheet is more, so it experiences large opposing force due to air. While the sheet crumpled into a ball experience less opposing force due to small area. This opposing force arises due to air resistance or air friction.

Q.12 Gravitational force on the surface of the moon is only (1/6)th as strong as gravitational force on the earth. What is the weight in Newton of a 10 kg object on the moon and on the earth?

Sol. Given, mass of the object, $m = 10$ kg

Weight on the earth, $w = mg$

$$= 10 \times 9.8$$

$$= 98 \text{ N}$$

Weight on the moon $= \frac{1}{6}$ of the weight on the earth

$$= \frac{1}{6} \times 98$$

$$= 16.33 \text{ N}$$

Q.13 A ball is thrown vertically upwards with a velocity of 49 m/s. Calculate

(i) the maximum height to which it rises.

(ii) the total time it takes to return to the surface of the earth.

Sol. Given, initial velocity, $u = 49$ m/s

(i) At the maximum height, velocity becomes zero.

$\therefore$ Final velocity, $v = 0$

From the third equation of upward motion,

$$v^2 = u^2 - 2gh$$

$$0 = (49)^2 - 2 \times 9.8 \times h$$

$$\therefore \quad h = \frac{(49)^2}{2 \times 9.8} = 122.5 \text{ m}$$

Maximum height attained = 122.5 m

(ii) Time taken by the ball to reach the maximum height.

From the first equation of motion, $v = u - gt$

or $$0 = 49 - 9.8 \times t$$

$$t = \frac{49}{9.8} = 5 \text{ s}$$

For the motion against gravity, the time of descent is same as the time of ascent. So, time taken by the ball to fall from maximum height is 5 s.

$\therefore$ Total time taken by the ball to return to surface of the earth $= 5 + 5 = 10$ s.

Q.14 A stone is released from the top of a tower of height 19.6 m. Calculate its final velocity just before touching the ground.

Sol. Given, height, $h = 19.6$ m

Initial velocity, $u = 0$ [$\because$ it starts from rest]

From the third equation of motion, $v^2 = u^2 + 2gh$

$$v^2 = 0 + 2 \times 9.8 \times 19.6 = 19.6 \times 19.6$$

$$\therefore \quad v = \sqrt{19.6 \times 19.6} = 19.6 \text{ m/s}$$

Final velocity of stone just before touching the ground is 19.6 m/s.

Q.15 A stone is thrown vertically upward with an initial velocity of 40 m/s. Taking $g = 10 \text{ m/s}^2$, find the maximum height reached by the stone. What is the net displacement and the total distance covered by the stone?

Sol. Given, initial velocity, $u = 40$ m/s

Final velocity becomes zero, i.e. $v = 0$

[at maximum height]

From third equation of upward motion,

$$v^2 = u^2 - 2gh$$

$$(0)^2 = (40)^2 - 2 \times 10 \times h$$

$$0 = 1600 - 20h$$

$$\Rightarrow \quad h = \frac{1600}{20} = 80 \text{ m}$$

$\therefore$ Maximum height reached by the stone = 80 m.

After reaching the maximum height, the stone will fall towards the earth and will reach the earth's surface covering the same distance.

So, distance covered by the stone = 80 + 80 = 160 m.

Displacement of the stone = 0.

Because, the stone starts from the earth's surface and finally reaches the earth's surface again, i.e. the initial and final positions of the stone are same.

Q.16 Calculate the force of gravitation between the earth and the sun. Given that the mass of the earth $= 6 \times 10^{24}$ kg and of the sun $= 2 \times 10^{30}$ kg. The average distance between the two is 1.5×10^{11} m.

Sol. The force of gravitation between the earth and the sun is given by $F = \dfrac{GM_sM_e}{r^2}$

where, $G = 6.67 \times 10^{-11} \text{ N-m}^2/\text{kg}^2$

Mass of the sun, $M_s = 2 \times 10^{30}$ kg

Mass of the earth, $M_e = 6 \times 10^{24}$ kg

Average distance between the earth and the sun,

$$r = 1.5 \times 10^{11} \text{ m}$$

$$F = \frac{6.67 \times 10^{-11} \times 2 \times 10^{30} \times 6 \times 10^{24}}{(1.5 \times 10^{11})^2} = 3.6 \times 10^{22} \text{ N}$$

Thus, the force between earth and sun is 3.6×10^{22} N.

Q.17 A stone is allowed to fall from the top of a tower 100 m high and at the same time, another stone is projected vertically upwards from the ground with a velocity of 25 m/s. Calculate when and where the two stones will meet.

Sol. Let after time t both stones meet and s be the distance travelled by the stone dropped from the top of tower at which the stones will meet.

Distance travelled by the stone dropped = s

$\therefore$ Distance travelled by the stone projected upwards = $(100 - s)$ m

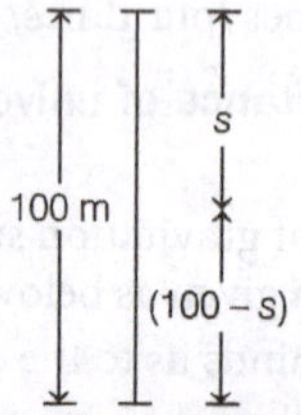

For the stone dropped from the tower,

$$s = ut + \frac{1}{2}gt^2 = 0 + \frac{1}{2}(10)t^2$$

[$u = 0$ because stone is dropped, i.e. it starts from rest]

$$s = 5t^2 \quad \text{...(i)}$$

For the stone projected upwards,

$$s' = ut - \frac{1}{2}gt^2$$

[due to upward motion, negative sign is taken]

$$(100 - s) = 25t - \frac{1}{2} \times 10t^2$$

$$\Rightarrow \quad 100 - s = 25t - 5t^2$$

Substituting value of s from Eq. (i), we get

$$100 - 5t^2 = 25t - 5t^2$$

$$25t = 100$$

$$\Rightarrow \quad t = 4 \text{ s}$$

So, the stones will meet after 4 s.

$$s = 5t^2 = 5 \times (4)^2 = 80 \text{ m}$$

So, the stones will be at a distance of 80 m from the top of tower or 20 m (100 m – 80 m) from the base of the tower.

Q.18 A ball thrown up vertically returns to the thrower after 6 s, find

(i) the velocity with which it was thrown up,

(ii) the maximum height it reaches

(iii) and its position after 4 s.

Sol. Total time taken = 6 s

$\therefore$ Time taken to reach the maximum height

$$= \frac{6}{2} = 3 \text{ s}$$

[$\because$ time of ascent = time of descent]

(i) From the first equation of motion, $v = u - gt$

[negative sign is taken due to upward motion]

$$0 = u - 9.8 \times 3$$

[$\because$ at maximum height, $v = 0$]

$$\Rightarrow \quad u = 29.4 \text{ m/s}$$

(ii) From the third equation of motion,

$$v^2 = u^2 - 2gh$$

[negative sign is taken due to upward motion]

$$0 = (29.4)^2 - 2 \times 9.8 \times h$$

$$\Rightarrow \quad h = \frac{(29.4)^2}{2 \times 9.8} = 44.1 \text{ m}$$

Maximum height attained by the ball is 44.1 m.

(iii) In initial 3 s, the ball will rise, then in next 3 s it falls toward the earth.

$\therefore$ The position after 4 s

= Distance covered in 1s in the downward motion

From the second equation of motion,

$$h = ut + \frac{1}{2}gt^2 = 0 + \frac{1}{2} \times 9.8 \times (1)^2 = 4.9 \text{ m}$$

Therefore, the ball will be at 4.9 m below from the top of the tower or the height of ball from the ground will be at $(44.1 - 4.9) = 39.2$

Q.19 In what direction, does the buoyant force on an object immersed in a liquid act?

Sol. The buoyant force on an object immersed in a liquid always acts in the vertically upward direction.

Q.20 Why does a block of plastic released under water, come up to the surface of water?

Sol. The upthrust or buoyant force acting on the block of plastic by the water is greater than the weight of the plastic block, so plastic block comes up to the surface of water.

Q.21 The volume of 50 g of a substance is 20 cm^3. If the density of water is 1 g cm^{-3}, will the substance float or sink?

Sol. Given, mass of substance, $m = 50$ g

Volume of substance, $V = 20 \text{ cm}^3$

$\therefore$ Density of substance,

$$\rho = \frac{\text{Mass}}{\text{Volume}} = \frac{50}{20} = 2.5 \text{ g cm}^{-3}$$

i.e. The density of the substance is greater than the density of water, so it will sink in water.

Q.22 The volume of a 500 g sealed packet is 350 cm^3. Will the packet float or sink in water, if the density of water is 1 g cm^{-3}? What will be the mass of the water displaced by this packet?

Sol. Given, mass of packet, $m = 500$ g

Volume of packet, $V = 350 \text{ cm}^3$

$\therefore$ Density of packet, $\rho = \frac{\text{Mass}}{\text{Volume}} = \frac{500 \text{ g}}{350 \text{ cm}^3} = 1.43 \text{ g cm}^{-3}$

i.e. The density of packet is greater than density of water, so it will sink in water.

Mass of water displaced by the packet

= Volume of packet × Density of water

$= 350 \times 1$

$= 350$ g

To Study NCERT Activities

Scan the Code

REVIEW EXERCISE

Including Competency Based Questions

Competency Focused (Objective) Questions

Multiple Choice Questions

1 The weakest force in the following is

(a) magnetic force (b) nuclear force
(c) gravitational force (d) electric force

Sol. (c) Gravitational force is the weakest force among given force.

2 Law of gravitation gives the gravitational force between

(a) the earth and a point mass only
(b) the earth and the sun only
(c) any two bodies having some mass
(d) two charged bodies only **NCERT Exemplar**

Sol. (c) Law of gravitation is applicable to all bodies having some mass and is given by $F = \frac{Gm_1m_2}{r^2}$

where, F = force of attraction between the two bodies,

m_1 and m_2 = masses of two bodies,

G = gravitational constant

and r = distance between the two bodies.

3 The atmosphere is held to the earth by **NCERT Exemplar**

(a) gravity (b) wind
(c) clouds (d) earth's magnetic field

Sol. (a) The atmosphere around earth has gases in it. These gases have mass, hence they are attracted by the gravitational force of earth.

Gravitational force is given by

$$F = \frac{Gm_1m_2}{r^2}$$

∴ We can say that atmosphere is held to the earth by its gravity.

4 In the relation $F = GMm/d^2$, the quantity G **NCERT Exemplar**

(a) depends on the value of g at the place of observation
(b) is used only when the earth is one of the two masses
(c) is greatest at the surface of the earth
(d) is universal gravitational constant of nature

Sol. (d) The quantity G is universal gravitational constant, where the value of $G = 6.67 \times 10^{-11} \text{Nm}^2/\text{kg}^2$

5 The value of quantity G in the law of gravitation

(a) depends on mass of the earth only
(b) depends on radius of earth only
(c) depends on both mass and radius of the earth
(d) is independent of mass and radius of the earth

NCERT Exemplar

Sol. (d) G is the constant of proportionality and is called the universal gravitational constant. It is independent of mass and radius of the earth.

6 The force of attraction between two unit point masses separated by a unit distance is called **NCERT Exemplar**

(a) gravitational potential
(b) acceleration due to gravity
(c) gravitational field
(d) universal gravitational constant

Sol. (d) The force of attraction between two unit point masses separated by a unit distance is called universal gravitational constant.

7 In given figure, two particles of masses m_1 and m_2 are at a separation r. The force of attraction F is

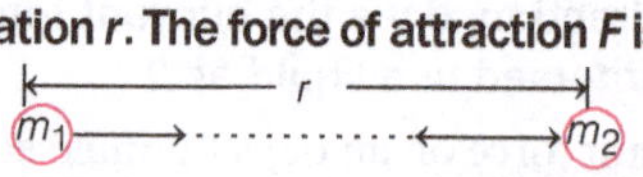

Competency Based Que.

(a) $F \propto \frac{m_1m_2}{r^2}$ (b) $F \propto \frac{m_1m}{r}$
(c) $F \propto \frac{m_1+m_2}{r^2}$ (d) zero

Sol. (a) According to gravitational force,

$$F = \frac{Gm_1m_2}{r^2}$$

$$\therefore \quad F \propto \frac{m_1m_2}{r^2}$$

8 An apple falls from a tree because of gravitational attraction between the earth and apple. If F_1 is the magnitude of force exerted by the earth on the apple and F_2 is the magnitude of force exerted by apple on earth, then **Competency Based Que.**

(a) F_1 is very much greater than F_2
(b) F_2 is very much greater than F_1
(c) F_1 is only a little greater than F_2
(d) F_1 and F_2 are equal.

Sol. (d) Newton's law of gravitation obey's Newton's third law of motion, i.e. forces of attraction between any two objects are equal and opposite. Hence, F_1 and F_2 are equal.

9 Which pair of objects will have the strongest force of gravity between them? **Competency Based Que.**

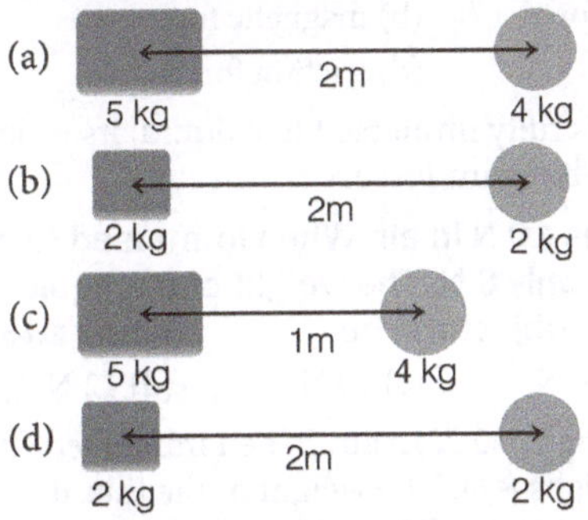

Sol. (*c*) Object that are closer together have the strongest force of gravity between them.

10 The gravitational force between two objects is *F*. If masses of both objects are halved without changing distance between them, then the gravitational force would become **NCERT Exemplar**

(a) $\frac{F}{4}$ (b) $\frac{F}{2}$ (c) F (d) $2F$

Sol. (*a*) As, $F = \frac{Gm_1m_2}{d^2}$, therefore when

$$m_1 \rightarrow \frac{m_1}{2}$$

and $m_2 \rightarrow \frac{m_2}{2}$, keeping d constant.

Then, $F' = \frac{G\left(\frac{m_1}{2}\right)\left(\frac{m_2}{2}\right)}{d^2} = \frac{F}{4}$

11 Identify the incorrect statement from the following

(a) The weight of an object on the Moon is one-sixth of its weight on Earth.
(b) Gravitational force acts only on objects with mass.
(c) Mass and weight are the same physical quantity and have the same units.
(d) The acceleration due to gravity is the same at all points on Earth.

Sol. (*c*) This is incorrect because mass is a scalar quantity, measured in kilograms, while weight is a force, measured in newtons.

12 A boy is whirling a stone tied with a string in an horizontal circular path. If the string breaks, the stone **Competency Based Que.**

(a) will continue to move in the circular path
(b) will move along a straight line towards the centre of the circular path
(c) will move along a straight line tangential to the circular path
(d) will move along a straight line perpendicular to the circular path away from the boy

Sol. (*c*) The stone will move along a straight line tangential to the circular path.

13 During free fall, maximum acceleration is experienced by a body **NCERT Exemplar**

(a) at poles (b) at equator
(c) at 23.6° latitude (d) None of these

Sol. (*a*) During free fall, value of g is maximum at the poles of the earth.

14 The value of gravitational acceleration (g) is

(a) highest at poles (b) highest at equator
(c) lowest at poles (d) lowest at equator

Sol. (*a*) Gravitational acceleration is given by $g = \frac{Gm_e}{R_e^2}$

where, G is gravitational constant, m_e is mass of earth and R_e is radius of earth.

Since, radius of earth at equator is greater than poles, hence value of g at poles is greater than equator.

15 Two objects of different masses falling freely near the surface of moon would **NCERT Exemplar**

(a) have same velocities at any instant
(b) have different accelerations
(c) experience forces of same magnitude
(d) undergo a change in their inertia

Sol. (*a*) Objects of different masses falling freely near the surface of the moon would have the same velocities at any instant because they will have same acceleration due to gravity.

16 The value of acceleration due to gravity **NCERT Exemplar**

(a) is same at equator and poles
(b) is least at poles
(c) is least at equator
(d) increases from pole to equator

Sol. (*c*) The value of g is less on equator than that of poles.

17 A car falls off a ledge and drops to the ground in 0.9 s. If the value of g is 10 m/s^2, then speed of car on striking the ground is

(a) 6 m/s (b) 8 m/s (c) 9 m/s (d) 18 m/s

Sol. (*c*) Initial velocity, $u = 0$

Acceleration due to gravity, $g = 10\ \text{m/s}^2$

Let v be the speed of car on striking the ground, then

$$v = u + gt$$
$$= 0 + 10 \times 0.9 = 9\ \text{m/s}$$

18 An object is thrown vertically upwards and rises to a height of 20 m, then the velocity with which the object was thrown upward is [take, $g = 10\ \text{m/s}^2$]

(a) 15 m/s (b) 25 m/s
(c) 10 m/s (d) 20 m/s

Sol. (*d*) Given, height, $h = 20$ m, $g = 10\ \text{m/s}^2$

At highest point, final velocity, $v = 0$

$\therefore$ From equation, $v^2 = u^2 - 2gh$

$$0 = u^2 - 2 \times 10 \times 20$$

Initial velocity, $u = \sqrt{400} = 20$ m/s

Thus, object was thrown upward with velocity 20 m/s.

19 Weight of an object of mass *m* can be represented by

(a) $\frac{GM}{R^2}$ (b) $\frac{GMm}{R^2}$ (c) $\frac{GMm}{2R^2}$ (d) $\frac{GM}{R^3}$

Sol. (*b*) Since, $w = mg$ and $g = \frac{GM}{R^2}$

So, $w = \frac{GMm}{R^2}$

20 The weight of an object at the centre of the earth of radius *R* is **NCERT Exemplar**

(a) zero

(b) infinite

(c) *R* times the weight at the surface of the earth

(d) $\frac{1}{R^2}$ times the weight at the surface of the earth

Sol. (*a*) The weight of an object at the centre of the earth of radius *R* is zero.

21 The relation between the weight of an object on the moon (w_m) and on the earth (w_e), is **NCERT Exemplar**

(a) $w_m = 6w_e$ (b) $w_e = \frac{1}{6}w_m$

(c) $w_m = w_e$ (d) $w_m = \frac{1}{6}w_e$

Sol. (*d*) The weight of an object on the moon is about one-sixth of its weight on the earth. This is because the values of acceleration due to gravity on the moon is about one-sixth on the earth.

22 A girl stands on a box having 60 cm length, 40 cm breadth and 20 cm width in three ways. In which of the following cases, pressure exerted by the brick will be

(a) maximum when length and breadth form the base

(b) maximum when breadth and width form the base

(c) maximum when width and length form the base

(d) the same in all the above three cases

Competency Based Que.

Sol. (*b*) According to question, when base is formed by breadth and width, area will be minimum. And so, pressure will be maximum.

23 Why the dam of water reservoir is thick at the bottom? **Competency Based Que.**

(a) Quantity of water increases with depth

(b) Density of water increases with depth

(c) Pressure of water increases with depth

(d) Temperature of water increases with depth

Sol. (*c*) The dam of water is made thick at the bottom, because due to maximum depth, the pressure of water is maximum at bottom and to bear this maximum pressure dam should be thick at the bottom.

24 When a ball is fully immersed in a liquid, its weight get decreased. It happens due to

(a) gravitational force (b) magnetic force

(c) buoyant force (d) friction force

Sol. (*c*) When a ball is fully immersed in a liquid, its weight decreases due to buoyant force.

25 An object weighs 10 N in air. When immersed fully in water, it weighs only 8 N. The weight of the liquid displaced by the object will be **NCERT Exemplar**

(a) 2 N (b) 8 N (c) 10 N (d) 12 N

Sol. (*a*) An object weighs 10 N in air. When immersed fully in a liquid, it weighs 8 N. The weight of the liquid displaced by the object will be 2 N.

26 The upward force exerted by the liquid displaced by the body when it is placed inside the liquid is called **NCERT Exemplar**

(a) buoyant force (b) gravitational force

(c) centripetal force (d) force of gravitation

Sol. (*a*) The upward force exerted by the liquid displaced by the body when it is placed inside the liquid is called buoyant force.

27 An object is put one by one in three liquids having different densities. The object floats with $\frac{1}{9}, \frac{2}{11}$ and $\frac{3}{7}$ parts of their volumes outside the liquid surface in liquids of densities d_1, d_2 and d_3, respectively. Which of the following statement is correct?

Competency Based Que.

(a) $d_1 > d_2 > d_3$ (b) $d_1 > d_2 < d_3$

(c) $d_1 < d_2 > d_3$ (d) $d_1 < d_2 < d_3$

Sol. (*d*) In a liquid of higher density, more part of the object remains outside the liquid. Since, the order of part of their volume outside the liquid is given by part of the body outside the liquid $\propto$ densities of liquid

$$\frac{1}{9} < \frac{2}{11} < \frac{3}{7}$$

Thus, the order of densities in increasing order is

$$d_1 < d_2 < d_3$$

28 Match Column A with Column B and select the correct option using the given codes.

Column A	Column B
1. Gravity	A. The amount of matter in an object.
2. Weight	B. The force with which earth attracts an object.
3. Mass	C. The force of attraction between two objects.
4. Free fall	D. Motion of an object.

Options

(a) 1-B, 2-C, 3-A, 4-D (b) 1-C, 2-D, 3-B, 4-A

(c) 1-D, 2-C, 3-A, 4-B (d) 1-A, 2-B, 3-C, 4-D

Sol. (*a*) 1-B, 2-C, 3-A, 4-D

Assertion–Reason Questions

Direction (Q.Nos. 1-8) ***In each of the following questions, a statement of Assertion is given by the corresponding statement of Reason. Of the statements, mark the correct answer as***

(a) If both Assertion and Reason are true and Reason is the correct explanation of Assertion.
(b) If both Assertion and Reason are true, but Reason is not the correct explanation of Assertion.
(c) If Assertion is true, but Reason is false.
(d) If Assertion is false, but Reason is true.

1 Assertion (A) The moon revolves around the earth due to gravitational force between moon and earth.
Reason (R) Gravitational force between moon and earth is calculated by Newton's law of gravitation.

Sol. (*b*) Moon revolves around the earth and centripetal force is obtained from gravitational force between moon and earth.
i.e. Gravitational force = Centripetal force
Gravitational force between moon and earth is calculated by Newton's law of gravitation.
Hence, both Assertion and Reason are true but Reason is not the correct explanation of Assertion.

2 Assertion (A) If the distance between two bodies of masses m_1 and m_2 is increased by a factor of 6, the gravitational force is reduced by $\frac{1}{36}$.
Reason (R) The gravitational force is inversely proportional to the square of the distance between two bodies.

Sol. (*a*) Gravitational force is given by the formula,
$$F = \frac{GMm}{R^2}$$
Gravitational force is inversely proportional to the square of the distance between two bodies.

3 Assertion (A) If a pendulum is suspended in a lift is falling freely, then its time period becomes infinite.
Reason (R) Free falling body has acceleration equal to acceleration due to gravity.

Sol. (*a*) If a pendulum is suspended in a lift and lift is moving downward with same acceleration *a*, then time period of pendulum is given by $T = 2\pi\sqrt{\frac{l}{g-a}}$.
In the case of free fall, $a = g$ then $T = \infty$, i.e. the time period of pendulum becomes infinite.

4 Assertion (A) At the centre of earth, a body has no centre of gravity.
Reason (R) This is because, $g = 0$ at the centre of earth.

Sol. (*a*) At the centre of earth, acceleration due to gravity, $g = 0$, i.e. a body has no weight and hence no centre of gravity.
Hence, both Assertion and Reason are true and Reason is the correct explanation of Assertion.

5 Assertion (A) On moon, a person feels lighter than earth.
Reason (R) It is due to more gravitational force exerted by moon on person.

Sol. (*c*) On moon, a person feels lighter as compared to earth because less gravitational force is exerted by moon on person.

6 Assertion (A) The effect of thrust on sand is larger while standing than lying.
Reason (R) Thrust is a force acting on an object perpendicular to the surface.

Sol. (*b*) Thrust on ground is more when a person is standing than that of lying because in case of standing, the effective area is less.

7 Assertion (A) When a body is dipped into water, then upthrust force acting on the body is equal to the weight of water displaced by the body.
Reason (R) A body will sink in water, if density of body is less than or equal to density of water.

Sol. (*c*) According to Archimedes' principle,
Upthrust force = Weight of water displaced
Hence, Assertion is true and Reason is false and the correct statement is, 'a body will sink in a liquid, if its density is more than that of the liquid'.

8 Assertion (A) Fluid is a substance which has the ability to flow.
Reason (R) Archimedes' principle is applicable for liquid as well as gases.

Sol. (*b*) Archimedes' principle is applicable for fluid which have the ability to flow.

Case Based/Source Based Questions

Direction (Q. Nos. 1-3) Answer the questions on the basis of your understanding of the following table and related studied concepts:

1 The gravitation is defined as the force of attraction between any two bodies in the universe. The earth attracts all objects lying on or near its surface towards its centre. The force with which the earth pulls the objects towards its centre is called gravitational force of the earth or gravity of the earth.

Gravitation theory was first stated by Galileo Gallilei in the late 16th and early 17th century, and he gave the way to Issac Newton in 1687 to discover the Newton theory of gravity, or the inverse-square law of gravitation. we can define gravitational force as a force that attracts any two objects with mass.

We say it is attractive because it always tries to pull the masses together, it never push them apart.

(i) A body of mass 50 kg weighs 220 N on mars. What is the acceleration due to gravity on mars? [1]

(ii) Is value of g same at different places on earth? Give reason for your answer. [1]

(iii) Why G is called gravitation constant? [1]

(iv) How the gravitation is different from gravity of earth? [1]

Sol. (i) Given, Mass = 50 kg, weight = 220 N

So, acceleration due to gravity $= \frac{220}{50} = 4.4 \text{ m/s}^2$

(ii) No, the value of g is maximum at the poles and minimum at equator. The variation is occurs because of the oblong shape of the earth and rotation about its own axis.

(iii) The constant G is universal because it is independent of the nature and size of bodies.

(iv) Gravitation is the force of attraction between any two bodies, while gravity refers to attraction between any body and the earth.

2. **Archimedes' principle, stated as follows: When a body is immersed fully or partially in a fluid, it experiences an upward force that is equal to the weight of the fluid displaced by it. The upward force is known as upthrust or buoyant force. In fact, all objects experience a force of buoyancy when they are immersed in a fluid. The magnitude of this buoyant force depends on the density of the fluid. Objects having density less than that of the liquid in which they are immersed float of the surface of the liquid. If the density of the object is more than the density of the liquid in which it is immersed, then it sinks in the liquid. Hence, body will float or sink depends upon difference between density of body and fluid.**

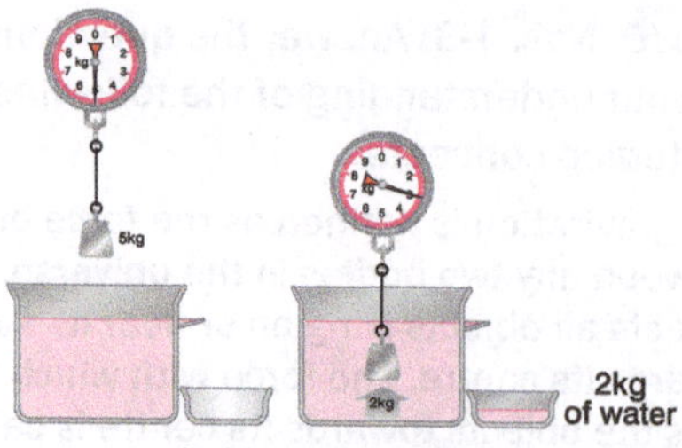

Archimede's principle

(a) Give answer of following questions:

(i) What happens, if the weight of the object is more than the weight of the water displaced by the object?

(ii) Who invented Archimede's principle?

(b) What are the application of Archimede's principle?

(c) A block of wood floats in which with ane third of its volume submerged. In ail, the block floats with two thirds of its volume submerged.

Find the density of

(i) wood

(ii) oil, if the density of water is 10^3 kg/m

Or

(c) Which is heavier cotton or iron and why?

Sol. (a) (i) According to the law of floatation, when the weight of the liquid displaced by immersed part of a body is equal to its weight, then a body starts floating. If the weight of the object is more than the weight of the liquid displaced, then the body sinks.

(ii) Archimedes' a Greek mathematician and physicist invented the Archimede's principle in the third century BC.

(b) The following are the applications of Archimede's principle

It helps in the design of ships and submarines.

Lactometers utilise it to test the purity of milk

(c) (i) Let V_0 be the total volume of the block of wood.

We have, density of body/density of fluid = Volume part of body/Total volume of body

When the fluid is water, then the volume of immersed part of the wooden block is $\frac{V_0}{3}$.

$$\because \frac{\text{Density of wood}}{\text{Density of water}} = \frac{\text{Volume of immersed part of the wooden block}}{\text{Total volume of the wooden block}}$$

$$\Rightarrow \frac{\text{Density of wood}}{10^3} = \frac{\left(\frac{V_0}{3}\right)}{V_0}$$

$$\Rightarrow \text{Density of wood} = \frac{10^3}{3} = 333.33 \text{ kg/m}^3$$

(ii) When the fluid is oil, then the volume of immersed part of the wooden block is $\frac{2V_0}{3}$.

Using the formula, Density of wood/Density of oil = Volume of immersed part of the wooden block/Total volume of the wooden block

$$\Rightarrow 333/\text{Density of oil} = \frac{\frac{2V_0}{3}}{V_0} = \frac{2}{3}$$

$$\Rightarrow \text{Density of oil} = 500 \text{ kg/m}^3$$

(c) The apparent weight of both is the same, but the buoyant force experienced by cotton is greater because the volume of cotton is greater than that of iron.

As a result, the weight of cotton is greater.

3 According to principle of floatation, an object will float in a fluid, if its density is less than that of the fluid.

When an object is partially or fully dipped into a fluid, the fluid exertes force on it. At any small portion of the surface of the object, the force by the fluid is perpendicular to the surface and is equal to the product of the pressure at the surface and surface area. The resultant of all these contact forces is called buoyant force (upthrust).

Archimedes' principle states that "any object partially or completely submerged in a fluid is buoyed up by a force equal to the weight of the fluid displaced by the object."

The buoyant force depends on the submerged volume of the object, be it partly or wholly immersed. The volume of the object immersed is same as the volume of the liquid displaced.

Therefore, buoyant force = $V \rho g$, where

V = volume of fluid displaced, ρ = density of fluid,

g = acceleration due to gravity

or Buoyant force = Weight of fluid displaced.

(i) An object weighs 36 g-wt in air and has a volume of 8.0 cm^3. What will be its apparent weight when immersed in water? [1]

(ii) A piece of metal weighs 9.25 g in air, 8.20 g in water and 8.36 g when immersed in gasoline. What is the density of the metal? [1]

(iii) What is the density of the gasoline? [½]

(a) $0.89 \text{ g}/\text{cm}^3$ (b) $0.85 \text{ g}/\text{cm}^3$

(c) $1.05 \text{ g}/\text{cm}^3$ (d) None of these

(iv) The density of water is $1 \text{ g}/\text{cm}^3$. Which of the following substance will float in water? [1]

Substance	Mass	Volume
(a)	6 g	3 cm^3
(b)	8 g	4 cm^3
(c)	10 g	2 cm^3
(d)	2 g	4 cm^3

(v) An object is immersed in two liquids A and B in succession. The extent to which the object sinks in liquid B is less than in liquid A. What conclusion can be derived from such an observation? [½]

(a) Density of liquid A is more than liquid B.

(b) Density of liquid B is more than liquid A.

(c) Upthrust exerted by liquid B is more than exerted by liquid A.

(d) Both (b) and (c) **CBSE DIKSHA**

Sol. (i) When immersed in water, the object is buoyed up by the mass of the water it displaces, which the mass of water displaced = 8 g (the density of water $= 1 \text{ g}/\text{cm}^3$). The upward (buoyancy) force is 8 g-wt.

The apparent weight will be

36 g-wt − 8 g-wt = 28 g - wt

(ii) When immersed in water, the metal object displaces $(9.25 - 8.20)$ g = 1.05g of water whose volume is $(1.05 \text{ g}) / (1.00 \text{ g}/\text{cm}^3) = 1.05 \text{ cm}^3$

The density of metal is 9.25 g/1.05 cm^3

$= 8.81 \text{ g cm}^3$

(iii) (b) The metal object displaces $(9.25 - 8.36)$ g = 0.89 g of gasoline, whose density must therefore be $(0.89 \text{ g}) / (1.05 \text{ cm}^3) = 0.85 \text{ g}/\text{cm}^3$.

(iv) (d) Substance d;

Density $= m/V = \frac{2}{4} = 0.5 \text{g}/\text{cm}^3$ which is less than density of water, so it will float.

(v) (d) Both (b) and (c)

More upthrust is exerted by liquid B, hence it is more denser than liquid A.

Constructed Response (Descriptive) **Questions**

Very Short Answer Type Questions

1 When do we use the term force of gravity rather than force of gravitation?

Sol. We use the term force of gravity rather than force of gravitation for the force of attraction between two bodies in which one body had infinitely large mass.

2 Which force keeps the moon in a uniform circular motion around the earth?

Sol. Gravitational force between the moon and the earth keeps the moon in a uniform circular motion around the earth.

3 The earth attracts an apple. Does the apple also attract the earth? If it does, why does the earth not move towards the apple? **Competency Based Que.**

Sol. The earth attracts an apple and similarly, the apple attracts the earth with an equal and opposite force. Mass of the earth is extremely massive as compared to that of the moon, so the acceleration experienced by earth is very small as compared to what experienced by the apple. Hence, the motion of the earth towards the apple is not noticeable.

4 The earth is acted upon by gravitation of the sun, even then it does not fall into the sun. Why? NCERT Exemplar

Sol. The earth does not fall into the sun because the earth remains in its circular orbit due to the gravitational force acting on it. This gravitational force is responsible for providing the centripetal force. Both forces are equal in magnitude but act in opposite direction, hence keeping earth in a fixed orbit.

5 Two objects kept in a room do not move towards each other as per the universal law of gravitation. Why?

Sol. The size of the bodies are very small, therefore the force of attraction between them is very small. So, both objects do not move towards each other.

6 Mention any two phenomena which successfully explain the basis of the universal law of gravitation?

Sol. The two phenomena are

(i) Tides in oceans are formed due to the gravitational force between the moon and water in oceans.

(ii) The atmosphere of the earth is only possible due to gravitational force.

7 Suppose gravity of the earth suddenly becomes zero, then which direction will the moon begin to move, if no other celestial body affects it? NCERT Exemplar

Sol. The moon will begin to move in a straight line in the direction in which it was moving at that instant because the circular motion of the moon is due to centripetal force provided by the gravitational force of the earth.

8 Two objects of masses m_1 and m_2 are dropped in vacuum from a height above the surface of the earth (m_1 is greater than m_2). Which one will reach the ground first and why?

Sol. Both will reach the ground at the same time because acceleration due to gravity is independent of the masses of freely falling bodies.

9 At which place on the earth, the acceleration due to gravity is zero?

Sol. At the centre of the earth, the acceleration due to gravity is zero.

10 A piece of paper takes much longer to fall than a stone through the same distance. Explain the reason? Competency Based Que.

Sol. A piece of paper takes much longer to fall than a stone through the same distance because the paper is lighter in weight and has a large surface area and therefore, experiences more friction due to air than a stone which has less surface area.

11 Why does a body reach the ground quicker at poles than at the equator when dropped from the same height? Competency Based Que.

Sol. The value of g, i.e. acceleration due to gravity is more at the poles than at the equator. The time taken for a body is less if the acceleration due to gravity is more. So, when we drop an object from the same height, a body reaches the ground quicker at the poles than at the equator.

12 Explain what happens to the force between two objects

(i) The mass of an object is doubled. [1]

(ii) The distance between the objects is doubled. [1]

Sol. (i) If the mass of an object is doubled, then

$$F_1 = G(2m_1)\frac{m_2}{r^2}$$

$$F_1 = 2\cdot Gm_1\frac{m_2}{r^2}$$

$$F_1 = 2F$$

$\therefore$ The gravitational force will be two times.

(ii) If the distance between the object is doubled, then

$$F_2 = \frac{G\cdot m_1\, m_2}{(2r)^2}$$

$$F_2 = \frac{1}{4}\cdot\frac{Gm_1m_2}{r^2}$$

$$F_2 = \frac{F}{4}$$

$\therefore$The gravitational force will one-fourth.

13 The astronauts in space feel weightless. Why?

Sol. They do not exert any force/weight on their spaceship in the absence of gravity in space.

14 Which of the two will double the pressure? Doubling the area or making the area half.

Sol. Making the area half, will double the pressure.

$$\left[\because p = \frac{F}{A}\right]$$

15 A bucket of water weightless inside the well water. Why?

Sol. Due to the upthrust exerted by the well water on the bottom of bucket in upward direction.

16 (i) A coin sinks when placed on the water surface. Give reason. [1]

(ii) A crumpled sheet of paper falls down faster through air as compare to plane sheet why? [1]

Sol. (i) The coin sinks when placed on the water surface because the density of the coin is greater than the density of water.

(ii) When a sheet of paper is crumpled, its surface area decreases. Hence, it experience less air resistance to its motion and it falls faster than the sheet of paper.

17 Rahul, a jeweller buys few grams of gold at the poles. He sells the same when he meets with a customer at the equator. Will the customer agree with the weight of gold? If not, why? **Competency Based Que.**

Sol. Customer will not agree with the weight of gold. Since the shape of the earth is not perfectly spherical, therefore the value of g on earth is maximum at the poles and minimum at the equator.

Thus, the weight of gold will be greater at the poles and smaller at the equator.

18 (i) The tip of the pin is sharp but the head is broad, explain why? [1]

(ii) Explain how does snow shoes stop you from sinking in the snow? [1]

Sol. (i) The tip of the pin is made sharp because tip has less area, therefore there is no more pressure, hence it pierces very easily. Head is made broad, so that the area of contact is more, therefore the pressure can be easily exerted.

(ii) Snow shoes stop you from sinking in the snow because snow shoes have broad base, so that there is more area of contact. Therefore, there will be less pressure on the snow and the person cannot sink.

19 Explain why does a plastic ball released under water comes up to the surface of water?

Sol. A plastic ball released under water comes up to the surface of water because the density of the plastic ball is less as compared to water. Hence, we can say that, the buoyant force is experienced by it under water. So, on releasing it comes to the surface of water.

20 Study the diagrams below

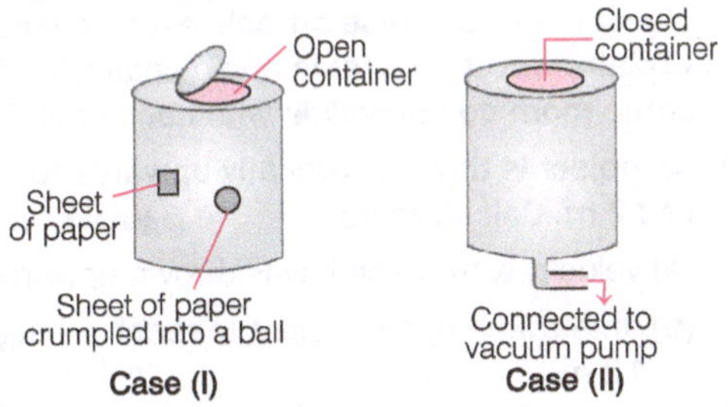

A sheet of paper and a crumpled paper are thrown down from the same height and time is noted. Answer the following questions:

(i) Will the time taken to reach the bottom the container be the same for the sheet of paper and crumpled paper? Why? Explain giving reason. [1]

(ii) What will happen in case (II)? [1]

Or Calculate the average density of the earth in terms of g, G and R.

Sol. (i) Since the area of a sheet of paper is more than the area of the paper crumpled into a small, therefore, a sheet of paper will experience a large opposing force due to air than the ball, while falling down. Hence, a sheet of paper falls slower than one that is crumpled into a ball.

(ii) Both will take same time to reach the bottom as there is no air resistance.

Or

We know that, $g = \frac{GM}{R^2}$ or $M = \frac{gR^2}{G}$

Average density of the earth, $D = \frac{\text{Mass}}{\text{Volume}} = \frac{gR^2}{G \times V_e}$

(where, V_e is the volume of the earth)

or $D = \frac{gR^2}{G\frac{4}{3}\pi R^3} = \frac{3g}{4\pi GR}$

21 On what factor does buoyant force depend?

Sol. Buoyant force depends upon

(i) Density of fluid

(ii) Volume of fluid displaced

(iii) Acceleration due to gravity at that point.

22 Density of glass is 3.5 g cm^{-3}. What does it mean?

Sol. 3.5 gcm^{-3} density of glass means that the volume of 3.5 g glass is 1 cm^3.

23 Name the instrument which is used to determine the density of liquid.

Sol. The instrument which is used to determine the density of liquid is "hydrometer."

24 Give a simple activity to prove how the objects of density less than that of liquid float on it.

Sol. First of all, take beaker and fill it with some water, then put an iron nail and cork in the beaker.
We observe that an iron nail sinks in water, whereas a cork floats on it. This is because the density of the iron nail is more than that of water, whereas that of a cork is less than water. **NCERT Exemplar**

Short Answer Type Questions

1 State the source of centripetal force that a planet requires to revolve around the sun. On what factors does the force depend? Suppose this force suddenly becomes zero, then in which direction will the planet begin to move, if no other celestial body affects it?

Sol. The source of centripetal force is the gravitational force. It depends upon the following factors

(i) Mass of the planet and the sun.

(ii) Distance between the planet and the sun.

If this force suddenly becomes zero, then the planet will begin to move in a straight line in the direction in which it was moving at that instant.

2 Identical packets are dropped from two aeroplanes, one above the equator and the other above the north pole, both at height *h*. Assuming all conditions are identical, will those packets take same time to reach the surface of earth? Justify your answer. NCERT Exemplar

Sol. The value of acceleration due to gravity is greater at the poles than at the equator.

Due to this difference in the acceleration due to gravity, the packet dropped at north pole from a height *h*, will accelerate more than the packet dropped at equator from the same height, and hence will reach the surface of the earth earlier.

3 (i) Seema buys few grams of gold at the poles as per the instruction of one of her friends. She hand over the same when she meets her at the equator. Will the friend agree with the weight of gold bought? If not, why? [1½]

(ii) If the moon attracts the earth, then why does the earth not move towards the moon? [1½]

Competency Based Que.

Sol. (i) No, her friend will not agree with the weight of gold bought because weight at poles is greater than the weight at equator.

(ii) We know that, the gravitational force is always attractive, still the moon does not fall on the earth because the gravitational force between the earth and the moon works as the necessary centripetal force for the moon to make it revolve around the earth.

4 Prove that, if a body is thrown vertically upwards, then the time of ascent is equal to the time of descent. Competency Based Que.

Sol. For the upward motion, equation of motion will be (final velocity, $v=0$)

$$v = u - gt_1,\quad 0 = u - gt_1,\quad t_1 = \frac{u}{g} \qquad \ldots\text{(i)}$$

and the downward motion,

$$v = u + gt_2$$
$$v = 0 + gt_2$$

The body falls back to the earth with the same speed as it was thrown vertically upwards.

$$\therefore \quad v = u,\quad u = 0 + gt_2 \Rightarrow t_2 = \frac{u}{g} \qquad \ldots\text{(ii)}$$

From Eqs. (i) and (ii), we get

$t_1 = t_2 \Rightarrow$ Time of ascent = Time of descent

5 On the earth, a stone is thrown from a height in a direction parallel to the earth's surface while another stone is simultaneously dropped from the same height. Which stone would reach the ground first and why? NCERT Exemplar

Sol. For both the stones,

initial velocity, $u=0$

Acceleration in downward direction $= g$

Now, from second equation of motion,

$$h = ut + \frac{1}{2}gt^2 \Rightarrow h = 0 + \frac{1}{2}gt^2$$

$$\Rightarrow h = \frac{1}{2}gt^2 \Rightarrow t = \sqrt{\frac{2h}{g}}$$

Both stones will take the same time to reach the ground because the two stones fall from the same height.

6 A ball is thrown with some speed *u* m/s. Show that under the free fall, it will fall on the ground with same speed.

Sol. When the ball is thrown upwards, then it will reach certain height *h* and starts falling. At maximum height *h*, the final velocity will be $v=0$.

Maximum height reached by the ball,

$$v^2 - u^2 = 2gh \qquad \text{[using equation]}$$
$$0 - u^2 = -2gh \qquad [\because \text{acceleration} = -g]$$
$$\Rightarrow h = \frac{u^2}{2g} \qquad \ldots\text{(i)}$$

In second case, when the ball starts to fall, then the initial velocity $u=0$. It will accelerate due to gravity, i.e. $a=g$ and reach ground with speed (say v_2).

Using equation, $v_2^2 - u^2 = 2gh$

$$\Rightarrow v_2^2 - 0 = 2gh$$
$$v_2^2 = 2g\left(\frac{u^2}{2g}\right) = u^2 \qquad \text{[from Eq. (i)]}$$
$$\Rightarrow v_2 = u$$

Thus, the ball reaches the ground with same speed.

7 (i) According to universal law of gravitation, every object in this universe attracts every other object. Explain, why then a table and a chair lying in the same room do not collide with each other? [1]

(ii) An object is thrown vertically upwards to a height of 12 m. Calculate its Competency Based Que.

(a) velocity with which it was thrown upwards. [1]

(b) time taken by the object to reach a height of 12 m. [1]

Sol. (i) Gravitational force is the weakest force in nature, yet it helps in holding massive bodies in place throughout the universe. Due to this reason, table and chair do not collide.

(ii) Given, height, $h = 12$ m

Final velocity, $v = 0$

Acceleration due to gravity, $g = -9.8\ \text{m/s}^2$

Initial velocity, $u = ?$ and time, $t = ?$

(a) $\therefore v^2 - u^2 = 2gh,\ 0 - u^2 = 2\times(-9.8)\times 12$

$$\Rightarrow u = 15.33\ \text{m/s}$$

(b) ∴ $v = u - gt$

$$\Rightarrow \quad t = \frac{u}{g} = \frac{15.33}{9.8} = 1.56 \text{ s}$$

8 Obtain a relation between the weight of an object on the surface of the earth and that on the moon.

Sol. Refer to text on page 213 (Weight of an object on the moon).

9 In a hypothetical case, if the diameter of the earth becomes half of its present value and mass becomes four times its present value, then how would the weight of any object on surface of the earth be affected?

Sol. ∴Weight, $w = mg$

As mass is a constant, then $w \propto g$

$$g = \frac{GM}{R^2} = 9.8 \text{ m/s}^2$$

Given, diameter of the earth becomes half of its present value, $d' = \frac{d}{2}$

Mass becomes four times its present value, $M' = 4M$

On bringing modifications,

$$g = \frac{G(4M)}{\left(\frac{R}{2}\right)^2} = 16\frac{GM}{R^2} = 16 \times 9.8$$

w becomes 16 times.

10 (i) When does an object show weightlessness? [1½]

(ii) In which situation, do we exert more pressure on ground when we stand on one foot or on the both feet? Justify your answer. [1½]

Sol. (i) An object has weight due to the attractive force of earth's gravity. If this force of attraction of the earth is somehow cancelled, or not present, then the body experiences no force towards the centre of earth. This condition is called weightlessness.

(ii) We exert more pressure on ground when we stand on one foot rather than on both feet, as the area of one foot is half than that of two feet. Since, $p \propto \frac{1}{A}$, standing on one foot will result in more pressure.

11 (i) Explain, why a completely immersed bottle in water bounces back on the surface. [2]

(ii) Why does a bucket of water weighs less inside the well water? [1]

Competency Based Que.

Sol. (i) Since, it is known that, a body can sink in water only when its weight is greater than the upthrust acting on it by the water. But in this case, the upthrust acting on the bottle is greater than its weight, thats why, it bounces back on the water surface.

(ii) A bucket of water weighs less inside the well water, it is because when the bucket is immersed in water fully, upthrust acts on it by water which reduces its actual weight.

12 Two different bodies are completely immersed in water and undergo the same loss in weight. Is it necessary that their weights in air should also be the same? Justify your answer. **Competency Based Que.**

Sol. No, it is not necessary that their weights in air should also be the same. This is because the two bodies have undergone the same loss in weight on completely immersing in water due to their equal volumes, not due to their equal weights. So, they may have different weights in air.

13 (i) Why does a bucket of water feel heavier when taken out of water? [1½]

(ii) Lead has greater density than iron and both are denser than water. Is the buoyant force on a lead object greater than, less than or equal to the buoyant force on an iron object of the same volume? [1½]

Competency Based Que.

Sol. (i) A bucket of water feels heavier when taken out of water because when immersed in water, an upward force, i.e. buoyant force acts on it which is equal to the weight of water displaced by the bucket.

(ii) The buoyant force on a lead object is lesser than the buoyant force on the iron object because lead has greater density, so it displaces lesser amount of water consequently lesser amount of buoyant force acts on it.

14 When a fresh egg is put into a beaker filled with water, it sinks in water. But when a lot of salt is dissolved in the water, the egg begins to rise and then floats. Why? **Competency Based Que.**

Sol. On dissolving a lot of salt in water, the density of salt solution becomes higher than that of pure water. Due to its much higher density, the salt solution exerts much more upward buoyant force on the egg, making the egg rise and then float.

15 Verify Archimedes' principle of buoyancy with an activity. For the activity, you are provided with a piece of stone, a rubber string and a container filled with water.

Sol. First of all, tie up the stone with the rubber string and hold it against a scale fixed on a wall. Put a mark on the elongated rubber string when stone is tied.

Repeat this experiment but this time suspend the stone in a beaker, filled with water. Now, compare the markings.

Explanation As the buoyant force is acting on the stone in upward direction, due to this, gravitational pull decreases and in turn, the stretch of the rubber is lost.

16 (i) **A piece of ice is placed on the water is surface in a glass, so that when the ice floats, the water comes up to the brim of the glass. What will happen to the level of water when the ice melts, will it overflow?** [1]

(ii) **What will happen, if we will replace the water with**

(a) a liquid denser than water [1]

(b) a liquid lighter than water. [1]

Sol. (i) According to Archimedes' principle when the ice melts, the volume of water formed will be equal to the volume of the displaced water. So, the level of water in the glass will remain unaffected.

(ii) (a) When the liquid denser than water is filled in the glass, then the volume of water formed by the melting of ice will be more than the volume of liquid displaced, so the level of water will rise. Therefore, the water will overflow from the glass.

(b) When the liquid lighter than water is filled in the glass, the level of water in the glass will come down. So, the water will not overflow from the glass.

Long Answer Type Questions

1 How does the force of attraction between the two bodies depend upon their masses and distance between them? A student thought that two bricks tied together would fall faster than a single one under the action of gravity. Do you agree with his hypothesis or not? Comment. NCERT Exemplar

Sol. As we know from Newton's law of gravitation, force of attraction between two bodies F is directly proportional to the product of their masses, and inversely proportional to the square of the distance between their centre.

i.e. $F \propto m_1 m_2$ and $F \propto \frac{1}{r^2}$

The hypothesis of the student is wrong. This is because acceleration due to gravity, with which bricks fall does not depend upon the mass of the body. So, the two bricks tied together would not fall faster than a single one.

2 (i) (a) **What is the expression for the acceleration due to gravity on the surface of the Earth?**

(b) **If the acceleration due to gravity on the surface of the earth is 9.8 m/s^2, calculate the acceleration due to gravity at a height equal to the radius of the Earth above its surface.**

(c) **If the acceleration due to gravity on the earth's surface is 9.8 m/s^2. Calculate the value of acceleration due to gravity at a depth of 1600 km below the earth's surface (Radius of the Earth = 6400 km).**

Or

(ii) (a) **What is weightlessness? Explain the concept with an example.**

(b) **An astronaut in a space station orbiting earth feels weightless. If the space station orbits at an altitude of 400 km, calculate the gravitational force experience by the astronaut of mass 70 kg. (Radius of the earth = 6400 km mass of the earth = 5.972×10^{24} kg, G = 6.674×10^{-11} Nm^2 kg^{-2}).**

(c) **What do you mean by free fall?**

Sol. (i) (a) The acceleration due to gravity, g at the surface of the earth can be derived using Newton's law of gravitation.

$$g = \frac{GM}{R^2}$$

where, G is the gravitational constant, M is the mass of the earth and R is the radius of the Earth.

(b) At a height equal to the radius of the earth above the surface, the distance from the centre of the earth is $2R$.

$$g' = \frac{GM}{(2R)^2} = \frac{GM}{4R^2} = \frac{g}{4}$$

$$g' = \frac{9.8}{4}$$

$$g' = 2.45 \text{ m/s}^2$$

(c) $g_d = g\left(1 - \frac{d}{R}\right)$

$$g_d = 9.8\left(1 - \frac{1600}{6400}\right)$$

$$g_d = 9.8(1 - 0.25)$$

$$g_d = 9.8 \times 0.75$$

$$g_d = 7.35 \text{ m/s}^2$$

Or

(ii) (a) Weightlessness is the condition in which an object or person experiences no net gravitational force. This occurs when they are in free fall, experiencing only the gravitational force, which is counteracted by their acceleration towards the centre of the earth.

Example An astronaut in orbit around the earth. The astronaut and the space station are both in free fall, moving with the same acceleration due to gravity, creating a sensation of weightlessness.

(b) The distance from the centre of the earth to the space station is

$$R = 6400 + 400 = 6800 \text{ km}$$

$$= 6.8 \times 10^6 \text{ m}$$

The gravitational force F is given by

$$F = \frac{GMm}{R^2}$$

$$F = \frac{6.674 \times 10^{-11} \times 5.972 \times 10^{24} \times 70}{(6.8 \times 10^6)^2}$$

$$F = 6.06 \times 10^2 \text{ N}$$

$$F \approx 606 \text{ N}$$

(c) When an object falls towards the earth under the effect of the earth's gravitational force alone, then such a motion of freely falling object is called free fall.

3 **(i) A steel needle sinks in water but a steel ship floats. Explain how?** [2]

(ii) Why do you prefer a broad and thick handle of your suitcase? [3]

Competency Based Que.

Sol. (i) Ship displaces more water than needle as volume of ship is more than that of needle. Since, upthrust depends on volume of object ($U = Vdg$), so more the volume of object, more upthrust acts on it and object floats.

(ii) Since, pressure acting on the body is inversely proportional to the surface area of contact, i.e.

$$p \propto \frac{1}{A}$$

It means that more the area of contact, less pressure will act on the body. As the broad and the thick handle of our suitcase has large area, due to which less pressure acts on our hand and it is very easy to take from one place to another.

4 **(i) A cube of side 5 cm is immersed in water and then in saturated salt solution. In which case, will it experience a greater buoyant force. If each side of the cube is reduced to 4 cm and then immersed in water, what will be the effect on the buoyant force experienced by the cube as compared to the first case for water. Give reason for each case.** [2½]

(ii) A ball weighing 4 kg of density 4000 kg m^{-3} is completely immersed in water of density 10^{3}kg m^{-3}. Find the force of buoyancy on it. [2½]
(Take, g = 10 ms^{-2})

Competency Based Que.

Sol. (i) The cube will experience a greater buoyant force in saturated salt solution than in water as the density of saturated salt solution is greater than that of water.

As, buoyant force = weight of liquid displaced by the object = ρVg

$$(m = \rho V)$$

As each side of the cube is reduced to 4 cm from 5 cm, so volume of cube decreases and hence, the buoyant force also decreases.

(ii) Mass of ball, $m = 4$ kg

Density of ball, $\rho = 4000 \text{ kg m}^{-3}$

Density of water, $\sigma = 10^3 \text{ kg m}^{-3}$

Volume of the ball

$$= \frac{\text{Mass of the ball}}{\text{Density of the ball}} = \frac{4}{4000} = 10^{-3} \text{ m}^3$$

The buoyant force exerted by the water of density 10^3 kg m^{-3} is given by

$$F_b = \sigma \times V \times g = 10^3 \times 10^{-3} \times 10 = 10 \text{ N}$$

Numerical Questions

1 **A stone dropped from a tree takes 2 s to reach the ground. Find its velocity on striking the ground.**

Sol. Given, initial velocity, $u = 0$, time, $t = 2$ s

Acceleration due to gravity, $a = g = 9.8 \text{ m/s}^2$

and final velocity, $v = ?$

From the first equation of motion,

$$v = u + at = 0 + 9.8 \times 2 = 19.6 \text{ m/s}$$

Thus, stone will strike the ground with velocity 19.6 m/s.

2 **A car falls off a ledge and drops to the ground in 0.5 s ($g = 10\text{ms}^{-2}$).**

(i) What is the speed on striking the ground? [1]

(ii) What is its average speed during 0.5 s? [1]

Sol. Given,

Time taken (t) = 0.5 s

$g = 10 \text{ m/s}^2, \quad u = 0$ (as free fall)

(i) $u = 0, a = g$ from equation of motion

$$v = u + gt$$
$$v = 0 + 10 \times 0.5$$
$$v = 5 \text{m/s}$$

(ii) Average speed $= \frac{u+v}{2} = \frac{0+5}{2} = 2.5$ m/s

3 **A coin is allowed to fall freely from a certain height. It reaches the ground after 0.5 s. What height was it thrown from?**

Sol. From Newton's equation of motion,

$$h = ut + \frac{1}{2}gt^2 \qquad (\text{as, } u = 0)$$

$$h = \frac{1}{2}gt^2 = 0.5 \times 10 \times (0.5)^2 = 1.25 \text{ m}$$

4 **A spacecraft carried a bucket containing soil weighing 60 N from the earth to the surface of moon. When he weighted the soil there on the surface of moon, he found that it was only 10 N. Calculate how much mass of the soil was lost and where did the rest of the soil go?** **Competency Based Que.**

Sol. Given that, the weight of the soil on the earth is 60 N

$g_{\text{earth}} = 10 \text{ ms}^{-2}$

Mass on the earth, $m_1 = \frac{60}{10} = 6\text{kg}$ $\left(m = \frac{W}{g_{earth}}\right)$

Weight of the soil on moon = 10N

$$g_{moon} = \frac{g_{earth}}{6} = \frac{10}{6} \text{ms}^{-2}$$

Mass on the moon, $m_2 = \frac{10 \times 6}{10}$ $\left(m = \frac{W}{g_{moon}}\right)$

$= 6$ kg

Since, $m_1 = m_2$, hence there will be no loss in mass of the soil on the surface of moon and decrease in weight was due to difference in the gravity.

5 A solid weighs 50 gf in air (where gf is gram force) and 44 gf when completely immersed in water. (Density $\rho = 1000 \text{ kg}/\text{m}^3$)

Calculate

(i) The upthrust [1]

(ii) The volume of the solid [1]

Sol. (i) Upthrust = Weight in air − Weight in water

$= 50 - 44$ (1 gf = 0.0098 N)

$= 6$ gf $= 0.0588$ N

(ii) Let V be the volume.

Upthrust $= V \rho g = V \times 1000 \times 9.8 = 9800\, V$

Now, $9800V = 0.0588$

or, $V = 0.000006 \text{ m}^3 = 6 \text{ cm}^3$

6 A force of 20 N is distributed uniformly on one surface of a cube of edge 10 cm. Find the pressure on this surface.

Sol. Force acting on one surface = Thrust $F = 20$ N

Area of one surface of cube, A

$= 10 \times 10 \times 10^{-4} \text{ m}^2$

$= 100 \times 10^{-4} \text{m}^2$

∴Pressure on this surface,

$$p = \frac{F}{A} = \frac{20}{100 \times 10^{-4}} = 2000 \text{ Pa}$$

7 Which will exert more pressure 100 kg of mass on an area of 10 m^2 or 50 kg of mass on an area of 4 m^2? (Take, $g = 10 \text{ m/s}^2$)

Sol. Given,

$m_1 = 100$ kg

$m_2 = 50$ kg

$A_1 = 10 \text{ m}^2$

$A_2 = 4 \text{ m}^2$

$F_1 = m_1 g = 1000$ N

$F_2 = m_2 g = 500$ N

$$p_1 = \frac{F_1}{A_1} = \frac{1000 \text{ N}}{10 \text{ m}^2} = 100 \text{ Pa}$$

$$p_2 = \frac{F_2}{A_2} = \frac{500}{4 \text{ m}^2} = 125 \text{ Pa}$$

50 kg mass on 4 m^2 exerts more pressure.

8 A ball of mass 8 kg and density 4000 kgm^{-3} is completely immersed in water of density 10^3kg m^{-3}. Find the buoyant force on the ball. (Take, $g = 10 \text{ms}^{-2}$)

Sol. Buoyant force = Weight of water displaced

= Density of water × Volume of water displaced (Volume of ball) × g

$= 1000 \times \frac{8}{4000} \times 10$ $\left[\because \text{Density} = \frac{\text{Mass}}{\text{Volume}}\right]$

$= 20$ N

9 A body weighs 25 kg on the surface of the earth. If the mass of the earth is 6×10^{24}kg, then the radius of the earth is 6.4×10^6m and the gravitational constant is $6.67 \times 10^{-11} \text{ N-m}^2/\text{kg}^2$.

Calculate

(i) the mutual force of attraction between the body and the earth. [1]

(ii) the acceleration produced in the body. [1]

(iii) the acceleration produced in the earth. [1]

Sol. Given, mass of earth, $M_e = 6 \times 10^{24}$ kg

Body weighs, $m = 25$ kg

Radius of earth, $R_e = 6.4 \times 10^6$ m

and gravitational constant,

$$G = 6.67 \times 10^{-11} \text{N-m}^2/\text{kg}^2$$

(i) ∴ Mutual force, $F = G\frac{M_e}{R_e^2}m$

$$= \frac{6.67 \times 10^{-11} \times 6 \times 10^{24} \times 25}{(6.4 \times 10^6)^2} = 244 \text{ N}$$

(ii) ∴ Acceleration produced in the body,

$$a = \frac{F}{m} = \frac{244}{25} = 9.8 \text{ m/s}^2$$

(iii) ∴ Acceleration produced in the earth,

$$a = \frac{F}{M_e} = \frac{244}{6 \times 10^{24}} = 4.06 \times 10^{-23} \text{ m/s}^2$$

10 Two bodies of masses 3 kg and 12 kg are placed at a distance 12 m. A third body of mass 0.5 kg is to be placed at such a point that the force acting on this body is zero. Find the position of that point.

Sol. Given, mass of first body, $m_1 = 3$ kg

and mass of second body, $m_2 = 12$ kg

Let the mass of third body, $m_3 = 0.5$ kg be placed at a distance of x from m_1 as shown in figure.

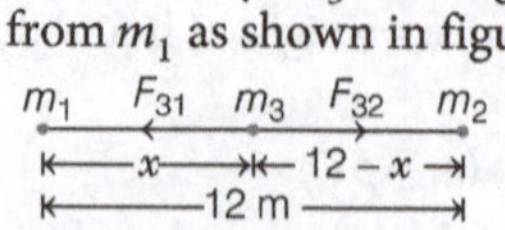

Then, force acting on m_3 due to m_1 is equal and opposite to the force acting on m_3 due to m_2.

$\therefore \quad F_{31} = F_{32}$

$$\frac{Gm_3m_1}{x^2} = \frac{Gm_3m_2}{(12-x)^2} \Rightarrow \frac{3}{x^2} = \frac{12}{(12-x)^2}$$

$$\Rightarrow \left(\frac{12-x}{x}\right)^2 = \frac{12}{3} = 4 \Rightarrow \frac{12-x}{x} = 2$$

$$\Rightarrow \quad 12 - x = 2x \quad \Rightarrow \quad 12 = 3x$$

$$\Rightarrow \quad x = 4 \text{ m}$$

The position of required point is at a distance 4 m from the mass 3 kg.

11 A ball is dropped from the edge of a roof. It takes 0.1s to cross a window of height 2.0 m. Find the height of the roof above the top of the window.

Competency Based Que.

Sol. Let AB be the window and suppose the roof is at a height y above A. Also, suppose it takes a time t_1, for the ball to reach A. The velocity of the ball at A,

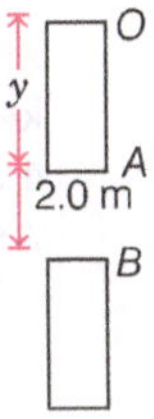

$$v_1 = 0 + gt_1 = 9.8t_1$$

Now, consider the motion of the ball from A to B.

Here, the initial velocity is v_1, the distance covered is 2 m and the time taken is 0.1 s.

From second equation of motion, $s = ut + \frac{1}{2}gt^2$

$$\Rightarrow 2.0 = v_1(0.1) + \frac{1}{2} \times 9.8 \times (0.1)^2 = 9.8t_1(0.1) + 0.049$$

$$\Rightarrow \quad t_1 = 1.99 \approx 2 \text{ s}$$

The height y is $y = \frac{1}{2}gt_1^2 = \frac{1}{2} \times 9.8 \times (2)^2 = 19.6$ m

The roof is at a height 19.6 m above the top of the window.

12 A firecracker is fired and it rises to a height of 1000 m. Find the

(i) velocity by which it was released. [1½]

(ii) time taken by it to reach the highest point. (Take, g = 9.8 m/s²) [1½]

Sol. Given, height, $h = 1000$ m

Final velocity, $v = 0$

Acceleration due to gravity, $g = 9.8 \text{ m/s}^2$

(i) From the third equation of motion, $v^2 = u^2 + 2gh$

$$\Rightarrow \quad 0 = u^2 - 2 \times 9.8 \times 1000$$

$$u = \sqrt{2 \times 9.8 \times 1000} = \sqrt{19600} = 140 \text{ m/s}$$

Velocity by which firecracker is released = 140 m/s

(ii) From the first equation of motion,

$$v = u + gt$$

$$\Rightarrow \quad 0 = 140 - 9.8t \Rightarrow t = \frac{140}{9.8} = 14.28 \text{ s}$$

Time taken, t = 14.28 s

13 A ball is thrown upwards from the ground of a tower with a speed of 20 m/s. There is a window in the tower at the height of 15 m from the ground. How many times and when will the ball pass the window? (Take, g = 10 m/s²) **Competency Based Que.**

Sol. Given, initial velocity, $u = 20$ m/s

Maximum height that the ball will reach, $h = ?$

From the third equation of motion, $v^2 = u^2 + 2gh$

[$\because$ at maximum height, $v = 0$]

$$\Rightarrow \quad h = \frac{-u^2}{2g} = \frac{-(20)^2}{2(-10)} = \frac{400}{20} = 20 \text{ m}$$

This means that ball will reach the height of 20 m and will come back. It will pass the window two times.

Now, to calculate the time that ball will take to reach 15 m height.

From the second equation of upward motion,

$$h = ut - \frac{1}{2}gt^2 \quad [\because g \text{ is in the downward direction}]$$

$$15 = 20t - \frac{1}{2}(10)t^2$$

$$\Rightarrow \quad 5t^2 - 20t + 15 = 0$$

$$t^2 - 4t + 3 = 0$$

$$t^2 - 3t - t + 3 = 0$$

$$t(t-3) - 1(t-3) = 0$$

$$(t-1)(t-3) = 0$$

$$\Rightarrow \quad t = 1, 3$$

Thus, ball will pass the window at 1 s and 3 s, respectively.

14 A ball is thrown up with a speed of 0.6 m/s.

(i) How high will it go before it begins to fall? [1½]

(ii) How long will it take to reach that height? [1½]

Sol. Initial speed, $u = 0.6$ m/s

Acceleration, $g = -9.8 \text{ m/s}^2$

Final speed, $v = 0$

(i) We know, $v^2 - u^2 = 2gh$

$$0 - (0.6)^2 = 2 \times (-9.8) \times h$$

$$-0.36 = -19.6h$$

$$h = \frac{0.36}{19.6} = 0.0183 \text{ m}$$

(ii) Putting the values in the formula,

$$v = u + gt$$

$$0 = 0.6 - 9.8t$$

$$t = \frac{0.6}{9.8} = 0.06 \text{ s}$$

15 What height above the surface of the earth, the value of g becomes 64% of its value at the surface of the earth? (Take, the radius of the earth = 6400 km)

Competency Based Que.

Sol. Let g = acceleration due to gravity at the earth surface.

g_h = acceleration due to gravity at height h

$$= \frac{64}{100} \times g = 0.64\, g$$

$\because$ $$g = \frac{GM}{R_e^2} \quad \text{...(i)}$$

Here, G is gravitational constant, R is radius of earth and M is mass.

Similarly, $$g_h = \frac{GM}{(R_e + h)^2} \quad \text{...(ii)}$$

From Eqs. (i) and (ii), we get

$\therefore$ $$g_h = \frac{gR_e^2}{(R_e + h)^2}$$

$\Rightarrow$ $$0.64\, g = \frac{gR_e^2}{(R_e + h)^2}$$

$\Rightarrow$ $$0.64\,(R_e + h)^2 = R_e^2$$

$\Rightarrow$ $$0.8\,(R_e + h) = R_e$$

$\Rightarrow$ $$0.8h = R_e - 0.8\, R_e = 0.2\, R_e$$

$$h = \frac{2 \times 6400}{8} = 1600 \text{ km} \quad [\because R_e = 6400 \text{ km}]$$

Thus, the height above the surface of the earth is 1600 km.

16 Find the ratio of the pressure exerted by a block of 400 N when placed on a table top along its two different sides with dimensions 20 cm × 10 cm and 10 cm × 15 cm.

Sol. Thrust = Weight = 400 N

Base area1 = 20 cm × 10 cm

$$A_1 = 0.2 \text{ m} \times 0.1 \text{ m} = 0.02 \text{ m}^2$$

Pressure, $$p_1 = \frac{w}{A_1} = \frac{400}{0.02} = 2 \times 10^4 \text{ Pa}$$

Base area 2 = 10 cm × 15 cm

$$A_2 = 0.1 \text{ m} \times 0.15 \text{ cm} = 0.015 \text{ m}^2$$

Pressure, $$p_2 = \frac{w}{A_2} = \frac{400}{0.015} = \frac{80000}{3}$$

$\therefore$ $$\frac{p_1}{p_2} = \frac{2 \times 10^4}{\frac{80000}{3}} = \frac{3}{4}$$

$\therefore$ $p_1 : p_2 = 3 : 4$

17 Shashank placed an iron cuboid of dimensions 4 cm × 7 cm × 10 cm on a tray containing fine sand. He placed the cuboid in such a way that it was made to lie on the sand with its faces of dimensions

(i) 4 cm × 7 cm (ii) 7cm × 10 cm

(iii) and 4 cm × 10 cm

If the density of iron is nearly 8 g cm^{-3} and g = 10 ms^{-2}, find the minimum and maximum pressure as calculated by Shashank. **Competency Based Que.**

Sol. $\therefore$ Mass of cuboid = Volume × Density

$$= (4 \text{ cm} \times 7 \text{ cm} \times 10 \text{ cm}) \times 8 \text{ g cm}^{-3}$$

[$\because$ Volume of cuboid = $l \times b \times h$]

$$= 2240 \text{ g} = 2.24 \text{ kg}$$

Force applied by the cuboid on the sand

$$= mg = 2.24 \times 10 = 22.4 \text{ N} \quad [\because g = 10 \text{ ms}^{-2}]$$

Pressure will be minimum when area of the face of cuboid kept on sand is maximum, i.e. in the case of face with 7 cm × 10 cm.

Area of the face = 7 cm × 10 cm = $\frac{7}{100}$ m × $\frac{10}{100}$ m

$$= 0.07 \text{ m} \times 0.1 \text{ m} = 0.007 \text{ m}^2$$

Minimum pressure $= \frac{\text{Force}}{\text{Area}} = \frac{22.4}{0.007} = 3200 \text{ Nm}^{-2}$

Pressure will be maximum when area of face of cuboid kept on the sand is minimum, i.e. in the case of face with 4 cm × 7cm.

Area of the face = 4 cm × 7 cm

$$= \frac{4}{100} \text{ m} \times \frac{7}{100} \text{ m} = 0.0028 \text{ m}^2$$

Maximum pressure $= \frac{\text{Force}}{\text{Area}} = \frac{22.4}{0.0028} = 8000 \text{ Nm}^{-2}$

18 A cubical tub of side 2 m is full of water. Calculate the total thrust and pressure at the bottom of tank due to water. (Take, density of water = 1000 kg m^{-3} and g = 10 m s^{-2})

Sol. $\therefore$ Volume of cubical tub = Length × Breadth × Height

Here, length = breadth = height = 2 m

$\therefore$ Volume = 2 × 2 × 2 = 8 m^3

Mass of water = Volume × Density of water

$$= 8 \times 1000 = 8000 \text{ kg}$$

$\therefore$ Weight of water

$$= \text{Mass} \times \text{Acceleration due to gravity} = 8000 \times 10 = 8 \times 10^4 \text{ N}$$

$\therefore$ Total thrust = Weight of water = 8×10^4 N

Area of bottom = Area of square shape of tub

$$= 2 \times 2 = 4 \text{ m}^2$$

$\therefore$ Pressure of water at the bottom $= \frac{\text{Force}}{\text{Area}} = \frac{\text{Weight}}{\text{Area}}$

$$= \frac{8 \times 10^4}{4} = 2 \times 10^4 \text{ Pa}$$

19 A boat of mass 50 kg is floating in the river with $\left(\frac{1}{2}\right)$ nd of its volume inside the water. Calculate the buoyant force acting on the boat. (Take, g = 10 ms^{-2})

Sol. Given, mass of the boat, m = 50 kg

As we know that, when a body floats in river, its apparent weight is zero.

Therefore, buoyant force = weight of body

$$= mg = 50 \times 10$$

i.e. Buoyant force = 500 N

20 A cubical object of side 4 cm has fallen in a well. If mass of the cube is 2 kg, then state whether this object will float or sink in water. (Take, density of water 1000 kg m^{-3})

Sol. Given that,

Mass of the object, $m = 2$ kg

Side of cube = 4 cm = 0.04 m $[\because 1\text{ m} = 100\text{ cm}]$

Since, volume of cube = $(\text{side})^3$

$\therefore$ Volume of the object, $V = (0.04\text{ m})^3 = 0.000064\text{ m}^3$

As we know that,

$$\text{Density} = \frac{\text{Mass of the object}}{\text{Volume of the object}}$$

$$\Rightarrow \text{Density} = \frac{2}{0.000064}\text{ kgm}^{-3}$$
$$= \frac{2000000}{64}\text{ kgm}^{-3} = 31250\text{ kgm}^{-2}$$

Here, density of the object (i.e. 31250 kg m^{-3}) is greater than the density of water (i.e. 1000 kg m^{-3}).

Therefore, the object will sink in water.

21 A ball filled with air has a volume of 500 cm^3. Calculate the minimum force applied by a child to put it completely inside the water. (Take, g = 10 ms^{-2})

Sol. Given that,

Volume, $V = 500\text{ cm}^3 = 500 \times 10^{-6}\text{ m}^3$,

$g = 10\text{ ms}^{-2}, F = ?$

Force required to put the ball inside the water
= Buoyant force
= Weight of water displaced $= mg$ ...(i)

Now, we know that,

Mass of water = Density of water × Volume

$m = \rho V$

On substituting this value in Eq. (i), we get

Force $= \rho V g$

$= (1000\text{ kg m}^{-3}) \times (500 \times 10^{-6}\text{ m}^3) \times (10\text{ ms}^{-2})$

$= 1000 \times 500 \times 10^{-6} \times 10\text{ N} = 5\text{ N}$

$\therefore$ Minimum force applied by a child to put the ball completely inside the water is 5 N.

22 (i) A person weighs 110.84 N on the moon, whose acceleration due to gravity is 1/6 of that the earth. If the value of g on the earth is 9.8 m/s^2, then calculate

(a) g' on the moon

(b) mass of person on the moon

(c) weight of person on the earth [3]

(ii) How is the value of g on the earth related to the mass of the earth and its radius? Derive it. [2]

Sol. (i) (a) g on the moon is given by

$$g' = \frac{g}{6} = \frac{9.8}{6} = 1.63\text{ m/s}^2$$

(b) Given, a person weighs on the moon = 110.84 N

Mass of the person on the moon,

$$m = \frac{110.84}{1.63} = 68\text{ kg}$$

(c) Weight of person on the earth $= mg$

$= 68 \times 9.8 = 666.4\text{ N-m}^2/\text{kg}^2$

(ii) Value of g on earth is related to the mass of the earth and its radius.

Derivation

From Newton's law of gravitation,

$$F = \frac{GMm}{R^2} \quad \text{...(i)}$$

Here, M is mass of earth, object having mass m is falling towards it and R is the distance between centres of earth and the object.

From second law of motion, force exerted on an object, $F = ma$

Since, $a = g$ (i.e. acceleration due to gravity)

$$F = mg \quad \text{...(ii)}$$

Equating RHS of Eqs. (i) and (ii), we get

$$mg = \frac{GMm}{R^2}$$

$$g = \frac{GM}{R^2}$$

23 The radius of the earth at the poles is 6357 km and the radius at the equator is 6378 km. Calculate the percentage change in the weight of a body when it is taken from the equator to the poles.

Sol. Let acceleration due to gravity at equator, $g_e = \frac{GM_e}{R_e^2}$

and acceleration due to gravity at poles, $g_p = \frac{GM_e}{R_p^2}$

The variation of acceleration due to gravity,

$$\Delta g = g_p - g_e = GM_e\left(\frac{1}{R_p^2} - \frac{1}{R_e^2}\right)$$

$$\text{Percentage variation in } g = \frac{GM_e\left(\frac{1}{R_p^2} - \frac{1}{R_e^2}\right)}{\frac{GM_e}{R_e^2}} \times 100$$

$$= \frac{R_e^2 - R_p^2}{R_e^2 R_p^2} \times 100 \times R_e^2 = \frac{R_e^2 - R_p^2}{R_p^2} \times 100$$

$$= \frac{(6378)^2 - (6357)^2}{(6357)^2} \times 100 \approx 0.7\%$$

$\therefore$ % variation in the weight of a body

% change in $g = 0.7\%$

24 (i) At some moment, two giant planets jupiter and saturn of the solar system are in the same line as seen from the earth. Find the total gravitational force due to them on a person of mass 50 kg on the earth. Could the force due to the planets be important? [3]

Mass of the jupiter $= 2\times 10^{27}$ kg

Mass of the saturn $= 6\times 10^{26}$ kg

Distance of jupiter from the earth

$= 6.3\times 10^{11}$ m

Distance of saturn from the earth

$= 1.28\times 10^{12}$ m

Gravitational constant,

$G = 6.67\times 10^{-11}$ N - m^2 / kg^2

Acceleration due to gravity on the earth

$= 9.8$ m / s^2

(ii) A bag of sugar weighs *w* at a certain place on the equator. If this bag is taken to Antarctica, then will it weigh the same or more or less. Give a reason for your answer. [2]

Competency Based Que.

Sol. (i) (a) Gravitational force acting on the 50 kg,

$mg = 50\times 9.8 = 490$ N

(b) Gravitational force acting on the 50 kg mass due to jupiter,

$$F_{\text{jupiter}} = \frac{G\times M_{\text{jupiter}}\times M_{\text{person}}}{(\text{Distance of jupiter from the earth})^2}$$

$$F_{\text{jupiter}} = \frac{6.67\times 10^{-11}\times 2\times 10^{27}\times 50}{6.3\times 10^{11}\times 6.3\times 10^{11}}$$

$$F_{\text{jupiter}} = \frac{6.67\times 2\times 50\times 10^{-11+27-22}}{6.3\times 6.3}$$

$$F_{\text{jupiter}} = 1.68\times 10^{-5}\text{ N}$$

(c) Gravitational force acting on the 50 kg mass due to saturn

$$F_{\text{saturn}} = \frac{G\times M_{\text{saturn}}\times M_{\text{person}}}{(\text{Distance of saturn from the earth})^2}$$

$$F_{\text{saturn}} = \frac{6.67\times 10^{-11}\times 6\times 10^{26}\times 50}{1.28\times 10^{12}\times 1.28\times 10^{12}}$$

$$F_{\text{saturn}} = \frac{6.67\times 6\times 50}{1.28\times 1.28}\times 10^{-11+26-24}$$

$$F_{\text{saturn}} = 0.12\times 10^{-5}\text{ N}$$

$\therefore$ Total gravitational force due to the jupiter and the saturn $= (1.68\times 10^{-5} + 0.12\times 10^{-5})$ N

$= 1.8\times 10^{-5}$ N

Thus, the combined force due to the planets jupiter and saturn (1.8×10^{-5}) N is negligible as compared to the gravitational force due to the earth.

(ii) We know that, g at equator is less than g at poles (Antarctica). Thus, weight at equator is less than weight at pole (Antarctica). A bag of sugar weighs w at a certain place on the equator. If this bag is taken to Antarctica, then it will weigh more due to greater value of g.

25 A stone is dropped from the edge of a roof.

(i) How long does it take to fall 4.9 m? [2]

(ii) How fast does it move at the end of that fall? [1]

(iii) How fast does it move at the end of 7.9 m? [1]

(iv) What is its acceleration after 1s and after 2 s? [1]

Sol. Given, initial velocity, $u = 0$

Acceleration, $g = 9.8$ m/s^2

Distance, $s = 4.9$ m

(i) We have, $s = ut + \frac{1}{2}gt^2$

$$4.9 = 0\times t + \frac{1}{2}\times 9.8\times t^2 \Rightarrow t^2 = \frac{9.8}{9.8} = 1 \Rightarrow t = 1\text{ s}$$

The stone takes 1 s to fall 4.9 m.

(ii) We have, $v^2 - u^2 = 2as$

$$v^2 - 0^2 = 2\times 9.8\times 4.9 \Rightarrow v = \sqrt{96.04} = 9.8\text{ m/s}$$

At the end of 4.9 m, stone will be moving at a speed of 9.8 m/s.

(iii) We have, $v^2 - u^2 = 2as$

$$v^2 - 0^2 = 2\times 9.8\times 7.9 \Rightarrow v = 12.44\text{ m/s}$$

The stone will be moving with a speed of 12.44 m/s at the end of 7.9 m

(iv) During the free fall, the acceleration produced in a body remains constant.

So, acceleration after 1 s $= 9.8$ m/s^2

Acceleration after 2 s $= 9.8$m/s^2

26 A particle weighs 120 N on the surface of the earth. At what height above the earth's surface will its weight be 30 N? (Radius of the earth = 6400 km)

Sol. Let the weight of the particle on the surface of the earth,

$$w = 120 = \frac{GMm}{R^2}$$

Hence, $$120 = \frac{GMm}{R^2} \quad \text{...(i)}$$

Let the height h above the earth's surface, where its weight will be 30 N.

Hence, $$30 = \frac{GMm}{(h+R)^2} \quad \text{...(ii)}$$

On dividing Eq. (i) by Eq. (ii), we get

$$\frac{120}{30} = \frac{GMm}{R^2}\times\frac{(h+R)^2}{GMm}$$

$$\frac{4}{1} = \frac{(h+R)^2}{R^2} \Rightarrow 2 = \frac{h+R}{R} \Rightarrow 2R = h + R$$

$\Rightarrow$ $h = 2R - R = R = 6400$ km (given)

$= 6.4\times 10^6$ m

ASSESSMENT EXERCISE

Competency Focused (Objective) Questions

Multiple Type Questions

1 Newton's law of gravitation is universal law because it
(a) acts on all bodies and particles on the earth
(b) acts on all the masses at all distances and not affected by the medium
(c) is always attractive
(d) None of the above

2 Gravitational force between two objects is 10 N. If masses of both objects are doubled without changing distance between them, then the gravitational force would become
(a) 2.5 N (b) 20 N
(c) 40 N (d) 10 N

3 Which of the given graphs correctly represents the variation of g on earth? **Competency Based Que.**

(a)
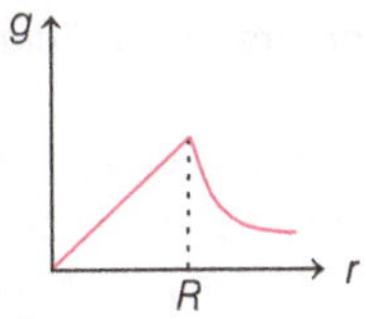

(b)
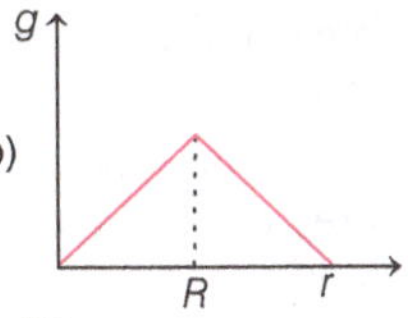

(c)
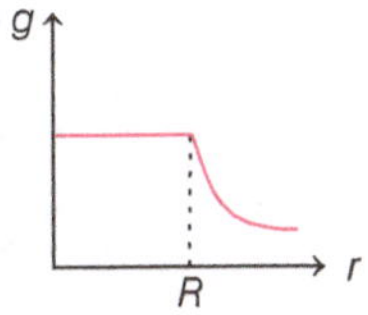

(d)
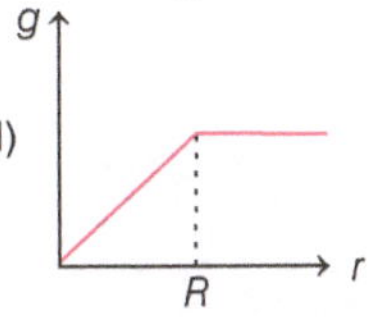

4 Three spheres have radii 1 cm, 2 cm and 3 cm, respectively. Which sphere exerts maximum pressure on earth ?
(a) First (b) Second
(c) Third (d) All are equal

5 When a body is dipped completely or partially into a liquid, then weight (w) of the liquid displaced by the body and upthrust force on the body into the liquid are related as
(a) $w = F$ (b) $w < F$
(c) $w > F$ (d) None of these

Assertion-Reason Questions

Direction (Q.Nos. 6-8) *In each of the following questions, a statement of Assertion is given by the corresponding statement of Reason. Of the statements, mark the correct answer as*

(a) If both Assertion and Reason are true and Reason is the correct explanation of Assertion.
(b) If both Assertion and Reason are true, but Reason is not the correct explanation of Assertion.
(c) If Assertion is true, but Reason is false.
(d) If Assertion is false, but Reason is true.

6 **Assertion** (A) At the centre of earth, the value of gravitational acceleration is zero.
Reason (R) On going below the earth surface, the value of gravitational acceleration increases.

7 **Assertion** (A) To float, a body must displace liquid whose weight is greater than actual weight of the body.
Reason (R) During floating, the body will experience no net downward force in that case.

8 **Assertion** (A) A balloon filled with hydrogen gas floats in the air.
Reason Upthrust acting on the balloon is greater than weight of the balloon.

Answers

1. (b) **2.** (c) **3.** (a) **4.** (a) **5.** (a) **6.** (c) **7.** (b) **8.** (a)

Case Based/Source Based Question

Direction (Q.No. 9) *Answer the question on the basis of your **understanding** of the following paragraph and related studied concepts:*

9 Weight is the force acting vertically downwards. Here, the force is acting perpendicular to the surface of the contact. The force acting on an object perpendicular to the surface is called thrust. When you stand on loose sand, the force that is the weight of your body is acting on an area equal to area of your feet. When you lie down, the same force acts on an area equal to the contact area of your whole body, which is larger than the area of your feet. Thus, the effects of forces of the same magnitude on different areas are different. The effect of thrust depends on the area on which it acts. The effect of thrust on sand is larger while standing than while lying.

(i) When you stand on loose sand, your feet go deep into sand and why?
(ii) According to given passage, when will the effect of thrust on sand be larger?
(iii) What happens when you lie down on loose sand?
(iv) When you stand on loose sand, then what is the direction of force acting on that area ?

Constructed Response (Descriptive) Questions

Very Short Answer Type Questions

10 Does the force of gravitation exist at all the places of the universe?

11 The gravitational force between two objects is *F*. How will the force change when the distance between them is reduced to (1/4)th? **Competency Based Que.**

12 Weight of an object at a given place can be measure of its mass. Comment.

13 Is the volume of liquid displaced always equal to the volume of the body immersed in the liquid?

14 An object is immersed in three different liquids. Will it experience same buoyant force due to all the liquids? **Competency Based Que.**

Short Answer Type Questions

15 A sphere of mass 40 kg is attracted by a second sphere of mass 15 kg when their centres are 320 cm apart with a force of 0.1 milligram weight. Calculate the value of gravitational constant. [**Ans.** 1.7×10^{-8} N-m^2/kg^2]

16 Does the acceleration of a freely falling object depend to any extent on the location, i.e. whether the object is on top of Mount Everest or in Death Valley of California? Explain. **Competency Based Que.**

17 Find the ratio of weights of a body on the earth and jupiter, given *g* on jupiter is 2.5 times that on the earth.

18 A man is asked to run with a bag containing 20 kg steel block. Will it be easier for him to run with 20 kg cotton replacing the block? Explain with reason.

19 A test tube floats in water with a small coin at its bottom. The mass of this test tube is equal to mass of seven coins and external volume is 16 cm^3. It just sinks when the third coin is added. Calculate the mass of each coin. (Density of water is 1g cm^{-3}) [**Ans.** 1.78 g] **Competency Based Que.**

Long Answer Type Questions

20 What is upthrust? What are the quantities that can vary upthrust? How does it account for the floating of a body? When a partially immersed body is pressed down a little, what will happen to the upthrust?

21 (i) How does a boat float in water?

(ii) State two factors on which magnitude of buoyant force acting on a body, immersed in a fluid depends.

(iii) A block of wood can float while a similar sized block of concrete can be used as an anchor. Why? **Competency Based Que.**

CHAPTER 10

Work and Energy

In this chapter, we will study about scientific conception of work and its mathematical formula along with we will also study two scientific concepts which are closely related to work, i.e. energy and power.

10.1 Work

Work is said to be done, when an object is displaced from its position by applying a force. Object is always displaced in the direction of net force.

Scientific Conception of Work

From the point of view of science, following two conditions need to be satisfied for work

(i) A force should act on an object.

(ii) The object must be displaced.

If any one of the above conditions does not exist, work is not done.

e.g. A girl pulls a trolley and the trolley moves through a distance. In this way, she has exerted a force on the trolley and it is displaced. Hence, the work is done.

Work Done by a Constant Force

Work done by a force on an object is equal to the magnitude of the force multiplied by the distance moved in the direction of force.

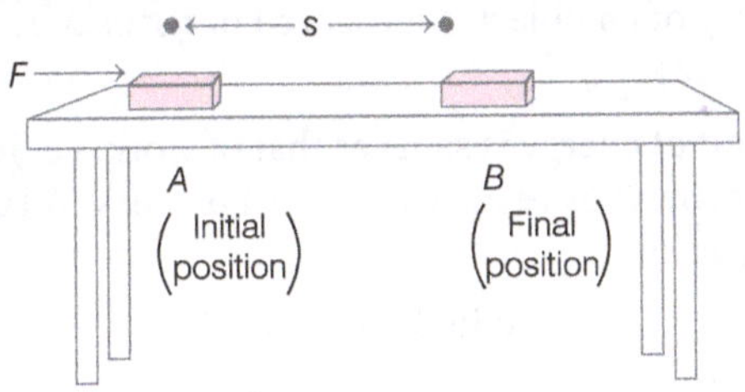

Work done by a force when the body moves in the direction of force

Let us assume that a constant force F acts on an object at point A (shown in the figure), due to which the object gets displaced through a distance s in the direction of the force and reaches at point B, then the work done (W) by force (F) on that object will be equal to the product of the force and displacement.

Work done = Force × Displacement in the direction of force

or $\quad W = F \times s \quad$ ...(i)

SI Unit of Work

The SI unit of work is **Newton-metre** (N-m) which is also called **Joule** (J).

If $F = 1$ N and $s = 1$ m, then the work done by the force will be 1 N-m or 1J.

Thus, 1 J is the amount of work done on an object when a force of 1 N displaces it by 1 m along the direction of net force.

$$1 \text{ Joule} = 1 \text{ Newton} \times 1 \text{ metre} \Rightarrow 1\text{J} = 1\text{N-m}$$

Work is a **scalar quantity**, it has only magnitude and no direction.

Example 1. **A force of 10 N is acting on an object. The object is displaced through 5 m in the direction of force. What is the work done in this case?**

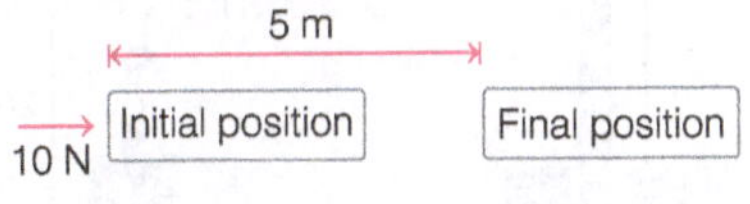

Sol. Given, force, $F = 10$ N, displacement, $s = 5$ m

$\therefore$ Work done, $W = F \times s = 10 \times 5 = 50$ N-m or 50 J

Positive, Negative and Zero Work

- When the force F and displacement s are in the same direction (angle between direction of force and displacement is 0°), work done will be **positive**, i.e. work is done by the force.
  e.g. a boy pulls an object towards himself.
  $$W = +F \times s$$
- When the force F and displacement s are in opposite direction (angle between direction of force and displacement is 180°), work done will be **negative**, i.e. work is done against the force.
  e.g. frictional force acts in the direction opposite to the direction of displacement, so work done by friction will be negative.
  $$W = -F \times s$$
- When the force and displacement are in perpendicular direction (angle between direction of force and displacement is 90°), work done is **zero**.
  e.g. a coolie carrying load on his head. In this case, gravitational force is acting vertically downward (weight of load) and displacement is along horizontal direction, i.e. force and displacement are perpendicular to each other.
  Thus, work done by gravitational force is zero.
  $$W = 0$$

Note When a body moves along a circular path, the angle between the force (along radius of circle) and the direction of motion (along tangent of circle) is 90°. Hence, no work is done by a body along circular path.

Example 2. **A crane lifts a crate upwards through a height of 20 m. The lifting force provided by the crane is 5 kN. How much work is done by the force?**

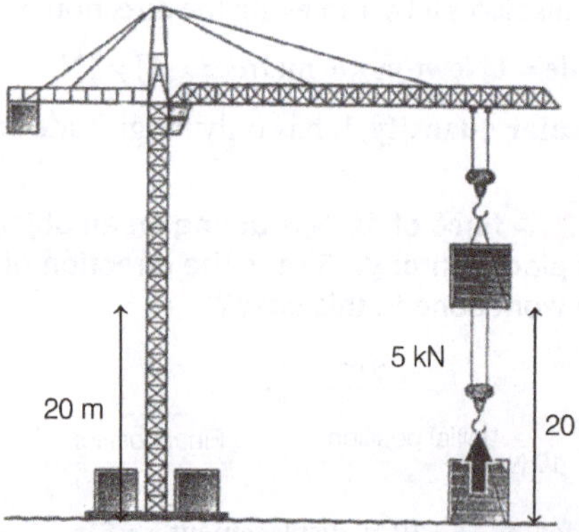

Sol. Given, force, $F = 5 \text{ kN} = 5000 \text{ N}$

Displacement, $s = 20$ m, Work done, $W = ?$

We know that work done, $W = Fs$

Here, force and displacement are in same direction.

So, $W = Fs \Rightarrow W = 5000 \times 20 = 100000$ J

So, the work done by the force is 100000 J or 100 kJ.

Example 3. **A cyclist comes to a skidding stop in 10 m. During the process the force on the cycle due to road is 200 N and is directly opposed to the motion. How much work is done by road on the cycle?**

Sol. Given, $F = 200$ N; $s = 10$ m

$$\theta = 180°$$
$$W = Fs\cos\theta = 200 \times 10 \times \cos 180°$$
$$= -200 \text{ J}$$

Example 4. **What is the work done by a man in carrying a suitcase weighing 30 kg over his head when he travels distance of 10 m in the horizontal direction?**

Sol. Here, $\theta = 90°$

So, work done $= Fs\cos\theta$

$$= Fs\cos 90°$$
$$= 0$$

Try These 10.1

1. **Give two necessary conditions without which work is not said to be done in science.**
2. **Fill in the blank.**
   .... work is done by a coolie to carry load on his head.
3. **What is the work done on a body for a displacement 100 cm against 10 N friction force.** [Ans. −10 N -m]
4. **When is the work done said to be negative?**
5. **A boy pushes wooden box and displaced it by 2 m with force of 50N, calculate the work done by boy on box.** [Ans. 100 N -m]

10.2 Energy

It is the ability to do work. It is always essential for performing any mechanical work.

The energy of an object is measured in terms of its capacity of doing work.

The SI unit of energy is same as that of work, i.e. **Joule** (J). 1 joule of energy is required to do 1 J of work. A larger unit of energy is kJ.

$$1 \text{kilo joule (kJ)} = 10^3 \text{ J}$$

The object which does the work, losses energy and the object on which work is done, gains energy.

Work done against a force is therefore stored as energy.

e.g. ▪ When a fast moving cricket ball hits a stationary wicket, the wicket is thrown away.

▪ When a raised hammer strikes on a nail placed on a piece of wood, it drives the nail into the wood.

The Sun is the biggest natural source of energy to us. We can also get energy from the nuclei of atoms, the interior of the Earth and the tides in the ocean.

Forms of Energy

Energy exists in various forms like mechanical energy (the sum of potential energy and kinetic energy), heat energy, chemical energy, electrical energy and light energy.

Kinetic Energy

The energy which is possessed by an object due to its motion is called kinetic energy. Its **SI unit** is joule **(J)**.

Kinetic energy of a body moving with certain velocity is equal to the work done on it to make it acquire that velocity. Kinetic energy of an object increases with its speed.

Some examples of kinetic energy are

- Due to kinetic energy, a bullet fired from a gun can pierce a target.
- A moving hammer, drives a nail into the wood. Due to its motion, it has kinetic energy or ability to do work.
- A running horse has kinetic energy.
- A flowing river possesses kinetic energy.

The kinetic energy possessed by an object of mass m, moving with a uniform velocity v is given by,

$$\text{KE (or } E_K) = \frac{1}{2}mv^2$$

Calculation of Kinetic Energy

The kinetic energy of an object moving with a certain velocity is equal to the work done on it to make it acquire that velocity.

Consider an object of mass m moving with a uniform velocity u. A force F is applied on it which displaces it through a distance s and it attains a velocity v.

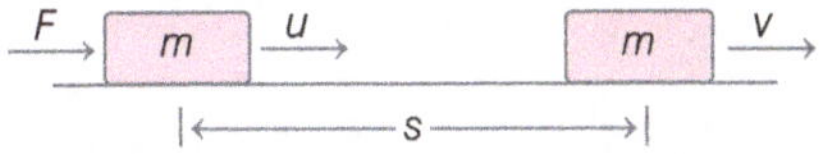

Then, work is done to increase its velocity from u to v.

$$W = Fs \quad \text{...(i)}$$

According to the third equation of motion,

$$v^2 - u^2 = 2as$$

$$\therefore \quad s = \frac{v^2 - u^2}{2a} \quad \text{...(ii)}$$

where, a is uniform acceleration, u is initial velocity and v is final velocity.

Also from, $F = ma$ ...(iii)

Substituting the values of F and s from Eqs. (ii) and (iii) in Eq. (i), we have

$$W = ma \cdot \frac{v^2 - u^2}{2a} \quad \text{or} \quad W = \frac{1}{2}m(v^2 - u^2)$$

This is known as **work-energy theorem** (i.e. total work is equal to change in kinetic energy).

If initial velocity, $u = 0$

Then, $W = \frac{1}{2}mv^2$

This work done is equal to the kinetic energy of the object.

$$\therefore \quad \text{KE (or } E_K) = \frac{1}{2}mv^2$$

Some important results can be derived from the formula $\text{KE} = \frac{1}{2}mv^2$, these are given below :

(i) If the mass of an object is doubled, its kinetic energy also gets doubled.

(ii) If the mass of an object is halved, its kinetic energy also gets halved.

(iii) If the speed of an object is doubled, its kinetic energy becomes four times.

(iv) If the speed of an object is halved, its kinetic energy becomes one-fourth.

(v) Heavy objects moving with high speed have more kinetic energy than small objects moving with same speed.

Example 5. A bullet of mass 8 g is fired with a velocity of 80 ms^{-1}. Calculate its kinetic energy.

Sol. Given, mass, $m = 8\text{ g} = \frac{8}{1000}$ kg and velocity, $v = 80\text{ ms}^{-1}$

$$\text{KE of the bullet} = \frac{1}{2}mv^2 = \frac{1}{2} \times \frac{8}{1000} \times (80)^2$$

$$= \frac{1}{2} \times \frac{8}{1000} \times 80 \times 80$$

$$= 25.6\text{ J}$$

Example 6. **If a body of mass 5 kg is moving along a straight line with velocity 10 ms^{-1} and acceleration 20 ms^{-2}. Find its kinetic energy (KE) after 10 s.**

Sol. Given, mass of the body, $m = 5$ kg

Initial velocity, $u = 10\ ms^{-1}$

Acceleration, $a = 20\ ms^{-2}$

Time, $t = 10$ s Velocity, $v = ?$; KE = ?

First, we use equation of motion, $v = u + at$ to find v.

Then, we use $KE = \frac{1}{2}mv^2$ to find kinetic energy.

So, $v = u + at\ ms^{-1}$ ...(i)

As we know, kinetic energy, $KE = \frac{1}{2}mv^2$ ...(ii)

So, $KE = \frac{1}{2}m \times (u + at)^2$ [from Eqs. (i) and (ii)]

$\Rightarrow KE = \frac{1}{2} \times 5 \times (10 + 20 \times 10)^2$

$\Rightarrow KE = \frac{1}{2} \times 5 \times 210 \times 210$

$= 110250$ J

Example 7. **What is the work done to increase the velocity of a van from 10 m/s to 20 m/s, if the mass of the van is 2000 kg?**

Sol. Given, $m = 2000$ kg, $v_1 = 10\ ms^{-1}$ and $v_2 = 20\ ms^{-1}$

The initial kinetic energy of the van

$KE_1 = \frac{1}{2}mv_1^2$ [$\because KE = \frac{1}{2}mv^2$]

$= \frac{1}{2} \times 2000 \times (10)^2 = 100000\ J = 100\ kJ$

Final kinetic energy of the van

$KE_2 = \frac{1}{2}mv_2^2 = \frac{1}{2} \times 2000 \times (20)^2$

$= 400000\ J = 400\ kJ$

The work done = Change in kinetic energy

$= 400 - 100 = 300\ kJ$

So, the kinetic energy of van increases by 300 kJ when it speeds up from 10 ms^{-1} to 20 ms^{-1}.

Potential Energy

The energy possessed by a body due to its change in position or shape is called **potential energy.** Its SI unit is **joule** (J).

We can say that, the potential energy possessed by a body is the energy present in it by virtue of its position or configuration, e.g. a stretched rubber band, spring, string on the bow, etc.

Now, we can say that a body possesses energy even when it is not in motion.

Some examples of potential energy are

- Water stored in dam has potential energy due to its position at the height.
- A stone lying on the roof of the building has potential energy due to its height.
- A wound spring of a watch has potential energy due to change in its shape.

Potential Energy of an Object at a Height

When an object is raised through a certain height above the ground, its energy increases. This is because work is done on it against gravity while it is being raised.

The energy present in such an object is the **gravitational potential energy.**

The gravitational potential energy of an object at a point above the ground is defined as the work done in raising it from the ground to that point against gravity.

Expression for Potential Energy

Consider an object of mass m, lying at a point A on the Earth's surface. Here, its potential energy is zero and its weight mg acts vertically downwards.

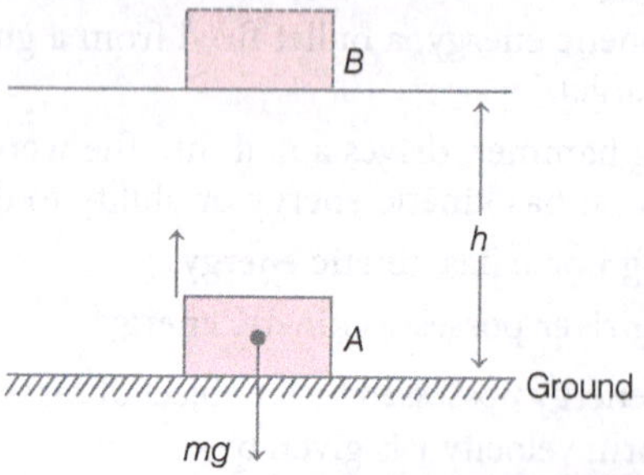

To lift the object to another position B at a height h, we have to apply a minimum force which is equal to mg in the upward direction. So, work is done on the body against the force of gravity. Therefore,

Work done = Force × Displacement

or $W = F \times s$

As, $F = mg$ [weight of the body]

Here, $s = h$

Therefore, $W = mg \times h = mgh$

i.e. $PE = mgh$

This work done is equal to the gain in energy of the body. This is the potential energy (PE) of the body.

$\therefore$ $PE \text{ (or } E_P) = mgh$

The potential energy of an object at a height depends on the ground level or the zero level we choose.

An object in a given position can have a certain potential energy with respect to one level and a different value of potential energy with respect to another level.

The work done by gravity depends on the difference in vertical heights of the initial and final positions of the objects and not on the path along which the object is moved. It is clear from the figure given below.

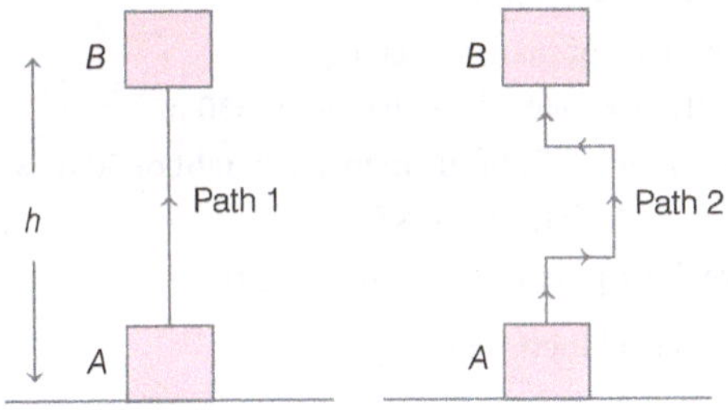

In both the above situations, the work done on the object is *mgh*.

Example 8. **Suppose you have a body of mass 1 kg in your hand. To what height will you raise it, so that it may acquire a gravitational potential energy of 1 J? (Take, $g = 10 \text{ ms}^{-2}$)**

Sol. Given, PE = 1 J, mass, $m = 1$ kg,

Acceleration due to gravity, $g = 10 \text{ ms}^{-2}$, $h = ?$

We know that, $PE = mgh$ or $1 = 1 \times 10 \times h$

$\therefore$ Height, $h = \frac{1}{1 \times 10} = 0.1 \text{ m} = 10 \text{ cm}$

Example 9. **A boy weighing 40 kg climbs up a vertical height of 200 m. Calculate the amount of work done by him. How much potential energy does he gain? (Take, $g = 9.8 \text{ ms}^{-2}$)**

Sol. Given that, mass, $m = 40$ kg

Acceleration due to gravity, $g = 9.8 \text{ ms}^{-2}$, height, $h = 200$ m

Work done by the body $= mgh = 40 \times 9.8 \times 200$

$= 78400 \text{ J} = 7.84 \times 10^4 \text{ J}$

Gain in PE = Work done $= 7.84 \times 10^4$ J

Example 10. **Suppose two bodies *A* and *B* having equal masses are kept at heights of *h* and 3 *h*, respectively. Find the ratio of their potential energies.**

Sol. Let the mass of each body be *m*.

PE of body $A = mgh$; PE of body $B = mg \times 3h$

Ratio of their potential energies $= \frac{mgh}{mg \times 3h} = \frac{1}{3} = 1:3$

Try These 10.2

1. **When is an object said to possess energy?**
2. **State True and False for the following statements:**
   (i) The kinetic energy of an object becomes one-third, if its speed is halved.
   (ii) When an object is raised through a certain height above the ground, its energy decreases.
3. **Name the type of energy possessed by the water stored in a dam.**
4. **Two persons reach the top of a building, one by using lift and other by using staircases of building. What will be the change in potential energy of the two?**
5. **If an engine supplies 100 J of energy to a mass of 200 g, how high can it be lifted? (Given, $g = 9.8 \text{ ms}^{-2}$)**

10.3 Law of Conservation of Energy

The law of conservation of energy states that **energy can neither be created nor be destroyed, it can only be transformed from one form to another.**

The total energy before and after transformation always remains constant.

Conservation of Energy During the Free Fall of a Body

Consider an object of mass *m*, lying at position *B*. It is made to fall freely from a height (*h*) above the ground, as shown in figure .

At point *B*

At the start, the potential energy is *mgh* and kinetic energy is zero (as its velocity is zero). i.e. $PE = mgh$

$KE = 0$

$\therefore$ Total energy, $TE = PE + KE = mgh$

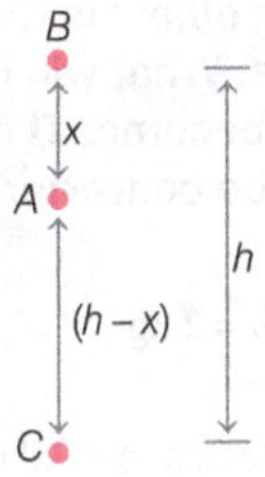

At point *A*

As it falls, its potential energy will change into kinetic energy. If v is the velocity of the object at a given instant, its kinetic energy would be $\frac{1}{2}mv^2$.

$$PE = mg\,(h - x)$$

From Newton's third equation of motion,

$$v^2 = u^2 + 2gx$$

$$\Rightarrow \quad v^2 = 2gx \qquad [\because u = 0]$$

$$KE = \frac{1}{2}\,mv^2 = \frac{1}{2}m \times 2gx = mgx \qquad [\because v^2 = 2gx]$$

$\therefore$ Total energy $= mg\,(h - x) + mgx = mgh$

Total energy, TE $= mgh$

At point C

As the fall of the object continues, the potential energy would decrease while the kinetic energy would increase. When the object is about to reach the ground, $h = 0$ and v will be the highest.

$$PE = 0$$

$$KE = \frac{1}{2}mv^2 = \frac{1}{2}m(2gh) = mgh \qquad [\because v^2 = 2gh]$$

$\therefore$ Total energy, TE $= mgh$

Thus, the sum of the potential energy and kinetic energy of the object would be the same at all points, i.e.

$$PE + KE = \text{constant}$$

or $\quad mgh + \frac{1}{2}mv^2 = \text{constant}$

This verifies the law of conservation of energy.

The sum of kinetic energy and potential energy of an object is also called **mechanical energy**.

We observe that, during the free fall of an object, the decrease in potential energy at any point in its path appears as an equal amount of increase in kinetic energy.

Thus, we can say that, there is a continuous transformation of gravitational potential energy into kinetic energy.

Example 11. **A 2 kg object is thrown vertically upward with a speed of 10 m/s. What will be its height at the point, where its speed becomes 0 m/s? (At this point, all the kinetic energy will be converted into potential energy)**

Sol. Given,

Mass of the object, $m = 2$ kg

Initial speed, $u = 10$ m/s

Gravitational acceleration, $g = 9.8$ m/s^2

The initial kinetic energy is given by:

$$KE = \frac{1}{2}mu^2$$

$$KE = \frac{1}{2} \times 2 \times (10)^2 = 100\text{ J}$$

At the highest point KE = 0, so all of the initial kinetic energy becomes potential energy.

$$PE = KE = 100\text{ J}$$

Potential energy is given by

$$PE = mgh$$

Substitute the values,

$$100 = 2 \times 9.8 \times h$$

$$100 = 19.6 \times h$$

$$h = \frac{100}{19.6} \approx 5.1\text{ m}$$

Example 12. **A man is moving with high velocity of 30 ms^{-1}. Determine the total mechanical energy of the man weighing 60 kg, if he is on a height of 50 m at this speed. (Take, g = 10 ms^{-2})**

Sol. Given, mass of man, $m = 60$ kg

Velocity, $v = 30$ ms^{-1} and height, $h = 50$ m

Total energy (TE) of the man at a height of 50 m is given by

$$TE = PE + KE \qquad \text{...(i)}$$

where, PE = potential energy $(= mgh)$

and $\quad$ KE = kinetic energy $\left(= \frac{1}{2}mv^2\right)$

$$TE = mgh + \frac{1}{2}mv^2 \qquad \text{[from Eq. (i)]}$$

$$= 60 \times 10 \times 50 + \frac{1}{2} \times 60 \times (30)^2$$

$$= 30000 + 27000 = 57000\text{ J}$$

Transformation of Energy
(Are Various Energy Forms Interconvertible?)

One form of energy can be converted into other form of energy and this phenomenon is called **transformation of energy**.

When an object is dropped from some height, its potential energy continuously converts into kinetic energy. When an object is thrown upwards, its kinetic energy continuously converts into potential energy.

Some examples of energy transformation are as follows.

(i) Green plants prepare their own food (stored in the form of chemical energy) by using solar energy through the process of photosynthesis.

(ii) When we throw a ball, the muscular energy which is stored in our body, gets converted into kinetic energy of the ball.

(iii) The wound spring in the toy car possesses potential energy. As the spring is released, its potential energy changes into kinetic energy due to which, toy car moves.

(iv) In a stretched bow, potential energy is stored. As it is released, the potential energy of the stretched bow gets converted into the kinetic energy of arrow which moves in the forward direction with large velocity.

Some Energy Transformations

S.No.	Devices	Transformations
1.	Electric motor	Electrical energy into mechanical energy.
2.	Electric generator	Mechanical energy into electrical energy.
3.	Steam engine	Heat energy into kinetic energy.
4.	Electric bulb	Electrical energy into light energy.
5.	Dry cell	Chemical energy into electrical energy.
6.	Solar cell	Light energy into electrical energy.

Try These 10.3

1 **What remains constant during free fall of a body?**

2 **Fill in the blank**

.... energy gets converted into kinetic energy, when we throw a ball.

3 **Which energy is converted to get heat from heaters during winter?**

4 **Name the device which converts chemical energy into electrical energy.**

5 **A ball is thrown up vertically with a velocity of 20 ms^{-1}. At what height will its kinetic energy be half of its original value?**

10.4 Rate of Doing Work : Power

The rate of doing work by an agent or a machine is called the power of the agent or the machine.

Thus, Power $= \dfrac{\text{Work}}{\text{Time}}$

If an agent does a total amount of work W by exerting a force on a body for a total time-interval t, then the average power delivered by the agent is given by

$$P = W/t$$

The unit of power is **watt (W)** in honour of **James Watt.** We express larger rate of energy transfer in **kilowatt (kW).**

$$1\text{ W} = 1\text{ Js}^{-1}$$

or $1\text{kW} = 1000\text{ W} = 1000\text{ Js}^{-1} \Rightarrow 1\text{ MW} = 10^6\text{ W},$

$1\text{ HP (horse power)} = 746\text{ W}$

Average Power

It is defined as the ratio of total work done by the total time taken.

An agent may perform work at different rates at different intervals of time. In such situation, average power is considered by dividing the total energy consumed by the total time taken.

$$\therefore \text{ Average power} = \frac{\text{Total energy consumed}}{\text{Total time taken}}$$

Example 13. **A boy does 400 J of work in 20 s and then he does 100 J of work in 2s. Find the ratio of the power delivered by the boy in two cases.**

Sol. *Case* I Work done by the boy, $W_1 = 400$ J

Time taken, $t_1 = 20$ s,

power, $P_1 = ?$

Case II Work done by the boy, $W_2 = 100$ J

Time taken, $t_2 = 2$ s,

power, $P_2 = ?$

$$\therefore \text{ Power, } P = \frac{\text{Work done }(W)}{\text{Time taken }(t)}$$

$$P_1 = \frac{W_1}{t_1} = \frac{400}{20} = 20\text{ W}$$

and $$P_2 = \frac{W_2}{t_2} = \frac{100}{2} = 50\text{ W}$$

So, $$\frac{P_1}{P_2} = \frac{20}{50} = 2:5$$

Example 14. **A boy of mass 55 kg runs up a staircase of 50 steps in 10 s. If the height of each step is 10 cm, find his power. (Take g =10 m/s^2).**

Sol. Weight of the boy $= mg$

$= 55 \times 10 = 550$ N

Height of the staircase, $h = \dfrac{50 \times 10}{100} = 5$ m

Time taken to climb, $t = 10$ s

Thus, power, $P = \dfrac{\text{Work done}}{\text{Time taken}} = \dfrac{mgh}{t}$

$= \dfrac{550 \times 5}{10} = 275$ W

Example 15. **The heart does 1.2 J of work in each heart beat. How many times per minute does it beat, if its power is 2 W?**

Sol. Here, work done in each heart beat $=1.2$ J

$t=1\text{ min}=60\text{ s}$, Power, $P=2\text{ W}=2\text{ Js}^{-1}$

Total work done $=P\times t=2\times 60=120$ J

Number of times heart beats per minute

$$=\frac{\text{Total work done}}{\text{Work done in each heart beat}}$$

$$=\frac{120}{1.2}=100\text{ times}$$

Example 16. **A horse exerts a pull on a cart of 500 N, so that horse cart system moves with a uniform velocity of 36 kmh^{-1}. What is the power developed by the horse in watt as well as in horse power?**

Sol. Given, Force, $F=500$ N

and Velocity, $v=36\text{ kmh}^{-1}=\frac{36\times 1000}{3600}=10\text{ ms}^{-1}$

As, $P=\frac{W}{t}=\frac{Fs}{t}$ $[\because W=Fs \text{ and } v=s/t]$

$=Fv=500\times 10=5000$ W

In horse power, $P=\frac{5000}{746}=6.70$ HP

Try These 10.4

1. **What do you mean by the rate at which energy is transformed to other form?**
2. **A machine gun fires 360 bullets per minute. Each bullet has a mass of 5 g and travels at 600 m/s. What is the power of the gun? (Assume no loss of energy 100% power transmission)** [Ans. 5400 W]
3. **What is the necessity of using term Average Power instead of Power?**
4. **What is the value of 1 MW power in terms of HP?** [Ans. 1340.48 HP]

Mind Map

WORK AND ENERGY

Work

Work is said to be done, if on applying a force on an object, it is displaced from its position in the direction of force.

- **Two conditions to satisfy for work done.**
  (i) A force should act on an object.
  (ii) The object must be displaced.

- **Mathematical Expression**

  $W = Fs$

  – It is scalar quantity.
  – SI unit of work is N-m or joule.

Positive, Negative and Zero Work

- **Positive Work done**
  Work done is + ve, when angle $\theta = 0°$ i.e., force and displacement are in same direction.
  $W = +Fs$
- **Negative Work done**
  Work done is – ve, when angle $\theta = 180°$ i.e. force and displacement are anti-parallel to each other.
  $W = -Fs$
- **Zero Work done**
  Work done is zero, when angle $\theta = 90°$ i.e. force and displacement are at right angle to each other.
  $W = 0$

Energy

– The capacity of doing work is called energy.
– SI Unit of energy is joule.

Forms of Energy

Energy exists in various forms like mechanical energy (kinetic + potential), heat energy, chemical energy, electrical energy, light energy, etc.

- **Kinetic Energy (KE)**
  – Energy possessed due to the motion of the body is called kinetic energy.
  – Kinetic energy of a body moving with a certain velocity is equal to the work done on it. Kinetic energy of an object increases with its speed.

  $KE = \frac{1}{2}mv^2$

- **Potential Energy (PE)**
  – Energy due to its change in position or shape of the body is called potential energy.
  – We can say that, the potential energy possessed by a body, is the energy present in it by virtue of its position or configuration.

  $PE = mgh$

- **Mechanical Energy (ME)**
  The sum of total kinetic energy and potential energy is called mechanical energy.

  $ME = PE + KE$

  $ME = mgh + \frac{1}{2}mv^2$

Power

– The rate of doing work or the rate at which energy is transferred or used or transformed other form is callled power.
– SI unit of power is watt.

$1W = 1 J/s$

$1kW = 1000 W$

- **Mathematical Expression**

  $\text{Power}(P) = \frac{\text{Work }(W)}{\text{Time taken}(t)}$

  $\text{Power}(P) = \text{Force}(F) \times \text{Velocity}(v)$

Law of Conservation of Energy

– Energy can neither be created nor be destroyed. It can only be transformed from one form to another.
– During the motion of a body total energy is always conserved if there is no loss of energy by the system.

$ME = KE + PE = \text{Constant.}$

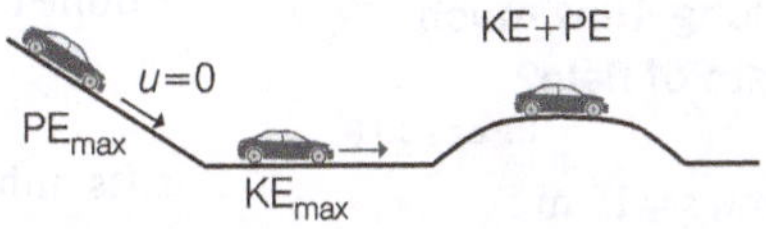

Transformation of Energy

– One form of energy can be converted into other forms of energy.

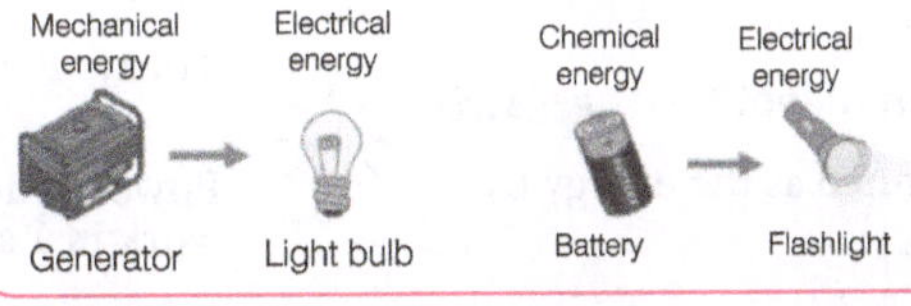

Work -Energy Theorem

Work done by external forces on a body is equal to the change in kinetic energy of the body.

$W = \frac{1}{2}m(v^2 - u^2)$

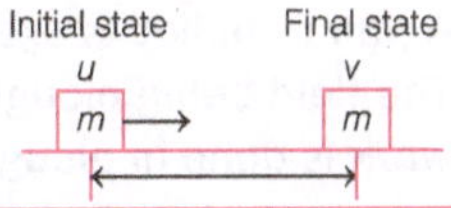

NCERT FOLDER

Complete Explanations of all NCERT's Questions

Intext Questions

Q.1 A force of 7 N acts on an object. The displacement is say 8 m, in the direction of the force. Let us take it that the force acts on the object through the displacement. What is the work done in this case? **Page 115**

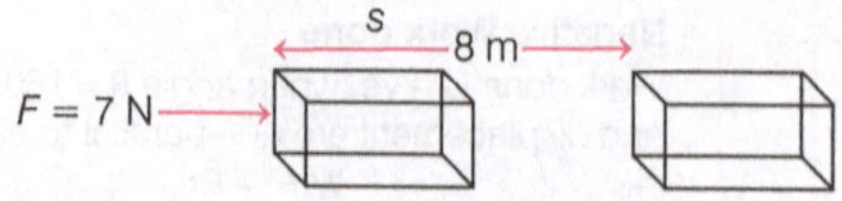

Sol. As work done,

$W = Fs$

[Work done is positive because force and displacement are in same direction]

$\therefore \quad W = 7 \times 8 = 56 \text{ J}$

Q.2 When do we say that work is done? **Page 116**

Sol. If a force acting on a body causes some displacement, then we can say that work is being done by the force on the body which is displaced.

Q.3 Write an expression for the work done when a force is acting on an object in the direction of its displacement. **Page 116**

Sol. Expression for the work done is given by

Work done, $W = Fs$ [F and s are in same direction]

where, F = force and s = displacement. So, $W = Fs$

Q.4 Define 1 J of work. **Page 116**

Sol. 1 J of work is defined as the amount of work done on an object when a force of 1 N displaces it by 1 m along the line of action of the force.

Q.5 A pair of bullocks exert a force of 140 N on a plough. The field being ploughed is 15 m long. How much work is done in ploughing the length of field? **Page 116**

Sol. Given, force, $F = 140$ N, displacement, $s = 15$ m

$\therefore$Work done, $W = +Fs$ [F and s are in same direction]

So, $= 140 \times 15$

$= 2100 \text{ J}$

Q.6 What is the kinetic energy of an object? **Page 119**

Sol. Kinetic energy of an object is defined as the energy by virtue of its motion.

Q.7 Write an expression for the kinetic energy of an object. **Page 119**

Sol. The expression for kinetic energy for an object is given by

$$\text{KE} = \frac{1}{2} mv^2$$

where, KE = kinetic energy, m = mass of the body

and v = velocity of the body.

Q.8 The kinetic energy of an object of mass m moving with a velocity of 5 ms^{-1} is 25 J. What will be its kinetic energy when its velocity is increased three times? **Page 119**

Sol. As from the question,

Kinetic energy (KE_i) initially is given by $\frac{1}{2} mv_i^2$

where, m = mass of the body, v_i = initial velocity

$$\text{KE}_i = \frac{1}{2} mv_i^2 \quad [\text{given, KE}_i = 25 \text{ J}, \; v_i = 5 \text{ ms}^{-1}]$$

$$\Rightarrow \quad 25 = \frac{1}{2} m(5^2)$$

$$\Rightarrow \quad m = \frac{25 \times 2}{5 \times 5} \Rightarrow \; m = 2 \text{ kg}$$

Now, as from question, final velocity (v_f) becomes 3 times of its initial velocity, i.e. $v_f = 3v_i$

$$\Rightarrow \quad v_f = 3 \times 5 = 15 \text{ ms}^{-1}$$

Now, kinetic energy,

$$\text{KE} = \frac{1}{2} mv_f^2 = \frac{1}{2} \times 2 \times 15 \times 15 = 225 \text{ J}$$

Q.9 What is power? **Page 123**

Sol. Power is defined as the rate of doing work. If the work done by an object in time t is W. Then, power,

$$P = \frac{W}{t}$$

Its unit is Js^{-1} or watt.

Q.10 Define 1 watt of power. **Page 123**

Sol. $\therefore$Power, $P = \frac{W}{t}$. If $W = 1$ J, $t = 1$ s

Then, $P = \frac{1 \text{ J}}{1 \text{ s}} = 1 \text{ W}$

Power of an object is said to be 1 watt, if it does 1 J of work in 1 s.

Q.11 A lamp consumes 1000 J of electrical energy in 10 s. What is the power? Page 123

Sol. Given, energy $= 1000\,J$

i.e. work done, $W = 1000\,J$

Time, $t = 10\,s$

$\therefore$ Power of lamp, $P = \frac{W}{t} = \frac{1000}{10} = 100\,W$

Q.12 Define average power. Page 123

Sol. Average power is defined as the ratio of total work done to the total time taken.

Exercise Questions

Q.1 Look at the activities listed below. Reason out whether or not work is done in the light of your understanding of the term 'work.'

(i) Seema is swimming in a pond.
(ii) A donkey is carrying a load on its back.
(iii) A wind mill is lifting water from a well.
(iv) A green plant is carrying out photosynthesis.
(v) An engine is pulling a train.
(vi) Food grains are getting dried in the Sun.
(vii) A sail boat is moving due to wind energy.

Sol. (i) Work is being done by Seema because she displaces the water by applying the force.

(ii) No work is being done by the gravitational force because, the direction of force, i.e. load is vertically downward and displacement is along horizontal. If displacement and force are perpendicular, then no work is done.

(iii) Work is done because wind mill is lifting the water, i.e. it is changing the position of water.

(iv) No work is done because there is no force and displacement.

(v) Work is done because engine is changing the position of train.

(vi) No work is done because there is no force and no displacement.

(vii) Work is done by of the force acting on the boat, because it starts moving.

Q.2 An object thrown at a certain angle to the ground moves in a curved path and falls back to the ground. The initial and the final points of the path of the object lie on the same horizontal line. What is the work done by the force of gravity on the object?

Sol. As we know that work done is the product of force and displacement and here in this case, displacement in the direction of gravitational force (change in height) is zero, so work done by the force of gravity on the object is zero.

Q.3 What is the work done by the force of gravity on a satellite moving around the Earth? Justify your answer.

Sol. Work done by the force of gravity on a satellite moving around the Earth is zero. Because the angle between force (centripetal) and displacement in case of circular motion.

So, work done, $W = 0$

Q.4 Can there be displacement of an object in the absence of any force acting on it? Think, discuss this question with your friends and teacher.

Sol. Yes, if an object moves with a constant velocity, i.e. there is no acceleration, then no force acts on it. As the object is moving, so it gets displaced from one position to another position.

Q.5 A person holds a bundle of hay over his head for 30 min and gets tired. Has he done some work or not? Justify your answer.

Sol. On holding a bundle of hay over the head, work done by the person is zero because there is no displacement.

Q.6 Soni says that the acceleration in an object could be zero even when several forces are acting on it. Do you agree with her? Why?

Sol. Yes, I am agree with Soni, the acceleration of an object can be zero even when several forces are acting on it, if the resultant of all the forces acting on object is zero.

Q.7 In each of the following, a force *F* is acting on an object of mass *m*. The direction of displacement is from West to East shown by the longer arrow. Observe the figures carefully and state whether the work done by the force is negative, positive or zero.

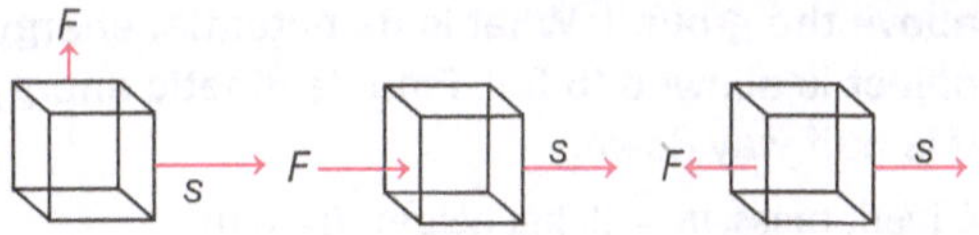

Fig. (I) Fig. (II) Fig. (III)

Sol. (i) In Fig. (I), angle between F and s is 90°, so work done is zero.

(ii) In Fig. (II), angle between F and s is 0°, so work done is positive.

(iii) In Fig. (III), angle between F and s is 180°, so work done is negative.

Q.8 Certain force acting on a mass 20 kg mass changes its velocity from 5 ms^{-1} to 2 ms^{-1}. Calculate the work done by the force.

Sol. Given, mass, $m = 20\,kg$

Initial velocity, $u = 5\,ms^{-1}$

Final velocity, $v = 2\ ms^{-1}$

$\therefore$ Work done by the force = Change in kinetic energy

= Final kinetic energy − Initial kinetic energy

$$= \frac{1}{2}mv^2 - \frac{1}{2}mu^2$$

$$= \frac{1}{2}m(v^2 - u^2) = \frac{1}{2} \times 20[(2)^2 - (5)^2]$$

$$= 10(4 - 25) = 10 \times (-21) = -210\ J$$

Q.9 A mass of 10 kg is at a point *A* on the table. It is moved to a point *B*. If the line joining *A* and *B* is horizontal, what is the work done on the object by the gravitational force? Explain your answer.

Sol. Here, both the initial and final positions are on the same horizontal line. So, there is no difference in height, i.e. $h = 0$. where, h = difference in the heights of initial and final positions of the object.

We know that work done by gravitational force,

$$W = mgh$$

$\therefore$ Work done, $W = mg \times 0 = 0$

Q.10 The potential energy of a freely falling object decreases progressively. Does this violate law of conservation of energy? Why?

Sol. It is true that the potential energy of freely falling object decreases progressively. But as the object falls down, its speed increases, i.e. the kinetic energy of the object increases progressively (kinetic energy will increase with the increase in speed).

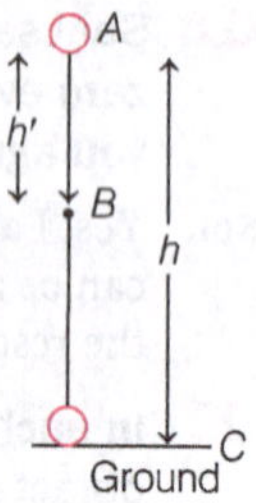

Now, we can say that the law of conservation of energy is not violated, because the decrease in potential energy results in the increase of kinetic energy.

Q.11 An object of mass 40 kg is raised to a height of 5 m above the ground. What is its potential energy, if object is allowed to fall. Find its kinetic energy when it is half way down.

Sol. Given, mass, $m = 40$ kg, height, $h = 5$ m

As potential energy is given by PE $= mgh$

So, PE $= 40 \times 10 \times 5 = 2000$ J $\quad [\because g = 10\ ms^{-2}]$

When it is allowed to fall, its PE gets converted into kinetic energy KE. So, when it reaches to the half-way, half of its PE gets converted to KE.

So, $mg\frac{h}{2} = \frac{1}{2}mv^2$ [where, v = velocity at the bottom]

So, $\text{KE} = mg\frac{h}{2} = 40 \times 10 \times \frac{5}{2} = 1000\ J$

Q.12 An object of mass *m* is moving with a constant velocity *v*. How much work should be done on the object in order to bring the object to rest?

Sol. Concept Change in kinetic energy (KE) = Work done

Given, mass $= m$, initial velocity, $u = v$

Final velocity, $v = 0$

So, $$W = \frac{1}{2}mv^2 - \frac{1}{2}mu^2$$

$\Rightarrow$ $$W = \frac{1}{2}m(0)^2 - \frac{1}{2}mv^2 = -\frac{1}{2}mv^2$$

Hence, the work that should be done in order to bring the object to rest is $\frac{1}{2}mv^2$.

Q.13 Calculate the work required to be done to stop a car of 1500 kg moving at a velocity to 60 kmh^{-1}.

Sol. Concept : Change in kinetic energy is equal to the work done W.

Given, initial velocity, $u = 60\ kmh^{-1}$

$$= 60 \times \frac{5}{18} = \frac{50}{3}\ ms^{-1}$$

$[\because 1\ kmh^{-1} = 5/18\ ms^{-1}]$

Final velocity, $v = 0$

So, magnitude of change in kinetic energy $= W$

$$= \frac{1}{2}mv^2 - \frac{1}{2}mu^2$$

$\Rightarrow$ $$W = \frac{1}{2}m(v^2 - u^2)$$

$$= \frac{1}{2} \times 1500 \times \left(\frac{-50 \times 50}{9}\right)$$

$$= -\frac{1}{2} \times \frac{1500 \times 50 \times 50}{9}$$

$$W = \frac{-625000}{3} = -208333.3\ J$$

Hence, the work required to be done to stop a car is 208333.3 J.

Q.14 A freely falling object eventually stops on reaching the ground. What happens to its kinetic energy?

Sol. When freely falling object strikes the ground, some sound and heat is produced. So, the kinetic energy of the object converts into sound energy and heat energy.

Q.15 A battery lights a bulb. Describe the energy changes involved in the process.

Sol. A battery contains chemicals and supplies electrical energy. So, a battery converts chemical energy into electrical energy. In an electrical bulb, the electrical energy is first converted into heat energy. This heat energy causes the filament of bulb to become white-hot and produce light energy.

Thus, the energy changes are

Chemical energy $\rightarrow$ Electrical energy $\rightarrow$ Heat energy $\rightarrow$ Light energy

Q.16 What are the various energy transformations that occur when you are riding a bicycle?

Sol. In case of riding a bicycle, the muscular energy is converted into the kinetic energy of the bicycle.

Q.17 Does the transfer of energy take place when you push a huge rock with all your might and fail to move it? Where is the energy you spend going?

Sol. When we push a huge rock, then the rock also exerts a large force on us (according to Newton's third law of motion). The muscular energy spent by us in the process is used to oppose the huge force acting on us due to the rock.

Q.18 Illustrate the law of conservation of energy by discussing the energy changes which occur when we draw a pendulum bob to one side and allow it to oscillate. Why does the bob eventually come to rest? What happens to its energy eventually? Is it a violation of the law of conservation of energy?

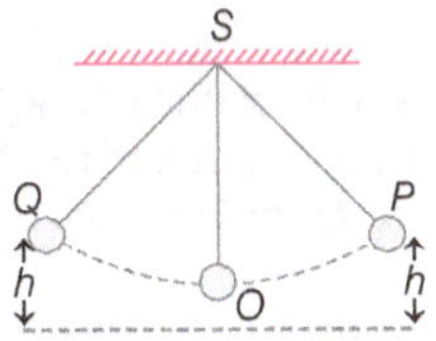

Sol. Let a simple pendulum be suspended from a rigid support S and OS be the equilibrium position of the pendulum. Let the pendulum be displaced to a position P, where it is at rest. At position P, the pendulum has potential energy (mgh). When the pendulum is released from position P, it begins to move towards position O. The speed of the pendulum increases and its height decreases that means the potential energy is converting into kinetic energy.

At position O, whole of the potential energy of the pendulum is converted into its kinetic energy.

Then, the pendulum swings to other side due to inertia of motion. As the pendulum begins to move towards position Q, the speed of pendulum decreases and height increases that means kinetic energy is converting into potential energy. At point Q, whole of the kinetic energy is converted into potential energy.

Thus, we find that the potential energy is converted into kinetic energy and *vice-versa* during the motion of the pendulum. But the total energy remains constant.

When the pendulum oscillates in air, the air friction opposes its motion. So, some part of kinetic energy of pendulum is used to overcome this friction. With the passage of time, energy of the pendulum goes on decreasing and finally becomes zero.

The energy of the pendulum is transferred to the atmosphere. So, energy is being transferred, i.e. converted from one form to another. So, no violation of the law of conservation of energy takes place.

Q.19 A certain household has consumed 250 units of energy during a month. How much energy is this in joules?

Sol. 1 unit of energy is equal to 1 kilowatt hour (kWh)

$$1 \text{ unit} = 1 \text{ kWh}$$

$$1 \text{ kWh} = 3.6 \times 10^6 \text{ J}$$

Therefore, 250 units of energy $= 250 \times 3.6 \times 10^6$

$$= 9 \times 10^8 \text{ J}$$

Q.20 An electric heater is rated 1500 W. How much energy does it use in 10 h?

Sol. Given, power of the electric heater, $P = 1500$ W

Time of use, $t = 10 \text{ h} = 36000$ s

$$\therefore \quad P = \frac{E}{t}$$

$$\Rightarrow \quad E = P \times t = 1500 \times 36000 = 54 \times 10^6 \text{ J}$$

The energy used by the heater in 10 h is 54×10^6 J.

Q.21 Find the energy in joules consumed in 10 h by four devices of power 500 W each.

Sol. Given, power rating of the device, $P = 500$ W

$$= 0.50 \text{ kW}$$

Time for which the device runs, $T = 10$ h

$$\therefore \text{ Power, } P = \frac{W}{T}$$

$\because$ Work done, W = Energy consumed by the device

$\therefore$ Energy consumed $= P \times T$

$$= 0.50 \times 10$$

$$= 5 \text{ kWh}$$

$$= 5 \times 3.6 \times 10^6 \text{ J}$$

Hence, the energy consumed by the four equal rating devices in 10 hs

$$= 4 \times 5 \times 3.6 \times 10^6 \text{ J}$$

$$= 72 \times 10^6 \text{ J}$$

To Study NCERT Activities

Scan the Code

REVIEW EXERCISE

Including Competency Based Questions

Competency Focused (Objective) Questions

Multiple Choice Questions

1 When a horse-pulls a cart, who does the work ?

(a) Cart (b) Wheels (c) Road (d) Horse

Sol. (*d*) When a horse-pulls a cart, work is being done by horse.

2 With the help of figure, write an expression for work in terms of force and displacement.

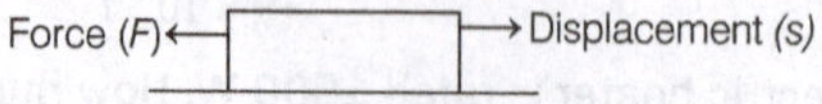

(a) $W = -F \times s$ (b) $W = F / s$

(c) $W = F \times s$ (d) $W = -\frac{F}{s}$

Sol. (*a*) When a force *F* displaces a body through a distance *s* in the opposite direction of applied force, then the work done *W* on the body is given by

Work done = – Force × Displacement

or $W = -F \times s$

3 If 10 N of force is applied to an object, but the object does not move, then how much work being done by the force ?

(a) Zero (b) 10 J (c) 10 N (d) 20 J

Sol. (*a*) If there is no displacement due to application of force, then net work done will be zero.

4 The work done on an object does not depend upon the

NCERT Exemplar

(a) displacement

(b) force applied

(c) angle between force and displacement

(d) initial velocity of the object

Sol. (*d*) The work done on an object depends upon the force applied, displacement and the angle between force and displacement.

Work done does not depend upon initial velocity of the object.

5 Which one of these is an example of scientific work done?

(a) Playing mobile games when sitting on a sofa.

(b) Studying for board exams.

(c) Pushing a wall and got tired.

(d) Climbing stairs of home.

Sol. (*d*) Climbing stairs of home involves displacement with the help of some force and scientific work done needs displacement and force acting on the body.

6 In case of negative work, the force acting on the body and displacement are **Competency Based Que.**

(a) perpendicular to each other

(b) parallel to each other

(c) inclined to an angle 30°

(d) anti-parallel to each other

Sol. (*d*) In case of negative work, force *F* and displacement *s* are in opposite direction. i.e., anti-parallel to each other.

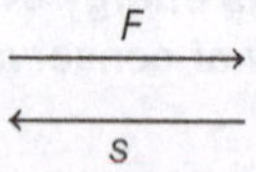

7 A girl is carrying a school bag of 3 kg mass on her back and moves 200 m on a levelled road. The work done against the gravitational force will be ($g = 10\ ms^{-2}$)

NCERT Exemplar

(a) 6×10^3 J (b) 6 J (c) 0.6 J (d) zero

Sol. (*d*) Zero, gravitational force acting perpendicular to the displacement i.e., angle between direction of force and displacement is 90°.

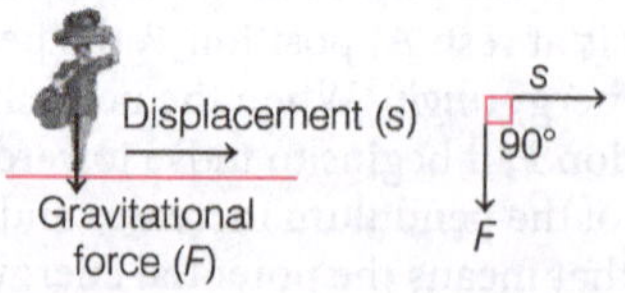

8 Which of the following statements is/are incorrect?

Competency Based Que.

I. Work and energy have different units.

II. Two bodies of unequal masses have equal acceleration at any instant of time when they are dropped from a cliff.

(a) II only (b) I only

(c) Both I and II (d) None of these

Sol. (*b*) I. Work and energy have same units i.e. joule.

II. Yes, they have equal acceleration i.e. acceleration due to gravity.

9 A ball is allowed to fall freely from a tower. Which energy is possessed at the middle point during the fall?

(a) Kinetic only

(b) Potential only

(c) Both potential and kinetic

(d) Heat only

Sol. (*c*) At middle point of fall, the ball has both kinetic and potential energies.

10 **An iron sphere of mass 10 kg has the same diameter as an aluminium sphere of mass is 3.5 kg. Both spheres are dropped simultaneously from a tower. When they are 10 m above the ground, they have the same** **NCERT Exemplar**

(a) acceleration (b) momentum
(c) potential energy (d) kinetic energy

Sol. (*a*) Momentum, kinetic energy and potential energy depend on the mass but acceleration which is acceleration due to gravity is independent of mass.

11 **When speed of the moving bus is tripled, then**

(a) kinetic energy is increased by nine-times.
(b) potential energy is increased by nine-times.
(c) momentum is increased by nine-times.
(d) acceleration is doubled.

Sol. (*a*) Kinetic energy, $KE = \frac{1}{2}mv^2$

$$KE' = \frac{1}{2}m(3v)^2 = 9\left(\frac{1}{2}mv^2\right) = 9\,KE$$

Potential energy does not depend on speed.
Momentum, $p = mv$

$$p' = m(3v) = 3(mv) = 3p$$

Momentum is increased by 3 times.

12 **If two stones *A* and *B* are dropped from a tower, then which one has maximum kinetic energy ?**

(a) Lighter stone (b) Heavier stone
(c) Both have equal (d) None of these

Sol. (*b*) If two stones are dropped from some height, then the heavier stone has greater kinetic energy w.r.t. lighter stone, because kinetic energy is directly proportional to mass.

13 **Which of the following case causes larger change in kinetic energy of a body?** **Competency Based Que.**

(a) Increasing mass two times.
(b) Increasing velocity two times
(c) Increasing its potential energy two times.
(d) Increasing mass three times.

Sol. (*b*) Formula of kinetic energy,
$KE = \frac{1}{2}mv^2$ (m = mass, v = velocity)

Changing mass two / three times increases KE only two/three times and there is no dependence of potential energy on kinetic energy.
But increases velocity two times,

$$KE' = \frac{1}{2}m\,(2v)^2 = 4\left(\frac{1}{2}mv^2\right) = 4KE$$

cause large change in KE

14 **Two particles of masses 20 g and 50 g have equal kinetic energies. What will be the ratio of squares of the momentum?** **Competency Based Que.**

(a) 5 : 2 (b) 5 : 3
(c) 2 : 5 (d) 1 : 5

Sol. (*c*) Kinetic energy,

$$E = \frac{1}{2}mv^2 = \frac{1}{2}\frac{m^2v^2}{m} = \frac{p^2}{2m} \qquad (\because p = mv)$$

So, $E_1 = \frac{p_1^2}{2m_1}$ and $E_2 = \frac{p_2^2}{2m_2}$

$$E_1 = E_2 \Rightarrow \left(\frac{p_1}{p_2}\right)^2 = \frac{m_1}{m_2} = \frac{\frac{20}{1000}}{\frac{50}{1000}} \qquad \left(1\text{g} = \frac{1}{1000}\text{kg}\right)$$

$$= \frac{20}{50} = 2:5$$

15 **When the kinetic energy of a body is increased by 800% the momentum of the body is increased by what percentage?**

(a) 2000% (b) 20%
(c) 200% (d) 100%

Sol. (*c*) $K_f = K_i + 800\%$ of K_i

$$\Rightarrow K_f = K_i + \frac{800}{100}K_i = \frac{900}{100}K_i$$

$$\Rightarrow K_f = 9K_i$$

$$\Rightarrow \frac{K_f}{K_i} = 9$$

From $KE = \frac{p^2}{2m} \Rightarrow p \propto \sqrt{K}$

$$\frac{p_f}{p_i} = \sqrt{\frac{K_f}{K_i}} = \sqrt{9} = 3$$

$$\Rightarrow p_f = 3p_i$$

Percentage increase in momentum

$$= \frac{p_f - p_i}{p_i} \times 100$$

$$= \frac{3p_i - p_i}{p_i} \times 100 = 200\%$$

16 **For given situation, find the potential energy of the ball.** **Competency Based Que.**

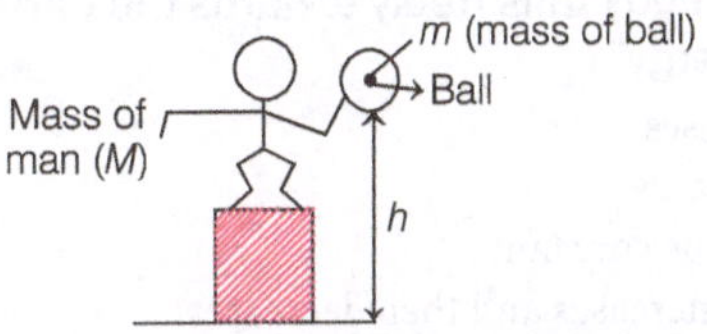

(a) $PE = mgh$ (b) $PE = \frac{1}{2}mv^2$
(c) PE = zero (d) $PE = Mgh$

Sol. (*a*) According to the figure,
PE of ball = Weight of ball × Height

$$= mg \times h = mgh$$

17 **Water stored in a dam possesses** NCERT Exemplar

(a) no energy
(b) electrical energy
(c) kinetic energy
(d) potential energy

Sol. (*d*) Potential energy is stored energy or the energy of position, so water stored in a dam possesses potential energy.

18 **An airplane is taking off from a field. Find the height at which it should be, so that its potential energy is 1.5×10^8 J. (Take, mass of plane $= 10^5$ kg)**

(a) 200 m
(b) 150 m
(c) 250 m
(d) 100 m.

Sol. (*b*) Here, mass, $m = 10^5$ kg,

Potential energy, $PE = 1.5 \times 10^8$ J.

$\therefore \quad PE = mgh$

$$h = \frac{(PE)}{mg} = \frac{1.5 \times 10^8}{10^5 \times 10} = 150 \text{ m}$$

19 **A body is falling from a height *h*. After it has fallen a height $\frac{h}{2}$, it will possess** NCERT Exemplar

(a) only potential energy
(b) only kinetic energy
(c) half potential and half kinetic energy
(d) more kinetic and less potential energy

Sol. (*c*) Velocity when it reaches a height $\frac{h}{2}$,

From equation of motion, $v^2 = u^2 + 2as$

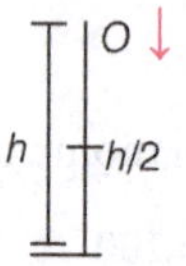

Here, $u = 0$ m/s, $a = g$, $s = \frac{h}{2}$

$$v^2 = gh$$

Kinetic energy, $KE = \frac{1}{2}mv^2 = \frac{mgh}{2}$ or $\frac{PE}{2}$

20 **When a body falls freely towards the earth, then its total energy** NCERT Exemplar

(a) increases
(b) decreases
(c) remains constant
(d) first increases and then decreases

Sol. (*c*) Since, total energy of the system is always conserved, so when a body falls freely towards the earth, then its total energy remains constant, i.e. the sum of the potential energy and kinetic energy of the body would be same at all points.

21 **A flying bird in the sky possesses which energy?**

(a) Only kinetic energy
(b) Only potential energy
(c) Neither potential nor kinetic energy
(d) Both potential and kinetic energy.

Sol. (*d*) A flying bird in the sky possesses potential energy by virtue of its position and since its flying with speed, so it also possesses kinetic energy.

22 **In solar cell, light energy is**

(a) converted into chemical energy
(b) converted into mechanical energy
(c) converted into electrical energy
(d) converted into gravitational energy

Sol. (*c*) In solar cell, light energy is converted into electrical energy.

23 **A horse does 5000 J of work in 100 s. What is its power ?**

(a) 50 W
(b) 50 J
(c) 10 W
(d) 10 J

Sol. (*a*) Given, work done, $W = 5000$ J

Time taken, $\quad t = 100$ s

We know that,

Power, $\quad P = \frac{W}{t}$

$$= \frac{5000}{100} = 50 \text{ J/s}$$

Thus, power, $\quad P = 50$ W

24 **If a 15 W bulb and a 10 W bulb are connected to a source of 250 V potential, the bulb glowing brighter is,**

(a) 10 W
(b) 15 W
(c) Both Bulb glowing bright equally
(d) cannot be determined

Sol. (*b*) 15 W, the bulb having greater power will be glowing brighter than 10 W bulb.

Assertion–Reason Questions

Direction (Q.Nos. 1-8) ***In each of the following questions, a statement of Assertion is given by the corresponding statement of Reason. Of the statements, mark the correct answer as***

(a) If both Assertion and Reason are true and Reason is the correct explanation of Assertion.
(b) If both Assertion and Reason are true, but Reason is not the correct explanation of Assertion.
(c) If Assertion is true, but Reason is false.
(d) If Assertion is false, but Reason is true.

1 Assertion (A) When the force opposes the motion of a body, the work done is zero.

Reason (R) The angle between the force and displacement is 180°.

Sol. (*d*) The work done is negative, when force opposes the motion of a body and the angle between them is 180°.

2 Assertion (A) A moving hammer drives a nail into the wall of house.

Reason (R) Work done in driving the nail is positive.

Sol. (*a*) The nail displaces in the direction of force applied. So, the work done is positive.

3 Assertion (A) A person driving the motorcycle increases the speed on approaching a hilly road.

Reason (R) To provide more potential energy to the motorcycle. So, that it may go up against gravity of earth.

Sol. (*c*) The person increases the speed, to provide more kinetic energy to the motorcycle, which gets converted to potential energy as it drives up on hilly road.

4 Assertion (A) The kinetic energy of a body with any reference, must always be positive.

Reason (R) The potential energy of a body can be positive/negative with the chosen reference.

Sol. (*b*) Expression for kinetic energy, $KE = \frac{1}{2}mv^2$

m and v^2 can't be negative in any reference.

Potential energy depends on the chosen reference level. So, it can be positive or negative.

5 Assertion (A) Total energy of freely falling body is constant at each point.

Reason (R) Kinetic energy of freely falling body is minimum, when it reaches at ground.

Sol. (*c*) According to law of conservation of energy, total energy of freely falling body remains conserved. Kinetic energy is maximum when body reaches at ground. Hence, Assertion is true, but Reason is false.

6 Assertion (A) Electric motor converts electrical energy into mechanical energy.

Reason (R) Mechanical energy is equal to kinetic energy.

Sol. (*c*) Electric motor converts electrical energy into mechanical energy. Mechanical energy is equal to sum of kinetic energy and potential energy.

Hence, Assertion is true but Reason is false.

7 Assertion (A) A truck and a bus does the same amount of work in 40 s and 60 s respectively. Truck is more powerful than the bus.

Reason (R) $\text{Power} = \frac{\text{Work done}}{\text{Time taken}}$

Sol. (*a*) $\text{Power} \propto \frac{1}{(\text{Time taken})}$

(As work done is same in both cases)

i.e., truck is more powerful than bus.

8 Assertion (A) An electric bulb consumes 200 J of electrical energy in 10s. Then, its power is 20 W.

Reason (R) To get power, energy consumed is divided by the time taken.

Sol. (*a*) $\text{Power of bulb} = \frac{(\text{Energy consumed})}{(\text{Time taken})}$

$$P = \frac{200}{10} = 20\text{W}$$

Case Based/Source Based Questions

Direction (Q.Nos. 1-3) ***Answer the question on the basis of your understanding of the following table and related studied concepts:***

1. Following table gives an approximate idea about the energy associated with different phenomena:

Phenomenon	Energy (in J)
Rotational energy of earth	10^{29}
Annual solar energy incident on the earth	5×10^{24}
Annual wind energy dissipated near earth's surface	10^{22}
Energy released from 15 megaton fusion bomb	10^{17}
Energy released in burning 1000 kg of coal	3×10^{10}
Kinetic energy of large jet aircraft	10^{9}
Daily food intake of a human adult	10^{7}
Typical energy of a proton in nucleus	10^{-13}
Typical energy of an electron in an atom	10^{-18}
Energy to break one bond in DNA	10^{-20}

(i) What is the ratio of the phenomenon of maximum energy to the phenomenon of minimum energy? [1]

(ii) Find the number of broken bonds in DNA to get 100 J of energy. [1]

(iii) Find the calorific value of coal. [1]

(iv) If mass of large jet aircraft is 1000 kg, then find the velocity of jet aircraft. [1]

Sol. (i) According to given table, maximum energy is given due to the phenomenon of rotation of earth

$\therefore \quad E_{max} = 10^{29}$ J

Minimum energy is given due to the phenomenon of breaking of one bond in DNA.

i.e. $\quad E_{min} = 10^{-20}$ J

$$\therefore \quad \frac{E_{max}}{E_{min}} = \frac{10^{29}}{10^{-20}} = 10^{49}$$

$$\therefore \quad E_{max} : E_{min} = 10^{49} : 1$$

(ii) $\therefore 10^{-20}$ J energy is obtained due to breaking of one bond in DNA.

$\therefore$ To obtain energy of 100 J, number of broken bonds is

$$\text{DNA} = \frac{100}{10^{-20}} = 10^{22}$$

(iii) From given table, Mass of burned coal, $m = 1000$ kg

Energy released, $E = 3 \times 10^{10}$ J

$$\therefore \text{Calorific value of coal} = \frac{E}{m} = \frac{3 \times 10^{10}}{1000} = 3 \times 10^{7} \text{ J/kg}$$

(iv) Given, $m = 1000$ kg

From table, kinetic energy of jet aircraft, $K = 10^9$ J

i.e. $\frac{1}{2}mv^2 = 10^9 \Rightarrow \frac{1}{2} \times 1000 \times v^2 = 10^9$

$\Rightarrow v = \sqrt{2} \times 10^3 = 1.414 \times 10^3 = 1414$ m/s

2. A ball is thrown vertically upward. When it rises, the gravitational force does negative work on it, decreasing its kinetic energy. As the ball descends, the gravitational force does positive work on it, increasing its kinetic energy. The ball falls back to the point of projection with same velocity and kinetic energy with which it was thrown up. The net work done by the gravitational force on the ball during the round trip is zero because work done by the gravity on displacing a body from one point to another points depends only on the ends positions of the body.

(i) Find the work done by the gravitational force on the ball, when it moves upward direction. [1]

(ii) When the ball moves vertically upward, then work done by gravitational force is negative. Why? [1]

(iii) Find the net work done by the conservative force during the round trip of a body. [1]

(iv) Name the energy of the ball which remains the same during round trip of the ball. [1]

Sol. (i) The ball is thrown vertically upward, the work done by the gravitational force on the ball will be negative.

(ii) When the ball moves vertically upward, then angle between the direction of gravitational force and displacement remains 180°.

$\therefore$ Work done, $W = Fs \cos 180° = -Fs$

Therefore, work done by gravitational force on the ball during upward movement is negative.

(iii) Work done by the conservative force depends only on initial and final position of the object. During round trip of a body, initial and final position of the body coincides, hence work done by the conservative force is zero.

(iv) Mechanical energy (sum of kinetic and potential energy).

3 When an object of mass *m*, is placed under the influence of gravitational force of earth (a conservative force) and some work is done upon the object by an external force, there will be a change in the total mechanical energy of the object. If only internal forces are doing work, there is no change in total mechanical energy (gravitational force between the mass and the earth are internal forces), it is said to be conserved. Thus, according to work energy theorem

Initial mechanical energy + Work done by external forces (Work done by against conservative force) = Final mechanical energy.

The work done by external forces can be a positive or a negative work. Whether the work is positive or negative, depends upon the angle between the force and the direction of motion. **CBSE DIKSHA**

(i) A trolley runs from *P* to *Q* along a track. At *Q* its potential energy is 50 kJ less than at *P*. At *P*, the kinetic energy of the trolley is 5 kJ. Between *P* and *Q* the work the trolley does against friction is 10 kJ. What is the kinetic energy of the trolley at *Q*? [1]

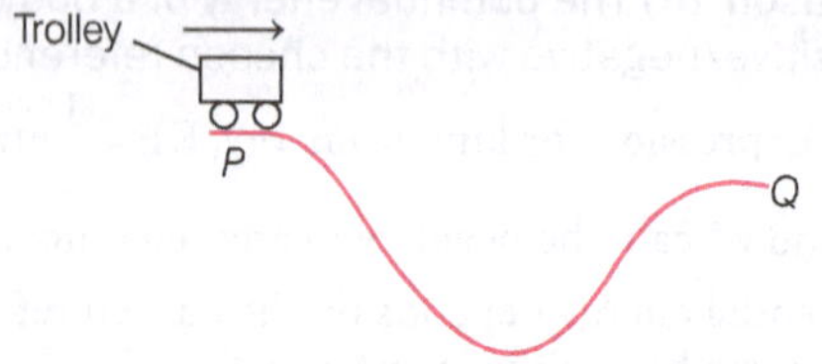

(a) 35 kJ (b) 45 kJ
(c) 55 kJ (d) 65 kJ

(ii) A car driver adjusts the pressure on a car's brakes, so that the car travels at constant speed down a hill from *P* to *Q*. The magnitude of the change in the car's kinetic energy is ΔE_K. The magnitude of the change in its gravitational potential energy is ΔE_p. Which statement is correct when the car reaches *Q*? [1]

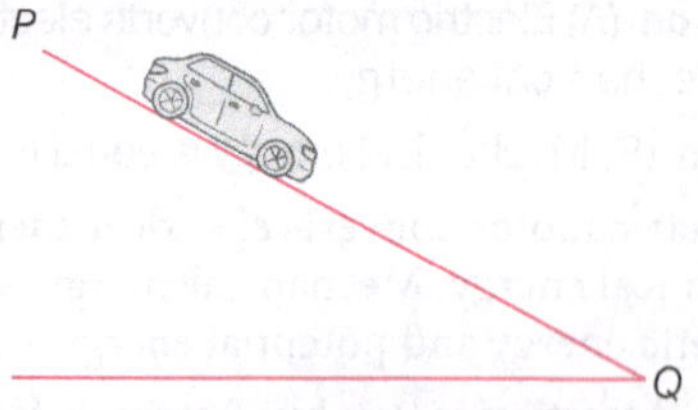

(a) $\Delta E_K > \Delta E_P$ (b) $\Delta E_K = \Delta E_P$
(c) $\Delta E_P > \Delta E_K > 0$ (d) $\Delta E_K = 0$

(iii) An object weighing 10 N is dropped from a height of 4 m above the ground. When it has fallen freely through a distance of 1 m, its total mechanical energy with respect to the ground is [1]

(a) 2.5 J (b) 10 J
(c) 30 J (d) 40 J

Use the following diagram to answer question (iv) and (v).

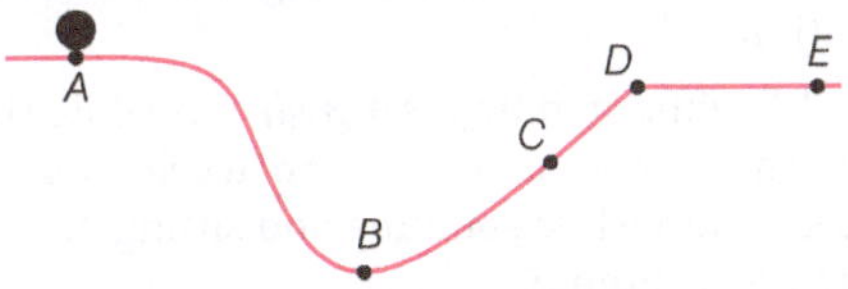

(iv) The object will have a minimum gravitational potential energy at which of the following point(s)? [1/2]

(a) *A* (b) *B* (c) *C* (d) *D* and *E*

(v) The object's kinetic energy at point *C* is less than its kinetic energy at which of the following point(s)? [1/2]

(a) *A* only (b) *A*, *D* and *E*

(c) *B* only (d) *D* and *E*

Sol. (i) (*b*) 45 kJ

Using law of conservation of energy,

$PE_P + KE_P +$ Work done against friction $= PE_Q + KE_Q$

Given, $PE_P - PE_Q = 50$ kJ

$KE_P = 5$ kJ

Work done against friction $= -10$ kJ

$\Rightarrow \quad 50 + 5 - 10 = KE_Q$

$KE_Q = 45$ kJ

(ii) (*d*) $\Delta E_k = 0$, since car is travelling at a constant speed from *P* to *Q*.

(iii) (*d*) 40 J

Mechanical energy is equal to potential energy at the top of height 4 m above the ground.

$PE = mgh$

$= 10 \times 4 = 40$ J

(iv) (*b*) *B* because, $h = 0$

(v) (*c*) *B* only, because KE is maximum at *B* due to maximum velocity at *B*.

Constructed Response (Descriptive) Questions

Very Short Answer Type Questions

1 Why do we say work done against gravity is negative?

Sol. It is because force and displacement are in opposite directions to each other.

2 A man is holding a suitcase in his hand at rest. What is the work done by him?

Sol. Zero, as displacement is zero.

3 A player throws ball straight to the wicket keeper having a 20 m distance between them. What is the work done by the force of gravity on cricket ball? Competency Based Que.

Sol. In the playground, even if the ball is thrown straight to the wicket keeper, force of gravity always acts vertically downward, i.e. displacement and force of gravity are perpendicular to each other. Work done is zero.

4 Is it possible that an object is in the state of accelerated motion due to external force acting on it, but no work is being done by the force. Explain it with an example. NCERT Exemplar

Sol. Yes, it is possible, when an object moves in a circular path. Centripetal force always act radially inward and the direction of displacement is perpendicular to this force. In this situation no work is being done by the force.

5 What will cause greater change in kinetic energy of a body? Changing its mass or changing its velocity.

Sol. Change in velocity will cause greater change in kinetic energy because $KE = \frac{1}{2}mv^2$

6 What will be the relationship between kinetic energy and momentum of a car having mass *m* and moving with velocity *v* m/s?

Sol. Let the kinetic energy of the car be,

$KE = \frac{1}{2}mv^2$ (m = mass of car, v = velocity of car)

Momentum, $p = mv$

Now, $KE = \frac{1}{2} \times mv^2 \times \frac{m}{m}$

$= \frac{(mv)^2}{2m}$

$KE = \frac{p^2}{2m}$

$KE \propto p^2$

Kinetic energy is directly proportional to the square of momentum.

7 If a body is thrown vertically upwards, its velocity goes on decreasing. What happens to its kinetic energy when it reaches at the top? Competency Based Que.

Sol. The whole of its kinetic energy gets converted into potential energy (mgh), where m is the mass of body, h is the height and g is the acceleration due to gravity.

8 In which situation, the potential energy of a spring is minimum?

Sol. When a spring is at its natural length (i.e. neither stretched nor compressed), the potential energy of a spring is minimum.

9 Can potential energy of a body be negative?

Sol. Yes, potential energy of a body can be negative also, when the potential energy of a body is calculated below the reference line.

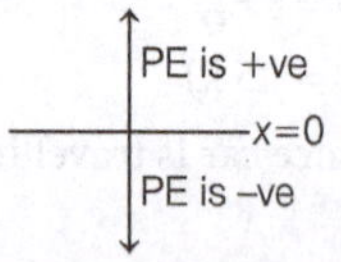

10 Can any object have mechanical energy even if its momentum is zero? **NCERT Exemplar**

Sol. Since, mechanical energy is the sum of kinetic energy and potential energy. And as given that, momentum of the body is zero, it means velocity of the body is zero, so it has kinetic energy equals to zero. But it may have potential energy. So, even if the momentum of the body is zero, it may have mechanical energy.

11 Name the type of energy stored in spring of a watch.

Sol. Elastic potential energy is stored in spring of a watch.

12 Are work and energy the same, although the unit of both is same? **Competency Based Que.**

Sol. An object having the capability to do work is said to possess energy. The object which does the work, losses energy and the object on which work is done, gains energy. So, work is transfer of energy with the help of force.

13 Explain why a bulb becomes hot after working for some time?

Sol. A bulb converts electrical energy to light energy, but not all electrical energy is converted to light, some amount goes to heat energy, that's why it becomes hot.

14 (i) How plants prepare their own food? [1]

(ii) What's the need of rubbing hand in winters? [1]

Sol. (i) By converting solar energy from sun to chemical energy, plants prepare their own food.

(ii) By rubbing hand, mechanical energy is converted to heat energy to prevent from cold.

Short Answer Type Questions

1 A girl sits and stands repeatedly for 6 min. Draw a graph to show the variation of potential energy of her body with time. **Competency Based Que.**

Sol.

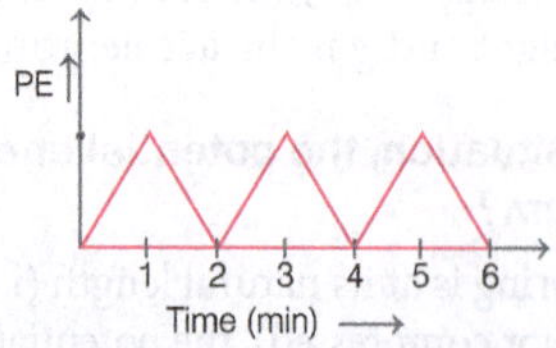

From the graph shown above, we can take the sitting position of the girl as the position of zero potential energy.

Let m be the mass of the girl and h be the position of centre of gravity while standing above the sitting position.

The PE while standing is $+ mgh$ and while sitting is zero. We can assume that there is no acceleration or deceleration while standing and sitting, this is repeated after every minute.

2 (i) Define potential energy. [1]

(ii) Give an example where potential energy is acquired by a body due to change in its shape. [1]

(iii) A skier of mass 50 kg stands at *A*, at the top of a ski jump. He takes off from *A* for his jump to *B*. Calculate the change in his gravitational potential energy between *A* and *B*. [1]

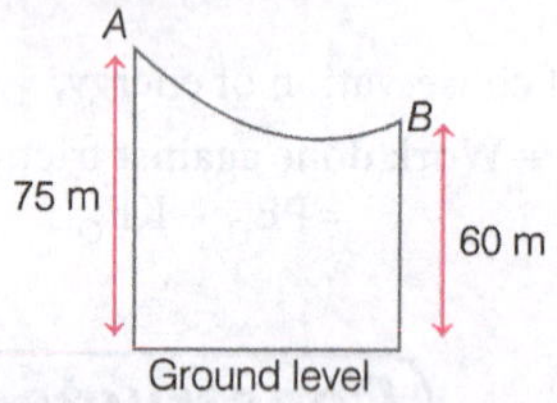

Sol. (i) **Potential Energy** It is the energy possessed by a body by virtue of its position or shape.

(ii) In a toy car, the wound spring possesses potential energy. When spring is released, its potential energy changes into kinetic energy due to which the toy car moves.

(iii) Given, $m = 50$ kg, $h_1 = 75$ m, $h_2 = 60$ m

At point A, $PE_1 = mgh_1 = 50 \times 10 \times 75 = 37500$ J

At point B, $PE_2 = mgh_2 = 50 \times 10 \times 60 = 30000$ J

Change in $PE = PE_1 - PE_2 = 37500 - 30000 = 7500$ J

3 (i) A body of mass *m* is raised to a vertical height *h* through two different paths *A* and *B* as shown in the figure. What will be the potential energy of the body in the two cases? Give reason for your answer. [1½]

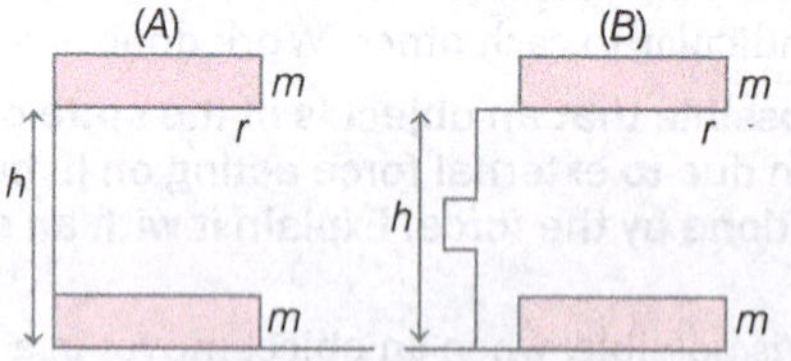

(ii) If two bodies *X* and *Y* having equal masses are kept at heights of 2*h* and 5*h*. Calculate the ratio of their potential energies. ($g = 10$ m/s^2) [1½]

Competency Based Que.

Sol. (i) The work done against gravity in both the cases is mgh. It is independent of the path along which the body is moved and it depends only on the initial and final positions of the body. Hence, potential energy of the body is same in both cases.

(ii) Potential energies of bodies X and Y,

$$PE_x = mgh_1 \text{ and } PE_y = mgh_2$$
$$PE_x = mg(2h) \text{ and } PE_y = mg(5h)$$

Comparing the PE_x and PE_y.

$$\frac{PE_x}{PE_y} = \frac{mg(2h)}{mg(5h)}$$

$$\Rightarrow \quad \frac{PE_x}{PE_y} = \frac{2}{5} = 2:5$$

4 Deduce the expression for kinetic energy of a body.

Sol. Refer to the text on page 245 (Calculation of Kinetic Energy).

5 Derive an expression and verify law of conservation of energy during the free fall of a body.

Sol. Refer to the text on page 247 (Law of Conservation of Energy).

6 (i) State and define SI unit of energy. [1]

(ii) A person carrying 10 bricks each of mass 2.5 kg on his head moves to a height 20 m in 50 s. Calculate power of the person spent in carrying bricks. (Given, $g = 10\ ms^{-2}$) [2]

Sol. (i) The SI unit of energy is Joule (J).

1 Joule is the energy required to do 1J of work

(ii) Given, mass of one brick = 2.5 kg

Mass of 10 bricks = 2.5 × 10 = 25 kg

Height, $h = 20$ m, time, $t = 50$ s, power, $P = ?$

$$\therefore \text{ Power, } P = \frac{mgh}{t} = \frac{25 \times 10 \times 20}{50} = 100\ Js^{-1}$$

Long Answer Type Questions

1 The velocity of a body moving in a straight line is increased by applying a constant force F for some distance in the direction of the motion. Prove that the increase in the kinetic energy of the body is equal to the work done by the force on the body. NCERT Exemplar

Sol. Consider an object of mass m moving with a uniform velocity u. Let, it now be displaced through a distance s, when a constant force F acts on it in the direction of its displacement.

From the third equation of motion, $v^2 = u^2 + 2as$

$$\Rightarrow \quad v^2 - u^2 = 2as$$

$$\Rightarrow \quad s = \frac{v^2 - u^2}{2a} \quad \text{....(i)}$$

We know that, work done by F is

$W = Fs$ [where, force and displacement are in same direction]

$$\therefore \quad W = ma \times s \quad [\because F = ma]$$
$$= ma \times \left(\frac{v^2 - u^2}{2a}\right) \quad \text{[from Eq. (i)]}$$
$$W = \frac{1}{2} m (v^2 - u^2) \quad \text{...(ii)}$$

If the object is starting from its stationary position, i.e. $u = 0$, from Eq. (ii), we get

$$W = \frac{1}{2} mv^2$$

It is clear that, the work done is equal to the increase in the kinetic energy of an object.

2 A freely falling object eventually stops on reaching the ground. What happens to its kinetic energy?

Sol. When a freely falling body eventually stops on reaching the ground, its kinetic energy appears in the form of

(i) Heat (the body and the ground become warmer due to collision).

(ii) Sound (produced due to collision of the body with the ground).

(iii) Potential energy of configuration of the body and the ground (the body may be deformed and the ground may be depressed at the place of collision).

The process in which the kinetic energy of a freely falling body is lost in an unproductive chain of energy changes is called dissipation of energy.

3 A motorcycle and a car are moving on a levelled horizontal road with equal kinetic energy. Both the vehicles are brought to rest by equal retarding forces applied by the brakes. Which of them will cover shorter distance to stop? Competency Based Que.

Sol. The kinetic energy is equal to the total work done by each vehicle before coming to rest.

i.e, Work done, W = Change in kinetic energy

$$-W = \frac{1}{2}m(0)^2 - \frac{1}{2}mu^2$$

$$W = \frac{1}{2}mu^2 \quad \text{... (i)}$$

Kinetic energy of the car E_C = Kinetic energy of the motorcycle, E_M let F be the retarding force applied by the brakes and x and y are the distances travelled by motorcycle and car before coming to rest.

Work done by motorcycle, $W_M = Fx$

Work done by car, $W_C = Fy$

From Eq. (i), Both the vehicles have equal kinetic energy,

i.e., $Fx = Fy$

Since, F is also same, $\Rightarrow x = y$

Both the vehicles will cover equal distances before coming to rest.

Numerical Questions

1 A car and a truck have the same speed of 60 ms^{-1}. If their masses are in the ratio 1 : 4. Find the ratio of their KE.

Sol. As, $\frac{KE_1}{KE_2}=\frac{(1/2)m_1v^2}{(1/2)m_2v^2}=\frac{m_1}{m_2}=\frac{1}{4}=1:4$

2 What will be the velocity of a particle of mass 5 kg having kinetic energy of 250 J.

Sol. Here, mass of particle, $m=5$ kg,

Kinetic energy, KE = 250 J

$v=?$ (to find)

$$KE=\frac{1}{2}mv^2$$

$$v^2=\frac{2KE}{m}$$

$$\Rightarrow \quad v=\sqrt{\frac{2KE}{m}}=\sqrt{\frac{2\times 250}{5}}=10 \text{ m/s}$$

3 What amount of energy will be required to stop a truck of 1200 kg moving at a velocity of 25 km/h.

Sol. Given, initial velocity, $u=25 \text{ km/h}=25\times\frac{5}{18}$ m/s

$$=\frac{125}{18} \text{ m/s}$$

and final velocity $v=0$

Work done by breaking force to stop truck is equal to the energy stored in truck.

Work done = Change in kinetic energy. (K_f-K_i)

$$=\frac{1}{2}m(0)^2-\frac{1}{2}mu^2$$

$$=-\frac{1}{2}\times 1200\times\left(\frac{125}{18}\right)^2$$

$$=-\frac{1}{2}\times 1200\times(6.94)^2=-28898.16 \text{ J.}$$

28898.16 J of energy will be required to stop truck.

(– ve sign indicate force will be opposite to displacement)

4 An object of mass 2 kg is dropped from a height of 1m. What will be its kinetic energy as it reaches the ground? (Take, g = 9.8 ms^{-2})

Sol. Given, mass, $m=2$ kg and height, $h=1$ m

On reaching the ground, the kinetic energy of object is converted into its potential energy such that

$$KE=PE=mgh=2\times 9.8\times 1=19.6 \text{ J}$$

5 If a stone of mass 3 kg is thrown up with a speed of 30 m/s. Calculate its maximum potential energy.

Sol. Mass of stone, $m=3$ kg

Speed with which it's thrown, $u=30$ m/s, $v=0$

From equation of motion,

$$v^2=u^2-2gh$$

$$gh=\frac{u^2}{2}=\frac{30^2}{2}=\frac{900}{2}=450$$

$$h=\frac{450}{g} \text{ m}$$

Maximum potential energy,

$$PE=mgh=3\times g\times\frac{450}{g}=1350 \text{ J}$$

6 If an electric iron of 1200 W is used for 30 min everyday, find electric energy consumed in the month of April. **NCERT Exemplar**

Sol. 1200 W means 1200 J/s.

For 30 min, 1200 × 30 × 60 = 2160000 J of energy consumed per day,

There are 30 days in the month of April,

Electric energy consumed in the month of April,

$$E=2160000\times 30$$

$$E=6.48\times 10^7 \text{ J}$$

7 A girl weighing 50 kg runs up a hill raising herself vertically 10 m in 20 s. What is the power expended by girl?

Sol. Power expended by girl $=\frac{\text{Work done by girl}}{\text{Time taken}}$

$$=\frac{F\times s}{t}=\frac{mg\times s}{t}=\frac{50\times 9.8\times 10}{20} \quad [\because F=mg]$$

$$=245 \text{ W}$$

8 An elevator with a load of 700 kg is moving down with a velocity of 0.5 m/s. The power produced by motor in horse power will be?
[1 HP = 746 W]

Sol. Power, $P=\frac{W}{t}=\frac{Fs}{t}=Fv$ (As $v=s/t$)

Power produced by motor, $P=700\times 10\times 0.5$

(As $F=mg$ on load) $P=3500$ W

In horse power, $P=\frac{3500}{746}=4.69$ HP

9 On the blades of a water turbine, water is falling at the rate of 6000 kg/h, from a height of 60m. Find the power given to the turbine. (Take, g = 10 m/s^2)

Sol. Potential energy stored in 6000 kg of water at height 60 m,

$$PE=mgh=6000\times 10\times 60=36\times 10^5 \text{ J}$$

This much amount of energy stored in water falls on turbine per hour and power is developed.

$$\text{Power}=\frac{\text{Energy (J)}}{\text{Time (s)}}=\frac{36\times 10^5}{60\times 60}=10^3 \text{ W}$$

10 A lift is designed in such a way to carry a load of 5000 kg through 12 floors of a building, on an average height is 9 m per floor in 30 s. Find the power of the lift. ($g = 10\ m/s^2$)

Sol. Height of the building, $h = 12 \times 9 = 108$ m

Potential energy at the top of building, PE $= mgh$

$PE = 5 \times 10^3 \times 10 \times 108 = 540 \times 10^4$ J

This amount of energy is transferred in 30 s with the help of lift.

Power of the lift, $P = \dfrac{540 \times 10^4}{30} = 18 \times 10^4$ W.

11 What will be the output power (in watt) of a 55 kg athelete who accelerates from 0 to 12 m/s in 4 s?

Sol. Here, $m = 55$ kg

From work-energy theorem,

Work done = Change in kinetic energy

$W = \dfrac{1}{2} m(12^2 - 0^2) = \dfrac{1}{2} \times 55 \times 144 = 3960$ J

Power output, $P = \dfrac{\text{Work}}{\text{Time}} = \dfrac{3960}{4} = 990$ W

12 A girl is carrying a bucket filled with water by applying a force of 15 N. She moves a horizontal distance 10 m and then climbs up a vertical distance of 20 m. Calculate the total work done by the girl. **Competency Based Que.**

Sol. For horizontal distance 10 m covered, force and displacement are perpendicular to each other, i.e. both make 90° angle.

So, work done will be zero in this case.

When the girl climbs up a vertical distance of 20 m, then the work done by her,

$$W = F \times s = 15 \times 20 = 300\ \text{J}.$$

Total work done $= 0 + W = 0 + 300$ J

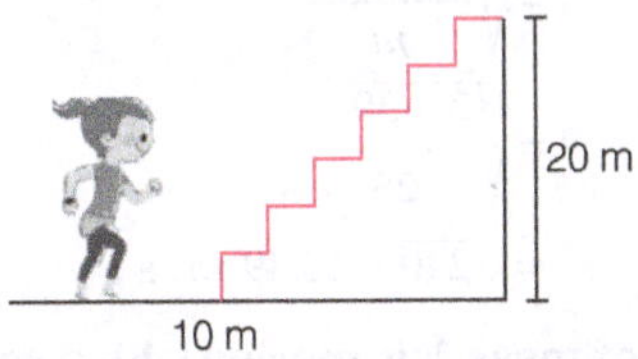

13 A labourer whose own mass is 50 kg carries a load of an additional 60 kg on his head to the top of a building 15 m high. Find the total work done by him. Also, find the work done by him, if he carries another additional block of mass 10 kg to the same height. (Take, $g = 10\ m\ s^{-2}$) **Competency Based Que.**

Sol. Given, total mass, $m = 50 + 60 = 110$ kg

Displacement, $s = 15$ m

Work done by him is given by $W = 0$

[since force and displacement are perpendicular to each other.]

If additional block of mass 10 kg is carried by him to the same height, then also work done by him remains zero because force and displacement are perpendicular to each other.

14 A girl having mass of 35 kg sits on a trolley of mass 5 kg. The trolley is given an initial velocity of $4\ ms^{-1}$ by applying a force.

The trolley comes to rest after traversing a distance of 16 m.

(i) How much work is done on the trolley? [1½]

(ii) How much work is done by the girl? [1½]

NCERT Exemplar

Sol. Given, $u = 4\ ms^{-1}$, $v = 0$ and $s = 16$ m

From the third equation of motion,

[$\because$ for retardation, the acceleration is negative, i.e. $a = -a$]

$$v^2 = u^2 - 2as$$

$$\Rightarrow \quad (0)^2 = (4)^2 - 2a \times 16$$

$$0 = 16 - 32a \Rightarrow a = \frac{16}{32} = 0.5\ ms^{-2}$$

where, u = initial velocity, v = final velocity,

a = acceleration and s = displacement.

(i) Total mass $= 35 + 5 = 40$ kg

Work is done on the trolley,

$W = F \cdot d = ma \cdot s$ [$\because F = ma$]

$= 40 \times 0.5 \times 16 = 320$ J

(ii) Given, mass of girl, $m = 35$ kg

Work done by the girl,

$W = F \cdot d = ma \cdot s = 35 \times 0.5 \times 16 = 280$ J

15 A boy is moving on a straight road against a frictional force of 5 N. After travelling a distance of 1.5 km he forgot the correct path at a round about (Fig.) of radius 100 m. However, he moves on the circular path for one and half cycle and then he moves forward upto 2.0 km.

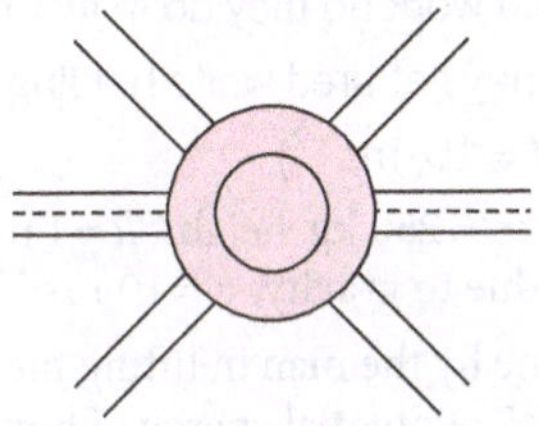

Calculate the work done by him. **Competency Based Que.**

Sol. Expression for work done, $W = F \times s$

where, F is the force acting on the body and s is the displacement of the body.

We know that, displacement is the smallest distance covered between the initial and final position of the body.

Here, in this displacement will be,

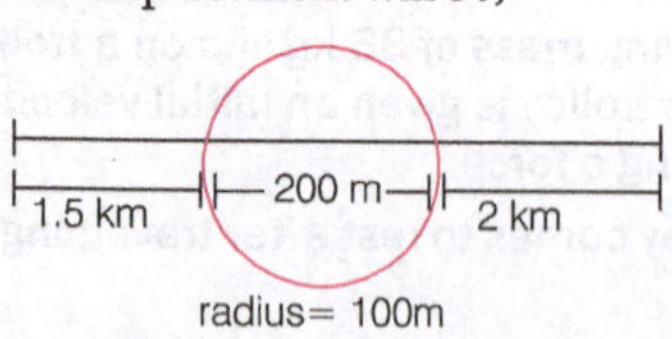

$$s = 1500 + 200 + 2000$$
$$= 3700 \text{ m}$$

Hence, the work done by boy,

$$W = F \times s = 5 \times 3700 = 18500 \text{ J}$$

16 On a level road, a scooterist applies brakes to slow down from a speed of 54 kmh^{-1} to 36 kmh^{-1}. What amount of work is done by the brakes? (Assuming, the mass of the empty scooter is 86 kg and that of the scooterist and petrol is 64 kg.)

Sol. Here, total mass, $m = 86 + 64 = 150$ kg

Initial velocity, $u = 54 \text{ kmh}^{-1}$

$$= \frac{54 \times 1000}{3600} = 15 \text{ ms}^{-1}$$

Final velocity, $v = 36 \text{ kmh}^{-1}$

$$= 36 \times \frac{1000}{3600} = 10 \text{ ms}^{-1}$$

Work done by brakes = KE lost by the scooter

= Final KE − Initial KE

$$= \frac{1}{2}mv^2 - \frac{1}{2}mu^2 = \frac{1}{2}m(v^2 - u^2)$$

$$= \frac{1}{2} \times 150[(10)^2 - (15)^2] = \frac{1}{2} \times 150(100 - 225)$$

$$= -75 \times 125 = -9375 \text{ J}$$

17 Four men lift a 250 kg box to a height of 1 m and hold it without raising or lowering it.

(i) How much work is done by the man in lifting the box? [1]

(ii) How much work do they do in just holding it? [1]

(iii) Why do they get tired while holding it? [1]

(Given, $g = 10 \text{ ms}^{-2}$) NCERT Exemplar

Sol. Given, mass, $m = 250$ kg, height, $h = 1$ m and acceleration due to gravity, $g = 10 \text{ ms}^{-2}$

(i) Work done by the man in lifting the box,

W = Potential energy of box

$W = mgh = 250 \times 10 \times 1 = 2500$ J

(ii) Work done is zero in holding a box because displacement is zero.

(iii) In holding the box, the energy of each man is lost. Due to the loss of energy, they feel tired.

18 A light and a heavy object have the same momentum. Find out the ratio of their kinetic energies. Which one has a larger kinetic energy? NCERT Exemplar

Sol. Suppose m_1 and m_2 are masses of a light and a heavy object respectively. As we know,

kinetic energy, $\text{KE} = \frac{1}{2}mv^2$ ...(i)

[where, v = velocity of objects.]

and momentum, $p = mv$ ...(ii)

On multiplying and dividing with m in Eq. (i), we get

So, $\text{KE} = \frac{1}{2}\frac{mv^2 \times m}{m}$

$\Rightarrow \text{KE} = \frac{1}{2}\frac{(mv)^2}{m}$ as from Eq. (ii) $[\because p = mv]$

So, $\text{KE} = \frac{p^2}{2m}$

We have, kinetic energy, $\text{KE} = \frac{p^2}{2m}$

$\because$ Momentum is same for light and heavy body.

So, kinetic energy, $\text{KE} \propto \frac{1}{m}$

Thus, kinetic energy is inversely proportional to the mass. So, lighter body has larger kinetic energy.

19 Calculate the velocity of a particle of mass 250 g having a kinetic energy of 30 J.

Sol. Given, mass of the body, $m = 250\text{g} = 0.25\text{kg}$

Kinetic energy, $\text{KE} = 30 \text{ J} = 30 \text{ N-m} = 30 \text{kg} - \text{m}^2/\text{s}^2$

$$\text{KE} = \frac{1}{2}mv^2$$

$$v^2 = \frac{2 \times (\text{KE})}{m}$$

$$v = \sqrt{\frac{2 \times (\text{KE})}{m}}$$

$$v = \sqrt{\frac{2 \times 30}{0.25}}$$

$$= \sqrt{240} = 15.49 \text{ m/s}$$

20 An object of mass M is moving with a constant velocity, v. How much work should be done on the object to bring the object to a constant velocity $\frac{v}{2}$?

Sol. From the work-energy theorem,

Total work done on the object = Change in kinetic energy of the object.

$$W = \frac{1}{2}mv_f^2 - \frac{1}{2}mv_i^2$$

$$= \frac{1}{2}m(v_f^2 - v_i^2)$$

Here, $v_f = \frac{v}{2}$ and $v_i = v$

$$W = \frac{1}{2}m\left[\left(\frac{v}{2}\right)^2 - (v)^2\right]$$

$$W = \frac{1}{2}m\left(\frac{v^2}{4} - v^2\right)$$

$$W = \frac{1}{2}mv^2\left(\frac{1}{4} - 1\right) = \frac{1}{2}mv^2\left(\frac{-3}{4}\right) = -\frac{3}{8}mv^2$$

Negative sign indicates that, the force is in opposite direction to the displacement of the object.

21 A body of mass 5 kg is thrown vertically upwards with an initial velocity of 50 ms^{-1}. What will be its potential energy at the end of 5 s?

Sol. Given, $m = 5\text{kg}$, $u = 50\,\text{ms}^{-1}$, $t = 5\,\text{s}$ and $g = -10\,\text{ms}^{-2}$

Height covered by the body in 5 s is $h = ut + \frac{1}{2}gt^2$

$$= 50 \times 5 - \frac{1}{2} \times 10 \times (5)^2$$

$$= 250 - 125 = 125\text{ m}$$

Therefore, PE of the body after 5 s

$$= mgh = 5 \times 10 \times 125 = 6250\text{ J}$$

22 The weight of a person on a planet *A* is about half that on the earth. He can jump up to 0.4 m height on the surface of the earth. How high he can jump on the planet *A*? **NCERT Exemplar**

Sol. It is given that, weight of person on the earth $= w$

(i.e. $w = mg$)

and as he can jump up to height, $h_1 = 0.4$ m

So, potential energy at this point

$$= mgh_1 = mg \times 0.4 \quad \text{...(i)}$$

And it is given that,

weight of the person on the other planet $= \frac{w}{2}$

And if he could jump to height (h_2), his potential energy would be

$$\frac{w}{2}h_2 = \frac{mg}{2}h_2 \quad \text{...(ii)}$$

Since, he applied same amount of effort in both the cases to lift his body, so his potential energy will be same.

From Eqs. (i) and (ii), we get

$$mg \times 0.4 = \frac{mg}{2}h_2$$

$$\Rightarrow \quad h_2 = 0.4 \times 2 = 0.8\text{ m}$$

23 300 J of work is to be done in lifting a bag of mass 5 kg in weight up to height of 4 m from the ground. What will be the acceleration with which the bag was raised? (Take, g =10 ms^{-2})

Sol. Given, mass, $m = 5$ kg, work, $W = 300$ J
$h = 4$ m, $g = 10\text{ ms}^{-2}$

Let a be the acceleration with which bag is lifted, then

Work done, $W = mgh + mah = m(g + a)h$

$$\Rightarrow \quad 300 = 5 \times (10 + a) \times 4$$

$$\Rightarrow \quad 300 = 20(10 + a)$$

$$\Rightarrow \quad 10 + a = \frac{300}{20} = 15$$

$$\Rightarrow \quad a = 15 - 10 = 5\text{ ms}^{-2}$$

24 A boy *X* can run with a speed of 8 ms^{-1} against the frictional force of 10 N and another *Y* can move with a speed of 3 ms^{-1} against the frictional force of 20 N. Find the ratio of powers of *X* and *Y*. **Competency Based Que.**

Sol. Given, distance travelled by the boy X in 1 s = 8 m

Distance travelled by the boy Y in 1 s = 3 m

As we know, work done by the boy X to run against the frictional force of 10 N = 10 N× 8 m = 80 J

So, power of 80 J of work done by $X = \frac{W}{t}$

$$= \frac{80\text{ J}}{1\text{s}} = 80\text{ W}$$

Similarly, work done by the boy Y to run against the frictional force of 20 N = 20 N× 3 m = 60J

$$\text{Power of } Y = \frac{60\text{ J}}{1\text{ s}} = 60\text{ W}$$

So, ratio of two values of powers is given by

$$\frac{\text{Power of } X}{\text{Power of } Y} = \frac{80}{60} = \frac{4}{3} = 4:3$$

25 Find the ratio of gravitational potential energy, if height of an object is doubled and mass is tripled. Also, find the ratio of work done by gravity in bringing the object to zero height in both cases. **Competency Based Que.**

Sol. Let an object of mass m be placed at height h from the ground level. As we know that the gravitational potential energy of the object is $PE_1 = mgh$.

When the height of the object is doubled and its mass is tripled, then its gravitational potential energy becomes

$$PE_2 = (3m) \times g \times (2h)$$
$$= 6\,mgh$$

$$\therefore \quad \frac{PE_2}{PE_1} = 6\left(\frac{mgh}{mgh}\right) = 6:1$$

When the object is at zero height, then its potential energy = 0 $\quad [\because h = 0]$

As, work done by the gravity to bring the object of mass m placed at height h to zero height is given by

$$W_1 = \text{change in energy}$$
$$= mgh - 0 = mgh$$

So, the work done by gravity to bring the object of mass $3m$ placed at height $2h$ to zero height is

$$W_2 = 6mgh - 0 = 6mgh$$

$$\therefore \quad \frac{W_2}{W_1} = \frac{6}{1} = 6:1$$

26 **A small child tends to mimic his father by lifting a mass of 10 kg on his head. As soon as he succeeds in lifting it, he loses the object that falls back to the ground. If the child has a height of 90 cm, find the kinetic energy**

(i) at half the height of the child, [1½]

(ii) with which the object strikes the ground. [1½]

Sol. Given, mass of the object, $m = 10$ kg

Height of the child, $h = 90 \text{ cm} = 0.9$ m

Total energy of the object at head of the child is given by

$$= \text{PE} + \text{KE} = mgh + 0 \quad [\because \text{KE} = 0, \text{ as } v = 0]$$
$$= mgh = 10 \times 9.8 \times 0.9 = 88.2 \text{ J}$$

(i) At half the height of child, i.e. at 0.45 m

Total energy, $\text{TE} = \text{PE} + \text{KE} = mgh + \text{KE}$

$$= 10 \times 9.8 \times 0.45 + \text{KE}$$

Now, from the law of conservation of energy,

$$\text{KE} + 10 \times 9.8 \times 0.45 = 88.2$$

or $\quad \text{KE} + 44.1 = 88.2$

$\therefore \quad \text{KE} = 88.2 - 44.1 = 44.1 \text{ J}$

(ii) When the object strikes the ground,

Total energy $= \text{PE} + \text{KE} = 0 + \text{KE} \quad [\because \text{PE} = 0, \text{ as } h = 0]$

$= \text{KE}$

$\therefore$ From the law of conservation of energy,

$$\text{KE} = 88.2 \text{ J} \quad [\because \text{TE} = 88.2 \text{ J}]$$

27 **At a height of 20 m above the ground, an object of mass 4 kg is released from rest. It is travelling at a speed of 20 ms^{-1} when it hits the ground. The object does not rebound and the gravitational field strength is 10 Nkg^{-1}.**

How much energy is converted into heat and sound on impact?

Sol. Given, height above the ground, $h = 20$ m

Mass of the ball, $m = 4$ kg

Speed of the ball while striking the ground, $v = 20 \text{ ms}^{-1}$

Acceleration due to gravity, $g = 10 \text{ Nkg}^{-1}$

According to law of conservation of energy, all the energy of the ball will be converted into sound and heat energy because the ball does not rebound.

$\therefore$ Energy of the ball,

$$= \frac{1}{2}mv^2 = \frac{1}{2} \times 4 \times (20)^2 = 800 \text{ J}$$

Hence, 800 J of energy will be converted into heat and sound.

28 **Two women are working on a construction site as shown in figure.**

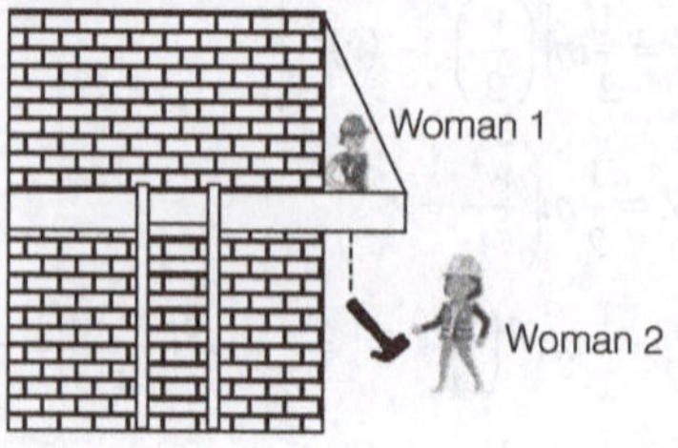

(i) **Woman 1 drops the hammer, which falls to the ground from a height of 3 m. Mass of hammer is 1 kg.**

(a) **Find the change in potential energy of the hammer, which falls to the ground.** [1]

(b) **What energy changes occur from the time the hammer leaves the hand of woman 1 and it is at rest on the ground.** [1]

(ii) **Woman 2 picks up the hammer and gives it back to the woman 1. She climbs the 2 m in 7 s. Her weight including the hammer is 600 N. Find the useful power which her legs are producing.** [1]

Competency Based Que.

Sol. (i) Mass of hammer, $m = 1$ kg.

(a) Height, $h = 3$m.

Change in potential energy,

$$= mgh = 1 \times 10 \times 3 = 30 \text{ J}$$

(b) Potential energy converted into kinetic energy and obtained heat + Sound energy

(ii) Weight, $mg = 600$ N (weight = woman + hammer)

Height, $h = 2$ m

Time taken, $t = 7$ s

$$\text{Power} = \frac{\text{Work done}}{\text{Time taken}} = \frac{(mg)h}{t} = \frac{600 \times 2}{7} = 171.42 \text{W}$$

29 **Mohan lifts his cellphone to a height of 1 m. He takes 1 s to do this. After lowering the phone, he then lifts it 2 m in 2 s. Has he generated more power in doing the second task? Give reason to justify your answer.**

Sol. Let, mass of cellphone be m kg

Work done (W) by Mohan $= mgh$

where, h = height at which cellphone is raised

and g = acceleration due to gravity.

$\Rightarrow \quad W = mg \times 1 = mg$

$$\therefore \text{ Power delivered } (P_1) = \frac{\text{Work done}(W)}{\text{Time}(t)} = \frac{mg}{1} = mg$$

Work done to lift cellphone by 2 m $= mg \times 2 = 2mg$

$$\text{Power delivered } (P_2) = \frac{\text{Work done}(W)}{\text{Time}(t)} = \frac{2mg}{2} = mg$$

So, in both cases power delivered by Mohan is same.

30 **A girl is drawing water from a well of 10 m depth in 25 s. Let the mass of her bucket be 3 kg. Find the power used by her. (Take, $g = 10\ m/s^2$)**

Sol. Here, mass of the bucket, $m = 3$ kg

Depth of the well, $h = 10$ m

Time taken to draw water, $t = 25$ s.

From the reference level, the girl is at a height 10 m above

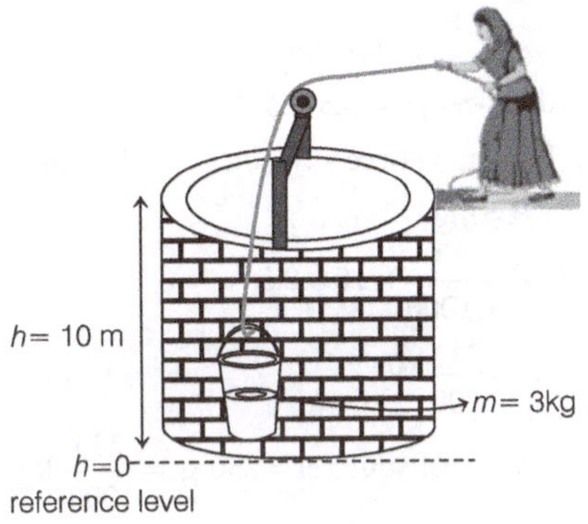

Work done by the girl is converted to increase in potential energy of the bucket.

Work done by the girl, $W = mgh$

$$= 3 \times 10 \times 10 = 300\ J$$

$\because$ Power used by her will be,

$$P = \frac{\text{Work done}}{\text{Time taken}} = \frac{300}{25} = 12\ W$$

31 **A boy of mass 50 kg runs up a staircase of 45 steps in 9 s. If the height of each step of the staircase is 15 cm, find the power of the boy. (Given, $g = 10\ ms^{-2}$)**

Sol. Given, mass of body, $m = 50$ kg

Height of each step = 15 cm

Total height of staircase,

$$h = 45 \times 15 = 675\ \text{cm} = 6.75\ m$$

$$t = 9\ s,\ g = 10\ ms^{-2}$$

$\therefore$ PE $= mgh = 50 \times 10 \times 6.75 = 3375$ J

So, the energy of the boy is 3375 J

$\therefore$ Power of the boy ,

$$P = \frac{PE}{\text{Time}} = \frac{3375}{9} = 375\ W$$

32 **A machine gun takes 10 s to fire 30 bullets with a velocity of 500 ms^{-1}. Find the power developed by the gun when each bullet has a mass of 100 g.**

Sol. Given, mass of 30 bullets = 30 × 100 = 3 kg

Velocity, $v = 500\ ms^{-1}$, time, $t = 10$ s

$\therefore$ Power developed by the gun, $P = \frac{W}{t}$

[here, work done by gun will be equal to the kinetic energy of all the bullets.]

$$\therefore \quad P = \frac{KE}{t} = \frac{\frac{1}{2}mv^2}{t} = \frac{mv^2}{2t} = \frac{3 \times (500)^2}{2 \times 10}$$

$$= \frac{3 \times 500 \times 500}{20} = 37500\ W$$

33 **The power of a motor pump is 2 kW. How much water per minute, the pump can raise to a height of 10 m? (Given, $g = 10\ ms^{-2}$)** NCERT Exemplar

Sol. Given, power of a motor

$$= 2\ kW = 2 \times 1000\ W = 2000\ W \quad [\because 1\ kW = 1000\ W]$$

$\therefore$ Power, $P = \frac{\text{Energy}}{\text{Time}}$

By putting the values, $P = \frac{mgh}{t}$

[where, m = mass of water]

$$2000 = \frac{m \times 10 \times 10}{60}$$

[here, $h = 10$ m and $t = 1$ min = 60 s]

$$\Rightarrow \quad m = \frac{2000 \times 60}{10 \times 10}$$

$$\Rightarrow \quad m = 1200\ kg$$

34 **Two boys *A* and *B* weighing 60 kg and 40 kg respectively, climb on a staircase each carrying a load of 20 kg on their head. The staircase has 10 steps, each of height 50 cm. If *A* takes 20 s to climb and *B* takes 10 s to climb, then** Competency Based Que.

(i) who possesses greater power? [1½]

(ii) find the ratio of their powers. [1½]

Sol. Given, mass of *A*, $m_A = 60$ kg

Mass of *B*, $m_B = 40$ kg

Mass of luggage, $m_L = 20$ kg

Height of staircase, $h = 0.5 \times 10 = 5$ m

So, work done by boy *A* to climb staircase $= mgh$

$$= (60 + 20) \times 9.8 \times 5 = 3920\ J$$

So, power of $A = \frac{\text{work}}{\text{time}} = \frac{3920}{20} = 196\ W$

Similarly, power of $B = \frac{\text{work}}{\text{time}} = \frac{mgh}{t}$

$$= \frac{[(40 + 20) \times 9.8 \times 5]}{10} = \frac{2940}{10}$$

$$= 294\ W$$

(i) *B* possesses greater power than *A*

(ii) So, the ratio is given by

$$\frac{\text{power of } A}{\text{power of } B} = \frac{196}{294} = 2:3$$

35 Define watt. Express kilowatt in terms of joule per second. A 150 kg car engine develops 500 W for each kg. What force does it exert in moving the car at speed of 20 ms^{-1}? **NCERT Exemplar**

Sol. (i) One watt is the power of a body which does work at the rate of 1 Js^{-1}.

i.e. $1 \text{ watt} = 1 \dfrac{\text{joule}}{\text{second}}$

(ii) 1 kilowatt = 1000 watt = 1000 Js^{-1}.

(iii) Given, $m = 150$ kg,

$P = 500$ W and $v = 20$ ms^{-1}

A car engine of 150 kg develops 500 W for each kg.

So, total power $= 150 \times 500 = 75000$ W

We have, power = force × speed

$= 75000 = F \times 20$

$\therefore$ Force, $F = \dfrac{75000}{20} = 3750$ N

36 How is the power related to the speed at which a body can be lifted? How many kilograms will a man working at the power of 100 W, be able to lift at constant speed of 1 ms^{-1} vertically? (Take, g =10 ms^{-2}) **NCERT Exemplar**

Sol. The power delivered to a body can also expressed in terms of the force F applied to the body and the velocity v of the body

Power, $P = \dfrac{\text{Work}}{\text{Time}} \Rightarrow P = \dfrac{F \cdot s}{t}$

where, F = force, s = displacement and t = time

$P = F \cdot v$ $\quad [\because W = F \cdot s]$

[where, v = velocity of the body] $\quad \left(\because v = \dfrac{s}{t}\right)$

Given, power, $P = 100$ W, $v = 1$ ms^{-1}

and $g = 10$ ms^{-2}

We know that, power,

$P = F \cdot v \Rightarrow P = mg \cdot v$ $\quad [\because F = mg]$

$100 = mg \cdot v$

$100 = m \times 10 \times 1$

$\Rightarrow m = \dfrac{100}{10}$

$\Rightarrow m = 10$ kg

Therefore, a man working at the power of 100 W can lift 10 kg.

37 Compare the power at which each of the following is moving upwards against the force of gravity? (Given, g =10 ms^{-2})

(i) A butterfly of mass 1 g that flies upward at a rate of 0.5 ms^{-1}. [1½]

(ii) A 250 g squirrel climbing up on a tree at a rate of 0.5 ms^{-1}. [1½]

NCERT Exemplar

Firstly, we find the power by using the formula $P = mg \cdot v$ in both parts and then by comparing both powers.

Sol. (i) Given, mass of butterfly, $m = 1\text{g} = \dfrac{1}{1000}$ kg, $\quad [\because 1 \text{ kg} = 1000 \text{ g}]$

$g = 10$ ms^{-2}

and speed, $v = 0.5$ ms^{-1}

$\therefore$ Power = Force × Speed $\quad [\because$ force, $F = mg]$

$P = mgv$

$\Rightarrow P = \dfrac{1}{1000} \times 10 \times 0.5$

$\Rightarrow P = \dfrac{1}{200}$ W

(ii) Given, mass of squirrel = 250 g $= \dfrac{250}{1000}$ kg $\quad [\because 1 \text{ kg} = 1000 \text{ g}]$

and speed = 0.5 m s^{-1}

$\therefore$ Power = Force × Speed $\quad [\because$ force, $F = mg]$

$P = mg \times v$

$\Rightarrow P = \dfrac{250}{1000} \times 10 \times 0.5 = \dfrac{250}{200}$ W

$\therefore P = \dfrac{250}{200}$ W

Therefore, a squirrel has more power than butterfly.

38 (i) A 4000 kg bus moving uniformly at a speed of 80 m/s stops after covering distance s. The force applied by the brakes is 30000 N. Calculate the distance covered s and work done by force applied by the brakes. [3]

(ii) A man is holding a suitcase in his hand of 5 kg while waiting for train on platform. Why he got tired while holding it? [2]

Sol. (i) Given, $u = 80$ m/s,

Force, $F = -30000$ N,

Mass of bus, $m = 4000$ kg

We know that,

$F = ma \Rightarrow a = \dfrac{F}{m} = \dfrac{-30000}{4000} = -\dfrac{30}{4}$ m/s^2

From equation of motion,

$v^2 - u^2 = 2as$

$0^2 - (80)^2 = 2\left(\dfrac{-30}{4}\right)s = \dfrac{2}{30} \times 80^2 = s$

$\Rightarrow s = 426.66$ m

So, work done by force applied by brakes,

$$W = F \times s = -30000 \times 426.66$$
$$= -12800000 = -1.28 \times 10^7 \text{ J}$$

Negative sign shows force and displacement are in opposite direction.

(ii) He got tired while holding it, because the muscles in his hand are continuously working against gravity to support the weight.

39 **A vehicle of 1 tonne travelling with a speed of 60 ms^{-1} notices a cow on the road 9 m ahead and applies brakes. It stops just infront of the cow.** **Competency Based Que.**

(i) Find out the KE of the vehicle before applying brakes. [1]

(ii) Calculate the retarding force provided by the brakes. [1]

(iii) How much time did it take to stop after the brakes were applied? [2]

(iv) What is the work done by the braking force? [1]

Sol. Given, mass of the vehicle, $m = 1$ tonne $= 1000$ kg

Initial speed, $u = 60$ ms^{-1}

Distance between vehicle and the cow, $s = 9$ m

Final velocity, $v = 0$

(i) KE of vehicle before applying brakes is given by

$$= \frac{1}{2} mu^2$$
$$= \frac{1}{2} \times 1000 \times 60 \times 60 = 1800000 \text{ J}$$

(ii) From the third equation of motion, $v^2 - u^2 = 2as$

$(0)^2 - (60)^2 = 2 \times a \times 9$

$\Rightarrow \quad a = -200 \text{ ms}^{-2}$

So, retarding force provided by the brakes

$$= ma = 1000 \times (-200)$$
$$= -200000 \text{ N}$$

(iii) Now, again from the second equation of motion,

$$s = ut + \frac{1}{2} at^2$$

$\Rightarrow \quad 9 = 60t + \frac{1}{2} \times (-200)\, t^2$

or $\quad 9 = 60t - 100t^2$

or $\quad 100t^2 - 60t + 9 = 0$

$\Rightarrow \quad (10t - 3)^2 = 0$

or $\quad 10t - 3 = 0$

$\Rightarrow \quad t = \frac{3}{10} = 0.3 \text{ s}$

(iv) So, work done by the braking force is given by

$$= Fs = -200000 \times 9 = -1800000 \text{ J}$$

40 **(i) What remains unchanged in the oscillation of pendulum, if it is released from point *A* as shown in the figure. Explain in brief.** [2]

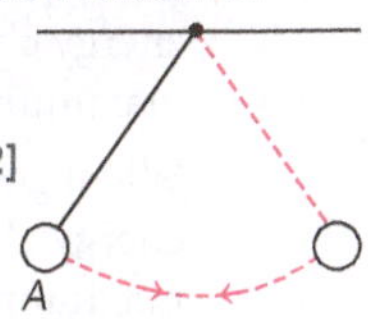

(ii) A man of mass 50 kg jumps from a height of 0.5 m. If $g = 10$ ms^{-2}, what will be his energy at the highest point? [1½]

(iii) Calculate the energy of a body of mass 20 kg moving with velocity of 0.1 ms^{-1}. [1½]

Sol. (i) The total mechanical energy remains unchanged at each point of the oscillation of pendulum.

Total mechanical energy (ME) = Kinetic energy (KE) + Potential energy (PE)

i.e., $\quad$ ME = KE + PE = constant.

or $\quad mgh + \frac{1}{2} mv^2 = \text{constant}$

This verifies the law of conservation of energy.

(ii) Given, $m = 50$ kg, $h = 0.5$ m, $g = 10$ ms^{-2}

At highest point, kinetic energy is converted into potential energy.

$\therefore \quad \text{PE} = mgh = 50 \times 10 \times 0.5 = 250 \text{ J}$

(iii) Given, $m = 20$ kg, $v = 0.1$ ms^{-1}

As we know that, a moving body has kinetic energy.

$\therefore \quad \text{KE} = \frac{1}{2} mv^2 = \frac{1}{2} \times 20 \times (0.1)^2$

$$= \frac{1}{2} \times 20 \times 0.1 \times 0.1 = 0.1 \text{ J}$$

41 **(i) A shell is fired from a canon vertically upwards from a point *X* as shown in the figure below. On reaching the highest point *Y*, it falls down. Give brief about the transformation of energy from *X* to *Y* and *Y* to *X*.** [2]

(ii) A shell of mass 2 kg is dropped from a height of 40 m. Calculate its kinetic energy and potential energy after **Competency Based Que.**

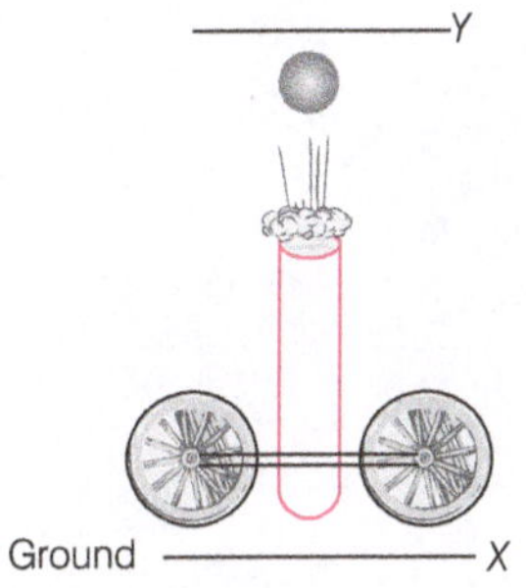

(a) 1st Second **(b) 2nd Second**
(c) 3rd Second ($g = 10$ m/s^2) [3]

Sol. (i) While going vertically upwards from ground, kinetic energy changes to potential energy and becomes maximum at point Y.

When going down from the highest point, potential energy changes to kinetic energy and it becomes maximum just before hitting the ground.

(ii) Total energy of the shell,

$$TE = mgh = 2 \times 10 \times 40 = 800 \text{ J}$$

(a) After 1st second,

$$= u + gt = 0 + 10 \times 1$$
$$= 10 \text{ m/s} \quad (\text{as } u = 0 \text{ at point } Y)$$

Kinetic energy, $KE = \frac{1}{2}mv^2$

$$= \frac{1}{2} \times 2 \times 10^2 = 100 \text{ J}$$

Potential energy, $PE = TE - KE$

$$= 800 - 100 = 700 \text{ J}$$

(b) After 2nd Second,

$$v = u + gt = 0 + 10 \times 2$$
$$v = 20 \text{ m/s}$$
$$KE = \frac{1}{2}mv^2$$
$$= \frac{1}{2} \times 2 \times 20^2 = 400 \text{ J}$$
$$PE = TE - KE$$
$$= 800 - 400$$
$$= 400 \text{ J}$$

(c) After 3rd second,

using, $s = ut + \frac{1}{2}gt^2$

$$40 = 0 \times t + \frac{1}{2} \times 10 \times t^2$$
$$\frac{80}{10} = t^2$$
$$t = \sqrt{8} = 2.82 \text{ s}$$

The shell falls back to ground in 2.82 s, so after 3 s, it will have energy equal to total energy due to law of conservation of energy.

42 **A bus of mass 800 kg is moving with a uniform speed of 20 m/s against a opposing force of 3000 N as shown in the figure,**

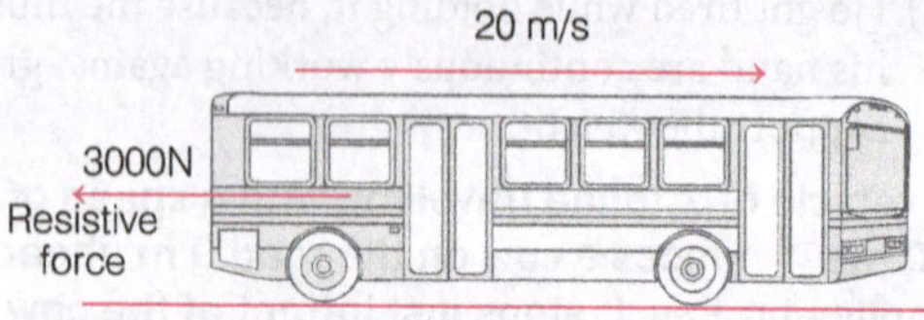

(i) A fuel used by the engine to drive the bus. What form of energy is in the fuel? [1]

(ii) Find the kinetic energy of the bus. [1½]

(iii) Find the energy used in 1s against the frictional force. [1½]

(iv) Calculate the minimum power that the bus engine has to deliver to the wheels? [1]

Competency Based Que.

Sol. (i) Chemical energy is the form of energy is in the fuel.

(ii) Kinetic energy of the bus,

$$KE = \frac{1}{2}mv^2$$
$$= \frac{1}{2} \times 800 \times (20)^2 = \frac{1}{2} \times 800 \times 400 = 160000 \text{ J}$$

(iii) Energy used is equal to the work done against the frictional force.

$$E = \text{Work done against frictional force}$$
$$= \text{Force} \times \text{Distance}$$
$$= 3000 \times 20 = 60000 \text{ J} = 60 \text{ kJ}$$

(iv) Minimum power that bus engine has to deliver to the wheels,

$$P_{min} = \frac{\text{Energy used}}{\text{Time taken}} = \frac{60000}{1} = 60000 \text{ W}$$
$$P_{min} = 60 \text{ kW}$$

ASSESSMENT EXERCISE

Competency Focused (Objective) Questions

Multiple Type Questions

1 In case of negative work, the angle between the force and displacement is **NCERT Exemplar**

(a) 0 (b) 45°
(c) 90° (d) 180°

2 A girl is carrying a school bag of 3 kg mass on her back and moves 200 m on a levelled road. The work done against the gravitational force will be ($g = 10 \text{ ms}^{-2}$) **NCERT Exemplar**

(a) 6×10^3 J (b) 6 J
(c) 0.6 J (d) zero

3 Mukesh drops a ball of 200 g from a tower of height 20 m. What will be its kinetic energy at the height of 5 m?

(a) 30 J (b) 50 J
(c) 60 J (d) 65 J

4 Figure shows the frictional force *versus* displacement for a particle in motion. The loss of kinetic energy (work done against friction) in travelling over s = 0 to s = 20 m will be **Competency Based Que.**

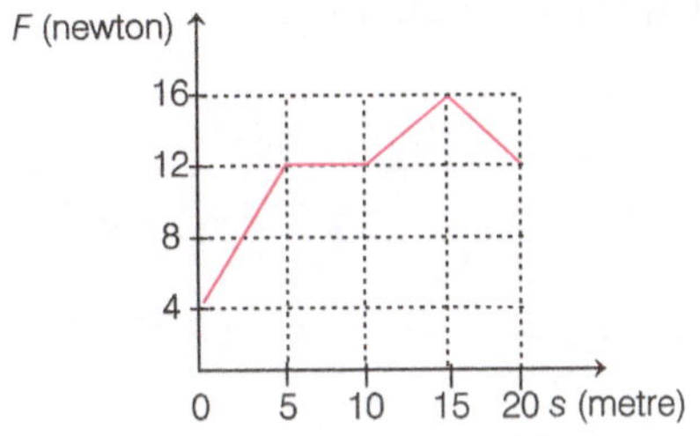

(a) 80 J (b) 160 J (c) 240 J (d) 24 J

5 Which of the following is unit of power?

(a) kilowatt-hour (b) horse power
(c) watt hour (d) All of these

Assertion-Reason

Direction (Q.Nos. 6-8) *In each of the following questions, a statement of Assertion is given by the corresponding statement of Reason. Of the statements, mark the correct answer as*

(a) If both Assertion and Reason are true and Reason is the correct explanation of Assertion.
(b) If both Assertion and Reason are true, but Reason is not the correct explanation of Assertion.
(c) If Assertion is true, but Reason is false.
(d) If Assertion is false, but Reason is true.

6 Assertion (A) Work done by a body is zero only, when displacement produced by the force is zero.

Reason (R) Work done by a force is negative, when displacement occurs in the opposite direction of applied force.

7 Assertion (A) In a stretched bow, potential energy is stored.

Reason (R) Mechanical energy of a moving body remains conserved.

8 Assertion (A) Steam engine converts heat energy into kinetic energy.

Reason (R) Steam engine works on the principle of conservation of energy.

Answers

1. (d) **2.** (d) **3.** (a) **4.** (c) **5.** (b)
6. (d) **7.** (b) **8.** (a)

Case Based/Source Based Questions

Direction (Q.Nos. 9) *Answer the question on the basis of your understanding of the following paragraph and related studied concepts*

9. Collision between two billiard balls or between two automobiles on a road are a few examples of collision from everyday life. Even gas atoms and molecules at room temperature keep on colliding against each other. In some collisions, momentum of the system is conserved but the kinetic energy is not conserved while in some collisions, both momentum and kinetic energy of the system are conserved. When two billiard balls collide to each other elastically, then their velocity of separation is equal to velocity of approach.

Similarly, in inelastic collision of two bodies, velocity of approach is less than the velocity of separation. In perfectly inelastic collision of two bodies, velocity of separation becomes zero.

(i) Which type of energy conserved in elastic collision of two billiard balls?

(ii) In perfectly inelastic collision, the two bodies move with a common velocity. Why?

(iii) In which type of collision, total energy and momentum both are conserved?

Constructed Response (Descriptive) Questions

Very Short Answer Type Questions

10 When is work done by a force zero?

11 Which will have more impact on kinetic energy—tripling mass or velocity?

12 Where does a pendulum have maximum

(i) potential energy? (ii) kinetic energy?

Competency Based Que.

13 If a stone is thrown upwards, what happens to its kinetic energy and potential energy?

14 A man of 50 kg jumps to a height of 3 m. What is the maximum PE that he will have? [Ans. 1.5×10^3 J]

Short Answer Type Questions

15 The velocity of a body moving in a straight line is increased by applying a constant force *F*, for some distance in the direction of the motion. Prove that the increase in the kinetic energy of the body is equal to the work done by the force on the body.

Competency Based Que.

16 What do you mean by gravitational potential energy? Show that gravitational potential energy is independent of the path followed.

17 (i) A mass *m* is dropped from a height *h*. At half-way to the ground, what is the total energy?

(ii) What happens to the work done by you, as you hit a football?

(iii) Write the relation between power, energy and time.

18 When water is flowing through a pipe, then its velocity changes by 5%. Find the percentage change in the power of water. [Ans. 5%]

19 A boy of mass 50 kg runs up a staircase of 50 steps in 10 s. If the height of each step is 15 cm, then find the his power. (Take, $g = 10\ ms^{-2}$) [Ans. 375 W]

Long Answer Type Questions

20 (i) What do you understand by the term "transformation of energy?" Explain with an example.

(ii) Explain the transformation of energy in the following case

(a) A ball thrown upwards

(b) A stone dropped from the roof of a buildings

21 (i) A force of 20N acts on a body of 3kg for 5 s. Find the kinetic energy produced by the body in 5 s. [Ans. 1666.6J]

(ii) Calculate the power of a pump which lifts 100 kg of water to a water tank placed at a height of 20 m in 10 s. (Take, $g = 10\ ms^{-2}$) [Ans. 2000 W]

CHAPTER 11

Sound

We hear sound from various sources, e.g. from humans, birds, machines, vehicles, TV, radio, etc. **Sound** is a form of energy which produces a sensation of hearing in our ears. In this chapter we are going to learn how sound is produced and how it is transmitted through a medium and received by our ears.

11.1 Production of Sound

Sound is produced by vibrating objects. **Vibration** means a kind of rapid to and fro motion of an object. The sound of human voice is also produced due to vibrations in the vocal cord.

We can produce sound by striking the tuning fork, by plucking, scratching, rubbing, blowing or shaking different objects. They all produce sound due to vibrations.

11.2 Propagation of Sound

Sound cannot travel without any medium. The medium can be defined as the matter or substance through which sound is transmitted. It can be solid, liquid or gas. Sound travels faster in solid than in any other medium.

When an object vibrates, it sets the particles of the medium (solid, liquid or gas) around it in vibrations. The particles do not travel all the way from the vibrating object to the ear. A particle of the medium in contact with the vibrating object is first displaced from its **equilibrium position.** It then exerts a force on the adjacent particle. As a result of which, the adjacent particle gets displaced from its position of rest.

After displacing the adjacent particle, the first particle comes back to its original position. This process continues in the medium till the sound reaches our ear.

The source of sound creates a disturbance in the medium which travels through it. The particles of the medium do not move forward but the disturbance is carried forward. This is propagation of sound in a medium, hence sound can be visualised as a wave. Sound waves require a medium to travel, so they are called **mechanical waves.**

Formation of Compression and Rarefaction in Air

When a vibrating object moves forward in air, it pushes and compresses the air infront of it, creating a **compression** which starts to move away from the vibrating object. When the vibrating object moves backwards, it creates **rarefaction.**

Compression is the part of a longitudinal wave in which the particles of the medium are closer to one another than they normally are and it is the region of high pressure. It is denoted by *C* in the figure given here.

Rarefaction is the part of a longitudinal wave in which the particles of the medium are farther apart than they normally are and it is the region of low pressure. It is denoted by *R* in the figure given here.

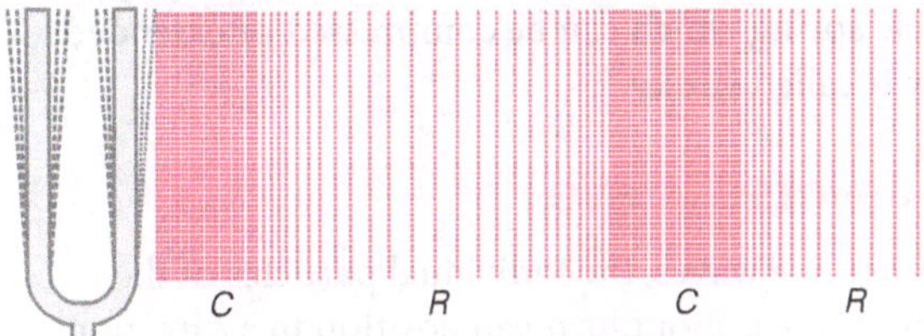

A vibrating object creating a series of compressions (C) and rarefactions (R) in the medium

As the object moves back and forth rapidly, a series of compressions and rarefactions is created in air.

Thus, propagation of sound can be visualised as propagation of density variations or pressure variations in the medium as pressure is related to the number of particles of a medium in a given volume.
More density of the particles in the medium gives more pressure and *vice-versa*.

In compression region, the density and pressure is higher than that of rarefaction.

11.3 Types of Waves

There are mainly two types of waves

Longitudinal Waves

In longitudinal waves, the individual particles of the medium move in a direction parallel to the direction of propagation of the disturbance.
The particles do not move from one place to another but they simply oscillate back and forth about their positions of rest.

This is exactly how a sound wave propagates, hence **sound waves are longitudinal waves**. These waves can be produced in all the three media such as solids, liquids and gases. The waves which travel along a spring when it is pushed and pulled at one end, are the longitudinal waves.

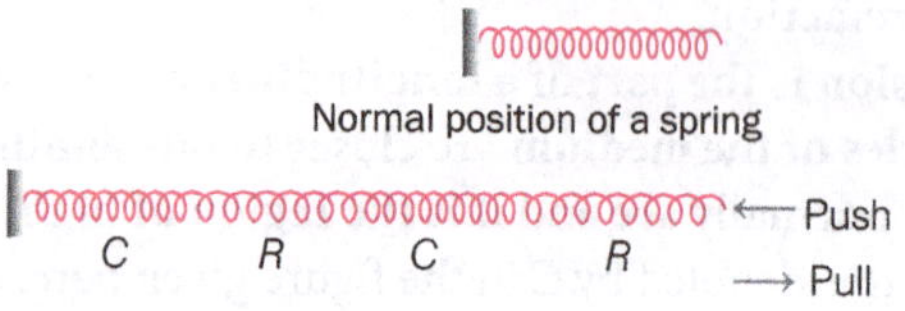

Longitudinal wave in a slinky

When coils are close together than normal, compressions (C) are observed in spring. When coils are farther apart than normal, rarefactions (R) are observed. A long flexible spring which can be compressed or extended easily is called **slinky**.

Transverse Waves

In transverse waves, the individual particles of the medium move about its mean position in a direction perpendicular to the direction of wave propagation.
e.g. Light is a transverse wave (but it is not a mechanical wave, i.e. it does not require a medium for its propagation). Transverse waves can be produced only in solids and liquids but not in gases.

The waves produced by moving one end of a long spring or rope, up and down rapidly, whose other end is fixed, are transverse waves.

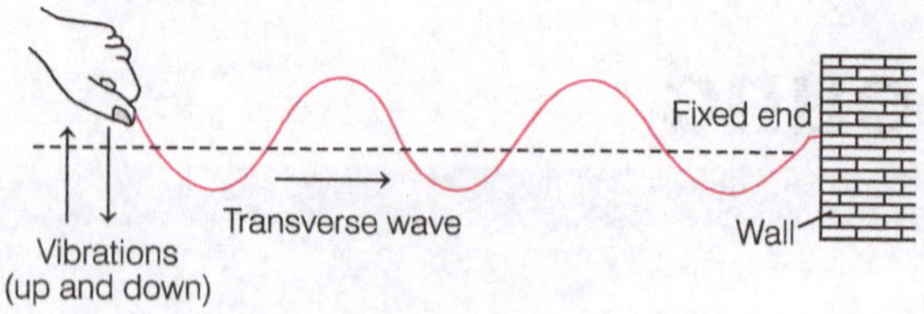

Transverse wave on a long spring or rope

Transverse wave with crest and trough is shown below

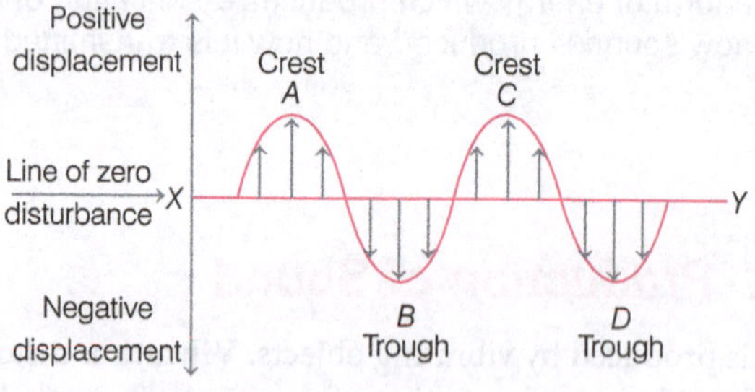

Crest and trough of a transverse wave

Note **Crest** The point of maximum positive displacement on a transverse wave.
Trough The point of maximum negative displacement on a transverse wave.

Try These 11.1

1. **Which form of energy produces a sensation of hearing in our ears?**
2. **In which wave a particles vibrate in direction perpendicular to that of wave propogation ?**
3. **Is it possible for a transverse wave to propagate without any medium?**
4. **Fill in the blanks**
   (i) **The nature of sound wave is ....**
   (ii) **Transverse waves can be produced only in ..... and ...... but not in ....**

11.4 Terms to Describe Sound Waves

Sound waves can be described by its

(i) wavelength (ii) frequency (iii) time period
(iv) amplitude (v) speed

Wavelength

The distance between the two consecutive compressions (C) or two consecutive rarefactions (R) is called the wavelength. Wavelength is the minimum distance in which a sound wave repeats itself.

In other words, it is the combined length of a compression and an adjacent rarefaction. It is represented by a Greek letter **lambda** λ. Its SI unit is **metre** (m).

Frequency

The number of complete waves (or oscillations) produced in one second is called frequency of the wave. It is the number of vibrations that occur per second.

Or the number of the compressions or rarefactions that cross a point per unit time.

The frequency of a wave is fixed and does not change even when it passes through different substances. It is denoted by ν. Its SI unit is **hertz** (symbol Hz) named in honour of **Heinrich Rudolf Hertz.**

Time Period

The time taken by two consecutive **compressions** or **rarefactions** to cross a fixed point is called the time period of the wave.

In other words, the time required to produce one complete wave (or oscillations) is called time period of the wave. It is denoted by symbol T. Its SI unit is **second** (s).

The time period of a wave is the reciprocal of its frequency,

i.e. $$\text{Time period } (T) = \frac{1}{\text{Frequency}(\nu)}$$

Amplitude

The maximum displacement of the particles of a medium from their original mean positions on passing a wave through the medium is called amplitude of the wave.

It is used to describe the size of the wave. It is usually denoted by the letter A. Its SI unit is metre (m).
The amplitude of a wave is same as the amplitude of the vibrating body producing the wave. The amplitude of the sound wave depends upon the force with which an object is made to vibrate.

Speed

The distance travelled by a wave in one second is called **speed of the wave** or **velocity of the wave.**
Under the same physical conditions, the speed of sound remains same for all frequencies.
It is represented by letter v.
Its SI unit is **metre per second** (m/s or ms^{-1}).

Relationship between speed, frequency and wavelength of a wave

$$\text{Speed} = \frac{\text{Distance travelled}}{\text{Time taken}}$$

Suppose distance travelled by a wave is λ (wavelength) in time T, then the speed is given by $v = \lambda / T$

We know that, frequency, $\nu = 1/T$

Therefore, $v = \lambda \times \nu$ or $v = \nu\lambda$

or Speed (velocity) = Frequency × Wavelength

Graphical Representation of a Sound Wave

When a sound wave passes through air, the density of air changes continuously.

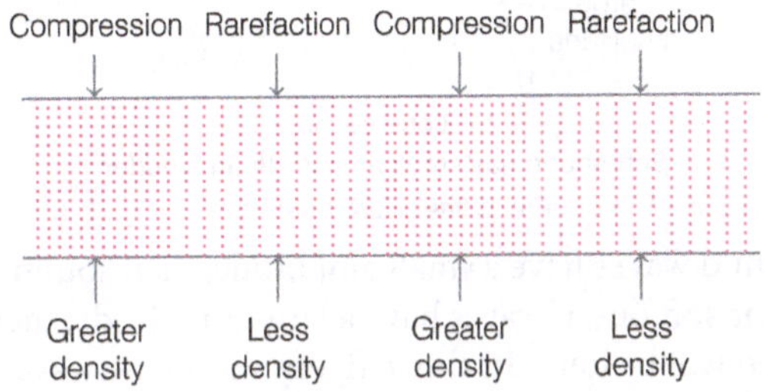

Representation of sound wave

A sound wave in air has been represented by means of a density-distance graph as shown below

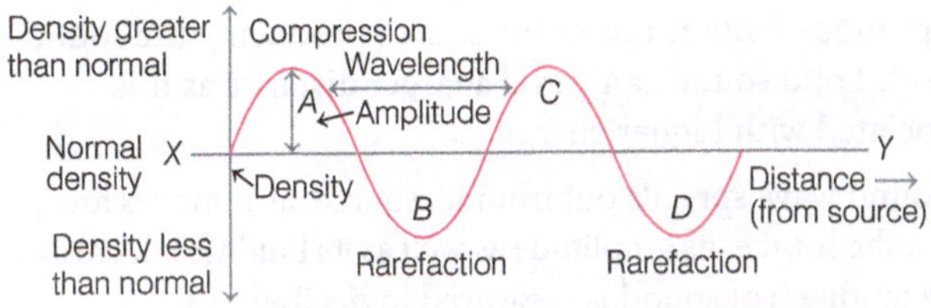

A sound wave in air by density-distance graph

Example 1. **Sound waves travel in air with speed of about 330 ms^{-1}. Calculate the wavelength of sound whose frequency is 550 Hz. Calculate time period of one oscillation.**

Sol. Given, frequency of sound, $\nu = 550$ Hz

Speed of sound wave, $v = 330\ ms^{-1}$

Wavelength of sound wave, $\lambda = ?$

Time period, $T = ?$

We know that, $v = \nu\lambda$ and $T = 1/\nu$

$$\Rightarrow \quad \lambda = \frac{v}{\nu} = \frac{330}{550} = \frac{3}{5} = 0.6 \text{ m}$$

Again, $$T = \frac{1}{\nu} = \frac{1}{550} = 0.001 \text{ s}$$

11.5 Characteristics of Sound

A sound has three characteristics. These are loudness, pitch and quality (or timbre).

(i) Loudness

It is the measure of the sound energy reaching the ear per second. Greater the sound energy reaching our ear per second, louder the sound will appear to be.

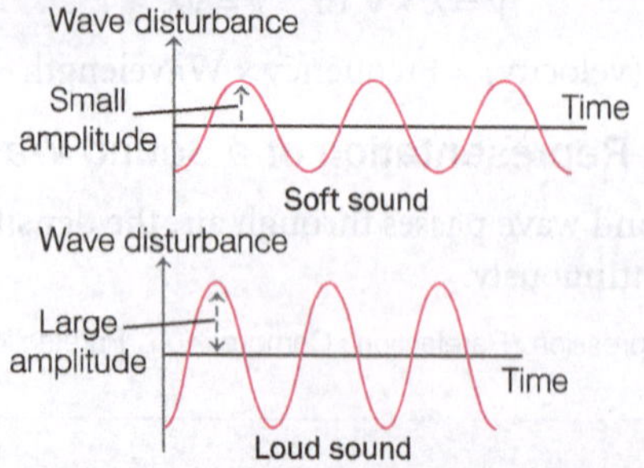

Soft sound has small amplitude and louder sound has large amplitude

If the sound waves have a small amplitude, then sound will be faint or soft but, if waves have a large amplitude, then the sound will be loud. In above figure shows the wave shapes of a loud and a soft sound of the same frequency.

Since, the amplitude of a sound wave is equal to the amplitude of vibrations of the source producing the sound waves, hence the loudness of sound depends on the amplitude of vibrations of the source producing the sound waves. Loud sound can travel a larger distance as it is associated with higher energy.

A sound wave spreads out from its source, as it moves away from the source, its amplitude as well as its loudness decreases. The loudness of sound is measured in **decibel** (dB). It depends on the sensitivity or the response of our ears.

(ii) Intensity

The amount of sound energy passing each second through unit area is known as the **intensity** of sound. Loudness and intensity are not the same terms.

Loudness is a measure of the response of the ear to the sound. Even when two sounds are of equal intensity, we may hear one as louder than the other, simply because our ear detects it in better way.

The SI unit of intensity is **watt per square metre** (W/m^2).

(iii) Pitch or Shrillness

It is that characteristic of sound by which we can distinguish between different sounds of the same loudness. Due to this characteristic, we can distinguish between a man's voice and woman's voice of the same loudness without seeing them.

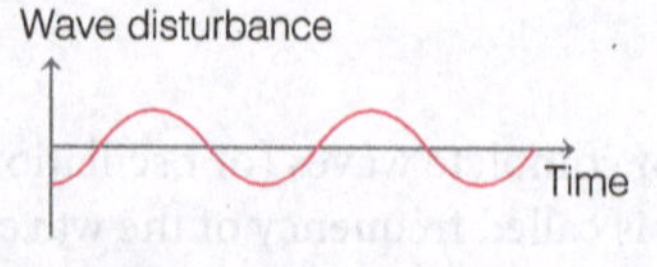

Wave shape for a low pitched sound

Pitch of a sound depends on the frequency of vibration. Greater the frequency of a sound, the higher will be its pitch.

In other words, the faster the vibration of the source, the higher is the frequency and hence, higher is the pitch, as shown in figure. Thus, a high pitch sound corresponds to more number of compressions and rarefactions passing through a fixed point per unit time. Low pitch sound has low frequency and high pitch sound has high frequency.

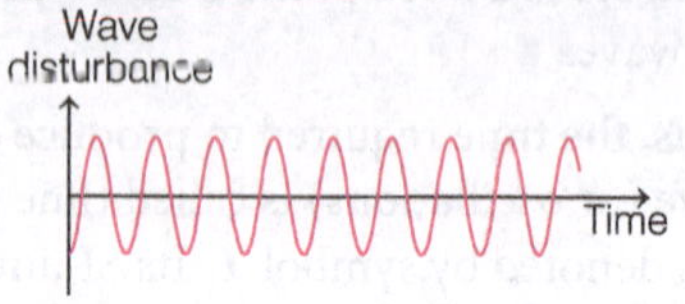

Wave shape for a high pitched sound

Objects of different sizes and conditions vibrates at different frequencies to produce sounds of different pitches.

(iv) Quality or Timbre

The quality or timbre of sound enables us to distinguish one sound from another having the same pitch and loudness.

A sound of single frequency is called a **tone**. The sound produced due to a mixture of several frequencies is called a **note** and is pleasant in listening too.
Noise is unpleasant to ear. Music is pleasant to ear and is of rich quality.

11.6 Speed of Sound and Light

The speed of sound in air is about 344 ms^{-1} at 22°C and 331 ms^{-1} at 0°C and the speed of light in air is 300000000 ms^{-1} or 3×10^8 ms^{-1}. Thus, speed of light is very high as compared to the speed of sound.

This is the reason why in the rainy season, the flash of lightning is seen first and the sound of thunder is heard a little later, though both are produced at the same time in clouds.

Speed of Sound in Different Media

The medium through which sound propagates can be a solid substance, a liquid or a gas. The speed of sound depends on the properties of medium through which it travels and the temperature of the medium.

The speed of sound decreases when we go from solid to gaseous state. If temperature of the medium increases, then speed of sound also increases.

Try These 11.2

1. **Wave of frequency 200 Hz is produced in a string as shown in the figure. Find amplitude, wavelength and velocity of the wave.**

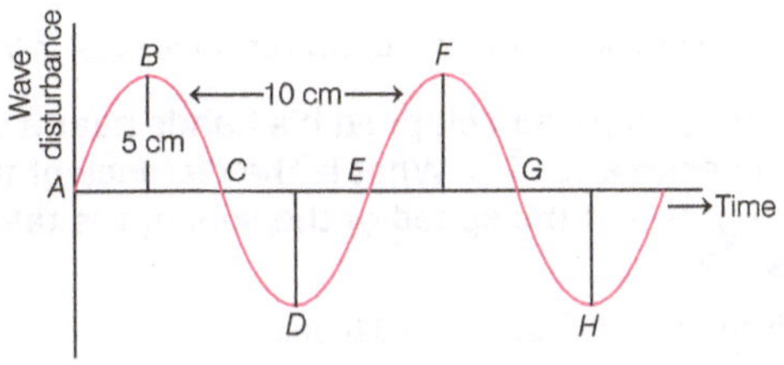

[**Ans.** Amplitude = 5 cm, wavelength = 10 cm and velocity = 20 m/s]

2. **An object is vibrating at 60 Hz. What is the time period ?** [**Ans.** 0.016 s]
3. **If a source of sound produces 200 compressions and 200 rarefactions in air in 20 s, find the frequency of sound produced.** [**Ans.** 10 Hz]
4. **State True and False for the following statement:**
   Pitch of sound wave helps us to distinguish between a man's voice and woman's voice without seeing them.
5. **What happens to the speed of sound when it goes from solid to gaseous state?**

11.7 Reflection of Sound Wave

The bouncing back of sound when it strikes a hard surface is known as **reflection** of sound.

It can be reflected from any surface whether it is smooth or rough. Sound is reflected in the same way as light and follows the same laws of reflection, which are as follows

(i) The incident sound wave (AO), the reflected sound wave (OB) and the normal (ON) at the point of incidence (O), all three lie in the same plane.

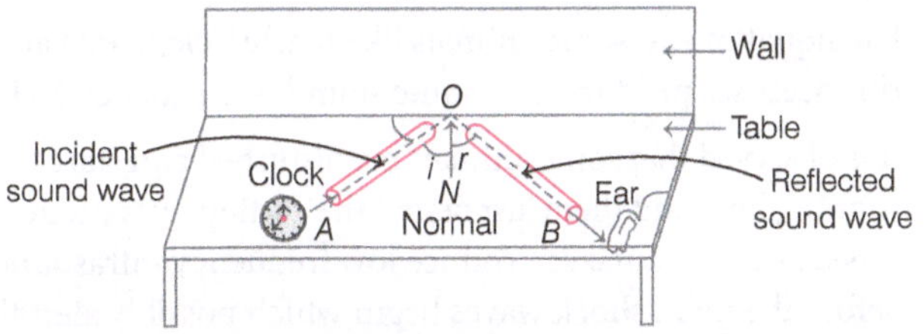

Reflection of sound

(ii) The angle of incidence ($\angle AON$) of sound is equal to the angle of reflection ($\angle NOB$) of sound.

Echo

When a person shouts in a big empty hall, we first hear his original sound, after that we hear the reflected sound of that shout. So, the repetition of sound caused by reflection of sound waves is called an echo.

The sensation of sound persists in our brain for about 0.1 s. Thus, to hear a distinct echo, the time interval between the original sound and the reflected one must be atleast 0.1 s.

Note If we take the speed of sound to be 344 m/s at a given temperature at 22°C in air, the sound must reflect at 90° angle to the obstacle and reach back the ear of the listener on reflection after 0.1s.

The distance travelled by the sound in 0.1 s

$= \text{speed} \times \text{time}$

$= 344 \times 0.1 = 34.4 \text{ m}$

So, echo will be heard, if the minimum distance between the source of sound and the obstacle is

$$= \frac{34.4}{2} \text{ m} = 17.2 \text{ m}$$

This distance will change with the change in temperature of air.

Echoes may be heard more than once due to successive multiple reflections. The rolling of thunder is due to successive reflections of sound from a number of reflecting surfaces, such as clouds and the land.

Reverberation

The persistence of a sound in a big hall due to repeated reflections from the walls, ceiling and floor of the wall is known as **reverberation**. This occurs when original sound and reflected sound overlaps. For reverberation to occur, (reflection occurs at less than 17 m distance).

A short reverberation is desirable in a concert hall, where music is being played, as it boosts the sound level. But excessive reverberation is highly undesirable because sound becomes blurred, distorted and confusing due to overlapping of different sounds.

To reduce reverberation, the roof and walls of the auditorium are generally covered with sound absorbent materials like compressed fibre board, rough plaster or draperies. The seat materials are also selected on the basis of their sound absorbing properties.

Uses of Multiple Reflection of Sound

The reflection of sound is used in the working of devices such as megaphone, horns, stethoscope and sound board. These devices involve multiple reflections of sound waves.

(i) Megaphone and Horn

Megaphone is a large cone shaped device used to amplify and send the voice of a person in particular direction who speaks into it.

When a person speaks into the narrow end of the megaphone tube, the sound waves produced are prevented from spreading by successive reflections from the wider end of the megaphone tube, hence sound of his voice can be heard over a longer distance.

(ii) Stethoscope

It is a medical instrument used by doctors to listen the sound produced within the heart and the lungs in human body. The sound of heartbeats (or lungs) reaches the doctors ears by the multiple reflections of sound waves through the stethoscope tube.

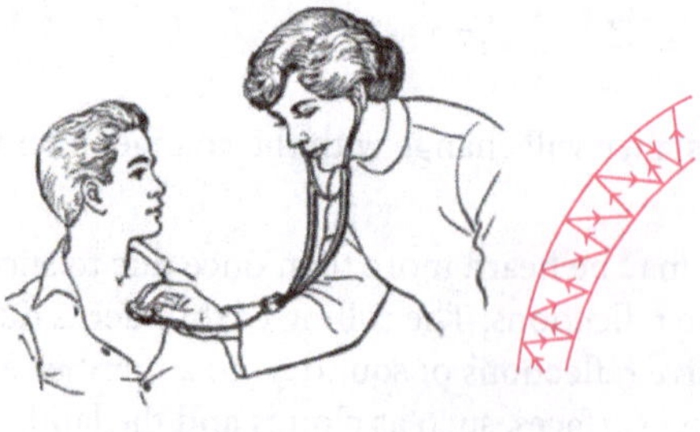

Stethoscope

(iii) Sound Board

It is a concave board (curved board) placed behind the stage in big halls, so that sound after reflecting from sound board, spreads evenly across the width of the hall.

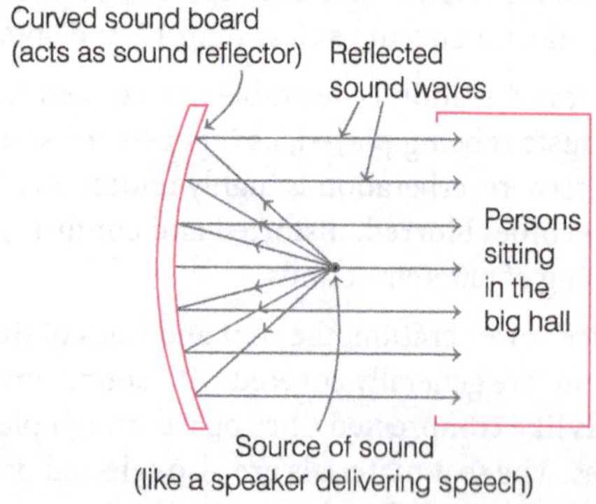

Curved sound board behind the speaker or the stage in big hall

Generally, the ceilings of the concert halls, conference halls and cinema halls are also curved, so that sound after reflection reaches all corners of the hall.

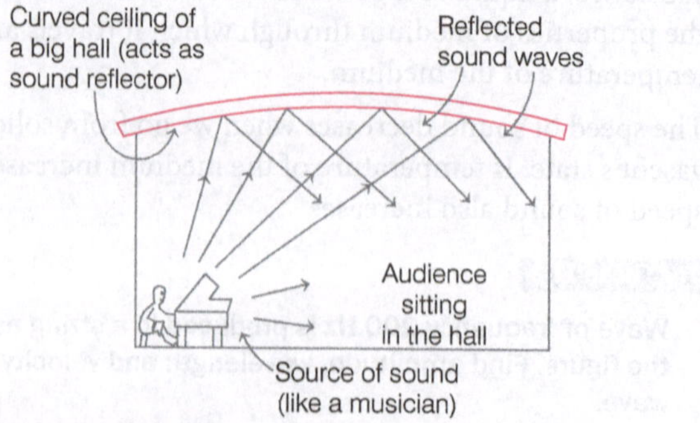

Curved sound board behind the speaker or the stage in big hall

Example 2. **A person clapped his hands near a cliff and heard the echo after 2 s. What is the distance of the cliff from the person if the speed of the sound, v is taken as 346 ms^{-1}?** **NCERT**

Sol. Given, speed of sound, $v = 346 \text{ ms}^{-1}$

Time taken for hearing the echo, $t = 2$ s

Distance travelled by the sound

$$= v \times t = 346 \text{ ms}^{-1} \times 2 \text{ s} = 692 \text{ m}$$

In 2 s sound has to travel twice the distance between the cliff and the person. Hence, the distance between the cliff and the person $= 692 \text{ m}/2 = 346$ m.

11.8 Range of Hearing

The average frequency range over which the human ear is sensitive is called **audible range.** The audible range of sound for human beings is from 20 Hz to 20000 Hz (20 kHz).

Children under the age of 5 and some animals such as dogs can hear up to 25000 Hz. As people grow older, their ears become less sensitive to higher and lower frequencies.

Infrasonic Sound

The sound of frequencies lower than 20 Hz are known as **infrasonic sounds** or infrasound, which cannot be heard by human beings.

Earthquakes and some animals like whales, elephants and rhinoceroses produce infrasonic sound of frequency 5 Hz.

It is observed that some animals get disturbed and start running here and there just before the earthquakes occur. This is because earthquakes produce low frequency infrasound before the main shock waves begin which possibly alert the animals and they get disturbed.

Ultrasonic Sound

The sounds of frequencies higher than 20000 Hz are called **ultrasonic sounds** or ultrasounds which cannot be heard by human beings. Dogs can hear ultrasonic sounds of frequency up to 50000 Hz. This is why dogs are used for detective work by the police. Bats, dolphins, and porpoises can produce ultrasonic sounds. Rats also play games by producing ultrasound.

> **Hearing Aid.**
>
> This is a device which is used by people who have difficulty hearing. It is an electronic, battery operated device. It receives sound through a **microphone** which converts the **sound waves** to **electrical signals**
>
> These electrical signals are amplified by an amplifier. The amplified electrical signals are given to a speaker of the hearing aid. The speaker converts the **amplified electrical signals** to **sound** and then sends it to the ear for clear hearing.

11.9 Ultrasound and Its Applications

Ultrasounds are high frequency waves. They travel in straight line without bending around the corners. They can penetrate into matter to a large extent. Due to these properties, ultrasound is used in industry and in hospitals for medical purposes.

Some of the important applications of ultrasound are given below

(i) In Cleaning Minute Parts of Machines

Ultrasound is used to clean parts located in hard-to-reach-places, such as spiral tubes, odd-shaped machines and electronic components, etc. Objects to be cleaned are placed in a cleaning solution and ultrasonic waves are sent into the solution.

Due to their high frequency, the ultrasound waves stirrup the solution, hence the particles of dust, grease and dirt vibrate too much, become loose, get detached from the object and fall into the solution. The objects, thus get thoroughly cleaned.

(ii) In Internal Investigation of Human Body

Ultrasound is used to investigate the internal organs of human body such as liver, gall bladder, pancreas, kidneys, uterus and heart, etc.

Ultrasound waves can penetrate the human body and different types of tissues get reflected in different ways from a region where there is a change of tissue density. In this way, ultrasound helps us to see inside the human body and to give pictures of the inner organs by converting into electrical signals.

These pictures or images are then displayed on a monitor or printed on a film. This technique is called **ultrasonography.** Ultrasonography is used for the examination of fetus during pregnancy to detect any growth abnormalities, which helps in taking the necessary action to rectify the abnormalities.

Ultrasonic scanner is an instrument that helps the doctor to detect abnormalities, such as stones in the gall bladder and kidney or tumours in different organs and many other ailments.

Ultrasound is also used for diagnosing heart diseases by scanning the heart from inside. This technique is known as **echocardiography.**

Ultrasound may be employed to break small stones formed in the kidneys into fine grains which later get flushed out with urine. This way, the patient gets relief from pain.

(iii) In Industries

Ultrasound is used in industry for detecting flaws (cracks, etc.) in metal blocks without damaging them.

Metal blocks are used in the construction of big structures like bridges, machines and scientific equipment, etc. If there are some cracks and flaws in the metal blocks, which are invisible from outside reduces the strength of the structure. These can be detected by using ultrasound. This is based on the fact that an internal crack (or hole) does not allow ultrasound to pass through it.

It reflects the ultrasound. Ultrasound waves are allowed to pass through one face of metal block (to be tested) and detectors are placed on the opposite face of the metal block to detect the transmitted ultrasound waves.

If there is even a small defect, the ultrasound waves gets reflected back indicating the presence of the flaw or defect, as shown in figure.

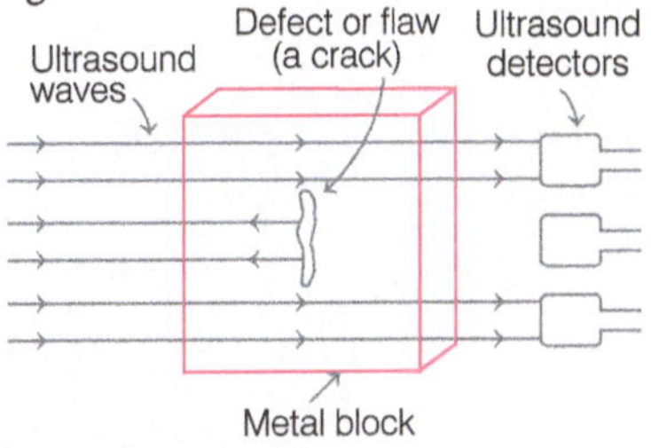

Ultrasound reflected from a part of block, which shows that this metal block has a flaw or defect (like a crack) inside it

Ordinary sound waves cannot be used for detecting the flaws in metal blocks because they will bend around the corners of the defective location and therefore, enter the detector.

Use of Ultrasonic Waves by Bats

Bats search out prey and fly in dark night by emitting and detecting reflections of ultrasonic waves. The method used by some animals like bats, tortoises and dolphins to locate the objects by hearing the echoes of their ultrasonic **squeaks** is known as **echolocation.**

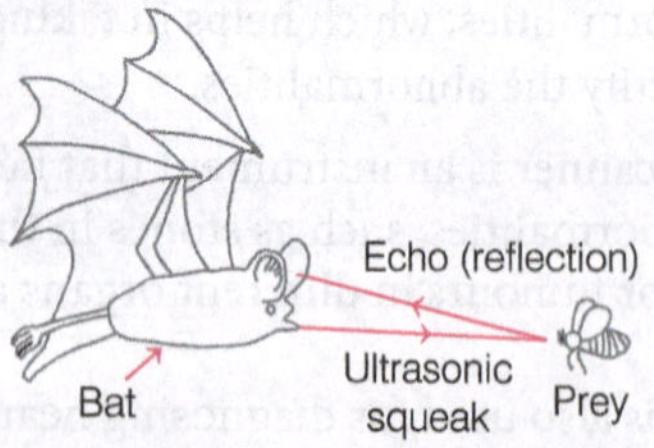

Bats can search their prey in the darkness of night by the method of echolocation

Bats emit high frequency or high pitched ultrasonic squeaks while flying and listen to the echoes produced by reflection of their squeaks from the obstacles or prey in their path. From the time taken by the echo to be heard, bats can determine the distance of the obstacle or prey and can avoid the obstacle by changing the direction or catch the prey.

However, certain moths can hear the high frequency ultrasonic squeaks of a bat and can know where the bat is flying nearby and are able to escape from being captured.

Try These 11.3

1. **In an experiment on studying the laws of reflection of sound, if the incident wave makes an angle of 35° with the rigid surface (wall), what will be the angle of reflection?** [Ans. 55°]
2. **An echo is returned in 6 s. What is the distance of reflecting surface from source? [given that speed of sound is 342 m/s]** [Ans. 1026 m]
3. **What should be the condition for obtaining reverberation?**
4. **Fill in the blank:**
   The sound absorbant materials used in concert hall is ....
5. **Which technique is used for the examination of fetus during pregnancy?**
6. **Name the sound waves of frequency which are too low to hear for human beings.**

Mind Map

SOUND

Speed of Sound Waves
The speed of sound wave in air is about 344 m/s at 22°C and 331 m/s at 0°C.

Speed of Sound in Different Media
- The medium through which sound propagates can be solid substance, a liquid or a gas.
- The speed of sound depends on the properties of medium and the temperature through which it travels.
- The speed of sound decrease when we go for solid to gaseous state. If the temperature of the medium increases, then speed of sound also increases.

Production of Sound
Sound is produced by vibrating objects. Vibration means a kind of rapid to and fro motion of an object.

Propagation of Sound
Propagation of sound waves takes place in material medium, so they are called mechanical waves.
- **Rarefaction**
  Part of longitudinal wave in which density of the particle is minimum.
- **Compression**
  Part of a longitudinal wave in which density of the particle is maximum.

Reflection of Sound
- Sound reflects as a light. The bouncing back of sound when it strikes a hard surface is known as reflection of sound. Laws of reflection are same for both.
  i.e. Angle of incidence = Angle of reflection.
- **Echo**
  The repetition of sound caused by reflection of sound is called echo. Condition for echo is distance between source of sound and obstacle must be 17.2 m.
- **Reverberation**
  - The persistence of sound in a big hall due to repeated reflection from the walls. ceilings and floor of the walls is known as reverberation.
  - To reduce it, sound absorbent materials like curtains, compressed fibreboard, etc, are used in cinema hall and auditorium.

Types of Waves
- **Longitudinal Waves**
  Individual particles move parallel to the propagation of disturbance. The particles do not move from one place to another, they only oscillate to their mean position.
  e.g. Sound wave.

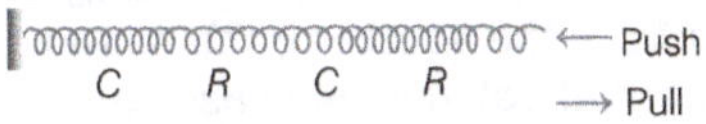

- **Transverse Waves**
  Individual particles of the medium move about their mean position in a direction perpendicular to direction of propagation of disturbance.
  e.g. Light wave.

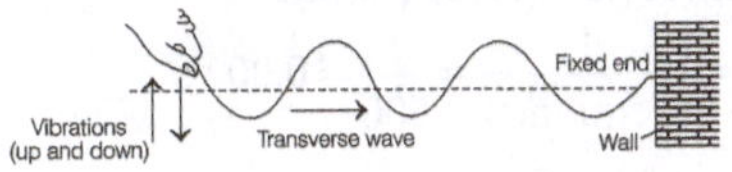

Uses of Multiple Reflection
- **Megaphone**
  It is large cone shaped device used to amplify and direct the voice of a person who speaks.
- **Stethoscope**
  It is medical instrument used to hear heartbeat and sounds of lungs.
- **Sound Board**
  It is a concave board placed behind the state in big halls so that sound after reflecting from sound board, spreads evenly across the width of the hall.

Terms to Describe Sound
- **Wavelength**
  - The distance between two consecutive compressions or two rarefactions is called wavelength (λ).
  - The SI unit of wavelength is metre (m).
- **Frequency**
  - The number of complete waves (or oscillations) produced in one second is called frequency (*n*).
  - The SI unit of frequency is hertz (Hz).
- **Time Period**
  - The time required to complete one full cycle of a wave is called time period (*T*).
  - The SI unit of time period is second (s)
  - The time period of a wave is the reciprocal of its frequency i.e, $T=\frac{1}{\nu}$
- **Amplitude**
  - The maximum displacement of the particles of medium from their original mean position on passing a wave through the medium is called amplitude (*A*)
  - The SI unit of amplitude is metre (m).
- **Speed**
  - The distance travelled by a wave in one second is called speed of wave (*v*).
  - The SI unit of speed is metre per second.
  - Relationship between speed, frequency and wavelength.
    $v=\nu\lambda$
    where, v=Speed of wave
    ν=Frequency
    λ=Wavelength

Graphical Representation of Sound Wave
- When a sound wave passes through air, the density of air changes continuously.

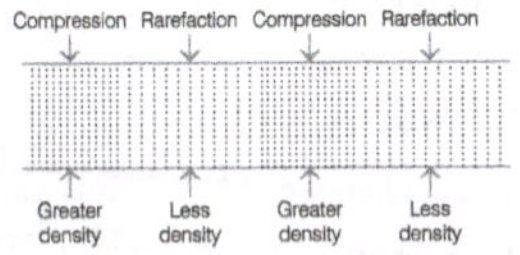

- A sound wave in air has been represented by means of a density-distance graph as shown below .

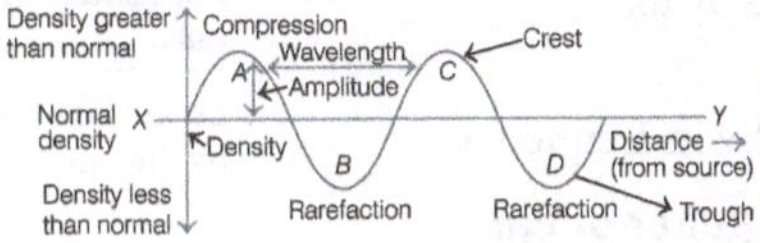

Range of Hearing
- **Audible Range**
  Range of sound which we can hear (20 Hz to 20000 Hz).
- **Infrasonic Sound**
  - Sound of frequency less than 20 Hz are known as infrasonic sound
  - During earthquake before main shock waves it is produced.
  - Some animals such as rhinoceros can hear infrasonic waves.
- **Ultrasonic Sound**
  - Sounds of frequency greater than 20000 Hz are called ultrasonic sound.
  - Used in investigation of internal organs of human body.
  - Used to clean parts located hard to reach places such as spiral tubes.
  - Used in detecting flaws (cracks) in industries.

Characteristics of Sound
- **Loudness**
  - It is the measure of sound energy reaching the ear per second.
  - Loudness ∝ amplitude

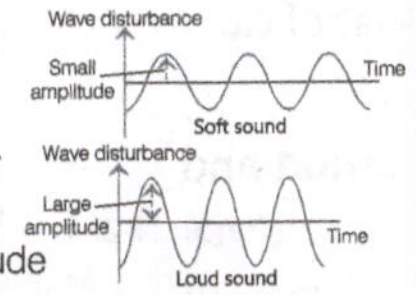

- **Intensity**
  The amount of sound energy passing each second through unit area is known as intensity of sound.

- **Pitch or Shrillness**
  - It is the characteristic by which we can distinguish between different sounds of same loudness.
  - Pitch ∝ Frequency

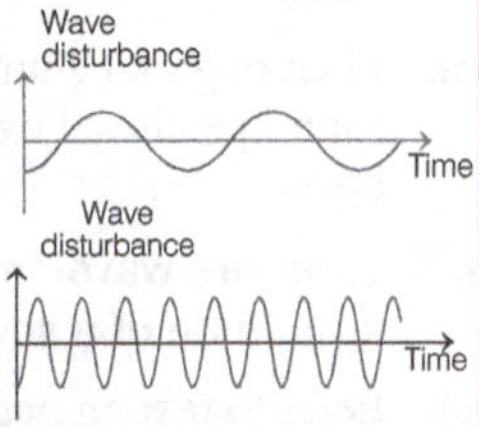

- **Quality**
  It is the characteristic which determines sound of same pitch and loudness.

NCERT FOLDER

Complete Explanations of all NCERT's Questions

Intext Questions

Q.1 How does the sound produced by a vibrating object in a medium reach your ear? **Page 129**

Sol. Sound is produced by vibrating objects. When an object vibrates, it sets the particles of the medium around it in vibration. These vibrations are passed or transmitted to neighbouring particles in all directions. When vibrations are transmitted by medium particles to our ear, we get sensation of hearing.

Q.2 Explain how sound is produced by your school bell. **Page 129**

Sol. The bell produces the sound when gong of the bell is struck by hammer. When the gong is struck by hammer, it starts vibrating. Since, the vibrating objects produce sound, so the bell produces sound.

Q.3 Why are sound waves called mechanical waves? **Page 129**

Sol. Sound waves are called mechanical waves because, they are produced by the motion of particles of a medium and require material medium for their propagation.

Q.4 Suppose you and your friend are on the Moon. Will you be able to hear any sound produced by your friend? **Page 129**

Sol. No, I will not be able to hear any sound produced by my friend because the sound waves require some material medium like air to travel. There is no atmosphere or air on the Moon, so the sound produced by my friend will not reaches to me and I will not be able to hear.

Q.5 Which wave property determines **Page 132**

(i) loudness (ii) and pitch?

Sol. (i) Loudness of sound wave is determined by its amplitude.

(ii) Pitch of the sound wave is determined by its frequency.

Q.6 Guess which sound has a higher pitch, guitar or car horn. **Page 132**

Sol. Pitch of guitar sound is higher because the frequency of sound produced by guitar is higher than that of car horn.

Q.7 What are wavelength, frequency, time period and amplitude of a sound wave? **Page 132**

Sol. Refer to text on pages 276 and 277 (Terms to Describe Sound Waves).

Q.8 How are the wavelength and frequency of a sound wave related to speed? **Page 132**

Sol. The relation between wavelength (λ), frequency (ν) and speed of wave (v) is $v = \nu\lambda$.

Q.9 Calculate the wavelength of a sound wave whose frequency is 200Hz and speed is 440 ms^{-1} in a given medium. **Page 132**

Sol. Given, frequency, $\nu = 200$ Hz, velocity, $v = 440\ ms^{-1}$

According to the relation, $v = \nu\lambda$

$$\Rightarrow \lambda = \frac{v}{\nu} = \frac{440}{200} = 2.2\ m$$

Q.10 A person is listening to a tone of 500 Hz sitting at a distance of 450 m from the source of the sound, what is the time interval between successive compressions from the source? **Page 132**

Sol. The time interval between two successive compressions or rarefactions is equal to the time period of the wave.

$\therefore$ Required time interval = Time period

$$= \frac{1}{\text{Frequency}} = \frac{1}{500} = 0.002\ s$$

$$= 2\times 10^{-3}\ s = 2\ ms$$

Q.11 Distinguish between loudness and intensity of sound. **Page 133**

Sol. Difference between loudness and intensity

Loudness	Intensity
It is a subjective quantity. A sound may be loud for one person but may be feeble for another person.	It is an objective physical quantity which does not change for person to person.
It cannot be measured as it is just a sensation which can be felt only.	It can be measured as a physical quantity.
Loudness of sound is measured by the unit decibel (dB).	Intensity of sound is measured by the unit watt per square metre (W/m^2).
It depends on the sensitivity of ears.	It does not depend on the sensitivity of ears.

Q.12 In which of the three media, air, water or iron, does sound travel the fastest at a particular temperature? **Page 133**

Sol. Sound travels fastest through iron. As the density increases, the speed of the sound also increases. Iron is solid, so it has high density.

Q.13 An echo returned in 3 s. What is the distance of the reflecting surface from the source, given that the speed of sound is 342 ms^{-1}? **Page 134**

Sol. Given, speed of sound, $v = 342$ ms^{-1}

Time taken, $t = 3$ s

So, distance travelled by sound $= v \times t = 342 \times 3 = 1026$ m

Hence, distance between reflecting surface and source should be $\frac{1026}{2} = 513$ m.

Q.14 Why are the ceilings of concert halls curved? **Page 135**

Sol. The curved ceiling of conference hall focuses reflection of sound from the walls to audience, so that every corner of the hall gets sound equivalently.

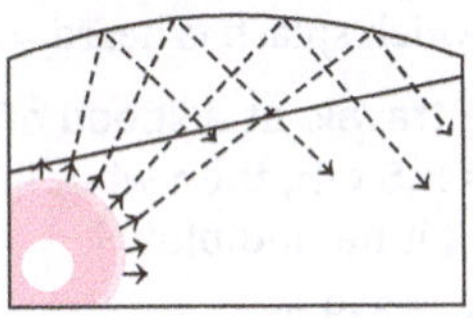

Q.15 What is audible range of the average human ear? **Page 136**

Sol. The audible frequency range for the average human ear is 20 Hz to 20000 Hz.

Q.16 What is the range of frequencies associated with **Page 136**

(i) infrasound

(ii) and ultrasound?

Sol. (i) Sound waves having frequencies less than 20 Hz and greater than zero are called **infrasound.**

(ii) Sound waves having frequencies more than 20000 Hz are called **ultrasound.**

Exercise Questions

Q.1 What is sound and how is it produced?

Sol. Sound is a form of energy, which produces the sensation of hearing in our ears. It is produced when an object is set to vibrate or we can say that vibrating objects produce sound.

Q.2 Describe with the help of a diagram, how compressions and rarefactions are produced in air near a source of sound.

Sol. When a vibrating object moves forward, it pushes the air infront of it creating a region of high pressure. This region is called **compression.** This compression starts to move away from the vibrating object. When the vibrating object moves backward, it creates a region of low pressure called **rarefaction.** As the object moves back and forth rapidly, a series of compressions and rarefactions is created. This make the sound wave to propagates through the medium.

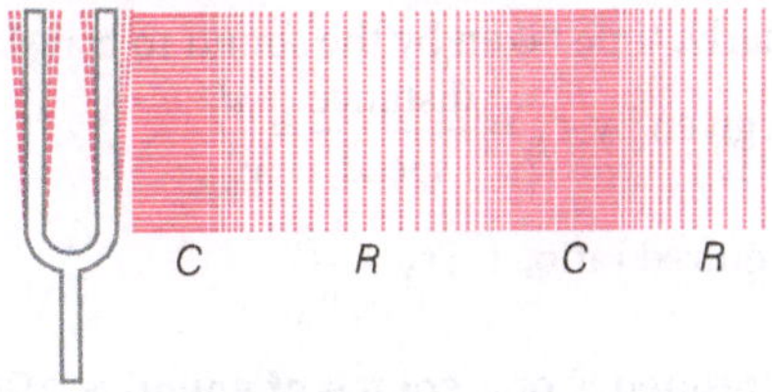

A vibrating object creating a series of compressions (C) and rarefactions (R) in the medium

Q.3 Why is sound wave called a longitudinal wave?

Sol. The sound wave is called longitudinal wave because on propagation of sound wave in a medium, the particles of the medium vibrate to and fro about their equilibrium positions and parallel to the direction of propagation of the wave.

Q.4 Which characteristic of the sound helps you to identify your friend by his voice while sitting with others in a dark room?

Sol. Timbre, a quality of sound is the characteristic by which we can identify the person by his voice.

Q.5 Flash and thunder are produced simultaneously. But thunder is heard a few seconds after the flash is seen, why?

Sol. Thunder is heard few seconds after the flash is seen because speed of light in atmosphere (or air) is 3×10^8 ms^{-1} which is very high as compared to the speed of sound which is only 330 ms^{-1}. So, sound of thunder reaches us later than the flash.

Q.6 A person has hearing range from 20 Hz to 20 kHz. What are the typical wavelengths of sound waves in air corresponding to these two frequencies? (Take, the speed of sound in air as 344 ms^{-1})

Sol. The relation between speed (v), wavelength (λ) and frequency (ν) of a wave is $v = \nu\lambda$

$$\lambda = \frac{v}{\nu}$$

(i) Here, $v = 344$ ms^{-1}, $\nu = 20$ Hz

$\therefore$ Corresponding wavelength, $\lambda = \frac{v}{\nu} = \frac{344}{20} = 17.2$ m

(ii) Here, $v = 344$ ms^{-1}, $\nu = 20$ kHz $= 20 \times 10^3$ Hz

$\therefore$ Corresponding wavelength,

$$\lambda = \frac{v}{\nu} = \frac{344}{20 \times 10^3}$$

$$= 1.72 \times 10^{-2} \text{ m}$$

Q.7 Two children are at opposite ends of an aluminium rod. One strikes the end of the rod with a stone. Find the ratio of time taken by the sound wave in air and in aluminium to reach the second child.

Sol. Let l be length of the rod.

Time taken by the sound to travel through the aluminium rod is given by

$$t_1 = \frac{\text{distance}}{\text{speed}} = \frac{d}{v_{Al}}$$

Similarly, time taken by the sound to travel through the air is given by $t_2 = \frac{\text{distance}}{\text{speed}} = \frac{d}{v_{air}}$

$\therefore$ Required ratio, $t_1 : t_2 = \frac{v_{air}}{v_{Al}}$

Q.8 The frequency of a source of sound is 100 Hz. How many times does it vibrate in a minute?

Sol. Given, frequency, $\nu = 100$ Hz

From the definition of frequency, we can say that

Number of oscillations in 1 s = 100

$\therefore$ Number of oscillations in 1 min or 60 s

$= 100 \times 60 = 6000$

Thus, the source of sound vibrates 6000 times in a minute.

Q.9 Does sound follow the same laws of reflection as light does? Explain.

Sol. Yes, sound wave follows the same laws as in case of laws of reflection of light.

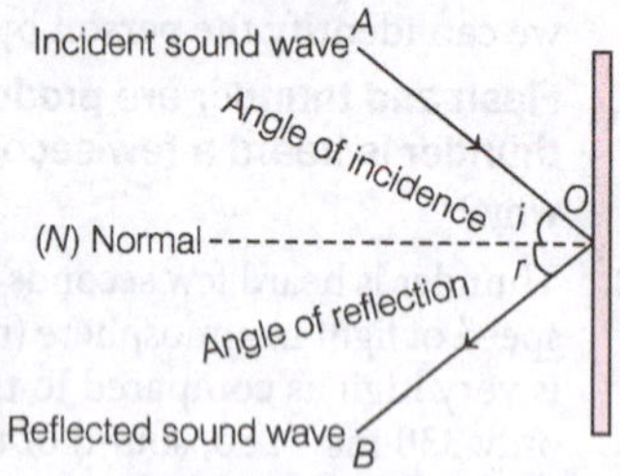

The laws of reflection of sound are as follows

(i) The incident sound wave (AO), the reflected sound wave (OB) and the normal (ON) at the point of incidence, all lie in the same plane.

(ii) The angle of incidence ($\angle AON$) of sound is equal to the angle of reflection ($\angle NOB$) of sound.

Q.10 When a sound is reflected from a distant object, an echo is produced. Let the distance between the reflecting surface and the source of sound production remains the same. Do you hear echo sound on a hotter day?

Sol. The time taken by echo to be heard, $t = \frac{2d}{v}$

where, d = distance between the reflecting surface and source of sound and v = speed of sound in air.

As we know that, speed of sound increases with increase in temperature, so on a hotter day, speed of sound will be higher, so the time after which echo is heard will decrease. If time taken by the reflected sound is less than 0.1s after the production of original sound, then echo will not be heard.

Q.11 Give two practical applications of reflection of sound waves.

Sol. Refer to text on page 280 (Uses of multiple reflection of sound).

Q.12 A stone is dropped from the top of a tower 500 m high into a pond of water at the base of the tower. When is the splash heard at the top? [Given, g = 10 ms^{-2} and speed of sound = 340 ms^{-1}]

Sol. Time after which the splash is heard = Time taken by the stone to reach the pond + Time taken by splash sound to reach the top of tower.

(i) For the time taken by the stone to reach the pond.

Here, $u = 0$ [$\because$ stone is dropped from rest]

From equation of motion, $h = ut + \frac{1}{2} gt^2$

$$500 = 0 \times t + \frac{1}{2} \times 10 (t)^2$$

$$500 = 5t^2 \Rightarrow t^2 = 100$$

$$\Rightarrow t = \sqrt{100} = 10 \text{ s}$$

(ii) Time taken by splash sound to reach the top of the tower, $t' = \frac{\text{Distance}}{\text{Speed}} = \frac{500}{340} = 1.47$ s

$\therefore$ Time after which splash is heard $= 10 + 1.47 = 11.47$ s

Q.13 A sound wave travels at a speed of 339 ms^{-1}. If its wavelength is 1.5 cm, then what is the frequency of the wave? Will it be audible?

Sol. Given, speed, v = 339 ms^{-1}

Wavelength, $\lambda = 1.5 \text{ cm} = 1.5 \times 10^{-2}$ m

$\therefore$ Frequency, $\nu = \frac{v}{\lambda} = \frac{339}{1.5 \times 10^{-2}} = 22600$ Hz

This frequency is greater than 20000 Hz, so it will not be audible. Audible range for human ear is 20 Hz to 20000 Hz.

Q.14 What is reverberation? How can it be reduced?

Sol. The persistence of a sound in a big hall due to repeated reflections from the walls, ceiling and floor of the wall is known as reverberation. It can be reduced by covering the roofs and walls of the hall by sound absorbing materials.

Q.15 What is loudness of sound? What factors does it depend on?

Sol. Loudness of a sound is a subjective quantity, it is the measure of the sound energy reaching the ear per second.

Loudness depends on

(i) the amplitude of the vibrating body

(ii) and the sensitivity of human ear.

Q.16 How is ultrasound used for cleaning?

Sol. Refer to text on page 281 (Ultrasound and its applications (i))

Q.17 Explain how defects in a metal block can be detected using ultrasound?

Sol. Refer to text on page 281 (Ultrasound and its Applications (iii))

To Study NCERT Activities

Scan the Code

REVIEW EXERCISE

Including Competency Based Questions

Competency Focused (Objective) Questions

Multiple Choice Questions

1 A tuning fork produces sound wave, because it creates

(a) heat (b) light
(c) vibration (d) None of these

Sol. (*c*) If tuning fork is vibrating, it produces sound.

2 Which of the following does not produce sound wave?

(a) Drum (b) Birds
(c) TV (d) Microwave oven

Sol. (*d*) Microwave oven is used to produce electromagnetic wave.

3 A mechanical wave can travel

(a) in a material medium but not in vacuum.
(b) in vacuum but not in a material medium.
(c) Both in vacuum and a material medium
(d) Neither in a material medium nor in vacuum.

Sol. (*a*) Mechanical wave can travel through material medium but not in vacuum.

4 Sound travels in air, if

(a) particles of medium travel from one place to another
(b) there is no moisture in the atmosphere
(c) disturbance moves
(d) both particles as well as disturbance travel from one place to another **NCERT Exemplar**

Sol. (*c*) When sound travels in air, then only disturbances created by the vibration of particle moves from one place to other.

5 A light string is suspended from a hook which is attached to a 1 kg weight at its lower end. If the string is pulled and then released, the disturbance produced in the spring is **Competency Based Que.**

(a) pulse (b) longitudinal wave
(c) transverse wave (d) None of these

Sol. (*c*) Transverse waves are produced in stretched string.

6 The frequency of a source of sound is 200 Hz. How many times does it vibrate in 2 min ?

(a) 2400 (b) 24000 (c) 24500 (d) 2450

Sol. (*b*) Given, frequency = 200 Hz

Number of oscillation in 1s = 200

[because frequency represents number of oscillations in 1s]

Number of oscillation in 2 min or 120 s

$= 200 \times 120 = 24000$

7 When we change feeble sound to loud sound, we increase its **NCERT Exemplar**

(a) frequency (b) amplitude
(c) velocity (d) wavelength

Sol. (*b*) The loudness or softness of a sound is determined by its amplitude. So for a loud sound, it must have higher amplitude.

8 Which of the following figures represent the soft sound? **Competency Based Que.**

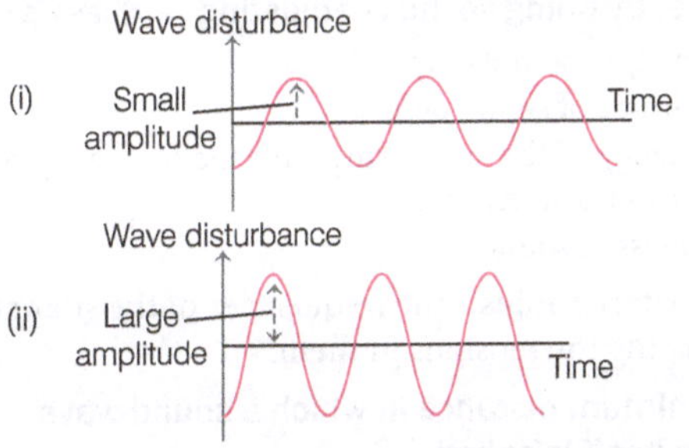

(a) (i) (b) (ii)
(c) (i) and (ii) both (d) None of these

Sol. (*a*) If the sound waves have a small amplitude, then sound will be faint or soft but if waves have a large amplitude, then the sound will be loud.

9 A man is beating a drum infront of a cliff, hears the echo after 4s. What is the distance of man from the cliff, if velocity of sound in air is 330 m/s? **Competency Based Que.**

(a) 660 m (b) 500 m
(c) 1000 m (d) 0.3 km

Sol. (*a*) Given, speed = 330 m/s and time = 4s

As we know that,
Distance, $s =$ Speed × Time $= 330 \times 4 = 1320$ m

As in 4s, sound has to travel twice distance between man and the cliff.

So, distance between man and cliff is $\frac{s}{2} = \frac{1320}{2} = 660$ m

10 **A key of a mechanical piano struck gently and then struck again but much harder this time. In the second case,**

(a) sound will be louder but pitch will not be different.
(b) sound will be louder and pitch will also be higher.
(c) sound will be louder but pitch will be lower.
(d) Both loudness and pitch will remain unaffected.

Sol. (*a*) When the key of a piano is struck harder, the sound will be louder as it vibrates with greater amplitude but the pitch will not be different as it does not depend on how hard the key is struck.

11 **In the curve, half the wavelength is** **Competency Based Que.**

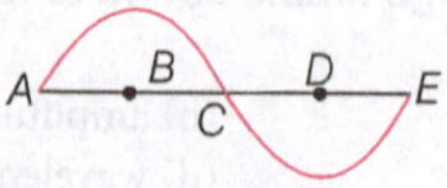

(a) *AB* (b) *BD*
(c) *DE* (d) *AE*

Sol. (*b*) In the given curve, half of the wavelength will be *BD*.

12 **Before playing the orchestra in a musical concert, a sitarist tries to adjust the tension and pluck the string suitable. By doing so, he is adjusting** **NCERT Exemplar**

(a) intensity of sound only
(b) amplitude of sound only
(c) frequency of the sitar string with the frequency of other musical instruments
(d) loudness of sound

Sol. (*c*) The sitarist adjusts the frequencies of the sitar strings by adjusting the tensions in them.

13 **The minimum distance in which a sound wave repeats itself is called**

(a) frequency (b) amplitude
(c) wavelength (d) time period

Sol. (*c*) The minimum distance in which sound wave repeats itself is called wavelength.

14 **A wave is slinky travelled to and fro in 5 s and the length of the slinky is 5 m. What will be the velocity of the wave ?**

(a) 10 m/s (b) 5 m/s
(c) 2 m/s (d) 25 m/s

Sol. (*c*) As the wave moves to and fro, so the total distance will be $d = 2 \times 5 = 10$ m

We have,

time, $t = 5$ s

$$\text{Velocity} = \frac{\text{Total distance}}{\text{Time}} = \frac{10}{5} \text{ m/s} = 2 \text{ m/s}$$

15 **What is the SI unit of loudness?**

(a) Dioptre (b) Metre
(c) Weber (d) Decibel

Sol. (*d*) The SI unit of loudness is decibel (dB).

16 **A man's voice and a woman's voice is differ by its**

(a) loudness (b) pitch
(c) intensity (d) amplitude

Sol. (*b*) Pitch is the characteristic of sound by which we can distinguish between different sounds of the same loudness.

17 **Note is a sound** **NCERT Exemplar**

(a) of mixture of several frequencies.
(b) of mixture of two frequencies only.
(c) of a single frequency.
(d) always unpleasant to listen.

Sol. (*a*) The sound produced due to a mixture of several frequencies is called a note.

18 **Which of the following statements is/are correct?** **Competency Based Que.**

I. Sound would travel faster on a hot summer day than on a cold winter day.
II. Velocity of sound is directly proportional to the square of its absolute temperature.

(a) I and II (b) Only I
(c) Only II (d) None of these

Sol. (*b*) The velocity of sound in a gas is directly proportional to the square root of its absolute temperature.

Since, temperature of a hot day is more than cold winter day, therefore sound travel faster on a hot summer day than on a cold winter day.

19 **Echo is caused by the phenomenon of**

(a) reflection (b) rarefaction
(c) refraction (d) reverberation

Sol. (*a*) An echo is the reflected sound waves.

20 **What is the range of audio waves ?**

(a) 20 kHz to 200 kHz (b) 20 Hz to 20 kHz
(c) 20 Hz to 20 MHz (d) 20 Hz to 20 MHz

Sol. (*b*) The range of audio waves is 20 Hz to 20 kHz.

21 **Infrasound can be heard by** **NCERT Exemplar**

(a) dog (b) bat
(c) rhinocerose (d) human beings

Sol. (*c*) Infrasound are the waves whose frequency is less than 20 Hz. Rhinoceroses communicate using infrasound of frequency as low as 5 Hz.

22 **In SONAR, we use** **NCERT Exemplar**

(a) ultrasonic waves (b) infrasonic waves
(c) radio waves (d) audible sound waves

Sol. (*a*) In SONAR, we use ultrasonic waves or ultrasound.

23 **Earthquake produces which kind of sound before the main shock wave begins** **NCERT Exemplar**

(a) ultrasound (b) infrasound
(c) audible sound (d) None of these

Sol. (*b*) Earthquake produces infrasound before the main shock wave begins.

24 Identify the correct representation of the audible range for human beings?

(a) 20Hz – 20kHz
(b) 0.02kHz – 20kHz
(c) 0.2kHZ – 20kHZ
(d) 0.02kHz – 2kHz.

Sol. (*a*) The audible range of sound for human beings is 20Hz to 20kHz.

25 Infrasonic (f_i), audible (f_a) and ultrasonic (f_u) frequencies of sound are related as

(a) $f_i < f_a < f_u$
(b) $f_a < f_i < f_u$
(c) $f_i > f_a > f_u$
(d) $f_a < f_u < f_i$

Sol. (*a*) Infrasonic, audible and ultrasonic frequencies of sound are related as

$$f_i < f_a < f_u$$

Assertion–Reason Questions

Direction (Q.Nos. 1-8) ***In each of the following questions, a statement of Assertion is given by the corresponding statement of Reason. Of the statements, mark the correct answer as***

(a) If both Assertion and Reason are true and Reason is the correct explanation of Assertion.
(b) If both Assertion and Reason are true, but Reason is not the correct explanation of Assertion.
(c) If Assertion is true, but Reason is false.
(d) If Assertion is false, but Reason is true.

1 Assertion (A) Sound wave is a longitudinal wave.

Reason (R) Sound wave can be produced in all the three media such as solids, liquids and gases.

Sol. (*b*) Sound wave is longitudinal wave which requires a medium (solid, liquid or gas) to travel through them. Hence, Assertion and Reason both are true, but Reason is not the correct explanation of Assertion.

2 Assertion (A) Velocity of sound wave of frequency 550 Hz and wavelength 0.6 m is 330 m/s.

Reason (R) Velocity of sound wave is given by Velocity = Frequency × Wavelength

Sol. (*a*) Velocity of sound wave = Frequency × Wavelength

$$= 550 \times 0.6$$
$$= 330 \text{ m/s}$$

Hence, Assertion and Reason both are true and Reason is the correct explanation of Assertion.

3 Assertion (A) On rainy day, sound travel slower than a dry day.

Reason (R) The density of air decreases when moisture is present in air .

Sol. (*d*) The density of moist air is less than the density of dry air. The speed of sound is inversely proportional to the square root of density of medium. So, sound travels faster on rainy days than on dry days.

4 Assertion (A) Pitch of sound is helpful to distinguish between a man's voice and woman's voice of the same loudness without seeing them.

Reason (R) Greater frequency of sound, the higher will be its pitch.

Sol. (*a*) Pitch of sound depends on the frequency of vibration. Greater the frequency of a sound, the higher will be its pitch which helps to distinguish between a man's voice and woman's voice of the same loudness. Hence, Assertion and Reason both are true and Reason is the correct explanation of Assertion.

5 Assertion (A) Echo is caused by the phenomenon of reflection.

Reason (R) The persistance of a sound in a big hall is due to echo.

Sol. (*c*) Echo is caused by the phenomenon of reflection. The persistance of sound in a big hall is due to reverberation. Hence, Assertion is true, but Reason is false.

6 Assertion (A) The audible range of sound for human beings is from 20 Hz to 20000 Hz.

Reason (R) For a human being, it is difficult to hear ultrasonic sound while easy to hear infrasonic sound.

Sol. (*c*) A human being can hear only audible range of frequency (20 Hz to 20000 Hz) but cannot hear infrasonic and ultrasonic sound.
Hence, Assertion is true, but Reason is false.

7 Assertion (A) Moths and bats move out freely even in night and search out prey.

Reason (R) Moths and bats send ultrasonic signals.

Sol. (*a*) Bats and moths send ultrasonic signals and receive it back after reflection from prey.
Hence, both Assertion and Reason are correct and Reason is the correct explanation of Assertion.

8 Assertion (A) Elephants and rhinoceroses communicate using infrasonic sound which is not audible for normal human.

Reason (R) Sound of frequency below 20 Hz is called infrasound.

Sol. (*a*) Elephants and rhinoceroses communicate using infrasound frequency of 5 Hz which is below 20 Hz and the audible frequency for human is 20 Hz to 20 kHz.

Case Based/Source Based Questions

Direction (Q. Nos. 1-4) Answer the questions on the basis of your understanding of the following table and related studied concepts:

1. The diagram shows the structure of the human ear. The three basic divisions are outer ear, middle ear and inner ear.

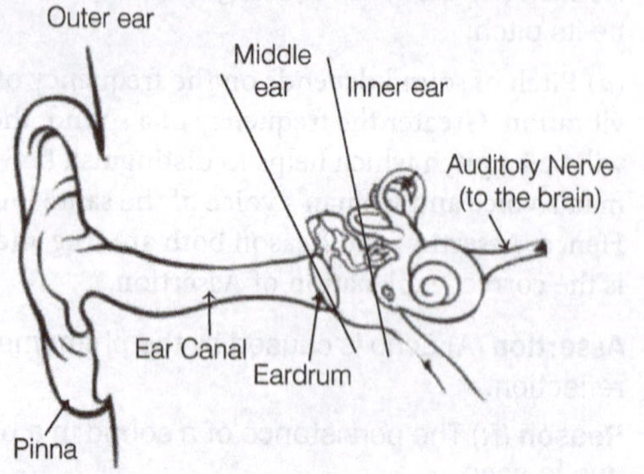

(i) Which division of the human ear contains bones? [1]

(ii) What is likely to cause loss of hearing when a pointed object is inserted into the ear? [1½]

(a) Cut in the ear canal

(b) Puncture in the pinna

(c) Rupture of the ear drum

(d) Rupture of the auditory nerve

(iii) In which of these conditions will an echo be heard? [1½]

(a) A man playing drums on a beach.

(b) A man reciting poems in a small room.

(c) A man shouting from the middle of an open farm.

(d) A man shouting from a place that is surrounded by hills.

Sol. (i) The middle of the human ear consists bones.

(ii) (*c*) Rupture of the ear drum is a serious condition that causes permanent hearing loss. When a pointed object inserted into the ear.

(iii) (*d*) A man shouting from a place that is surrounded by hills heard an echo because, the repetition of sound caused by reflection on sound waves.

2. The picture shows for sound waves.

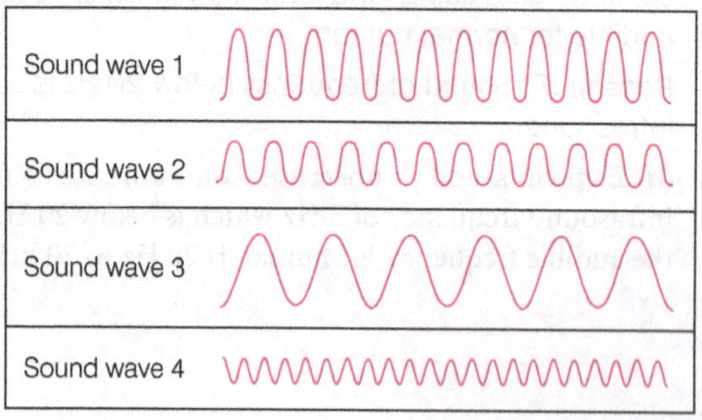

(i) Which sound wave has the highest frequency? [1½]

(a) Sound wave 1 (b) Sound wave 2

(c) Sound wave 3 (d) Sound wave 4

(ii) Which two sound waves have almost the same loudness? [1½]

(a) Sound wave 1 and sound wave 2

(b) Sound wave 2 and sound wave 4

(c) Sound wave 1 and sound wave 3

(d) Sound wave 3 and sound wave 4

(iii) Which of these is the frequency of an infrasound? [1]

(a) 10 Hz (b) 75 Hz

(c) 15000 Hz (d) 35000 Hz

Sol. (i) (*d*) The number of complete waves produced in given time is the highest in sound wave 4 therefore, sound wave 4 has the highest frequency.

(ii) (*c*) In sound wave 1 and sound wave 3 both have the same amplitude. Therefore, option (c) is correct.

(iii) (*a*) The sound of frequencies lower than 20 Hz are known as infrasound. Therefore, option (a) is correct.

3. Hearing range describes the range of frequencies that can be heard by humans or other animals though it can also refer to the range of levels.

Range of frequency of sound

	Frequency
Audible range for human	20Hz to 20000 Hz
Infrasonic sound	less than 20 Hz
Ultrasonic sound	greater than 20 kHz

People with hearing loss need a hearing aid. A hearing aid is an electronic, battery operated device. The hearing aid receives sound through microphone using this hearing aid people able to hear clear sound.

(i) In which range, whales and elephants produce frequency of sound? [1]

(ii) What do you mean by audible range for human beings? [1]

(iii) What type of aid used by people suffering from hearing loss? [1]

(iv) Name the sound having frequency range less than 20 Hz. [1]

Sol. (i) Whales and elephants produce sound in the infrasound range, i.e. less than 20 Hz.

(ii) The audible range for human beings means the range of frequencies that can be heard by human. Audible range for human is 20 Hz to 20000 Hz.

(iii) People suffering from hearing loss need a hearing aid. A hearing aid is an electronic battery operated device.

(iv) Infrasonic sound.

4. **Bats search out prey and fly in dark night by emitting and detecting reflections of ultrasonic waves. The method used by some animals like bats, tortoise and dolphins to locate objects by hearing the echoes of their ultrasonic squeaks is known as echolocations.**

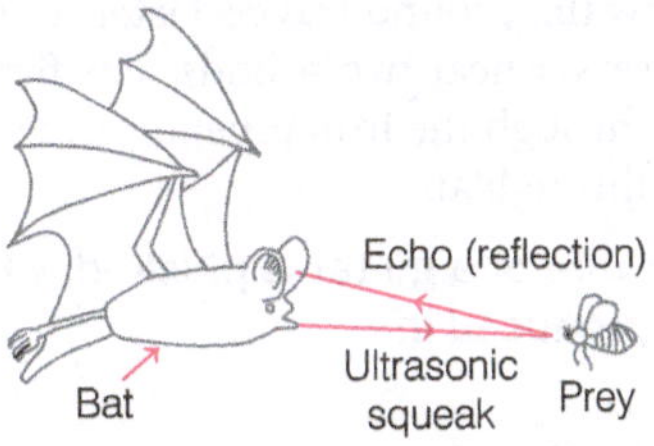

Bats emit high frequency or high pitched ultrasonic squeaks while flying and listen to the echoes produced by reflection of their squeaks from the obstacles or prey in the path. From the time taken by the echo to be heard, bats can determine the distance of the obstacle or prey and can avoid the obstacle by changing the direction or catch the prey.

However, certain moths can hear the high frequency ultrasonic squeaks of a bat and can know where the bat is flying nearby and are able to escape from being captured.

(i) Define echolocation. [1]

(ii) How bats can determine the distance of the obstacle? [1]

(iii) What is the frequency of ultrasonic waves? [1]

(iv) Bats can detects reflection of which type of wave? [1]

Sol. (i) The methods used by bats, dolphins to locate the objects or prey by hearing the echos of their ultrasonic squeaks is known as echolocations.

(ii) From the time taken by the echo to be heard, bats can determine the distance of the obstacle.

(iii) The frequency of ultrasonic waves is more than 20 kHz.

(iv) Bats can detects reflection of ultrasonic waves. The frequency range of this wave is higher than 20 kHz.

Constructed Response (Descriptive) Questions

Very Short Answer Type Questions

1 **Why can't we hear the sound of an explosion on the surface of the Moon?**

Sol. There is no atmosphere on the Moon and we know that sound waves need a medium to travel. Thus, we do not hear the sound of an explosion on the surface of the Moon.

2 **On what factor does the quality of the sound depend?**

Sol. Quality of the sound depends on the shape of the sound wave.

3 **Among air, water and steel, in which medium, the sound wave will travel faster?**

Sol. The sound wave will travel faster in steel because speed of sound is the fastest in the solids.

4 **If a freely suspended vertical spring is pulled in downward direction and then released, which type of waves are produced in the spring?**

Sol. In this situation, longitudinal waves will produce in spring.

5 **Give one example of transverse and longitudinal waves.**

Sol. Transverse wave — Light
Longitudinal wave — Sound

6 **When vertically jerk is given to a string, transverse waves are formed. Give three features of these waves.** **Competency Based Que.**

Sol. The features of transverse waves are

(i) The transverse waves needs a medium to travel and cannot travel through vacuum.

(ii) When the transverse waves travels, they create alternate crests and troughs.

(iii) The particles of medium vibrates at right angles to the direction of propagation of wave.

7 **Which characteristics of the sound helps you to identify your friend by his voice while sitting with other in a dark room?**

Sol. Timbre and pitch are the characteristics of sound which help you to identify the sound of different voices. Therefore, because of timbre and pitch, a person can identify the voice of other while sitting in the dark room.

8 **Give the correct picture of reflection of sound marked with the angle of incidence, angle of reflection and the normal.** **Competency Based Que.**

Sol.

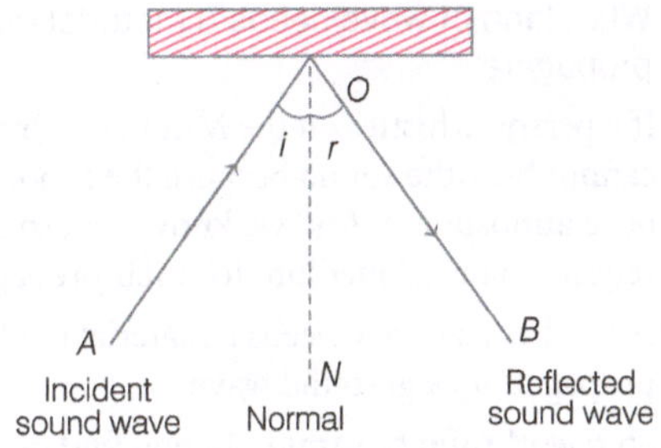

$\angle i$ = angle of incidence
and $\angle r$ = angle of reflection.

9 From which type of surfaces, the reflection of sound is better?

Sol. Hard surface is better reflector of sound.

10 At 20°C, what should be minimum distance of a person from a sound reflecting surface to hear an echo? **Competency Based Que.**

Sol. The minimum distance from sound reflecting surface to hear an echo should be atleast 17.2 m.

11 Why are roofs and walls of an auditorium/hall generally covered with sound absorbent materials?

Sol. To reduce reverberation, the roofs and walls of an auditorium or hall are generally covered with sound absorbent materials.

12 Waves of higher frequencies are used to measure depth of the sea.

(i) Name these waves. [½]

(ii) Give the frequency range of these waves. [½]

(iii) Give one more use of these waves. [1]

Sol. (i) Ultrasonic waves

(ii) Waves of frequency is greater than 20 kHz.

(iii) These waves are used in medical science for echo cardiography and ultrasonography.

These are also used to detect flaws in metal blocks and ultrasonic cleaning.

13 Mention one application of ultrasound in

(i) industries [1]

(ii) medical field [1]

Sol. (i) In industries, ultrasound is used to detect crack and flaws in metal blocks.

(ii) In medical field, ultrasound is used to break the stones in gall bladder and kidney.

Short Answer Type Questions

1 (i) Suppose a person whistles standing on the Moon. Will the person standing nearby hear the sound? Explain giving reason. [1½]

(ii) What kind of wave needs a material medium to propagate? [1½]

Sol. (i) If a person whistles on the Moon, nearby person cannot hear the sound because the Moon does not have atmosphere. And we know that, sound waves require material medium for their propagation.

(ii) A mechanical wave needs a material medium for its propagation, e.g. sound wave.

2 When a workman hammers to one end of the long iron pipeline, an observer places his ear on the other end of pipeline. How he can distinctly hear two sounds? Justify your answer. **Competency Based Que.**

Sol. Due to propagation of sound through solids such as iron, the sound of hammering to one end will be heard by the observer in the other end of the pipeline. Also, the sound of hammering will be propagated through air to reach the observer.

As we know that, sound travels faster in iron than in air. So, the observer hear two sounds. The first one, travelling through the iron pipeline and the second travelling through air.

3 When the wire of a guitar is plucked, what types of wave are produced in

(i) air [1½]

(ii) and wire ? [1½]

Give reasons in support of your answer.

Sol. (i) When the wire of a guitar is plucked, a longitudinal wave is produced in air due to the to and fro motion of string of guitar.

(ii) In the wire of guitar, transverse wave is produced as the particle vibrates perpendicular to the direction of motion.

4 Through what type of medium, can

(i) the transverse waves [1½]

(ii) and the longitudinal waves be transmitted? [1½]

Explain in brief.

Sol. (i) Since, transverse waves travel in the form of crests and troughs, they involve changes in the shape of medium. So, they can be transmitted through a medium having elasticity of shape. As solids and liquids have elasticity of shape, hence transverse waves can be transmitted through solids and liquids.

(ii) Since, longitudinal waves travel in the form of compressions and rarefactions, they involve changes in the volume and density of medium. As all media, i.e. solids, liquids and gases have elasticity of volume. Hence, these waves (longitudinal waves) can be transmitted through all the three types of media.

5 A railway track which is discussed has a length of 200 m. A person puts his ear at one end of the rail and suddenly another person hits the other end with a metal hammer, as shown in figure. **Competency Based Que.**

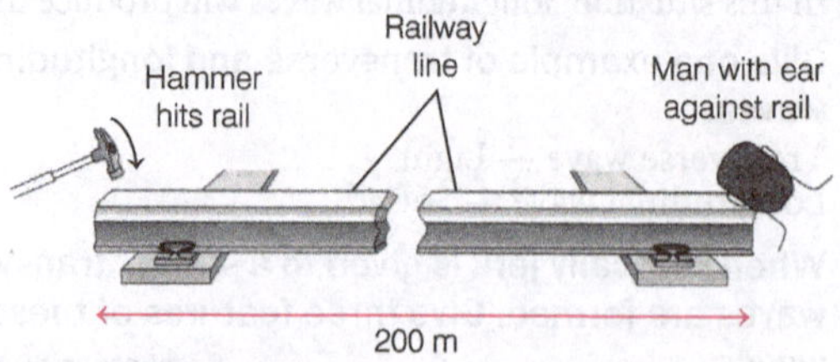

(i) (a) State an approximate value for the speed of sound in air. [1/2]

(b) Sound travels 6000 m/s in steel. Calculate the time it takes for the sound travel with the rail. [1/2]

(ii) The person with his ear actually hear two sounds from the metal hammer, which is separated by short interval. Give reason why the person hears two sound ? [2]

Sol. (i) (a) The approximate value for the speed of sound in air is 344 m/s.

(b) Given,

Distance = 200 m, speed = 6000 m/s

$$\therefore \text{Time taken} = \frac{\text{Distance}}{\text{Speed}} = \frac{200}{6000} = 0.03 \text{ s}$$

(ii) We all know that, the speed of sound is different in different materials. The man hears two sounds because sound travels about 15 times faster in steel as compared to air. Therefore, man hears one sound through air and another one through railway line made of steel.

6 Name the types of waves and two examples associated with

(i) compressions and rarefactions [1½]

(ii) crests and troughs. [1½]

Sol. (i) The waves which travel along a slinky when it is pushed and pulled at one end, are the longitudinal waves. The following figure shows longitudinal waves

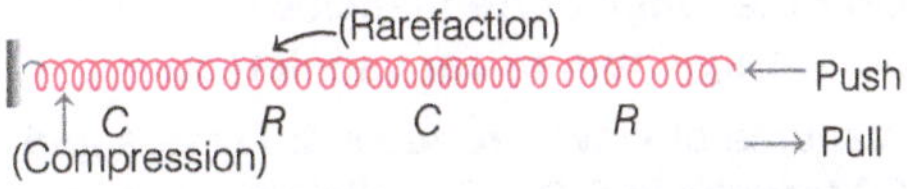

Longitudinal wave in a slinky

(ii) The waves produced by moving one end of a long rope (or spring) up and down rapidly whose other end is fixed, are transverse wave as shown in figure below

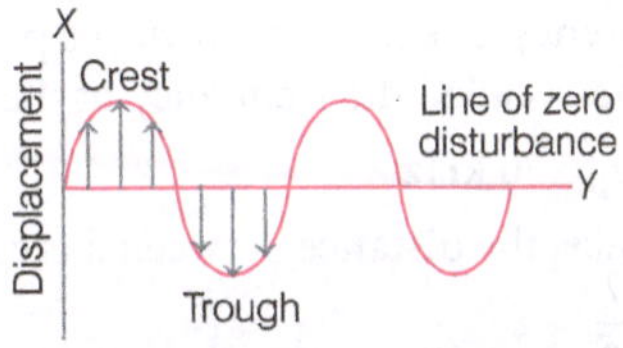

Crest and trough of a transverse wave

7 Figure shows a trace of a sound wave which is produced by a particular tuning fork.

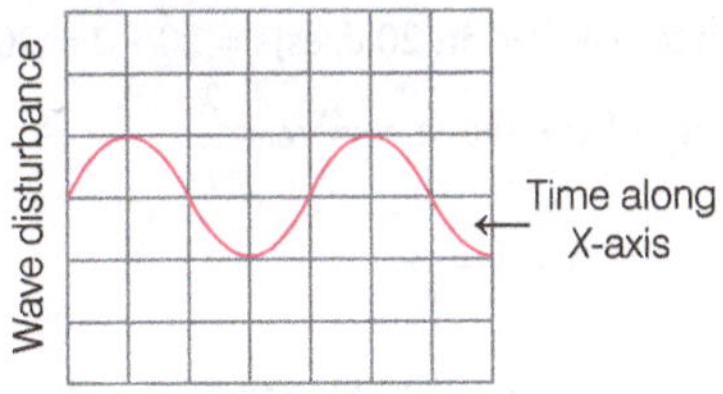

(i) Draw a trace of the sound wave which has a higher frequency than that shown in figure. [1½]

(ii) Draw a trace of the sound wave which has a larger amplitude than that shown in figure. [1½]

Competency Based Que.

Sol. (i)

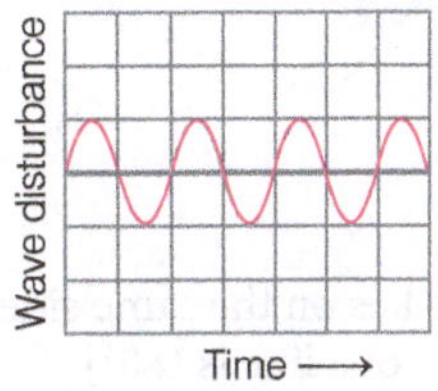

(ii)

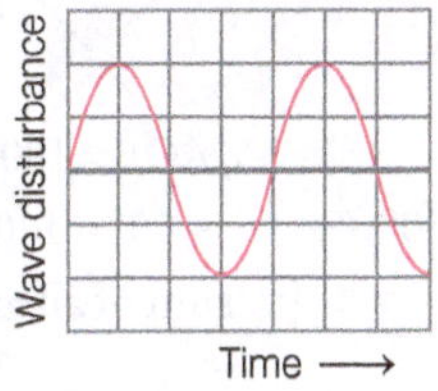

8 Find the distance of cloud from you when you hear a thunder 3 s after the lightning is seen. Given, speed of light $= 3 \times 10^8$ ms^{-1}, speed of sound $= 330$ ms^{-1}. Why is lightning before the thunder is heard during a thunderstorm?

Sol. Given, time, $t = 3$ s

and speed of sound in air $= 330$ ms^{-1}

Therefore, the distance from the cloud will be calculated as

Distance = Speed × Time = 330 × 3 = 990 m

As the speed of light in air (i.e. 3×10^8 ms^{-1}) is much greater than the speed of sound in air (i.e. 340 ms^{-1}). So, this is a reason why lightning is seen before the thunder is heard during thunderstorm.

9 (i) In summer when the day is hot, will the speed of sound will increase or decrease why? [1½]

(ii) Determine the minimum distance between the listener and reflector for an echo to be heard distinctively of sound propagating with speed of v m/s ? ($v = 340$ ms^{-1}) [1½]

Sol. (i) In summer when the day is hot, the speed of sound increases, because the speed of sound depends upon the temperature.

(ii) The sensation of sound persists in our brain is about 0.1 s, to hear a distinct echo, the time interval between the original sound and the reflected one must be equal to 0.1 s.

So, each will be heard, if the minimum distance between the listener and reflector will be 17.2 m.

10 For hearing the loudest ticking sound heard by the ear, find the angle x in the given figure.

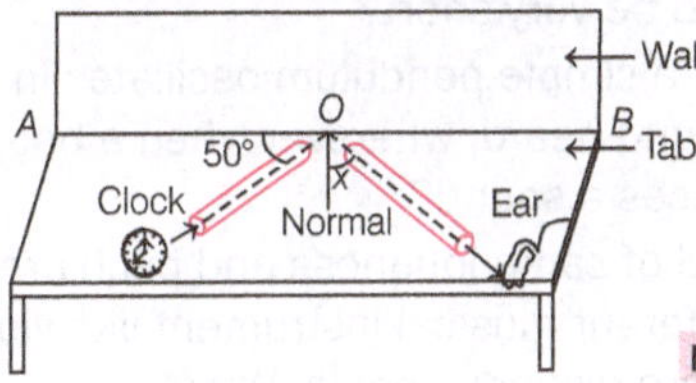

NCERT Exemplar

Sol. We know that in laws of reflection, the angle of incidence (x) is always equal to the angle of reflection (x). Since, AOB is a straight line.

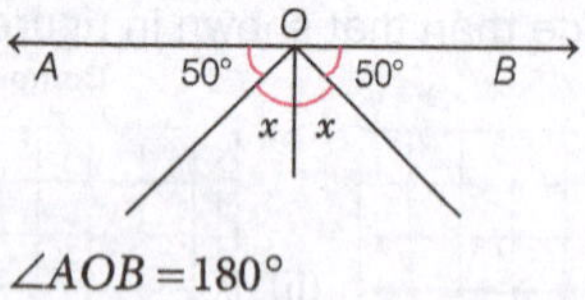

$\therefore \quad \angle AOB = 180°$

$\therefore 50° + x + x + 50° = 180°$

[∵ sum of all angles lies on the same side of a line is 180°]

$2x + 100° = 180°$

$\Rightarrow \quad 2x = 180° - 100° \Rightarrow \quad 2x = 80°$

$\Rightarrow \quad x = \frac{80°}{2} \Rightarrow x = 40°$

Hence, the value of x is 40°.

11 An echo is heard on a day when temperature is about 22°C. Will echo be heard sooner or later, if the temperature increases to 40°C? **Competency Based Que.**

Sol. Echo will be heard sooner than the echo heard when temperature was 22°C. Because speed of sound increases with increase in temperature.

Also, speed of sound in air $= \frac{\text{distance}}{\text{time}}$

i.e. If speed of sound increases, then time after which the echo will be heard decreases.

12 (i) **Why the stage of an auditorium has curved background curtains, carpets and false ceiling?** [1½]

(ii) **Why the sound of ringing bell inside a vacuum chambers cannot be heard?** [1½]

Sol. (i) The auditorium stage background is curved, because it is arranged in such manner that it can reflect sound evenly across the width of hall. So that the sound is clearly heard. Curtains, carpets all these help to reflect the sound.

(ii) It cannot be heard because sound waves are mechanical waves and mechanical waves cannot pass through vacuum.

13 Give reason for the following **Competency Based Que.**

(i) **The auditorium hall which are used for function and speeches in that hall why reverberation time should be very short?** [1]

(ii) **When a simple pendulum oscillates in air, there is no sound heard, wherever when a body vibrates it produces a sound?** [1]

(iii) **Sound of same loudness and pitch are produced by different musical instrument like violin and flute are distinguishable. Why?** [1]

Sol. (i) The reverberation time is short because, if the reverberation time of a auditorium hall will be long, then the multiple echoes will interfere with original sound. As a result, nothing will be heard distinctly.

(ii) When a simple pendulum oscillates in air, there is no sound heard because its frequency is less than 20 Hz. Whereas, when a body vibrates it produces sound because its frequency is more than 20 Hz and less then 20,000 Hz.

(iii) Due to the characteristics of quality of timbre of sound waves, the two sound waves are distinguishable.

14 How is it that, bats are able to fly at night without colliding with other objects? **Competency Based Que.**

Sol. Bats search out prey and fly at night by emitting and detecting reflections of ultrasonic waves.

Bats emit high frequency ultrasonic squeaks while flying and listen to the echoes produced by reflection of their squeaks from the obstacle i.e. prey or object in their path. From the time taken by the echo to be heard, bats can determine the distance of the object and can avoid the object by changing the direction without colliding with it.

Long Answer Type Questions

1 (i) **What is meant by frequency of sound waves?** [1]

(ii) **Give the range of frequencies of sound waves that an average human ear can detect.** [1]

(iii) **A source of wave produces 20 crests and 20 troughs in 0.2 s. The distance between a crest and next trough is 50 cm. Find the**

(a) wavelength, [1]

(b) frequency and [1]

(c) time period of the wave. [1]

Sol. (i) **Frequency** The number of waves produced per second is called the frequency of the wave.

(ii) 20 Hz to 20 kHz

(iii) (a) Since, the distance between a crest and next trough is $\frac{\lambda}{2}$.

Therefore, $\frac{\lambda}{2} = 50$ cm (given)

$\lambda = 100$ cm or 1 m

(b) Distance covered in 20 crests = 20 × 1 = 20 m

Velocity of the wave, $v = \nu\lambda = \frac{\lambda}{t}$

$\nu \times 1 = \frac{20}{0.2}$ [$\because t = 0.2$ s]

$\therefore \quad \nu = 100$ Hz or

$\because$ 1 crest and 1 trough = 1 wave

$\therefore$ 20 crest and 20 trough = 20 waves

$\therefore$ Frequency $= \dfrac{\text{Number of waves}}{\text{Time}} = \dfrac{20}{0.2}$

$= 100 \text{ Hz}$

(c) $\therefore$ Time period, $T = \dfrac{1}{\nu} = \dfrac{1}{100} = 0.01 \text{ s}$

2 Establish the relationship between speed of sound, its wavelength and frequency. If velocity of sound in air is 340 ms^{-1}. Calculate

(i) wavelength when frequency is 256 Hz [2½]

(ii) frequency when wavelength is 0.85 m. [2½]

NCERT Exemplar

Sol. The speed of sound is defined as the distance which a point on a wave, such as a compression or a rarefaction, travels per unit time.

We know that, speed,

$$v = \frac{\text{distance}}{\text{time}} = \frac{\lambda}{T}$$

where, λ is the wavelength of the sound wave.
It is the distance travelled by the sound wave in one time period (T) of the wave.

$$v = \lambda \times \frac{1}{T}$$

We know that, $\nu = \dfrac{1}{T}$ [where, ν = frequency]

$$v = \lambda \nu$$

i.e. Speed = Wavelength × Frequency

Given, speed of sound in air, $v = 340 \text{ ms}^{-1}$
and frequency, $\nu = 256$ Hz

(i) Speed = Wavelength × Frequency

$\Rightarrow \quad 340 = \lambda \times 256$

$\Rightarrow \quad \lambda = \dfrac{340}{256} = 1.33 \text{ m}$

(ii) Given wavelength, $\lambda = 0.85$ m

Then, frequency of sound in air,

$$\nu = \frac{\text{Speed}}{\text{Wavelength}}$$

$\Rightarrow \quad \nu = \dfrac{340}{0.85} = \dfrac{340 \times 100}{85} = 400 \text{ Hz}$

Thus, frequency of sound is 400 Hz.

3 Draw a curve showing density or pressure variations with respect to distance for a disturbance produced by sound. Mark the position of compression and rarefaction on this curve. Also, define wavelengths and time period using this curve. **Competency Based Que.**

Sol. We have a curve showing density or pressure variations with respect to distance for a disturbance produced by sound.

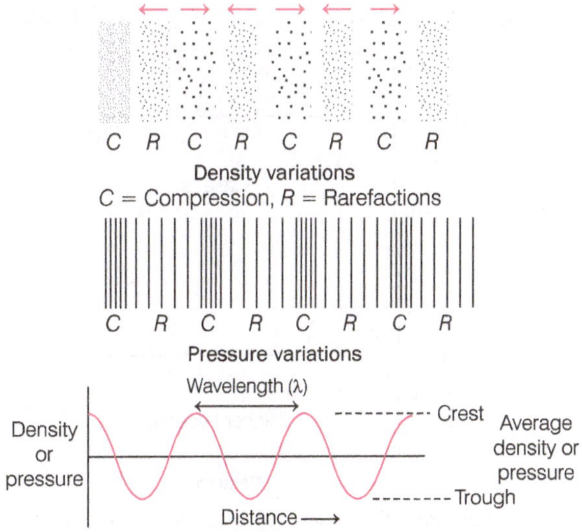

Wavelength can be defined as the distance between two successive compressions or rarefactions. It is denoted by λ.
Time taken by the waves to complete one full cycle, so that its particles are in same phase is called time period. It is denoted by T.

4 Represent graphically by two separate diagrams in each case.

(i) Two sound waves having the same amplitude but different frequencies. [1½]

(ii) Two sound waves having the same frequency but different amplitudes. [1½]

(iii) Two sound waves having different amplitudes and also different wavelengths. [2] **NCERT Exemplar**

Sol. (i)

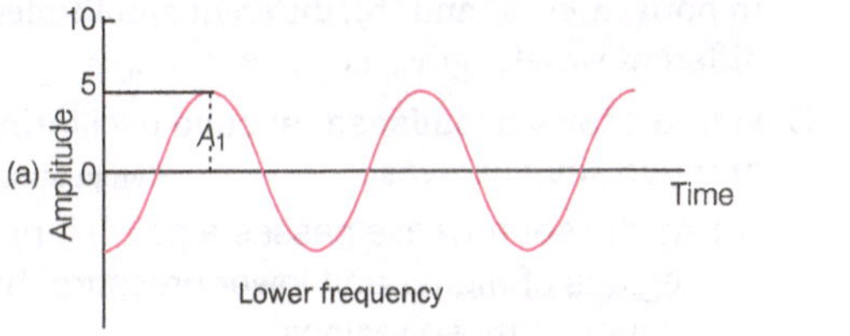

Case (a)

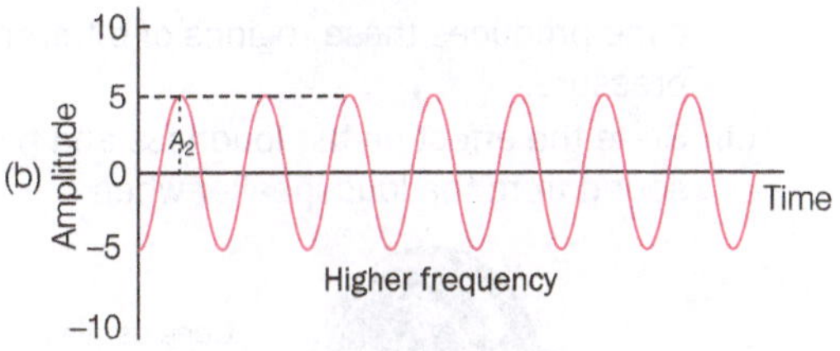

Case (b)

In both cases (a) and (b), same amplitude and different frequencies, i.e. ($A_1 = A_2$).

(ii)

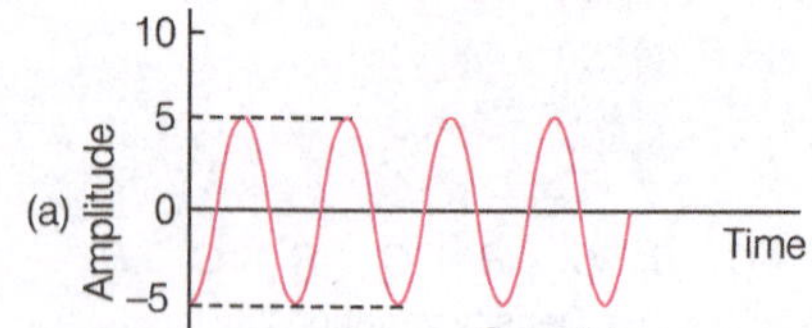

Case (a)

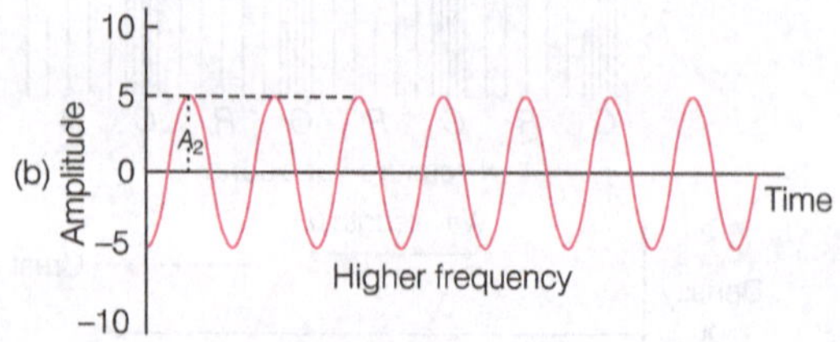

Case (b)

In both the cases. (a) and (b), same frequency and different amplitudes, i.e. $(A_1 \neq A_2)$.

(iii)

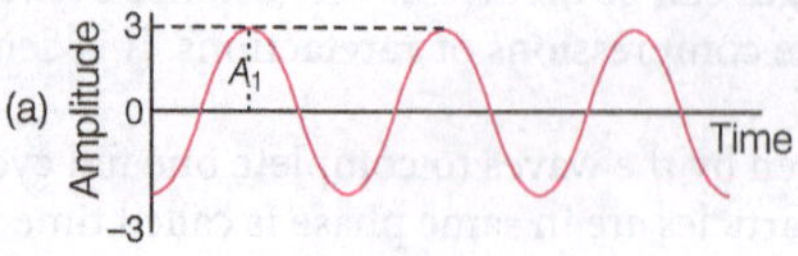

Case (a)

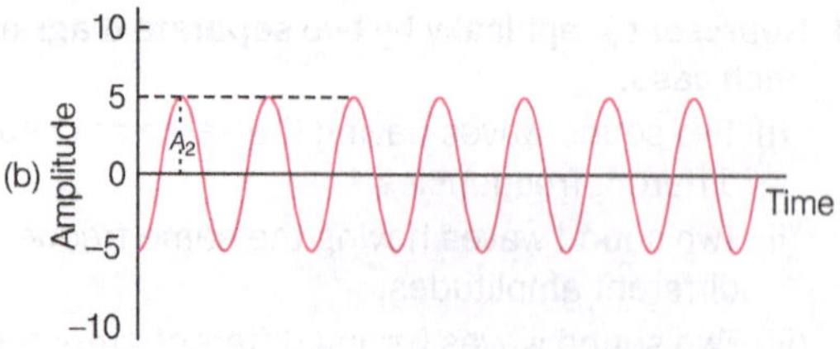

Case (b)

In both cases (a) and (b), different amplitudes and different wavelengths, i.e. $A_1 \neq A_2, \lambda_1 \neq \lambda_2$.

5 Figure shows a loudspeaker cone oscillating to produce sound waves **Competency Based Que.**

(i) As the sound wave passes a point, it produces regions of higher and lower pressure. State the names of these regions. [1]

(ii) Describe how the movement of the loudspeaker cone produces these regions of different pressure. [2]

(iii) State the effect on the loudness and pitch of the sound from the loudspeaker when

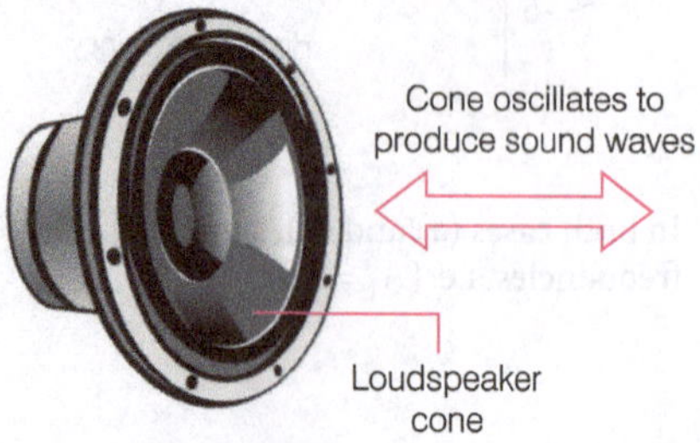

(a) The amplitude increases but the frequency of the sound stays the same. [1]

(b) The amplitude stays the same but the frequency increases. [1]

Sol. (i) **Region of high pressure** Compression

Region of low pressure Rarefaction

(ii) When the loudspeaker cone moves forward. i.e, in the direction of propagation of wave, it pushes the layer of air closer. Similarly, this layer pushes the next air layer and the process goes on. In this way, the layers of air near the cone are compressed to form a compression, this is the region of high pressure.

(iii) (a) Loudness increases as greater the amplitude of sound waves, because it depends on frequency but pitch remains same.

(b) Loudness remains same but pitch increases as the pitch of sound is directly proportional to frequency.

Numerical Questions

1 A human heartbeats 72 times in a minute. Calculate its frequency.

Sol. Given, number of heartbeats = 72

Time = 1 min = 60 s

$$\therefore \text{Frequency} = \frac{\text{Number of beats}}{\text{Total time (in second)}}$$

$$= \frac{72}{60} = 1.2 \text{ Hz} \qquad [\because 1 \text{ min} = 60 \text{ s}]$$

2 A sound wave travels at a speed of 342 m/s. If the wavelength is 2.5 cm, what is the frequency of the wave?

Sol. Wavelength, $\lambda = 2.5 \text{ cm} = 0.025 \text{ m}$

Speed, $v = 342$ m/s

$$\text{Frequency, } \nu = \frac{v}{\lambda} = \frac{342}{0.025} = 13680 \text{ Hz}$$

3 30 Vibrations are produced in a slinky in 15 s, when a jerk is given to it. Find its time period and frequency ?

Sol. Number of vibrations in 15 second = 30

Number of vibration in 1 second = 30 / 15 = 2

Frequency = 2 Hz

$$\text{Time period} = \frac{1}{\nu} = \frac{1}{2} = 0.5 \text{ s}$$

4 A radar signal is received in 2×10^{-5} s after it was sent and reflected by an aeroplane. How far is the aeroplane if speed of wave is 3×10^8 m/s?

Sol. Given,

Speed of wave, $v = 3 \times 10^8$ m/s

Time taken for receiving the radar signal

$t = 2 \times 10^{-5}$ s

Distance travelled by the wave

$$= v \times t = 3 \times 10^8 \times 2 \times 10^{-5}$$
$$= 6 \times 10^3 \text{ m}$$

In this time, wave has to travel twice the distance between the aeroplane and the receiver. Hence, the distance of the aeroplane $= 3 \times 10^3$ m.

5 Raman hears the echo of his own voice from a distant mountain after 0.6 s. If the speed of sound in air is 340 m/s, calculate the distance of mountain from the Raman. **Competency Based Que.**

Sol. Let, s be the distance of the mountain from the Raman and t is the time of to and fro journey of sound waves, then from relations.

Distance = Velocity × Time

We have, $2s = vt$

$$s = \frac{vt}{2}$$

Here, $v = 340$ m/s, $t = 0.6$ s

$$s = \frac{340 \times 0.6}{2}$$

$$s = 340 \times 0.3 \text{ m} = 102 \text{ m}$$

6 A person has a hearing range from 20 Hz to 20 kHz. What are the typical wavelength of sound waves in air corresponding to these two frequencies?

Sol. The wavelength for 20 Hz sound waves would be

$$v = n \times \lambda \quad \text{(where } n \text{ is frequency)}$$

$$\lambda = \frac{v}{n} = \frac{344}{20} = 17.2 \text{ m}$$

For 20 kHz sound waves the wavelength would be

$$v = n \times \lambda$$

$$\lambda = \frac{v}{n} = \frac{344}{20000} = 0.0172 \text{ m}$$

7 Ram is standing in front of wall at distance of 85 m produces 2 claps per second. He notices that the sound of his clapping coincides with the echo. The echo is heard only one when clapping is stopped. Calculate the speed of sound. **Competency Based Que.**

Sol. Here, distance of Ram from the wall, $d = 85$ m

time taken by the echo to be heard, $t = \frac{1}{2}\text{s} = 0.5$ s

If d is distance between Ram and the wall, the total distance travelled by sound is going and coming back $= 2d$

$$\therefore \ 2d = vt \text{ or, } v = \frac{2d}{t} = \frac{2 \times 85}{0.5} = 340 \text{ m/s}$$

8 A boat is moving with velocity 20 ms^{-1} in a sea is rocked by waves. If its crests are 80 m apart, then at what time the boat bounces up?

Sol. Given that, wavelength, $\lambda = 80$ m

(distance between two consecutive crests and troughs is equal to the wavelength.)

Velocity, $v = 20 \text{ ms}^{-1}$, time, $T = ?$

As we know that, $T = \frac{\lambda}{v} = \frac{80}{20} = 4$ s

9 A construction worker's helmet slips and falls when he is 78.4 m above the ground. He hears the sound of the helmet hitting the ground 4.23 s after it slipped. Find the speed of sound in air. **Competency Based Que.**

Sol. Here, s = distance travelled by the helmet to reach the ground = 78.4 m

and t = total time taken for hearing the sound of the helmet hitting the ground = 4.23 s.

Let t be the time taken by helmet in reaching the ground.

So, we know that, according to equation of motion,

$$s = ut + \frac{1}{2}gt^2 \left[\begin{array}{l}\text{where, } u = \text{initial velocity} \\ \text{and } g = \text{acceleration due to gravity.}\end{array}\right]$$

$$\Rightarrow \quad 78.4 = 0 \times t + \frac{1}{2} \times 9.8 \times t^2$$

$$\Rightarrow \quad 78.4 = \frac{1}{2} \times 9.8 \times t^2$$

$$\Rightarrow \quad t^2 = 16 \Rightarrow t = 4 \text{ s}$$

So, time taken by the sound wave to travel distance 78.4 m.

$\Rightarrow 4.23 \text{ s} - 4 \text{ s} = 0.23$ s.

So, speed of sound in air $= \frac{78.4 \text{ m}}{0.23 \text{ s}} = 340.86 \text{ ms}^{-1}$

10 A sound wave travels at a speed of 340 ms^{-1}. If its wavelength is 1.5 cm. What is the frequency of the wave? Will it be audible?

Sol. Given that, speed of sound, $v = 340 \text{ ms}^{-1}$

Wavelength, $\lambda = 1.5 \text{ cm} = \frac{1.5}{100}$ m Frequency, $\nu = ?$

Using the formula, $v = \nu\lambda$

$$\Rightarrow \quad \nu = \frac{v}{\lambda} = \frac{340}{\left(\frac{1.5}{100}\right)} \text{ ms}^{-1} = \frac{340 \times 100}{1.5}$$

$$= 22666.6 \text{ Hz}$$

We know that, audible range of frequencies is 20 Hz to 20000 Hz.

So, the given frequency (i.e. 22666.6 Hz) is not audible.

11 A sound wave has a frequency of 2 kHz and a wavelength of 45 cm. It takes 4 s to travel. Calculatethe distance it travels.

Sol. Here, frequency of sound wave,

$$\nu = 2\text{ kHz} = 2\times 10^3\text{ Hz}$$

Wavelength of the wave, $\lambda = 45\text{ cm} = 0.45\text{ m}$

Velocity of the wave, $v = \nu\lambda$

$$= 2\times 10^3 \times 0.45 = 900\text{ ms}^{-1}$$

Time to travel = 4 s

Distance travelled by the wave $= vt = 900 \times 4 = 3600$ m

12 A person strikes the end of the iron rod with a stone, a boy places his ear on the other end of the iron rod. What is the ratio of time taken by sound wave in air and in iron rod to reach the boy? (Given, $v_{iron} = 5950\text{ ms}^{-1}$ and $v_{air} = 346\text{ ms}^{-1}$)

Sol. As we know that, time taken $= \dfrac{\text{distance}}{\text{speed}}$

$$\Rightarrow \quad t = \frac{\lambda}{v}$$

$$\Rightarrow \quad t \propto \frac{1}{v}$$

$\Rightarrow$ t is inversely proportional to $\dfrac{1}{v}$.

$$\therefore \quad \frac{\text{Speed of sound in iron rod}}{\text{Speed of sound in air}} = \frac{t_{air}}{t_{iron}}$$

$$\Rightarrow \quad \text{Ratio} = \frac{t_{air}}{t_{iron}} = \frac{5950}{346} = 17.2 : 1$$

13 Aditi clapped her hands near a cliff and heard the echo after 4 s. What is the distance of the cliff from her, if the speed of sound is taken as 346 ms^{-1}?

Sol. Given, speed of sound, $v = 346\text{ ms}^{-1}$

Time taken for hearing the echo, $t = 4$ s

$\therefore$ Distance travelled by the sound $= v\times t$

$$= 346 \times 4 = 1384\text{m}$$

In 4 s, sound has to travel twice the distance between the cliff and Aditi. Therefore, the distance between the cliff and Aditi is $\dfrac{1384}{2} = 692$ m.

14 A ship sends out ultrasound that returns from the sea bed and is detected after 1.71 s. If the speed of ultrasound through sea water is 1531 ms^{-1}, what is the distance of the sea bed from the ship?

Sol. Given, time between transmission and detection, $t = 1.71$ s

Speed of ultrasound through sea water,

$$v = 1531\text{ ms}^{-1}$$

Distance travelled by the ultrasound

$$= 2\times \text{ Depth of the sea} = 2d$$

or $2d = v\times t = 1531\times 1.71 = 2618.01$ m

$$d = \frac{2618.01}{2} = 1309\text{ m}$$

Hence, the distance of the sea bed from the ship is 1309 m.

15 A child hears an echo from a cliff, 4 s after the sound from a powerful cracker is produced. How far away is the cliff from the child? (Take, velocity of the sound in air as 330 ms^{-1}.)

Sol. The time taken by echo to be heard, $t = \dfrac{2d}{v} = 4$ s

(In case of echo, sound covers twice the distance between sound source and reflector.)

Velocity of sound in air, $v = 330\text{ ms}^{-1}$

$$\frac{2d}{v} = 4 \quad \text{or} \quad 2d = 330\times 4$$

$$\Rightarrow \quad d = \frac{330\times 4}{2} = 660\text{ m}$$

Thus, the distance of the cliff from the child is 660 m.

16 A boy is standing in the middle of a big square field. There is a tall building on one side of the field. He explodes a cracker and hears its echo 0.4 s later. What is the size of the square field? (Given, speed of sound in air is 330 ms^{-1})

Competency Based Que.

Sol. Given, speed of sound in air, $v = 330\text{ ms}^{-1}$

Time taken for hearing the echo, $t = 0.4$ s

As we know, distance travelled by the sound

$$= v\times t = 330\times 0.4 = 132\text{ m}$$

As in 0.4 s, sound has to travel twice the distance between the boy and the building.

Hence, the distance between the boy and the building is

$$= \frac{d}{2} = \frac{132}{2} = 66\text{ m}$$

Side of the square field = Twice the distance between the boy and the building

Side of the square field

$$= 2\times 66\text{ m} = 132\text{ m}$$

So, size of the square field = (side of the square field)^2

$$= (132\text{ m})^2 = 17424\text{ m}^2$$

17 **The given graph shows the displacement *versus* time relation for a disturbance travelling with velocity of 1500 ms^{-1}. Calculate the wavelength of the disturbance.**

NCERT Exemplar

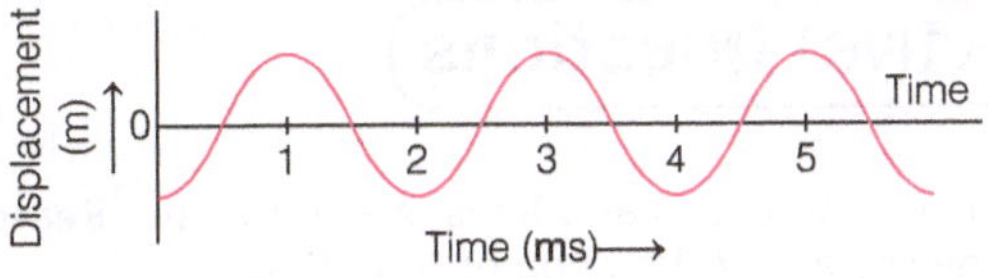

Sol. Given, velocity, $v = 1500 \text{ ms}^{-1}$

Time taken in one complete cycle is 2 μs.

Time, $T = 2\ \mu s = 2 \times 10^{-6}$ s $[\because 1\ \mu s = 10^{-6}\ s]$

We know that, $v = \nu\lambda$ $\left[\because \nu = \frac{1}{T}\right]$

So, $v = \frac{\lambda}{T}$

$\Rightarrow \lambda = vT$

where, λ = wavelength, ν = frequency

and T = time period.

So, $\lambda = 1500 \times 2 \times 10^{-6}$

$= 3000 \times 10^{-6}$

$= 3 \times 10^{-3}$ m

18 **A girl is sitting in the middle of a park of dimension $12 \text{ m} \times 12$ m. On the left side of it, there is a building adjoining the park and on right side of the park, there is a road adjoining the park. A sound is produced on the road by a cracker. Is it possible for the girl to hear the echo of this sound ? Explain your answer.**

Competency Based Que.

Sol. If the time gap between the original sound and reflected sound received by the listener is around 0.15 , only then the echo can be heard.

Speed of sound in air, $v = 344 \text{ms}^{-1}$

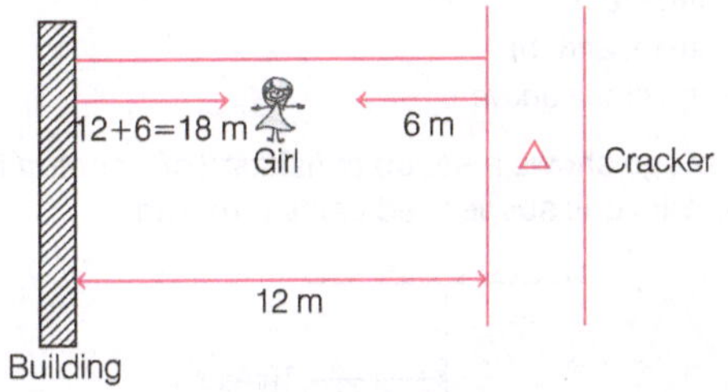

The time gap between the original sound and the reflected sound received by the girl.

$$= \frac{18}{344} - \frac{6}{344} = 0.035 \text{ s}$$

As 0.035 s < 0.1 s, therefore no echo will be heard by the girl.

ASSESSMENT EXERCISE

Competency Focused (Objective) Questions

Multiple Type Questions

1 Sound waves transfer
(a) energy
(b) momentum
(c) Both (a) and (b)
(d) None of the above

2 The image shows a set up consisting of a tuning fork and a metallic ball suspended using a thread.

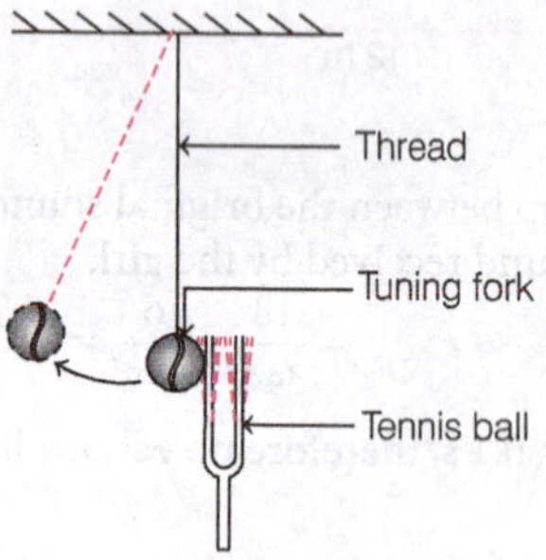

What happens when the metallic ball hits the tuning fork?
(a) The tuning fork vibrates the ball to produce sound.
(b) The tuning fork vibrates to and fro to produce sound.
(c) The tuning fork gets heated by the collision of the ball.
(d) The tuning fork generates heat by the vibrating to and fro.

3 Which medium will have sound waves propagating at a higher speed? **Competency Based Que.**
(a) A liquid medium at 25°C temperature.
(b) A liquid medium at 50°C temperature.
(c) A gaseous medium at 50°C temperature.
(d) A gaseous medium at 25°C temperature.

4 Which wave property determines the loudness of sound ?
(a) Frequency (b) Pitch
(c) Speed (d) Amplitude

5 The sensation of sound persists for 0.1 s in our brain. As a result, a clap near a tall building can be heard again. At what temperature of the air would the minimum distance required for differentiating the original sound of clap from its reflection be the greatest?
(a) 0°C (b) 10°C
(c) 20°C (d) 30°C

Assertion-Reason

Direction (Q.Nos. 6-8) *In each of the following questions, a statement of Assertion is given by the corresponding statement of Reason of the statements, mark the correct answer as*

(a) If both Assertion and Reason are true and Reason is the correct explanation of Assertion.
(b) If both Assertion and Reason are true, but Reason is not the correct explanation of Assertion.
(c) If Assertion is true, but Reason is false.
(d) If Assertion is false, but Reason is true.

6 **Assertion** (A) Sound wave is an longitudinal wave.
Reason (R) Speed of sound in solid is less than air.

7 **Assertion** (A) The loudness of sound is measured in decibel.
Reason (R) If sound waves have a large amplitude, then the sound will be loud.

8 **Assertion** (a) Ultrasonic sound is used in industry for detecting flaws (cracks etc) in metal blocks without damaging them.
Reason (R) An internal crack (or hole) does not allow ultrasound to pass through it.

Answers

1. (c)	**2.** (b)	**3.** (b)	**4.** (d)	**5.** (d)	**6.** (c)
7. (b)	**8.** (a)				

Case Based/Source Based Question

Direction (Q.No. 9) *Answer the question on the basis of your understanding of the following paragraph and related studied concepts*

9. Sound travels about 5 times faster in water than in air. The speed of sound in sea water is very large about 1500m/s. Thus, two whales in the sea which are hundreds of kilometres away can talk to each other easily through sea water. Similarly, sound travels about 15 times faster in iron (or steel) than in air.

Since, the speed of sound in steel is very very large (being about 5310 m/s which is more than 1800 km/h), we can hear the sound of an approaching train by putting our ear to the railway line made of steel even when the train is far away.

(i) Give reason, when we put our ears to a railway line, we can hear sound of an approaching train even when it is far off.
(ii) What is the speed of sound in steel?
(iii) Find the distance of a gun from a man, if the flash of a gun is seen by a man 3s before the sound is heard. (Speed of sound in air is 332 m/s)
(iv) Out of solids, liquids and gases in which medium sound travels slowest?

Constructed Response (Descriptive) Questions

Very Short Answer Type Questions

10 What is the nature of the ocean waves in deep water?

11 Which physical quantity remains unchanged after reflection of a sound wave?

12 Give the principle involved in megaphone.

13 The window panes of houses sometimes crack when a bomb explodes even at a large distance. Why? **Competency Based Que.**

14 How do submarines know the depth of a sea?

Short Answer Type Questions

15 What is compression and rarefaction in longitudinal wave? Explain.

16 Why does the amplitude of oscillation get reduced over a period of time? Explain with diagram. **Competency Based Que.**

17 What is the intensity of sound wave? Give its relation with amplitude.

18 A bat can hear sound at frequencies up to 130 kHz. What is the wavelength of sound?
(speed of sound is 344 ms^{-1} in air) [**Ans.** 2.65×10^{-3} m]

19 What is the difference between infrasonic and ultrasonic?

Long Answer Type Questions

20 Given below are some examples of wave motion. State in each case, if the wave motion is transverse, longitudinal or a combination of both. **Competency Based Que.**

(i) Motion of a kink in a long coil spring produced by displacing one end of the string side ways.

(ii) Wave produced in a cylinder consisting a liquid by moving its piston back and forth.

(iii) Waves produced by a motor boat sailing in water.

(iv) Light waves travelling from the Sun to the Earth.

(v) Ultrasonic waves in air produced by a vibrating quartz crystal.

21 Answer the following.

(i) Can transverse waves travel in glasses?

(ii) At any instant, a compression is formed at a point. After how much time,
(a) a rarefaction
(b) and a compression will be formed at the same point?

CHAPTER 12

Improvement in Food Resources

All living organisms need energy for carrying out various life processes. They obtain this energy from food. The food supplies various nutrients like proteins, fats, lipids, carbohydrates, vitamins, minerals, etc., which are required for body development, growth and good health. Both plants and animals are considered as major sources of food for us. We obtain most of this food from agriculture and animal husbandry.

Need for Improvement in Food Resources in India

India is a populous country. Its population is over one billion and it is still growing. To fulfill the need of such a vast and increasing population, there is a need to increase food production.
But India is already intensively cultivated. So, there is no scope of increasing the area of land under cultivation. It is therefore, necessary to increase our production efficiency for both crops and livestock.

To meet these requirements, many efforts were made in the past to increase the food production. Majority of them comes under green revolution and white revolution.

(i) **Green revolution** has contributed in increasing the food grain production.

(ii) **White revolution** has led to better availability of milk.

However, these revolutions have also increased the chances of intensive use of our natural resources. Due to this, there are more chances of depletion of natural resources.

Therefore, it is important that we should increase food production without degrading our environment. This can be done by incorporating sustainable practices in agriculture and animal husbandry.

12.1 Crops

These are the plants that are cultivated by human beings on a large scale for food, fodder and other materials.

Types of Crops

The important types of crops are

(i) **Cereal crops** These plants are cultivated to provide **carbohydrate** for daily energy requirements, e.g. wheat, rice, maize, millets and *Sorghum*.

(ii) **Pulses** These are the seeds of crops that can be eaten to fulfill **protein** requirement, e.g. gram (chana), pea (matar), black gram (urad), green gram (moong), pigeon pea (arhar), lentil (masoor), etc.

(iii) **Oilseed crops** These plants provide us with necessary fats and oils, e.g. soybean, groundnut, sesame, castor, mustard, linseed and sunflower, etc.

(iv) **Vegetables, spices and fruits** These fulfill the requirement of a variety of vitamins and minerals along with small quantities of proteins, carbohydrates and fats, e.g. cabbage, onion, pepper, etc.

(v) **Fodder crops** These plants are raised as food for the livestock, e.g. berseem, oats or sudan grass, etc.

Climatic Conditions for Crops

Different crops require different climatic conditions like, **temperature** and **photoperiods** (i.e. related to the duration of sunlight) for their growth and completion of life cycle. Since, plants manufacture their food in sunlight by the process of photosynthesis, growth of plants and flowering depend on the duration of sunlight.

Classification of Crops

Based on the seasons crops can be classified as

(i) **Kharif crops** These crops are grown in hot and rainy season (Kharif season) from the month of June to October, e.g. paddy, soybean, pigeon pea, maize, cotton, green gram, groundnut, black gram, etc.

(ii) **Rabi crops** These crops are grown in dry and winter season (Rabi season) from the month of November to April, e.g. wheat, gram, peas, mustard, linseed, barley, etc.

12.2 Improvement in Crop Yield

The practices involved in increasing crop yield are categorised into three major groups as

(i) **Crop variety improvement** which includes the choice of seeds for planting.

(ii) **Crop production management** which includes nurturing of the crop plants.

(iii) **Crop protection management** which includes the protection of the growing and harvested crops from loss.

Crop Variety Improvement

It is the technique of bringing together various useful characters from different varieties of crop plants into one crop variety.

The main aim of this practice is to find a variety of crop, that produces high yield and can withstand different conditions like high soil salinity, diverse climatic conditions drought, flood and water availability.

Varieties or strains of crops can be selected by breeding for various traits such as disease resistance, response to fertilisers, product quality and high yields. A new variety developed with all such features is highly acceptable.

Methods of Crop Variety Improvement

There are two methods to incorporate desirable characteristics into crop varieties.

These are as follows

(i) **Hybridisation** It refers to the crossing between the genetically dissimilar plants to produce a new type (hybrid) or High Yielding Variety (HYV).

It is further of the following types

(a) **Intervarietal** The cross done between two plants belonging to different varieties of crops. It is the most common method used in plant breeding.

(b) **Interspecific** The cross done between two plants belonging to different species of the same genus.

(c) **Intergeneric** The cross done between plants belonging to different genera.

(ii) **Genetically modified crops** It involves the incorporation of new genes in crop plants to increase their yield, improve quality, sustainability, etc., and provide desired characteristics in the crop.

Significance of Crop Variety Improvement

Some of the important factors for which crop variety improvement is done are as follows

(i) **Higher yield** Variety improvement is done to increase the productivity of the crop per acre.

(ii) **Improved quality** The definitions of quality is different for different crops. For example, baking quality is important in wheat, protein quality in pulses, oil quality in oilseeds and preserving quality in fruits and vegetables.

(iii) **Biotic and abiotic resistance** Biotic stresses (diseases, insects and nematodes) and abiotic stresses (drought, salinity, water logging, heat, cold and frost) affect crop production negatively. Varieties resistant to such conditions are always preferred as they help to improve crop production.

(iv) **Change in maturity duration** Short duration of time between sowing and harvesting makes a crop more economical. It allows the farmers to grow multiple rounds of crops in a year. It also reduces the cost of crop production. Uniform maturity makes the harvesting process easy. It also reduces losses during the harvesting.

(v) **Wider adaptability** Developing varieties that can grow and adapt to different environmental conditions help in stabilising crop production. Thus, a single variety can be grown in different regions having different climatic conditions.

(vi) **Desirable agronomic characteristics** Plants showing higher productivity and good growth are preferred more than others, e.g. tallness and profuse branching are preferred characters for fodder crops. Dwarfness is desired in cereals, so that less nutrients are consumed by these crops.

Try These 12.1

1 Which revolution had contributed in increasing the food grain production?

2 Name the nutrient provided by cereal crops like wheat, maize and rice, etc.

3 Which type of plants are raised as food for the livestock?

4 Mention the time period during which pigeon pea crop is grown. Also mention its type.

5 State the term given to the cross made between two plants belonging to different varieties of crops.

12.3 Crop Production Management

It refers to the management of crop production by the use of different farming practices and agricultural technologies. It depends upon the financial conditions of the farmers.

There is a correlation between higher inputs and yields. The purchasing capacity of farmer for inputs decides cropping system and production practices.

Thus, the production practices can be grouped at three levels, i.e. 'no cost', 'low cost' and 'high cost' production practices.

Crop production management includes the management of nutrients, irrigation and cropping patterns, which are as discussed below

1. Nutrient Management

Nutrients are the inorganic elements, which are required by plants for their growth and development. Nutrients are supplied to plants by air, water and soil. There are total 16 essential nutrients for plants.

Plants Nutrients with their Sources

Sources	Nutrients
Air	Carbon and oxygen
Water	Hydrogen and oxygen
Soil	Macro and micronutrients

Soil supplies following 13 nutrients that are divided into two major categories as

(i) **Macronutrients** These are required by plants in large quantities, hence known as macronutrients. These include six nutrients *viz.*, nitrogen, phosphorus, potassium, calcium, magnesium and sulphur.

(ii) **Micronutrients** These are required by plants in small quantities and include seven nutrients *viz.*, iron, manganese, boron, zinc, copper, molybdenum and chlorine.

The deficiency of any of these nutrients affects physiological processes in plants including reproduction, growth and susceptibility to disease.

Nutrients can be supplied to the soil in the form of manure and fertilisers. It helps to increase the yield of crops.

Manure

It is a natural fertiliser. It contains large quantities of organic substances formed by the decomposition of animal excreta and plant wastes. It supplies small quantities of nutrients to the soil.

Based on the type of biological material used, manure can be classified as

(i) **Compost and vermicompost** The process in which farm waste material like livestock excreta (cow dung, etc.), vegetable waste, animal refuse, domestic waste, sewage waste, straw, eradicated weeds, etc., are decomposed in pits is known as **composting.**

The **compost** is rich in organic matter and nutrients. Compost is also prepared by using earthworms to hasten the process of decomposition of plants and animals refuse. This process is called **vermicomposting.**

(ii) **Green manure** Some plants like sunn hemp or guar are grown and mulched by ploughing them into the soil before sowing of the crop seeds. These green plants turn into green manure which helps in increasing the content of **nitrogen** and **phosphorus** in the soil.

Advantages of manure are as follows

(i) It enriches soil with nutrients and organic matter (called **humus**).

(ii) It increases soil fertility and decreases the harmful effects of pesticides and insecticides on soil.

(iii) The bulk of organic matter helps in improving the soil structure by increasing the water holding capacity in sandy soils. In clayey soil, large quantity of organic matter helps in drainage and in avoiding water logging.

(iv) By the use of biological waste material (manure), we can protect the environment from excessive use of fertilisers.

(v) It also helps in the recycling of farm waste.

Fertilisers

These are commercially produced plant nutrients. Fertilisers supply nitrogen, phosphorus and potassium (NPK) to the soil.

Advantages of fertilisers are as follows

(i) These are easily available, easy to use and store.

(ii) These help in the higher yields of high-cost farming.

(iii) These are used to ensure good vegetative growth (leaves, branches and flowers) and give rise to healthy plants.

Disadvantages of fertilisers are as follows

(i) Fertilisers can cause water pollution as they get washed away, since they are not absorbed fully by the plants due to excessive irrigation. Hence, they should be used and applied carefully in terms of proper dose, time and after observing the pre and post application carefully.

(ii) The continuous use of fertilisers in any area can eventually destroy fertility of a soil because the organic matter in the soil does not get replenished. Also microorganisms present in the soil are harmed by the use of fertilisers.

(iii) They provide short-term benefits. Thus, for maintaining soil fertility, both short-term benefits of using fertilisers and long-term benefits of using manure must be considered, while aiming for the optimum yields in crop production.

Organic Farming

It is an environment friendly farming system that characterises the following

- Minimal or no use of fertilisers, herbicides, pesticides, etc.
- Maximum use of organic manures, recycled farm wastes (straw and livestock excreta).
- Use of biofertilisers and biopesticides like culture of blue-green algae and neem leaves, respectively.
- Following healthy cropping systems like mixed cropping, intercropping and crop rotation.

Try These 12.2

1. **To which category of plant nutrients does nitrogen belong?**
2. **Mention any two methods by which minerals can be replenished in the soil.**
3. **What does the process of making manure from kitchen waste termed as?**
4. **State the term used for making manure from plants and animal refuse using earthworms.**
5. **Which term is used for the type of farming which requires minimal or no usage of any type of chemicals substances?**

2. Irrigation

The process of supplying water to crop plants in fields by the means of canals, reservoirs, wells, tubewells, etc., is called irrigation.

Most agricultural practices in India are mainly rain fed. The success of a crop in most areas is mainly dependent upon the timely monsoons and sufficient rainfall spread through a particular growing season.

In order to ensure that water is supplied to the crops at right stages and in required amounts, farmers depend on various natural resources like ponds, wells, canals, etc., for the irrigation of their farmlands.

Irrigation Systems

In India, a wide variety of water resources and a highly varied climate is found. Under such conditions, several different kinds of irrigation systems are adopted depending on the type of water resources available for agricultural purposes. These are as follows

(i) **Wells** These are constructed wherever groundwater is available for irrigation. These are of two main types

(a) **Dug wells** In these wells water is collected from water bearing strata. This water is lifted by mechanical means, like bullock operated device.

(b) **Tube wells** In these wells, water can be lifted from deeper strata using pumps.

(ii) **Canals** These are usually an elaborate and extensively used method of irrigation. In this system canals receive water from reservoirs like dam or from rivers. The main canal is divided into other branch canals that have further distributaries to irrigate fields.

(iii) **River lift systems** This method is used in areas where canal flow is insufficient or irregular due to insufficient reservoir release. Here, water is directly drawn from the rivers for supplementing irrigation in areas close to rivers.

(iv) **Tanks** These are small storage reservoirs, which intercept and store the run-off of smaller catchment areas.

Modern Techniques of Irrigation

Fresh initiatives are also taken for increasing water availability for agriculture by augmenting groundwater levels. These mainly includes the following

(i) **Rainwater harvesting** In this, rainwater is collected into the ground by digging tunnels, etc. This water percolates into the soil, thus maintaining the water table.

(ii) **Watershed development** Small check-dams are built to increase groundwater levels. The purpose of check-dams is to stop the rainwater from flowing away and also to reduce soil erosion.

Drought

It is the condition that occurs because of scarcity or irregular distribution of rains. It poses a threat to rain-fed farming areas, where farmers do not use irrigation for crops production and depend only on rain. Hence, poor monsoons in such areas cause crop failure.

Light soils like sandy soil have less water retention capacity. In areas with light soils, crops get adversely affected by drought conditions. Scientists have developed some crop varieties, which can tolerate drought conditions.

3. Cropping Patterns

It involves raising crops so as to obtain maximum benefit from the same piece of land. It reduces the risk of crop failure, diseases, etc. For this purpose, crops can be grown in different ways. Some of these are as follows

I. Mixed Cropping

It is the practice of growing two or more crops simultaneously on the same piece of land. For example, wheat + gram, wheat + mustard, groundnut + sunflower, etc. Some advantages of mixed cropping are

(i) Improves soil fertility.

(ii) The risk of total crop failure due to uncertain monsoon is reduced.

(iii) Gives some insurance against failure of one of the crops.

II. Intercropping

It is the practice of growing two or more crops simultaneously on the same field in a definite pattern. A few rows of one crop alternate with a few rows of other crop.

The crops are selected on the basis of their nutrient requirements. Two crops must have different nutrient requirements from each other. For example, soybean + maize, finger millet (bajra) + cowpea (lobia), etc.

Some advantages of intercropping are

(i) It ensures maximum utilisation of supplied nutrients and therefore better returns.

(ii) It prevents the spread of pests and diseases to all the plants of one crop in a field.

(iii) Both crops give better returns in it.

III. Crop Rotation

It is the practice of growing different crops on a piece of land in a pre-planned succession. The crop combination depends upon the duration of crops.

One crop is grown on a field and after its harvest, a second crop is grown on the same field. This can also follow a third crop. The crop to be chosen after one harvest depends upon the availability of moisture and irrigation facilities.

Some advantages of crop rotation are

(i) It improves the fertility of soil.

(ii) It minimises pest infestation and diseases.

(iii) It prevents the change in the chemical nature of the soil.

(iv) It avoids depletion of a particular nutrient from the soil.

(v) If done properly, two or three crops can be grown in a year with good harvest.

Try These 12.3

1. **Name the type of irrigation system where water is drawn from deeper strata by using pumps.**
2. **Which system of irrigation is used in areas where canal flow is insufficient?**
3. **State the type of irrigation system used purposely to stop rainwater from flowing away and reduce soil erosion.**
4. **What is the term used for growing wheat and gram together in a field at the same time?**
5. **Give the term used for growing different crops on a piece of land in a pre-planned succession.**

12.4 Crop Protection Management

It is a management strategy that includes methods to minimise infestation caused by weeds, pests, insects and related diseases, in order to get maximum yield.

Various threats to crops include

1. Weeds

These are the unwanted plants in the cultivated field. They usually compete with the crops for food, space and light.

Weeds take up nutrients and reduce the growth of the crop. Therefore, they should be removed during early stages of crop growth in order to obtain good harvest.

Some examples of weeds are

Xanthium (gokhroo), *Parthenium* (gajar ghas), *Cyperinus rotundus* (motha), *Amaranthus, Chenopodium,* wild oat, etc.

Following methods are used to control weeds

(i) **Mechanical methods** Such as uprooting.

(ii) **Preventive methods** Proper seed bed preparation, timely sowing of crops, intercropping and crop rotation.

(iii) **Chemical methods** Use of weedicides.

2. Insect Pests

These are destructive organisms that negatively affect the health of crop and thus reduce its yield.

Insect pests attack the plants in following ways

(i) They cut the root, stem and leaf, e.g. locusts.

(ii) They suck the cell sap from various parts of the plant, e.g. aphids.

(iii) They bore into stems and fruits, e.g. shoot borer larvae.

The pests can be controlled in many ways such as

(i) By the use of resistant varieties.

(ii) Summer ploughing (fields ploughed deep during summers to destroy weeds and pests).

3. Crop Diseases

Diseases in plants are caused by different pathogens such as bacteria, fungi and viruses. These pathogens are present in the environment and transmitted through the soil, water and air.

Crop diseases can be controlled by the use of pesticides like herbicides, insecticides and fungicides. They are sprayed on crop plants in limited amounts or used for treating seeds and soil.

Excessive use of these chemicals can be poisonous to plants and animals. It also causes environmental pollution.

Storage of Grains

During storage of grains, high losses can occur in agricultural produce. Factors responsible for such losses can be categorised as

(i) **Biotic factors** These include rodents, fungi, insects, mites and bacteria.

(ii) **Abiotic factors** These include inappropriate moisture and temperature conditions in the place of storage.

Possible effects of these factors on grains include

(a) Degradation in quality.

(b) Poor germinative capacity.

(c) Discolouration of the produce.

(d) Loss in weight.

All these lead to poor marketability and heavy economic losses. These factors can be controlled by

(i) Proper treatment and systematic management of warehouses.

(ii) The proper storage of grains can be done by

(a) Strict cleaning of the produce before storage.

(b) Proper drying of the produce in sunlight and then in shade.

(c) Periodic fumigation on a regular basis to kill pests.

Try These 12.4

1 **Give two examples of unwanted plants that grow in the cultivated field.**

2 **Mention the methods to control the growth of unwanted plants. (Any two)**

3 **What term is given to the ploughing of field to destroy weeds and pests in summer?**

4 **State the factors which are responsible for losses of agricultural produce during storage.**

5 **Give one possible effect of factors that are responsible for agricultural losses in storage of grains.**

12.5 Animal Husbandry

The scientific management of animal livestock is termed as animal husbandry. It can be defined as the science of rearing, feeding, breeding, disease control and utilisation of animals.

The animal, based farming mainly includes cattle, goat, sheep, poultry and fish farming.

Need for Animal Husbandry

(i) It is required to meet the increasing demands of animal based goods like milk, meat, eggs, leather, etc., due to an increase in the size of the population and its living standards.

(ii) It sets guidelines for proper management and systematic approach to animal rearing.

Nutritional Values of Animal Products

Animal products	Percent (%) nutrients					
	Fats	Proteins	Sugar	Minerals	Water	Vitamins
Milk (Cow)	3.60	4.00	4.50	0.70	87.20	B_1, B_2, B_{12}, D, E
Egg	12.00	13.00	*	1.00	74.00	B_2, D
Meat	3.60	21.10	*	1.10	74.20	B_2, B_{12}
Fish	2.50	19.00	*	1.30	77.20	Niacin, D, A

Cattle Farming

It is the raising of cattle for two purposes, milk and draught labour for agricultural work (such as tilling, irrigation and carting).

Cattle in India belong to two different species

(i) *Bos indicus* (cows)
(ii) *Bos bubalis* (buffaloes).

On the basis of work done by them, cattle can be divided into two categories

(i) **Draught animals** These are used to do labour work in farms.
(ii) **Milch animals** These are milk producing females or dairy animals. Milk production largely depends on the duration of the **lactation period.** It is the period of milk production after the birth of a calf. We can increase the milk production by increasing the lactation period.

Cattle and their Breeds

The breeds of cattle are as follows

(i) **Indigenous or Local breeds** They are selected because of their excellent resistances to disease, e.g. Red Sindhi and Sahiwal.
(ii) **Exotic or Foreign breeds** They are selected because of their long lactation period, e.g. Jersey and Brown Swiss.

These two breeds can be cross-breed to get animals with both the desirable qualities.

Farm Management for Cattle

Efficient farm management is essential for human farming, better health of animals and production of clean milk.

Various measures for farm management are as follows

(i) To provide proper cleaning and shelter facilities for cattle.
(ii) Regular brushing of animals to remove dirt and loose hair.
(iii) The cattle should be sheltered under well-ventilated roofed sheds in order to protect them from rain, heat and cold.
(iv) The floor of the cattle shed should be sloping, so that it stays dry and facilitates cleaning.

Food Requirements of Cattle

Food is required for dairy cattle for following two purposes

(i) **For maintenance** Food is required to support the animal to live a healthy life.
(ii) **For producing milk** This type of food is required during the lactation period.

Animal feed includes

(a) **Roughage** This is largely fibrous and contain low nutrients, e.g. green fodder, silage, hay and legumes.
(b) **Concentrates** These are low in fibre. They contain relatively high levels of proteins and other nutrients. Apart from the above mentioned products, some feed additives containing micronutrients promote the health and milk output of dairy animals. It should also be noted that cattle should be given balanced rations with all the nutrients in proportionate amounts.

Diseases in Cattle

Like other animals, cattle also suffer from a number of diseases. These diseases besides causing death, also reduce milk production. The parasites of cattle can be of following types

(i) **External parasites** They live on the skin and cause skin diseases, e.g. lice, mites, etc.
(ii) **Internal parasites** They include worms that affect stomach and intestine and flukes that damage the liver.

Cattle can also get infectious diseases from various bacteria and viruses. As a preventive measure, vaccinations are given to farm animals against many viral and bacterial diseases.

Poultry Farming

It is the rearing of domestic fowl for the production of eggs and chicken meat. In this, improved poultry breeds are developed and farmed to produce **layers** for eggs and **broilers** for meat.

Measures taken to Improve Poultry Breeds

For the improvement of poultry breeds, cross-breeding is done successfully between Indian or indigenous (e.g. Aseel) and foreign or exotic (e.g. Leghorn) breeds. These cross- breeding programmes focus to develop desirable traits like

(i) Quality and quantity (number) of chicks.
(ii) Dwarf broiler parent for commercial chick production.
(iii) Summer adaptation capacity/tolerance to high temperature.

(iv) Low maintenance requirements.

(v) Reduction in the size of egg-laying bird with the ability to utilise more fibrous and cheaper diets. This diet is formulated using agricultural byproducts.

Egg and Broiler Production

Broiler chickens are fed with vitamin-rich supplementary feed for good growth rate and better feed efficiency.

Care is taken to avoid mortality and to maintain feathering and carcass quality. They are produced as broilers and sent to market for meat purposes.

Broilers and egg layers have different housing, nutritional and environmental requirements.

The diet of broilers is rich in protein with adequate fat. In the poultry feed, the level of vitamins-A and K is kept high.

Farm Management for Poultry Birds

The following practices are required for the maintenance of shelter for poultry birds

(i) Proper cleaning and sanitation of the shelter.

(ii) Maintenance of temperature and hygiene in the shelter.

(iii) Proper ventilation.

(iv) Prevention and control of diseases and pests.

Poultry Diseases and their Prevention

Poultry fowl suffer from various diseases caused by virus, bacteria, fungi and parasites. They also suffer from nutritional deficiency diseases.

These diseases can be prevented by

(i) Providing nutritional diet to poultry birds.

(ii) Proper cleaning and sanitation of shelter.

(iii) Proper and periodic vaccination of poultry birds.

(iv) Spraying of disinfectants at regular intervals in the shelter.

Try These 12.5

1. **Name the term used for feeding, breeding, disease control and management of animals.**
2. **Which category do the cattle belong to when used for ploughing the field?**
3. **Give an example of a breed of cattle that has long lactation period.**
4. **A low fibre but protein rich diet is given to cattle. Name it.**
5. **What are the chickens specially developed for obtaining meat called?**

Fish Production

Fish is a cheap source of animal protein for our food. Production of fish includes both finned true fish as well as shell fish like prawns and molluscs.

The two ways of obtaining fish are

(i) **Capture fishing** It is a method of obtaining fish from natural resources.

(ii) **Culture fishery** It is the method of obtaining fish from fish farming or **pisciculture**.
Both the methods can be used for fishing in marine and freshwater (i.e. river and ponds) ecosystems.

Marine Fisheries

Marine fishes are caught using many kinds of fishing nets from fishing boats. Examples of popular marine fishes are pomfret, mackerel, tuna, sardines and Bombay duck. India's marine fishery resources include 7500 km of coastline and deep seas beyond it.
Marine fishes of high economic value that are farmed in sea water are as follows

(i) **Finned fishes** Mullets, bhetki and pearl spots.

(ii) **Shell fishes** Prawns, mussels, oysters as well as seaweeds. Oysters are also cultivated for the pearls they produce.

The yield of fishes can be increased by locating large schools of fish in the open sea with the use of satellites and echo sounders.

Mariculture

As marine fish stocks get further depleted, the demand for more fish can only be met by culture fisheries. This practice is called **mariculture**. The marine fishes are cultivated in coastal waters of India on commercial basis. It includes mullets, bhetki, eel, milkfish, etc.

Inland Fisheries

It includes fishery in freshwater and brackish water.

(i) **Freshwater resources** include canals, ponds, reservoirs and rivers.

(ii) **Brackish water resources** are those where seawater and freshwater mix together, e.g. estuaries and lagoons. These are important fish reservoirs.

The yield of capture fishing is not high in such inland water bodies. Thus, most fish production from these resources is done through aquaculture.

Sometimes fish culture is done in combination with rice crops. In this, paddy crop gets ample of water and fishes get food.

Composite Fish Culture Systems (Polyculture)

It includes a combination of 5 or 6 fish species cultivated in a single pond having different food habits. Due to this, they do not compete for food with each other. Thus, it helps in more intensive fish farming.

Advantages of composite fish culture are as follows

(i) Both local and imported fish species are used.

(ii) Due to different food habits all the food in pond is consumed by the fishes.

(iii) The fish yield from pond is high as there is no competition for food. For example, *Catla* is surface feeder, rohu feeds in the middle-zone of the pond, mrigal and common carps are bottom feeders, grass carp feeds on weeds in the pond.

Disadvantages of composite fish culture are as follows

(i) One of the major problem of fish farming is the lack of availability of good quality fish seed because most of the fishes breed only during monsoon.

(ii) To overcome this problem, fishes are bred in ponds using hormonal stimulation. It ensures the supply of pure fish seed in desired quantities.

Beekeeping

It is the method of rearing, care and management of honeybees for obtaining bee products like honey, beewax (used in medicinal preparations), etc. For commercial honey production, apiaries or bee farms are established.

The advantages of beekeeping are as follows

(i) Requires low investment.

(ii) Provides varied products like honey (for eating or making other products), wax (used in medicinal and cosmetic preparations), bee venom, etc.

(iii) Acts as an additional source of income for farmers.

(iv) Helps in increasing crop yield by better pollination.

Varieties of Bees used for Commercial Honey Production

Scientific names	Common names
Apis cerana indica	Indian bee
Apis dorsata	Rock bee
Apis florae	Little bee
Apis mellifera	Italian bee

Out of the above mentioned species, *A. mellifera* has been brought in India in order to increase the yield of honey. This is the main variety used for the commercial honey production.

Advantages of Italian Bees

- They have high honey collection capacity.
- They sting somewhat less.
- They can stay in a given beehive for long periods and breed well.

Honey

It is a widely used product that is obtained from apiculture (beekeeping)

- **Value of honey** It depends on pasturage or flowers available to bees for nectar and pollen collection.
- **Taste of honey** It depends on adequate quantity of pasturage and kind of flowers available.

Try These 12.6

1 Give any two examples of fishes found in marine waters.

2 What is the increase in the production of fish and shell fish called?

3 What term is referred to the culture of several species of fish in a single pond?

4 Name the species of bee that has been brought in the country to increase the yield of honey.

5 State any one factor on which the taste of honey depends.

Mind Map

Improvement in Food Resources

To meet the requirement of food, it is essential to increase our food production without degrading the environment and disturbing its balance.

In plants

Improvement in Crop Yield

It is necessary to ensure food security, meet growing population demands.

Crop Variety Improvement

The main aim of this practice is to find a variety of crop which can withstand different situations like soil quality, weather quality, water availability (drought and flood) and can ultimately give good yield.

Ways to improve crop variety

- **Hybridisation**: It refers to the cross between genetically dissimilar plants.
- **Genetically Modified Crops**: A gene that would provide the desired characteristics is introduced into the crop.

Crop Protection Management

- Includes technique of protecting and growing crops.
- Also allows preserving of agricultural products from natural enemies, such as insects, weeds, etc.

- Pest control
- Disease control
- Weed control
- Storage of grains

Crop Production Management

- **Nutrient Management**
  - **Manure**: Organic substances formed by the decomposition of animal excreta and plant waste, which supply small quantities of nutrients to soil.
    - **Compost**: Formed by the process of decomposition of farm waste materials in pits and by using earthworms (vermicomposting).
    - **Green Manure**: Formed by ploughing plants like sunn hemp or guar into the soil prior to sowing seeds.
  - **Fertilisers**: Commercially produced organic or inorganic compound containing one or more essential plant nutrients. These are used for increasing soil fertility.
- **Irrigation**: The process of supplying water to crop plants in field by means of canal, reservoirs, wells and tubewells.
- **Cropping Patterns**

  Includes

  - **Mixed Cropping**: It involves growing of two or more crops simultaneously on the same piece of land.
  - **Intercropping**: It involves growing of two or more crops on the same field in different pattern.
  - **Crop Rotation**: Different crops are grown on a piece of land in pre-planned succession. It depends upon the duration of crops.

In animals

Animal Husbandry

Scientific management of animal livestock.

- **Cattle Farming**: It is done for milk and draught labour by cattle.
- **Poultry Farming**: It is the method of production of fowl for meat and egg. It aims at improving poultry breeds.
- **Fish Production**: It is the capture and culture of fish for supplement of animal protein for humans. It is a cheap source of animal protein for our food.
  - Marine fisheries
  - Inland fisheries
- **Beekeeping**: Scientifically known as apiculture. It is rearing, care and management of honey for obtaining honey and beeswax, etc. For commercial honey production apiaries or bee farms are established.

NCERT FOLDER

Complete Explanations of all NCERT's Questions

Intext Questions

Q.1 What do we get from cereals, pulses, fruits and vegetables? Page 141

Sol. Cereals (wheat, rice, maize, etc.) are the source of carbohydrates, which provide energy. Pulses (pea, gram and soybean, etc.) are the source of proteins. Vegetables and fruits provide us vitamins and minerals in addition to small amount of carbohydrates, proteins and fats.

Q.2 How do biotic and abiotic factors affect crop production? Page 142

Sol. Factors which affect crop production are as follows

(i) Biotic factors that cause loss of grains are rodents, pests, insects, etc.

(ii) Abiotic factors that affect crop production includes drought, salinity, water logging, heat, cold and frost.

Both biotic and abiotic factors causes stress on crop and affect crop production in the following ways

(a) Poor seed germination

(b) Infestation of insects

(c) Low yield

(d) Discolouration of leaves

Q.3 What are the desirable agronomic characteristics for crop improvements? Page 143

Sol. Desirable agronomic characteristics in crop plants help to give higher productivity. For example,

(i) Tallness and profused branching are desirable characters for fodder crops.

(ii) Dwarfness is desired in cereals, because tall crop plants cannot resist strong winds.

Q.4 What are macronutrients and why are they called macronutrients? Page 142

Sol. Macronutrients are essential nutrients required for growth, functioning and survival of plants. They are called so because they are required in large amounts by plants. They are six in number, i.e.

(i) nitrogen (ii) phosphorus
(iii) potassium (iv) calcium
(v) magnesium (vi) sulphur

Q.5 How do plants get nutrients? Page 143

Sol. Most of the nutrients to the plants are supplied by soil, which are absorbed by roots of plants. Some nutrients are provided by air and water too. Air supplies carbon and oxygen, hydrogen comes from water.

Q.6 Compare the use of manure and fertilisers in maintaining soil fertility. Page. 144

Sol. Effects of the use of manure in maintaining soil fertility are as follows

(i) Manures provide a lot of organic matter (humus) to the soil. Humus helps to restore water retention capacity of sandy soil and drainage in clayey soil.

(ii) It is also a source of soil organisms like friendly bacteria and earthworm.

Effects of fertilisers on soil quality are

(i) Fertilisers are inorganic compounds and fulfill nutrient requirement of soil.

(ii) Due to continuous use of fertilisers, the organic matter decreases. It reduces porosity of the soil and the plant roots do not get sufficient oxygen.

Q.7 Which of the following conditions will give the most benefits? Why? Page 145

(i) Farmers use high quality seeds, do not adopt irrigation or use fertilisers.

(ii) Farmers use ordinary seeds, adopt irrigation and use fertilisers.

(iii) Farmers use quality seeds, adopt irrigation, use fertilisers and use crop protection measures.

Sol. Condition (iii) will give most benefits because of the following reasons

(a) good quality seeds will give good yield.

(b) irrigation methods will overcome drought and flood situation.

(c) fertilisers fulfill the nutrient requirement of the soil, providing high yield.

(d) crop protection method protects the plants from weeds, pests and pathogens. Thus, farmers will get maximum benefit of their input in the form of good seeds and agronomic approaches.

Q.8 Why should preventive measures and biological control methods be preferred for protecting crops? Page 146

Sol. Preventive measures and biological control methods should be preferred for protecting crops because

(i) They are simple and target specific.

(ii) They are economical as they involve less financial investment.

(iii) They minimise pollution and are ecologically safe.

(iv) They minimise the adverse effects on soil fertility.

(v) They are harmless to other living organisms.

Q.9 What factors may be responsible for losses of grain during storage? Page 146

Sol. The major factors responsible for losses of grain during storage are

(i) **Biotic factors** They include attack from insects, rodents, fungi, mites and bacteria.

(ii) **Abiotic factors** They include inappropriate moisture and temperature conditions in the place of storage.

Q.10 Which method is commonly used for improving cattle breeds and why? Page 147

Sol. Cross breeding method is commonly used for improving cattle breeds. It is the process in which indigenous varieties of cattle are crossed with exotic breeds to get a cross-breed which is of desired qualities.

Q.11 Discuss the implications of the following statement. "It is interesting to note that poultry is India's most efficient converter of low fibre food stuff (which is unfit for human consumption) into highly nutritious animal protein food". Page 148

Sol. Poultry birds are efficient converters of agricultural byproducts and fibrous wastes into high quality meat, as the waste which is unfit for human consumption can be formulated into cheaper diets for poultry birds. Also, they help in providing eggs, feather and nutrient rich manure. So, the mentioned statement is implicit for poultry birds.

Q.12 What management practices are common in dairy and poultry farming? Page 148

Sol. The common management practices include

(i) Keeping the shelter well-designed, ventilated and hygienic.

(ii) The animals and birds are given healthy feed with balanced nutrition.

(iii) Both animals and birds must be protected from various diseases. Regular check-ups should be done.

Q.13 What are the differences between broilers and layers and in their management? Page 148

Sol. A broiler is a poultry bird specially kept for obtaining meat. Layer is a poultry bird that gives eggs. There is a difference in their housing, nutrition and environmental requirements.

The daily food requirement of broilers is slightly different from those of layers. Broilers require protein rich food with adequate fat and high amount of vitamin-A and K. Layers require feed with vitamins, minerals and micronutrients, enough space and proper lighting.

Q.14 How are fishes obtained? Page 150

Sol. Fishes are obtained either by capturing them from their natural resources (Capture fishing) or by culturing them by fish farming (Culture fishery).

Q.15 What are the advantages of composite fish culture? Page 150

Sol. Advantages of composite fish culture are as follows

(i) Fishes selected for this culture differ in their feeding habits and thus avoid competition for food between them.

(ii) All these species together use all the food in the pond without competing with each other.

(iii) This increases the total fish yield from the pond.

Q.16 What are the desirable characters of bee varieties suitable for honey production? Page 150

Sol. The desirable characters of bee required for honey production are as follows

(i) The bee should have good honey production capacity.

(ii) They should be stingless and breed very well.

(iii) They should be able to stay in a beehive for long periods.

Q.17 What is pasturage and how is it related to honey production? Page 150

Sol. Pasturage includes the flowering plants and trees found around an apiary. From them, nectar and pollen are collected by bees to form honey.

Pasturage plays an important role in determining the quantity and quality of honey.

Exercise

Q.1 Explain any one method of crop production which ensures high yield.

Sol. Intercropping is a method of crop production, which ensures high yield. During this, two or more crops having different nutrient requirements are grown simultaneously on the same field in a definite pattern.

Q.2 Why are manures and fertilisers used in fields?

Sol. Manures and fertilisers are used to improve soil fertility and increase the crop productivity. They replenish deficient nutrients in the soil.

Q.3 What are the advantages of intercropping and crop rotation?

Sol. Advantages of intercropping are as follows

(i) Crops selected in this method differ in their nutrient requirements. This ensures maximum utilisation of the supplied nutrients.

(ii) It prevents pests and diseases from spreading to all the plants belonging to one crop in a field.

Advantages of crop rotation are as follows

(i) It makes the soil fertile and increases the yield from a single field.

(ii) It reduces the use of fertilisers. For example, use of nitrogenous fertilisers is not required as leguminous plants, that are grown in crop rotation help in biological nitrogen-fixation.

(iii) It helps in the replenishment of soil fertility.

Q.4 What is genetic manipulation? How is it useful in agricultural practices?

Sol. Genetic manipulation is the incorporation of desirable characters into an organism by hybridisation, mutation, DNA recombination, etc. By genetic manipulation, improved varieties of seeds can be obtained. These varieties have desirable characters like high yield, disease resistance and better adaptability.

Q.5 How do storage grain losses occur?

Sol. During the storage of grains both biotic and abiotic factors cause losses to the grain. Biotic factors such as insects, rodents, mites, fungi, bacteria, etc., and various abiotic factors such as moisture, temperature, lack of sunlight, etc., are responsible for losses of grains.

Q.6 How do good animal husbandry practices benefit farmers?

Sol. Animal husbandry involves the scientific management of the farm animals. Its benefits the farmers in the following ways

(i) Improvement of the breeds having good desirable characters.

(ii) Better yield in quantity and quality.

(iii) Reduction of the input cost.

Q.7 What are the benefits of cattle farming?

Sol. Main benefits of cattle farming are as follows

(i) Acquring milk and various milk-based products from cattle.

(ii) Cattle can be employed for labour work in agricultural fields such as tilling, irrigation and carting.

Q.8 For increasing production, what is common in poultry, fisheries and beekeeping?

Sol. Cross-breeding is the most important practice to increase the production and desired characteristics in poultry, fisheries and beekeeping.

Q.9 How do you differentiate between capture fishing, mariculture and aquaculture?

Sol. Differences between capture fishing, mariculture and aquaculture are as follows

Capture fishing	Mariculture	Aquaculture
It is the practice of obtaining fish from natural resources like ponds, canals, rivers, etc.	It is a practice of culture of marine fish varieties in the coastal waters.	It is the production of fish from freshwater resources like canals and brackish water resources like estuaries and lagoons.
Fishes can be located easily and then caught using fishing net.	Satellites and echo-sounders are used for locating fish and then caught using many kinds of fishing nets.	Fishes can be located easily and are caught using simple fishing nets.

REVIEW EXERCISE

Including Competency Based Questions

Competency Focused (Objective) Questions

Multiple Choice Questions

1 The revolution associated with increased food grain production is

(a) white revolution (b) golden revolution
(c) green revolution (d) blue revolution

Sol. (c) Green revolution has lead to increase in stocks of food grains, improvement in economic conditions of farmers and increased employment opportunities.

2 Find out the wrong statement from the following. **Competency Based Que.**

(a) White revolution is meant for increase in milk production
(b) Blue revolution is meant for increase in fish production
(c) Increasing food production without compromising with environmental quality is called as sustainable agriculture
(d) None of the above

Sol. (d)

3 To solve the food problem of the country, which among the following is necessary?

(a) Increased production and storage of food grains
(b) Easy access of people to the food grains
(c) People should have money to purchase the grains
(d) All of the above

Sol. (d)

4 Select the correct statement out of the following given in regard to variety improvement **NCERT Exemplar**

(a) Quality consideration of crop products are similar
(b) Crop production goes down due to biotic and abiotic strains
(c) The longer duration of the crop from sowing to harvesting the more economical is the variety
(d) Dwarfness is desired in fodder crops

Sol. (b)

5 Refer to the Venn diagram given below showing two types of crops.

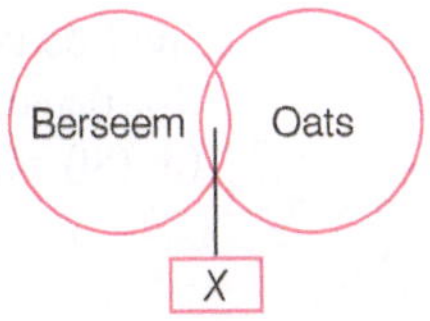

Identify X and choose the feature that correctly relates to it. **Competency Based Que.**

	Berseem	Features
(a)	Fodder crops	Raised as food for livestock
(b)	Oil seeds	Provides oil and fat
(c)	Pulses	Cultivated for carbohydrate
(d)	Cereal	Fulfill protein requirement

Sol. (a) In the above Venn diagram, X is to be identified as fodder crops. These plants are raised as food for the livestock.

6 The study aims to explore the growth needs of crop. Focusing on mustard seeds. These seeds were planted in various locations, each subjected to specific temperature, as detailed in the table. **Competency Based Que.**

Location	Temperature conditions
A	15°C to 18°C
B	35°C to 38°C
C	–1°C to 2°C
D	45° to 48°C

At which location would the mustard grow most effectively?

(a) Location A (b) Location B
(c) Location C (d) Location D

Sol. (a) In location A mustard will grow effectively. As mustard is a Rabi crop, it thrives in a dry, chilly climate. The temperature range needed for the mustard crop is from 10°C to 25°C.

7 Find out the correct sentence.

(i) Hybridisation means crossing between genetically dissimilar plants.
(ii) Cross between two varieties is called as inter specific hybridisation.
(iii) Introducing genes of desired character into a plant gives genetically modified crop.

(iv) Cross between plants of two species is called as inter varietal hybridisation.

(a) (i) and (iii) (b) (ii) and (iv)
(c) (ii) and (iii) (d) (iii) and (iv)

Sol. (a) Statements (i) and (iii) are correct about hybridisation.

Statements (ii) and (iv) can be corrected as

Cross between two varieties is called inter varietal hybridisation.

Whereas cross between plants of two species is called interspecific hybridisation.

8 Developing crop varieties with wider adaptability will help in enhancing crop production because

(a) a single variety can be grown under different climatic conditions in different regions
(b) that variety will have resistance to a wide variety of pests
(c) that variety will be higher yielding than many other varieties
(d) that variety can be grown under same climatic conditions

Sol. (a)

9 Crop *X* is cultivated in limited regions because of its specific temperature needs. To enhance the yield of crop *X*, it is advisable to create various varieties. What characteristics should be incorporated in the development of these varieties to boost productivity? **Competency Based Que.**

(a) Developing varieties with strong resistance
(b) Developing varieties with less dependence on water
(c) Developing varieties with extended maturity duration
(d) Developing varieties adaptable to different climatic conditions

Sol. (d)

10 Which of the following pairs are not correctly matched with respect to the type of nutrients?

(a) Calcium and sulphur
(b) Boron and zinc
(c) Phosphorus and molybdenum
(d) Chlorine and copper

Sol. (c) Pair given in option (c) is not correctly matched as phosphorus is a macronutrient, whereas molybdenum is a micronutrient. Rest other pairs are correct.

11 Find out the correct statement about manure.

(i) Manure contains large quantities of organic matter.
(ii) It increases the water holding capacity of sandy soil.
(iii) It helps in draining out of excess of water from clayey soil.
(iv) The excessive use of manure pollutes environment because it is made of animal excretory waste. **Competency Based Que.**

(a) (i) and (iii) (b) (i) and (ii)
(c) (ii) and (iii) (d) (iii) and (iv)

Sol. (b) Manure is an eco-friendly method as it is rich in organic matter that provides essential nutrients to the soil. Also, manure increases the water holding capacity of soil. Therefore, it cannot be responsible for draining out excess water.

12 Which one of the following nutrients is not available in fertilisers? **NCERT Exemplar**

(a) Nitrogen (b) Phosphorus
(c) Iron (d) Potassium

Sol. (c)

13 Fertilisers are the commercially produced plant nutrients. The correct reason for this is

(a) they supply nitrogen, phosphorus and potassium
(b) they ensure good vegetative growth
(c) they give rise to healthy plants
(d) All of the above

Sol. (d)

14 Weeds affect the crop plants by **NCERT Exemplar**

(a) killing of plants in field before they grow
(b) dominating the plants to grow
(c) competing for various resources of crops (plants) causing low availability of nutrients
(d) All of the above

Sol. (c) Weeds are unwanted plants, which compete with main crop plants for nutrients and reduce the growth of crops.

15 Preventive and control measures adopted for the storage of grains include

(a) strict cleaning (b) proper disjoining
(c) fumigation (d) All of these

Sol. (d)

16 Cattle husbandry is done for the following purposes

(i) Milk production increase **NCERT Exemplar**
(ii) Agricultural work
(iii) Meat production
(iv) Egg production

(a) (i), (ii) and (iii) (b) (ii), (iii) and (iv)
(c) (iii) and (iv) (d) (i) and (iv)

Sol. (a)

17 Which of the following are Indian cattle?

(i) *Bos indicus* **(ii) *Bos domestica***
(iii) *Bos bubalis* **(iv) *Bos vulgaris***

(a) (i) and (iii) (b) (i) and (ii)
(c) (ii) and (iii) (d) (iii) and (iv)

Sol. (a) Indian cattle belongs to two different species, *Bos indicus* (cows) and *Bos bubalis* (buffaloes).

18 Which of the following are exotic breeds? NCERT Exemplar

(i) Brawn **(ii) Jersey**
(iii) Brown Swiss **(iv) Jersey Swiss**

(a) (i) and (iii) (b) (ii) and (iii)
(c) (i) and (iv) (d) (ii) and (iv)

Sol. (b)

19 The table lists the characteristics of few milch breed of cattle.

Milch breed of cattle	Characteristics
Jersey	Long lactation period
Sahiwal	Resistant to diseases
Brown Swiss	Long lactation period
Red Sindhi	Resistant to diseases

Based on the characteristics listed in the table, what will be the characteristics of the new breed if Sahiwal and Brown Swiss are cross-breed? Competency Based Que.

(a) The new breed will have a long lactation period and will be resistant to diseases
(b) The new breed will have a small lactation period, but will be resistant to diseases
(c) The new breed will have a long lactation period, but will not be resistant to diseases
(d) The new breed will have a small lactation period and will not be resistant to diseases

Sol. (a)

20 Poultry farming is undertaken to raise following. NCERT Exemplar

(i) Egg production **(ii) Feather production**
(iii) Chicken meat **(iv) Milk production**

(a) (i) and (iii) (b) (i) and (ii)
(c) (ii) and (iii) (d) (iii) and (iv)

Sol. (a) Poultry farming is undertaken to raise domestic fowl for egg production and chicken meat. Therefore, improved poultry breeds are developed.

21 The table lists four types of food for broiler chickens.

Types of food	Nutritional values
A	Rich in fats
B	Rich in proteins
C	Rich in fats with low levels of vitamin-A
D	Low levels of fats and vitamin-K.

Which kind of food is suitable for broiler chickens?

(a) Food A (b) Food B
(c) Food C (d) Food D

Sol. (b) Food B will be suitable for broiler chickens as the daily food requirement for broiler is protein rich with adequate fat.

22 Oysters are cultivated in inland water bodies for food. What else can be obtained from the cultivation of oysters?

(a) Pearl (b) Sponge
(c) Platinum (d) Aluminium

Sol. (a)

23 Which one of the following fishes is a surface feeder? NCERT Exemplar

(a) Rohu (b) Mrigal
(c) Common carp (d) Catla

Sol. (d) Surface feeder fishes have a back that is perfectly straight, this allows for their upturned mouths to easily get right on the surface and scoop up the food. Catla possess all these characters, thus is a surface feeder.
Rohu feed in the middle zone of the pond and mrigal and common carp are bottom feeders.

24 The management and production of fishes for commercial use is called

(a) pisciculture
(b) apiculture
(c) mariculture
(d) monoculture

Sol. (a) Pisciculture is the rearing, management and production of fishes for commercial utilisation.

25 Which type of honeybees are useful to increase the yield of honey in India?

(a) *Apis florae* (b) *Apis mellifera*
(c) *Apis dorsata* (d) *Apis indica*

Sol. (b) *Apis mellifera* is the best suited in India for apiculture industries. It can be easily domesticated because of gentle nature and have high honey production capacity.

Assertion-Reason Questions

Direction (Q. Nos. 1-5) ***In each of the following questions, a statement of Assertion (A) is given by the corresponding statement of Reason (R). Of the statements, mark the correct answer as***

(a) Both A and R are true and R is the correct explanation of A
(b) Both A and R are true, but R is not the correct explanation of A
(c) A is true, but R is false
(d) A is false, but R is true

1 Assertion (A) Cultivation practices and crop yields are related to environmental conditions.

Reason (R) Climatic conditions such as temperature and photoperiod influence a plant's life cycle.

Sol. (a) Both A and R are true and R is the correct explanation of A.

2 Assertion (A) Tallness and profuse branching are desirable characters of cereals.

Reason (R) Developing varieties of desired agronomic characters help to give higher productivity.

Sol. (d) A is false, but R is true. A can be corrected as Dwarfness is a desirable character of cereals.

3 Assertion (A) Manures contain large quantities of organic matter.

Reason (R) The excessive use of manure leads to water pollution.

Sol. (c) A is true, but R is false. R can be corrected as The excessive use of fertilisers leads to the water pollution.

4 Assertion (A) Poor monsoons cause crop failure in India.

Reason (R) India has a wide variety of water resources.

Sol. (b) Both A and R are true, but R is not the correct explanation of A.

Most of the agriculture in India is rain fed, that is the success of crops in most areas is dependent on timely monsoons and sufficient rainfall spread through most of the growing season.

5 Assertion (A) Inspite of large population of cattle, milk production is meagre in India.

Reason (R) Poor quality feed is given to cattle.

Sol. (a) Both A and R are true and R is the correct explanation of A.

Case Based/Source Based Questions

1 ***Read the following passage and answer the questions that follows***

In the diagram given below, *A* farmer has grown millet along with *X* crops simultaneously on his field. These crops are planted in alternating rows to ensure efficient use of resources and reduce the risk of crop failure.

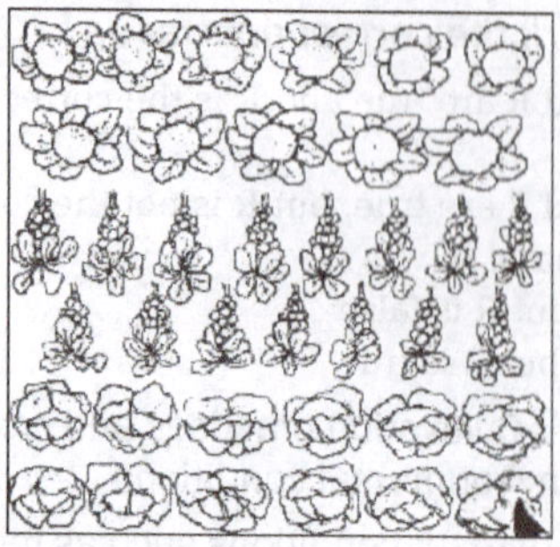

(i) Name the cropping pattern showing in the diagram.

Sol. The cropping pattern in the given diagram is intercropping. [1]

(ii) Identify the crop *X* in the given paragraph.

Sol. *X* is cowpea or lobia. [1]

(iii) State two advantages of the cropping pattern shown in the above diagram.

Sol. (a) This cropping pattern ensures maximum utilisation of nutrients supplied to the crops.

(b) It prevents pests and diseases from spreading to all plants of the same crop in the field. [2]

2 ***Study the diagram given below and answer the questions that follows***

The picture shows how organic manure and chemical fertiliser are used by plants.

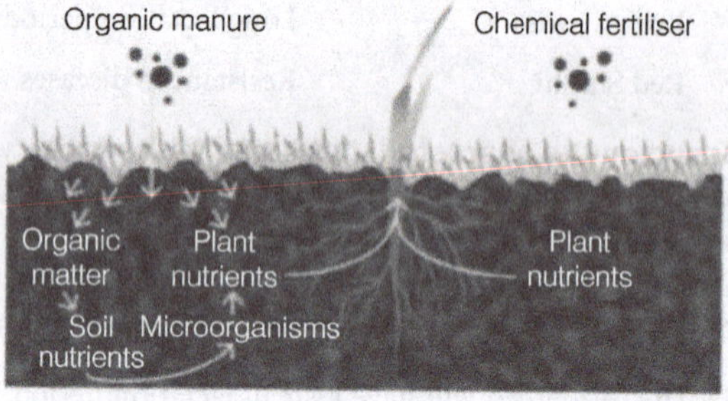

(i) Name two micronutrients and two macronutrients.

Sol. Two micronutrients-Iron and manganese.

Two macronutrients - Nitrogen and phosphorus. [1 + 1]

(ii) Why do we add manures and fertilisers to the soil?

Sol. Manures and fertilisers are added to the soil to enrich the soil with the nutrients, in order to increase the yield of crop. [1]

(iii) How is manure particularly useful for clayey and sandy soil?

Sol. Manure increases the water holding capacity in sandy soil. In clayey soil, it helps in drainage and avoids water logging. [1]

3 ***Observe the graph given below and answer the questions that follows***

Figure shows the two crop fields [plots *A* and *B*] that have been treated by manures and chemical fertilisers, respectively, keeping other environmental factors same.

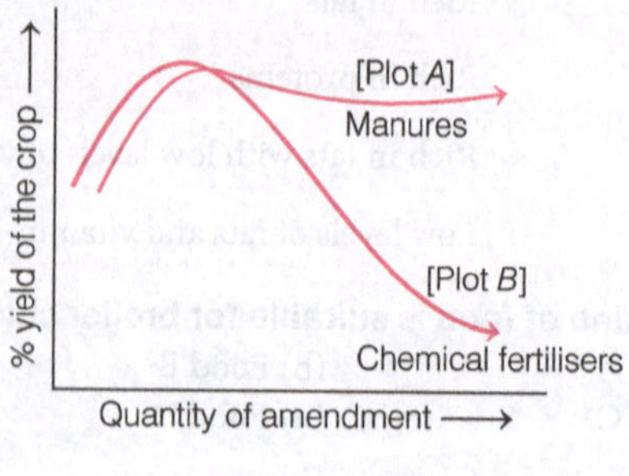

(i) Why does plot *B* shows sudden increase and then gradual decrease in yield?

Sol. With the addition of chemical fertilisers, there is a sudden increase in yield due to the release of nutrients like N, P, K, etc., in high quantity. The gradual decline in the graph is due to continuous use of high quantity of chemicals. It has killed microbes useful for replenishing the organic matter in the soil. This results in reducing the soil fertility. Thus, the decrease in yield. [2]

(ii) Why is the highest peak in plot *A* graph slightly delayed?

Sol. Manures supply small quantities of nutrients to the soil slowly as it contains large amounts of organic matter. It takes time to mix with the soil. It increases water holding capacity and aeration of soil, thereby increasing soil fertility continuously. [1]

(iii) What is the reason for the different patterns of the two graphs?

Sol. The difference in the two graphs is because of the fact that use of manure is beneficial for longer duration in cropping. The yield gets high when the quantity of manure increases. In case of plot *B*, the chemical fertilisers may cause various problems, when used continuously for long time. Loss of microbial activity reduces decomposition of organic matter. As a result, soil fertility is lost that affects the yield. [1]

4 ***Read the following passage and answer the questions that follows***

In summer vacation, the students of IX standard were given an investigating project. They were asked to visit a dairy farm and note down their observation. Mahi took information from internet and made project. Ruchi visited a dairy, saw how and what cattle were feed with and how much milk they give per day. She also learned about diseases they suffer from and how they are cleaned and taken care of.

(i) To increase the milk production, what kind of feed is given to cattle?

Sol. Feed including roughage and concentrates should be given to cattle for increasing milk production. [1]

(ii) Write down two symptoms of sick animal.

Sol. (a) The animal looks tired, inactive and tries to remain isolated.

(b) Urine is often coloured while dung is loose or watery. [1]

(iii) Write down the method of farm management.

Sol. The cattle should be sheltered in well ventilated and properly roofed sheds in order to protect them from rain, heat and cold. [1]

(iv) Give example of internal parasites that caused disease in cattles. [1]

Sol. Fluke is a parasite that damage the liver in cattle.

5 ***Observe the diagram given below and answer the questions that follows***

Composite fish culture is a process of growing different types of fish in the same pond. The diagram shows a composite fish culture pond.

(i) Give example of each, i.e. surface dweller, mid level dweller and bottom dweller.

Sol. Example of the following are given below

Surface dweller – Catla

Mid level dweller – Rohu

Bottom dweller – Mrigal [1]

(ii) Discuss one problem that arise during composite fish culture and also a method to over come it.

Sol. The major problem in fish farming is the lack of availability of good quality seeds. To over come this problem, several ways have been worked out to breed these fish in ponds using hormonal stimulation. [2]

(iii) On what basis, different species of fishes are selected in composite fish culture?

Sol. In a composite fish culture, species of fishes are selected in a way that they do not compete for food among them. [1]

Constructed Response (Descriptive) Questions

Very Short Answer Type Questions

1 Identify two crops from the following, which provide us carbohydrates for energy requirement.
Black gram, wheat, lentil and rice. **Competency Based Que.**

Sol. Wheat and rice are cereals which provide us carbohydrates. [1 + 1]

2 Name the type of nutrient that we get from mustard seeds and linseed.

Sol. Mustard seeds and linseed provide us with fats.

3 Give examples of two protein containing Rabi crops.

Sol. Grams and peas are two protein containing Rabi crops. [1+1]

4 Improved varieties can be produced in both animals and plants. How? **Competency Based Que.**

Sol. Hybridisation and genetic modification are the two processes used for the production of new and improved species in both animals and plants.

5 What are the two advantages of selecting seeds of crops with wider adaptability for agriculture?

Sol. The two advantages of selecting seeds of crops with wider adaptibility for agriculture are as follows

(i) It helps in stabilising the crop production under different environmental conditions.

(ii) Selecting seeds with wider adaptability enhances resistance to both biotic stresses and abiotic stresses. [1+1]

6 List two desirable traits for fodder crops.

Sol. (i) Tall plants (ii) Profuse branching [1+1]

7 What are exotic breeds in terms of cattle?

Sol. Exotic breeds are not native to that place, e.g. Brown Swiss and Jersey, breeds that are the exotic breeds of cow in India.

8 Which type of food is required by dairy animals?

Sol. Dairy animals require two types of food

(i) Roughage – Largely fibrous

(ii) Concentrates – Low in fibre and contain relatively high level of proteins and other nutrients [1+1]

9 White Leghorn is an exotic breed of an animal. Name the animal.

Sol. It is popular exotic breed of hen that produces long, white eggs and requires less amount of feed.

10 Which two vitamins, are usually added in the poultry feed?

Sol. Vitamin-A and K are added in the poultry feed. [1 + 1]

11 What is mariculture?

Sol. Cultivation of marine fishes like mullets, pearl spots, etc., in coastal waters on commercial scale is known as mariculture.

12 Why fish culture is done with a combination of rice?

Sol. Fish culture is done with a combination of rice, so that fishes get ample food in the paddy field and the latter can get water.

13 Give two advantages of apiculture.

Sol. Two advantages of apiculture are

(i) It produces honey and wax.

(ii) It is a low investment additional income generating activity for farmers. [1 + 1]

14 Give one example of each, local variety and foreign variety of bee.

Sol. **Local variety** *Apis cerana indica*

Foreign variety *Apis mellifera* [1 + 1]

15 Given below is pie chart representation of animal livestock management. Identify '*N*' and write any one application in the industry. **Competency Based Que.**

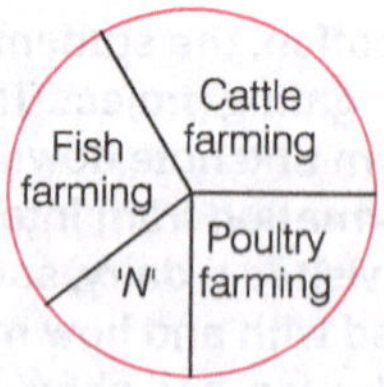

Sol. '*N*' is to be identified as bee farming. [1]

Industrial application Apiculture is a source of beeswax that is used in various medicinal preparations. [1]

Short Answer Type Questions

1 Group the following and tabulate them as energy yielding, protein yielding, oil yielding and fodder crops. Wheat, rice, berseem, maize, gram, oats, pigeon gram, sudan grass, lentil, soybean, groundnut, castor and mustard. **NCERT Exemplar**

Sol. (i) **Energy yielding crops** Wheat, rice, maize and oats.

(ii) **Protein yielding crops** Gram, lentil and pigeon gram.

(iii) **Oil yielding crops** Groundnut, castor, soybean and mustard.

(iv) **Fodder crops** Berseem and sudan grass.

2 Why has improving crop yields become more important these days?
List the major group of activities for improving crop yields. Which one of these activities is the most important and why? **Competency Based Que.**

Sol. Due to continuously growing population, requirement of food is also increasing every year to feed this population. Extra farming land is not available in our country to increase production. Therefore, it is necessary to increase crop yield to meet growing demands for food. [1]

The major activities for improving crop yields include

(i) crop variety improvement
(ii) crop production improvement
(iii) crop protection management [1]

Out of these three activities, crop variety improvement is very important. It helps to attain the crops of good yield, improved quality and resistant to various, stresses. [1]

3 Discuss the role of hybridisation in crop improvement. **Competency Based Que.**

Sol. Hybridisation is a method of crossing between genetically dissimilar plants. It is of three types

(i) **Intervarietal cross** between two different varieties.
(ii) **Interspecific cross** between two different species of same genus.
(iii) **Intergeneric cross** between two different genera.

In plant breeding, intervarietal hybridisation is mostly used to improve the crop variety.

Improved varieties are high yielding and resistant to diseases and pests. They have better quality and various other desirable traits. Thus, they play an important role in crop improvement.

4 (i) Name the month during which Kharif crop is grown.
(ii) List any two factors for which crop variety improvement is done.

Sol. (i) Kharif crop is grown during the months from June to October. [1]

(ii) Two factors for which crop variety improvement is done are

(a) **Higher yield** To increase productivity of crop per acre.
(b) **Improved quality** The definition of quality is different for different crops, e.g. baking quality is important in wheat, protein quality in pulses, etc. [1 + 1]

5 In agriculture practices, higher input gives higher yield. Discuss how? **Competency Based Que.**

Sol. In agriculture, higher yield can be obtained by using higher yielding varieties, modern technologies, improved farm practices with latest agricultural machines. All these require high cost and knowledge of new techniques.

Finance also, plays a very important role as the cost of input decides the outcome of cropping. Therefore, higher input gives higher yield in agricultural practices.

6 What is manure? State two advantages of using manure. How does green manure differ from ordinary manure?

Sol. Manure is an organic substance obtained through the decomposition of plant wastes like straw and animal wastes like cow dung. The decomposition is brought about by microbes. [1]

Advantages of using manure are

(i) It enriches soil with nutrients without causing any pollution.
(ii) It improves soil texture.
(iii) It increases water holding capacity of soil by adding organic matter to it. [1]

Green manure is different as it is obtained by growing green plants such as sunn hemp and guar, which are then mulched by ploughing them into the soil. Later on, it forms green manure and enrich the soil with nitrogen and phosphorus. [1]

7 Differentiate between compost and vermicompost.

Sol. Differences between compost and vermicompost are as follows

Compost	Vermicompost
It is prepared from all types of organic wastes like sewage, animal refuse, farm waste, etc.	It is prepared from domestic waste, vegetable waste, etc.
It takes 3-6 months to prepare.	It takes 1-2 months to prepare.
Organic remains are decomposed by microbes.	Organic remains are decomposed by earthworms.

8 Define the following.
(i) Vermicompost **(ii) Green manure**
(iii) Biofertilisers **NCERT Exemplar**

Sol. (i) **Vermicompost** is a manure rich in organic matter and nutrients. The compost is prepared by using earthworms to hasten the process of decomposition of plants and animals refuse. [1]

(ii) **Green manure** is prepared by growing green plants in the field itself. It helps in enriching the soil with nitrogen and phosphorus content, e.g. sunn hemp is grown in fields, mulched by ploughing and allowed to decompose in field for the preparation of green manure. [1]

(iii) **Biofertilisers** are living organisms used as fertilisers to supply nutrients to crop plants, e.g. nitrogen-fixing blue-green algae and nitrogen-fixing bacteria, which fix nitrogen in the soil. [1]

9 Give some advantages of mixed cropping.

Sol. Advantages of mixed cropping are as follows

(i) Chances of pest infestation is greatly reduced.

(ii) By growing two or more crops simultaneously, soil fertility is improved.

(iii) The risk of total crop failure due to uncertain monsoon is reduced. [1×3]

10 If there is low rainfall in a village throughout the year, what measures will you suggest to the farmers for better cropping? **NCERT Exemplar**

Sol. Suggestions to farmers for better cropping in low rainfall area are

(i) Enrich soil with humus, as it increases water holding capacity of soil.

(ii) Use of drought resistant and early maturing varieties of crops.

(iii) Better irrigation facilities and methods to conserve water. [1×3]

11 Observe the following figure and answer the questions that follows.

***A* – First type of crop**

***B* – Second type of crop**

Box represents the agricultural field in which crops are grown.

A	*A*	*A*	*A*	*A*	*A*
A	*A*	*A*	*A*	*A*	*A*
B	*B*	*B*	*B*	*B*	*B*
B	*B*	*B*	*B*	*B*	*B*
A	*A*	*A*	*A*	*A*	*A*
A	*A*	*A*	*A*	*A*	*A*

(i) Which type of cropping pattern is seen in picture?

(ii) Discuss this cropping pattern.

(iii) What should be kept in mind regarding the types of crops, while following this cropping method? **Competency Based Que.**

Sol. (i) Intercropping is seen in the given picture. [1]

(ii) In this cropping pattern, two or more crops are grown simultaneously in a definite pattern on a field. [1]

(iii) The nutritional requirements of the selected plants should be different. It ensures maximum utilisation of the nutrients supplied. [1]

12 Discuss various methods of weed control. **NCERT Exemplar**

Sol. The various methods of weed control are as follows

(i) **Mechanical method** Uprooting, weeding, ploughing, burying and flooding.

(ii) **Cultural method** Proper seed bed preparation, timely sowing of crops, intercropping and crop rotation.

(iii) **Chemical method** Spraying of chemicals like herbicides or weedicides.

(iv) **Biological control** Use of insects or some organisms, which consume and destroy the weed plants, e.g. prickly-pear cactus (*Opuntia*) is controlled by insects and aquatic weeds are controlled by grass carp.

13 Discuss, why pesticides should be used in very accurate concentration and in very appropriate manner? **NCERT Exemplar**

Sol. Pesticides should be used in accurate concentration as they are very harmful to the environment. They are non-biodegradable and can accumulate in organisms (biomagnification).

Run-off during monsoons can carry pesticides into aquatic bodies and causes water pollution.

Wind can carry them to other fields, grazing areas and human settlements and undeveloped areas and potentially affect other species. These can further affect land and water bodies adversely.

14 The food available is decreasing, day by day, both in quantity and in quality. What steps can be employed to improve this condition, when the population is increasing drastically? **Competency Based Que.**

Sol. The following steps can be taken to improve the condition of food for present as well as for future generations

(i) By selecting good variety of crops having desirable agronomic traits. Such varieties can be developed using hybridisation technique and by genetic modification of crops.

(ii) The field should be kept fertile and nutrient rich by using manure, fertilisers, etc.

(iii) By using high yielding variety of seeds for high yield per acre.

(iv) By using a beneficial cropping pattern such as mixed cropping, crop rotation, etc.

(v) By improving irrigation facilities and bringing more agricultural land under irrigation.

(vi) By protecting crops from weeds, diseases, etc. [½ ×6]

15 Give one word for the following.

(i) **Farming without use of chemicals as fertilisers, herbicides and pesticides is known as ....**

(ii) **Growing of wheat and groundnut on the same field is called ....**

(iii) **Planting soybean and maize in alternate rows in the same field is called ....**

(iv) **Growing different crops on a piece of land in pre-planned succession is known as ....**

(v) ***Xanthium* and *Parthenium* are commonly known as ....**

(vi) **Causal organism of any disease is called ....**

NCERT Exemplar

Sol. (i) organic farming (ii) mixed cropping
(iii) intercropping (iv) crop rotation
(v) weeds (vi) pathogen [½ ×6]

16 Explain the factors that are to be considered before deciding the nature of feed for cattle.

Sol. Following factors should be considered before deciding the nature of feed for cattle

(i) Food requirements of dairy animals are of two types
  (a) **Maintenance requirement** Food required to support the animal to live a healthy life.
  (b) **Milk producing requirement** Food type required during lactation period.

(ii) Animal feed includes
  (a) **Roughage** Largely fibrous.
  (b) **Concentrates** High levels of proteins and other nutrients.

(iii) The food requirements of cattle are different for every age and type of work they do. [1+ 1+ 1]

17 (i) What is poultry farming? How does it help in solving food and nutrition problems?

(ii) Name two desirable traits for variety improvement in poultry farming.

Sol. (i) Poultry farming is the method to rear domestic fowl for the production of eggs and meat. It helps in solving food and nutrition problem by providing a balanced diet for the human population. It also converts agricultural byproducts into high quality meat. [1+ 1]

(ii) (a) Quality and quantity (number) of chicks.
  (b) Dwarf broiler parents for commercial chick production. [½ + ½]

18 Suggest some preventive measures for the diseases of poultry birds. **NCERT Exemplar**

Sol. Poultry fowl suffers from various diseases. These are caused by different agents found in nature and can affect the growth, quality and quantity of chicks.

Fowls also suffer from nutritional deficiencies. These diseases can be prevented by

(i) providing nutritional diet to poultry birds.
(ii) cleaning and sanitation of shelter.
(iii) appropriate vaccination of poultry birds.
(iv) spraying disinfectant at regular intervals in the shelter.

19 Cross-breeding programme is successfully done in poultry farming for variety improvement. Enlist some desirable traits for which cross-breeding is done in poultry birds.

Sol. The cross-breeding programmes between Indian breeds like Aseel and foreign breeds like Leghorn are carried out for variety improvement. It focusses on developing new varieties for the following desirable traits

(i) **Number and quality of chicks** The cross-breed variety should produce good quality chicks in large quantity.
(ii) **Dwarf broiler parent** They help in commercial chick production.
(iii) **Summer adaptation capacity** The variety should be adaptable to survive in high temperature and different climatic conditions.
(iv) **Low maintenance requirement** It should decrease the investment charges.
(v) Reduction in the size of the egg-laying bird with the ability to utilise more fibrous and cheaper diets that is formulated using agricultural byproducts.

20 Differentiate between layers and broilers. What type of food should be given to broilers?

Sol. Differences between layers and broilers are as follows

Layers	Broilers
These are egg-laying birds, managed for the purpose of getting eggs.	These are maintained for getting meat.
They require restricted and calculated feed with vitamins, minerals and micronutrients.	Their daily food requirement is rich in proteins and vitamins-A and K. The fat content should also be adequate.

21 Write a short note on marine fisheries.

Sol. India's marine fishery resources area includes long coastline and deep seas beyond it. Marine fishes are caught using many kinds of fishing nets from fishing boats. The yields are increased by locating large schools of fish in open sea by using satellites, etc.

Popular marine fish varieties are pomfret, mackerel, tuna, sardines and Bombay duck.

High economic value marine fishes are as follows

(i) **Finned fishes** Mullets, bhetki and pearl spots.

(ii) **Shell fishes** Prawns, mussels and oysters.

(iii) **Oysters** are also cultivated for the pearls they produce.

22 What is honey? What does the quality of honey depend upon?

Sol. Honey is a dense sweet liquid. It contains natural sugars, small amount of minerals and vitamins. The quality of honey depends upon the pasturage or flowers available to the bees for nectar and pollen collection. [1+2]

23 What are the advantages of beekeeping?

Sol. Following are the main advantages of beekeeping

(i) Along with getting honey on a commercial scale, other products like wax and royal jelly are also obtained from beekeeping. [1]

(ii) It requires low investments, due to which farmers use it as an additional income generating activity. [1]

(iii) It helps in cross-pollination. Pollens are transferred from one flower to another by bees, while collecting nectar. [1]

24 An Italian bee variety *Apis mellifera* has been introduced in India for honey production. Write about its merit over the other varieties. **NCERT Exemplar**

Sol. Merits of Italian bee variety *Apis mellifera* are as follows

(i) It is stingless.

(ii) It stays in beehives for long period of time and breeds very well.

(iii) It has high honey collection capacity.

25 Differentiate between

(i) Inland fishery and marine fishery

(ii) Apiculture and aquaculture.

Sol. (i) Differences between inland and marine fisheries are as follows

Inland fishery	Marine fishery
It consists of fishing in freshwater and brackish water.	It consists of fishing in sea water along the coastline and deep sea beyond it.
Most of the fish production is through a practice called aquaculture.	Most of the fish production is through a practice called mariculture.

(ii) Difference between apiculture and aquaculture is as follows

Apiculture	Aquaculture
It is the rearing and maintenance of honeybees for obtaining honey, wax and other substances.	It is the production of high economic value aquatic plants and animals under controlled situations by proper utilisation of available water.

26 Differentiate between the following.

(i) Capture fishery and culture fishery.

(ii) Beekeeping and poultry farming. **NCERT Exemplar**

Sol. (i) Differences between capture and culture fisheries are as follows

Capture fishery	Culture fishery
It is a way of obtaining fish from natural resources.	It is a way of obtaining fish from fish farming.
There is no seeding and raising of fish.	The fish is reared.
It is undertaken in both inland and marine waters.	It is undertaken mostly inland and near seashore.

(ii) Differences between beekeeping and poultry farming are as follows

Beekeeping	Poultry farming
It is a practice of rearing and management of honeybee.	It is the practice of raising domestic fowl.
Bees obtain food (nectar) from flower.	Poultry birds are provided food by the rearers.
It provides honey and wax, etc.	It provides eggs and meat (flesh).

27 Give an example of exotic and indigenous breeds of the following.

(i) Poultry **(ii) Milk cattle**

(iii) Bees

Sol.

Animals	Exotic breeds	Indigenous breeds
Poultry	White Leghorn	Aseel
Milk cattle	Jersey	Red Sindhi
Bees	*Apis mellifera*	*Apis cerana indica*

Long Answer Type Questions

1 How can crop variety improvement methods help farmers facing repeated crop failure? Describe three factors for which they could do crop improvement. Which is the most common method of obtaining improved varieties of crops? Explain briefly.
Competency Based Que.

Sol. Crop variety improvement basically focuses on developing a crop variety that can provide a good yield, resistant to diseases and pests and is adaptable. Thus, it can lead to better crop produce. [1]

Factors for which crop improvement can be done are as follows

(i) **Higher yield** Every farmer involved in agriculture needs to get a good yield to be economically stable. Crops need to be improved, so that they provide good productivity per acre.

(ii) **Improved quality** The quality considerations of crop products vary from crop to crop. For example, baking quality in wheat, protein quality in pulses and oil quality in oilseeds should be given consideration, while selecting an improved variety.

(iii) **Wider adaptability** Varieties having wider adaptability can stabilise their growth in different environmental conditions. [1×3]

There are two ways of getting a variety with desirable characteristics

(i) **Genetic manipulation** A gene is introduced in plant that provides the desirable characters.

(ii) **Hybridisation** The most common method of obtaining improved variety of crops is hybridisation. It is defined as a cross between genetically dissimilar plants.

It can be of three types

(i) **Intervarietal** Cross between two different varieties.

(ii) **Interspecific** Cross between two different species of the same genus.

(iii) **Intergeneric** Cross between two different genera. [1]

2 Mention the modern initiatives undertaken in India to supply water to the fields.

Sol. Poor monsoons cause crop failure. The crops should be given adequate amount of water at appropriate stages of life for the increase in the expected yield of crops. Under such circumstances, different kinds of irrigation systems are developed. It ensures the supply of water to the agricultural lands. Depending on the type of water resources, the irrigation systems are as follows

(i) **Wells** They are of two types.

(a) **Dug wells** In this type of well, water is collected from water bearing strata.

(b) **Tube wells** In this type of well, water is lifted by pumps from deeper strata for irrigation.

(ii) **Canals** In this system, canal receives water from one or more reservoirs or from rivers. The main canal is divided into branch canals with many distributaries to irrigate fields.

(iii) **River lift system** It is most common in those areas, where canal flow is irregular or insufficient due to less number of reservoirs released. In lift system, water is directly drawn from rivers for irrigation in areas near to rivers.

(iv) **Tanks** These are small storage reservoirs intercepting and storing the run-off of smaller catchment areas.

3 (i) The black and the white dots in the given picture are an indication of two different types of cropping patterns. Identify the cropping patterns.

(ii) Mention one advantage of each cropping pattern.

(iii) How are the two cropping patterns different from each other?
Competency Based Que.

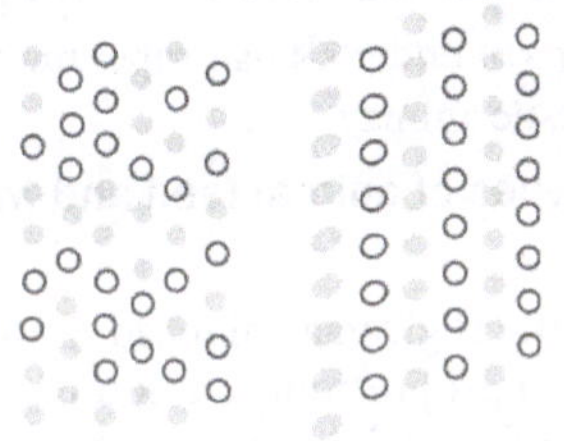

A *B*

Sol. (i) *A*–Mixed cropping, *B*–Intercropping [1]

(ii) *A*–Such cropping pattern gives insurance against failure of one of the crops.

B–It ensures maximum utilisation of nutrients supplied. [1+1]

(iii) Intercropping differs from mixed cropping in several ways, which are as follows

Intercropping	Mixed cropping
It is a practice of growing two or more crops simultaneously in definite pattern.	It is a practice of growing two or more crops simultaneously on the same piece of land.
Its main target is to increase the productivity per unit area.	Its main target is to minimise the risk of total crop failure.
Both crops are easily threshed and harvested separately.	Harvesting and threshing of both crops separately is not possible.

[2]

4 (i) Which factors are responsible for causing loss of storage grains? State some preventive measures for storage of food grains.

(ii) What do you mean by animal husbandry? State any two advantages of it.

Sol. (i) Factors responsible for the loss during storage of grains are as follows

(a) **Biotic factors** includes insects, rodents, birds, mites and bacteria, etc.

(b) **Abiotic factors** includes moisture content, temperature, etc. [1]

Preventive measures for the storage of food grains include

- Drying
- Maintenance of hygiene
- Fumigation
- Improved storage structure. [1]

(ii) **Animal husbandry** It is the science of rearing, feeding, caring, breeding and utilisation of animals. Advantages of animal husbandry are

(a) It is beneficial for farmers as increased yield brings more income and raises their living standard.

(b) It helps in undertaking proper management of domestic animals. [3]

5 Name two types of animal feed and write their functions. NCERT Exemplar

Sol. The dairy cattle is given a balanced ration. It contains all nutrients in proportionate amounts. A ration is the amount of food, which is given to the animal during a twenty four hour period.

The animal feed includes two types of substances

(i) **Roughage** It largely contains fibres such as green fodder, hay (straw of cereals) and legumes, (e.g. berseem and cowpea).

(ii) **Concentrates** The concentrates used in feed of cattle and buffaloes are a mixture of substances. These are rich in one or more nutrients. For example, cotton seeds, oil seeds, grains of maize, oats, barley, jowar, bajra and gram.

Besides above mentioned nutritious food material, dairy animals require certain additive feeds. They promote the growth of the animals. They contain antibiotics, minerals and hormones. They facilitate good yield of milk and meat and protect them from diseases.

6 Mention some measures taken to improve poultry breeds.

Sol. Refer to text on page no. 308 and 309.

7 What do you understand by composite fish culture? Describe in detail with its advantages and disadvantages. NCERT Exemplar

Sol. Composite fish culture system is adopted for intensive fishing. [1]

Characteristics of composite fish culture These are as follows

(i) Both local as well as imported fish species can be used in such systems.

(ii) Combination of five or six fish species is used in a single fish pond.

(iii) These species have different feeding habits.

(iv) The species are selected, so that they do not compete for food among them because of their different food habits. Some examples are

- **Catla** Surface feeders.
- **Rohu** Feeds in the middle zone of the pond.
- **Mrigal and Common carps** Bottom feeders.

Grass carps Weed feeders. [2]

Advantages of composite fish culture are as follows

(i) All the food available in the pond is utilised.

(ii) There is no competition for food.

(iii) There is an increase in the fish yield from the pond.

One of the disadvantages of composite fish culture is the lack of availability of good quality fish seeds. [2]

8 You are living in an area with abundant greenery and pasturage. A farmer living near your home is not satisfied with the income he gets from his agricultural land. Which additional income generating activity will you suggest to him in such a scenario? Competency Based Que.

Sol. Beekeeping is the best suited activity in such a scenario that I would suggest to him. It is a low investment, additional income generating activity.

It is the method of rearing, care and management of honeybees for obtaining honey, wax and other substances. Utilities of this activity are as follows

(i) Honey is used for the consumption and manufacturing of other useful products.

(ii) Beeswax is used in various medicinal preparations.

(iii) Bees help in cross-pollination of crops as bee transfers pollen grain from one flower to another, while collecting nectar.

One can also suggest him to use following varieties of bees in apiculture

(i) ***Apis cerana indica*** Commonly known as Indian bee.

(ii) ***Apis dorsata*** Commonly known as rock bee.

(iii) ***Apis florea*** Commonly known as little bee.

(iv) ***Apis mellifera*** Commonly known as Italian bee that has been brought to increase the yield of honey.

The advantages of Italian bees are as follows

(i) They have good honey collection capacity.

(ii) They are stingless.

(iii) They stay in a given beehive for long periods and breed very well.

(iv) They are very good for commercial production of honey.

He should also take care of the pasturage around the apiary as the value or quality of honey depends on it.

9 (i) What is the term used for the scientific management of livestock?

(ii) What do you mean by the term apiary and pasturage?

(iii) Mention any two desirable traits, for which cross-breeding programmes between Indian and foreign breeds are undertaken in poultry farming.

Sol. (i) **Animal husbandry** It is the term used for scientific management of livestock. [1]

(ii) **Apiary** (Bee farm), which is established for the commercial production of honey, etc., is known as apiary. [2]

Pasturage It is the flora (flowers) present in the surroundings of apiary that provide nectar to bees. Quantity and quality of honey directly depends upon the pasturage.

(iii) Two desirable traits for which cross-breeding between Indian and foreign breeds are undertaken in poultry farming are

(a) Number and quality of chicks.

(b) Tolerance to high temperature. [2]

ASSESSMENT EXERCISE

Competency Focused (Objective) Questions

Multiple Type Questions

1 Which one is an oil yielding plant among the following?
(a) Pigeon pea (b) Linseed
(c) *Sorghum* (d) Berseem

2 Choose the example of green manure out of the following given options.
(a) Blue-green algae
(b) Leguminous plants
(c) *Parthenium*
(d) Sunn hemp

3 What according to you one should adopt out of the following practices for a sustained livelihood? **Competency Based Que.**
(a) Intercropping
(b) Mixed farming
(c) Integrated farming practices
(d) All of the above

4 Which out of these is a breed of cattle?
(a) Jersey (b) Scampi
(c) Ghagus (d) Kadaknath

5 Select the correct sign which signifies that an animal is in a healthy condition.
(a) Good apetite
(b) Normal pH
(c) Normal body temperature
(d) Both (a) and (c)

Assertion–Reason Questions

Direction (Q. Nos. 6-10) *In each of the following questions, a statement of Assertion (A) is given by the corresponding statement of Reason (R). Of the statements, mark the correct answer as*

(a) Both A and R are true and R is the correct explanation of A
(b) Both A and R are true, but R is not the correct explanation of A
(c) A is true, but R is false
(d) A is false, but R is true

6 Assertion (A) Developing varieties for wider adaptability will help in stabilising crop production.
Reason (R) One variety can then be grown under different climatic conditions in different areas.

7 Assertion (A) In intercropping, two or more crops are grown together on same land.
Reason (R) It ensures maximum utilisation of nutrients supplied.

8 Assertion (A) It is necessary to adopt some preventive and control measures before storing grains.
Reason (R) Storage losses in agricultural produce are very high.

9 Assertion (A) *Bos indicus* and *Bos bubalis* are the exotic species of the cattle.
Reason (R) Milk production depends on the duration of the lactation period.

10 Assertion (A) *A. mellifera*, an exotic bee species is commercially employed in apiaries.
Reason (R) It produces high yield of honey.

Answers

1. (b)	**2.** (d)	**3.** (d)	**4.** (a)	**5.** (d)
6. (a)	**7.** (a)	**8.** (a)	**9.** (d)	**10.** (b)

Case Based Questions

Direction (Q. Nos. 11-14) ***Answer the questions on the basis of your understanding of the following passage and related studied concepts.***

Cattle farming is one of the most common practice of animal industry in India. Cattle animals includes cows, bulls and buffaloes, etc. There are 26 breeds of cattle and 7 breeds of buffaloes in India. They differ in colour, general body build, horns, geographical distribution, etc. The best cattle breeds occur in the drier regions of the country. On the basis of work or their utility cattles are classified into following groups, i.e. milch and draught. The exotic or foreign breeds are often mated to obtain new and different offspring.

11 In India for what purposes cattle farming is done on such a large scale ?

12 Name any two indigenous and exotic breeds of cattle.

13 What is the idea behind mating an indigenous breed of cattle with an exotic breed in cattle farming?

14 Your family is planning to open up a cattle farm, what measures would you advise them to adapt for a successful and financially benefitting practice?

Constructed Response (Descriptive) Questions

Very Short Answer Type Questions

15 Write the factors on which irrigation requirements depend.

16 Which crop is generally grown between cultivation of two cereal crops to restore the fertility of soil?

17 What is common in poultry, fisheries and beekeeping with respect to increase in the production of animals?

Short Answer Type Questions

18 What are the reasons behind the occurrence of the green revolution and the white revolution?

19 In last few decades, the production of food from animal sources has increased. Justify this statement.

20 How can poultry and fish farming help in solving the food and nutrition problems?

21 ***Refer to the given figure and answer the questions that follows*** **Competency Based Que.**

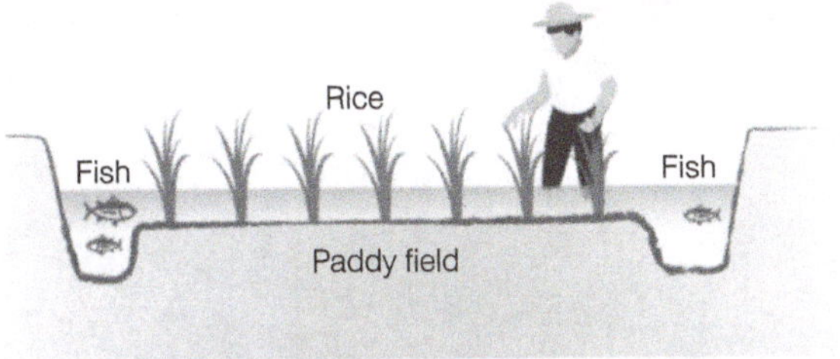

(i) Which type of fish farming is shown in the given figure?

(ii) Name any two fish that are suitable for this type of farming.

(iii) Give any two properties of fish used for this type of culture.

Long Answer Type Questions

22 Mention any two desirable agronomic characters for crop improvement. Explain how farmers get desired characters incorporated into new varieties produced? List two conditions necessary for the new varieties to be accepted.

23 There is a water reservoir (river) near a village. Due to insufficient rain, farmers are worried about their crops. Suggest and explain the irrigation practice that can be adopted to supply water to the entire agricultural land in the village.

24 ***Refer to the given figure and answer the questions that follows*** **Competency Based Que.**

(i) The wax glands of worker bees secrete wax. How is it beneficial for humans?

(ii) Among indigenous and exotic breeds, which one would you choose for beekeeping and why?

(iii) Even though both worker bees and queen bees develop from fertilised eggs, but only queen bees lay eggs. Give reason.

(iv) 'Worker bees are more laborious than drones'. Justify the statement.

CHAPTER TO BE ASSESSED FORMATIVELY

CHAPTER 13

Health and Diseases

Health is the state of proper functioning of body and mind. Any malfunctioning at the level of cells, organs or organ systems can be caused by various agents/factors. These could be infections by microorganisms, stress or any other agent leading to the state of illness and health failure. This condition is known as disease. In order to ensure smooth functioning of our body, we must understand the various aspects of health and disease.

13.1 Health

Health is a state of complete physical, mental and social well-being. It is not merely the absence of disease or infirmity as defined by the WHO (World Health Organisation; 1948). Thus, being healthy means that one should feel good physically, mentally and socially.

Significance of Health

Good health has following advantages:

(*i*) It increases our working efficiency. It helps us to perform various activities at our best.

(*ii*) It helps us to cope up with the social and mental pressures without much difficulty.

(*iii*) It contributes to overall well-being, making life more joyful and fulfilling.

13.2 Personal and Community Health Issues

The health of every individual depends on his personal habits, economic status and physical environment. Personal health refers to the overall well-being of an individual.

But human beings live in communities therefore, the health of the community is also an important factor for an individual's health.

Community health refers to the maintenance, protection and improvement (overall well-being) of the whole community in which an individual lives.

The following factors explain the relation between community and individual health.

(*i*) **Social environment** Our physical environment is decided by our surrounding. The place where we live (i.e., villages, towns or cities) is an important factor in our individual health.

(*ii*) **Public cleanliness** The possibility of poor health increases if no agency ensures that garbage is collected and disposed. Open drain-water lying stagnant around us also causes health issues. Therefore, public cleanliness is important for individual health.

(*iii*) **Good economic conditions and jobs** Hygienic food can be earned by doing work. For this, work oppurtunities should be available. This ensures good individual health.

(*iv*) **Social equality and harmony** In order to keep ourselves healthy, we need to be happy. For this, we should maintain good relations with our society. We should not mistreat each other.

Distinctions between Healthy and Disease-Free

The word disease, i.e. **disturbed ease** means being uncomfortable and not at ease. A condition is referred as disease when it has a specific and particular cause leading to discomfort. However, being disease-free does not necessarily mean being healthy. The differences between the two conditions are tabulated below:

Healthy	*Disease-Free*
It is a state of complete physical, mental and social well-being.	It is a state of absence of discomfort or dearrangement of body parts and their functions.
It depends upon the individual as well as on the physical and social environmental factors (societies and communities).	It is related to the individual only.
A healthy person will be disease-free.	A disease-free person can be healthy or unhealthy.
Healthy person is energetic and able to perform as per requirement.	Performance of a disease-free person depends upon environment and personal attitude.

Try These 13.1

1. **Define the term health.**
2. **Give the full-form of WHO.**
3. **Give one significance of good health.**
4. **Why social harmony is needed for a person to achieve good individual health?**
5. **What is disease?**

13.3 Disease and Its Causes

Disease refers to any condition that disturbs or modifies the normal functioning of the living organisms. Each organ system of our body has specific organs to perform particular functions. In the presence of a disease, functioning or the appearance of one or more systems of the body may change. These changes give rise to symptoms and signs of disease.

Symptoms of diseases are the indications of something being wrong or unusual, cold, headache, cough, loose motions, etc. These indicate that there may be a disease but, they do not exactly indicate what the disease is. For example, a headache may rarely mean meningitis, it can simply means just official stress or any other disease.

Signs of a disease give more definite indications of the presence of a particular disease. They help the doctors (physicians) to diagnose the disease.

Acute and Chronic Diseases

The manifestation of diseases will be different depending upon various factors. Depending on the duration of infection, diseases may be of following two types:

(*i*) **Acute diseases** are the diseases that last only for very short period of time. Thus, they do not cause long-term harmful effects on human health. In these diseases, patients recover completely after the cure, e.g. common cold, cough, etc.

(*ii*) **Chronic diseases** are the diseases, which last for a long time, even as much as a lifetime. They cause drastic long-term effects on human health, e.g. elephantiasis (an infection caused by filarial worm), cancer, Tuberculosis (TB), etc.

Chronic Diseases and Poor Health

Acute and chronic diseases have different effects on our health. Any disease that causes poor functioning of one part of the body affects our general health because for general health, all body parts should work properly. Acute diseases do not have time to cause major effects on general health. Chronic diseases cause major effects because they are long-term diseases. They can cause serious distress to health as compared to acute diseases.

Causes of Diseases

Most of the diseases will have many causes, rather than one single cause.

These causes of diseases are classified into two types:

(*i*) **Immediate causes** These are the real or primary causes, also called **first level of cause.** Various microorganisms like bacteria, virus, fungi, protozoans, etc., that can cause infectious diseases are included in this category.

(*ii*) **Contributory causes** These are also called **intrinsic or internal factors**. They do not lead to a disease themselves.

These can be of following types:

- **Poor health due to inadequate diet** It occurs due to deficiency of one or more nutrient, making the person unhealthy or susceptible to diseases, e.g. Kwashiorkor, a nutritional deficiency disease occurring due to low protein diet. So, lack of good nourishment becomes **second level of cause of disease.**

- **Genetic disorders** These are present since birth and pass down from parents to offsprings.
- **Lack of public services or poor economic conditions** Poverty also contributes to the cause of disease. These causes become the **third level causes of disease.**

Infectious and Non-Infectious Causes

Immediate causes of diseases belong to two distinct types. One group of diseases is caused by infectious agents like microorganisms. With the spread of these microbes, disease caused by them also spreads. Hence, these diseases are known as **infectious diseases.** The second group of diseases is not caused by infectious agents. These diseases are restricted only to the persons, who are suffering from them. As they do not spread from infected person to a healthy person, these are called **non-infectious diseases** or **non-communicable diseases.** For e.g., some cancers are caused by genetic abnormalities or by exposure to certain carcinogenic chemicals and radiations. High blood pressure can be caused by excessive weight and lack of exercise, etc.

Try These 13.2

1. **What does help a physician to confirm a disease?**
2. **When compared to an acute disease patient, a chronic disease patient recovers after a longtime. Is it true? Give one reason.**
3. **Name the diseases that spread to healthy people after coming in contact with a sick person.**
4. **Name the type of disease that remain restricted only to a particular person.**

13.4 Infectious Diseases

Infectious diseases are caused by some biological agents (pathogens) such as viruses, bacteria, fungi and single-celled animals, i.e. protozoans, etc. These can rapidly spread from one person to another by various means such as water, air, food, insects (vectors) or by physical contact.

Infectious Agents

The unicellular or multicellular organisms that cause infection are called **infectious agents.** These disease causing organisms are also called **pathogens** and they are classified into a wide range of categories. Some of them are viruses, bacteria, fungi, protozoans, nematodes, etc.

Various types of diseases and their pathogens are as follows:

- Diseases caused by viruses include common cold, influenza, dengue fever and AIDS. For instance, SARS virus causes respiratory disorder.
- Diseases like typhoid fever, cholera, tuberculosis and anthrax are caused by bacteria. For instance, *Staphylococci* bacteria can cause acne.
- Manl common skin infections are caused by different kinds of fungi. For instance, *Trichophyton* is a fungus that causes ringworm in humans
- Protozoan microbes cause many familiar diseases, such as malaria and kala-azar (caused by *Leishmania*). For instance, *Trypanosoma* is responsible for sleeping sickness
- Intestinal worm infections, as well as diseases like elephantiasis caused by different species of worms. For instance, *Ascaris lunbricoides* cause an intestinal infection called ascariasis.

Note
- Viruses, bacteria and fungi multiply very quickly, while worms multiply very slowly in comparison.
- The purpose of dividing infectious agents into different categories is to decide the kind of treatment to use because the same drug will not work against a microbe belonging to a different group.

Antibiotics

These are the chemical substances produced mainly by microorganisms (bacteria and fungi). At low concentration they have the ability to inhibit the growth of other microorganisms. They commonly block the **biochemical pathways** important for bacteria, e.g. penicillin.

The antibiotic penicillin blocks the formation of cell wall in bacteria. This cell wall helps in the protection of bacteria. Due to penicillin, bacteria become unable to make the cell wall and die easily.

Many antibiotics can work against many species of bacteria rather than simply working against one.

Antibiotics do not work against viral infections because viruses do not use the same pathway as that of bacteria. Therefore, taking antibiotics during common cold does not reduce the severity or duration of disease.

Peptic Ulcers and the Nobel Prize

Two Australians, **Robin Warren** and **Barry Marshall** discovered that a bacterium *Helicobacter pylori* was responsible for peptic ulcers disease. Previously, it was thought that peptic ulcers were caused due to stressful lifestyle. Due to this discovery, peptic ulcer no longer remained a chronic disease as it can be treated by a short period of treatment with antibiotics. For this discovery, both of them received the Nobel Prize in physiology and medicine in the year 2005.

Means of Spread

Infectious diseases can spread from an infected person to a healthy person by various ways and therefore, are also called **communicable diseases.** Diseases spread through various modes like air, water, sexual contact, vectors, etc. These are discussed below.

(i) Airborne Diseases

Causative microbes of such diseases spread through air. Little droplets are thrown out by an infected person on sneezing or coughing. These droplets can be breathed in by someone standing close and the microbes get a chance to start new infection. For e.g. common cold, cough, pneumonia and tuberculosis.

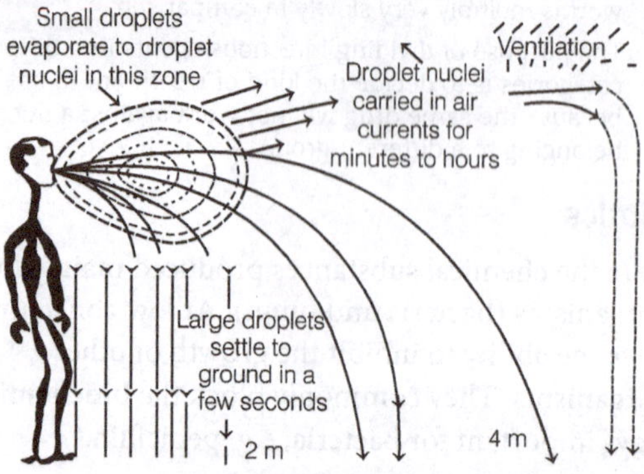

Air-transmitted diseases

Air-transmitted diseases are easy to catch if we are closer to the infected person. In closed areas, the droplet nuclei recirculate and pose a risk for everyone. Overcrowded and poorly ventilated housing is a major factor in spreading airborne diseases.

(ii) Waterborne Diseases

In such diseases, microbes spread through water. If the excreta from someone suffering from an infectious gut disease, such as cholera, gets mixed with the drinking water used by people living nearby, it results in waterborne disease. Cholera causing microbes enter new hosts through the water they drink and can cause disease in them. Such diseases are much more likely to spread in the absence of safe supply of drinking water.

(iii) Sexually Transmitted Diseases (STDs)

These are microbial diseases, that can be transmitted by sexual contact from one partner to the other. However, STDs do not spread by casual physical contacts, like hugs, handshakes, sports such as wrestling or by any other way in which we touch each other socially. Syphilis and AIDS are the common examples of sexually transmitted diseases.

Note AIDS virus can also spread through blood transfusion, from an infected mother to her baby during pregnancy and through breastfeeding.

(iv) Spread of Diseases through Vectors

Many animals which live around us in the environment can transmit diseases (germs) from sick person to a healthy person (another potential host).

These animals act as an intermediaries and are known as **vectors** (carrier of the disease or infection), e.g.

Mosquitoes such as *Anopheles* (female)–malaria, *Culex*–filariasis, *Aedes*–yellow fever, dengue.

Flies such as housefly–typhoid, tse-tse fly–sleeping sickness, sandfly–kala-azar.

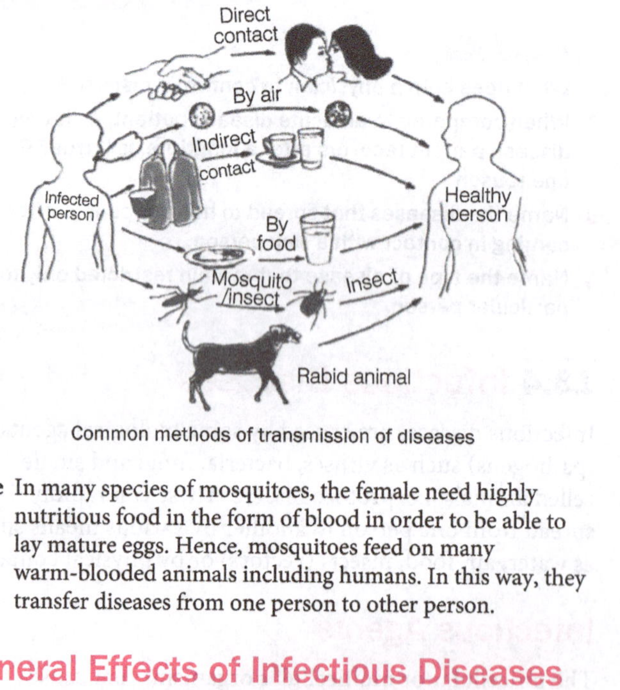

Common methods of transmission of diseases

Note In many species of mosquitoes, the female need highly nutritious food in the form of blood in order to be able to lay mature eggs. Hence, mosquitoes feed on many warm-blooded animals including humans. In this way, they transfer diseases from one person to other person.

General Effects of Infectious Diseases

Immune system is essential for our health. It is the defence system that protects body against various types of microbes. It also keeps the body safe by killing infectious microbes.

When infectious microbes enter the body, the immune system gets activated in response to infection. An active immune system recruits many cells to the affected area and kill off the disease-causing microbes. This recruitment process is called **inflammation.** Due to this process, there may be local effects like swelling, pain and general effects like fever.

Sometimes, **allergy** (heightened sensitivity to a foreign substance causing body's defence system to over react) may also occur in response to allergens.

In some cases the tissue specificity of the infection leads to general seeming effects. For e.g., AIDS virus, HIV reaches the immune system and damages its function. Due to this body is not able to fight with even minor infections like cold or diarrhoea. This may lead to death.

The **severity** of disease manifestations indirectly depends on the number of microbes (pathogens) in the body. If the number of microbes is very small, the disease manifestations may be minor or unnoticed. But if the number of microbes is large, the disease can be severe enough to be life-threatening. The importance of the immune system can thus be well-understood from the fact that it is a major factor that determines the number of microbes surviving in the body.

Organ-Specific and Tissue- Specific Manifestations

Our body is very large as compared to the microbes. So they can reach several places in the body through various routes and affect particular tissues or organs. The selection for the site of microbe's habitat (home) is related to their point of entry,
e.g.

- If they enter from the air through nose, they are likely to reach the lungs. This is how tuberculosis causing bacterium enters the body.
- If they enter through mouth, they can stay in the gut lining, e.g., typhoid causing bacteria. They can also go to the liver like jaundice causing virus.
- If they enter through sexual contact, they spread to lymph node all over the body like HIV.
- If they enter through mosquito bites, they may enter the liver and then to Red Blood Cells (RBCs) like malaria causing microbes. They may reach to brain like Japanese encephalitis virus that causes brain fever.

Thus, the signs and symptoms of a disease will depend upon the tissue or organ targeted by microbes, e.g.

- If the target is the lungs, the symptoms will be cough and breathlessness.
- If the target is liver, then jaundice may occur.
- If the target is brain, then headache, vomiting, fits or unconciousness may occur.

In addition to these organ-specific and tissue-specific effects of infectious diseases, there are other common effects too, which depend on body's **immune system.**

Try These 13.3

1. **Which female mosquito feed on blood of warm-blooded animals like human beings?**
2. **Keeping in mind about the property of organ-specific diseases, mention the location of the microbes when they enter through mouth and sexual contact, respectively.**
3. **A person complaints of frequent headache, vomiting and becomes unconscious frequently. Which organ is most likely to be affected?**
4. **Which system of human body is a major factor determining the number of microbes in body?**
5. **Do you agree that the severity of disease manifestations indirectly depends on the number of microbes in the body? Answer simply Yes or No?**

Principles of Treatment

When an infectious disease occur, a doctor prescribes various medicines, each working differently for treatment.

Following are the two ways to treat infectious diseases:

- **To reduce the effects of the disease** By providing a particular treatment, so that symptoms can be reduced. The symptoms are usually because of inflammation. For example, we can take medicines that bring down fever, reduce pain or loose motions or take complete rest to conserve energy. But, it will not kill the disease causing microorganisms. Therefore, disease would not be cured completely.
- **To kill the cause of the disease** Taking medicines that kill microbes is the best way for complete recovery from a particular disease. It is essential that medicine specific to disease causing microbe is taken. For e.g. for the treatment of bacterial disease, antibiotics can be taken by the patient that block essential biochemical pathways of bacteria (these may be pathways for synthesis of new substances or respiration) without affecting our own.

Similarly, there are drugs that can kill protozoans, such as malarial parasite. It is harder to make anti-viral medicines because viruses have very few biochemical mechanisms of their own. They enter our cells and use our machinery for completing their life processes. This means that there are relatively few virus-specific targets to aim at. However, effective anti-viral drugs like the drug that keeps HIV infection under control are now available.

Principles of Prevention

Due to modern technology and advancement in science, we have antibiotics and other medicines to cure many diseases. But there are few limitations that are normally faced while treating an infectious disease.

These limitations are as follows

- Once someone has disease, his body functions are damaged and may never recover completely.
- The treatment will take time. It means that someone suffering from a disease is likely to be bedridden for sometime, even if proper treatment is given.
- The person suffering from an infectious disease can serve as the source for further spread of infection to other people. Thus, multiplying the difficulties mentioned above.

Because of above limitations, prevention of disease is better than cure.

Methods to Prevent Diseases

There are two ways to prevent diseases. These are described below:

(*i*) **General Ways of Preventing Infectious Diseases**
These ways are mostly related to prevent exposure to infectious microbes. Public hygiene is also necessary for the prevention of infectious diseases.
The practices adopted for preventing the to exposure disease causing microbes are given in table below

Microbes	Practice
Airborne microbes	By providing living conditions that are not over-crowded.
Waterborne microbes	By providing safe drinking water. This is done by treating the water to kill any microbial contamination.
Vector-borne microbes	By providing clean environment which would prevent breeding of mosquitoes, etc.

Some other general principles for prevention are:

(*a*) **Strong immune system** The immune system of our body normally fights against the microbes that enter into our body and kills them. The cells of the immune system kill off the microbes before it can take on major proportions. As we know, if number of injecting microbes is less, the manifestations of disease will be minor. In other words, becoming exposed to or infected with an infectious microbe does not necessarily mean developing noticeable disease.

(*b*) **Balanced diet** Immune system will not function properly if sufficient amount of food and nourishment is not available. Therefore, availability of proper and sufficient food for everyone is the second basic principle of prevention.

(*ii*) **Specific Ways of Preventing Infectious Diseases**
It includes adopting the practice of immunisation.

Immunisation

When the immune system first sees an infectious microbe, it responds against it and then remembers it specifically. So, the next time when that particular microbe or its close relatives enter the body, the immune system responds with greater vigour. It eliminates the infection more quickly than the first time around. This is the basic principle of immunisation.

Smallpox

Although, there is no smallpox in the world today, but a hundred years ago, epidemics of this disease were common. There was, however one group of people, who provided nursing care for the disease victims and did not fear of catching the disease. This was group, who had smallpox earlier and survived it. Thus, having the disease once means prevention from subsequent attacks of the same disease. This is due to the memory ability of the immune system.

Vaccination

This term is derived from Latin word *Vaccinia* meaning cowpox where the word *Vacca* means cow. It is the process of injecting dead microbes into the body of a healthy person in order to develop immunity against a particular disease caused by that microbe.

This eliminates the infection because when the immune system first sees an infectious microbe, it responds against it and then remembers it specifically. So, the body develops a memory of the particular infection by putting something into the body that mimics the microbes we want to vaccinate against.

Vaccine is a preparation of weakened or killed infectious agents or their products. They stimulate the immune system to produce antibodies against particular disease. The first vaccine was discovered by **Edward Jenner** against smallpox disease.

Many vaccines are available for preventing infectious diseases and provide disease-specific means of prevention.

The diseases against which vaccines are available, are given below:

- Diphtheria, Pertussis, Tetanus — DPT (Hib vaccine)
- Poliomyelitis — OPV (Oral Polio Vaccine)
- Hepatitis-B — Hepatitis vaccine
- Tuberculosis — BCG (Bacillus Calmette Guerin)

These vaccines are available under child immunisation programme for preventing infectious diseases. Vaccines has to be provided at proper age, e.g. a vaccine against hepatitis-A is available in the market. Hepatitis virus cause jaundice and transmitted through water. Majority of children in many parts of India are already immune to hepatitis-A by the time they are five years old. This is because they are exposed to the virus through water.

Pulse Polio Programme

India launched the Pulse Polio Immunisation (PPI) programme in 1995 as a result of World Health Organisation's (WHO) Global Polio Eradication Initiative. Under this programme, all children under 5 years are given 2 drops of Oral Polio Vaccine (OPV) until polio is eradicated. PPI was initiated with the objective of achieving hundred per cent coverage. India has been declared polio-free by WHO. However, pulse polio programme is continuing to eliminate any chance of its comeback.

Try These 13.4

1. **What is the one principle for treating infectious diseases?**
2. **Are anti-viral medicines are difficult to make than anti-bacterial medicines? Yes or No.**
3. **State the major practice one should adopt in order to reduce vector-borne microbes.**
4. **Name one severe infectious disease that represents the failure of the immune system.**
5. **Hepatitis-A vaccine was given to a child of 8 years. Will it be helpful?**

Summary of Some Infectious Diseases

Diseases Caused by Protozoans

Disease	*Causal organism*	*Means of spread*	*Symptoms*	*Prevention and control*
Malaria	*Plasmodium* (enters liver)	Female *Anopheles* mosquito	Headache, nausea and muscular pain. High fever with specific pattern of cold, hot and sweating stage.	Use mosquito nets and insect repellents to prevent mosquito bite. Do not allow collection of water anywhere. Sprinkle kerosene oil in open drainage or any place where uncovered water is collected. Wire-gauze should be used on doors and windows. Doses of quinine are prescribed to control malaria.
Sleeping sickness	*Trypanosoma brucei*	Bite of tse-tse fly	Anxiety, fever, headache, itching, insomnia, mood changes, sleep pattern changes, etc.	Using insect repellents, wearing long-sleeved clothing, avoiding tse-tse fly dense areas. Doses of drug Eflornithine.
Kala-azar or **Leishmaniasis**	*Leishmania donovani*	Bite of infected sandflies	Difficulty in breathing. Skin sores, which may become skin ulcers. Ulcers in mouth, tongue, gum, lips and nose. Abdominal discomfort.	Use insect repellent. Stay in well-screened areas. Antibodies containing compound is the main drug for treating this disease.

Diseases Caused by Bacteria

Disease	*Causal organism*	*Means of spread*	*Symptoms*	*Prevention and control*
Tuberculosis (TB)	*Mycobacterium tuberculosis*	Inhaling infected droplets released by coughing, sneezing or talking to infected person.	Loss of appetite and weight. **Lung TB** It includes continuous fever, persistant cough and blood stained sputum, chest pain, breathlessness. **Lymph gland TB** It includes swelling, secretion through skin. Prolonged low grade fever arises in afternoon.	Avoid over-crowded areas, isolation of patient, covering mouth while coughing, maintain good hygiene and sanitary conditions. Immunisation with BCG for prevention, ATT(Anti-tubercular Therapy) for control.
Cholera	*Vibrio cholerae*	Flies, contaminated water and food.	Watery diarrhoea, vomiting without nausea and shrunken eyes. Great loss of mineral salts leads to kidney failure.	Boiled water and cooked food should be consumed, maintenance of personal hygiene and good sanitation. Immunisation by cholera vaccine, ORS (Oral Rehydration Solution) controls dehydration, antibiotic tetracycline kills bacteria.
Typhoid	*Salmonella typhi*	By ingestion of water, food contaminated with faecal matter, by houseflies, etc.	Headache, fever that rises in afternoon and keeps increasing for 7-8 days. High fever in second week, gradually decline during 3rd-4th week.	Proper sanitation and disposal of faecal matter. TAB vaccination, typhoral oral vaccine, chloromycetin drug cures typhoid.
Diarrhoea	Mainly bacteria, such as *Escherichia coli*, *Shigella*, *Salmonella*, etc., and some also caused by **viruses** (rotavirus, enterovirus), **protozoans** (*Entamoeba histolytica*) and **nematodes** (*Ascaris*).	Contaminated food , water, hands, clothes, etc.	Frequent loose motions, vomiting, weight loss, abdominal cramps and dehydration.	Proper personal hygiene and sanitary conditions. Stale food should be avoided. Give ORS to control dehydration. ORS can be prepared by adding sugar and small amount of salt in water. Dose of antibiotics and anti-diarrhoeal drug.

Diseases Caused by Virus

Disease	Causal organism	Means of spread	Symptoms	Prevention and control
Influenza	*Myxovirus influenzae*	Through contact and by droplet infection *via* sneezing, coughing or talking to infected person.	Sudden chills, discharge from nose, sneezing, fever, headache, coughing, inflammation of respiratory mucosa and weakness.	Try to keep away from the patient. Anti-viral drugs are taken for cure.
Jaundice or **Hepatitis-A** and **B**	Hepatitis virus or Hepatitis-A and B virus	Food and water contaminated with hepatitis virus.	Dark yellow urine and light yellow stool. High fever, nausea, vomiting, headache, loss of appetite and joint pain.	Use chlorinated boiled water. Avoid stale food. Hepatitis-A and B vaccination and interferon injection. Intake of high calorie diet such as juice of sugarcanes, radish with jaggery.
AIDS (Acquired Immuno Deficiency Syndrome)	Retrovirus HIV (Human Immuno Deficiency Virus)	Through blood transfusion, sexual contact, use of contaminated needles from infected person to healthy person, from mother to child through placenta.	Swollen lymph node, regular fever and sweating at night, weight loss, loss of memory and ability to speak and think. Frequent occurrence of viral, bacterial and fungal infection.	Keeping knowledge about AIDS transmission. Avoid sexual contact with unknown person. Avoid use of common needles and razors. No effective treatment is known so far. Some anti-viral drugs are given to the patient to keep HIV infection under control.
Rabies (Hydrophobia)	Rabies virus	By bite of rabid cat, dog and monkey.	Severe headache and high fever. Painful contraction of muscles of throat and chest. Fear of water (hydrophobia) is developed. Excessive salivation, difficulty in taking food and damage of central nervous system. Mental depression for a short period.	Cleaning of wound with medicated soap. Course of anti-rabies vaccine. Compulsory immunisation of stray cats and dogs. No treatment if disease occurs.
Dengue	Dengue virus	*Aedes* mosquito (it lands with the head and tip of abdomen pointing towards the surface)	High fever with headache, nausea, vomiting, weakness and joint pains.	Maintenance of hygienic conditions in community, preventing the mosquito breeding sites and public awareness programmes should be conducted.
Polio or Poliomyelitis	Polio virus	Contaminated food, water and milk.	Sore throat and headache. Fever, vomiting, muscular pain, stiffness in neck and tingling sensation in limbs. Ultimately paralysis of lower body (paraplegia).	Complete rest and physiotherapy (helpful in beginning). Maintenance of hygiene by proper sanitary disposal. OPV (Oral Polio Vaccine) is given orally. Following pulse polio programme controls polio.

NCERT FOLDER

Complete Explanations of all NCERT's Questions

INTEXT QUESTIONS

Q.1 State any two conditions essential for good health.

Sol. Two conditions essential for good health are

(*i*) Availability of sufficient and nutritious food.

(*ii*) Better sanitation or clean surroundings.

Q.2 State any two conditions essential for being free of disease.

Sol. The conditions essential for being free of diseases are

(*i*) Taking good food (balanced diet).

(*ii*) Maintaining personal and public hygiene.

Q.3 Are the conditions essential for maintaining good health and being free of diseases same or different? Why?

Sol. Essential conditions for maintaining good health and being free of diseases are different, but interconnected. If the conditions that are essential for good health are maintained, then the chances of getting a disease will be minimised automatically. But, being disease-free does not mean being healthy. (The former means not suffering from any disease while, the latter means complete physical, mental and social well-being).

Q.4 List any three reasons, why you would think that you are sick and ought to see a doctor. If only one of these symptoms was present, would you still go to the doctor? Why or why not?

Sol. Three

(*i*) Cough, cold and high fever

(*ii*) Having diarrhoea (loose motions)

(*iii*) Having a wound with pus

These symptoms indicate disease but do not tell what the disease is. So, it is advisable to go to the doctor to diagnose the disease. If the symptom is mild, such as a slight fever or minor body pain, it can often be managed at home with rest and proper hydration. However, if the symptom is severe like difficulty in breathing or a high fever, immediate medical attention is necessory to prevent complications and ensure appropriate treatment.

Q.5 In which of the following case do you think the long-term effects on your health are likely to be most unpleasant?

(*i*) If you get jaundice.

(*ii*) If you get lice.

(*iii*) If you get acne.

Why?

Sol. Lice and acne will not cause long lasting effects on our body. But in case of jaundice, there will be severe long lasting effects, e.g.

(*i*) High temperature, headache and joint pain

(*ii*) Feeling of nausea and vomiting

(*iii*) Irritating rashes

The patient will suffer from poor health and will only recover by taking complete bed rest for some time.

Q.6 Why are we normally advised to take bland and nourishing food when we are sick?

Sol. In case of illness, the normal functions of the body get disturbed and immune system is weakened. So, a nourishing food is required, which is easily digestable and contains all the nutrients. Therefore, bland and nourishing food is advised to be taken during sickness.

Q.7 What are the different means by which infectious diseases are spread?

Sol. Different means by which infectious diseases spread are:

(*i*) **Through Air** When an infected person coughs, sneezes, or talks, droplets carrying germs can spread through the air and infect others (e.g., tuberculosis, common cold, COVID-19).

(ii) **Through Water** Contaminated water can carry disease-causing microbes, leading to infections when consumed (e.g., cholera, typhoid, dysentery).

(iii) **Through Sexual Contact** Certain infections spread through unprotected sexual contact with an infected person (e.g., HIV/AIDS, syphilis, gonorrhea.

(iv) **Through Vectors** Insects and animals act as carriers of diseases and transmit them to humans (e.g. malaria by mosquitoes, dengue by, *Aedes* mosquitoes, plague by rats).

Q.8 What precautions can you take in your school to reduce the incidence of infectious diseases?

Sol. To prevent the incidence of infectious diseases in school, following precautions can be taken:

(*i*) Avoid contact with students suffering from airborne diseases like common cold, cough, eye flu, etc.

(*ii*) By checking the availability of clean drinking water in school.

(*iii*) By maintaining cleanliness to protect against flies and mosquitoes.

(*iv*) Starting immunisation programmes in schools.

Q.9 What is immunisation?

Sol. **Immunisation** is the process of making a person resistant to a specific infectious disease by administering a vaccine. The vaccine stimulates the body's immune system to recognise and fight the disease-causing organism if exposed in the future. This helps in preventing infections and reducing the severity of diseases.

Q.10 What are the immunisation programmes available at the nearest health centre in your locality? Which of these diseases are the major health problems in your area?

Sol. The following immunisation programmes are available at the nearest health centre in our locality:

(*i*) **Immunisation for infants** DPT, BCG, polio, measles and MMR.

(*ii*) **Immunisation for children** Typhoid, TT, DT, smallpox and TAB.

(*iii*) **Immunisation for pregnant women** TT and hepatitis-B.

The diseases like typhoid, polio, measles, tetanus, etc., are the major health problems in our locality. To prevent these diseases, the government has initiated expanded immunisation programme all over the country.

REVIEW EXERCISE

Including Competency Based Questions

Competency Focused (Objective) Questions

Multiple Choice Questions

1 Which of the following statements about health and community well-being is correct?

(a) An individual's health is independent of the health of the community
(b) Public health measures like sanitation and vaccination improve overall health
(c) Social health does not affect an individual's well-being
(d) Community health is only affected by government policies, not individuals

Sol. (*b*) Public heath measures like sanitation and vaccination play a crucial role in preventing diseases and improving overall community health. They help reduce infections, enhance quality of life and promote longevity.

2 Which of the following diseases is considered acute?

(a) Tuberculosis
(b) Hypertension
(c) Asthma
(d) Common cold

Sol. (*d*) The common cold is an acute disease because it has a sudden onset, lasts for a short duration (typically a few days to a couple of weeks) and resolves on its own or with minimal treatment.

3 How do chronic diseases typically affect a person's health over time?

(a) They cause immediate severe symptoms and disappear quickly
(b) They gradually weaken the body and reduce overall functioning
(c) They have no impact on a person's quality of life
(d) They always lead to death within a few months

Sol. (*b*) Chronic diseases develop slowly and persist over a long period, often for years or even a lifetime. Unlike acute diseases that resolve quickly, chronic conditions gradually weaken the body.

4 Which one of the following has a long term effect on the health of an individual?

(a) Common cold
(b) Chicken pox
(c) Chewing tobacco
(d) Stress

Sol. (*c*) Chewing tobacco has long term effects on health, including an increased risk of oral cancer, gum disease, heart disease and addiction due to nicotine.

5 Which of the following is a major cause of infectious diseases?

(a) Deficiency of nutrients
(b) Genetic mutations
(c) Pathogens like bacteria, viruses and fungi
(d) Excessive physical exercise

Sol. (*c*) Infectious diseases are primarily caused by pathogens such as bacteria, viruses, fungi and Protozoa.

6 Which of the following diseases is caused by a protozoan?

(a) Tuberculosis
(b) Kala-azar
(c) Influenza
(d) Acne

Sol. (*b*) Kala-azar is caused by a protozoan parasite called *Leishmania donovani*. It is transmitted through the bite of infected sandflies and affects the spleen, liver and bone marrow.

7 Which of the following statements is true about bacteria and viruses?

(a) Both have similar life processes as viruses
(b) Bacteria live inside host cells like viruses
(c) Bacterial diseases can be treated with antibiotics, but virus cannot
(d) Viruses can multiply outside host cells like bacteria

Sol. (*c*) Bacteria are living organisms that can be treated with antibiotics, while viruses are non-living outside a host and require antiviral drugs or vaccines for prevention and control. Antibiotics are ineffective against viruses.

8 Which of the following diseases is spread through air?

(a) Malaria
(b) Tuberculosis
(c) Cholera
(d) Dengue

Sol. (*b*) Tuberculosis (TB) is an airborne disease caused by *Mycobacterium tuberculosis*. It spreads when an infected person coughs or sneezes, releasing bacteria into the air, which others can inhale.

9 If you live in a overcrowded and poorly ventilated house, it is possible that you may suffer from which of the following diseases. NCERT Exemplar

(a) Cancer
(b) AIDS
(c) Air borne diseases
(d) Cholera

Sol. (*c*) Overcrowded and poorly ventilated spaces increase the risk of airborne diseases like tuberculosis, influenza, and the common cold, as germs spread easily through the air.

10 Choose the wrong statement. **NCERT Exemplar**

(a) High blood pressure is caused by excessive weight and lack of exercise.

(b) Cancers can be caused by genetic abnormalities

(c) Peptic ulcers are caused by eating acidic food

(d) Acne is not caused by *Staphylococci*

Sol. (*c*) Peptic ulcers are primarily caused by *Helicobacter pylori* bacteria and prolonged use of Non-steroidal Anti-inflammatory Drugs (NSAIDs), not by consuming acidic food

11 Which of the following is not a way in which sexually transmitted diseases spread?

(a) Unprotected sexual contact

(b) Sharing needles with infected persons

(c) Hugging and shaking hands

(d) Blood transfusion from an infected person

Sol. (*c*) Sexually Transmitted Diseases (STDs) do not spread through casual contact like hugging or shaking hands. They primarily transmit through unprotected sexual contact, infected needles and contaminated blood transfusions.

12 Which of the following is an example of general prevention of diseases?

(a) Taking antibiotics

(b) Getting proper nutrition and maintaining hygiene

(c) Waiting for symptoms to appear before taking action

(d) Ignoring minor infections

Sol. (*b*) Good nutrition and hygiene strengthen the immune system and reduce the risk of infections. These general prevention measures help maintain overall health and protect against various diseases.

13 What is the main purpose of immunisation?

(a) To cure diseases after infection

(b) To strengthen the body's immune system against specific diseases

(c) To kill all microbes in the body

(d) To delay the spread of diseases

Sol. (*b*) Immunisation prepares the body's immune system to recognise and fight specific pathogens, preventing infections before they occur.

Assertion-Reason Questions

Direction (Q.Nos. 1-5) In each of the following questions, a statement of Assertion (A) is given by the corresponding statement of Reason (R). Of the statements, mark the correct answer as

(a) Both A and R are true and R is the correct explanation of A.

(b) Both A and R are true, but R is not the correct explanation of A.

(c) A is true, but R is false.

(d) A is false, but R is true.

1 Assertion (A) Malnutrition can lead to diseases even in the absence of infection.

Reason (R) Lack of proper nutrients affects the body's ability to function and fight infections.

Sol. (*a*) Both A and R are true and R is the correct explanation of A.

Malnutrition weakens the immune system, making the body more vulnerable to infections. Even without infection, nutrient deficiency can lead to diseases such as anaemia or rickets.

2 Assertion (A) Cholera is a water-borne disease.

Reason (R) Cholera is caused by a virus that multiplies in the intestines.

Sol. (*c*) A is true, but R is false.

Cholera is caused by the bacterium *Vibrio cholera*.

3 Assertion (A) AIDS (Acquired Immunodeficiency Syndrome) is caused by the Human Immunodeficiency Virus (HIV).

Reason (R) The HIV virus is only spread through sexual contact.

Sol. (*c*) A is true, but R is false.

HIV/AIDS can be transmitted from an infected mother to her baby during pregnancy, childbirth or breastfeeding. However, it is also spread through blood contact, not just sexual transmission.

4 Assertion (A) Antibiotics are effective in treating bacterial infections.

Reason (R) Antibiotics block bio-chemical pathways essential for bacterial survival.

Sol. (*a*) Both A and R are true and R is the correct explanation of A.

Antibiotics work by blocking bacterial bio-chemical pathways, preventing their growth and survival.

Since viruses do not use these pathways, antibiotics are ineffective against viral infections.

5 Assertion (A) Vaccination is an effective method to prevent certain infectious diseases.

Reason (R) Vaccines prepare the immune system to fight against specific pathogens.

Sol. (*a*) Both A and R are true and R is the correct explanation of A.

Vaccination introduces a weakened or inactive pathogen into the body, prompting the immune system to recognise and remember it. This helps in preventing future infections by the same pathogen.

Case Based/Source Based Questions

1 Two HIV-infected siblings, Vini and Prabhat were expelled from their school. Only after the intervention of an NGO, they were readmitted.

Read the above passage and answer the following questions:

(*i*) Which disease are the two children suffering from?

(*ii*) Write any three modes of transmission of this disease.

(*iii*) What is your viewpoint about both the steps taken by the school as well as the NGO? What value is shown by the NGO?

Sol. (*i*) AIDS (caused by HIV virus)

(*ii*) Three modes of transmission of this disease are:

(*a*) Blood transfusion

(*b*) Sexual contact with infected person

(*c*) Carrier mother to her fetus

(*iii*) School was wrong in its action as AIDS does not spread by casual contact.

The NGO on the other hand showed the value to fight against injustice.

2 Shashank and Vipul are two close friends, who spend most of their time together. Shashank observed that Vipul is behaving differently since last week. He gets tired and sits on the bench after playing for 5-10 minutes. Shashank asked Vipul if he was not feeling well. Vipul just looked at Shashank with his pale eyes and complained of nausea and vomiting. Shashank advised him to visit the doctor. Read the above passage and answer the following questions:

(*i*) Name the disease that is reflected in Vipul's situation?

(*ii*) Which causative organism is responsible for it?

(*iii*) Name two other disease caused by the same group of causative organisms as this disease.

(*iv*) Write any one characteristic feature of causeative organism of this group.

Sol. (*i*) Jaundice

(*ii*) Hepatitis virus

(*iii*) Jaundice is caused by the virus. Two other viral diseases are Rabies and Polio

(*iv*) Viruses do not have their own metabolic system, they depend on host cell machinery to reproduce.

Constructed Response (Descriptive) Questions

Very Short Answer Type Questions

1 Public cleanliness is considered more important for individual's health. Do you agree? Give reason.

Sol. Yes, public cleanliness is more important for individual's health because open drainage, garbage on street, stagnant water, etc are the places where disease causing microbes multiply and mosquitoes and flies breed. In this way, diseases may spread in community and hence, affect individual's health.

2 Give any four factors necessary for a healthy person. **NCERT Exemplar**

Or **List any four essential factors that must be taken care of by an individual for keeping good health.**

Sol. Four factors necessary for a healthy person are:

(*i*) Balanced diet

(*ii*) Clean surrounding environment

(*iii*) Social harmony

(*iv*) Good economic conditions

3 How is personal health and community health connected?

Sol. Personal health refers to the overall well-being of an individual whereas community health is the maintenance, protection and improvement of the whole community in which an individual lives. Human beings live in communities, interacting and affecting other individuals. Therefore, the health of the community becomes an important factor for maintaining individual's health.

4 Which disease is more harmful, acute or chronic disease? Why?

Sol. Chronic disease is more harmful as it lasts for a long time and causes drastic long term effects on human health, e.g. diabetes, TB, etc. On the contrary, acute disease lasts for a very short period of time, e.g. common cold, cough, etc.

5 Classify the following diseases as infectious and non-infectious: **NCERT Exemplar**

(*i*) AIDS (*ii*) Tuberculosis

(*iii*) Cholera (*iv*) High blood pressure

(*v*) Heart disease (*vi*) Pneumonia

(*vii*) Cancer

Sol.
- **Infectious diseases** AIDS, Tuberculosis, Cholera, Pneumonia.
- **Non-infectious diseases** High blood pressure, Heart disease, Cancer.

6 Which bacterium causes peptic ulcers? Who discovered the pathogen for the first time? NCERT Exemplar

Sol. Bacterium *Helicobactor pylori* causes peptic ulcers. Robin Warren and Barry Marshall discovered the pathogen for the first time.

7 Identify the microorganism and its type. Name the disease it causes and the means of its spread.

Sol. The given microorganism is *Trypanosoma*. It is a protozoan that causes sleeping sickness in humans.

It spreads through the bite of tse-tse fly.

8 Roshni visited her friend suffering from malaria. What are the chances of her contracting the disease?

Sol. Malaria does not spread by direct contact. It can only be transferred to healthy person by vectors like *Anopheles* mosquito. So, there are less chances of Roshni to contracting the disease.

9 Name two types of diseases caused by regularly breathing in the polluted air?

Sol. Pneumonia, tuberculosis, common cold, bronchitis (any two).

10 What is an antibiotic? Give two examples. NCERT Exemplar

Sol. An antibiotic is a biochemical compound produced by a microorganism, such as bacteria or fungi. It kills or blocks the growth of other microorganisms (pathogens) by blocking their life processes without harming human cells, e.g. penicillin, streptomycin, etc.

11 'Air, water, food and personal contact'– choose the odd one out with respect to hepatitis virus.

Sol. Air is the odd one. Rest are the medium through which hepatitis virus gets transmitted.

12 A lady suffering from AIDS is pregnant. What is the most likely route for the child to get the disease?

Sol. AIDS spreads through the exchange of body fluids. So, the virus from infected mother to child occurs through placenta.

13 Explain, why antibiotics do not work against viruses, but work against many groups of bacteria.

Or **Why are antibiotics not effective for viral diseases?** NCERT Exemplar

Sol. Antibiotics work against bacteria but not viruses because bacteria have specific structures like cell walls and ribosomes, which antibiotics target. Viruses, however, lack these structures and replicate inside host cells, making antibiotics ineffective. Viral infections require antiviral drugs instead of antibiotics.

14 Name

(*i*) A worm which is found in our small intestine.

(*ii*) Bacteria responsible for causing cholera.

Sol. (*i*) *Ascaris*

(*ii*) *Vibrio cholerae.*

15 Name the disease in which

(*i*) patient fears water

(*ii*) skin becomes yellowis.

Sol. (*i*) Rabies (*ii*) Hepatitis

16 Why does intake of penicillin not affect human cells?

Sol. Penicillin inhibits the formation of cell wall, which is present in bacteria but is absent in human cells. So, it does not affect human cells.

17 List the causative organisms for the following diseases.

(*i*) Kala-azar, (*ii*) Sleeping sickness,

(*iii*) Acne, (*iv*) AIDS

Sol. The causative organisms are:

(*i*) Protozoan (*Leishmania*) — Kala-azar

(*ii*) *Trypanosoma* — Sleeping sickness

(*iii*) Bacteria (*Staphylococci*) — Acne

(*iv*) HIV virus — AIDS

18 How do diseases spread through water?

Sol. Diseases spread through water when contaminated water containing pathogens is consumed or used for cooking. This occurs due to sewage contamination, poor sanitation, or unsafe drinking water. Waterborne diseases like cholera, typhoid and dysentery are caused by bacteria, viruses, or parasites present in polluted water.

19 Explain, what is organ specific manifestation?

Sol. Organ specific manifestation is the ability or adaptation of a microbe, to infect specific organ of an organism in a particular type of disease. For e.g., in case of TB, the infected organ is lung.

20 Write the symptoms and diseases associated with the following:

(*i*) When microbes attack the lungs

(*ii*) When the virus enters the liver

Sol. (*i*) When microbes attack the lungs, tuberculosis may occur. It is caused by bacterium *Mycobacterium tuberculosis*. Its symptoms are:

(*a*) Cough, chest pain and blood stained sputum.

(*b*) Prolonged low fever

(*ii*) When virus enters the liver, jaundice may occur, which is caused by hepatitis virus.

Its symptoms are:

(*a*) High fever and headache.

(*b*) Loss of appetite and dark yellow urine.

21 What is inflammation? Write the symptoms of this in human body.

Sol. **Inflammation** is the body's natural response to injury, infection, or harmful stimuli.

It helps in healing and protecting tissues from further damage.

Symptoms of inflammation Redness, swelling, pain, heat, and loss of function in the affected area.

22 Why does a person suffering from HIV-AIDS die, even due to small infection?

Sol. In case of HIV infection, the virus reaches the immune system and damages its functions. Due to this body will not be able to fight with even small infections like cold and may lead to death.

23 High fever, headache, nausea, vomiting and joint pains are some of the symptoms seen in a patient.

Which disease he might be suffering from? How does it spread?

Sol. The symptoms are pointing towards dengue disease. It spreads *via Aedes* mosquito.

24 A patient has been recommended to take Oral Rehydration Solution (ORS) multiple times a day. Which disease is he likely to be suffering from.

Sol. The patient must be suffering from diarrhoea.

25 Name any two groups of microorganisms from which antibiotics could be extracted? **NCERT Exemplar**

Sol. Two groups of microorganism from which antibiotics could be extracted are:

(*i*) Bacteria (*ii*) Fungi.

26 Name the scientist, who discovered smallpox vaccine. Give the basic principle of vaccination.

Sol. Edward Jenner discovered smallpox vaccine. Basic principle of vaccination is memory of pathogen retained by the cells of immune system.

27 How do children in many parts of India get immune to hepatitis-A by the time they are five years old?

Sol. Children in many parts of India are already immune to hepatitis-A by the time they are five years old because they are exposed to the virus through water.

28 Which part of the body is attacked by the bacteria causing tuberculosis? If they enter

(*i*) through the nose

(*ii*) through the mouth

Sol. (*i*) *Via* the nose-lungs.

(*ii*) Through the mouth-gut lining liver.

29 Why do some children fall ill more frequently than others living in the same locality? **NCERT Exemplar**

Sol. Children fall ill more frequently due to (*i*) poor personal hygiene; (*ii*) poor domestic hygiene; (*iii*) unclean food; (*iv*) lack of proper nutrition and balanced diet.

All these factors result in the weakening of the immune system. It makes these children more susceptible to disease.

30 Why is it that one is advised to avoid closed, crowded places like cinema halls during changing weather?

Sol. During changing weather, one is advised to avoid crowded places because changing seasons are the time when infectious agents are most prevalent. Closed crowded places provide the moist conditions that favour the fast growth of pathogen. Thus, chances of getting infection increase.

31 A virus enters the immune system of a patient and damages its function. Answer the following questions.

(*i*) Name the disease patient is suffering from.

(*ii*) Name the pathogen and two modes of transmission of this virus.

Sol. (*i*) AIDS (Acquired Immuno Deficiency Syndrome)

(*ii*) HIV (Human Immuno Deficiency Virus)

Two modes of transmission of AIDS are:

(*i*) Sexual contact

(*ii*) Blood transfusion

32 A mother, who had suffered from chickenpox in her childhood, is now taking care of her child, who is suffering from the same disease. What are the chances of the mother having chickenpox? Explain.

Sol. The chances of mother having chickenpox are nil because she has became immune to this disease. When the immune system first encounters an infectious microbe, it responds against it and then remembers it specifically. So, the next time when that particular microbe enters into the body, the immune system responds with greater vigour and eliminates infection more quickly. Thus, eliminating any chance of further infection.

Short Answer Type Questions

1 Becoming exposed to or infected with a microbe does not necessarily mean developing noticeable disease. Explain. NCERT Exemplar

Sol. Becoming exposed to or infected with a microbe does not necessarily lead to noticeable disease because an infectious microbe can cause illness only if the immune system fails to defend against it. Many individuals have a strong immune system or acquired immunity against the pathogen. In such cases, immune cells eliminate the microbe before it multiplies significantly. As a result, despite exposure to the infectious microbe, the person does not develop the disease.

2 What is a disease? How many types of diseases have you studied? Give examples. NCERT Exemplar

Sol. Disease refers to any condition that impairs normal functioning of the living organisms. It may be a response to environmental factors, specific infective agents or inherent defects of the organism only.

Types of diseases are as follows:

(i) **Acute or chronic** (on the basis of duration). Examples of acute diseases are common cold and cough. Examples of chronic diseases are diabetes and elephantiasis.

(ii) **Infectious** and **non-infectious** (on the basis of causative agent). Examples of infectious diseases are influenza and pneumonia. Examples of non-infectious diseases are cancer and diabetes.

3 What do you mean by disease symptoms? Explain by giving two examples? NCERT Exemplar

Or **What is symptom of a disease?**

Sol. Symptoms are the evidences or physical indications that point the presence of a disease. They are visible in the form of either structural or functional changes in our body or any of its parts. On the basis of these symptoms doctors search for definite clues or signs of a particular disease.

For example, symptoms for malaria and typhoid are same like fever, weakness, headache, etc. But signs for the disease are different as malaria fever manifests through chills and typhoid fever shows rashes, stomach pain, etc.

4 Give two examples for each of the following:

(*i*) Acute diseases

(*ii*) Chronic diseases

(*iii*) Infectious diseases

(*iv*) Non-infectious diseases NCERT Exemplar

Sol. (*i*) Acute diseases last for short period of time and do not cause long term effects, e.g. cold and cough.

(*ii*) Chronic diseases last for long period of time even for whole life and also cause long term effects on health, e.g. tuberculosis and arthritis.

(*iii*) Infectious diseases are caused by the attack of pathogens and can pass from one person to another, e.g. malaria and chickenpox.

(*iv*) Non-infectious diseases are caused by the factors other than living pathogens and are not transmitted from one person to other, e.g. diabetes and goitre.

5 A baby from a poor family is suffering from loose motions. Predict the first, second and third level cause of the disease in the given case.

Sol. As the baby suffering from loose motions, the **first** or the **immediate cause** is a virus. The virus could have come from unclean drinking water.

The baby suffered because he was not well-nourished and so the virus from water attacked his body system. Thus, lack of good nourishment becomes **second level cause**. The baby was not properly fed because he belongs to a poor family. Thus, poor public services providing unclean drinking water and poverty becomes the **third level cause** of the disease.

6 Construct a table showing category of agents which cause infection and one disease/ infection caused by each.

(*i*) Virus

(*ii*) Fungus

(*iii*) Bacteria

(*iv*) Protozoan

(*v*) Worm

State the importance of categorisation of infection causing agents.

Sol.

Disease Causing Agent	Disease/ Infection Caused
(*i*) Virus	AIDS
(*ii*) Fungus	Ringworm
(*iii*) Bacteria	Tuberculosis
(*iv*) Protozoa	Malaria
(*v*) Worm	Elephantiasis

Importance of categorisation of infection causing agents It helps to decide the kind of treatment to use because the same drug will not work against a microbe belonging to a different group.

7 Name any three diseases transmitted by vectors. NCERT Exemplar

Sol. Diseases caused by various vectors are as follows:

Insect Vector	Disease Transmitted
Mosquitoes	
(*i*) *Anopheles* (female)	Malaria
(*ii*) *Culex*	Filariasis
(*iii*) *Aedes*	Yellow fever, dengue
Flies	
(*i*) Housefly	Typhoid, diarrhoea, dysentery, cholera, tuberculosis and conjunctivitis (an eye disease).
(*ii*) Sandfly	Kala-azar
(*iii*) Tse-tse fly	Sleeping sickness.

8 List any three ways of preventing the spread of airborne diseases.

Sol. The measures of preventing airborne diseases include

(*i*) Avoiding direct contact with the infected persons.

(*ii*) Not sharing articles used by infected persons.

(*iii*) Use of mask/gloves/handkerchief.

9 Explain, how body reacts after the entry of microbes in the body.

Sol. When virus, bacteria or other microbes enter our body, they begin to multiply and cause infection. As a result of infection, the cells of our body get damaged and signs and symptoms of illness appear.

Our immune system comes into action in response to infection. It recruits many cells to affected tissue to kill off the disease causing microbes. This recruitment process is called inflammation. Due to the effect of this process swelling, pain and fever occur.

10 A person was bitten by a stray dog. After some days his nature gets irritated, he started fearing water.

(*i*) Name the disease.

(*ii*) Is there any vaccine available?

(*iii*) Is there any plan of your local authority for the control of this disease?

Sol. (*i*) Rabies is the disease which spreads by the bite of an infected stray dog.

(*ii*) Yes, a course of anti-rabies vaccine is available.

(*iii*) Yes, the local authority makes efforts to immunise all stray dogs.

11 A person is suffering from loss of appetite with feeling of nausea and is passing dark yellow urine. Identify the disease and suggest any two methods of preventing it and two methods of controlling it.

Sol. The person is suffering from jaundice.

Two methods for prevention are:

(*i*) Use chlorinated boiled water.

(*ii*) Hepatitis-A vaccine should be taken to prevent the disease.

Two methods for controlling are:

(*i*) Application of interferon injection on the advice of doctor will control the disease.

(*ii*) The patient should take high calorie diet such as juice of sugarcane, radish with jaggery.

12 Give cause and remedy of

(*i*) Hepatitis (*ii*) AIDS (*iii*) Malaria

Sol.

Disease	Cause and Remedy
(*i*) Hepatitis	▪ Hepatitis virus. ▪ Avoid stale food, Hepatitis-A and B vaccination.
(*ii*) AIDS	▪ HIV. ▪ Avoid used razors/needles /blades and sexual contact with unknown person.
(*iii*) Malaria	▪ *Plasmodium*. ▪ Hygienic conditions and not letting water stagnate for mosquito breeding, use mosquito repellant.

13 Given below are few situations:

(*i*) Geeta of class IX was having common cold. She sits with Sarika who also develops the disease.

(*ii*) Animesh of class IX shifted to a new residence, with his family, where water purification system has not been installed yet. He develops cholera and dysentery.

Associate these situations with their mode of transmission and assign appropriate category to them.

Sol. The mode of transmission in both the cases are

(*i*) through air (*ii*) through water

Both the cases are related to communicable diseases.

14 (*i*) What are vectors?

(*ii*) Which of these is an acute ailment and why? Tuberculosis, cancer, diarrhoea elephantiasis

(*iii*) When is a disease categorised as a communicable disease? Give example.

Sol. (*i*) Vectors or intermediates are animals that carry the infecting agents from a sick person to a healthy person.

Anopheles mosquito (for malaria), housefly (for typhoid), rat flea (for plague) are the examples of vectors.

(*ii*) Diarrhoea is an acute ailment as it is a short term disease and does not cause any persistent effects on person's health.

(*iii*) When the microbial agent causing a disease moves from an affected person to a healthy person through air, water or vector, it is categorised as a communicable disease, e.g. pneumonia, cholera.

15 Give an account of malaria, giving its causative agent, symptoms and control measures.

Sol. Malaria is caused by a protozoan *Plasmodium* and spreads by female *Anopheles* mosquito.
Symptoms of malaria are:
(*i*) High fever with specific pattern of cold, hot and sweating stage.
(*ii*) Severe bodyache (muscular pain).
The control measures of malaria include:
(*i*) Use insect repellent and mosquito net.
(*ii*) Cover open drain with kerosene oil.
(*iii*) Use prescribed dose of quinine to control the diseases.

16 With diagram only depict the common methods of transmission of diseases.

Sol. Refer to diagram on Pg 336.

17 (*i*) **If penicillin is given to a patient suffering from Jaundice, it does not have any effect on the infection. Why?**
(*ii*) **Name a disease which has been eradicated from the world.**
(*iii*) **State the principle behind its eradication.**

Sol. (*i*) Penicillin given to a patient suffering from jaundice will have no effect. Jaundice is caused by a virus.
(*ii*) Smallpox has been eradicated from the world.
(*iii*) The principle behind its eradication is immunisation.

18 Why is AIDS considered to be a 'syndrome' and not a disease? NCERT Exemplar

Sol. **Syndrome** is a group of symptoms, signs, physical and physiological disturbances that are due to a common cause.

AIDS is also a complex of diseases and symptoms. It develops due to the failure of body to fight against even minor infections, such as cold.

HIV that causes AIDS damages immune system of the patient.

As a result, even small cold leads to the development of pneumonia. A slight gut infection leads to severe diarrhoea and blood loss. Likewise, skin rashes develop into ulcers. Thus, it leads to a group of symptoms.

19 Why is immune system essential for our health? NCERT Exemplar

Sol. Immune system is body's defence system against various types of pathogens.

Immune system keeps the body healthy by killing infectious microbes, and remembers the microbe for better action against any subsequent encounters. It is also important as it decides on the severity of disease manifestations by determining the number of microbes surviving in the body.

20 Who discovered 'vaccine' for the first time? Name any two diseases which can be prevented by using vaccines. NCERT Exemplar

Sol. A 'vaccine' is a biological preparation that improves immunity to a particular disease.

An English physician Edward Jenner (1749-1823), made the first vaccine against smallpox using the microbes of cowpox, a similar, but less severe disease. The modern term 'vaccination' comes from the Latin words *Vacca* which means cow and *Vaccinia* meaning cowpox.

Diseases which can be prevented by vaccines are diphtheria, pertussis, tetanus and measles.

21 A person is suffering from chest pain, breathlessness, loss of body weight, persistent cough and produces blood stained sputum.
(*i*) **Name the disease and its causative agent.**
(*ii*) **Mention any mean of its transmission.**
(*iii*) **Name the vaccine used to prevent this disease.**

Sol. (*i*) The disease is Tuberculosis (TB) and its causative agent is *Mycobacterium tuberculosis.*
(*ii*) Inhaling infected droplets released by coughing, sneezing or talking to infected person.
(*iii*) Vaccine used to prevent this disease is BCG (Bacillus Calmette Guerin).

22 Name and give an example of each.
(*i*) **The disease causing factors within the body.**
(*ii*) **The non-cellular disease causing microorganism.**
(*iii*) **The substance introduced in body to confer immunity against subsequent infection.**

Sol. (*i*) **Intrinsic factors**, e.g. excessive weight, hormonal imbalance.
(*ii*) **Virus**, e.g. AIDS, influenza.
(*iii*) Weakened or killed antigens introduced through vaccination confer immunity against specific infections, e.g. polio vaccine.

23 Educating parents would help a lot in reducing the incidences of diseases in children. Justify the statement with five reasons.

Sol. (*i*) Educated parents understand the importance of healthy and balanced diet for the their children which will prevent nutritional deficiency disorders and will also help in the proper functioning of immune system.
(*ii*) They know about modes of spread of diseases so, will maintain hygienic conditions.
(*iii*) Parents will provide only safe uncontaminated water to avoid water-borne diseases.
(*iv*) Educated parents can provide symptomatic treatment first and then go for further doctor's consultation to kill the cause of the disease.

(*v*) Educated parents can educate a sense of social and moral responsibility in their children to maintain clean environment to prevent spread of infections.

Long Answer Type Questions

1. Explain by giving reasons. **NCERT Exemplar**

(*i*) Balanced diet is necessary for maintaining healthy body.

(*ii*) Health of an organism depends upon the surrounding environmental conditions.

(*iii*) Our surroundings should be free from stagnant water.

(*iv*) Social harmony and good economic conditions are necessary for good health.

Sol. (*i*) A balanced diet is the first and foremost condition necessary for good health. A balanced diet provides all the nutrients, e.g. proteins, carbohydrates, fats, vitamins and minerals required by the body in correct proportions. When our diet lacks one or more of these nutrients, we get deficiency diseases or nutritional disorders, e.g. if our diet lacks the mineral iron, we may get a disease called anaemia. Excessive or inadequate intake of food and nutrients leads to conditions such as obesity, kwashiorkor and rickets, e.g. vitamin-A causes hypervitaminosis-A and calcium causes rickets. A balanced diet prevents deficiency diseases. It also increases our ability to fight against infections in general.

(*ii*) Our health depends on the cleanliness of our surroundings. Flies and mosquitoes carry germs that cause diseases. Flies breed in rotting garbage and mosquitoes breed in pools of stagnant water. So, people fall ill quite often if the area in which they live or work has garbage, stagnant water or open drains.

Clean air is also a part of our surrounding and a basic requirement for good health.

(*iii*) This is so because many waterborne diseases causing insect vectors flourish in stagnant water, which cause diseases such as malaria, dengue, etc., in human beings.

(*iv*) Social harmony and good economic conditions are necessary for good health. Social harmony involves each other's participation in joys and sorrows, helping others, etc. If we mistreat each other, we cannot be happy or healthy. Proper earning is necessary to provide adequate and nutritious food and clean environment for living. Thus, good economic condition is also a necessary factor for good health.

2 Explain the following statements.

(*i*) Being disease-free is not the same as being healthy.

(*ii*) Community health is essential for good individual health.

(*iii*) Villagers suffer from cholera more than urban people.

Sol. (*i*) A person who is free from any disease may still be unhealthy due to poor nutrition, lack of physical fitness, mental stress, or an unhealthy lifestyle. Health is not just the absence of disease but a complete state of physical, mental and social well-being. For example, a person who does not have a disease but suffers from weakness, stress, or unhappiness cannot be considered truly healthy.

(*ii*) An individual lives in a society where factors like cleanliness, availability of clean water, proper waste disposal and disease control affect their well-being. Even if one person maintains hygiene, they can still get sick if their surroundings are polluted or if infectious diseases spread within the community. For example, if garbage is left in open areas, it can attract mosquitoes and cause diseases like malaria or dengue, affecting many people in the area. Therefore, a healthy community ensures better health for individuals.

(*iii*) In villages, people often defecate in open and the water is also taken from handpumps, etc., for use. This increases the chances of water getting contaminated. As cholera is transmitted by water, the villagers are more likely to suffer from the disease.

3 (*i*) Name two airborne diseases. How does the disease causing microbes spread through air?

(*ii*) How does HIV virus spread from a patient to a healthy person?

(*iii*) How does the immune system of our body works?

Sol. (*i*) Pneumonia and common cold are two airborne diseases. Spreading of disease-causing microbes occurs through the little droplets thrown out by an infected person, when he sneezes or coughs. Someone standing close by can breathe in these droplets and microbes get a chance to start new infection.

(*ii*) Refer to theory on Pg 336.

(*iii*) The immune system protects the body by identifying and fighting harmful microbes like bacteria and viruses. It detects these invaders and activates white blood celis to destroy them. The immune system also produces antibodies that help in neutralizing pathogens and preventing future infections. Once the body fights off an infection, it remembers the microbe, providing long-term protection. This defence mechanism helps keep us healthy by preventing and controlling diseases.

4 Mr. Iyer had cold and throat infection. Doctor prescribed an antibiotic.

(*i*) Which pathogen could have caused the infection?

(*ii*) What is the mode of action of antibiotics? Mr. Iyer recovered from cold but he still had throat infection. Would the doctor continue the antibiotic further? State yes or no giving reason.

Sol. (*i*) Cold is commonly caused by a virus while soar throat can be due to bacterial infection or allergy.

(*ii*) Antibiotics act on bacteria and kill them by inhibiting their metabolic reactions (e.g. cell wall formation, ribosome functioning, etc.).
Yes, the doctor can continue the antibiotics for 3-4 days more because bacterial sore throat takes about 10 days to heal.

5 (*i*) State two examples of viral diseases.

(*ii*) After an injury, an injection is given immediately. What is it and why is it given?

(*iii*) What type of food is advised when we fall sick and why?

Sol. (*i*) AIDS and dengue fever.

(*ii*) The injection is of anti-tetanus serum. It is given immediately after injury because the bacteria that cause tetanus enter the body through a cut or wound in the skin. So, to avoid its infection, the injection is given immediately.

(*iii*) Bland and nourishing food is advised during sickness because such food is easily digestible, provides sufficient energy and nutrients for the regeneration of cells and tissues.

6. Explain the statement by giving two examples: 'It is not necessary that the pathogen may affect an organ or tissue depending upon the point of entry.'

Sol. The pathogen does not necessarily affect an organ or tissue depending on the point of entry. It may invade the body at the easiest accessible route and then makes it's way to the target organ/tissue. The examples of such instances are:

(*i*) **AIDS causing virus** enters through sexual contact but spreads to lymph nodes all over the body.

(*ii*) **Japanese encephalitis** virus enters blood through mosquito bite but reaches brain.

(*iii*) **Malaria** protozoan *Plasmodium* enters blood through mosquito bite but reaches liver and then passes into the RBC. (Any two) (5)

7 What precautions will you take to justify 'prevention is better than cure'? NCERT Exemplar

Or **How can you justify the statement prevention of diseases is better than cure?**

Sol. The statement "Prevention is better than cure" emphasizes that it is always better to avoid diseases rather than treating them after they occur. Preventing a disease reduces suffering, saves time and money, and protects overall health. Simple measures like maintaining personal hygiene, eating a nutritious diet, getting vaccinated, drinking clean water and ensuring proper sanitation can help prevent many illnesses.

On the other hand, once a person falls sick, treatment may involve medications, hospital visits and even long recovery periods. Some diseases, like diabetes, heart disease, or severe infections, can lead to long-term complications, making prevention even more important.

Additionally, prevention benefits not just individuals but also the entire community. For example, vaccination programs help control the spread of infectious diseases like polio and measles, protecting both individuals and society. Therefore, focusing on preventive healthcare ensures a healthier and safer life for everyone.

8 What are the causes and symptoms of malaria? How can it be prevented and controlled?

Sol. Malaria is caused by the protozoan parasite *Plasmodium*. This disease spreads through the bite of an insect vector, i.e. the female *Anopheles* mosquito, which feeds on human blood.

Its symptoms are:

(*i*) Fever, headache, nausea and muscular pain.

(*ii*) Each malarial attack lasts for 6-10 h duration and consists of the three stages. These three stages are

(*a*) **Cold stage** Feeling extreme cold and shivers.

(*b*) **Hot stage** High fever, fast respiration and heartbeats are increased.

(*c*) **Sweating stage** Profuse sweating occurs, leading to a drop in body temperature and relief from fever.

The only way to prevent malaria is to take precaution against mosquito bites. We can protect ourselves from bite of mosquitoes by the following methods

(*i*) Mosquito repellent should be used to prevent mosquito bite.

(*ii*) Mosquito larvae can be killed by sprinkling kerosene oil in open drainage, water coolers or any uncovered waterbodies. Adult mosquitoes can be killed by spraying insecticides, e.g. BHC, malathion.

(*iii*) One should sleep under mosquito nets.

(*iv*) Wire-gauze should be used on doors and windows of houses to prevent entry of mosquitoes.

9 Fill in the table with appropriate term

Disease	Microbe	Target Organ	Mode of Transmission
Meningitis	Virus	__(i)__	Faecal contamination
Hepatitis	__(ii)__	__(iii)__	Contaminated water
__(iv)__	Bacteria	Lungs	__(v)__
Ringworm	Fungus	__(vi)__	Indirect contact
__(vii)__	Virus	Lungs	__(viii)__
Dengue fever	__(ix)__	Whole body	__(x)__

Sol. (*i*) Brain

(*ii*) Virus

(*iii*) Liver

(*iv*) Tuberculosis

(*v*) Air contaminated by droplets of cough, sneeze, etc.

(*vi*) Skin

(*vii*) Influenza

(*viii*) Contact and droplet infection.

(*ix*) Virus

(*x*) Vector mediated transmission, i.e. the bite of *Aedes* mosquito. (½ × 10)

10 About a hundred years ago, when smallpox persisted, a group of people who had this disease earlier and had survived it had no chance of suffering from it again. So having the disease once was a means of preventing subsequent attacks of the same disease.

(*i*) Why does this happen? Explain.

(*ii*) We can 'fool' the immune system. Clarify.

(*iii*) Name this principle of prevention of diseases.

Sol. (i) When a person gets infected with smallpox, their immune system produces memory cells that recognize and destroy the virus if it enters the body again. This provides long-term immunity, preventing reinfection.

(ii) We can 'fool' the immune system. Vaccination mimics an actual infection by introducing a weakened or inactive form of the pathogen. This stimulates the immune system to produce memory cells without causing the disease, preparing the body for future attacks.

(iii) This principle is called immunization or vaccination.

11 A person is suffering from watery diarrhoea, effortless vomiting without nausea and loss of several litres of fluid takes place within hours.

(*i*) Name the disease and its causal organism.

(*ii*) Suggest some preventive measures to avoid this disease.

(*iii*) Can the spread of this disease be controlled? If yes, how?

Sol. (*i*) The person is suffering from cholera and it is caused by bacterium *Vibrio cholerae.*

(*ii*) Preventive measures to avoid this disease are:

(*a*) Boiled water and cooked food should be taken in cholera prone areas. Good personal hygiene and proper sanitation in the community is necessary for protection against cholera.

(*b*) People should be immunised by cholera vaccine. One dose of immunisation lasts for about six months.

(*iii*) Control measures for this disease are:

(*a*) For prevention, dehydration therapy with ORS (Oral Rehydration Solution) should be done.

(*b*) Antibiotics such as tetracycline kills the bacteria of cholera.

ASSESSMENT EXERCISE

Competency Focused (Objective) Questions

Multiple Choice Questions

1 Choose the odd one out from the list of diseases given below w.r.t their causative agent.
(a) Measles (b) Rabies
(c) Smallpox (d) Pneumonia

2 Warren and Marshall discovered
(a) *Helicobacter* which causes peptic ulcers
(b) Typhoid causing bacteria
(c) *Trypanosoma* which causes sleeping sickness
(d) DPT a triple vaccine

3 Among the options given below, a non-infectious disease is
(a) tuberculosis (b) cancer
(c) pneumonia (d) cholera

4 Making anti-viral drugs is more difficult than making anti-bacterial medicines because:
(a) viruses make use of host machinery
(b) viruses are on the border line of living and non-living
(c) viruses have very few biochemical mechanisms of their own
(d) viruses have a protein coat

5 Complete the analogy given below and choose the correct option.
Typhoid: Bacterial disease: Polio: ....
(a) Protozoan
(b) Bacterial disease
(c) Viral disease
(d) Worm disease

6 Which of the following infectious agents is listed in "Emerging Infectious Diseases", a journal of CDC, U.S.?
(a) *Leishmania*
(b) *Staphylococci*
(c) *Ascaris*
(d) SARS virus

Assertion-Reason Questions

Direction (Q.Nos. 7-9) *In each of the following questions, a statement of Assertion (A) is given by the corresponding statement of Reason (R). Of the statements, mark the correct answer as*
(a) Both A and R are true and R is the correct explanation of A.
(b) Both A and R are true, but R is not the correct explanation of A
(c) A is true, but R is false
(d) A is false, but R is true

7 Assertion (A) Practicing both personal and public hygiene is essential for preventing diseases and promoting good health.
Reason (R) Good health can be maintained by following personal hygiene practices and ensuring a clean and safe environment at the public level.

8 Assertion (A) Non-communicable diseases can be transmitted from one person to another.
Reason (R) These diseases are mainly caused by lifestyle factors like diet, exercise and smoking.

9 Assertion (A) Tuberculosis (TB) can be spread through the air when an infected person coughs or sneezes.
Reason (R) Tuberculosis (TB) is caused by a virus that weakens the immune system.

Answers

1. (d)	**2.** (a)	**3.** (b)	**4.** (c)	**5.** (c)
6. (d)	**7.** (b)	**8.** (d)	**9.** (c)	

Case Based/Source Based Questions

Observe the diagram given below and answer the following questions.

10 What is the common cause of the disease shown in the diagram?

11 Given two preventive measures for this disease.

12 What are the carriers of this disease?

Very Short Answer Type Questions

13 State any two causes of a non-infectious disease.

14 What are carriers in communicable diseases? How do they transmit diseases?

15 Name the disease caused by contaminated food and water.

16 Give reason, why our surroundings should be free from stagnant water.

17 Write down the modes of transmission of tuberculosis.

18 Discuss a few strategies that can be used as preventive measures to reduce the occurrence of any infectious disease.

Short Answer Type Questions

19 Give an account of diseases caused by viruses.

20 Is prevention of disease more desirable than its successful treatment? Explain.

21 Explain, how antibiotics are able to check growth of microbes in diseases that are caused by bacteria?

22 Why are you more likely to suffer from an infection when you travel through public transport?

Long Answer Type Questions

23 Describe community issues that influence health.

24 What principles should be taken in account for the prevention of diseases?

25 Tuberculosis is a highly infectious disease. Justify. Also comment on its prevention and treatment.

26 Explain in detail about vaccination

EXPERIMENT 1

Experiment 1 (a)

Objective To prepare a true solution of common salt, sugar and alum.

Materials Required Powdered samples of **common** salt (sodium chloride. i.e. NaCl), sugar (sucrose, $C_{12}H_{22}O_{11}$), alum (potassium aluminium sulphate, $KAl(SO_4)_2 \cdot 12H_2O$, distilled water, test tubes (3), pipette, test tube stand and spatula.

Theory A true solution is obtained when a low molecular mass, soluble substance is dissolved in any solvent.

Procedure

(*i*) Take three clean test tubes. Label these as *A*, *B* and *C* respectively. Place the test tubes on a stand.

(*ii*) Pour 10 mL of distilled water in each of the test tubes *A*, *B* and *C*, with the help of a pipette.

(*iii*) Add about 0.5 g of common salt in test tube *A*, 0.5 g of sugar in test tube *B* and 0.5 g of alum in test tube *C*, with the help of a spatula.

(*iv*) Hold the test tubes one-by-one in your right hand and shake the contents of each tube.

(*v*) Label each test tube with the name of the solution viz, Common salt + Water in test tube *A*

Sugar + Water in test tube *B*

Alum + Water in test tube *C*

(*vi*) The process of preparing a true solution of common salt and water is shown below:

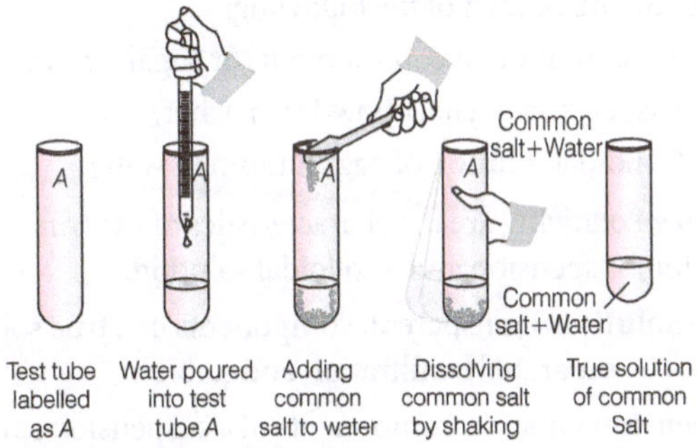

Process of preparing a true solution

Results/Conclusion

(*i*) The solution in test tube *A* is a true solution of common salt.

(*ii*) The solution in test tube *B* is a true solution of sugar.

(*iii*) The solution in test tube *C* is a true solution of alum.

Precautions

(*i*) Use powdered sample of the given substance because it dissolves faster than the big crystals/lumps.

(*ii*) Do not take more than 1 g of substance for making a true solution.

(*iii*) Shake the contents thoroughly.

(*iv*) Clean the spatula every time before use.

Experiment 1 (b)

Objective To prepare a suspension of soil, chalk powder and fine sand in water.

Materials Required Small samples of soil, powdered chalk, fine sand, test tubes (3), pipette, test tube stand, spatula and distilled water.

Theory A suspension can be prepared by shaking vigorously a finely powdered and insoluble substance in water.

Procedure

(*i*) Take three clean test tubes. Label them as *A* (soil + water), *B* (chalk powder + water) and *C* (fine sand + water).

(*ii*) Place these test tubes on the test tube stand.

(*iii*) Pour about 10 mL of distilled water in each of these test tubes with the help of a pipette.

(*iv*) Add about 0.5 g of soil in test tube *A*, 0.5 g of powdered chalk in test tube *B* and 0.5 g of fine sand in test tube *C*, with the help of a spatula. Clean the spatula every time before use.

(*v*) Hold the test tubes one-by-one in your right hand and shake the contents of each test tube.

(*vi*) Place these test tubes on the test tube stand.

(*vii*) The process of preparing a suspension of soil in water is shown below

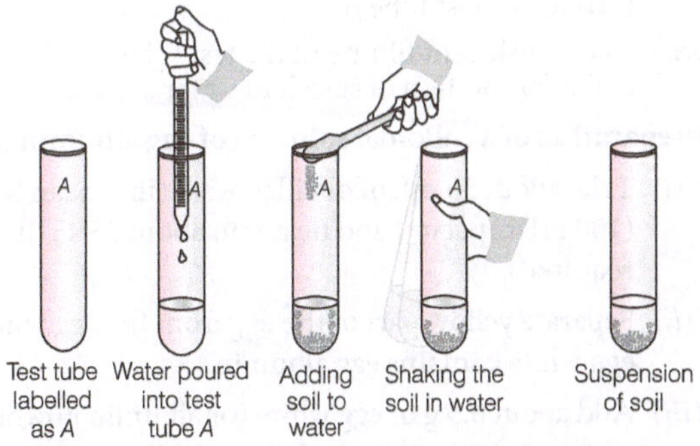

Process of preparing a suspension

Result/Conclusion

(*i*) Test tube *A* contains the suspension of soil in water.

(*ii*) Test tube *B* contains the suspension of chalk in water.

(*iii*) Test tube *C* contains the suspension of fine sand in water.

Precautions

(*i*) While measuring a certain volume of solvent, such as water, read the lower meniscus.

(*ii*) The substance whose suspension in water is to be prepared must be sieved to remove larger particles.

Experiment 1 (c)

Objective To prepare a colloidal solution of

(*i*) starch in water and (*ii*) egg albumin/milk in water.

Materials Required Beakers (100 mL capacity) (2), test tubes (2), glass rod (2), water bath, Bunsen burner, thermometer, funnel, filter paper, starch powder, egg albumin powder (or an egg) and distilled water.

Theory A material can be brought into colloidal state by dispersion method. In simple dispersion method, the bulk material is shaken vigorously with the solvent.

Procedure

I. **Preparation of colloidal solution of starch in water**

(*i*) Take three clean test tubes. Label them as *A*, *B* and *C* respectively. Place the test tubes on a stand.

(*ii*) Pour about 50 mL of distilled water in a clean beaker (100 mL capacity) and heat it to about to 50°C.

(*iii*) Take about 0.5 g of starch powder in test tube *A* and add a little water to make a thin paste like slurry.

(*iv*) Pour the starch slurry into hot water (in beaker) and stir it vigorously with a glass rod.

(*v*) Continue heating and stirring the contents of the beaker for about 10 min.

(*vi*) Allow it to cool at room temperature.

(*vii*) Filter the colloidal solution of starch in water to remove any suspended particles/lump and collect the filtrate in a test tube *B*.

(*viii*) The translucent filtrate in the test tube *B* is the colloidal solution of starch in water.

II. **Preparation of a colloidal solution of egg albumin in water**

(*i*) Take about 30 mL of distilled water in a clean beaker (100 mL capacity) and heat it to about 35°C (if required).

(*ii*) Separate yellow part of the egg from the egg white. The egg white contains egg albumin.

(*iii*) Add about 0.5 g of egg white (or albumin powder) which is obtained by drying egg white to water in the beaker and stir it vigorously for about 1 min with the help of a glass rod.

(*iv*) Add another 0.5 g of egg albumin to the solution in the beaker and stir it vigorously for another 1 min.

(*v*) Filter the turbid solution and collect the filtrate in a clean test tube *C*/beaker.

(*vi*) This translucent/turbid solution is the colloidal solution of egg albumin in water.

(*vii*) Same procedures can be used for the preparation of calloidal solution of milk.

Result/Conclusion

(*i*) Egg albumin is the major protein constituent of white egg.

(*ii*) Commercially, available egg albumin should be stored at 2-8°C.

Precautions

(*i*) While adding starch slurry into warm water, stirring must be continued.

(*ii*) Dry starch should never be added to warm water to prevent lump formation.

(*iii*) While preparing the colloidal solution of egg albumin, temperature of water should be controlled (≈ 35°C) properly.

(*iv*) Use a separate glass rod for stirring the contents of the different beakers.

Experiment 1(d)

Objective To distinguish between a true solution, a suspension and a colloidal solution on the basis of

(*i*) transparency (*ii*) filtration criterion

(*iii*) stability

Materials Required Test tubes (3), boiling tubes (3), beakers (100 mL capacity), test tube stand , funnels (3) and filter papers.

About 30 mL of each of the following:

(*i*) True solution of common salt (or sugar) in water.

(*ii*) Suspension of chalk powder in water.

(*iii*) Colloidal solution of egg albumin in water.

Theory Following are the characteristics of the true solution, suspension and a colloidal solution.

True Solution Transparent, components of a true solution cannot be separated by filtration and stable.

Suspension Opaque, components of a suspension can be separated by filtration and unstable.

Colloidal Solution Translucent, component of a colloidal solution cannot be separated by filtration and stable.

Procedure

(*i*) Take three test tubes and label them as *A*, *B* and *C*.

(*ii*) Mark each test tubes in the lower half with a sign of cross (X).

(*iii*) Place these test tubes on a test tube stand such that the mark (X) is on your opposite side.

(*iv*) Perform the experiments and record your observations and conclusions/inferences in the tabular form.

Property	Experiment	Observation	Inference
Transparency	Fill half of the test tube *A* with common salt solution.	The mark (×) is clearly visible when seen through the test tube *A*.	The common salt solution is transparent.
	Fill half of the test tube *B* with the suspension of chalk.	The mark (×) is not visible when seen through the test tube *B*.	The suspension of chalk is opaque.
	Fill half of the test tube *C* with colloidal solution of egg albumin.	The mark (×) is faintly visible when seen through the test tube *C*.	The colloidal solution of egg albumin is translucent.
Filtration criterion	Filter the contents of each test tube separately through a filter paper and collect the filtrate in a boiling tube. (Observe the filtrate and the residue left on the filter paper, if any).	In the case of test tube *A*, a clear filtrate is obtained and no residue is left on the filter paper.	Common salt cannot be separated from its solution in water by filtration.
		In the case of test tube *B*, a clear filtrate is obtained and some residue (chalk powder) is left on the filter paper.	Chalk powder can be separated from its suspension in water by filtration.
		In the case of test tube *C*, a translucent filtrate is obtained and no residue is left on the filter paper.	Egg albumin cannot be separated from its colloidal solution in water by filtration.
Stability	Pour about 10 mL of the true solution of common salt in water into test tube *A* and leave the test tube undisturbed for 5 minutes.	The solute particles in test tube *A* do not settle down.	The solution of common salt in water is stable.
	Pour about 10 mL of the suspension of chalk powder in water into test tube *B* and leave for 5 minutes.	Bigger particles tend to settle down at the bottom of test tube *B*.	The suspension of chalk in water is unstable.
	Pour about 10 mL of the colloidal solution of egg albumin in water into test tube *C* and leave the content undisturbed for 5 minutes.	The contents of test tube *C* remain unchanged and no solid particles settle down.	The colloidal solution of egg albumin in water is stable.
	Pour about 10 mL of the colloidal solution of egg albumin into test tube *C*.	The contents of test tube *C* remain unchanged and no solid particles settle down.	The colloidal solution of egg albumin in water is stable.

Leave these test tubes on a test tube stand undisturbed for about 5 min, and note your observations and inference.

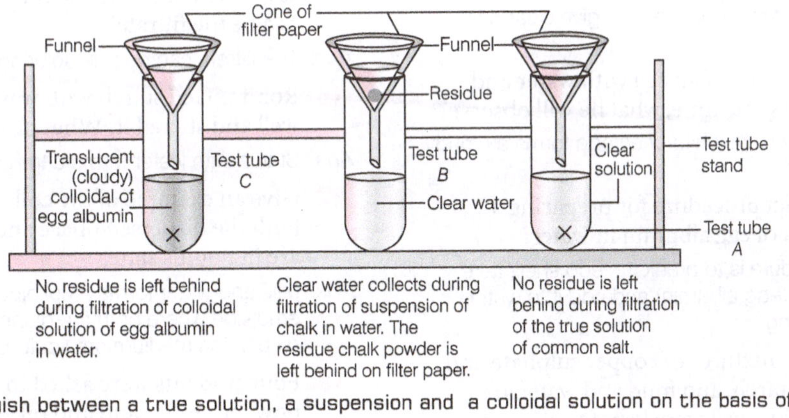

To distinguish between a true solution, a suspension and a colloidal solution on the basis of filtration

Result/Conclusion

(*i*) Common salt solution is transparent, stable and its components cannot be separated by filtration.

(*ii*) The suspension of chalk in water is opaque, unstable and its components can be separated by simple filtration.

(*iii*) The colloidal solution of egg albumin in water is translucent, stable and its components cannot be separated by simple filtration.

QUESTIONS

1. **Give an example of suspension.**

Ans. Copper sulphate in water is a suspension.

2. **Give an example where tyndall effect can be observed?**

Ans. Tyndall effect is observed in colloidal solution. It can be seen in starch and water solution as it is a colloidal solution.

3. **If sugar is dissolved in water, which type mixture would be the resulting solution appears?**

Ans. It will appear as a homogeneous mixture.

4. **Three students Avani, Sudesh and Hari were given funnels, filter paper, test tubes, test tube stands, common salt, chalk powder and starch. They prepared true solution, suspension and colloidal solution. Test tubes were arranged as shown in the figure.**

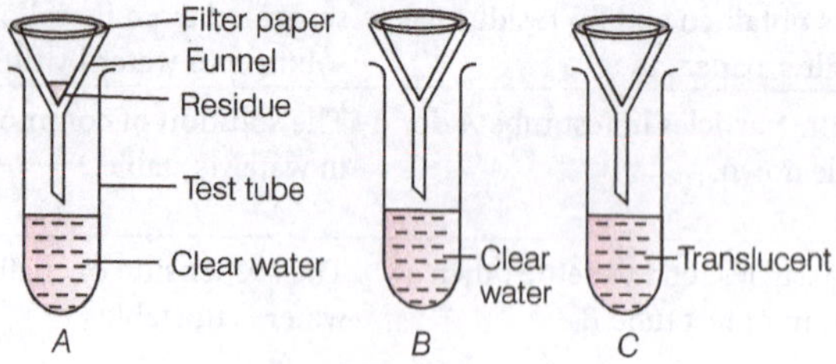

What conclusion they will draw from the above figure?

Ans. *A* is suspension, *B* is true solution and *C* is colloid.

5. **Four students prepared mixtures in water by taking sodium chloride, sand, chalk powder and starch respectively, in four different test tubes. After stirring the mixture, in which solution mixture will appear clear and transparent?**

Ans. Sodium chloride dissolves in water to give clear and transparent solution.

6. **A student mixes white of an egg with water and stirs it well. After some time, what he will observe?**

Ans. Student will observe that white of an egg forms a cloudy solution with water.

7. **What is the correct procedure for preparing a colloidal solution of egg albumin in water?**

Ans. The correct procedure is to break the egg shell, take only white portion (egg albumin) and add it to water with constant stirring.

8. **Three unlabelled mixtures of copper sulphate and water, milk and starch, and mud and water are taken. After stirring well were kept for observation and a student was asked to identify. Which solution mixture is opaque translucent and transpaternt, respectively?**

Ans. Copper sulphate and water forms a transparent solution. Milk and starch with water forms a translucent solution and mud with water forms a opaque solution.

9. **What would be the first step to prepare a colloidal solution of starch?**

Ans. To prepare a colloidal solution of starch, one should first add a thin paste of starch powder to boiling water and stir.

10. **What is the particle size of suspension?**

Ans. Suspensions have particles greater than 100 nm (10^{-7} m).

11. **If common salt is added to the unsaturated solution of water and common salt. What will happen?**

Ans. If common salt is added to the unsaturated solution of water and common salt, the solution will remain a true solution.

12. **In an experiment to separate the components of a mixture of sand, common salt and ammonium chloride dissolved in water. Which component will be removed by filtration?**

Ans. Sand dissolved in water is removed by filtration.

13. **How can a suspension of chalk in water be prepared?**

Ans. A suspension of chalk in water can be prepared by placing powdered chalk in water and shaking it vigorously.

14. **Among which of the following is most stable? True solution, colloidal, suspension**

Ans. True solution is transparent, stable and its components cannot be separated by filtration.

15. **A student was asked to prepare a true solution of sugar in water. By chance, he added sugar in excess. He stirred the solution for quite some time but some sugar settled down. He filtered the contents. What can be the filtrate?**

Ans. The filtrate can be true solution or colloidal solution.

16. **Rohit mixed starch with water, boiled the mixture well and stirred it. What he observed?**

Ans. Starch with water forms a translucent solution.

17. **Give an example of the colloidal solution where both the dispersed phase and the dispersion medium are in liquids state.**

Ans. Milk and water forms a colloidal solution also known as emulsion where both the dispersed phase and the dispersion medium are liquids.

18. **Four students were asked to add water to chalk powder, milk, sand and oil. They were asked in which sample there was no suspension when added to water?**

Ans. Milk and oil in water form emulsion. Chalk powder and sand in water form suspension.

EXPERIMENT 2

Objective To prepare

(*i*) a mixture and (*ii*) a compound

using iron filings and sulphur powder and distinguish between these on the basis of

(*a*) appearance, i.e. homogeneity and heterogeneity.

(*b*) behaviour towards a magnet.

(*c*) behaviour towards carbon disulphide as a solvent.

(*d*) effect of heat.

Materials Required China dish, petri dish, pestle-mortar, watch glass, test tubes, glass rod, Bunsen burner, magnifying glass, bar magnet, funnel, filter paper, iron filings (10 g), sulphur (5 g), carbon disulphide (5 mL), dilute hydrochloric acid or dilute sulphuric acid.

Theory A mixture is obtained by mixing two or more substances in any proportion. A compound is obtained by the chemical combination of two or more elements in a fixed ratio. Mixtures and compounds differ in their appearance, composition, properties such as behaviour towards magnet, solubility and reaction with dilute acids. The constituents of a compound cannot be separated by physical processes, whereas the constituents of a mixture can be separated by physical means.

Procedure

I. Preparation of a mixture of iron filings and sulphur powder

Take a small amount of fine iron filings and sulphur in a pestle and mortar. Grind them thoroughly. The powder so obtained is a mixture of iron and sulphur. Keep it aside in a petri dish.

II. Preparation of the compound of iron filings and sulphur powder

Take 5.6 g of iron filings and 3.2 g of sulphur in a pestle and mortar. Grind the two components together. Transfer this mixture to a China dish. Heat the China dish on a low flame until the reaction starts. Continue stirring while heating the reaction mixture.

$$\underset{\text{Iron}}{Fe\,(s)} + \underset{\text{Sulphur}}{S\,(s)} \xrightarrow{\text{Heat}} \underset{\substack{\text{Iron sulphide} \\ [\text{Fe(II) sulphide}]}}{FeS}$$

When the reaction is over and the whole mass in the China dish turns black, stop heating. Allow it to cool to room temperature. Grind the solid black mass in a clean pestle and mortar to a fine powder. Keep it aside in a petri dish.

III. To distinguish between the mixture and compound containing iron and sulphur

Perform the following experiments and record your observations and inferences in tabular form.

S.No.	Test/Property	Experiment	Observations	Inference
1.	Appearance (Homogeneity and heterogeneity)	Take a small quantity of the mixture prepared on a watch glass. Observe it first with the naked eye and then with a magnifying glass.	Particles of iron and sulphur are seen clearly even with the naked eye.	The mixture is heterogeneous. 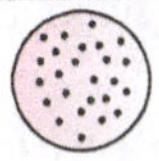 Sulphur and iron particles are seen clearly.
		Take a small quantity of the compound of iron and sulphur on a watch glass. Observe it first with the naked eye and then with a magnifying glass.	The whole mass appears uniform in colour.	The compound is homogeneous. 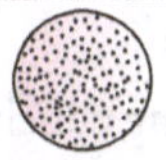 All particles of the compound are black in colour and uniformly distributed.
2.	Behaviour towards a magnet	Move a bar magnet over the prepared mixture of iron and sulphur.	Iron particles get attracted towards the magnet and sulphur is left behind.	The components of a mixture can be separated by simple physical methods. 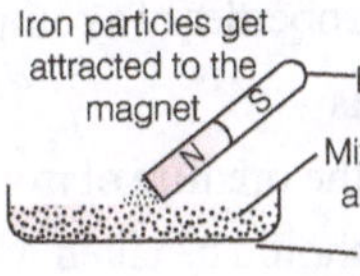

S.No.	Test/Property	Experiment	Observations	Inference
		Move a bar magnet over the prepared compound of iron and sulphur.	The black coloured particles of the compound do not get attracted by the magnet.	The components forming a compound cannot be separated by a magnet. 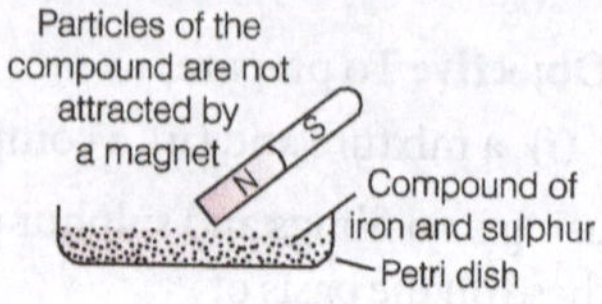
3.	Behaviour towards carbon disulphide	Take a little mixture of iron and sulphur in a test tube. Add 1-2 mL of carbon disulphide. Shake well and filter. Collect the filtrate in a China dish. Let carbon disulphide evaporate.	Carbon disulphide dissolves sulphur and iron particles are left on filter paper. Yellow sulphur crystals can be seen in the China dish after carbon disulphide has evaporated.	In a mixture, each component retains its own properties. Sulphur is soluble in carbon disulphide but iron does not.
		Take a small quantity of the compound of iron and sulphur in a test tube. Add 1-2 mL of carbon disulphide to it and shake well.	The compound of iron and sulphur does not dissolve in carbon disulphide.	In a compound, the constituents lose their characteristic properties and the compound shows altogether different properties.
4.	Effect of heat	Take a small quantity of the prepared mixture in a test tube and heat it.	At higher temperature, iron and sulphur react to form a black substance which does not show the properties of iron and sulphur.	The components of the mixture, iron and sulphur react on heating to give a compound called iron sulphide.
		Take a small quantity of the prepared compound in a test tube and heat it.	No reaction occurs. The substance, on strong heating starts glowing and on cooling, it returns to its original colour.	The compound iron sulphide remains chemically unchanged on heating.
5.	Reaction with dilute sulphuric acid [$H_2SO_4(aq)$]	Take a small quantity of the mixture in a test tube. Add 1-2 mL of dil. H_2SO_4 and heat it.	Bubbles of a colourless and odourless gas are evolved. The gas burns with a blue flame with a pop sound. Yellow powder (sulphur) remains unreacted.	Iron reacts with dil. H_2SO_4 to give hydrogen gas. $2Fe(s) + 3H_2SO_4(aq) \longrightarrow Fe_2(SO_4)_3(aq) + 3H_2(g)$

Conclusion

The following conclusions can be drawn from the experiments performed

(i) A mixture can be obtained by just mixing/ grinding the various components together in any ratio.

(ii) A chemical compound is formed only when the required components react chemically with each other.

(iii) Each component of a mixture retains its properties in a mixture.

(iv) The properties of a compound are altogether different from the properties of its constituents.

Precautions

(i) Heat the mixture of iron and sulphur in hard glass test tubes only.

(ii) Care should be taken while heating iron and sulphur.

(iii) Carbon disulphide is inflammable, so keep it away from the flame.

(iv) Do not inhale gases evolved directly.

QUESTIONS

1. **Aqueous solutions of zinc sulphate and iron sulphate were taken in test tubes I and II by Mr. Bean. Metal pieces of iron and zinc were dropped in the two solutions. After several hours what observation would be recorded by Mr. Bean?**

Ans. The observation recorded by Mr. Bean

$$Fe + ZnSO_4 \longrightarrow \text{No reaction}$$

It is because iron is less reactive than zinc.

$$\underset{\text{Zinc}}{Zn} + \underset{\text{Green solution}}{FeSO_4} \longrightarrow \underset{\text{Colourless solution}}{ZnSO_4} + \underset{\text{Black}}{Fe}$$

The solution becomes colourless and black iron gets deposited.

2. **In an experiment, carbon disulphide was added to a test tube containing a mixture of iron filings and sulphur powder. Draw the correct figure for this observation.**

Ans. Carbon disulphide dissolves sulphur and iron filings remain in the solution.

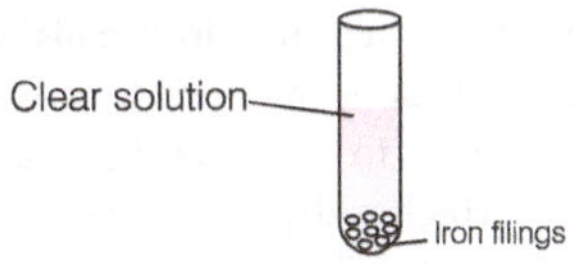

3. **Iron sulphide and a mixture of iron filings and sulphur powder were taken in different China dishes. Which of the following mixtures is heterogeneous and homogeneous?**

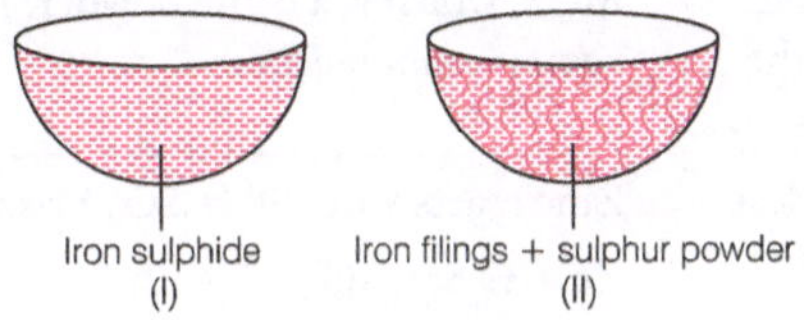

Ans. Iron sulphide is homogeneous but the mixture of iron filings and sulphur is heterogeneous.

4. **Rama heated a mixture of iron filings and sulphur in a hard glass test tube for some time till a grey-black product was formed. He cooled the test tube and then added 2 mL of carbon disulphide in it and stirred the contents of the test tube. In this experiment, what observation had he made?**

Ans. The compound of iron and sulphur, i.e. iron sulphide (FeS) does not dissolve in carbon disulphide.

5. **A student takes a substance *A*, which is attracted by a magnet and reacts with acids. He takes another substance *B*, which dissolves in carbon disulphide. He heats *A* and *B* together in a test tube to form product *AB*. What is the substances *A* and *B* and the product *AB* are respectively**

Ans. Iron filings (*A*) are attracted towards a bar magnet and reacts with dilute hydrochloric acid or dilute sulphuric acid to liberate hydrogen. Sulphur (*B*) is soluble in carbon disulphide. Iron filings and sulphur powder react to form iron sulphide (*AB*) which is black in colour.

6. **China dish *A* contains mixture of iron filings and sulphur powder. In China dish *B*, same portion of the mixture is heated till the two components combine together to form a compound. Umesh added carbon disulphide to both the China dishes. What he would observe?**

Ans. In China dish *A*, there is a mixture, so sulphur gets dissolved in carbon disulphide. Iron is insoluble in it. In China dish *B*, compound FeS is formed. Though, sulphur is soluble in carbon disulphide, but the compound FeS is not soluble in it.

7. **Rahul takes two substances *X* and *Y*. *X* is a mixture of iron filings and sulphur and *Y* is a product obtained by heating the mixture *X* and crushing it to a fine powder. On bringing a magnet over both *X* and *Y*, What will happen?**

Ans. *X* contains iron filings (magnetic material) while *Y* is a compound of iron and sulphur (FeS, non-magnetic material).

8. **What is the purpose of separating the components of a mixture?**

Ans. The purposes of separating the components of a mixture are as follows

(i) Separation makes it possible to study and use the individual components of the mixture.

(ii) It is helpful in removing any harmful or undesirable constituents.

(iii) It is helpful in obtaining a pure sample of a substance.

9. **When you mix iron filings with sulphur powder thoroughly and spread the mixture evenly on a white sheet. How do the particles in the mixture appear?**

Ans. In a mixture of iron filings and sulphur powder, sulphur and iron filings are separately visible but are not homogeneous.

10. **Dil. HCl is added separately to**

I. mixture of iron filings and sulphur.

II. iron sulphide.

What would happen?

Ans. In a mixture of iron filings and sulphur, iron reacts with dil. HCl to liberate hydrogen gas.

11. **What is formed, when iron filings heated with sulphur?**

Ans. Heating iron filings with sulphur forms ferrous sulphide.

$$Fe + S \xrightarrow{\Delta} FeS$$

12. **When a mixture of iron filings and sulphur powder is dissolved in carbon disulphide, how do the resulting solution will appear?**

Ans. Here, sulphur powder dissolves in carbon disulphide and iron filings are deposited at the base of the test tube.

EXPERIMENT 3

Objective Perform the following reactions and classify them as physical or chemical changes.

(*i*) Iron with copper sulphate solution in water.
(*ii*) Burning of magnesium in air.
(*iii*) Zinc with dilute sulphuric acid.
(*iv*) Heating of copper sulphate crystals.
(*v*) Sodium sulphate with barium chloride in the form of their solutions in water.

Materials Required Test tubes, test tube holder, test tube stand, China dish, conical flask, beaker dropper, Bunsen burner, iron nails, copper sulphate solution, magnesium ribbon, zinc metal, dilute sulphuric acid, sodium sulphate solution, barium chloride solution and water.

Theory Anything that may undergo different look, composition, colour, position, size or shape due to some internal or external factor is called change. These changes are classified into two categories:

(*i*) **Physical changes** Changes in which the original constituents do not change their properties, and there is no formation of new substance or compound takes place are called physical changes.

(*ii*) **Chemical changes** Changes in which the original constituents undergo change to form a new substance or compound with different properties, are known as chemical changes.

Procedure

S. No.	Experiment	Observation	Inference
1.	Take about 10 mL of $CuSO_4$ solution in a clean, dry test tube and drop iron nails into it. Keep the test tube undisturbed for about 10 min.	The blue coloured solution becomes light green in colour. The iron nails gets coated with a reddish-brown deposit.	On reaction of iron nails with $CuSO_4$ solution, $FeSO_4$, is formed which is light green in colour and free Cu is formed which is deposited over the iron nails as a reddish-brown deposit. It is a *displacement reaction.*
2.	Clean a piece of magnesium ribbon (5 cm) with a sand paper and hold it with a pair of tongs. Keep a China dish below it, burn magnesium ribbon in air with a burner.	The magnesium ribbon on heating with a burner catches fire. It burns with a dazzling white flame to form a white powder which keeps dropping till the ribbon is burning.	Mg burns with O_2 with a dazzling white flame, it forms a new chemical compound MgO, which is a white powder. It is a *combination reaction.*
3. (*i*)	Take a clean and dry conical flask and add small pieces of granulated zinc in it. Put about 5 mL of dil. H_2SO_4 in it. Keep the conical flask undisturbed for about 5 min.	A gas is evolved briskly, the colourless bubbles of which can be seen in the conical flask. It is also seen that the reaction mixture appears to be boiling and the conical flask and its contents become hot.	Zinc reacts with dil. H_2SO_4 briskly. $Zn + H_2SO_4(dil.) \longrightarrow ZnSO_4 + H_2$
(*ii*)	Bring a burning matchstick near the mouth of the conical flask.	The gas evolved burns with a 'pop' sound (cracking sound).	Gas evolved is H_2. It is a *displacement reaction.*
4.	Take $CuSO_4 \cdot 5H_2O$ in a dry test tube and fix cork with delivery tube and clamp it. Take crushed ice in a beaker and set other end of delivery tube in test tube. Heat the test tube first slowly and then strongly.	On heating at 110°C, $CuSO_4 \cdot 5H_2O$ changes to dirty white. At 250°C, dirty white changes to white. Finally at 720°C, anhydrous copper sulphate changes to black CuO with the evolution of SO_3 gas.	The heating process occur at 110°C and 150°C is a physical change. The heating process occur at 250°C is a *thermal decomposition reaction*, and also a chemical change. Since, new substance (CuO and SO_3) are formed which have different properties.
5.	Take a clean test tube and add about 5 mL of Na_2SO_4 in it. Now, add about 5 mL of $BaCl_2$ solution in it. Keep the test tube undisturbed for sometime.	A white precipitate is formed which gradually settles at the base of the test tube.	Na_2SO_4 reacts with $BaCl_2$ solution to form insoluble $BaSO_4$. It is a *double displacement reaction.*

Chemical Reactions Involved

(*i*) Reaction of iron nails and copper sulphate solution

$$\underset{\text{(Nail)}}{\underset{\text{Iron}}{Fe(s)}} + \underset{\text{(Blue solution)}}{\underset{\text{Copper sulphate}}{CuSO_4(aq)}} \xrightarrow[\text{reaction)}]{\text{(Displacement}} \underset{\text{(Light green solution)}}{\underset{\text{Ferrous sulphate}}{FeSO_4(aq)}} + \underset{\text{Copper}}{Cu(s)}$$

(*ii*) Burning of magnesium ribbon in air

$$\underset{\text{(Ribbon)}}{\underset{\text{Magnesium}}{2\,Mg(s)}} + \underset{\text{Oxygen}}{O_2(g)} \xrightarrow[\text{(Combination reaction)}]{\Delta} \underset{\text{(White powder)}}{\underset{\text{Magnesium oxide}}{2MgO(s)}}$$

(*iii*) Action of zinc with dilute sulphuric acid

$$\underset{\text{Zinc}}{Zn(s)} + \underset{\text{Sulphuric acid}}{\text{Dil. } H_2SO_4(aq)} \xrightarrow[\text{reaction)}]{\text{(Displacement}} \underset{\text{Zinc sulphate}}{ZnSO_4(aq)} + \underset{\text{Hydrogen}}{H_2(g)\uparrow}$$

(*iv*) Heating of hydrated copper sulphate

$$\underset{\text{sulphate (Blue)}}{\underset{\text{Hydrated copper}}{CuSO_4\cdot 5H_2O}} \xrightarrow[\text{(Decomposition reaction)}]{110°C} \underset{\text{monohydrate}}{\underset{\text{Copper sulphate}}{CuSO_4\cdot H_2O}} + 4H_2O$$

$$CuSO_4\cdot H_2O \xrightarrow{250°C} \underset{\text{sulphate (White)}}{\underset{\text{Anhyd. copper}}{CuSO_4}} + H_2O$$

$$\underset{\text{sulphate}}{\underset{\text{Anhyd. cupper}}{CuSO_4}} \longrightarrow \underset{\text{(Black)}}{\underset{\text{Copper oxide}}{CuO}} + \underset{\text{trioxide}}{\underset{\text{Sulphur}}{SO_3\uparrow}}$$

(*v*) Reaction of sodium sulphate solution and barium chloride solution

$$\underset{\text{sulphate}}{\underset{\text{Sodium}}{Na_2SO_4(aq)}} + \underset{\text{chloride}}{\underset{\text{Barium}}{BaCl_2(aq)}} \xrightarrow[\text{displacement reaction}]{\text{Double}} \underset{\text{(White ppt.)}}{\underset{\text{sulphate}}{\underset{\text{Barium}}{BaSO_4(s)\downarrow}}} + \underset{\text{chloride}}{\underset{\text{Sodium}}{2NaCl(aq)}}$$

Result/Conclusion

(*i*) Iron reacts with copper sulphate solution in water is a **displacement reaction** and is a chemical change.

(*ii*) Burning of magnesium in air is a **combination reaction** and is a chemical change.

(*iii*) Zinc with dilute sulphuric acid is a **displacement reaction** and is a chemical change.

(*iv*) Heating of hydrated copper salt at low temperature is a physical change.
- Heating of hydrated copper sulphate at higher temperature is a **decomposition reaction** and is a chemical change.

(*v*) Reaction between sodium sulphate and barium chloride solution is a double displacement reaction and is a chemical change.

Precautions

(*i*) Always take a clean and dry test tube.

(*ii*) The test tube should always be held over the flame with the help of a test tube holder.

(*iii*) Use tongs to hold the magnesium ribbon over the flame.

(*iv*) Do not use excess of chemicals.

(*v*) Clean the iron nails and magnesium ribbon by rubbing with sand paper.

QUESTIONS

1. When zinc reacts with dilute sulphuric acid, which gas is evolved?

Ans. Hydrogen gas is evolved, which is colourless, odourless and burns with a pop sound. Reaction involved is

$$Zn + \underset{\text{(Dilute)}}{H_2SO_4} \longrightarrow ZnSO_4 + H_2\uparrow$$

2. Ankur was doing an experiment to carry out the reaction of zinc granules with dilute sulphuric acid. He observed that a gas is being evolved. Name the gas.

Ans. Small amount of hydrogen gas escapes from the delivery tube.

3. An iron nail is placed in a beaker containing copper sulphate solution. In the beaker, a sensitive thermometer is suspended and the temperature of copper sulphate solution is recorded. The nail is taken out after 10 min and the temperature is again recorded. What happen at the end of experiment records.

Ans. The thermometer records high temperature due to small amount of heat produced in the chemical reaction.

4. On burning magnesium ribbon in air, a white ash is obtained. What is the product and the type of change are respectively?

Ans. It is a chemical change. A new compound called magnesium oxide is formed on burning of magnesium ribbon in air.

$$\underset{\text{(Ribbon)}}{\underset{\text{Magnesium}}{2Mg}} + O_2 \xrightarrow{\text{Heat}} \underset{\text{(White powder)}}{\underset{\text{Magnesium oxide}}{2MgO}}$$

5. When solution of sodium sulphate is added to the solution of barium chloride what is the product obtained?

Ans. When aqueous solutions of sodium sulphate and barium chloride are mixed, a white precipitate of barium sulphate is formed by double displacement.

$$\underset{\text{sulphate}}{\underset{\text{Sodium}}{Na_2SO_4(aq)}} + \underset{\text{chloride}}{\underset{\text{Barium}}{BaCl_2(aq)}} \longrightarrow \underset{\text{sulphate}}{\underset{\text{Barium}}{BaSO_4(s)}} + \underset{\text{Sodium chloride}}{2NaCl\ (aq)}$$

6. Sketch a diagram for correct way of burning of magnesium ribbon during an experiment.

Ans. Magnesium ribbon burns with a dazzling white flame. It should be held with a pair of tongs.

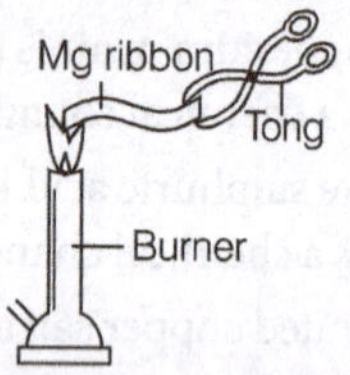

7. What leads to low heating of crystals of hydrated copper sulphate?

Ans. $CuSO_4 \cdot 5H_2O \xrightarrow{\text{Heat}} CuSO_4 + 5H_2O$

Hydrated copper sulphate (Blue) → Anhydrous copper sulphate (White) + Water

8. Label the diagram.

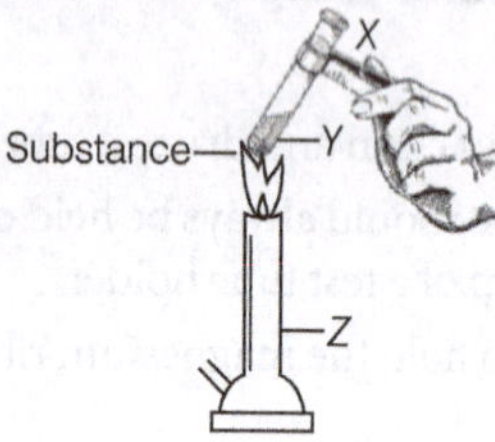

Ans. The labellings are:

X = Test tube holder

Y = Test tube

Z = Burner

9. Write three points that is observed when zinc granules are added to dilute sulphuric acid in a test tube?

Ans. (*i*) Release of bubbles of gas from the test tube.

(*ii*) Gradual decrease in the size of the granules.

(*iii*) Heat energy evolved in the reaction.

10. You are asked to study the reaction between zinc and dilute sulphuric acid. Name the apparatus required for this experiment.

Ans. Conical flask, delivery tube, rubber stopper, and matchbox.

11. Which type of the possible changes that may occur on strongly heating of crystals of copper sulphate?

Ans. It is a chemical and irreversible change.

$$CuSO_4 \xrightarrow{720\,^\circ C} CuO + SO_3$$

12. Student *X* puts iron nails in $CuSO_4$ solution while the other student *Y* puts Cu pieces in $FeSO_4$ solution. Who made the observation that solution turns green from blue colour is reported?

Ans. Fe displaces copper (Cu) from $CuSO_4$ solution and the solution turns green from blue colour.

$$\underset{\text{Iron}}{Fe} + \underset{\text{(Blue solution)}}{CuSO_4} \longrightarrow \underset{\text{(Light green)}}{FeSO_4} + \underset{\text{Copper}}{Cu}$$

13. It is advised to rub magnesium ribbon with sand paper before burning it in air. Why?

Ans. After rubbing, any layer of its oxide etc., deposited on it is removed and then magnesium comes in direct contact with air.

14. Aqueous solutions of sodium sulphate and barium chloride are mixed together in a beaker. What would be observed?

Ans. When aqueous solutions of sodium sulphate and barium chloride are mixed together in a beaker, a white precipitate of barium sulphate is formed.

15. What is physical or chemical effect on rubbing of magnesium ribbon with sand paper or any other abrasive?

Ans. After rubbing, magnesium ribbon, any layer of its oxide deposited on it.

16. When barium chloride solution is added to sodium sulphate solution. What is obtained as precipitate?

Ans. When barium chloride solution is added to sodium sulphate solution, white precipitate of barium sulphate is formed.

$$Na_2SO_4(aq) + BaCl_2(aq) \longrightarrow BaSO_4(s) + 2NaCl(aq)$$

EXPERIMENT 4

Experiment 4 (a)

Objective To prepare stained, temporary mount of onion peel and to study its cells.

Materials Required An onion bulb, slide, coverslip, two watch glasses, needle, brush, forceps, razor blade, compound microscope, blotting paper, methylene blue (or safranin) solution, glycerine and water.

Theory All living organisms are composed of cells. Thus, cell is the structural and functional unit of life. The new cells arise by the division of pre-existing cells. In plants, cells have an outermost rigid cell wall beneath which is a cell membrane that encloses cytoplasm, cell organelles and a nucleus.

Procedure

(*i*) Take a fleshy scaly leaf of an onion. Using a pair of forceps, pull out a thin membranous peel adhering to the inner surface of the leaf. This is the epidermal peel.

(*ii*) Place the peel in a watch glass containing water and cut it into small rectangular pieces.

(*iii*) Mix 1 or 2 drops of methylene blue or safranin in a small quantity of water taken in another watch glass and transfer the peel into it. Leave the peel for about 3 minutes. Dip the peel in water to remove excess stain.

(*iv*) Take a clean slide with a drop of glycerine in the middle and using a brush, transfer the washed and stained peel on to it.

(*v*) Place a cover slip over it by slowly lowering it with a needle. Avoid entry of air bubbles.

(*vi*) Remove excess glycerine from the edges of cover slip with the help of a piece of blotting paper.

(*vii*) Observe the slide under the microscope, first in low power (10x) and then in high power (45x).

(*viii*) Draw a labelled diagram of the cells as seen under microscope.

(*ix*) Observe and record its features.

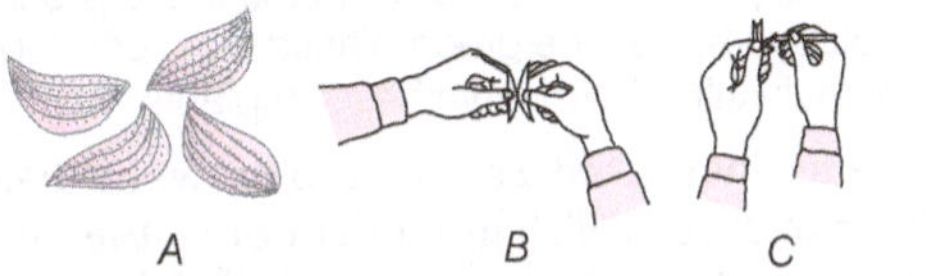

A, B, C- Method of removing peel from onion

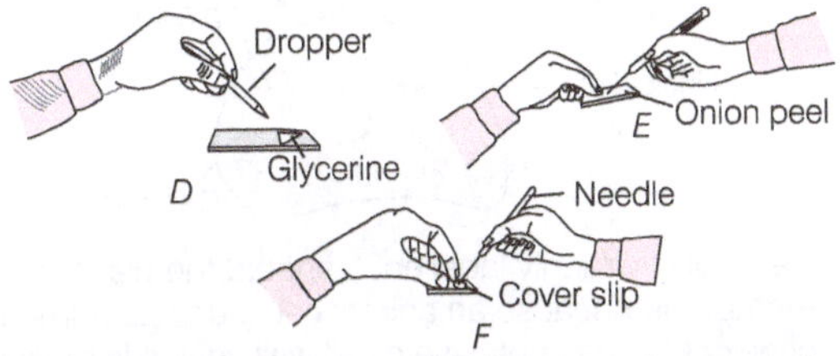

D, E, F Steps for showing mounting procedure

Observations

- There are large number of brick-shaped (rectangular) epidermal cells lying side by side (compactly arranged).
- Each cell has a distinct cell wall and there are no intercellular spaces.
- A distinct darkly stained nucleus is present in each cell.
- A prominent vacuole is seen in the centre and cytoplasm is present in the periphery of every cell.

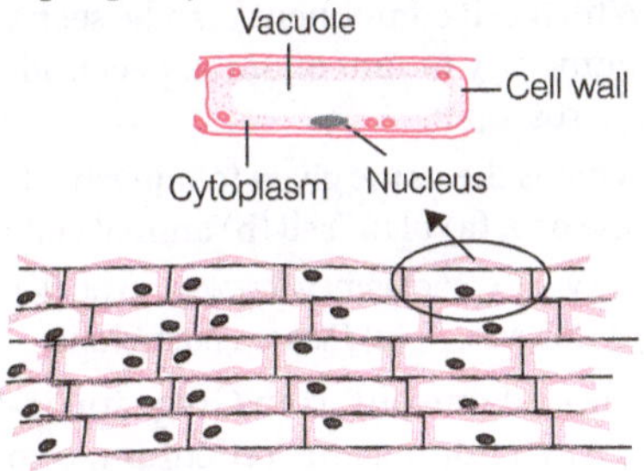

Cell structure of an onion peel

Conclusion The cells observed under microscope are plant cells as each cell has a distinct cell wall and a large central vacuole. The cells that forms the outer layer of the leaf known as epidermis.

Precautions

(*i*) Always hold the slide from its edges.

(*ii*) The slide and coverslip should be cleaned before use.

(*iii*) Staining of peel should be appropriate. Avoid understaining or excessive staining of the peel.

(*iv*) Keep the coverslip gently so as to avoid the entry of air bubbles.

(*v*) Extra glycerine from the edges of the cover slip should be soaked with blotting paper.

(*vi*) Use a brush to transfer the peel on the slide.

Experiment 4 (b)

Objective To prepare a temporary mount of human cheek cells and to study their characteristics.

Materials Required Methylene blue stain, glycerine, a compound microscope, slide, cover slip, a clean spatula or a toothpick, a brush, a needle and a piece of blotting paper.

Theory Like plants, the body of all animals including humans is composed of cells. Unlike plant cells, animal cells do not have cell wall. The outermost covering of an animal cell is called cell membrane. The cytoplasm, nucleus and other cell organelles are enclosed in it. Epithelial tissue is the outermost covering of most organs and cavities of an animal body.

Procedure

(*i*) Rinse your mouth with freshwater.

(*ii*) With the help of a clean spatula or a toothpick, gently scrape the inner side of your cheek.

(*iii*) Transfer the scrapped material into a drop of water taken on a clean slide.

(*iv*) With the help of a needle, spread the material uniformly.

(*v*) Add a drop of methylene blue stain. After about 3 minutes put a drop of glycerine over it.

(*vi*) Place a clean cover slip over the glycerine. And remove the excess glycerine from the edges of cover slip with the help of a piece of blotting paper.

(*vii*) Examine the slide under microscope, first under low power (10x) and then under high power (45x).

(*viii*) Draw diagrams of cells as seen under the microscope. Observe and record the features.

Observations

(*i*) A large number of flat polygonal cells arranged compactly are observed under the microscopic field.

(*ii*) Each cell is bounded by a thin cell membrane.

(*iii*) A darkly stained distinct nucleus is observed in each cell.

(*iv*) Cytoplasm is granular.

(*v*) Cells lack cell wall and large vacuoles.

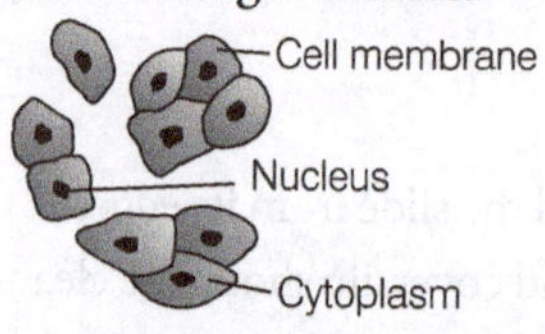

Cheek epithelial cells

Conclusion The cells observed under microscope are animal cells as each cell has a cell membrane as outer boundary enclosing a distinct nucleus and dense cytoplasm. Cell wall and central prominent vacuoles are absent.

Precautions

(*i*) Clean your mouth cavity with warm water before scraping the cheek.

(*ii*) Scrape the cheek gently to avoid bleeding.

(*iii*) Scraping should be properly spread so that the cells are widely separated.

(*iv*) The cover slip should be kept gently to avoid entry of air bubbles.

(*v*) Always hold the slide by its edges to avoid fingerprints.

(*vi*) Avoid overstaining or understaining of the material.

QUESTIONS

1. Which scientist discovered 'cell'?

Ans. Robert Hooke discovered 'cell' in 1665. It is the basic unit of life.

2. Which is the largest known cell?

Ans. Ostrich egg is the largest known cell.

3. Write the name of the smallest human cell.

Ans. Sperms are the smallest known human cells whereas neuron is the largest cell in a human body.

4. Which is called as the 'powerhouse of the cell' ?

Ans. Mitochondria are known as the 'powerhouse of the cell'. They possess enzymes necessary for the oxidation of carbohydrates. This process releases energy in the form of ATP and hence, they are referred to as powerhouse.

5. Draw the diagram of the cells of an onion peel.

Ans.

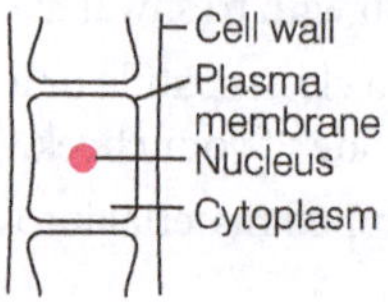

6. Which cell organelle is known as protein factory of the cell?

Ans. Ribosome is known as protein factory of the cell, as it is involved in the synthesis of proteins.

7. How many type of plastids are found in plant cells?

Ans. In plant cells, plastids are of three main types, i.e. leucoplasts, chloroplasts and chromoplasts. Leucoplasts are colourless plastids, chloroplasts are green plastids and chromoplasts are variously coloured plastids.

8. Give the name of a single membranous organelle?

Ans. Lysosome is a single membranous organelle. It is also known as suicide bag of the cell.

9. Which part of a typical plant cell is non-living?

Ans. The only non-living part of a plant cell is a cell wall. It is rigid, permeable, composed of cellulose and provides strength and rigidity to the cell.

10. Which organelle helps in the photosynthesis in plant cells?

Ans. Plastids present in plant cells helps in the process of photosynthesis. The green plastids, i.e. chloroplasts are the main site of photosynthesis in plants.

11. The teacher asked a student to draw the diagram of human cheek cell. The student draw the following diagram. Identify the part wrongly labelled by him.

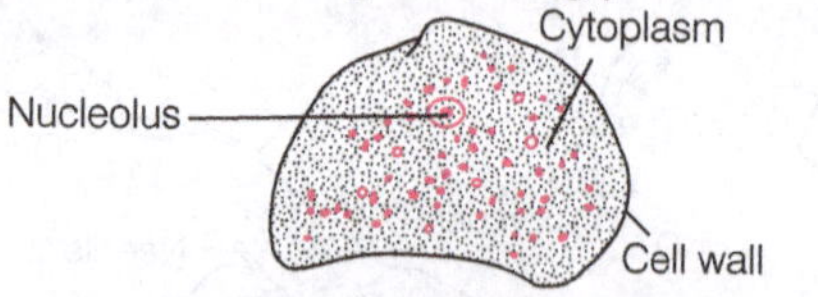

Ans. Cell wall is wrongly labelled. It should the plasma membrane because an animal cell (such as human cheek cell) does not have a cell wall. Infact, is present only in plant cells.

12. Which cell organelle regulates the growth of a cell?

Ans. The growth of the cells is regulated by nucleus.

13. (i) **Which stain will you prefer to prepare a temporary mount of onion peel?**

(ii) **Why glycerine is used for mounting material?**

Ans. (i) Safranin.

(ii) Glycerine being hygroscopic does not allow the mounted material to lose water and become dry.

14. (i) **Which cell components can be seen clearly in a temporary mount of onion peel under compound microscope?**

(ii) **What is the name given to outermost covering in case of a, (a) plant cell (b) animal cell ?**

Ans. (i) Cell wall, cytoplasm, vacuole and nucleus.

(ii) (a) Cell wall, (b) Plasma membrane.

15. Pick the odd one out from Golgi apparatus, cytoplasm, endoplasmic reticulum, lysosomes. Explain.

Ans. Cytoplasm form the structural part of the cell, while ER, lysosomes and Golgi apparatus are the organelles present in cytoplasm.

EXPERIMENT 5

Experiment 5 (a)

Objective To identify parenchyma, collenchyma and sclerenchyma tissues in plants from prepared slides and draw their labelled diagrams.

Materials Required Permanent slides of parenchyma, sclerenchyma tissues and compound microscope.

Theory Plant tissues are broadly classified into meristematic and permanent tissues. Permanent tissues may be, simple tissues like parenchyma, collenchyma and sclerenchyma or complex tissues like xylem and phloem. The structural features of tissues like wall characteristics, cell size, lumen size and cytoplasmic contents vary in different types of permanent tissues.

Procedure Focus the prepared slides of parenchyma and sclerenchyma tissues one by one, under the compound microscope. Observe their characteristic features. Draw labelled diagrams and note down your observations.

Observations

1. **Parenchyma Tissue Identifying Features**

- Parenchyma cells are isodiametric, oval or round in shape.
- Each cell has a prominent nucleus, a large vacuole, thin cell wall and peripheral cytoplasm.
- Intercellular spaces are present in between the parenchyma cells.

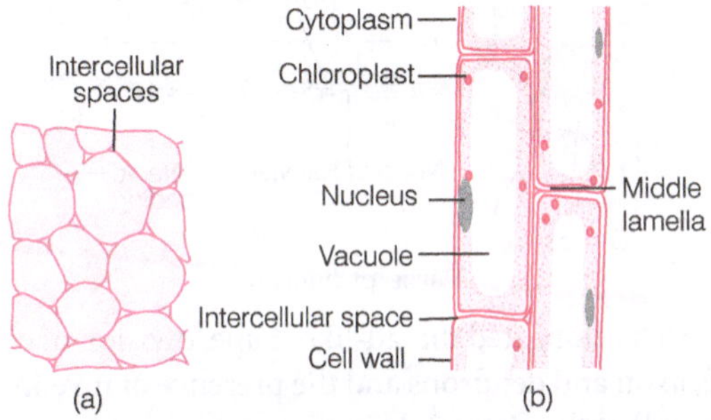

Parenchyma tissue; (a) Transverse section and (b) Longitudinal section

Functions

- Keeping the cells turgid they provide rigidity to the plant.
- It stores food materials in the form of proteins, starch, oil and fats.
- Chlorophyll containing parenchyma (chlorenchyma) helps in photosynthesis.

Conclusion As cells are thin-walled, isodiametric and have intercellular spaces, the given slide is of parenchyma tissue. It is a simple and permanent plant tissue.

2. **Collenchyma Tissue**

Identifying Features

- Cells appear oval, spherical or polygonal.
- Cells are elastic, living and mechanical tissue.
- Cells are closely packed hence, there is no intercellular space.
- Cell walls of these cells possess thickenings at the corners.

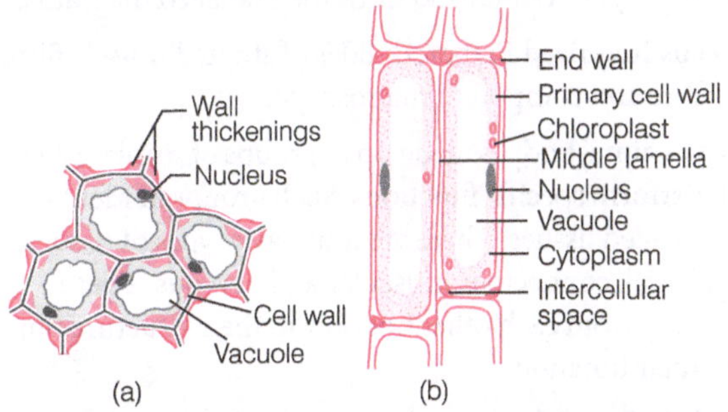

Collenchyma tissue : (a) Transverse section and (b) Longitudinal section

Functions

- This tissue gives mechanical strength to young plant parts.
- It prevents tearing of leaves and resists bending of stems.

Conclusion Since, the cells of the tissue are living, oval or spherical in shape and not have intercellular spaces, the given slide is of collenchyma tissue. It is a simple and permanent plant tissue.

3. **Sclerenchyma Tissue**

Identifying Features

- Cells appears polygonal, oval or circular in transverse section.
- Cells are dead and devoid of protoplasm.
- Cells have a thick lignified cell wall perforated with pits.
- Cells are closely packed hence, there is no intercellular space.
- The sclerenchyma tissue has two types of cells, i.e. fibres and sclereids. Fibres are long, narrow and pointed at both ends. Sclereids are short, isodiametric and are also called grit or stone cells.

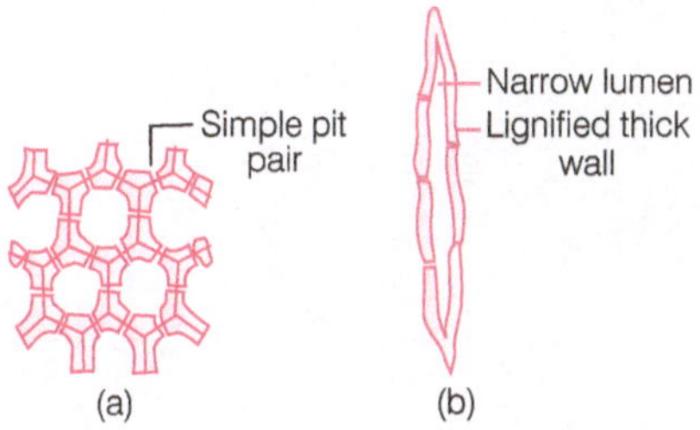

Sclerenchyma tissue; (a) Transverse section and (b) Longitudinal section

Function This tissue provides mechanical strength to the plant.

Conclusion Since, the cells of the tissue are thick-walled and highly lignified, it is sclerenchyma tissue. It is a simple permanent plant tissue.

Experiment 5 (b)

Objective To identify striated muscle fibre and nerve cells from the prepared slides and draw their labelled diagrams.

Materials Required Prepared slides of striated muscle fibre, nerve fibre and compound microscope.

Theory Animal body is made up of groups of similar cells which perform specific functions. Such groups of identical cells are called tissues. There are four basic types of tissues, i.e. epithelial, connective, muscular and nervous. These tissues vary from each other not only in their structure but also in their functions.

Procedure Focus the given slides first under the low power of microscope and then under high power. Observe their characteristic features, draw labelled diagrams and note down your observations.

Observations

1. Striated Muscle Fibre

Identifying Features

- The muscle cells are long, cylindrical and unbranched.
- These fibres show alternate light and dark bands or transverse striations.
- Each muscle cell is multinucleated and nuclei lie at the periphery.
- The cytoplasm of muscle cell is known as sarcoplasm and the plasma membrane is called sarcolemma.
- These muscles are attached to the bones hence, are also called skeletal muscles.
- Striated muscles are controlled by our will. Therefore, they are called voluntary muscles.
- These muscles are found in arms, legs, tongue, pharynx etc.

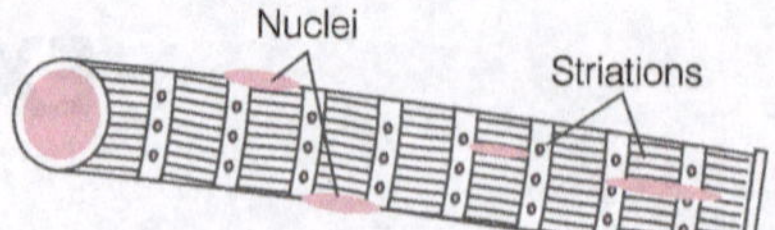

Striated muscle fibre

Conclusion The observed slide is of striated muscles as muscle fibres are long, cylindrical, multinucleated and show transverse striations.

Nerve Fibres

Identifying Features

- Each typical nerve cell or neuron has three main parts:
  (*i*) Cell body or cyton (*ii*) Axon (*iii*) Dendrites.
- Cyton or cell body has a prominent nucleus and cytoplasm.
- In the cytoplasm, granules are present, which are called Nissl's granules.
- The cell body gives out several branches called dendrons, which further divide and form dendrites.
- Axon is a single elongated branch given out from the cell body. Its ends are called axon endings.
- Axon is covered with a myelin sheath or medullary sheath in some cells. It is interrupted at places. There are gaps called node of Ranvier. Such nerve fibres are called myelinated nerve fibres.
- The loose connection between the axon endings of one nerve cell and dendrons and cell body of other nerve cell is called synapse.

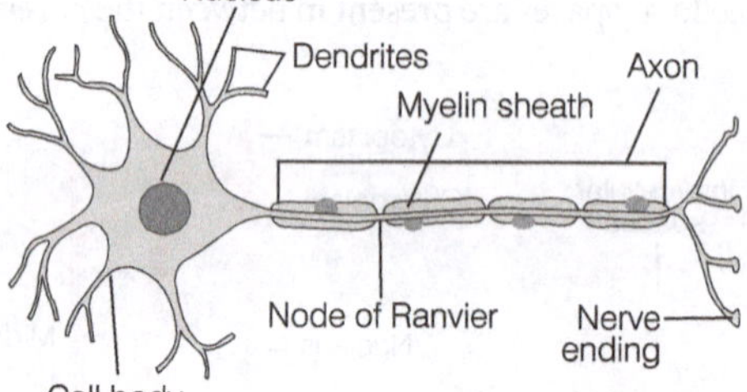

Parts of neuron

Conclusion The elongated thread-like shape, division of cell into cyton, axon and dendrons and the presence of myelin sheath shows that the given slide is of a nerve cell or neuron.

QUESTIONS

1. **Name the branch of biology which deals with the study of tissues.**

Ans. The branch of biology which deals with the study of tissues is called histology.

2. **A student was observing a slide. He observed long unbranched cells with striations and many nuclei. Identify the slide.**

Ans. The given features are of striated muscle fibres, i.e. multinucleated cells that are long and unbranched and show striations.

3. **Give the name of a simple, permanent living tissue of plants, which has wall thickenings.**

Ans. Collenchyma is a living tissue. It consists of living cells with wall thickenings at the corners.

4. **Name the tissue which provide mechanical strength as well as elasticity to the plants.**

Ans. Collenchyma provide mechanical strength as well as elasticity to the plants.

5. **Identify the part labelled as '*C*' in the given diagram.**

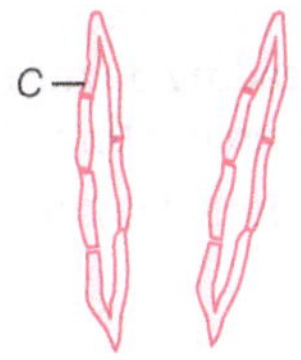

Ans. The given figure is of a sclerenchyma fibre. In the given diagram '*C*' is narrow lumen.

6. **Identify the tissue (*A*) and (*B*).**

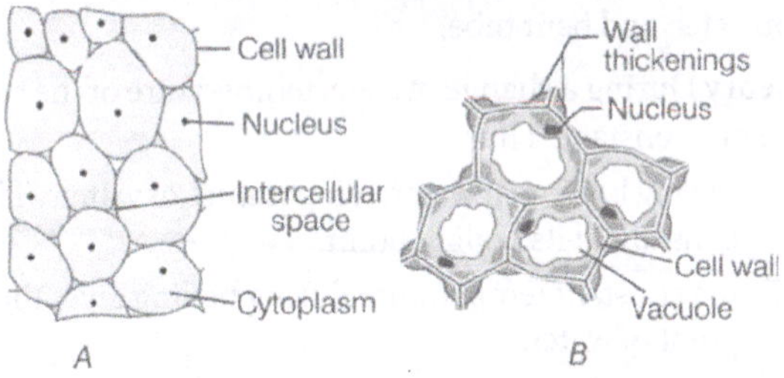

Ans. In the given diagram,

A – Parenchyma tissue, *B* – Collenchyma tissue.

7. **Which chemical substances are deposited in the walls of collenchyma cell/tissue?**

Ans. Pectin and cellulose are the chemical substances been deposited in the walls of collenchyma.

8. **Which plant tissue is present in seed coat of almond?**

Ans. Sclerenchyma, mainly sclereids (stone cells) are present in seed coat of almond and makes it very hard.

9. **Which plant cells have perforated cell wall?**

Ans. Vessels have perforated cell walls.

10. **The figure shows the longitudinal section of a plant tissue. Which cell type is represented by this figure?**

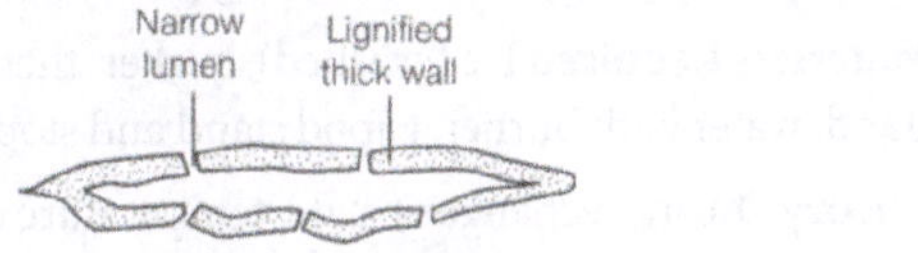

Ans. The cell is of sclerenchyma tissue as the walls are long and narrow and are thickened due to lignin. The cell walls are so thick that there is very little internal space inside the cell.

11. **Identify the given two slides *A* and *B* as a parenchyma or sclerenchyma. Sclerenchyma can be identified by which characteristic?**

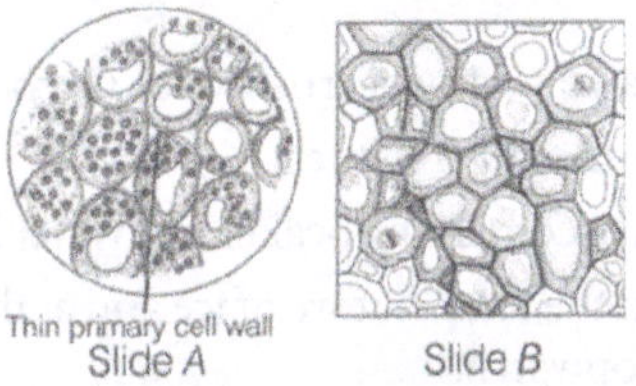

Ans. Slide *A* represents the parenchyma cells and slide *B* represents the sclerenchyma cells.
Sclerenchyma can be identified by the presence of thick cell walls, closely packed cells without intercellular spaces and presence of conspicuous middle lamella between two sclerenchymatous cells.

12. **Which muscles are involved in the movement of arms?**

Ans. The muscles involved in the movement of arms are striated muscles.

13. **Give the diagram of the striated muscle fibre as seen under the microscope? Give reason supporting your answer.**

Ans. Under microscope, striated muscles show alternate light and dark bands on striations when stained appropriately. Also, the nucleus in them lies at periphery.

Striated muscle fibre

14. **Identify the type of tissue based on characteristics given.**

(i) **Attached to bones, help in body movements. Alternate light and dark bands are present in them.**

(ii) **Involved in rhythmic contraction and relaxation of the heart.**

Ans. (i) Skeletal or striated muscle tissue.
(ii) Cardiac muscle tissue.

EXPERIMENT 6

Experiment 6 (a)

Objective To determine the melting point of ice.

Materials Required Ice (crushed), beaker, thermometer, iron stand, water bath burner, tripod stand and stopwatch.

Theory During a change of state, temperature of the substance remains constant. Thus,

(*i*) during melting of ice, temperature of ice will remain constant at its melting point until the entire solid converts into liquid.

(*ii*) the constant temperature during melting gives the melting point of ice.

Procedure

(*i*) Take a small quantity of crushed ice in a beaker.

(*ii*) Place a thermometer in the ice.

(*iii*) Place this ice containing beaker in a water bath.

(*iv*) Note down the temperature of ice and at the same time, start the stopwatch.

(*v*) Now, start heating the water bath on a low flame.

(*vi*) Note down the temperature of ice after every half minute and record it in a tabular form.

(*vii*) Continue until the whole ice gets melted.

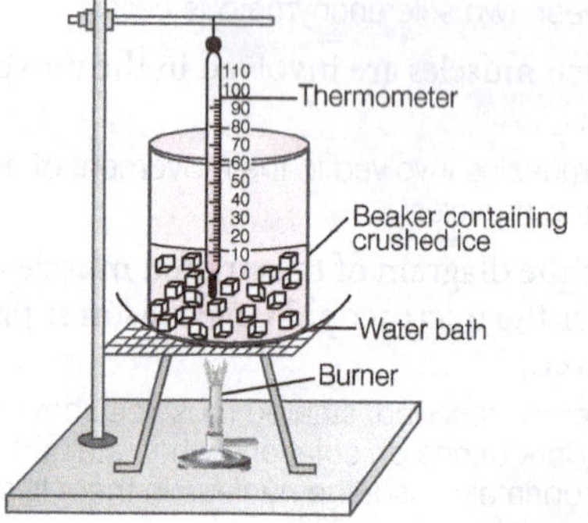

Determination of the melting point of ice

Observations

S. No.	Time (min)	Temperature (°C)
1.	0.0	....
2.	0.5	....
3.	1.0	....
4.	1.5	....
5.	2.0	....
6.	2.5	....
7.	3.0	....
8.	3.5	....
9.	4.0	....
10.	4.5	....
11.	5.0	....
12.	5.5	....
13.	6.0	....
14.	6.5	....
15.	7.0	....

Result Since, during the melting of ice, the temperature of ice remains constant at its melting point. Therefore, from the values given in the table

Melting point of ice = ... °C or .... K

Precautions

(*i*) Immersed only the bulb of the thermometer in the crushed ice.

(*ii*) While taking the reading on the thermometer, keep your eye at the level of mercury thread.

(*iii*) The thermometer should not touch the wall of the beaker.

Experiment 6 (b)

Objective To determine the boiling point of water.

Materials Required Distilled water, round bottom flask, thermometer, iron stand, sand bath, tripod stand, burner, stopwatch and bent tube.

Theory During a change of state, temperature of the substance remains constant. Thus,

(*i*) during boiling of water, temperature of water will remain constant at its boiling point.

(*ii*) the constant temperature during boiling gives the boiling point of water.

Procedure

(*i*) Take about 50 mL of water in a round bottom distillation flask.

(*ii*) Fix up a thermometer and a bent tube in the cork of the flask as shown in the figure.

(*iii*) Heat the flask on a sand bath kept on a tripod stand.

(*iv*) Start the stopwatch and read temperature on the thermometer.

(*v*) Keep recording the temperature after every one minute until water starts boiling.

(*vi*) Continue recording the temperature on the thermometer for few more minutes.

(*vii*) Record all observations in a tabular form.

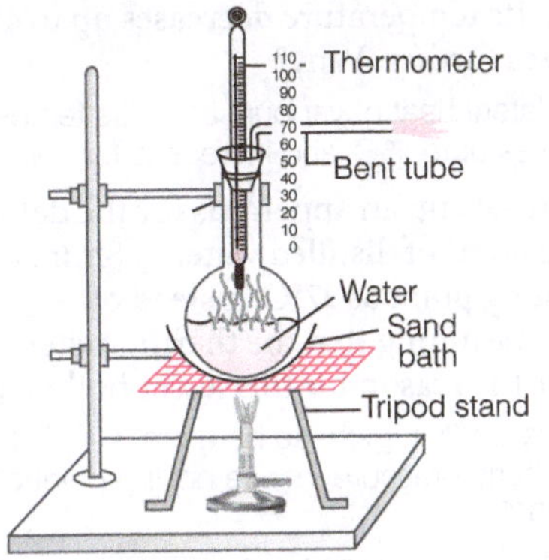

Determination of boiling point of water

Observations

S. No.	Time (min)	Temperature (°C)
1.	0	....
2.	1	....
3.	2	....
4.	3	....
5.	4	....
6.	5	....
7.	6	....
8.	7	....
9.	8	....
10.	9	....
11.	10	....
12.	11	....
13.	12	....
14.	13	....
15.	14	....

Result/Conclusion

Since, during the boiling of water, the temperature of water remains constant at its boiling point. Therefore, from the values given in the table

Boiling point of water = ... °C or .... K

Precautions

(*i*) The bulb of the thermometer should be kept outside the water.

(*ii*) While taking the reading on the thermometer, keep your eye at the level of mercury thread.

QUESTIONS

1. Sketch a diagram representing is the correct method of finding the melting point of ice?

Ans.

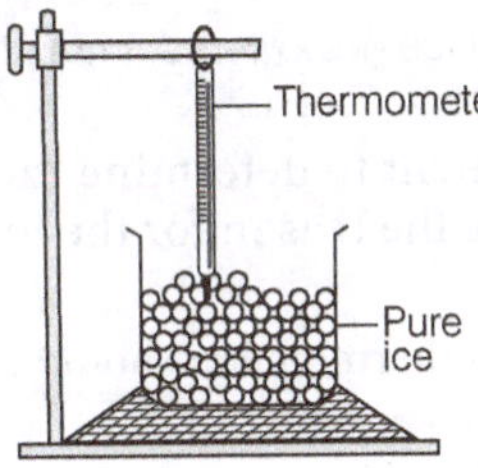

The bulb of the thermometer should be dipped completely inside the crushed ice.

2. You are given ice at −10°C. It is supplied with heat at a constant rate. The temperature of ice changes with the heat supplied. Represent this observation in graph.

Ans.

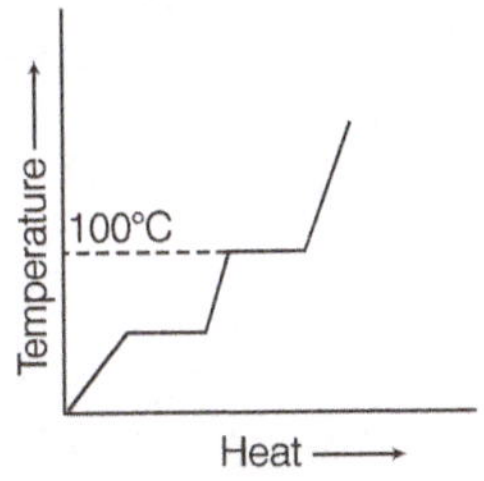

3. What do you mean by melting of a substance?

Ans. Melting point of a substance is that constant temperature at which the melting of substance starts and remain same until the entire solid converts into liquid.

4. Liquid *A* boils at 60°C, while liquid *B* boils at 80°C. Which is more volatile?

Ans. Low boiling point refers to high volatility. Hence, liquid *A* is more volatile.

5. Draw a set up representing the determination of boiling point of water.

Ans.

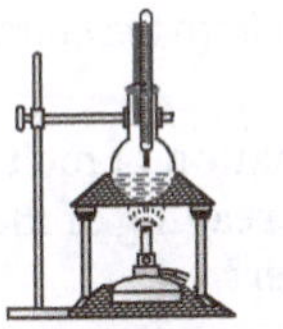

The bulb of the thermometer should be just above the surface of water and delivery tube should be above in space.

6. Consider the following graph.

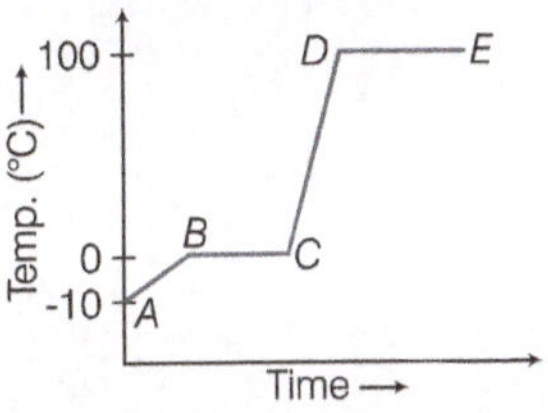

Which portion of temperature-time graph showing heating of ice at $-10°C$ to water at $100°C$ represent the change of state on heating?

Ans. *BC* represents the change of state of ice from solid to liquid and *DE* represents the change of state of water from liquid to steam (gas).

7. **In an experiment to determine the melting point of ice, Rakshita observes no change in the temperature, when she heats the ice till the whole ice melts. What could be the reason of no rise in temperature.**

Ans. During melting, the temperature remains constant until the entire ice changes into water as the heat supplied to ice is used to change the ice from its solid to liquid state.

8. **Name the set of apparatus required to determine the boiling point of water.**

Ans. Round bottom flask, burner, thermometer, wire gauze, stand with clamp, cork with two holes and glass tube.

9. **At room temperature, a student sets up an apparatus to determine the melting point of ice. He takes a beaker half-filled with crushed ice and dips a mercury thermometer in it. After this, what would he observed?**

Ans. Once a solid attains its melting temperature, the temperature remains same until entire solid converts into liquid.

10. **A student sets up an apparatus for the determination of boiling point of a sample of water supplied to him in his laboratory. He recorded the boiling point as 102℃. Assuming that the thermometer is accurate. What is reason for the error in the determined value of boiling point?**

Ans. Distilled water should be selected for determining the boiling point of water more accurately.

11. **During melting of ice, cooling effect is produced. Why?**

Ans. Ice absorbs heat from the surroundings, resulting in a cooling effect.

12. **In the determination of melting point of ice, when will the correct reading of melting point is noted in the thermometer?**

Ans. Melting point is the constant temperature at which the ice converts into water.

13. **Water in a container is heated uniformly from $0°C$ to $100°C$. Its temperature decreases up to 4°C and increases further. Why?**

Ans. Due to latent heat of vapourisation, its temperature decreases upto $4°C$ and increases further.

14. **Prakhar sets up an apparatus for the determination of boiling point of distilled water at Shimla. He recorded the boiling point as 97℃, instead of $100°C$. Assuming that the thermometer is accurate. What is the reason for this lesser boiling point?**

Ans. Shimla is a hilly region, so here pressure is less than atmospheric pressure, hence boiling point of water is less than 100℃.

15. **While heating a liquid, it has to be stirred properly. Why?**

Ans. During heating, if it is stirred properly, the liquid gets uniform temperature throughout.

16. **What would be the reading of a thermometer, when it is kept in the ice?**

Ans. The temperature of ice decreases gradually and after reaching at 0℃ (melting point), it becomes constant.

17. **In an experiment to determine the boiling point of water, mention two important precautions that should be taken.**

Ans. (*i*) Constant stirring must be done so that heating may be uniform.

(*ii*) Bulb of the thermometer must not dip in water.

18. **If in the determination of melting point of ice, ice is contaminated with some non-volatile impurity like common salt, how the melting point of ice is affected?**

Ans. Melting point of ice get lowered. Impurities always lower than melting point of solid.

19. **In an experiment to determine the boiling point of water, state the reason for the following precautions:**

(*i*) The bulb of thermometer should not touch the sides of beaker.

(*ii*) While boiling water, pumice stones should be added.

Ans. (*i*) The sides of the glass beaker are at higher temperature than the contents present inside the beaker. Therefore, the reading given by the thermometer touching the sides of the beaker does not give correct result.

(*ii*) Pieces of pumice stone are added to boiling water in order to avoid any bumping.

EXPERIMENT 7

Objective To verify the laws of reflection of sound.

Materials Required

(*i*) Two glass tubes of 3 ft in length and 2 inches in diameter.

(*ii*) Vertical reflector (polished wooden drawing board).

(*iii*) Sounding body (Gallon's whistle or clock).

Theory

(*i*) **Reflection of Sound** When sound travels in a given medium, it strikes the surface of another medium and bounces back in some other direction, this phenomenon is called reflection of sound.

(*ii*) **First Law of Reflection of Sound** It states that incident sound wave, the reflected sound wave and the normal at the point of incidence, all lie in the same plane.

(*iii*) **Second Law of Reflection of Sound** The angle of incidence of sound is equal to the angle of reflection of sound.

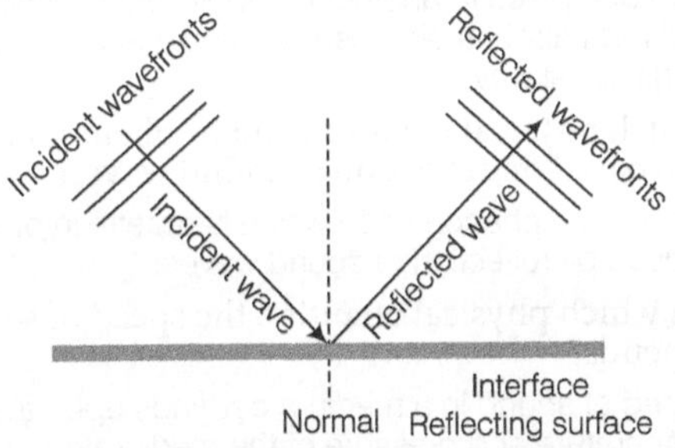

(*iv*) **Speed of Sound** It depends upon the nature of the medium through which the waves pass. Presence of moisture increases the velocity of sound in air because density of dry air is greater than the density of moisture.

Procedure

(*i*) Arrange two glass tubes *AB* and *CD* horizontally at same angle in front of a vertical reflector $R_1 R_2$.

(*ii*) At the mouth *A*, of tube *AB*, place a sounding body (a tuning fork or a clock).

(*iii*) Adjust the inclination of the tube *CD* with respect to the reflector $R_1 R_2$, so that sound is distinctly and loudly heard when the ear is placed at *D*.

(*iv*) Mark the position of tubes *AB* and *CD*.

(*v*) Draw a dotted line from the centre of diameter of tube *AB* and *CD* and extend upto reflector board. Draw normal.

(*vi*) Measure the angle between the sound waves coming from the tube *AB* and the normal (i.e. the angle of incidence of sound waves).

(*vii*) $\angle AON$ is called angle of incidence ($\angle i$).

(*viii*) Then, measure the angle of reflection ($\angle r$), i.e. angle between normal and the central line drawn from the tube *CD*, when sound is distinctly and loudly audible. This is the angle of reflection of sound wave ($\angle r$), i.e. $\angle DON$.

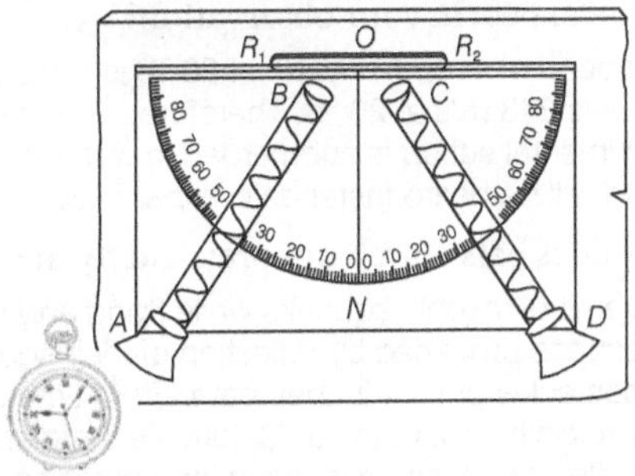

Observation Table

S. No.	Angle of incidence ($\angle i = \angle AON$)	Angle of reflection ($\angle r = \angle DON$)
1.		
2.		
3.		

Inference (Result)

(*i*) When glass tube *CD* (through which sound is heard) is lifted vertically or obliquely, then the sound of clock either weakens or diminishes completely. It shows that the reflected wave should lie in the same plane of incidence, which verifies first law of reflection of sound.

(*ii*) The angle of incidence and the angle of reflection of sound are found to be equal, which verifies second law of reflection of sound.

Precautions

(*i*) The inner surface of metallic tube should be highly polished.

(*ii*) Metal plate should be polished.

(*iii*) Tuning fork or clock should be closed to the tube, but it should not touch the tube.

(*iv*) There should be complete silence in the laboratory, so that sounds from other sources do not interfere.

QUESTIONS

1. What is the value of difference between the angle of reflection and angle of incidence?

Ans. We know that,

Angle of incidence = Angle of reflection

or $\angle i = \angle r$

Now, difference between angle of reflection and angle of incidence $= \angle r - \angle i = \angle r - \angle r = 0$

2. Suppose the whole experimental set up of this experiment is submerged in water. What changes do you expect in your observation?

Ans. The speed of sound in water at 20 °C is 1482 m/s while in air it is 343 m/s at 20 °C. Therefore, when the whole experimental set up is submerged in water, the reflected sound will be heard faster as compared to air.

3. How does bats search out prey and fly in dark night?

Ans. Bats emit ultrasonic squeaks while flying and listen to the echoes produced by reflection of their squeaks from the obstacles or prey in their path. From time taken by echo to be heard, bats can determine the distance of obstacle or prey and can avoid the obstacles or can catch the prey.

4. What will be the direction of sound, while performing the experiment on reflection of sound?

Ans. It is a precaution to keep the position of the ticking clock (source of sound) through which incident sound is coming, along the axis of tube which specifies that ear, ticking clock (source of sound) and reflecting surface all lie in the same plane.

5. Ramjeet, while verifying the laws of reflection of sound measured the angle between the incident sound wave and reflected sound wave to be 130°. Find the angle of incidence?

Ans. Since, angle of incidence = angle of reflection

or $\angle i = \angle r$

$\therefore \quad \angle i = \frac{\angle i + \angle r}{2} = \frac{130°}{2} = 65°$

6. In which medium, the reflection of sound does not occur?

Ans. Since, propagation of sound requires medium. So, reflection of sound does not occur in vacuum.

7. If the reflecting surface and the source of sound both are in the plane of the table, the position of the ear of the observer should be where?

Ans. From first law of reflection of sound, source of sound through which incident sound wave is coming, reflecting surface through which normal is drawn and position of the ear of an observer at which reflected sound wave reaches, all lie in the same plane.

8. When the sound wave propagates, which physical quantity changes in the medium?

Ans. Propagation of sound can be visualised as propagation of density variations or pressure variations in the medium as pressure is related to number of particles in the medium in a given volume. More density of particles in the medium gives more pressure and *vice-versa*.

9. While doing experiment on verifying the law of reflection of sound, four students measured the angles $\angle i$ and $\angle r$ as shown in the diagram below. Sketch the correct measurements of angle of incidence and angle of reflection done by student.

Ans. The angle of incidence is the angle, which the incident wave makes with the normal to the surface. Also, the angle of reflection is the angle, which reflected wave makes with the normal to the surface.

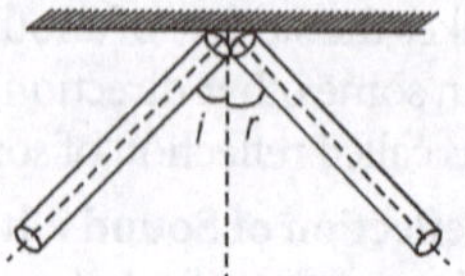

10. Sound wave is also known as longitudinal wave. Why?

Ans. Sound travels in the form of longitudinal wave. In longitudinal wave, the individual particles of the medium move in a direction parallel to the direction of propagation of disturbance. The particles do not move from one place to another but they simply oscillate back and forth about their mean position. Hence, it is longitudinal wave.

11. Which physical phenomenon or phenomena is/are also based on reflection of sound waves?

Ans. Echo is the phenomenon which is repetition of sound caused by reflection of sound waves.

12. On which physical quantity, the speed of sound depends?

Ans. Speed of sound in a medium depends upon the temperature and pressure of the medium.

13. The given figure represents the graph between the angle of incidence and angle of reflection for a sound wave. What conclusion can be drawn from it?

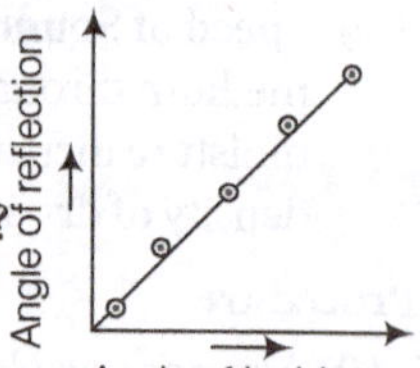

Ans. The conclusion is that angle of incidence is always equal to angle of reflection, i.e. $\angle i = \angle r$, which is second law of reflection of sound.

14. A student does the experiment on verifying the law of reflection of sound. He records the following values of the angle of incidence ($\angle i$) and angle of reflection ($\angle r$).

S.No.	1	2	3	4	5
Angle of incidence	30°	40°	45°	50°	60°
Angle of reflection	60°	50°	45°	40°	30°

Which reading/s among 1, 2, 3, 4 and 5 is/are correct?

Ans. Only 3 is correct, as $\angle i = \angle r$.

EXPERIMENT 8

Objective To determine the density of a solid (denser than water) by using a spring balance and a measuring cylinder.

Materials Required

(*i*) A solid block (whose density is to be measured).
(*ii*) Spring balance (0–100 g-f)
(*iii*) Measuring cylinder (100 mL)
(*iv*) Iron stand
(*v*) Glass stopper
(*vi*) Fine cotton thread
(*vii*) Beaker containing water

Theory

(*i*) **Density** It is defined as mass per unit volume of a substance.

$$\text{Density} = \frac{\text{Mass of a substance}}{\text{Volume of a substance}}$$

SI unit of density is kg m^{-3}.

(*ii*) **Principle of spring balance** It states that the extension produced in a spring is directly proportional to the stretching force applied, provided the elastic limit of the spring is not exceeded.

(*iii*) **Graduated measuring cylinder** It is made from hard glass, so that it can withstand variations in temperature. Its side is marked in mL or cc. The volume of a liquid in mL or cc can be read directly by pouring the liquid in it.

Procedure

This experiment can be completed in two steps

I. **To determine the mass of the solid block by using a spring balance.**

(*i*) Take spring balance capable of weighing upto 100 g.
(*ii*) Suspend the spring balance vertically on an iron stand and note down the position of its pointer on the scale. Record its zero error.
(*iii*) Suspend the given solid block from the lower hook of the spring balance and note down the position of the pointer on the scale. Record the reading on the scale.
(*iv*) Calculate the corrected mass of solid block.
(*v*) Remove solid block from the spring balance and reload it. Note down the reading again.
(*vi*) Repeat this atleast three times.
(*vii*) Record your observations in tabular form.

II. **To determine the volume of the solid block using measuring cylinder.**

(*i*) Note down the least count of the measuring cylinder.
For a 100 mL capacity cylinder, usually the least count is 1 mL.
(*ii*) Pour some water into measuring cylinder and place it on a table.
(*iii*) Note the level of water in the cylinder by reading the lower meniscus.
(*iv*) Attach the solid block with a few cm long thread and lower it gently into the water, so that it is completely immersed in water.
(*v*) Note down the new reading.
(*vi*) Take difference between the two readings that give the volume of the solid block.

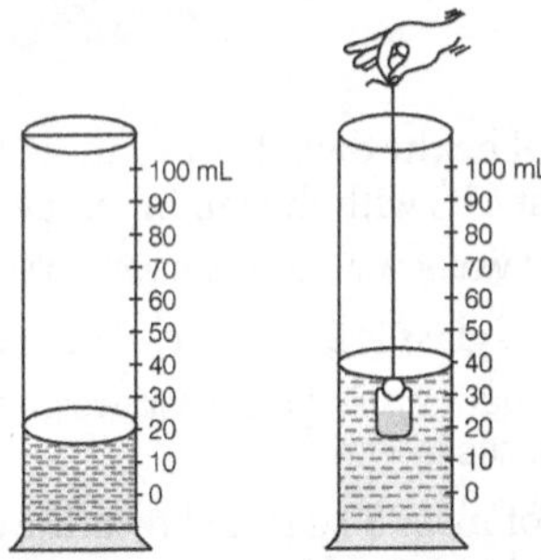

(*vii*) Repeat this experiment atleast three times.
(*viii*) Record your observations in tabular form.

Observations

(*i*) Least count of spring balance = ... g-f.
(*ii*) Zero error of the spring balance = ... g-f.

Observation Table

(A) Weight of the given solid block

S. No.	Weight of the given solid block		Mean value of the corrected weight of the solid block
	Observed	Corrected	
1			
2			
3			

(*iii*) Mean mass of solid block = m g.
(*iv*) Least count of measuring cylinder = ... mL.

(B) Reading of water level in measuring cylinder

S. No.	Initial level of water (V_1)	Final level of water (V_2)	Volume of solid block ($V_2 - V_1$)	Mean volume of solid block (mL)
1				
2				
3				

Calculations

(*i*) Mean volume of solid block = V mL

(*ii*) Density of solid block

$$= \frac{\text{Mean mass of solid block}}{\text{Mean volume of solid block}} = \frac{m}{V} \text{ g/mL}$$

Result

Density of the given solid block at .... °C

= .... g/mL

= .... kg/m^3

Precautions

(*i*) The pointer of spring balance should move freely on the scale.

(*ii*) The solid block should be fully immersed in water and should not touch the sides and bottom of measuring cylinder.

(*iii*) While reading the level of water in the measuring cylinder, keep your eye at the level of the lower meniscus and read the lower meniscus.

(*iv*) The pointer on the scale should be read only after it becomes steady.

Sources of Error

Mass and volume of solid block can be measured only upto the least counts of spring balance and measuring cylinder. So, the result obtained in the experiment may not be absolutely correct.

QUESTIONS

1. What will be the density of water with respect to its density at 4°C with the fall in temperature?

Ans. Density of water will decrease with fall in temperature.

2. Density of glass is 2.5 g/ cm^3. What does it mean?

Ans. It means that 1 cm^3 of glass will weigh 2.5 g or volume of 2.5 g glass is 1 cm^3.

3. A stone of mass 50 g is tied to a fine cotton thread and then immersed in water contained in measuring cylinder. Find the density of stone.

Ans. Given

$V_1 = 25$

$V_2 = 40$

We know that density $= \frac{M}{V}$

Volume of water displaced $= (V_2 - V_1)$cc

$= (40 - 25)$ cc $= 15$ cc

$\therefore \; D = \frac{50}{15} = 3.33$ g/cc $\quad [\because M = 50 \text{ g}]$

4. Mass of the body = 62.4 g

(i) Reading of water level in measuring cylinder without solid body (V_1) = 16.4 mL

(ii) V_2 (with solid body) = 24.4 mL

Based on the above observation, what is the density of material in g/cc?

Ans. We know that, $D = \frac{M}{V}$

$V = V_2 - V_1 = (24.4 - 16.4)$ cc $= 8$ cc

$\therefore \quad D = \frac{62.4}{8}$ g/cc

$= 7.8$ g/cc

5. Spring balance is based on which principle?

Ans. As the scale of spring balance is linear.

$\therefore$ Extension of spring $\propto$ stretching force.

6. A metal cylinder is melted and the whole mass is cast in the shape of cube. What will happen to its density?

Ans. In both the cases, the volume displaced by metallic cylinder and cube will be same. So, mass per unit volume does not change. Hence, the density of both cube and metallic cylinder will be same.

7. In a spring balance, the space between 0 and 25 g marking is divided into 10 equal parts. What will be the least count of spring balance?

Ans. Least count of spring balance $= \frac{25}{10} = 2.5$ g-wt

8. If we want to determine the volume of a solid by immersing it in water, what should be the nature of solid?

Ans. To determine the volume of a solid by immersing it in water, the solid should be heavier than water and insoluble in it.

9. While determining the density of a solid, a student is provided with four different combinations

Measuring cylinder

S. No.	Range	LC
1.	0-100 mL	1 mL
2.	0-200 mL	5 mL
3.	0-100 mL	2 mL
4.	0-200 mL	2 mL

Spring balance

S. No.	Range	LC
1.	0-100 g-wt	1 g-wt
2.	0-200 g-wt	5 g-wt
3.	0-100 g-wt	2 g-wt
4.	0-200 g-wt	2 g-wt

The student should choose which combination?

Ans. The student should choose 1-1,
i.e. Measuring cylinder 0-100 mL and LC = 1 mL
Spring balance 0-100 g-wt and LC = 1 g-wt

10. Density of gold is 19600 kg / m^3. What will be its density in CGS system?

Ans. Density of gold in CGS system

$$= \frac{\text{Density of gold}}{1000}$$

$$= \frac{19600}{1000} = 19.6\,\text{g cm}^{-3} \text{ (or g/cm}^3\text{)}$$

11. What is the relation between density D, mass M and volume V of the body ?

Ans. The correct relation between density (D), mass (M) and volume (V) of the body is

$$D = \frac{M}{V}.$$

EXPERIMENT 9

Objective To establish the relation between the loss in weight of a solid when fully immersed in

(*i*) tap water (*ii*) strongly salty water, with the weight of water displaced by it, by taking atleast two different solids.

Materials Required

(*i*) A spring balance (0-100 g-f).
(*ii*) A glass stopper (about 50 g).
(*iii*) A brass weight (50 g).
(*iv*) Thin cotton thread.
(*v*) An overflow jar.
(*vi*) A wooden block.
(*vii*) A pre-weighed beaker, showing its weight on the label affixed to it, 250 cc beaker containing tap water, 250 cc beaker containing strong salty water and a common compression balance.

Theory

(*i*) **Archimedes' Principle** It states that when a body is partly or wholly immersed in a fluid (i.e. liquid or gas), it experiences an apparent loss in weight, which is equal to the weight of the fluid displaced by it.

(*ii*) The apparent loss in weight can be calculated by weighing the body, firstly in air and then completely immersing it in water, with the help of a spring balance. The difference in weights, gives the apparent loss of weight of the body in water.

(*iii*) The water displaced can be calculated as under weight of water displaced is found by collecting it in a pre-weighed beaker, then reweighing it.

(*iv*) It is found that weight of water displaced by the solid is always equal to the apparent loss of weight of the solid in water. This verifies Archimedes' principle.

(*v*) **Buoyant force** An upward force experienced by a solid, when partly or wholly immersed in a fluid.

Procedure (A)

(*i*) Take a clean glass stopper and tie it with a fine thread. Make a loop on the other end of the cotton thread.

(*ii*) Check the spring balance for zero error and record it. Let, the zero error be x g-f.

(*iii*) Suspend the glass stopper from the hook of the spring balance. Read and record its weight in air. Let, the weight be w g-f.

(*iv*) Calculate the true weight of the glass stopper in air, by subtracting the zero error from the observed weight of the glass stopper in air.

(*v*) Place the overflow jar on the wooden block and slowly pour tap water in it, till the water just starts overflowing through its spout.
At this moment, stop pouring water. In a few moments, the water from the spout stops overflowing. In this situation, the water in the overflow jar is at the verge of overflowing.

(*vi*) Place the clean and dry pre-weighed beaker (say its weight is P g-f) under the spout of the overflow jar.

(*vii*) Now, gently lower the glass stopper (which is suspended from the hook of the spring balance) into the water in the overflow jar till it gets completely immersed. Also, at the same time, the water overflows through the spout and gets collected in the measuring pre-weighed beaker.

(*viii*) Read and record the weight of the glass stopper when fully immersed in water by subtracting the zero error from the observed weight.

(*ix*) Weigh the pre-weighed beaker alongwith the displaced water on the common compression balance. Let, the weight be P_1 g-f.

(*x*) Calculate the loss of weight of water displaced by the glass stopper when fully immersed in water.

(*xi*) Calculate the weight of water displaced by the glass stopper.

(*xii*) It is noticed that

(*a*) Loss of weight of the glass stopper in water = Weight of water displaced by glass stopper

(*b*) Repeat the above experiment by immersing the glass stopper in salty water. It is noticed that;
Loss of weight of glass stopper in salty water
= Weight of salty water displaced by the glass stopper

(*c*) Repeat the experiment by using brass weight and immersing it fully in tap water. It is noticed that;
Loss of weight of brass weight in water = Weight of water displaced by brass weight

(*d*) Repeat the experiment by using brass weight and immersing it fully in salty water. It is noticed that; Loss of weight of brass in salty water = Weight of salty water displaced by brass weight.

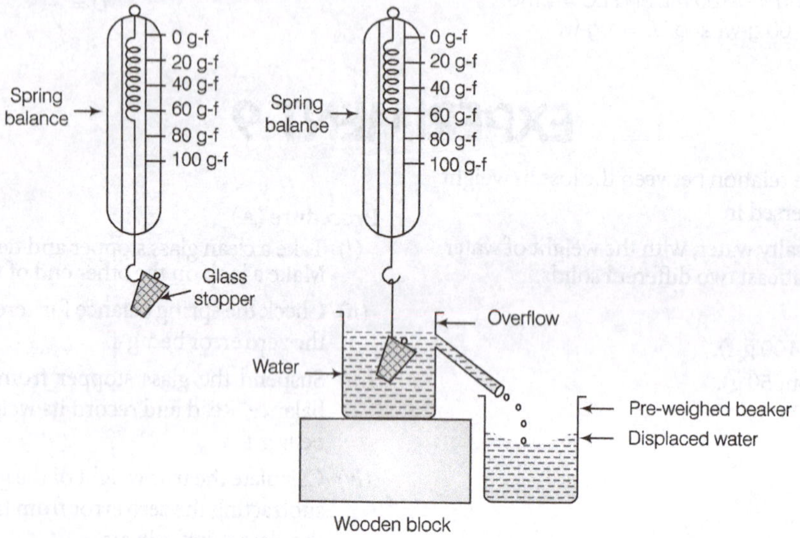

Observation Table

(*i*) Least count of the spring balance = ... g-f. (*ii*) Zero error of spring balance = ± *x*.

(A) Weight of the solid block in air and in tap water

S. No.	Weight of solid in air: Observed weight w_1 (g-f)	Weight of solid in air: Corrected weight $w'_1 = [w_1 - (\pm x)]$ (g-f)	Weight of solid in tap water: Observed weight w_2 (g-f)	Weight of solid in tap water: Corrected weight $w'_2 = [w_2 - (\pm x)]$ (g-f)	Apparent loss in weight of solid $(w'_1 - w'_2)$ (g-f)
1.					
2.					
3.					

(B) Volume of tap water displaced by solid block

S. No.	Initial level of water, V_1 (mL)	Final level of water, V_2 (mL)	Volume of tap water displaced, $(V_2 - V_1)$ (mL)
1.			
2.			
3.			

Mean volume of water displaced = ... mL.

(C) Weight of solid block in air and in salty water

S. No.	Weight of solid block in air		Weight of solid block in salty water		Apparent loss in weight of solid block $(w'_1 - w'_2)$ (g-f)
	Observed weight w_1 (g-f)	Corrected weight $w'_1 = [w_1 - (\pm x)]$ (g-f)	Observed weight w_2 (g-f)	Corrected weight $w'_2 = [w_2 - (\pm x)]$ (g-f)	
1.					
2.					
3.					

(D) Volume of the common salt solution displaced by solid block

S. No.	Initial level of salt in water, V_1 (mL)	Final level of salt solution, V_2 (mL)	Volume of the displaced salt solution, $(V_2 - V_1)$ mL
1.			
2.			
3.			

Mean volume of salty solution displaced = ...

(E) To determine density of salt solution

- Weigh accurately a dry beaker (100 mL) on a physical balance.
- Pipette out 50 mL of salt water and weigh it again.
- Mass of 50 mL of salt solution can be obtained from the above weighing.

Then, $$D = \frac{\text{Mass of salt solution (g)}}{50 \text{ mL}}$$

S. No.	Mass of empty beaker m_1 (g)	Mass of beaker +50 mL of salty water m_2 (g)	Mass of salt solution $=(m_2 - m_1)$ (g)	$D = \frac{(m_2 - m_1)}{50}$ (g/mL)
1.				
2.				
3.				

Mean value of density = ... g/mL.

Calculations (From Tables A and B)

(*i*) Apparent loss in weight of solid block in tap water = ... g - f.

(*ii*) Volume of tap water displaced by the solid block = ... mL.

(*iii*) Density of tap water = 1 g/mL.

(*iv*) Mass of tap water displaced by the solid block = Mean volume × Density = $(V_2 - V_1) \times 1$ g/mL.

(*v*) Weight of tap water displaced by solid block = ... g - f.

(*vi*) (From tables C and D) Apparent loss in weight of solid block in salt solution = ... g - f.

(*vii*) Mean volume of salt solution displaced by solid block = ... mL.

(*viii*) Density of salt solution, (as obtained experimentally), ρ = ... g/mL.

(*ix*) Mass of salt solution displaced by the solid block = mean volume × density = ... g.

(*x*) Weight of salt solution displaced by solid block = ... g - f.

Result

(i) Apparent loss in weight of solid block in tap water = Weight of tap water displaced by the solid block

(ii) Apparent loss in weight of solid block in salty water = Weight of salty water displaced by solid block

(iii) Apparent loss in weight of solid block when dipped in salt solution > Apparent loss in weight of solid block when dipped in tap water.

Conclusion

(i) The apparent loss in weight of a body when placed in a liquid is equal to the weight of liquid displaced by the body.

(ii) If the same body is immersed completely in two different liquids, the apparent loss in its weight is more in denser liquid. The liquid having higher density is called denser.

Precautions

(i) Use a sensitive spring balance.

(ii) Read and record zero error.

(iii) The water/salty water in the overflow jar should be at the verge of overflowing.

Sources of Error

(i) The spring balance can generally measure weight upto 1 g. Any change in weight less than 1 g will not be measured by it. Thus, there can be an error of ± 1 g in the weight of the glass stopper/brass weight.

(ii) While using pre-weighed beaker in subsequent experiments, if it is not thoroughly cleaned and dried, it can give wrong weight of water/salty water displaced.

QUESTIONS

1. When an object is immersed in different fluids, what will be the buoyant force acting on it.

Ans. This is so because different fluids have different densities.

2. What will be the effect on density, when a man adds salt in water present in a bucket?

Ans. Density of salt is greater than that of water. When salt is mixed in water, its density will increase.

3. What will be the level of water in a beaker, when a piece of ice is floating on water surface in a beaker?

Ans. Level of the water in a beaker will remain same because while floating, ice displaces water equal to its own weight. Hence, there is no rise in level of water.

4. When a body is immersed in a liquid, in which direction the buoyant force acts on the body?

Ans. Buoyant force exerted by the fluids always acts in vertically upward direction.

5. An object weighing 5 N in air, weighs 4.5 N in liquid. What will be the buoyant force experienced by the object?

Ans. Buoyant force = Weight in air – Weight in liquid

$= (5 - 4.5)$ N

$= 0.5$ N

6. Name the physical quantity in which apparent loss is observed when a solid object is immersed in a liquid.

Ans. Apparent loss is observed in a force and is measured in terms of weight.

7. While performing the experiment 'Archimedes principle' Rama took a glass stopper of 10 cm^3 volume and observed its weight as 40 g-wt. using a spring balance. Then, she immersed the glass stopper completely in tap water. What will be the weight of glass stopper?

Ans. We know that,

Apparent loss in weight = Weight of water displaced $= 10\ cm^3$

$\therefore$ Upthrust = 10 g

$\therefore$ Apparent weight in water $= (40 - 10) = 30$ g-wt.

8. The weight of body in air is 1500 N, when the body is immersed completely in a liquid of density d_1 it weighs 1000 N, while in another liquid of density d_2, it weighs 800 N. What will be the ratio of d_1 and d_2?

Ans. $\dfrac{\text{Density of liquid } A}{\text{Density of liquid } B} = \dfrac{d_1}{d_2} = \dfrac{\text{Upthrust due to } A}{\text{Upthrust due to } B} = \dfrac{500}{700} = \dfrac{5}{7}$

$\therefore$ Ratio of $d_1 : d_2 = 5 : 7$

9. A boat floats in water with $\frac{2}{5}$th of its volume outside water. If density of water is 10^3 kg/m^3, what will be the density of the material of this boat?

Ans. Volume of boat inside water $= 1 - \dfrac{2}{5} = \dfrac{3}{5}$

$\therefore$ Density of material of boat

$= \dfrac{\text{Volume of boat inside water}}{\text{Total volume of boat}}$

$= \dfrac{3}{5 \times 1} = 0.6\ g/cm^3$

Density of material of boat in SI system

$= 1000 \times 0.6$

$\therefore$ Density of material of boat is 0.6×10^3 kg/m^3.

10. If the density of the object placed in a liquid is equal to the density of the liquid. Wheather the object float or not?

Ans. As the density of object and liquid is same, it will float.

11. In what factor, the buoyant force on an object submerged in a fluid depends on?

Ans. As we know that,

Buoyant force $= V\rho g$

where, ρ = density of fluid

g = acceleration due to gravity

V = volume of fluid displaced

So, buoyant force depends on density of fluid, volume of fluid displaced and acceleration due to gravity.

12. What is the density of a block of wood which floats with 0.2 of its volume above water?

Ans. Volume of wood inside water $= (1-0.2) = 0.8\,\text{cm}^3$

$\therefore$ Density of wood

$$= \frac{\text{Volume of wood inside water}}{\text{Total volume of wood}}$$

$$= \frac{0.8}{1} = 0.8\ \text{g/cm}^3$$

13. Who discovered that the weight of the water displaced by a body is equal to the apparent loss of weight of a body in water?

Ans. Archimedes' discovered that the weight of the water (liquid) displaced by a body is equal to apparent loss of weight of a body in water.

14. Why is it more difficult to swim in the river water compared to sea water?

Ans. The density of sea water is more than river water. Thus, the swimmer experiences more upthrust in sea water than in the river water as the upthrust is directly proportional to the density of the liquid. Thus, it is easier to swim in the sea water as compared to the river water.

15. Four students have taken readings to verify Archimedes' principle. Which of the following students has taken the correct reading?

	Weight of the object in air	Weight lost by the object	Buoyant force	Weight of the water displaced
Student 1	100 N	30 N	70 N	30 N
Student 2	100 N	30 N	30 N	70 N
Student 3	80 N	30 N	30 N	30 N
Student 4	80 N	30 N	50 N	50 N

Ans. Student 3.

As, weight lost by the object = buoyant force = weight of water displaced.

EXPERIMENT 10

Objective

To determine the speed of a pulse propagated through a stretched helical spring.

Materials Required

(*i*) Flat wire helical spring of copper.

(*ii*) A metre rod.

(*iii*) A stopwatch.

(*iv*) A small wooden board.

Theory

(*i*) **Pulse** It is defined as the wave produced by a small disturbance in a medium.

(*ii*) **Helical spring** Long flexible spring is called slinky.

(*iii*) **Velocity of a pulse** It is defined as total distance travelled by the pulse from point *A* to *B* and back from *B* to *A* with respect to time.

i.e. $$v = \frac{\text{Total distance travelled by pulse}}{\text{Time taken}} = \frac{2d}{t}$$

Procedure

(*i*) Mark a line on the floor. From this line, measure a distance of 6 m with the help of metre rod and mark another line *AB* on the floor.

(*ii*) Let, one of the students (say S_1) hold the helical spring at point *A*.

(*iii*) Let, the other student (say S_2) stretch the helical spring to point *B*.

(*iv*) At point *A*, let student S_1 place a wooden block or a hard bound book parallel to the end of helical spring. This wooden block or hard bound book acts as a stopper.

(*v*) Let, the student S_1 pull the helical spring to position *C*, which is 10 cm from *A* and then give it a sharp push towards *A*, such that the motion of his hand stops at *A*, because of the wooden block. A pulse is produced in the helical spring, which travels towards *B*. It is then reflected towards *A* and again towards *B*. Practice it 5-10 times, till you are sure that you can generate a pulse and see it moving forward and backward.

(*vi*) Student S_2 will hold the stopwatch. When S_1 generates a pulse, student S_2 will watch the pulse to travel towards him. When the pulse reaches *B*, the student S_2 will start the stopwatch. This pulse on reflection will move towards point *A* and again towards *B*. As soon as the pulse again reaches *B*, the student S_2 will stop the stopwatch and will record the time for the pulse to travel from *B* to *A* and then back to *B*.

(*vii*) Repeat the experiment three more times.

(*viii*) Calculate the velocity of the pulse.

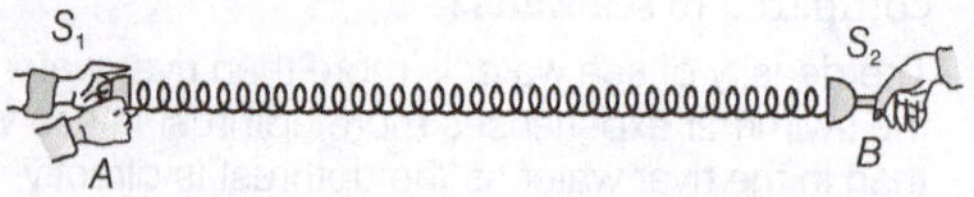

Observation Table

S. No.	Length between points A and B	Total distance travelled by pulse from B to A and back to B	Time taken	Velocity of pulse $= \frac{\text{Total distance}}{\text{Total time}}$
1.	...... m	2 × ...... m = ... m	...... s	v_1 = ... m/s
2.	...... m	2 × ...... m = ... m	...... s	v_2 = ... m/s
3.	...... m	2 × ...... m = ... m	...... s	v_3 = ... m/s
4.	...... m	2 × ...... m = ... m	...... s	v_4 = ... m/s

Calculation Average velocity of pulse $= \frac{v_1 + v_2 + v_3 + v_4}{4}$

= ......m/s

Result Velocity of pulse = ... m/s

Precautions

(*i*) Helical spring should be made of flat wire of copper.

(*ii*) Measure distance between points *A* and *B* very accurately.

(*iii*) Give a very sharp push to generate a pulse. Practice for atleast 5 to 10 times till you are sure that a pulse can be generated.

(*iv*) Make sure to arrest the push by a wooden block or a hard bound book, so that it does not overshoot point *A*.

(*v*) Experiment should be performed on a smooth floor or on a smooth table.

Sources of Error

(*i*) The student who starts and stops the stopwatch can be slow or fast and hence may record wrong time.

(*ii*) The push should not exceed the limit of 10 cm as it will reduce the distances between points *A* and *B*.

QUESTIONS

1. **When a pulse is formed on a helical spring, how medium oscillate?**

Ans. When a pulse is formed on a helical spring, the medium oscillates for a short while and then returns to its original position.

2. **If the air in the room cools down, what will be effect on the speed of sound?**

Ans. Speed of sound decreases with the fall in temperature.

3. **How can we sense a compression in a spring?**

Ans. When turns in a slinky are close to one another, it signifies compressions.

4. **While performing experiment to determine the velocity of pulse through helical spring, four students *A, B, C and D* did it by stretching the slinky given to each of them of length 4 m, 10 m, 3.5 m, 2.8 m, respectively. Which student will get the most correct result?**

Ans. Student *B* will get the most correct result because time can be measured more accurately in larger helical spring.

5. **The stopwatch used by a student to measure velocity of a pulse in a slinky was of least count 0.1s. He stops the stopwatch, when a pulse has made 3 journeys from one end to the other of the slinky. He finds seconds hand to be at 47th division. What will be correct time?**

Ans. Time = Number of divisions × Least count = 47 × 0.1

∴ Time = 4.7 s

6. **Following figure shows a pulse generated in a string which moves through it and strikes a rigid pole.**

What will be the direction of reflected pulse?

Ans. The reflected pulse after striking the rigid pole will be as follows:

7. **If a stopwatch makes '*t*' second, when pulse moves '*n*' times to and fro, what will be the time period of the motion of pulse?**

Ans. Time period = Total time ÷ number of oscillations

$= \frac{t}{n}$

8. **A weight suspended from a spring is pulled downward and then released. Which type of wave is produced in the spring?**

Ans. A periodic wave is produced.

9. **A pulse was created in a stretched string of length 5 m by four students *A, B, C* and *D*. They observed that the pulse returned after reflection at the point of creation 5 times in 10 s and calculated the speed as given below.**

Student	*A*	*B*	*C*	*D*
Speed m/s	0.5	2.5	5	10

Which student's observation is correct?

Ans. We know that velocity of pulse $= \frac{2d}{t} = \frac{2 \times 5 \times 5}{10}$
$= 5$ m/s

$\therefore$ Student *C*'s observation is correct.

10. Write the factor in which the speed of propagation of a pulse in a helical spring depends on?

Ans. It depends on
(i) dimensions of helical spring
(ii) material of helical spring
(iii) length of helical spring

11. To find the velocity of the pulse produced in a string. What will be needed?

Ans. To find the velocity of the pulse produced in a string, we need (i) measuring scale and (ii) stopwatch.

12. Two slinkies *A* and *B* of same length are made up of two different materials. The time taken by 20 pulses to travel through both of them and then come back are 70 s and 90 s, respectively. What does it conclude?

Ans. From the above statement, it can be concluded that in slinky *B*, pulse takes larger time to travel than in *A* and hence moves slower.

13. While determining the velocity of propagation of pulse, which type of pulse is generated on the helical spring in the experiment?

Ans. Longitudinal pulse is produced as the pulse and the particles of medium travel in the same direction.

14. In the experiment for determining the velocity of a pulse propagating along the length of string. We prefer a long thick cotton string. Why?

Ans. We prefer long thick cotton string, because longer the string, more accurately we can measure the time.

15. A weight is suspended from a flexible spring which is tied rigidly to a wall. It is released and then left. What will be the disturbance produced to the spring called?

Ans. The disturbance produced in the spring will be called pulse.

16. What is the velocity of a pulse for the slinky when it takes 5 s to travel from point *A* to *B* and back to *A*. The distance between *A* and *B* is 5 m.

Ans. $v = \frac{2d}{t} = \frac{2 \times 5}{5} = 2$ m/s

17. When a stone is dropped in water, what is produced at the point of impact?

Ans. A pulse is produced at the point of impact on dropping a stone in water.

18. The distance between compression and rarefaction of a sound is 7 cm. So, what will be its wavelength?

Ans. Wavelength is the distance between two compressions or two rarefactions. In other words, wavelength is a combined length of a compression and an adjacent rarefaction, i.e. 2×7 cm $= 14$ cm.

19. Shyam was calculating the velocity of wave using a slinky. What should be the features of spring to be used?

Ans. It should be long, soft and flexible. With more elastic and lengthier spring, velocity of the wave can be studied better.

20. A student sets up a slinky on a smooth table top in the manner shown below. If he gives a jerk to its free end, then in what direction, he can produce a pulse in the helical spring?

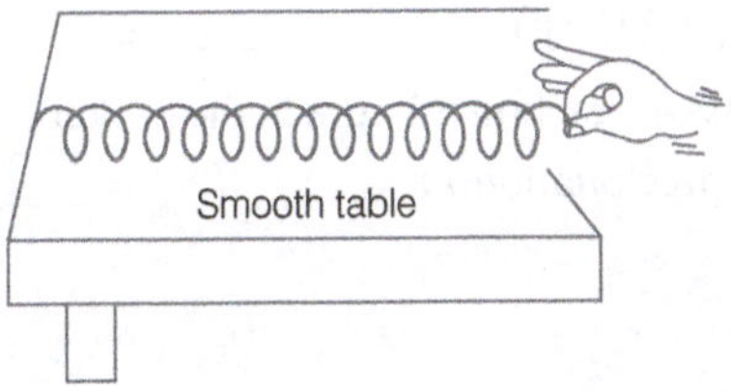

Ans. Backward and forward along the length of the helical spring.

EXPERIMENT 11

Objective To verify the law of conservation of mass in a chemical reaction.

Materials Required Barium chloride ($BaCl_2 \cdot 2H_2O$), sodium sulphate ($Na_2SO_4 \cdot 10H_2O$), distilled water, two beakers (150 mL), one beaker (250 mL), physical balance, spring balance (0–500 g) and a polythene bag, two watch glasses of known masses and a glass stirrer.

Theory

- Law of conservation of mass is also known as **law of indestructibility of mass.**
- It states that during a chemical reaction, matter is neither created nor destroyed.
- Thus, in a chemical reaction, total mass of the reactants is equal to the total mass of the products or we can say that mass remains conserved during a chemical reaction.

Procedure

(*i*) Pour 100 mL distilled water in two beakers (150 mL).
(*ii*) Using the physical balance and a watch glass of known mass, weigh 7.2 g of $BaCl_2 \cdot 2H_2O$ and dissolve it in a beaker (150 mL) containing 100 mL distilled water.
(*iii*) Similarly, weigh 16.1 g of $Na_2SO_4 \cdot 10H_2O$ in another watch glass of known mass and dissolve it in another beaker (150 mL) containing 100 mL distilled water.

(iv) Take the third beaker (250 mL) and weigh it using a spring balance and polythene bag.

(v) Both solutions are mixed in the third beaker and contents are stirred using a glass stirrer.

(vi) The beaker containing the reaction mixture is weighed again for determining the mass of reaction products.

(vii) Compare the masses of reactants and products before and after the chemical reaction.

Observations

(i) Mass of 100 mL distilled water = 100.0 g
(The density of distilled water is 1 g/mL)

(ii) Mass of $BaCl_2 \cdot 2H_2O$ = 7.2 g

(iii) Mass of $BaCl_2$ solution = 107.2 g

(iv) Mass of $Na_2SO_4 \cdot 10H_2O$ = 16.1 g

(v) Mass of Na_2SO_4 solution = 116.1 g

(vi) Total mass of reactants (solutions of $BaCl_2$ and Na_2SO_4) = 223.3 g

(vii) Mass of empty 250 mL beaker, m_1 = ____ g

(viii) Initial mass of reaction mixture and empty beaker (before the precipitation),
$m_2 = (m_1 + 223.3\text{g})$ = ____ g

(ix) Final mass of reaction mixture in the beaker after the precipitation, m_3 = ____ g

Observation Table

Experiment	Observation	Inference
Dissolve separately solid $BaCl_2 \cdot 2H_2O$ and $Na_2SO_4 \cdot 10\,H_2O$ in distilled water taken in separate beakers.	A clear solution is formed in both the beakers.	
Mix the above two solutions in a separate beaker.	A white precipitate of $BaSO_4$ is formed.	$BaCl_2(aq) + Na_2SO_4(aq) \longrightarrow BaSO_4(s) + 2NaCl(aq)$ (white ppt.)

Result On comparison of the masses of the reaction mixture before and after the reaction, it is found that,

Total mass before reaction = Total mass after reaction

Conclusion Above results verifies the law of conservation of mass.

Precautions

(i) The spring balance should be held vertically while taking measurements.

(ii) Before using the spring balance, ensure that the pointer is at zero mark.

(iii) The readings of the spring balance should be noted only when its pointer comes to rest.

(iv) Mixing of barium chloride and sodium sulphate solutions should be done slowly with constant stirring.

QUESTIONS

1. 4 g of calcium completely react with 1.6 g of oxygen. What will be the mass of calcium oxide formed?

Ans. $\underset{\substack{\text{Calcium}\\ 4\text{ g}}}{2\,Ca} + \underset{\substack{\text{Oxygen}\\ 1.6\text{ g}}}{O_2} \longrightarrow \underset{\substack{\text{Calcium oxide}\\ x}}{2\,CaO}$

According to the law of conservation of mass,

Mass of reactants = Mass of product

$\therefore \quad 4\text{g} + 1.6\text{ g} = x \Rightarrow x = 5.6\text{g}$

2. "The mass can neither be created nor destroyed in a chemical reaction".
Which law is described by this statement?

Ans. Law of conservation of mass states that "mass can neither be created nor destroyed in a chemical reaction". Law of constant proportion deals about the ratio by which atoms are combined. Dalton's atomic theory deals about indivisibility of atom. Avogadro's law say, one mole of any substance have equal number of constituent particles.

3. 1.25 g of copper carbonate was added to a beaker containing 20 g of HCl. After completion of chemical reaction, the mass of the beaker and its contents were less than 21.25 g. Why does this happen?

Ans. Chemical equation for the above reaction can be written as

$\underset{\substack{\text{Copper}\\ \text{carbonate}}}{CuCO_3} + \underset{\substack{\text{Dil.}\\ \text{hydrochloric}\\ \text{acid}}}{2HCl} \longrightarrow \underset{\substack{\text{Copper}\\ \text{chloride}}}{CuCl_2} + \underset{\substack{\text{Carbon}\\ \text{dioxide}}}{CO_2} + \underset{\text{Water}}{H_2O}$

Since, CO_2 gas escapes in air and hence, its mass goes unrecorded. This explains, why the recorded mass is less than 21.25 g.

4. 3 g of magnesium ribbon burns completely in 2 g of oxygen to form magnesium oxide. What is the mass of magnesium oxide thus formed?

Ans. $2Mg + O_2 \longrightarrow 2MgO$

$3\text{g} + 2\text{g} \longrightarrow x$

According to the law of conservation of mass, we can write

$x = 3 + 2 = 5\,g$

$\therefore$ Mass of MgO = 5 g

5. **2 g of zinc metal is completely burned in air to form zinc oxide. It was found that mass of zinc oxide is 2.5 g. Find the mass of oxygen used to form zinc oxide.**

Ans. $\underset{2\,g}{2Zn} + \underset{x\,g}{O_2} \longrightarrow \underset{2.5\,g}{2\,ZnO}$

$\therefore$ From law of conservation of mass

$2 + x = 2.5$

$\Rightarrow \quad x = (2.5 - 2)\,g = 0.5\,g$

6. **10 g of $CaCO_3$ on complete decomposition gives 4.4 g of CO_2. What will be the mass of the residue left behind?**

Ans. The chemical equation for the above reaction can be written as

$$CaCO_3(s) \xrightarrow{\Delta} CaO(s) + CO_2(g)$$

Mass of residue = Mass of $CaCO_3$ − Mass of CO_2

$= (10 - 4.4)\,g = 5.6\,g$

7. **To verify the law of conservation of mass in the case of a chemical change, in which form of sodium sulphate and barium chloride should be used?**

Ans. Aqueous solutions are used because precipitation reactions take place only when reactants are in aqueous states.

8. **For which types of changes law of conservation of mass is applicable?**

Ans. Law of conservation of mass is applicable to all physical and chemical changes.

9. **To verify law of conservation of mass, name the type of reaction which is commonly preferred?**

Ans. In precipitation reaction, one product precipitates and other one is soluble in solution hence, it is convenient to measure weight before and after the reaction. In other reactions, there is a possibility of the formation of one or more gaseous product which might escape out, thus making comparison of masses inconvenient.

10. **4.0 g of hydrogen completely reacts with 32 g of oxygen. What will be the mass of water thus formed?**

Ans. Equation for formation of water is as follows

$$\underset{4\,g}{2H_2} + \underset{32\,g}{O_2} \longrightarrow \underset{x}{2H_2O}$$

According to the law of conservation of mass,

Mass of reactants = Mass of products

Amount of water formed is $x = (4 + 32)\,g = 36\,g$

11. **4.90 g of $KClO_3$, when heated produced 1.94 g of oxygen. What will be the mass of residue left?**

Ans. $\underset{4.90\,g}{2KClO_3} \xrightarrow{\Delta} \underset{x}{2KCl} + \underset{1.94\,g}{3O_2}$

According to the law of conservation of mass,

Mass of reactants = Mass of products

$4.9 = x + 1.94$

$\therefore \quad x = (4.9 - 1.94)\,g = 2.96\,g$

$\therefore$ Mass of residue left is 2.96 g.

12. **Two reactants kept in beaker as aqueous solution, weighs 200 g altogether. If beaker weighs 100 g, then find the total mass of product formed.**

Ans. From law of conservation of mass,

Mass of (2 reactants + beaker) = Mass of product + Mass of beaker

200 g = Mass of product + 100 g

Mass of product = 100 g

13. **$\underset{10\,g}{AgNO_3(aq)} + \underset{5\,g}{NaCl(aq)} \longrightarrow \underset{7\,g}{AgCl(s)} + NaNO_3(aq)$**

In the above reaction, find the amount of $NaNO_3$?

Ans. According to the law of conservation of mass,

Mass of ($AgNO_3$ + NaCl) = Mass of (AgCl + $NaNO_3$)

$\therefore \quad (10 + 5)\,g = (7 + x)\,g$

$\therefore \; x = 15 - 7 = 8\,g$

$\therefore$ Mass of $NaNO_3$ is 8 g.

14. **170 g of silver nitrate ($AgNO_3$) reacts with 58 g of sodium chloride (NaCl) to produce 143 g of silver chloride precipitate and 85 g of sodium nitrate. Verify that the reaction is in agreement with the law of conservation of mass.**

Ans. The chemical equation for the above reaction is as follows

$$\underset{170\,g}{AgNO_3(aq)} + \underset{58\,g}{NaCl(aq)} \longrightarrow \underset{143\,g}{AgCl(s)} + \underset{85\,g}{NaNO_3(aq)}$$

Total mass of reactants = 170 + 58 = 228 g

Total mass of products = 143 + 85 = 228 g

$\because$ The total mass of the reactants are equal to the total mass of the product, therefore, the given reaction is in accordance with the law of conservation of mass.

15. **Give two precautions which should be taken while performing the experiment to verify the law of conservation of mass.**

Ans. (*i*) The spring balance should be held vertically while taking measurements.

(*ii*) Before using the spring balance, ensure that the pointer is at zero mark.

16. **To verify the law of conservation of mass in a chemical reaction a student takes a known amount of solution of $BaCl_2$ in a small test tube and hanged it in a sealed conical flask, containing Na_2SO_4 solution. The flask is slightly tilted, so that the two solutions mix with each other and a chemical reaction occurs. What is the relation between the masses of the chemical involved?**

Ans. Barium chloride ($BaCl_2$) solution reacts with the solution of sodium sulphate (Na_2SO_4) to give the precipitate of barium sulphate ($BaSO_4$)and a solution of sodium chloride (NaCl).

The reaction involved is as follows

$$BaCl_2(aq) + Na_2SO_4(aq) \longrightarrow BaSO_4(s) + 2NaCl(aq)$$

$\therefore$ Mass of ($BaCl_2$ + Na_2SO_4) = Mass of ($BaSO_4$ + NaCl)

17. **On complete combustion of a hydrocarbon in 0.22g oxygen, 0.9g of water and 0.44g of CO_2 is produced. Calculate the mass of hydrocarbon used.**

Ans. The chemical equation for the above reaction is as follows

$$\underset{\substack{\text{(Hydrocarbon)} \\ x}}{C_nH_{2n+2}} + \underset{\substack{\text{(Oxygen)} \\ 0.22\text{ g}}}{O_2} \longrightarrow \underset{\substack{\text{(Water)} \\ 0.9\text{ g}}}{H_2O} + \underset{\substack{\text{(Carbon} \\ \text{dioxide)} \\ 0.44\text{ g}}}{CO_2}$$

From law of conservation of mass, we have

$$x + 0.22 = 0.9 + 0.44$$

$$x = 1.34 - 0.22 = 1.12 \text{ g}$$

18. **If law of conservation of mass holds good, predict how much the residue would weigh when 96 g of $CaCO_3$ is heated and 12.2 g of CO_2 is released?**

Ans. Mass of reactant = 96g

Total mass of products = $(x + 12.2)$g

$\because$ Mass of reactant = Mass of product

(law of conservation of mass)

$\therefore \quad 96 = x + 12.2$

$\Rightarrow \quad x = 83.8$ g

Sample Question Paper 1 (Unsolved)
Science

Time : 3 hrs	M.M. : 80

General Instructions

1 The question paper consists of 39 questions.
2 All questions are compulsary. There is no overall choice. However, an internal choice is provided in some questions.
3 This question paper is divided into five sections A, B, C, D and E.
4 Only one of the alternatives has to be attempted in such question.
3 **Section A** - Consists of 20 Multiple Choice Questions carrying 1 mark each.
4 **Section B** - Consists of 6 Very Short Answer Type Questions carrying 2 marks each. Answer to these questions should be in the range of 30 to 50 words.
5 **Section C** - Consists of 7 Short Answer Type Questions carrying 3 marks each. Answer to these questions should be in the range of 50 to 80 words.
6 **Section D** - Consists of 3 Long Answer Type Questions carrying 5 marks each. Answer to these questions should be in the range of 80 to 120 words.
7 **Section E** - Consists of 3 Source Based/Case Based units of assessment of 4 marks each with sub-parts.

Section A

In this section, questions no. 1 to 20 are multiple choice questions. All questions are compulsory.

1. Consider the following.

Granite, sodium chloride, muddy water, milk of magnesia

How many of them are pure substance?

(a) 1 (b) 2 (c) 3 (d) 4

2. A sound wave is reflected from a brick wall. Compared with the incident wave, the reflected wave has

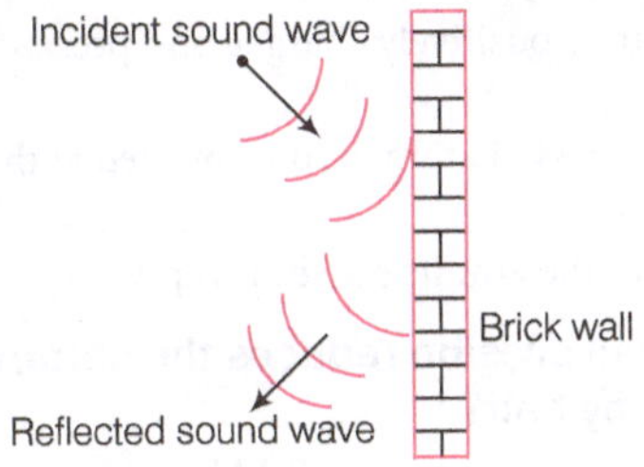

(a) a greater amplitude
(b) a shorter wavelength
(c) the same speed
(d) the same velocity

3. In the given ultrastructure of the animal cell, identify the organelle where ATP formation takes place.

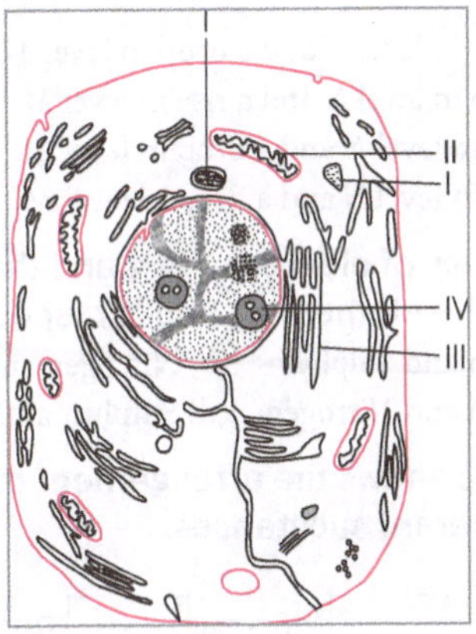

(a) I and II (b) Only III
(c) Only II (d) I, II, III and IV

4. The formula of chloride of metal *M* is MCl_3, then formula of the phosphate of metal *M* will be

(a) MPO_4 (b) M_2PO_4
(c) $M(PO_4)_3$ (d) $M_2(PO_4)_3$

5. Match Column I with Column II and select the correct option.

Column I		Column II	
1.	Work	A.	Energy due to motion
2.	Kinetic energy	B.	Work done per unit time
3.	Potential energy	C.	Force x Displacement x cos θ
4.	Power	D.	Energy due to height or position

(a) 1 → C, 2 → A, 3 → D, 4 → B
(b) 1 → B, 2 → A, 3 → C, 4 → D
(c) 1 → D, 2 → C, 3 → A, 4 → B
(d) 1 → A, 2 → D, 3 → C, 4 → B

6. Given below figure represents demonstration of osmosis by egg membrane osmoscope. After few days, which of the following would have occurred?

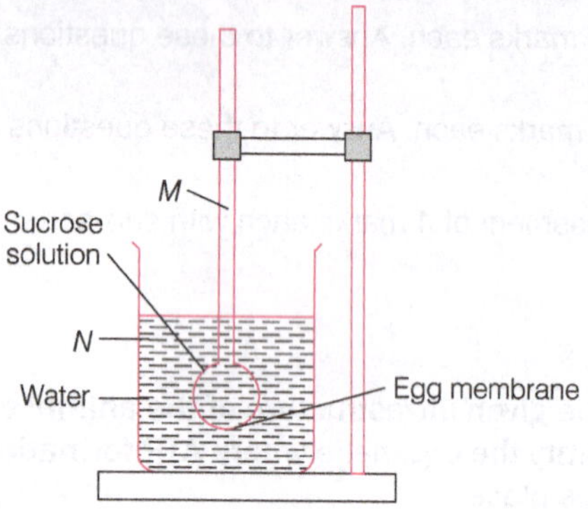

(a) A drop in level *N* and a drop in level *M*.
(b) A drop in level *N* and a rise in level *M*.
(c) A rise in level *N* and a drop in level *M*.
(d) A rise in level *N* and a drop in level *M*.

7. The valency of element *X* is 4 and that of *Y* is 2. Identify the elements *X* and *Y*, respectively.

(a) Carbon and Sulphur (b) Nitrogen and Chlorine
(c) Carbon and Nitrogen (d) Sulphur and hydrogen

8. The figure shows the arrangement of particle in three different substances.

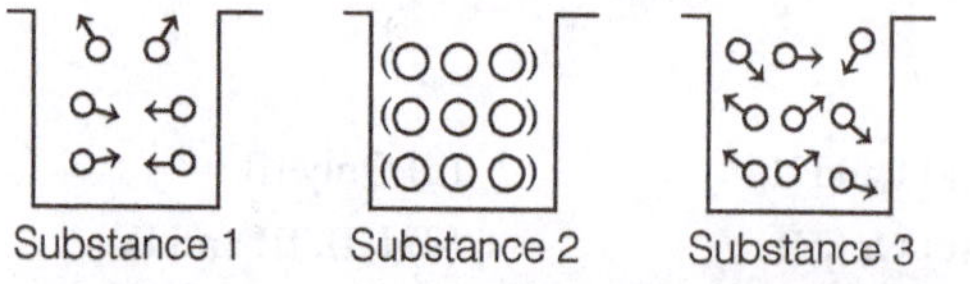

Which of the following is correct regarding the state of the substances 1,2 and 3, respectively?

(a) Solid, liquid and gas (b) Gas, liquid and solid
(c) Liquid, gas and solid (d) Gas, solid and liquid

9. A person met with an accident in which two long bones of hand were dislocated. Which among the following may be the possible reason?

(a) Ligament break
(b) Tendon break
(c) Break of skeletal muscle
(d) Areolar tissue break

10. The symbol of helium is

$$He_2^4$$

It shows that

(a) helium contains two electrons.
(b) an atom of helium has 2 protons and 4 neutrons in its nucleus.
(c) helium has a atomic number of 4.
(d) helium is as a diatomic molecule.

11. Which of the following helps in the repair of tissue and fills up the space inside the organ?

(a) Tendons (b) Adipose tissue
(c) Areolar tisssue (d) Cartilage

12. A solution contains 50 g of common salt in 450 g of water. The concentration of the solution is

(a) 500% (b) 50% (c) 10% (d) 80%

13. In the given experiment shown in diagram below.

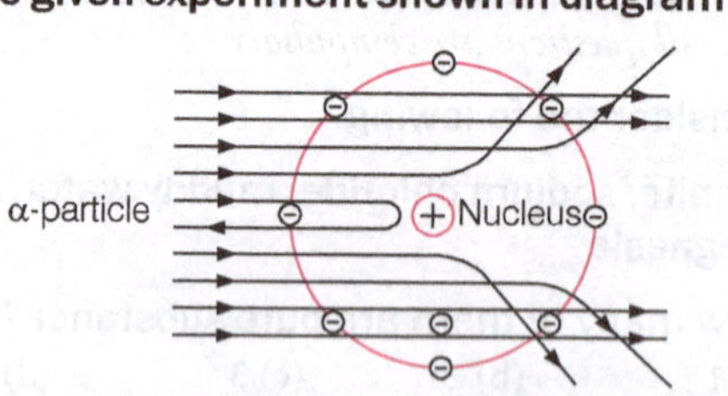

Most of α-particles pass through gold foil without any deviation. This indicates that

(a) the atom is spherical.
(b) nucleus is positively charged and present at centre of atom.
(c) entire mass of atom is concentrated at the nucleus of the atom.
(d) most of the atomic space is empty.

14. Which cell division reduces the chromosome number by half?

(a) Mitosis (b) Meiosis
(c) Both (a) and (b) (d) None of these

15. Which of the following is not a micronutrient?

(a) Iron (b) Nitrogen
(c) Zinc (d) Copper

16. Flexibility in plants is due to ....
(a) collenchyma
(b) sclerenchyma
(c) parenchyma
(d) chlorenchyma

Direction (Q.Nos. 17-20) In each of the following questions, a statement of Assertion is given by the corresponding statement of Reason. Out of the given statements, choose the correct one.
(a) If both A and R are true and R is the correct explanation of A.
(b) If both A and R are true, but R is not the correct explanation of A.
(c) If A is true, but R is false.
(d) If A is false, but R is true.

17. Assertion (A) Hybridisation is a way to obtain new and improved varieties of plants and animals.

Reason (R) Crossing may be done between two different varieties, two different species of same genus or different genus.

18. Assertion (A) Pure substances in which molecules are made up of only one kind of atoms are known as elements.

Reason (R) Hydrogen, oxygen and nitrogen are elements.

19. Assertion (A) A body can float only if it displaces liquid whose weight is equal to the actual weight.

Reason (R) The body will experience zero downward force in that case.

20. Assertion (A) Fish and other aquatic animals are used as food by man.

Reason (R) Fish and other varieties of sea food is a good source of protein.

Section B

Question Nos. 21 to 26 are very short answer type questions. Each question carries 2 marks.

21. (i) What do you understand by inertia?
(ii) Give one example each for the inertia of rest and inertia of motion.

22. (i) Helium atom has an atomic mass of 4 u and two protons in its nucleus. How many neutrons does it have?
(ii) Write the distribution of electrons in carbon and sodium atoms.

23. (i) In which medium, speed of the sound is maximum?

Or

(ii) Why we cannot hear an echo in a small room?

24. (i) Name the following :
(a) Tissue that forms inner lining of mouth.
(b) Tissue that transports food in plants.

Or

(ii) What happens to the cells formed by meristematic tissue?

25. Observe the diagram and answer the following questions.

(i) Name the muscles which helps in locomotion.
(ii) Explain the structure of these muscles.
(iii) Name the organs in which these muscles are present.

26. In agricultural practices, higher input gives higher yield. Discuss how?

Section C

Question Nos. 27 to 33 are short answer type questions. Each question carries 3 marks.

27. Define
(i) Vermicompost
(ii) Green manure
(iii) Biofertiliser

28. (i) Name the type of colloids in each of the following in which the dispersed phase and the dispersion medium are respectively.
(a) Liquid and gas
(b) Liquid and liquid
(c) Liquid and solid

Also, give one example of each.

Or

(ii) (a) What is meant by concentration of a solution? How will you prepare a 10% solution of sugar ?

(b) Explain, why particles of colloidal solution do not settle down when left undisturbed, while in case of a suspension they do.

(c) Tincture of iodine has antiseptic properties. How it is prepared ?

29. Name the tissue responsible for the flexibility in plants. How would you differentiate it from other permanent tissues?

30. (i)

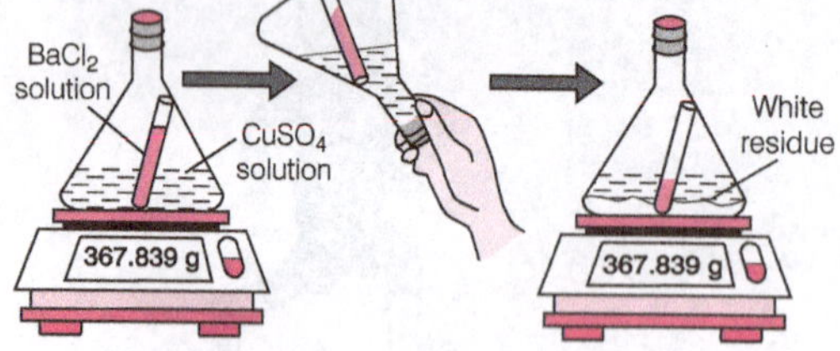

In the above given experiment, does the reaction follow law of conservation of mass? Justify your answer.

(ii) Write the formulae for the following compounds

(a) Caustic potash

(b) Limestone

(c) Common salt

31. When dried raisins are placed in plain water, raisins swell up. Also, when same swelled raisins are placed in concentrated salt solution, raisins shrunk.

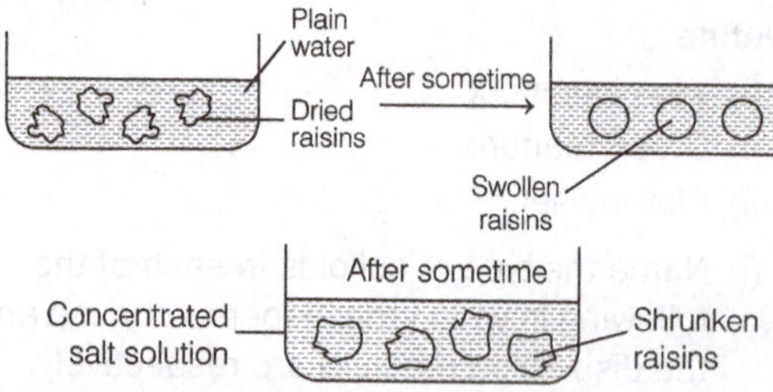

Analyse and compile the facts for the above experiment and write the whole process in your own words.

32. (i) Calculate the kinetic energy of a car of mass 400 kg moving with a velocity of 72 km/h.

(ii) If a passenger of mass 50 kg sites in the car, calculate the total kinetic energy of the car and passenger system.

33. Figure shows the distance-time graph of three objects *A*, *B* and *C*. Study the graph and answer the following questions.

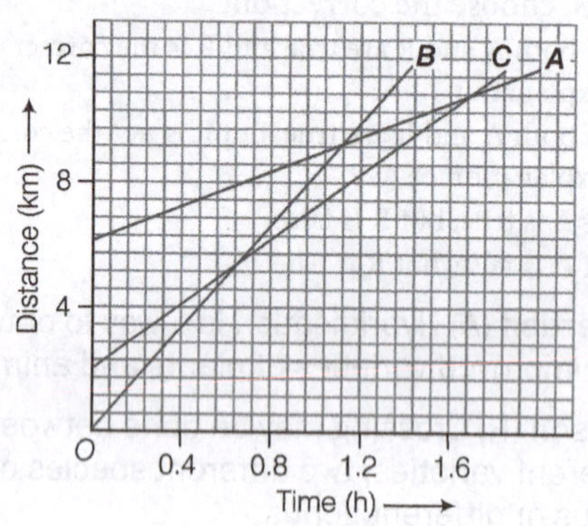

(i) Which of the three is travelling the fastest?

(ii) Are all three ever at same point on the road?

Section D

Question Nos. 34 to 36 are long answer type questions. Each question carries 5 marks.

34. (i)

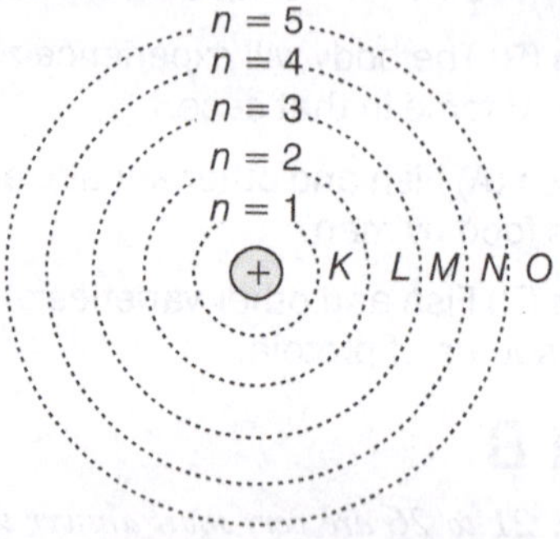

(a) What is the maximum number of electrons that can be accommodated in the outermost shell of an atom?

(b) What characteristic feature is seen in the configuration of chemically inactive elements?

(c) How are ions formed? Explain with example.

Or (ii) (a) Explain, why the number of atoms in one mole of hydrogen gas is double the number of atoms in one mole of helium gas?

(b) Explain atomic mass unit.

(c) How many atoms are present in

I. MnO_2 molecule

II. CO molecule?

35. (i) Observe the figure and answer the following questions:

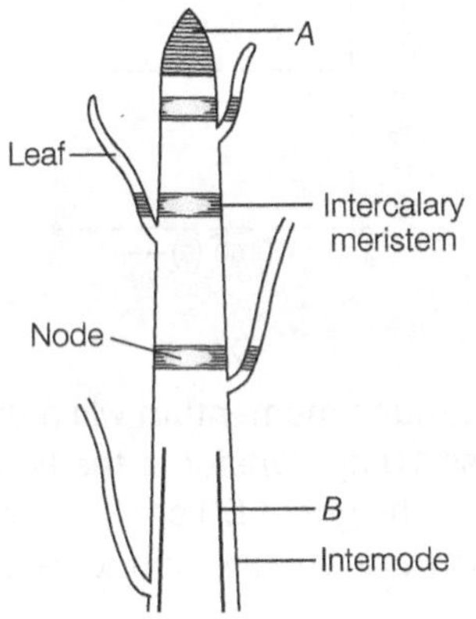

(a) What does the figure represents ?

(b) Write the function of *A* and *B*.

(c) Which part is responsible for increase in growth of internode?

Or

(ii) Give reasons for

(a) Meristematic cells have a prominent nucleus and dense cytoplasm but they lack vacuole.

(b) Intercellular spaces are absent in sclerenchymatous tissues.

(c) We get a crunchy and granular feeling, when we chew pear fruit.

(d) Branches of a tree move and bend freely in high wind velocity.

(e) It is difficult to pull out the husk of a coconut tree.

36. (i) An insect moves along a circular path of radius 10 cm with a constant speed. It takes 1 min to move from a point on the path to the diametrically opposite point, find (a) the distance covered, (b) the speed, (c) the displacement and (d) the average velocity.

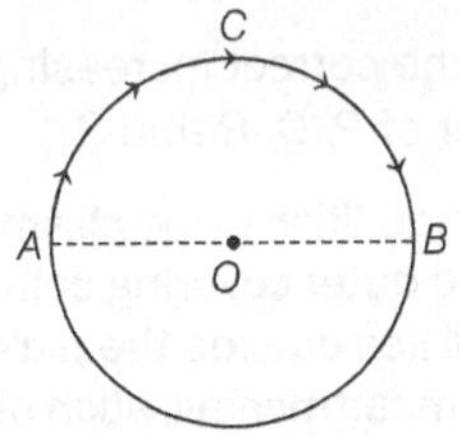

Or

(ii) The distance-time graph of two trains are shown in figure. The trains start simultaneously in the same direction.

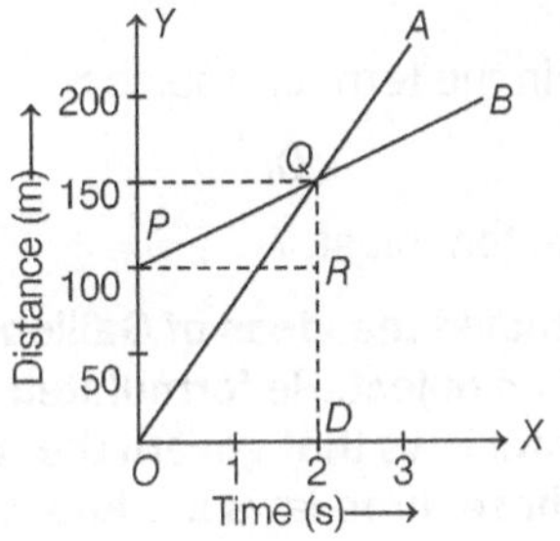

(a) How much *A* is ahead of *B* when the motion starts?

(b) What is the speed of *B*?

(c) When and where will *A* catch *B*?

(d) What is the difference between speeds of *A* and *B*?

(e) Is the speed of both the trains uniform or non-uniform ? Justify your answer.

Section E

Question Nos. 37 to 39 are case/source based questions. Each question carries 4 marks.

37.

Elements	Protons	Neutrons	Electrons
P	19	21	19
Q	20	20	20
R	17	18	17
S	17	20	17

(i) Find the nature of element *R* in above table.

(ii) Define the term isobar and which two elements from the above given table form a pair of isobar?

Or

(ii) Write the correct increasing order of atomic number of *P*, *Q*, *R* and S.

38. **Plant cells, in addition to the plasma membrane, have another rigid outer covering called the cell wall. The cell wall lies outside the plasma membrane. An extensive compartmentalisation of cytoplasm is seen through the presence of membrane-bound organelles. Cell organelles like plastids, vacuoles are present in plant cell but absent in animal cell.**

(i) Name the main constituent of cell wall.

(ii) Name the types of plastids found in plant cells.

(iii) Explain the term protoplasm.

Or

(iii) Define tonoplast.

39. **Newton studied the ideas of Galileo regarding the motion of an object. He formulated three fundamental laws that govern the motion of objects. These three laws are known as Newton's laws of motion.**

The first law of motion states that an object will continue to remain in its state of rest or of uniform motion along a straight line path unless an external force acts on it. This means, all objects resist change in their state.

The second law of motion states that the rate of change of momentum of an object is directly proportional to the applied external force and takes place in the direction in which external force acts.

The third law of motion states that whenever an object exerts a force on another object, then the second object exerts an equal and opposite force on the first object.

(a) Name the physical quantity which corresponds to the rate of change of momentum.

(b) Give two examples of effects of force.

(c) Velocity-time graph of a moving particle of mass 1 kg is shown below. What is the force acting on the particle?

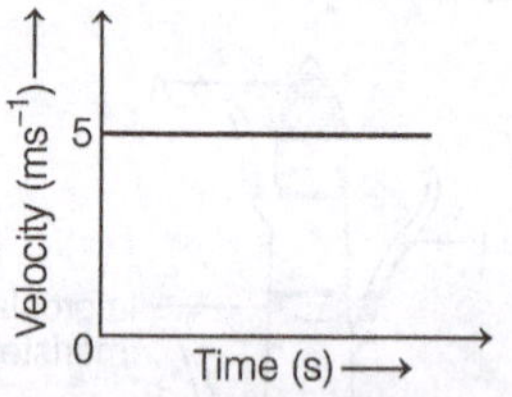

Or

(c) How much momentum will a dumb bell of mass 10 kg transfer to the floor, if it falls from a height of 80 cm ? [Take, its downward acceleration to be 10 ms^{-2}]

Answers

1. (a) **2.** (c) **3.** (c) **4.** (a) **5.** (a) **6.** (c) **7.** (a) **8.** (d) **9.** (a) **10.** (a) **11.** (c) **12.** (c) **13.** (d) **14.** (b) **15.** (b) **16.** (a) **17.** (a) **18.** (b) **19.** (b) **20.** (a)

32. (i) 80000 J (ii) 90000 J

36. (a) 31.4 cm (b) 31.4 cm/min
(c) 20 cm and (d) 20 cm/min

Or (a) 100 m (b) 25 ms^{-1}
(c) 2s, 150 m
(d) 50 ms^{-1}

Sample Question Paper 2 (Unsolved)
Science

Time : 3 hrs	M.M. : 80

General Instructions

1 The question paper consists of 39 questions.
2 All questions are compulsary. There is no overall choice. However, an internal choice is provided in some questions.
3 This question paper is divided into five sections A, B, C, D and E.
4 Only one of the alternatives has to be attempted in such question.
3 **Section A** - Consists of 20 Multiple Choice Questions carrying 1 mark each.
4 **Section B** - Consists of 6 Very Short answer Type Questions carrying 2 marks each. Answer to these questions should be in the range of 30 to 50 words.
5 **Section C** - Consists of 7 Short Answer Type Questions carrying 3 marks each. Answer to these questions should be in the range of 50 to 80 words.
6 **Section D** - Consists of 3 Long Answer Type Questions carrying 5 marks each. Answer to these questions should be in the range of 80 to 120 words.
7 **Section E** - Consists of 3 Source Based/Case Based units of assessment of 4 marks each with sub-parts.

Section A

In this section, questions no. 1 to 20 are multiple choice questions. All questions are compulsory.

1. $\underset{\text{(Liquid)}}{\text{Water}} \rightleftharpoons \underset{\text{(Solid)}}{\text{Ice}}$

The solid form of water floats on the surface of water because

(a) it is heavier than water.
(b) the density of water is same as that of ice.
(c) it is lighter than water.
(d) None of the above

2. Which of the following statements is incorrect about gravitation?

(a) Gravitational force between two objects is inversely proportional to the square of the distance between them.
(b) Gravitational force between two objects is independent of the masses of the objects.
(c) Gravitational force is always attractive in nature.
(d) The value of acceleration due to gravity is approximately 9.8 m/s^2 near the surface of the earth.

3. The following figure shows two crop field (plot *A* and plot *B*) which have been treated by manures and chemical fertilisers respectively, keeping other environmental factors same.

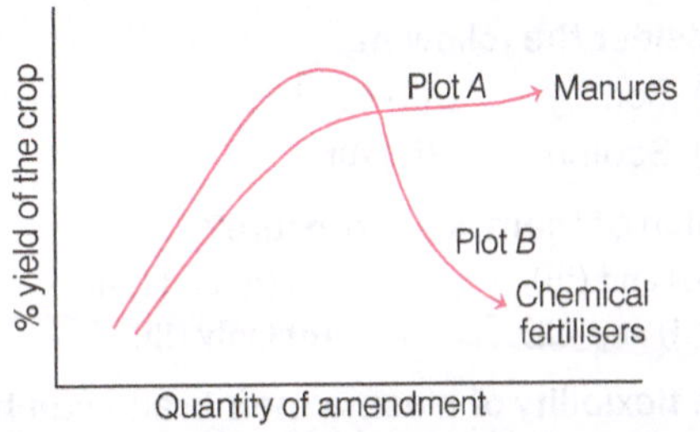

Which of the following option is best suited to show the reason of delay in highest peak in plot *A* graph as compared to *B*.

(a) Manure decay slowly so that release of minerals is also delayed
(b) Manure decay fastly so that fast release of minerals occurs that shows delayed
(c) Leaching
(d) None of the above

4. Solid $\underset{B}{\overset{A}{\rightleftharpoons}}$ Liquid $\underset{D}{\overset{C}{\rightleftharpoons}}$ Gas

Identify the process *A, B, C* and *D*.

	A	*B*	*C*	*D*
(a)	Fusion	Freezing	Vapourisation	Condensation
(b	Freezing	Vapourisation	Fusion	Condensation
(c)	Condensation	Vaporisation	Fusion	Freezing
(d)	Vapourisation	Condensation	Fusion	Freezing

5. Madhur while going home from his school applies brake to slow down his speed. The direction of velocity and acceleration in the given case are

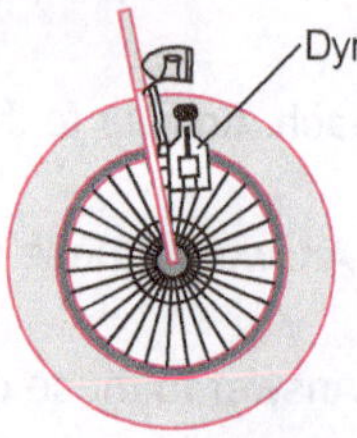

(a) opposite (b) same
(c) perpendicular (d) not related

6. Which of the following is not the function of epidermis?
(a) Protection from adverse condition
(b) Gaseous exchange
(c) Conduction of water
(d) Transpiration

7. Consider the following.
(i) Soil (ii) Coal
(iii) Sodium (iv) Air

Which of them is not mixture?
(a) (i) and (iii) (b) (ii) and (iv)
(c) (ii) and (iii) (d) Only (iii)

8. The flexibility of plasma membrane can be contributed to the presence of
(a) proteins (b) lipids
(c) nucleic acids (d) Both (a) and (b)

9. The number of electrons in an element *X* is 15 and the number of neutrons is 16. Which of the following is the correct representation of the element?
(a) ${}^{31}_{15}X$ (b) ${}^{31}_{16}X$ (c) ${}^{16}_{15}X$ (d) ${}^{15}_{16}X$

10. Which of the following is not a chemical change?
(a) Decaying of wood (b) Burning of wood
(c) Sawing of wood (d) Burning of candle

11. The number of nuclei present in striped muscle fibre is
(a) one (b) many
(c) two (d) None of these

12. Choose the correct statement of the following.
(a) Conversion of solid into vapours without passing through the liquid state is called vapourisation.
(b) Conversion of solid into vapours without passing through the liquid state is called sublimation.
(c) Conversion of vapours into solid without passing through the liquid state is called freezing.
(d) Conversion of solid into liquid is called sublimation.

13. Match the Column I with Column II and select the correct option using the given codes

	Column I (Formula of compound)		Column II (Molecular mass)
(a)	NaCl	(i)	32 u
(b)	SO_2	(ii)	58.5 u
(c)	NH_3	(iii)	17 u
(d)	CH_3OH	(iv)	64 u

(a) A→(i), B→(ii), C→(iii), D→(iv)
(b) A→(ii), B→(iv), C→(iii), D→(i)
(c) A→(ii), B→(iv), C→(i), D→(iii)
(d) A→(iii), B→(i), C→(iv), D→(ii)

14. The revolution associated with increased food grain production is
(a) white revolution (b) golden revolution
(c) green revolution (d) blue revolution

15. The term protoplasm was coined by ....
(a) Purkinje
(b) Robert Hooke
(c) Virchow
(d) Robert Brown

16. Which type of honeybees has high honey collection capacity?
(a) *Apis florae* (b) *Apis mellifera*
(c) *Apis dorsata* (d) *Apis indica*

Direction *(Q.Nos. 17-20) In each of the following questions, a statement of Assertion (A) is given by the corresponding statement of Reason (R). Out of the given statements, choose the correct one.*
(a) If both A and R are true and R is the correct explanation of A.
(b) If both A and R are true, but R is not the correct explanation of A.
(c) If A is true, but R is false.
(d) If A is false, but R is true.

17. **Assertion** (A) Circular motion is an example of uniform accelerated motion.

Reason (R) A uniform circular motion, there is no acceleration.

18. **Assertion** (A) Air is a mixture of gases.

Reason (R) The composition of air includes gases like N_2, O_2, CO_2 and water vapour.

19. **Assertion** (A) Chromosomes are composed of DNA and protein.

Reason (R) These are thread-like structures present in nucleus.

20. **Assertion** (A) Axon and dendrites are special feature of neurons.

Reason (R) They help in rapid conduction of nerve impulses.

Section B

Question Nos. 21 to 26 are very short answer type questions. Each question carries 2 marks.

21. What is manure? State two advantages of using manure.

22. A player throws a ball upwards with an initial speed of 19.6 m/s.

(i) What is the direction of acceleration of the ball during the upward motion?

(ii) What are the velocity and acceleration of the ball at highest point of its motion?

23. (i) Write three differences between epithelial tissue and connective tissue.

Or

(ii) Draw the diagram of areolar tissue and label the following parts

(a) Reticular fibre

(b) Fibroblast

(c) Collagen fibre

24. (i) Classify each of the following as a homogeneous or heterogeneous mixture : soda water, wood, air, soil, vinegar.

(ii) Write any two properties of suspension.

25. The average atomic mass of a sample of an element X is 16.2 u. What are the percentages of isotopes $^{16}_{8}X$ and $^{18}_{8}X$ in the sample?

Or

Give example of two atoms

(i) having same number of neutrons but different atomic numbers.

(ii) having same valency but different valence electrons.

26. Observe the picture given below.

Mention any two benefits of using the given cropping pattern.

Section C

Question Nos. 27 to 33 are short answer type questions. Each question carries 3 marks.

27. Waves of higher frequencies are used for cleaning hard to reach the places. These are also used to detect and find the distance of object underwater.

(i) Name the type of waves.

(ii) Mention the frequency of these waves.

(iii) Write another important use of these waves.

28. (i) Dheeraj has been cultivating wheat crop year after next. However, he observed a steady decline in crop yield for past few years. Agriculture inspector then advised him to cultivate soybean or chickpea crop for next year before planting wheat crop.

Comment on the logic and validity of this suggestion.

Or

(ii) Crop protection management aims at reducing the kind of infestations caused by weeds, insect pests, crop diseases, etc. Explain how?

29. Explain why, the motion of a body which is moving with constant speed in a circular path is said to be accelerated.

30. (i) Distinguish between mass and weight of an object.
(ii) Give reason, why objects with different masses take same time to fall from a fixed height.

31. (i) Differentiate between phagocytosis and exocytosis.
(ii) What are chromosomes? List their one function.

32. (i) Many substances are said to be actively transported across the cell membrane. Elaborate how?
(ii) Present any two reasons supporting the fact that transport across cell membrane is vital to a cell.

33. (i) An element X has a valency of 2. Write the chemical formula for
(a) bromide of the element
(b) oxide of the element
(ii) Define formula unit mass of a substance.

Section D

Question Nos. 34 to 36 are long answer type questions. Each question carries 5 marks

34. (i) (a) Explain the three states of matter on the basis of the following properties.
I. Intermolecular force
II. Arrangement of molecule
(b) Liquids generally have lower density as compared to solids but ice floats on water, why? Explain in brief.
(c) Comphor disapears with time without leaving any solid. Justify the statement.

Or (ii) (a) Write any three factors which affect the rate of evoporation.
(b) What is the physical state of water at 350°C?
(c) What temperatrue in kelvin scale is equal to 30°C?

35. (i) (a) What are mitochondria? Give its detailed structure along with a labelled diagram
(b) State any two important functions of mitochondria.

Or (ii) (a) Study the diagram below and name the parts marked as A, B and C. Mention the role played by part A and B in it.

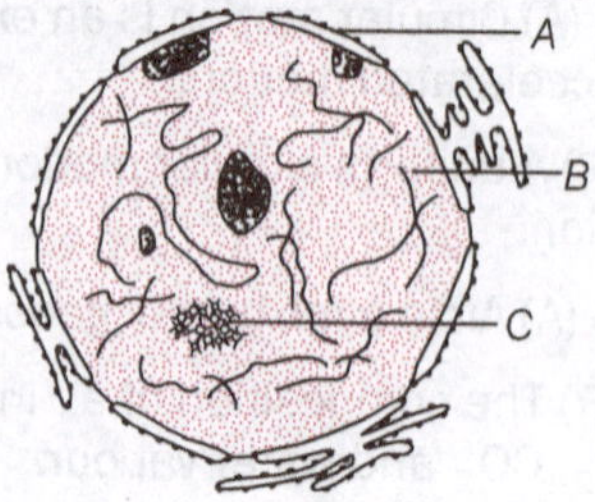

(b) Write any three important functions of nucleus in a cell.

36. (i) A vehicle of 1 tonne travelling with a speed of 60 ms^{-1} notices a cow on the road 9 m ahead, applies brakes. It stops just infront of the cow.
(a) Find out the KE of the vehicle before applying brakes.
(b) Calculate the retarding force provided by the brakes.
(c) How much time did it take to stop after the brakes were applied?
(d) What is the work done by the breaking force?

Or (ii) Establish the relationship between speed of sound, its wavelength and frequency. If velocity of sound in air is 340 ms^{-1}. Calculate
(a) wavelength when frequency is 256 Hz
(b) frequency when wavelength is 0.85 m.

Section E

Question Nos. 37 to 39 are case/source based questions. Each question carries 4 marks.

37. The symptoms of acidity are controlled by an antacid. Commercially available antacids consist of magnesium hydroxide, sugar and flavouring agents. The hydrochloric acid in the stomach is neutralised by the magnesium hydroxide to form salt and water. The mass of salt and water formed is equal to combined mass of base and acid reacted.

(i) Which law of chemical combination is mentioned in the above passage? Explain it by giving an example.
(ii) What is the combined mass of acid and antacid reacted to produce 9.5 g of salt and 3.6 g of water?

Or

(iii) If 2.0 g of sodium carbonate reacts with 10g of hydrochloric acid, it results in the formation of 3.5g of carbon dioxide and 8.5g of sodium chloride solution. Show that these results are in accordance to the above given law.

38. Observe the given figures of cell division.

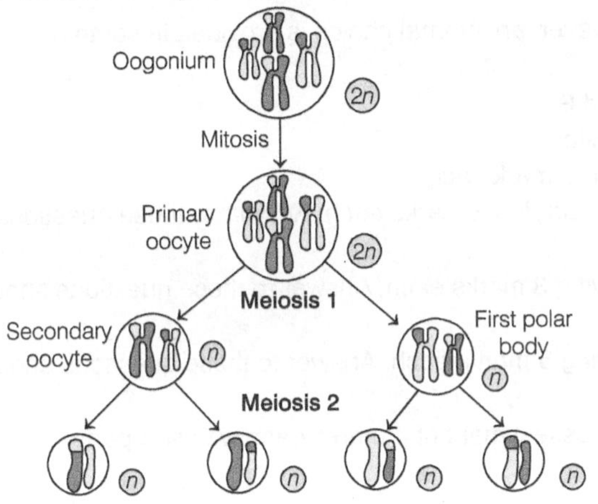

X

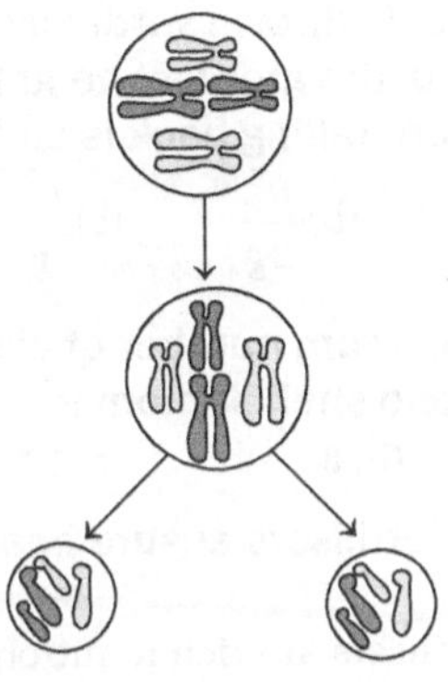

(i) Identify the type of cell division shown in the figure *X*.

Or

(ii) Identify the type of cell division shown in the figure *Y*.

(iii) Compare the division shown in the figure *X* or *Y*.

(iv) Name the type of cells that exhibit division shown in the figure *X*.

39. The distance travelled by a body is the actual length of the path covered by it, irrespective of the direction in which body travels. It is a scalar quantity.

The displacement of a body is the change in the position of the object when it moves from a given position to another position. It is equal to the length of the shortest path measured in the direction from the initial position to the final position of the object. It is a vector quantity.

(i) In which condition, will the magnitude of the displacement be equal to the distance travelled by an object?

(ii) The velocity *versus* time graph of a body in motion is shown below. What will be the displacement of the body?

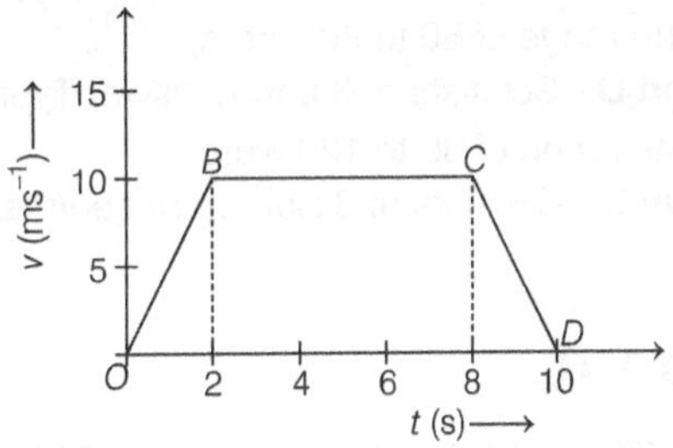

(iii) A particle starting from origin, moves 3 m North, 4 m East, 5 m South and then returns back to its initial position. What will be the displacement of the particle?

Or

(iv) A body travels a distance of 15 m from *A* to *B* and then moves a distance of 20 m at right angle to *AB*. What will be the displacement of the body?

Answers

1. (c) **2.** (b) **3.** (a) **4.** (a) **5.** (a) **6.** (c) **7.** (d) **8.** (d) **9.** (a) **10.** (c) **11.** (b) **12.** (b) **13.** (b) **14.** (c) **15.** (a) **16.** (b) **17.** (c) **18.** (a) **19.** (b) **20.** (a)

22. (ii) 0 m/s, 9.8 m/s^2

37. (ii) 13.1 g

Sample Question Paper 3 (Unsolved)
Science

Time : 3 hrs	M.M. : 80

General Instructions

1 The question paper consists of 39 questions.
2 All questions are compulsary. There is no overall choice. However, an internal choice is provided in some questions.
3 This question paper is divided into five sections A, B, C, D and E.
4 Only one of the alternatives has to be attempted in such question.
3 **Section A** - Consists of 20 Multiple Choice Questions carrying 1 mark each.
4 **Section B** - Consists of 6 Very Short answer Type Questions carrying 2 marks each. Answer to these questions should be in the range of 30 to 50 words.
5 **Section C** - Consists of 7 Short Answer Type Questions carrying 3 marks each. Answer to these questions should be in the range of 50 to 80 words.
6 **Section D** - Consists of 3 Long Answer Type Questions carrying 5 marks each. Answer to these questions should be in the range of 80 to 120 words.
7 **Section E** - Consists of 3 Source Based/Case Based units of assessment of 4 marks each with sub-parts.

Section A

In this section, questions no. 1 to 20 are multiple choice questions. All questions are compulsory.

1. The symbol for potassium is $^{39}_{19}K$. What can be concluded about potassium from the symbol?

(a) It contains 19 neutrons.
(b) It has a velency 2.
(c) It's electronic configuration is 2,8,8,1
(d) It contains 20 protons.

2. Radha observed the cell parts of two cells, i.e. cell *X* and cell Y under a light microscope. She recorded her observation in the table below. From her observations, identify cell *X* and cell *Y*.

	Cell *X*		Cell *Y*	
Organelles	Present	Absent	Present	Absent
Cell wall	✓			✓
Cytoplasm	✓		✓	
Nucleus	✓		✓	
Cell membrane	✓		✓	
Chloroplast		✓		✓

(a) *X*- Animal cell, *Y*-Plant cell
(b) *X*- Plant cell, *Y*- Animal cell
(c) *X*-Fungus cell, *Y*-Plant cell
(d) *X*-Fungus cell, *Y*-Animal cell

3. An object is thrown vertically upwards with a velocity *u*, the greatest height *h* to which it will rise before falling back is given by

(a) $\frac{u}{2g}$ (b) $\frac{u^2}{2g}$ (c) $\frac{u^2}{g}$ (d) $\frac{u}{g}$

4. The maximum number of electrons present in the second shell of atom is

(a) 2 (b) 8 (c) 10 (d) 18

5. How do fertilisers ensure healthy growth of plant ?

(a) Fertilisers are rich in nitrogen, carbon and oxygen
(b) Fertilisers are rich in nitrogen, phosphorus and potassium
(c) Fertiliser are rich in phosphorus, calcium and oxygen
(d) All of the above

6. Identify the incorrect statement about gravitational force.

(a) Gravitational force acts between any two objects having mass.
(b) Gravitational force decreases as the distance between two objects increases.
(c) Gravitational force depends only on the masses of the two objects.
(d) Gravitational force is always attractive in nature.

7. Match the Column I with Column II and select the correct option using the given codes.

Column I	Column II
(A) Symbol of potassium	(i) Ferrum
(B) Latin name of iron	(ii) P
(C) Latin name of gold	(iii) K
(D) Symbol of phosphrous	(iv) Aurum

(a) A→(i), B→(ii), C→(iii), D→(iv)
(b) A→(iii), B→(i), C→(iv), D→(ii)
(c) A→(ii), B→(i), C→(iii), D→(iv)
(d) A→(iv), B→(iii), C→(ii), D→(i)

8. Which pair of cells keep changing their shapes?
(a) Fat and bone cells
(b) WBCs and RBCs
(c) Sperm cells and ovum
(d) *Amoeba* and WBCs

9. The boiling points of diethyl ether, acetone and *n*-butyl alcohol are 35°C, 56°C and 118°C, respectively. Which one of the following correctly represents their boiling points in Kelvin scale?
(a) 306 K, 329 K, 391 K (b) 308 K, 329 K, 392 K
(c) 308 K, 329 K, 391 K (d) 329 K, 392 K, 308 K

10. $A \rightarrow CaCO_3$, $B \rightarrow NaCl$

The anionic part in *A* and *B* are respectively.

	A	B
(a)	Ca^{2+}	Cl^-
(b)	Ca^{2+}	Na^+
(c)	CO_3^{2-}	Na^+
(d)	CO_3^{2-}	Cl^-

11. Which of the following tissue covers the most of the organ and cavities within the body?
(a) Epithelial tissue
(b) Muscular tissue
(c) Nervous tissue
(d) Connective tissue

12. Which of following is a pure substance?
(a) Air
(b) Distilled water
(c) Steel
(d) Brass

13. The atom of an element has 40 protons, 40 electrons and 40 neutrons, then the atomic number of the element is
(a) 20 (b) 40
(c) 60 (d) 80

14. Two bones can be connected to each other by another type of tissue called
(a) ligaments
(b) tendons
(c) areolar tissue
(d) adipose tissue

15. The management and production of fishes for commercial use is called ....
(a) pisciculture
(b) apiculture
(c) mariculture
(d) monoculture

16. Kranti, Pusa Agarni and Pusa Bold are improved varieties of
(a) urad bean
(b) sunflower
(c) chick pea
(d) mustard

Direction *(Q.Nos. 17-20) In each of the following questions, a statement of Assertion (A) is given by the corresponding statement of Reason (R). Out of the given statements, choose the correct one.*
(a) If both A and R are true and R is the correct explanation of A.
(b) If both A and R are true, but R is not the correct explanation of A.
(c) If A is true, but R is false.
(d) If A is false, but R is true.

17. Assertion (A) Work done by a force on a body is positive when displacement is in the direction of applied force.

Reason (R) Work done W on a body is calculated by $W = Fs\cos\theta$, where θ is the angle between force F and displacement s.

18. Assertion (A) If the dispersed phase is liquid and dispersion medium is solid, then colloid is known as gel.

Reason (R) Whipped cream is an example of gel.

19. Assertion (A) The presence of genetic material as nucleoid is the characteristic of a prokaryotic cell.

Reason (R) The genetic material in these cells is not present in nucleus.

20. Assertion (A) Cultivation practices and crop yields are related to environmental conditions.

Reason (R) Climatic conditions such as temperature, photoperiod influence a plant's life cycle.

Section B

Question Nos. 21 to 26 are very short answer type questions. Each question carries 2 marks.

21. An object is moving with a uniform speed in a circle of radius *r*. Calculate the distance and displacement

(i) when it completes half the circle.

(ii) when it completes full the circle.

22. A cell organelle is responsible for energy production and is often reffered to as the power house. What could this organelle and why is it called so?

23. (i) When a constant force is applied to a body moving with constant acceleration, is the power of the force constant? If not, how would force have to vary with speed for the power to be constant?

Or

(ii) Find the relation between acceleration due to gravity (*g*) and the gravitational constant (*G*).

24. Sucrose (sugar) crystals obtained from sugarcane and beetroot are mixed together. Will it be a pure substance or a mixture? Give reasons for the same.

25. (i) (a) Explain how do cell walls permit the cells to withstand very dilute external media without bursting?

(b) Why does the skin of your fingers shrink when you wash clothes for a long time?

Or (ii) Explain the basic criteria for classification of permanent tissue in plants.

26. (i) Name the month during which Kharif crop is grown.

(ii) List any two factors for which crop variety improvement is done.

Section C

Question Nos. 27 to 33 are short answer type questions. Each question carries 3 marks.

27. On what factors do the following physical quantities depend?

(i) Inertia (ii) Momentum (iii) Force

28. (i) (a) Define atomic mass unit.

(b) Give the difference between a cation and an anion.

(c) Calculate the formula unit mass of $Al_2(CO_3)_3$.

Or (ii) (a) Define isotopes.

(b) Give any two uses of isotopes in the field of medicine.

(c) Chlorine occurs in nature in two isotopic forms with masses 35u and 37u. The percentage of ^{35}Cl is 75%. Find the average atomic mass of chlorine atom.

29. Animals of colder regions and fishes of cold water have thicker layer of subcutaneous fat. Describe why?

30. (i) List two differences between thrust and pressure.

(ii) What is meant by one pascal and one newton? How will the pressure change, if area of contact is doubled?

31. (i) Name two complex permanent tissues in vascular plants. What are these commonly called?

(ii) Where would you find striated muscle in human body? What is their function?

32. (i) What information do you get from the figure about the valency of atoms *X*, *Y* and *Z*?

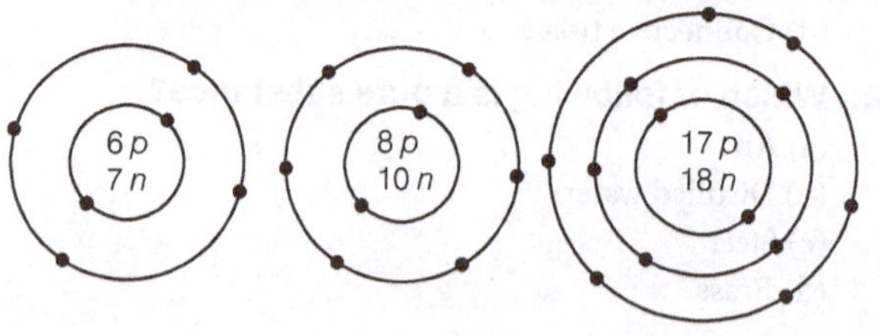

(ii) Draw atomic structure of an atom with same number of electrons in L and M-shells

33. The motion of a body of mass 5 kg is shown in the velocity-time graph.

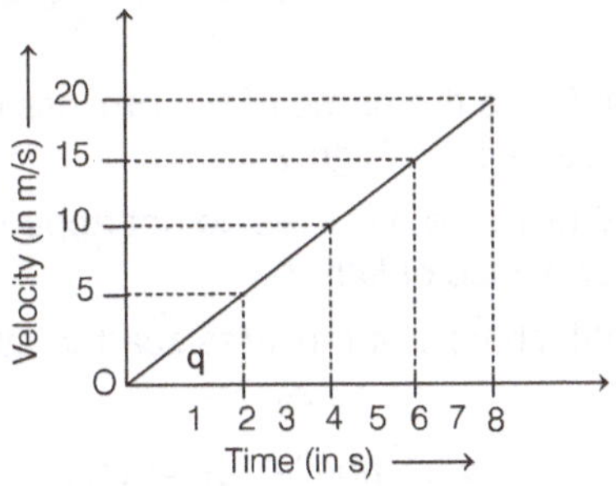

Find from the graph.

(i) It's acceleration.

(ii) The force acting on the body.

Section D

Question Nos. 34 to 36 are long answer type questions. Each question carries 5 marks

34. (i) (a) Differentiate between isotopes and isobars giving suitable examples.

(b) Why the atomic mass of Cl is 35.5u, even though no single atom has this mass ?

(c) Both ^{35}Cl and ^{37}Cl have the same valency. Why?

Or (ii) (a) An atom contains six protons and seven neutrons. What are the atomic number and mass number ?

(b) Helium, neon and argon have zero valency. Justify the statement.

(c) Write the difference between atomic mass and average atomic mass.

35. (i)(a) Differentiate between hypotonic and hypertonic solution.

(b) With the help of a diagram, explain the structure of nucleus.

Or (ii) Study the diagram given below and name the parts marked as X, Y and Z. Mention the function of X and Z.

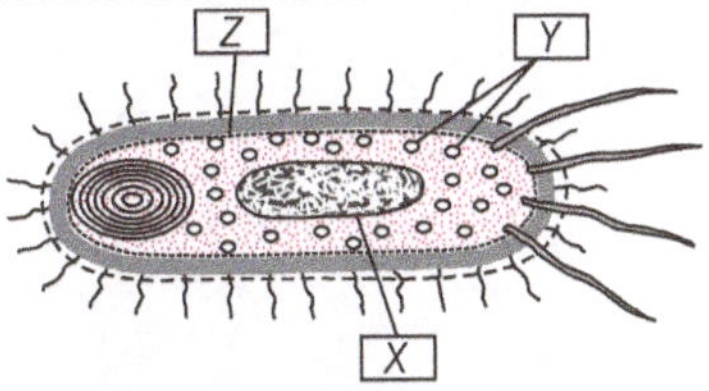

36. (i) A body weight 25 kg on the surface of the earth. If the mass of the earth is 6×10^{24} kg, the radius of the earth is 6.4×10^{6} m and the gravitational constant is 6.7×10^{-11} N- m^{2}kg^{-2}. Calculate

(a) the acceleration produced in the body.

(b) the acceleration produced in the earth.

Or

(ii) (a) The dimensions of a metallic cuboid are 30cm × 20cm × 15cm and its mass is 30kg. If the acceleration due to gravity is 10m/s^2. Calculate the pressure exerted by the cuboid when it rests on the face with sides 20cm × 15 cm on the table.

(b) In which of the following situations do we exert more pressure on the ground? Whether standing on the foot or standing on both feet? justify the answer.

Section E

Question Nos. 37 to 39 are case/source based questions. Each question carries 4 marks.

37. Energy exists in many different forms. The change of one form of energy into another form of energy is known as transformation of energy. When a body is released from a height, then the potential energy of the body is gradually transformed (or changed) into kinetic energy. When a body is thrown upwards, the kinetic energy of the body is gradually transformed into potential energy.

Some examples of the energy converters which make our life more comfortable are electric motor, electric generator, electric iron, electric bulb and solar cell.

When energy changes from one form to another, there is no loss or gain of energy. The total energy before and after transformation remains the same, i.e. energy can neither be created nor be destroyed.

(i) In case of riding a bicycle, which energy is converted into the kinetic energy of the bicycle?

(ii) Find the velocity of a body of mass 100 g having a kinetic energy of 20 J.

Or

(iii) Figure shows the frictional force *versus* displacement for a particle in motion. Find the loss of kinetic energy (work done against friction) in travelling over s = 0 to s = 20 m?

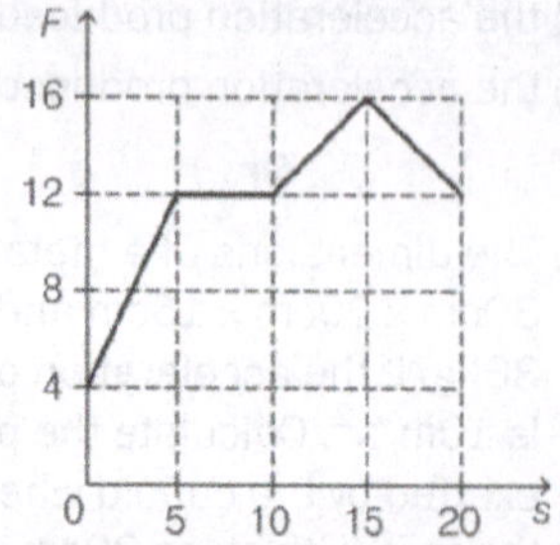

Or

(iv) How much work is done in lifting 200 kg of a mass through a vertical distance of 6 m ?

38. Lysosomes are membrane bound sac that are filled with digestive enzymes. These enzymes are made by rough endoplasmic reticulum. Lysosomes are also called the suicidal bags of a cell.

(i) What will happen if lysosomes malfunctions in a cell?

(ii) What is the fate of foreign material entering the cell?

(iii) Why are lysosomes considered the 'garbage trucks' of a cell?

Or

(iii) The lysosomal membrane is rich in which compound?

39. Manu went to watch a movie with his parents. In the dark, he found a small beam of light within which millions of tiny particles were dancing. He thought, when there was light, no such beam appears. He was very surprised. He asked about this from his science teacher who told him that it, was due to scattering of light.

(i) What is the name of the process of scattering of light?

(ii) Why these particles do not appear in the presence of light?

(iii) Which type of mixtures scatter light?

Or

(iv) Draw a well labelled diagram showing the process of scattering of light.

Answers

1. (c) **2.** (d) **3.** (b) **4.** (b) **5.** (b) **6.** (c) **7.** (b) **8.** (d) **9.** (c) **10.** (d) **11.** (a) **12.** (b) **13.** (b) **14.** (a) **15.** (a) **16.** (d) **17.** (a) **18.** (c) **19.** (a) **20.** (a)

21. (i) For half circle distance $= \pi r$

displacement $= 2r$

(ii) For complete circle, distance $= 2\pi r$

displacement $= 0$

33. (i) $2.5\ m/s^2$

(ii) 12.5 N

34. *Or* (ii) (a) Atomic number = 6,

Mass number = 13

36. (i) $9.81\ m/s^2$

(ii) $4.09 \times 10^{-23}\ m/s^2$

37. (ii) 20 m/s (iii) 160 J (iv) 12000J